KU-260-487

# Mauritius, Réunion & Seychelles
## a travel survival kit
### Robert Strauss
### Deanna Swaney

**Mauritius, Réunion & Seychelles – a travel survival kit**

2nd edition

**Published by**
**Lonely Planet Publications**
Head Office:  PO Box 617, Hawthorn, Vic 3122, Australia
Branches:     155 Filbert St, Suite 251, Oakland, CA 94607, USA
              10 Barley Mow Passage, Chiswick, London W4 4PH, UK
              71 bis rue du Cardinal Lemoine, 75005 Paris, France

**Printed by**
Colorcraft Ltd, Hong Kong
Printed in China

**Photographs by**
Robert Strauss (RS)
Deanna Swaney (DS)
Robert Willox (RW)
Front cover: typical boat, Guido A. Rossi (Image Bank)

**First Published**
December 1989

**This Edition**
September 1993

Although the authors and publisher have tried to make the information as accurate as possible, they accept no responsibility for any loss, injury or inconvenience sustained by any person using this book.

National Library of Australia Cataloguing in Publication Data

Strauss, Robert
Mauritius, Réunion & Seychelles – a travel survival kit.

2nd ed.
Includes index.
ISBN 0 86442 188 5.

1. Mauritius – Guidebooks. 2. Réunion – Guidebooks. 3. Seychelles – Guidebooks. I. Swaney, Deanna. II. Willox, Robert. III. Title. (Series: Lonely Planet travel survival kit).

916.9804

text & maps © Lonely Planet 1993
photos © photographers as indicated 1993
climate charts compiled from information supplied by Patrick J Tyson, © Patrick J Tyson, 1993

All rights reserved. No part of this publication may be reproduced, stored in a retrieval system or transmitted in any form by any means, electronic, mechanical, photocopying, recording or otherwise, except brief extracts for the purpose of review, without the written permission of the publisher and copyright owner.

## Robert Strauss

Robert was born in England. In the early 1970s he took the overland route to Nepal and then studied, taught and edited in England, Germany, Portugal, and Hong Kong. For Lonely Planet he has worked on travel survival kits to *China, Tibet, Japan, Brazil,* and *Bolivia* and has contributed to their shoestring guides for South America, North-East Asia and Europe. He has also written the *Trans-Siberian Rail Guide* (Compass Publications, UK).

## Deanna Swaney

A hopeless travel addict, Deanna Swaney escaped encroaching yuppiedom in the vibrant heart of mid-town Anchorage and made a break for South America to write Lonely Planet's *Bolivia – a travel survival kit.* Subsequent wanders led through an erratic circuit of wildlife encounters and island paradises – Arctic and tropical – and resulted in four more travel survival kits: *Tonga, Samoa, Iceland, Greenland & the Faroe Islands* and *Zimbabwe, Botswana & Namibia.*

She has also co-authored the second edition of *Brazil – a travel survival kit* and contributed to Lonely Planet's shoestring guides to Africa, South America and Scandinavia.

For this book, she covered Réunion and wrote the trekking information for all three places. Her immediate plans include a real holiday in a cheap beach resort in eastern Siberia.

## This Book

The 1st edition of of *Mauritius, Réunion & Seychelles* was written by Rob Willox in 1989. This edition was fully updated by Deanna Swaney and Robert Strauss.

## From the Authors

For help and assistance with our research we'd like to thank a host of friends and acquaintances. In Mauritius, Arthur Hooper; Louis Hein de Charmoy; Michel Zaragoza, 'un vrai pistard'; Chris Poulos & Francisco; Carl Jones, Duncan Chard, Greg Middleton and Bob Burn; and Nanda Appadoo (Mauritius). In Réunion, we were helped by Mr Nassor at Pension du Centre.

In the Seychelles, we were assisted by Mr & Mrs Albert Chung Faye; Ricardo (Brazil); Katrina (France/Italy); Guy (Belgium); Tony Mathiot; Heather Adams; Peter Driessel; and

René and Marlyse von Kaenel who provided amiable trekking company and motivation on Silhouette.

A general vote of thanks goes to Mikael Parkvall (Sweden) for copious notes on language, literature, and more; Gisela Treichler (Switzerland); Dendy Barker (UK); and Julie Bannister (Travel Bug UK).

The following readers contributed useful information in letters: Eva von Pottelberg & Christine Krols (Belgium), Bryan & Charmaine Roche (South Africa), Peter & Ginette Scott (UK), Dr Ronald Ti (Australia), Mike Steane (UK), Brigitte Beller (France), Kenneth Burton (USA), Mikael Parkvall (Sweden), Colin & Sheila Messenger (UK), Gillian Chambers (UK), Frederick Belton (USA), R Stratford (Canada), Stephen Clarke (UK), Julian Burke (Réunion), A.E. Vickers (South Africa), Tim & Marianne Goodell (UK), and Susan Russell (UK).

## From the Publisher

This edition was edited at the Lonely Planet office in Australia by Sally Steward. Jacqui Schiff was responsible for design, illustrations and maps, with additional maps from Margaret Jung, Tamsin Wilson and Sally Woodward. Margaret Jung was responsible for the cover design.

## Warning & Request

Things change – prices go up, schedules change, good places go bad and bad places go bankrupt – nothing stays the same. So if you find things better or worse, recently opened or long since closed, please write and tell us and help make the next edition better. Your letters will be used to help update future editions and, where possible, important changes will also be included in a Stop Press section in reprints.

We greatly appreciate all information that is sent to us by travellers. Back at Lonely Planet we employ a hard-working readers' letters team to sort through the many letters we receive. The best ones will be rewarded with a free copy of the next edition or another Lonely Planet guide if you prefer. We give away lots of books, but, unfortunately, not every letter/postcard receives one.

# Contents

# RÉUNION

# Map Legend

## BOUNDARIES

| | |
|---|---|
| —·—·—·— | ........ International Boundary |
| — ·· — ·· — | ............... Internal Boundary |
| +++++++++++ | .... National Park or Reserve |
| — — — — — | ......................... The Equator |
| ................. | ......................... The Tropics |

## SYMBOLS

| | |
|---|---|
| ◉ NATIONAL | ......................... National Capital |
| ● PROVINCIAL | ........ Provincial or State Capital |
| ● Major | ............................. Major Town |
| ● Minor | ............................. Minor Town |
| ■ | ......................... Places to Stay |
| ▼ | ............................ Places to Eat |
| ⊠ | ................................ Post Office |
| ✈ | ........................................ Airport |
| i | .................... Tourist Information |
| ⊖ | ............ Bus Station or Terminal |
| 66 | ............ Highway Route Number |
| ☾ ✚ ⛪ ✝ | ...... Mosque, Church, Cathedral |
| ∴ | ......................... Temple or Ruin |
| ✚ | .................................... Hospital |
| ☀ | ..................................... Lookout |
| Å | .......................... Camping Area |
| ⊼ | .............................. Picnic Area |
| ⌂ | ............................. Hut or Chalet |
| ▲ | ....................... Mountain or Hill |
| +—■—+ | ....................... Railway Station |
| ═══ | ............................. Road Bridge |
| +++++ | .......................... Railway Bridge |
| ⇒ ⇐ | ............................. Road Tunnel |
| ⇥ ⇤ | .......................... Railway Tunnel |
| ⏦⏦⏦ | .................... Escarpment or Cliff |
| ‿ | .......................................... Pass |
| ⊓⊔⊓⊔ | ............. Ancient or Historic Wall |

## ROUTES

| | |
|---|---|
| ——————— | ....... Major Road or Highway |
| - - - - - - - | ......... Unsealed Major Road |
| ——————— | ....................... Sealed Road |
| – – – – – | ..... Unsealed Road or Track |
| ════════ | ........................... City Street |
| +++++++++++ | ................................ Railway |
| ■—◉—■ | ................................. Subway |
| ................. | ..................... Walking Track |
| – – – – – | ......................... Ferry Route |
| ++++++++ | ........ Cable Car or Chair Lift |

## HYDROGRAPHIC FEATURES

| | |
|---|---|
| | .................... River or Creek |
| | ............. Intermittent Stream |
| | ........ Lake, Intermittent Lake |
| | ........................... Coast Line |
| | ................................. Spring |
| | ............................. Waterfall |
| | ................................. Swamp |
| | ............... Salt Lake or Reef |
| | ................................. Glacier |

## OTHER FEATURES

| | |
|---|---|
| | Park, Garden or National Park |
| | ....................... Built Up Area |
| | ... Market or Pedestrian Mall |
| | ......... Plaza or Town Square |
| | ............................. Cemetery |

Note: not all symbols displayed above appear in this book

# Introduction

The islands of the Indian Ocean are just as interesting, exciting and beautiful as the South Pacific islands, yet it's the South Pacific that gets the sizzling romances, the war stories, the high adventures and the news headlines. The fact is, the Indian Ocean islands have an image problem – they don't have one.

The main islands of the Indian Ocean lie hidden in the shadow of East Africa and are often wrongly labelled as African. Even some intrepid travellers don't know where they are and many English-speaking people confuse them with Fiji or Tahiti or Hawaii because they can't place Mauritius or the Seychelles and have never heard of Réunion. The French, however, are reasonably *au fait* with the Indian Ocean region, because France once controlled it.

The British ended up with most of it in 1814 as a prize for defeating Napoleon. They dutifully, stiffly, almost reluctantly, governed Mauritius and the Seychelles, but did little to alter the implanted French language or influence the evolving Créole culture.

Both Mauritius and the Seychelles have been independent nations for some time now, and are doing reasonably well considering the fate of their liberated big cousins in Africa. Réunion has stuck relatively comfortably with France.

Each of the three islands has developed differently and each is a country of contrasts in itself – they're melting pots of races, religions and cultures that peacefully coexist for the most part. This is perhaps the main reason that the islands don't present one image to the rest of the world.

The mixes on all three islands are similar, but they vary in degree. In Mauritius, Indian culture dominates; a Créole identity has been valiantly forged in the Seychelles; and Réunion follows European ways.

There are also great physical differences between the islands. Réunion is the surprise package, with a live volcano and exhilarating alpine scenery. The island is virtually unexplored by all but the French. The Seychelles is surrounded by wonderful lagoons and beaches. Mauritius has both coastal and plateau attractions, and high population density.

To put it very simply, go to the Seychelles for the beaches, to Réunion for the mountains and to Mauritius for the people and culture. But try to get to them all. We couldn't pick a favourite.

The visitor has so much to choose from that the image one person takes away is bound to be different from another's.

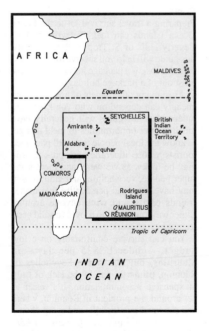

# Facts for the Visitor

### VISAS

Apart from an onward ticket, there are no entry requirements for Mauritius or the Seychelles, but those who require a French visa will need one for Réunion. It will be much easier to get one before you leave home. If you're planning to visit Madagascar or the Comoros as well, bring along a stock of passport-size photos.

### MONEY

Travellers' cheques in any of the major currencies may be changed without ado in Mauritius, Réunion and the Seychelles, though French francs are probably the best, especially for Réunion. Credit cards are widely accepted on all three islands.

### Costs

Preparing a travel survival kit to the Indian Ocean Islands can feel like writing about Beverly Hills or St Tropez. But hopefully, this guide will help you survive for much less than the cost of a package holiday (or get the most out of a package holiday).

As in many other facets of life, travelling cheaply can depend on who you know and independent travellers will generally have much greater opportunities to meet and get to know the local people than will packaged tourists whose itineraries are pre-set. You may be lucky, as we were, and meet some super people, very helpful and kind; or you may have a terrific personality that makes friends easily and wins anyone around. Either way, our aim is to provide a solid basis from which to work.

You can survive comfortably on a low budget – under US$25 per day – in Mauritius, but not in the Seychelles or Réunion, primarily due to the lack of truly inexpensive accommodation. It's easier to get around the problem in Réunion, where you can head into the hills and camp or stay in mountain huts or *chambres d'hôte* (family-run pensions) – in fact it would be a

waste not to since most of Réunion's interest lies in its wilderness. It's also advisable to bring from home all the equipment and clothing you'll be needing in Réunion since imports are subject to a 30.5% import tax. This could keep your average costs down to around US$25 per day. For more information, see the Accommodation section in the Réunion – Facts for the Visitor chapter.

In the Seychelles it's more difficult because accommodation is regulated by the tourist board; camping is forbidden and prices, availability and the standard of accommodation are fixed. If you keep to the less expensive guesthouses, you may just scrape by on around US$50 per day.

### WHAT TO BRING

The happiest travellers are those who pack lightly and can slip all their luggage under their plane seats. If you plan to use buses in Mauritius or Réunion, remember there's little space to stow luggage.

Backpacks with detachable daypacks make a versatile combination. Travel packs are backpacks which can be converted into more civilised-looking suitcases. They are cleverly compartmentalised, and have internal frames and special padding.

### Clothes

Keep clothing light and in cotton wherever possible; this applies especially to socks if you intend to do lots of tramping.

Anything as formal as a suit is unnecessary, but it's good to have a smart shirt and pair of trousers, or a smart dress or skirt for dinners out; don't forget good shoes too. Such an outfit can also help at customs and immigration, when entering or leaving a country. If nothing else, it makes you feel more respectable and authoritative (and thus respected) if trouble arises, than you would feel in shorts, T-shirt and thongs (flip-flops).

Make sure you have protection from the sun. Bring a hat and an appropriate-strength sun block. Take it easy to begin with when you go about exposing yourself to the fiery elements. It's so easy to get badly burnt, even when it's overcast, because you don't notice the damage until it's too late.

At the other extreme, a light wrap-up plastic cape or mac will stop a downpour from ruining the odd day or week. It's a must during the wet season. Also, remember to take precautions to keep your camera equipment and personal gear dry. Pack everything in plastic bags before you leave home.

At night it cools down a bit on the coast, but not enough to need woolly blankets and thick jumpers. It's a different story on the plateau around Curepipe in Mauritius or high in the cirques of Réunion. The temperature can drop to freezing and you'll definitely need warm clothing at night. Also, intending trekkers should bring good, solid footwear.

### Emergency Kit

If you're going to be roughing it away from the resort accommodation and living with islanders or in guesthouses, you should bring a torch (with spare batteries), toilet paper, a small mirror, a Swiss Army-type multi-purpose knife, a first aid kit (for information on a basic medical kit see the Health section in this chapter), a sewing kit, safety pins, cellophane tape and a small padlock (for locking rooms or luggage). That doesn't add up to much extra weight; if you're looking to save weight, bring only a thin towel.

### HEALTH

Travel health depends on predeparture preparations, day-to-day attention to health-related matters, and the manner of handling medical emergencies if they do arise. Although the following health section may seem like a who's who of dreadfully unpleasant diseases, your chances of contracting a serious illness in Mauritius, Réunion or the Seychelles are slight. You will, however, be exposed to different environmental factors, foods and sanitation standards, but if you take the recommended jabs, faithfully pop your antimalarials (where appropriate) and

use common sense, there shouldn't be any problems.

This rundown of health risks includes some preventative measures, symptom descriptions and suggestions about what to do if there is a problem. It isn't meant to replace professional diagnosis or prescription and visitors should discuss with their physician the most up-to-date methods used to prevent and treat the threats to health which may be encountered.

### Predeparture Preparations

**Health Insurance** A travel insurance policy to cover theft, loss and medical problems is a wise idea. Before heading abroad travellers should get up-to-date information. There is a wide variety of policies; contact your travel agent for further information. When buying a policy, it's important to check the small print:

- Some policies specifically exclude 'dangerous activities' which can include scuba diving, motorcycling or even trekking. If these activities are on your agenda, such a policy would be of limited value.
- You may prefer a policy which pays doctors or hospitals directly rather than requiring you to pay first and claim later. If you must claim after the fact, however, be sure you keep all documentation. Some policies ask you to phone (reverse charges) to a centre in your home country where an immediate assessment of the problem will be made.
- Check on the policy's coverage of emergency transport or evacuation back to your home country. If you have to stretch out across several airline seats, someone has to pay for it!

**Travel Health Information** In the USA you can request a health and safety information bulletin on the countries of the Indian Ocean by contacting the Overseas Citizens Emergency Center, or by writing to the Bureau of Consular Affairs Office, State Department, Washington, DC 20520. This office also has a special telephone number for emergencies while abroad, (202) 632-5525.

Read the Center for Disease Control's *Health Information for International Travel* supplement of *Morbidity & Mortality Weekly Report* or the World Health Organisation's

*Vaccination Certificate Requirements for International Travel & Health Advice to Travellers.* Both of these sources (CDC and WHO) are superior to the *Travel Information Manual* published by the International Air Transport Association.

International Association for Medical Assistance to Travelers (IAMAT) at 417 Center Street, Lewiston, New York, NY 14092 can provide you with a list of English-speaking physicians in the Indian Ocean countries.

In the UK, contact Medical Advisory Services for Travellers Abroad (MASTA), Keppel Street, London WC1E 7HT (☎ 071-6314408). MASTA provides a wide range of services including a choice of concise or comprehensive 'Health Briefs' and a range of medical supplies. Another source of medical information and supplies is the British Airways Travel Clinic (☎ 071-8315333). The Department of Health publishes leaflets SA40/41 on travellers' health requirements, and operates a phone service Freephone 0800 555777.

In Australia, contact the Traveller's Medical and Vaccination Centre in Sydney (☎ 02-221 7133) for general health information pertaining to Indian Ocean countries.

**Pharmacies & Medications** It's not necessary to take with you every remedy for every illness you might conceivably contract during your trip. Just about everything available at home can also be found in Mauritian, Réunion and the Seychelles pharmacies, and pharmaceutical drugs are available without a prescription. They are a bit lax about storage however, so be sure to check expiry dates before buying. It's also a good idea to take a sufficient supply of any prescriptions that you must take habitually, including contraceptive pills and vitamin tablets.

In addition, all travellers should be aware of any drug allergies they may have and avoid using them or their derivatives while travelling in Mauritius. Since common names of prescription medicines in the Indian Ocean are likely to be different from the ones you're used to, ask a pharmacist before taking anything you're not sure about.

**Medical Kit**
It's a good idea to carry a small, straightforward medical kit which may include:

- Aspirin or paracetamol – for pain or fever
- Antihistamine (such as Benadryl) – useful as a decongestant for colds and allergies, to ease itching from insect bites, or to prevent motion sickness
- Antibiotics – useful if you're travelling off the beaten track. Most antibiotics are prescription medicines.
- Kaolin and pectin preparation such as Pepto-Bismol for stomach upsets and Imodium or Lomotil to bung things up in case of emergencies during long-distance travel
- Rehydration mixture – for treatment of severe diarrhoea. This is particularly important when travelling with children.
- Antiseptic liquid or cream and antibiotic powder for minor injuries
- Calamine lotion – to ease irritation from bites and stings
- Bandages and Band-aids
- Scissors, tweezers, and a thermometer – but remember that you cannot transport mercury thermometers on airlines
- Insect repellent, sun block (15+), suntan lotion, chapstick and water purification tablets (or iodine)

For sources of requisite medical supplies, refer to the Travel Health Information section.

Ideally, antibiotics should be administered only under medical supervision and should never be taken indiscriminately. Overuse of antibiotics can weaken your immune system and reduce the drug's efficacy in the future. Take only the recommended dosage at the prescribed intervals and continue using the antibiotic for the prescribed period, even if you're feeling better sooner. Antibiotics are quite specific to the infections they will react with so if you're in doubt about a drug's effects or suffer any unexpected reactions, discontinue use immediately.

**Health Preparations** Make sure you're healthy before embarking on a long journey, have your teeth checked and if you wear glasses or contacts, bring a spare pair and a copy of your optical prescription.

At least one pair of good-quality sunglasses is essential, as the glare is terrific and dust and blown sand can get into the corners of your eyes. A hat, sun block and lip protection are also important.

If you require a particular medication, take an adequate supply as it may not be available locally. Take the prescription with the generic rather than brand name so it will be universally recognisable. It's also wise to carry a copy of the prescription to prove you're using the medication legally. Customs and Immigration officers may get excited at the sight of syringes or mysterious powdery preparations. The organisations listed under Travel Health Information can provide medical supplies such as syringes, together with multilingual customs documentation.

**Immunisations** Vaccinations provide protection against diseases you may encounter along the way. A yellow fever vaccination and related documentation is only necessary if you arrive from an infected area. Other commonly recommended jabs for travel to the Indian Ocean region are typhoid, tetanus DPT, and polio vaccines as well as gammaglobulin as protection against hepatitis. Some physicians will occasionally also recommend a cholera vaccine but its effectiveness is minimal.

*Cholera* Although many countries require this vaccine, it lasts only six months, and is not recommended for pregnant women.

*Tetanus DPT* Boosters are necessary at least every 10 years and are highly recommended as a matter of course.

*Typhoid* Protection lasts for three years and is useful if you are travelling for longer periods in rural tropical areas. The most common side effects from this vaccine are pain at the injection site, fever, headache, and a general unwell feeling.

*Gammaglobulin* Gammaglobulin is not a vaccination but a ready-made antibody which has proven successful in reducing the chances of contracting infectious hepatitis (hepatitis A). Because it may interfere with the development of immunity, it should not be given until at least 10 days after

administration of the last vaccine needed and as near as possible to departure due to its relatively short-lived effectiveness – normally about six months.

A new hepatitis A vaccine (administered as a course of two doses one month apart) has recently become available. The long-term protection offered by this vaccine should prove particularly useful for regular or long-term travellers.

## Basic Rules

**Food & Water** Care in what you eat and drink is the most important health rule; stomach upsets are the most common travel health problem but the majority of these upsets will be minor. Don't be paranoid about sampling local foods – it's all part of the travel experience and shouldn't be missed.

As a general rule, tap water in Mauritius, Réunion and the Seychelles is safe to drink and pleasant tasting, but care should be taken immediately following a cyclone or bad cyclonic storm. The simplest way to purify suspect water is to boil it for eight to 10 minutes. Simple filtering won't remove all dangerous organisms so if you can't boil suspect water, it should be treated chemically. Chlorine tablets (Puritabs, Steritabs and other brand names) will kill many but not all pathogens. Iodine is very effective and is available in tablet form (such as Potable Aqua) but follow the directions carefully and remember that too much iodine is harmful.

If you can't find tablets, tincture of iodine (2%) or iodine crystals may be used. Add two drops of tincture of iodine per litre or quart of water and let stand for 30 minutes. Iodine crystals can also be used to purify water but this is a more complicated and dangerous process since you first must prepare a saturated iodine solution. Iodine loses its effectiveness if exposed to air or damp so keep it in a tightly sealed container. Flavoured powder will disguise the normally foul taste of iodine-treated water and is an especially good idea for those travelling with children.

When it's hot, be sure to drink lots of

liquids. Excessive sweating can lead to loss of salt and cause muscle cramping. Failure to urinate or dark yellow urine is a sign of dehydration. Always carry a bottle of water on long trips.

Salads and fruit should be washed with purified water or peeled where possible. Ice cream is usually OK but beware of ice cream that has melted and been refrozen. Thoroughly cooked food is safest but not if it has been left to cool or if it has been reheated. Take great care with shellfish or fish and avoid undercooked meat. If a place looks clean and well run and the vendor also looks clean and healthy, then the food is probably all right. In general, look for places that are packed with locals.

### Diseases of Insanitation
**Diarrhoea** There is no escaping the fact that plain old travellers' diarrhoea can happen to you anywhere.

This problem is not caused by lack of sanitation or 'bad' food but primarily by a change in diet and a lack of resistance to local strains of bacteria. The first thing to remember is that every case of diarrhoea is not dysentery, so don't panic and start stuffing yourself with pills. If you've spent all your life living out of sterilised, cellophane-wrapped packets and tins from the supermarket, you'll have a hard time until you adjust.

If and when you get a gut infection, avoid rushing off to the chemist and loading up on antibiotics. In this case, taking antibiotics can do more harm than good. If the bacteria in your body are able to build up immunity to them, the antibiotics may not work when you really need them. Try to starve out the bugs first. If possible, eat nothing, rest and avoid travelling (or pop an Imodium or Lomotil). Drink lots of liquids – diarrhoea will cause dehydration and may result in stomach cramps due to a salt imbalance in the blood. If you can't hack starvation, keep to a light diet of dry toast, biscuits and black tea. To keep up your liquids, drink bottled water or lemonade. Once you're headed towards recovery, try some yoghurt but stay

away from sweets, fruit, and dairy products. If you don't recover after a couple of days, it may be necessary to visit a doctor to be tested for other problems which could include giardia, dysentery, cholera and so on.

**Giardia** This is first characterised by a swelling of the stomach, pale-coloured faeces, diarrhoea, frequent gas, headache and later by nausea and depression. Many doctors recommend Flagyl (metronidazole) tablets (250 mg) twice daily for three days. Flagyl, however, can cause side effects and some doctors prefer to treat giardiasis with two grams of Tinaba (tinadozole), taken in one fell swoop to knock the bug out hard and fast. If it doesn't work the first time, the treatment can be repeated for up to three days.

**Dysentery** This serious illness is caused by contaminated food or water and is characterised by severe diarrhoea, often with blood or mucus in the stool, and painful gut cramps. There are two types: bacillary dysentery, which is uncomfortable but not enduring; and amoebic dysentery which, as its name suggests, is caused by amoebas. This variety is much more difficult to treat and is more persistent.

Bacillary dysentery hits quickly and because it's caused by bacteria it responds well to antibiotics and is usually treated symptomatically with a kaolin and pectin or a bismuth compound. On the other hand, since the symptoms themselves are actually the best treatment – diarrhoea and fever are both trying to rid the body of the infection – it may be best to just hole up for a few days and let it run its course. If activity or travel is absolutely necessary during the infection, you can take either Imodium or Lomotil to 'plug the drain', so to speak, until reaching a more convenient location to R & R (rest and run).

*Amoebic dysentery*, or amoebiasis, is a much more serious variety. It is caused by protozoans, or amoebic parasites, called *Endamoeba histolytica* which are also transmitted through contaminated food or water. Once they've invaded, they live in the lower intestinal tract and cause heavy and often bloody diarrhoea, fever, tenderness in the liver area and intense abdominal pain.

If left untreated, ulceration and inflammation of the colon and rectum can become very serious. If you see blood in your faeces over two or three days, seek medical attention. If that's not possible, try the antiparasitic Flagyl (metronidazole). You'll need three tablets three or four times daily for 10 days to rid yourself of the condition. Flagyl should not be taken by pregnant women.

The best method of preventing dysentery is, of course, to avoid eating or drinking contaminated items.

**Cholera** The cholera vaccine is between 20% and 50% effective according to most authorities, and can have some side effects. Vaccination is not usually recommended, nor is it legally required in Mauritius, Réunion or the Seychelles.

Cholera is characterised by a sudden onset of acute diarrhoea with 'rice water' stools, vomiting, muscular cramps and extreme weakness. You need medical attention but your first concern should be rehydration. Drink as much water as you can – if it refuses to stay down, keep drinking anyway. If there is likely to be an appreciable delay in reaching medical treatment, begin a course of tetracycline which, incidentally, should not be administered to children or pregnant women. Be sure to check the expiry date since old tetracycline can become toxic.

**Viral Gastroenteritis** This is not caused by bacteria but, as the name implies, a virus. It is characterised by stomach cramps, diarrhoea, vomiting and slight fever. All you can do is rest and keep drinking as much water as possible.

**Hepatitis** This incapacitating disease is caused by a virus which attacks the liver. Type A can be caught by eating food, drinking water or using cutlery, crockery or toilets contaminated by an infected person. The victim's eyes and skin turn a sickly yellow and urine orange or brown. An infected

person will also experience tenderness in the right side of the abdomen and a loss of appetite.

If you contract infectious hepatitis (hepatitis A) during a short trip to the Indian Ocean, you probably should make arrangements to go home. If you can afford the time, however, and have a reliable travelling companion who can bring food and water, the best cure is to stay where you are, find a few good books and only leave bed to go to the toilet. After a month of so, you should feel like living again. Drink lots of fluids and keep to a diet high in proteins and vitamins. Avoid alcohol and cigarettes absolutely.

The best preventative measures available are either the recently introduced long-term hepatitis A vaccine; or a gammaglobulin jab before departure from home and booster shots every three or four months thereafter while you're away (beware of unsanitary needles!). A jab is also in order if you come in contact with any infected person; and if *you* come down with hepatitis, anyone who has been in recent contact with you should take the shot too.

Hepatitis B, formerly known as serum hepatitis, can only be caught through having sex with an infected person or by skin penetration such as tattooing or using the same syringe. If type B is diagnosed, fatal liver failure is a real possibility and the victim should be sent home and/or hospitalised immediately. Gammaglobulin is not effective against hepatitis B.

A vaccine does exist for hepatitis B, but it is not readily available and is extremely expensive. It consists of a course of three shots over a period of six months.

A variant of the B strain, called hepatitis C, now also exists. Transmission and symptoms are similar to hepatitis B; however there is presently no vaccine against hepatitis C. It is not very common, though, and should not be of too much concern to travellers.

**Typhoid** Contaminated food and water are responsible for typhoid fever, another gut infection that travels the faecal-oral route.

Vaccination against typhoid isn't 100% effective. Since it can be very serious, medical attention is necessary.

Early symptoms are like those of many other travellers' illnesses – you may feel as though you have a bad cold or the flu combined with a headache, sore throat and fever. The fever rises slowly until it exceeds 40°C while the pulse slowly drops. These symptoms may be accompanied by nausea, diarrhoea or constipation.

In the second week, the fever and slow pulse continue and a few pink spots may appear on the body. Trembling, delirium, weakness, weight loss and dehydration set in. If there are no further complications, the fever and symptoms will slowly fade during the third week. Medical attention is essential, however, since typhoid is extremely infectious and possible complications include pneumonia or peritonitis (burst appendix).

When feverish, the victim should be kept cool. Watch for dehydration. The recommended antibiotic is chloramphenicol but ampicillin causes fewer side effects.

## Insect-Borne Diseases

**Malaria** Opinions vary as to the prevalence of malaria on Mauritius, but malaria prophylaxis is generally advised. At present, Réunion and the Seychelles are free of malaria.

Malaria is caused by the blood parasite *plasmodium* which is transmitted by the nocturnal *anopheles* mosquito. Only the females spread the disease but you can contract it through a single bite from an insect carrying the parasite. Malaria sporozites enter the bloodstream and travel to the liver where they mature, infect the red blood cells and begin to multiply. This process takes between one and five weeks. Only when the infected cells re-enter the bloodstream and burst do the dramatic symptoms begin. For this reason, malaria can be extremely dangerous because the victim by this time has often left the malarial area, so the disease is not suspected and therefore is improperly treated.

There are four types of malaria: plasmodium falciparum, the deadliest, plasmodium malariae which is still universally sensitive to chloroquine, and finally plasmodium vivax and plasmodium ovale which are harboured outside the blood and can recur. The drug-resistant status of different malarial strains in different parts of the world is constantly in flux.

Diagnosis is confirmed by a blood test in which the plasmodium and its strain may be identified. Some strains, particularly *plasmodium falciparum*, can be fatal if not immediately and properly treated. Malarial symptoms include (in this order) gradual loss of appetite, malaise, weakness, alternating shivering and hot flashes, diarrhoea, periodic high fever, severe headache, vomiting and hallucinations.

The most effective form of malaria prevention, of course, is to avoid being bitten. Since the mosquitoes bite at dusk, you can avoid bites by covering bare skin and using an insect repellent. Sleep under a mosquito net or at least light a mosquito coil. Next best – but hardly 100% effective – is a course of antimalarials which are normally taken two weeks before, during and several weeks after travelling in malarial areas.

The malaria parasite mutates rapidly and although pharmacology manages to keep one step ahead of it, advice on which antimalarials you'll need to take goes out of date very quickly. Your doctor or travellers' health clinic will have access to the latest information. Currently, the recommended prophylaxis is chloroquine. If you develop malarial symptoms, seek medical advice immediately. If you have plasmodium falciparum and reach the headache stage, you may be in serious danger.

If you are not within reach of medical attention, the treatment for all strains (until you can reach a doctor) is one single dose of four tablets (600 mg) of chloroquine followed by two tablets (300 mg) six hours later and two tablets on each subsequent day. As an alternative (requisite for chloroquine-resistant strains) take a single dose of three tablets of Fansidar. *Never* use Fansidar as a prophylaxis. Halfan is another drug recently introduced for this type of emergency, but it may be difficult to obtain abroad – consult your doctor prior to departure.

**Worms** Worms are common in most humid tropical areas and a stool test when you return home isn't a bad idea if you think you may have contracted them. They can live on unwashed vegetables or in undercooked meat or you can pick them up through your skin by walking barefoot. Infestations may not be obvious for some time and although they are generally not serious, they can cause further health problems if left untreated. Once the problem is confirmed, over-the-counter medication is available to rid yourself of it.

The most common form you're likely to contract is hookworms. They are usually caught by walking barefoot on infected soil. They bore through the skin, attach themselves to the inner wall of the intestine and proceed to suck the blood, resulting in abdominal pain and sometimes anaemia.

Threadworms, or *strongyloidiasis*, are also found in low-lying areas and operate very much like hookworms, but symptoms are more visible and can include diarrhoea and vomiting.

Worms may be treated with thiabendazole or mabendazole taken orally twice daily for three or four days. As usual, however, medical advice is best because the symptoms of worms so closely resemble those of other, more serious conditions.

**Typhus** Typhus is spread by ticks, mites or lice and begins as a severe cold followed by a fever, chills, headache, muscle pains and rash. There is often a large and painful sore at the site of the bite and nearby lymph nodes become swollen and painful.

Trekkers may be at risk from cattle or wild game ticks. Seek local advice on areas where ticks are present and check yourself carefully after walking in those areas. A strong insect repellent can help and regular bushwalkers should consider treating boots and trousers with repellent.

## Cuts, Bites & Stings
**Cuts & Scratches** The warm, moist conditions of the tropical lowlands invite and promote the growth of 'wee beasties' that would be thwarted in more temperate climates. Because of this, even a small cut or scratch can become painfully infected and lead to more serious problems.

Since bacterial immunity to certain antibiotics can build up, it's not wise to take these medicines indiscriminately or as a preventative measure. The best treatment for cuts is to frequently cleanse the affected area with soap and water and apply Mercurochrome or an antiseptic cream. Where possible, avoid using bandages, which keep wounds moist and encourage the growth of bacteria. If, despite this, the wound becomes tender and inflamed then use of a mild, broad-spectrum antibiotic may be warranted.

**Insects** Ants, gnats, mosquitoes, bees and flies are just as annoying in the Indian Ocean as they are at home. Cover yourself well with clothing and use insect repellent on exposed skin. Burning incense and sleeping under mosquito nets in air-conditioned rooms or under fans also lowers the risk of being bitten. If you're going walking in humid or densely-foliated areas, wear light cotton trousers and shoes, not shorts and sandals or thongs (flip-flops). Regardless of temperature, never wear shorts or thongs in the forest and remember to carry an effective insect repellent.

Bee and wasp stings are usually more painful than dangerous. Calamine lotion offers some relief and ice packs will reduce pain and swelling.

## Diseases Spread by People & Animals
**Tetanus** This potentially fatal disease is found in underdeveloped tropical areas and is difficult to treat but is easily prevented by vaccination. Tetanus occurs when a wound becomes infected by a bacterium which lives

in human or animal faeces. Clean all cuts, punctures, and bites. Tetanus is also known as lockjaw and the first symptom may be difficulty in swallowing, a stiffening of the jaw and neck followed by painful convulsions of the jaw and whole body.

**Rabies** Avoid any animal that appears to be foaming at the mouth or acting strangely. Dogs are particularly notable carriers. Any bite, scratch or even lick from a mammal should be cleaned immediately and thoroughly. Scrub with soap and running water and then clean with an alcohol solution. If there is any possibility that the animal is infected, help should be sought. Even if the animal isn't rabid, all bites should be treated seriously as they can become infected or result in tetanus. A rabies vaccination is now available and should be considered if you spend a lot of time around animals.

The rabies virus incubates slowly in its victim, so while medical attention isn't urgent, it shouldn't be delayed.

**Diptheria** Diptheria can appear as a skin infection or a more serious throat infection. It is spread by contaminated dust coming in contact with the skin or being inhaled. About the only way to prevent the skin infection is to keep clean and dry – not always easy. The throat infection is prevented by vaccination.

**Gonorrhoea, Syphilis & Mauritius Rose** Sexual contact with an infected partner spreads a number of unpleasant diseases. While abstinence is 100% effective, use of a condom will lessen your risk considerably. The most common of these diseases are gonorrhoea and syphilis which in men first appear as sores, blisters or rashes around the genitals and pain or discharge when urinating. Symptoms may be less marked or not evident at all in women. The symptoms of syphilis eventually disappear completely but the disease continues and may cause severe problems in later years. Antibiotics are used to treat both syphilis and gonorrhoea.

One danger you will not usually be warned about is Mauritius Rose, a virulent form of VD. Take precautions. Mauritius is hardly a permissive society and prostitution is not rife. But there are many young girls who choose to supplement the family income in that manner and may appear a little over-hospitable at the disco. The unofficial red light district for Mauritians is at Pointe aux Sables. Tourists are not encouraged there.

Some pensions, or boarding houses, rent out rooms to couples for a 'little rest', but these are not to be seen as bring-your-own brothels. As families are usually big, unmarried couples have nowhere to go to get better acquainted. Travellers staying in such a place should check the bed linen thoroughly.

**AIDS** AIDS is another issue. In 1992, Mauritius reported nine AIDS cases and Réunion had 49. All visitors should be aware of the seriousness of this disease. At present, AIDS is a death sentence and will continue to be until a cure is found – and that may not be for a while. Although in the West it is most commonly spread through intravenous drug abuse and male homosexual activity, it is now also increasingly being transmitted through heterosexual activity.

Most people affected by the AIDS virus are not aware they have it and hospitals are likely to diagnose their symptoms as something more mundane. The obvious way to best avoid the disease is to remain celibate. Not everyone can – or is inclined to be – so if you do have sex, cut the risk by using a condom – the most effective preventative next to abstinence.

You can also pick up AIDS through blood transfusions and it is possible to contract the virus through injection with an unsterilised needle. If you must have an injection, either provide your own sterilised syringe or make absolutely sure it's either new or properly sterilised.

### Hypothermia

Hypothermia is a dangerous lowering of the body temperature. It is caused by exhaustion and exposure to cold, wet or windy weather, which can occur, for example, when hiking round the cirques in Réunion. The best precautions are to dress in layers; wear a hat, as heat is lost through the head; and have a strong, waterproof outer layer, as keeping dry is vital. Carry basic supplies, including food that contains simple sugars to generate heat quickly, and lots of fluid to drink.

Symptoms of hypothermia are exhaustion, numb skin, shivering, slurred speech, irrational or violent behaviour, lethargy, stumbling, dizzy spells, muscle cramps and violent bursts of energy. The best treatment is of course to get the victim to shelter and give them warm drinks and a warm (but not hot) bath if possible. Wet clothing should be changed or removed – no clothing at all is better than wet garments.

The patient should lie down, wrapped in a sleeping bag or blanket to preserve body heat. Another person may lie down with them in order to provide as much warmth as possible. If no improvement is noticed within a few minutes, seek help but don't leave the victim alone while doing so. The body heat of another person is of more immediate importance than medical attention.

### Sun, Heat & Exertion

**Sunburn** Mauritius, Réunion and the Seychelles lie within the humid tropics, where the sun's rays are more direct and concentrated than in temperate zones. Even in the cooler highland areas, everyone (particularly fair-skinned people) will be susceptible to hazardous UV rays. Don't neglect to apply sun block to any area of exposed skin, especially if you're near water.

Sun block is unfortunately quite expensive in all three countries, so you may want to bring some from home. In addition, a hat will serve to shade your face and protect your scalp. Sunglasses will prevent eye irritation (especially if you wear contact lenses).

**Prickly Heat** Prickly heat is an itchy rash caused by excessive perspiration trapped under the skin. It usually strikes those newly arrived in a hot climate whose pores have not opened enough to accommodate profuse sweating. Frequent baths and application of talcum powder will help relieve the itch.

**Heat Exhaustion** Heat combined with humidity and exposure to the sun can be oppressive and leave you feeling lethargic, irritable and dazed. A cool swim or lazy afternoon in the shade will do wonders to improve your mood. You'll also need to drink lots of liquids and eat salty foods in order to replenish your supply of these products lost during sweating.

Serious dehydration or salt deficiency can lead to heat exhaustion. Take time to acclimatise to high temperature and again, be sure to drink sufficient liquids. Salt deficiency, which can be brought on by diarrhoea or nausea, is characterised by fatigue, lethargy, headaches, giddiness and muscle cramps. Salt tablets will probably solve the problem. Anhidrotic heat exhaustion, caused by inability to sweat, is quite rare but can strike even those who have spent some time in hot climates.

**Heatstroke** This serious, sometimes fatal, condition can occur if the body's thermostat breaks down and body temperature rises to dangerous levels. Continuous exposure to high temperatures can leave you vulnerable to heatstroke. Alcohol intake and strenuous activity can increase chances of heatstroke, especially in those who've recently arrived in a hot climate.

Symptoms include minimal sweating, a high body temperature (39°C to 40°C), and a general feeling of unwellness. The skin may become flushed and red. Severe throbbing headaches, decreased coordination, and aggressive or confused behaviour may be signs of heatstroke. Eventually, the victim will become delirious and go into convulsions. Get the victim out of the sun, if possible, remove clothing, cover with a wet towel and fan continually. Seek medical help as soon as possible.

**Motion Sickness** If you're susceptible to motion sickness even on short trips, you should be prepared because the roads on Mauritius aren't exactly smooth, while those on Réunion are worse. If Dramamine works for you, take some along. Eating very lightly before and during a trip will reduce the chances of motion sickness. Try to find a place that minimises disturbance, near the wing on aircraft or near the centre on buses. Fresh air almost always helps but reading or cigarette smoking normally makes matters worse.

Commercial motion sickness preparations, which can cause drowsiness, have to be taken before the trip; after you've begun feeling ill, it's too late. Dramamine tablets should be taken three hours before departure and scopolamine patches (which are available only by prescription in most places) should be applied 10 to 12 hours before departure. Scopolamine will dilate the pupils if it accidentally comes in contact with the eyes and has been known to cause drowsiness, so caution should be exercised. Ginger can be used as a natural preventative and is available in capsule form.

### Women's Health
**Gynaecological Problems** Poor diet, lowered resistance due to use of antibiotics, and even contraceptive pills can lead to vaginal infections when travelling in hot climates. To prevent the worst of it, keep the genital area clean, wear cotton underwear and skirts or loose-fitting trousers.

Yeast infections, characterised by a rash, itch and discharge, can be treated with a vinegar or lemon juice douche or with yoghurt. Nystatin suppositories are the usual medical prescription. Trichomonas is a more serious infection which causes a discharge and a burning sensation when urinating. Sexual partners must also be treated and if a vinegar and water douche is not effective, medical attention should be sought. Flagyl is the most frequently prescribed drug.

**Pregnancy** Most miscarriages occur during the first trimester of pregnancy so this is the most risky time to be travelling. The last three months should also be spent within reasonable reach of good medical care since serious problems can develop at this stage as well. Pregnant women should avoid all unnecessary medication but vaccinations and malarial prophylactics should still be taken where possible. Additional care should be taken to prevent illness and particular attention to diet and proper nutrition will significantly lessen the chances of complications.

### Back Home
Be aware of illness after you return; take note of odd or persistent symptoms of any kind, get a check-up and remember to give your physician a complete travel history. Most doctors in temperate climes will not suspect unusual tropical diseases. If you have been travelling in malarial areas, have yourself tested for the disease.

### DANGERS & ANNOYANCES
### Security
Visitors to Mauritius, Réunion and the Seychelles are unlikely to have problems with security. The few problems we heard about included petty theft on beaches or from unlocked rooms, and pickpocketing in crowded markets and buses. However, don't leave vital documents, money or valuables in your room or in your suitcase while travelling.

**Predeparture Precautions** Travel insurance is essential for replacement of valuables and the cost of a good policy is a worthwhile price to pay for minimum disturbance or even abrupt termination of your travel plans.

Be prepared for the worst – make copies of your important records: a photostat of your passport (page with passport number, name, photograph, location where issued and expiry date; all visas); travellers' cheque numbers; credit card numbers; airline tickets; essential contact addresses, etc. Keep one copy on your person, one copy with your belongings and exchange one with a travelling companion.

Credit cards are useful in emergencies and for regular purchases. Make sure you know the number to call if you lose your credit card and be quick to cancel it if lost or stolen. New style credit card coupons do not have carbon paper inserts and offer more protection against misuse. If you sign an old style coupon, be sure to ask for the carbon inserts and destroy them after use. Similarly, destroy any coupons which have been filled out incorrectly. These are worthwhile precautions against unwanted duplication of your credit card!

Don't keep all your valuables together: distribute them about your person and baggage to avoid the risk of losing everything in one fell swoop.

**Security Accessories** Various types of money belt are available to be worn around the waist, neck or shoulder; and leather or cotton material is more comfortable than synthetics. Such belts are only useful if worn *under* clothing – pouches worn outside clothing are easy prey and attract attention. Determined thieves are wise to conventional money belts, and some travellers now also use cloth pouches sewn into trousers or attached inside with safety pins. Other methods include belts with concealed zipper compartment; and bandages or pouches worn around the leg.

Get used to keeping small change and a few banknotes in a shirt pocket so that you can pay bus tickets and small expenses without extracting large amounts of money which could quickly attract attention.

**Security Precautions in Hotels & on Beaches** Don't leave vital documents, money or valuables in your room. If you consider your hotel to be reliable, place valuables in its safe and get a receipt. Make sure you package your valuables in a small, double-zippered bag which can be padlocked, or use a large envelope with a signed seal which will easily show any tampering. Count money and travellers' cheques before and after retrieving them from the safe – this should quickly identify any attempts

to extract single bills or cheques which might otherwise go unnoticed.

Don't bring any valuables to the beach – and never tempt a passing thief by leaving your belongings unattended. Just take the minimum: swimsuit, towel, hat, T-shirt, suncream and enough money for a meal and drinks.

### Marine Dangers

Unless you know about marine life, don't touch the coral, shells or fish – some of them sting, cut and occasionally kill. In particular, watch out for sea urchins; the gaudy and easily recognisable lionfish with its poisonous spined fins; and cleverly camouflaged – and exceptionally poisonous – stonefish. Make sure you wear full-shoe fins when diving; and sailing shoes, plastic shoes or other suitably tough footwear when windsurfing, snorkelling, etc. Don't swim or let yourself drift too far away from the boat or shore in case you get caught in a strong current. Keep away from the surf breaking on the reef edge or anywhere else for that matter. One big wave and you could be fish fodder. Sharks are the least of your worries.

### Coconut Trees

Take care when walking under coconut trees and don't lie beneath them: in recent years there have been some tragic accidents with plummeting coconuts.

### BOOKS

If you intend to do a lot of reading, bring paperbacks from home and hope you can swap. There are plenty of expensive paperbacks on sale in the Seychelles and good book exchanges in Port Louis, Mauritius. On Réunion, however, you'll find English language books are very rare, but *Time* and *Newsweek* are normally available in bookshops *(librairies)*.

First time shoestring travellers may want to prepare for their trip by reading *The Tropical Traveller* by John Hatt (Pan, 1982).

See the Books & Maps section in the Facts for the Visitor chapter of each country for a rundown of available maps and a few pertinent reading suggestions.

## FILM & PHOTOGRAPHY

Points worth remembering include the heat, humidity, very fine sand, tropical sunlight, equatorial shadows and the great opportunities for underwater photography. If you're shooting on beaches, it's important to adjust for glare from water or sand; and keep sand and salt water well away from your equipment. Don't leave your camera for long in direct sunlight and don't store used film for long in the humid conditions, as it will fade.

Useful accessories would include a small flash, a cable release, a polarising filter, a lens cleaning kit (fluid, tissue, aerosol), and silica-gel packs to protect against humidity. Also, remember to take spare batteries for cameras and flash units. Make sure your equipment is insured.

The best times to take photographs on sunny days are the first two hours after sunrise and the last two before sunset. This brings out the best colours. At other times, the harsh sunlight and glare washes everything out, though you can use filters to counter the glare.

Photographing people, particularly dark-skinned people, requires more skill than snapping landscapes. Make sure you take the light reading from the subject's face, not the background. It also requires more patience and politeness. Many islanders, particularly the older Muslims and Hindus, are offended or frightened by snap-happy inquisitors. You should always ask first, ingratiate yourself, or snap discreetly from a distance.

Don't take photographs of airports or anything that looks like police or military equipment or property.

Finally, if you are worried about X-ray security machines at airports ruining your film, despite assurances that they won't, simply remove your camera and film stock from your luggage and take them through separately for inspection.

## Underwater Photography

Of course the urge to take underwater photographs is going to affect many Indian Ocean snorkellers and divers. In recent years underwater photography has become much easier. At one time it required complex and expensive equipment, whereas now there are a variety of reasonably priced and easy to use underwater cameras available. Very often it's possible to rent cameras, including underwater video cameras, from diving operators.

As with basic cameras above surface level the best photos taken with the simplest underwater cameras are likely to be straightforward snapshots. You are not going to get superb photographs of fish and marine life with a small, cheap camera but on the other hand photos of your fellow snorkellers or divers can often be terrific.

More than with other types of photography the results achieved underwater can improve dramatically with equipment expenditure, particularly on artificial lighting. As you descend natural colours are quickly absorbed, starting with the red end of the spectrum. You can see the same result with a picture or poster that has been left in bright sunlight for too long, soon the colours fade until everything looks blue. It's the same underwater, the deeper you go the more blue things look. Red has virtually disappeared by the time you're 10 metres down.

The human brain fools us to some extent by automatically compensating for this colour change, but the camera doesn't lie. If you are at any depth your pictures will look cold and blue.

To put the colour back in you need a flash and to work effectively underwater it has to be a much more powerful and complicated flash than above water. Thus newcomers to serious underwater photography soon find that having bought a Nikonos camera they have to lay out as much money again for flash equipment to go with it. With the right experience and equipment the results can be superb.

Generally the Nikonos cameras work best with 28 or 35 mm lenses, longer lenses do not work so well underwater. Although objects appear closer underwater with these short focal lengths you have to get close to achieve good results. Patience and practice will eventually enable you to move in close to otherwise wary fish. The Underwater photography opens up whole new fields of interest to divers and the results can often be startling. Flash photography can reveal colours which simply aren't there for the naked eye.

## ACTIVITIES
### Diving & Snorkelling
The Seychelles has the best diving locations and schools. Scuba is also popular in Mauritius and Réunion but there it isn't so much for the serious diver as for casual or learning divers.

Most of the instructors are members of the US-based Professional Association of Diving Instructors (PADI) and provide safety and tuition of a high standard. The other major diving organisation is the Federation of Australian Underwater Instructors (FAUI). If the school does not possess either of these qualifications, then you may be taking a risk with instruction and equipment.

As well as successfully completing the course remember that your ability, health and qualifications should be checked before any operator sells you courses or takes you out on an introductory dive. This is done through a check in a swimming pool or lagoon. All beginners must be able to swim at least 200 metres before proceeding. Certain medical conditions, such as asthma (or having a cold), do not go with diving. Also, you must remember that you should allow at least 24 hours between doing a dive and taking a flight.

Don't let having a certificate lull you into thinking that you know everything. Like any activity, experience is vitally important. As well as your diving certificate every diver has a log book in which they should record every dive they make. If a proposed dive is deep or difficult a good dive operator should check your log book to ensure experience is sufficient. A high proportion of diving accidents happen to inexperienced divers getting out of their depth.

More details of sites, schools and courses may be found under each country.

**Snorkelling** For the little paddlers, like us, who are content with snorkelling, watch out for sunburn, especially on your back. Wear a light T-shirt or slop on the water-resistant sun block creams and lotions.

### Surfing
Some of the surfing spots around Tamarin in Mauritius have been described as 'the perfect set up', with up to two metre waves. Other good surfing locations are near the Baie du Cap; 'Lefts and Rights', which is further south by Ilot Sancho; and one opposite the public gardens in Souillac. The surfing season is from June to August.

The only surf spots in Réunion are around St-Gilles-les-Bains. The best is said to be a reef break near the Club Med, but it is dangerous. Another good location is by the river near the Le Corail turtle farm in St-Leu. The most popular spot and surfing centre is Roches Noires beach at St-Gilles-les-Bains itself.

### Deep-Sea Fishing
Tourist bodies and beach hotels of each country continue to expand and heavily promote opportunities for deep-sea angling. For those who enjoy this 'sport', information has been provided where appropriate (check the Index for references).

### Other Water Sports
Other water sports, such as windsurfing, water-skiing, kayaking, pedalos, etc, are offered by the main beach hotels and often made available to nonresidents for a price.

See the Facts for the Visitor chapter of each country for lists of clubs and organisations that can help with information, hire equipment and organise marine recreation for visitors.

### Horse Riding
Horse riding opportunities on Mauritius are limited to Domaine Les Pailles, an estate run as a tourist attraction, including its own riding centre, Les Écuries du Domaine. For a list of horse riding centres in Réunion, see

the Activities section in the Réunion – Facts for the Visitor chapter.

Horse riding in the Seychelles is only available at the plush Barbarons Estate on the west coast of Mahé, near the hotel of the same name.

### Hunting

The hunting season for Java deer is from June to September. Hunting on estates is by invitation only. An exception to this rule is Domaine du Chasseur (☎ 6319259), Mauritius, an estate on the south-east coast where visitors can hunt deer either by stalking or from miradors (observation posts). More details about Domaine du Chasseur are provided in the South Mauritius chapter.

### Other Activities

See the Activities section in the Facts for the Visitor chapter for each country for information on other activities such as mountain bike riding, golf, abseilling and rock climbing. Tennis courts are available at most of the major hotels.

### MARINE LIFE

The Indian Ocean is a fascinating place for anybody with an interest in marine life. Coral reefs provide a home and shelter for an enormous variety of life. Most evident are, of course, the often fantastically colourful reef fish – but fish are only one of a host of species to be seen. Glass-bottom or semi-submersible boat trips, snorkelling or, best of all, scuba diving, will all help to open the door to the magical world below the surface.

### Coral

Coral is highly varied in its types but almost all the polyp skeletons are white – it's the living polyps which give coral its colourful appearance. During the day most polyps retract to the protection of their hard skeleton, so it's only at night that the full beauty of the hard corals can be seen. Hard coral is, however, only half the story. There is an equally varied assortment of soft corals. Like hard corals they are animals which gather in

colonies but they do not have the hard lime skeleton of their reef-building relations. For more information, see the Coral aside in this section.

### Fish

The Indian Ocean has several thousand species of fish and this remarkable variety includes everything from tiny diamond fish, the smallest backboned animals, to huge whale sharks. Some fish are seen in the day while others shelter in crevices and caverns in the coral and only emerge at night. Some are grazers, others hunters. Some huddle together in groups for protection while others move around by themselves. There are territorial species, guarding their own patch of reef fiercely, while others are free ranging.

### Echinoderms

The widely varied group of creatures known as echinoderms includes sea urchins, starfish or sea stars, brittle stars, feather stars and sea cucumbers. It appears to be a curiously diverse group but they all share basic structural similarities.

Starfish are highly visible since they have few natural enemies and do not hide away during daytime. Sea cucumbers, also known as bêche-de-mer, are also easy to see.

### Crustaceans

Hard-shelled crabs, shrimps, prawns and lobsters form another colourful and diverse group of reef creatures. The variety of shrimps is particularly large and many of them engage in the symbiotic relationships which are of such interest on the reef. Several types of shrimps act as cleaners – removing parasites, dead tissue and other waste matter from fishes.

### Molluscs

Like the echinoderms, molluscs include members that scarcely seem to bear any relationship to each other. Molluscs include a variety of shelled creatures or gastropods, the oysters, scallops and clams known as bivalves and also the cephalopods, a group which includes octopus and squid.

The mollusc family includes the many clams which appear to be embedded in the coral. Their fleshy mantles are seen in a spectacular array of colours.

Nudibranchs, or sea slugs, are snails which have abandoned their shells and put on their party clothes. They're some of the most colourful and graceful reef creatures you can see.

While some of the shells found in the Indian Ocean are incredibly beautiful there are some varieties, such as the cone shell, which can fire out a deadly poisonous barb.

## Whales & Dolphins

Fish are not the only creatures to be seen swimming around the waters of the Indian Ocean. The inviting waters are home to dolphins which can often be seen sporting around boats. After decades of being hunted almost to extinction, whales are returning to the region in increasing numbers. The shy and homely dugong is also found in shallow waters around reefs but it's a rare and now protected creature.

## Turtles

Several types of turtles are found in the Indian Ocean and although they are no longer present in the huge numbers of the

---

## Sex & Coral

Coral's sex life may be infrequent (it only happens once a year) but when it does it's certainly spectacular. Some coral polyps are all male or all female, while other colonies' polyps are hermaphrodite, that is they are both male and female. In a few types of coral these polyps can produce their own young which are released at various times over the year. In most cases, however, an hermaphrodite polyp's sperm cannot fertilise its own eggs or other eggs from the same colony.

Although the mass spawning which creates new coral only takes place once a year, the build-up to the big night lasts for six months or more. During that time the polyps ripen their eggs which are initially white but then change to pink, red, orange and other bright colours. At the same time the male testes form in the polyps and develop the sperm.

The big night comes in late spring or early summer, beginning a night or two after a full moon and building to a crescendo on the fourth, fifth and sixth nights. At this time the water temperature is right and tidal variation is at a minimum. Within the coral the eggs and sperm are formed into bundles and a half hour before spawning time the bundles are 'set', that is they are held ready at the mouth of the polyp, clearly visible through the thin tissue. Then these tiny bundles are released and float towards the surface.

The remarkable thing is that all over the reef this spawning takes place at the same time. Different colonies release their egg and sperm bundles, single sex polyps eject their sperm or their eggs, everything floats up. The egg and sperm bundles, big enough to be seen with the naked eye, are a spectacular sight. It's been described as looking like a fireworks display or an upside down snowstorm and since the event can be so accurately predicted divers are often able to witness it.

Once at the surface the bundles break up and the sperm swim off to find eggs of the same coral type. Obviously corals of the same type have to spawn at the same time in order for sperm from one colony to reach eggs from another, but the phenomenon is in all the corals spawning at once. It's far from easy for an individual sperm to find the right egg when the water is swarming with them but scientists think that by all spawning at once they reduce the risk of being consumed by the many marine creatures that would prey on them. By spawning soon after the full moon the reduced tidal variation means there is more time for fertilisation to take place before waves and currents sweep them away.

Once fertilisation has taken place the egg cells begin to divide, and within a day have become swimming coral larvae known as *planulae*. These are swept along by the sea but after a few days the planulae sink to the bottom and if the right spot is found, the tiny larvae become coral polyps and a new coral colony is begun. ■

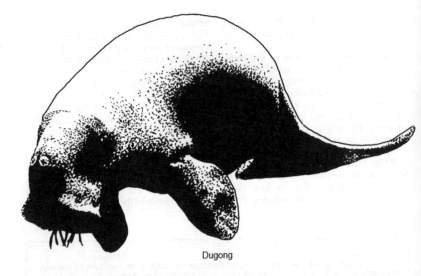

Dugong

past, there are a number of islands where they still come ashore to lay their eggs. Sea snakes, such as the yellow-bellied sea snake, are also present, but they're rarely seen by divers.

### Other Reef Life

Like coral, sponges are an animal and their basic form has changed very little over hundreds of millions of years. The Indian Ocean hosts a variety of worms, many of them colourful and strangely shaped creations totally unlike the typical terrestrial worm. Also found in the region are jellyfish, which are coelenterates and thus belong to the same family as coral and anemones.

### CONSERVATION

We strongly urge you not to buy anything made of turtle shell nor to buy or take shells from the beach. Stocks of turtles and many of the most beautiful shells have been cleared in many areas and some are actually endangered. Throughout much of the Indian Ocean, coral is being decimated by a plague of the crown of thorns starfish and the blame has been placed on the decimation of the

starfish's primary natural enemy, the lovely – and popular – triton's trumpet shell. Governments are trying to curb trade in and export of tortoiseshell, coral, shells and other natural products; please don't contribute to the problems by providing market incentives for the collectors.

### Marine Turtles

Throughout the Indian Ocean marine turtles still occur, albeit in dwindling numbers. Marine turtle species found in the Indian Ocean include the loggerhead turtle *(Caretta caretta)*, the green turtle *(Chelonia mydas)*, the leatherback turtle *(Dermochelys coriacea)*, and the hawksbill turtle *(Eretmochelys imbricata)*.

The downfall of many of these turtle species has been their edible flesh (and eggs), highly prized by local fishermen, and their carapace (tortoiseshell), which humans turn into fashionable ornaments. According to CITES (Convention on International Trade & Endangered Species), marine turtles are amongst the most endangered species, threatened by pollution and human exploitation.

For more information, contact the following publications and organisations:

*Marine Turtle Newsletter*
Karen & Scott Eckert, Hubbs-Sea World Research Institute, 1700 South Shores Road, San Diego, California 92109, USA
*Conservation International*
1015 Eighteenth St, NW Suite 1000, Washington, DC 20036, USA
*Greenpeace*
Canonbury Villas, London N1 2PN, England

You can play a positive role in ensuring that marine turtles have a future. If you visit a country where sea turtle products are available or where sea turtles nest, please do not eat turtle meat or soup; do not buy any sea turtle product souvenirs, such as hawksbill shell (commonly known as 'tortoiseshell') jewellery, ornaments, or stuffed turtles; take care not to disturb turtles or hatchlings and avoid using white light (for example, car headlights or torches) which can frighten nesting females and attract hatchlings away from the safety of the sea; and never throw plastic litter into the sea or coastal waterways because some turtles eat plastic bags (mistaking them for jellyfish) and suffer fatal intestinal problems as a result.

## Coral Reef Conservation

Most of the coastlines of Mauritius, the Seychelles, and the west coast of Réunion are fringed by coral reefs, fragile environments of calcareous deposits secreted by tiny marine animals known as coral polyps. The glorious white sand beaches of the Indian Ocean islands are composed of dead coral, shells and marine algae; without reefs, the beaches will erode and disappear. The reefs also provide shelter and habitat for numerous fish, shells, crustaceans, sea urchins and other marine life which in turn provide a food source for larger fish as well as humans, both directly and indirectly.

### Starfish

Starfish, *asteroids* or sea stars, are the most visible members of the very large group known as *echinoderms*. There are five distinct types of echinoderms including sea urchins, from which the group's name is derived. The other four are starfish, brittle stars, feather stars and sea cucumbers or bêche-de-mer. It is difficult to believe that creatures as different looking as the starfish and the sea cucumber are closely related but the group all share three distinct characteristics. These are a five-armed body plan, a skeleton of plates and tube feet which are operated by hydraulic pressure. The five-armed plan of the starfish is easy to see and the sea cucumber has the same plan, although it's hard to believe.

Starfish are bottom dwellers, like most echinoderms, and are very visible as they are often brightly coloured, do not move rapidly and in many cases don't hide away during the day. Generally they have five distinct arms, although some may have more – crown-of-thorns starfish usually have 15 or 16 but may have even more. In other starfish, like the rotund pincushion-looking sea star, the arms are not distinct at all but the five-cornered shape is still immediately apparent.

The five arms of a starfish each contain the full quota of organs for respiration, digestion, motion and reproduction. Along the underside of each arm is a groove from which emerge the tiny tube feet. These hydraulically operated feet are the starfish's actual means of locomotion, not the much larger arms. The starfish's mouth, with a surprisingly complex jaw, is at the bottom centre but some starfish, including the crown-of-thorns, can also consume their prey by a method known as 'stomach eversion'. The stomach is pulled out through the mouth and wrapped over the prey which is digested before the stomach is pulled back inside. Most starfish are carnivorous and can even force open the shells of a bivalve like an oyster, then evert their stomach into the opening to digest the bivalve.

Echinoderms in general have strong powers of regeneration and can often regenerate the entire creature from a single broken off arm. A regenerating starfish is known as a comet, since the newly regenerated parts do indeed look like a small star trailing a long, comet-like tail – the original larger arm. ■

A number of reef species engage in interesting symbiotic relationships, where two unrelated species get together in some activity for their mutual good.

The best recorded and, to the casual onlooker, most visible of these relationships is probably that of the anemone fish and the anemone. The brightly coloured anemone fish are a type of damselfish which have become acclimatised to living amongst the stinging tentacles of anemones. The bright orange clown anemone with its white vertical stripes edged with black is one of the most instantly recognisable fishes on the reef. A typical group of anemone fish will consist of several males and one larger female fish. They spend their entire life around the anemone, emerging briefly to feed then diving back into the protective tentacles at the first sign of danger. Anemone fish are not naturally immune to the anemone's sting, it is thought they gradually acquire immunity by repeatedly brushing themselves against the tentacles. Possibly they coat themselves with a layer of the anemone's mucus and the anemone does not sting the fish, just as its tentacles avoid stinging one another.

The relationship between anemone fish and the anemone is probably somewhat one-sided. The anemone fish may attract other fish within the anemone's grasp but an anemone can live without the anemone fish, the anemone fish are never seen without a protective anemone nearby.

Cleaner fish are another interesting reef relationship. The small cleaner wrasse performs a service job on larger fish. They set themselves up at 'cleaner stations' and wait for customers. The cleaners perform a small 'dance' to indicate they're ready for action and then zip around the larger fish nibbling off fungal growth, dead scales, parasites and the like. They will actually swim right into the mouth of larger fish to clean their teeth! Obviously this must be a tempting opportunity for the larger fish to get a quick free meal but cleaner fish are not threatened while they're at work.

The cleaner stations are an important part of reef life; some fish will regularly travel considerable distances for a clean and brush up and experimental removal of the cleaner fish from a section of reef has resulted in an increase in diseased and unhealthy fish and a fall in the general fish population. Certain varieties of shrimps also act as fish cleaners but in nature every situation presents an opportunity for some other creature and the reef also has false cleaners. These tiny fish masquerade as cleaners and then quickly take a bite out of the deceived larger fish. They've been known to take a nip at swimmers!

Even coral itself takes part in a symbiotic relationship. Within the cells of coral polyps are tiny single cell plants known as *zoocanthellae*. Like other plants they utilise sunlight to create energy and they also consume carbon dioxide produced by the coral. Their presence enables coral to grow much faster.

In the interest of preserving this vital environment, visitors participating in diving, snorkelling, sailboarding and other marine sports are requested to observe the following guidelines:

- Avoid touching or breaking coral branches, whether or not they appear to be dead.
- Don't practise sailboarding or boating in shallow lagoons where coral is present.
- Leave shells, starfish, sea urchins and other creatures where you find them.
- If at all possible, avoid walking on coral beds; swim or stick to the sandy bottoms.
- Don't fish in reef areas; hooks, harpoons, nets and other fishing apparatus are deadly to coral.
- Avoid throwing rubbish into the sea from either the shore or from boats. It winds up fouling reefs and beaches.
- Resist buying shells, coral jewellery and other marine products, regardless of their origin. By avoiding this largely illegal trade, you're preserving the reefs in other parts of the world.

## LANGUAGE

Along with local and Créole dialects, French is spoken on all three islands. The following concise list contains French words which

---

### Sponges

Sponges are amongst the most primitive of multi-celled creatures, in fact reefs were probably formed from sponge skeletons long before coral took over the reef construction business. Sponges still play a part in the growth of a reef as they bore into the coral and are a major factor in breaking down the limestone in a reef to eventually form the sand which can grow into a coral cay.

Sponges feed by filtering bacteria out of the water, which they do in amazing volume and with phenomenal efficiency. A sponge can typically handle their own volume of water every five to 20 seconds, and continue doing that 24 hours a day. As the water passes through their body, up to 99% of the bacteria is filtered out.

Despite this efficiency sponges have to look for additional ways to handle the nutrition they need. Some sponges have a form rather like a chimney and passing currents draw water up through the sponge. Most sponges also act as a home to blue-green algae, which pay rent by providing the host sponge with a share of their photosynthetic nutrient production. Other less welcome tenants also find that sponges make a good home – small crabs, shrimps, worms and even brittle stars often take up residence in a sponge's tubes and passages. ∎

---

may prove useful when looking for accommodation.

You'll find that menus in the Indian Ocean are mostly in French, with Créole variations in some cases. Included here is a list of French and Créole words which often turn up on menus.

| | |
|---|---|
| price, tariff | *prix, tarif* |
| included | *compris* |
| not included | *non compris* |
| per day | *par jour* |
| per week | *par semaine* |
| per month | *par mois* |
| bedroom | *chambre* |
| air-conditioned | *climatisé(e)* |
| single room | *chambre simple* |
| double room | *chambre double* |
| double bed | *grand lit* |
| extra bed | *lit supplémentaire* |
| twin beds | *lits jumeaux* |
| half board | *demi-pension* |
| full board | *pension complète* |
| meal | *repas* |
| breakfast | *petit déjeuner* |
| lunch | *déjeuner* |
| dinner | *dîner* |
| bathroom | *salle de bain* |
| shower | *douche* |
| toilet | *WC (pronounced 'doobla vay say')* |
| hot water | *eau chaude* |

| | |
|---|---|
| towels | *serviettes* |
| washbasin | *lavabo* |
| deposit | *dépôt de garantie, caution* |
| kitchen | *cuisine* |
| dining room | *salle à manger* |
| swimming pool | *piscine* |
| terrace, balcony | *terrasse* |
| facilities | *facilités* |
| with | *avec* |
| without | *sans* |
| on request | *sur demande, sur commande* |

### Seafood

| | |
|---|---|
| fish | *poisson* |
| trout | *truite* |
| tuna | *thon* |
| seafood | *fruits de mer* |
| lobster | *homard* |
| octopus | *poulpe* |
| sea urchins | *ourites* |
| giant prawn | *langouste* |
| prawns, shrimps | *crevettes* |
| squid | *calmar* |

### Meat

| | |
|---|---|
| meat (generic) | *viande* |
| beef | *boeuf* |
| chicken | *poulet* |
| duck | *canard* |

| | |
|---|---|
| goat | *chèvre* |
| kid | *cabri* |
| ham | *jambon* |
| rabbit | *lapin* |
| hare | *lièvre* |
| mutton | *mouton* |
| pork | *porc* |

## Vegetables

| | |
|---|---|
| vegetables | *légumes* |
| beans | *haricots* |
| cassava | *manioc* |
| chips | *pommes frites* |
| onions | *oignons* |
| potato | *pomme de terre* |
| sweet potato | *patate* |

## Fruit

| | |
|---|---|
| fruit | *fruit* |
| apple | *pomme* |
| banana | *banane* |
| coconut | *noix de coco* |
| custard apple | *corossol* |
| guava | *goyave* |
| lemon | *citron* |
| mango | *mangue* |
| orange | *orange* |
| passionfruit | *grenadelle* |
| pineapple | *ananas* |
| star fruit | *carambol* |

## Desserts

| | |
|---|---|
| dessert | *dessert* |
| cake | *gâteau* |
| cheese | *fromage* |
| ice cream | *glace* |
| jam | *confiture* |
| pastries | *pâtisseries* |
| sugar | *sucre* |

## Drinks

| | |
|---|---|
| drinks | *boissons* |
| milk | *lait* |
| fruit juice | *jus de fruit* |
| tea | *thé* |
| coffee | *café* |
| beer | *bière* |
| wine | *vin* |
| lemonade | *limonade* |

## Condiments

| | |
|---|---|
| chilli | *piment* |
| curry | *carri* |
| ginger | *gingembre* |
| pepper | *poivre* |
| salad dressing | *vinaigrette* |
| salt | *sel* |
| sweet and sour | *aigre-doux* |

## Miscellaneous

| | |
|---|---|
| bread | *pain* |
| butter | *beurre* |
| eggs | *oeufs* |
| noodles | *mines* |
| spring roll | *nems* |
| rice | *riz* |
| glass | *verre* |
| plate | *assiette* |
| cup | *tasse* |
| spoon | *cuiller* |
| knife | *couteau* |
| fork | *fourchette* |
| napkin | *serviette* |
| bill | *facture, addition* |
| daily special | *plat du jour* |
| vegetarian | *végétarien* |

## Time & Dates

| | |
|---|---|
| today | *aujourd'hui* |
| tomorrow | *demain* |
| yesterday | *hier* |
| in the morning | *le matin* |
| in the afternoon | *l'après-midi* |
| in the evening | *le soir* |
| | |
| Monday | *lundi* |
| Tuesday | *mardi* |
| Wednesday | *mercredi* |
| Thursday | *jeudi* |
| Friday | *vendredi* |
| Saturday | *samedi* |
| Sunday | *dimanche* |
| | |
| January | *janvier* |
| February | *février* |
| March | *mars* |
| April | *avril* |
| May | *mai* |
| June | *juin* |
| July | *juillet* |

| | | | |
|---|---|---|---|
| August | *août* | 13 | *treize* |
| September | *septembre* | 14 | *quatorze* |
| October | *octobre* | 15 | *quinze* |
| November | *novembre* | 16 | *seize* |
| December | *décembre* | 17 | *dix-sept* |
| | | 18 | *dix-huit* |
| **Numbers** | | 19 | *dix-neuf* |
| 0 | *zéro* | 20 | *vingt* |
| 1 | *un* | 21 | *vingt-et-un* |
| 2 | *deux* | 22 | *vingt-deux* |
| 3 | *trois* | 30 | *trente* |
| 4 | *quatre* | 40 | *quarante* |
| 5 | *cinq* | 50 | *cinquante* |
| 6 | *six* | 60 | *soixante* |
| 7 | *sept* | 70 | *soixante-dix* |
| 8 | *huit* | 80 | *quatre-vingts* |
| 9 | *neuf* | 90 | *quatre-vingt-dix* |
| 10 | *dix* | 100 | *cent* |
| 11 | *onze* | 1000 | *mille* |
| 12 | *douze* | one million | *un million* |

# Getting There & Away

This general discussion is designed to give you some basic ideas on how to reach the Indian Ocean area. More specific information is provided in the individual countries' Getting There & Away chapters.

## AIR
### Buying a Plane Ticket

Your plane ticket will probably be the single most expensive item in your budget, and buying it can be an intimidating business. There is likely to be a multitude of airlines and travel agents hoping to separate you from your money, and it is always worth putting aside a few hours to research the current state of the market. Start early: some of the cheapest tickets have to be bought months in advance, and some popular flights sell out early. Talk to other recent travellers – they may be able to stop you making some of the same old mistakes. Look at the ads in newspapers and magazines (not forgetting the press of the ethnic group whose country you plan to visit), consult reference books and watch for special offers. Then phone round travel agents for bargains. (Airlines can supply information on routes and timetables; however, except at times of inter-airline war, they do not supply the cheapest tickets.) Find out the fare, the route, the duration of the journey and any restrictions on the ticket. Then sit back and decide which is best for you.

You may discover that those impossibly cheap flights are 'fully booked, but we have another one that costs a bit more...' Or the flight is on an airline notorious for its poor safety standards and leaves you in the world's least favourite airport in mid-journey for 14 hours. Or they claim only to have the last two seats available for that country for the whole of July, which they will hold for you for a maximum of two hours. Don't panic – keep ringing around.

Use the fares quoted in this book as a guide only. They are approximate and based on the rates advertised by travel agents at the time of going to press. Quoted airfares do not necessarily constitute a recommendation for the carrier.

If you are travelling from the UK or the USA, you will probably find that the cheapest flights are being advertised by obscure bucket shops whose names haven't yet reached the telephone directory. Many such firms are honest and solvent, but there are a few rogues who will take your money and disappear, to reopen elsewhere a month or two later under a new name. If you are suspicious about a firm, don't give them all the money at once – leave a deposit of 20% or so and pay the balance when you get the ticket. If they insist on cash in advance, go somewhere else. And once you have the ticket, ring the airline to confirm that you are actually booked on the flight.

You may decide to pay more than the rock-bottom fare by opting for the safety of a better known travel agent. Firms such as STA, who have offices worldwide, Council Travel in the USA, or Travel CUTS in Canada are not going to disappear overnight, leaving you clutching a receipt for a non-existent ticket, but they do offer good prices to most destinations.

Once you have your ticket, write its number down, together with the flight number and other details, and keep the information somewhere separate. If the ticket is lost or stolen, this will help you get a replacement.

It's sensible to buy travel insurance as early as possible. If you buy it the week before you fly, you may find, for example, that you're not covered for delays to your flight caused by industrial action.

### Air Travellers with Special Needs

If you have special needs of any sort – you've broken a leg, you're vegetarian, travelling in

Top Left: Madame Paton (cattle egret), Victoria market, Mahé, Seychelles (RS)
Top Right: Aldabra tortoise, l'Islette, Mahé, Seychelles (RS)
Middle: Wright's skink, Cousin Island, Seychelles (RS)
Bottom: Mauritius kestrel, Domaine du Chasseur, Mauritius (RS)

Top: Carnivorous pitcher plant, Mont Pot à Eau, Silhouette, Seychelles (RS)
Bottom Left: Wild pineapple, Mahé, Seychelles (RS)
Bottom Right: Coco de Mer palms, Vallée de Mai, Praslin, Seychelles (DS)

a wheelchair, taking the baby, terrified of flying – you should let the airline know as soon as possible so that they can make arrangements accordingly. You should remind them when you reconfirm your booking (at least 72 hours before departure) and again when you check in at the airport. It may also be worth ringing round the airlines before you make your booking to find out how they can handle your particular needs.

Airports and airlines can be surprisingly helpful, but they do need advance warning. Most international airports will provide escorts from check-in desk to plane where needed, and there should be ramps, lifts, accessible toilets and reachable phones. Aircraft toilets, on the other hand, are likely to present a problem; travellers should discuss this with the airline at an early stage and, if necessary, with their doctor.

Guide dogs for the blind will often have to travel in a specially pressurised baggage compartment with other animals, away from their owner, though smaller guide dogs may be admitted to the cabin. All guide dogs will be subject to the same quarantine laws (six months in isolation, etc) as any other animal when entering or returning to countries currently free of rabies, such as the UK or Australia.

Deaf travellers can ask for airport and in-flight announcements to be written down for them.

Airlines will usually carry babies up to two years of age at 10% of the relevant adult fare, and some carry them free of charge. Reputable international airlines usually provide nappies (diapers), tissues, talcum and all the other paraphernalia needed to keep babies clean, dry and half-happy. For children between two and 12 years of age, the fare on international flights is usually 50% of the regular fare or 67% of a discounted fare. These days, most fares are considered to be discounted. 'Skycots' should be provided for infants by the airline if requested in advance; these will take a child weighing up to about 10 kg. Push chairs can often be taken as hand luggage.

## Student Travel

Worldwide, there are a number of student travel organisations which offer bargain-basement airfares to out-of-the-way destinations the world over, including the Indian Ocean and East Africa. Organisations which offer student services include:

Australia
    STA, 224 Faraday St, Carlton, Victoria, 3056
    (☎ (03) 347 6911)
    STA, 1A Lee St, Railway Square, Sydney, NSW
    (☎ (02) 212 1255)
Canada
    CHA 333 River Rd, Vanier, Ottawa, Ontario K1L
    8H9
    Canadian International Student Services, 80
    Richmond St W #1202 Toronto, Ontario M5H
    2A4 (☎ (416) 364 2738)
New Zealand
    STA, 10 High St, Auckland (☎ 390 458)
UK
    STA, 74 Old Brompton Rd, London SW7 3LQ
    (☎ 071-937 9971)
USA
    Whole World Travel, Suite 400, 17 East 45th St,
    New York, NY 10017 (☎ (212) 986 9470)
    Council on International Educational Exchange,
    205 East 42nd St, New York, NY 10017
    STA, 166 Geary St, San Francisco, CA 94108
    (☎ (415) 391 8407)
    STA, Suite 507, 2500 Wilshire Blvd, Los
    Angeles, CA 90057 (☎ (213) 380 2184)

## To/From the USA

In the USA, the best way to find cheap flights is by checking the Sunday travel sections in major newspapers such as the *Los Angeles Times*, *San Francisco Examiner* or *Chronicle* on the west coast and the *New York Times* on the east coast. The student travel bureaus – STA or Council Travel – are also worth a go but in the USA you'll have to produce proof of student status and in some cases be under 26 years of age to qualify for their discounted fares.

North America is a relative newcomer to the bucket-shop traditions of Europe and Asia, so ticket availability and the restrictions attached to them need to be weighed against what is offered on the standard Apex or full economy (coach) tickets. Do some homework before setting off. The magazines specialising in bucket-shop advertisements in London (see the discussion under To/From Europe) will post copies so you can study current pricing before you decide on a course of action. Also recommended is the newsletter *Travel Unlimited* (PO Box 1058, Allston, MA 02134) which publishes details of the cheapest airfares and courier possibilities for destinations all over the world from the USA.

**Non-Discounted Tickets** Due to excessive competition between carriers and a lot of governmental red tape in determining fare structures, flights originating in the USA are subject to numerous restrictions and regulations. This is especially true of bargain tickets; anything cheaper than the standard tourist or economy fare must be purchased at least 14 days, and sometimes as much as 30 days, prior to departure.

In addition, you'll have to book departure and return dates in advance and these tickets will be subject to minimum and maximum stay requirements: usually seven days and six months, respectively. It's often cheaper to purchase a return ticket and trash the return portion than to pay the one-way fare. From the USA, open tickets which allow an open return date within a 12-month period are generally not available, and penalties of up to 50% are imposed if you make changes to the return booking.

Travellers from the USA to the Indian Ocean region will probably have to think in terms of flying via Paris. On whatever bargain-basement trans-Atlantic carrier is currently operating, you can hop across the pond for about US$130 one way.

From the USA the major carrier gateway city to Europe is naturally New York, but there are also direct flights from nearly every other major city in the country, including Los Angeles, Houston, Miami and Boston. Economy fares must often be purchased two weeks in advance, with a requirement of a minimum stay of two weeks and a maximum stay of three months usually applied.

## To/From Canada
Travel CUTS has offices in all major Canadian cities. The *Toronto Globe & Mail* carries travel agents' ads. The magazine *Great Expeditions* (PO Box 8000-411, Abbotsford BC V2S 6H1) is useful. Travellers interested in booking flights with Canadian courier companies should obtain a copy of the *Travel Unlimited* newsletter mentioned in the To/From the USA section.

## To/From Europe
**Finding Discounted Tickets** There are bucket shops by the dozen in London, Paris, Amsterdam, Brussels, Frankfurt and a few other places. In London, several magazines with lots of bucket-shop ads can put you on to the current deals. In these magazines, you'll often find discounted fares to Nairobi or Mauritius. A word of warning, however: don't take the advertised fares as gospel truth. To comply with advertising laws in the UK, companies must be able to offer *some* tickets at their cheapest quoted price, but they may only have one or two of them per week. If you're not one of the lucky ones, you'll be looking at higher priced tickets. The best thing to do is begin looking for deals well in advance of your intended departure so you can get a fair idea of what's available. Following is a list of publications and organisations which have travel information for budget travellers:

*Trailfinder*
> This magazine is put out quarterly by Trailfinders (☎ 071-938 3939/3366) from 9 am to 6 pm Monday to Friday UK time or fax 071-938 3305 anytime), 42-48 Earls Court Rd, London W8 6EJ, UK. It's free if you pick it up in London but if you want it mailed, it costs UK£6 for four issues in the UK or Ireland, and UK£10 or the equivalent for four issues in Europe or elsewhere (airmail). Trailfinders can fix you up with all your ticketing requirements as well. They've been in business for years, their staff are friendly and we highly recommend them.

*Time Out*
> Tower House, Southampton St, London WC2E 7HD (☎ 071-836 4411). This is London's weekly entertainment guide and contains travel information and advertising. It's available at bookshops, newsagents and newsstands. Subscription enqui-

ries should be addressed to Time Out Subs, Unit 8, Grove Ash, Bletchley, Milton Keynes MK1 1BZ, UK.

*TNT Magazine*
52 Earls Court Rd, London W8, UK (☎ 071-937 3985). This free magazine can be picked up at most London Underground stations and on street corners around Earls Court and Kensington. It caters to Aussies and Kiwis working in the UK and is therefore full of travel advertising.

*Globe*
*Globe* is a newsletter published for members of the Globetrotters' Club (BCM Roving, London WC1N 3XX). It covers obscure destinations and can be handy to help find travelling companions.

Look also for travel agents' ads in the Sunday papers, travel magazines and listings magazines such as *City Limits*.

To initiate your price comparisons, you could contact travel agents such as Trailfinders (☎ 071-938 3939/3366); STA (☎ 071-937 9971) in London; or the highly recommended Travel Bug (☎ 061-721 4000) in Manchester. For courier flight details, contact Polo Express (☎ 081-759 5383) or Courier Travel Service (☎ 071-351 0300).

On the continent, the newsletter *Farang* (La Rue 8 à 4261, Braives, Belgium) deals with exotic destinations, as does the magazine *Aventure au Bout du Monde* (116 Rue de Javel, 75015 Paris).

### To/From Australia & New Zealand

Travel between Australasia and the western Indian Ocean has recently become more convenient with the addition of the Air Mauritius flight Sydney/Perth/Mauritius. Alternatively, take a Singapore Airlines flight to Mauritius via Singapore (you may be able to arrange a stop-over in Singapore if you want). You can also arrange it so that you fly to Singapore and, once there, catch either a connecting Air Seychelles flight to the Seychelles, or a flight to Mauritius aboard Air Mauritius or South African Airways. Another option is to go to Kuala Lumpur in Malaysia and then catch a connecting Air Mauritius flight to Mauritius.

Another option for Australasians is an RTW (round-the-world) ticket via Africa, visiting the Indian Ocean as an add-on from either Harare or Nairobi. RTW tickets with various stopovers can still be found for as little as A$2100, but often these include only northern hemisphere stopovers; surcharges are levied if the traveller wants to include Africa.

If coming from Australia, New Zealand or Asia, you can fly out of Singapore to the Seychelles on Tuesdays with Air Seychelles. An excursion fare from Singapore is S$1200. A return fare from Melbourne to the Seychelles via Singapore is A$1800 during the low season (16 January to 21 November) and A$2300 during the high season (22 November to 15 January). Return fares from Melbourne to Europe with a stopover in the Seychelles range between A$2800 and A$3000 depending on the season. Or you can fly to Mauritius with Singapore Airlines and up to the Seychelles with British Airways or Air France (see Getting There chapter in the Mauritius section for details).

The best publications for finding good deals are the Saturday editions of the daily newspapers such as the *Sydney Morning Herald* and the Melbourne *Age*. Alternatively, try STA which has branches at universities and in all state capitals.

### To/From Africa

You can fly to Mauritius direct from Johannesburg or Durban in South Africa, Harare (Zimbabwe), Antananarivo (Madagascar), Moroni (Comoros) or Nairobi (Kenya).

Air France has flights to Réunion from Paris via Madagascar, Moroni, Nairobi and Djibouti, and the same airline also serves the French island of Mayotte in the Comoros.

Air Kenya and British Airways fly to the Seychelles from Nairobi; Air France has six flights a week from Paris to the Seychelles via Djibouti.

### To/From Asia

Singapore, Kuala Lumpur and Bombay have good air links with Mauritius, and there is a once-weekly flight from Singapore to the Seychelles. To get to Réunion, you have to go via Mauritius or the Seychelles.

**To/From Other Indian Ocean Countries**

Once you get into the region, the island-hopping, if that's not too light a term in this case, becomes easier and cheaper. The best way of covering all three islands is with a round-trip air ticket using several airlines. The only condition is that you must continue the route in a circle; ie, you can't double back. This means you can also take in Madagascar, Comoros and Kenya. These round-trip air tickets are good bargains if you have the time.

Make all enquiries and bookings through a major tour operator or travel agency such as Rogers in Port Louis, Mauritius, or Bourbon Voyages in St Denis, Réunion, but not directly through the airlines. You'll have a better shot at a good deal. The same applies in your own country.

Refer to the islands' individual Getting There chapters for costs and more specific details of air and sea travel.

**BOAT**

Opportunities for sea travel to Mauritius, the Seychelles and Réunion are limited to passing cruise liners, yachts and the very occasional cargo-passenger ship. The cost is high, unless you can work your way as crew. The cruise liners usually only stop for a day or two. Sea travel between the Seychelles, Mauritius and Réunion is out of the question unless you have your own yacht or enough money and time to charter one.

If you want to try crewing onto a yacht, it is possible but your chances are slim. Remember that even if you do strike it lucky and find someone who is looking for crew, they'll be very fussy about whom they'll take.

Yacht skippers normally look for someone with a bit of cash money as well as sailing experience; you must reckon on paying a minimum of US$10 or the equivalent per day for expenses. There is no such thing as a free ride, unless you come across a rich playboy or playgirl who likes the cut of your jib. You must also have the right temperament, as conditions are difficult aboard a yacht. There's no privacy, nowhere to escape to if tension breaks and no buts about it – the skipper is boss.

Cruising time between the island countries varies depending on the weather conditions and the direction you're heading in. About 160 km in 24 hours is a rough rule of thumb. But there is no long-distance sailing between or around Mauritius and Réunion during the cyclone season (November to April). The Seychelles lies outside the cyclone zone.

# Mauritius

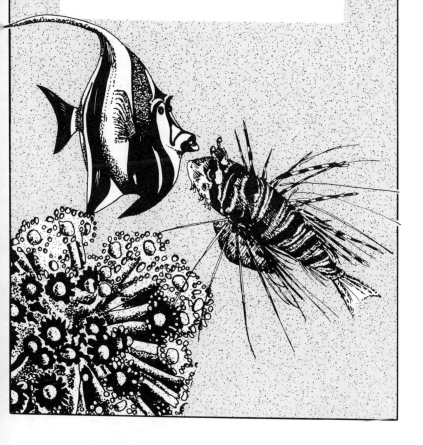

# Facts about the Country

It's hard to sing the praises of Mauritius when comparing it with other Indian Ocean countries. That's not to say it's second best – far from it. Perhaps the best thing about Mauritius is that it grows on you. Its beauties and pleasures are not immediate. Mauritius has industries and overpopulation. It is as green and lush as the Seychelles, but not as beautiful to look at. The mountains are pretty, but not as spectacular as those of Réunion. The beaches are good, but not great.

However, there are more things to do and see in Mauritius. Even better, it is cheaper to stay, eat and get around in Mauritius than in Réunion or the Seychelles. For the cost of a week in Réunion, you can stay three weeks in Mauritius. This makes Mauritius an excellent, relatively untapped destination for the traveller. The life style is active, but not hectic, so rather than try to get away from it all, you have to dive into it. Although tourism is on the rise again, most visitors tend to stay in luxury hotels and only venture out on occasional sightseeing or shopping trips.

With 60% of the population Hindu, the flavour is distinctly Indian. But the Franco-Mauritians, Créoles, Chinese and Muslims each play a large part in the economy, society and administration of the country, which is done mostly on a British model, thus giving visitors the best of several worlds.

## HISTORY

Mauritius has a colonial history. It has experienced four changes of 'ownership' and name between being first inhabited, in 1598, and independence, in 1968.

Understandably, the presently ruling Indian community does not take great pride in much of the past. Following the liberation of African slaves in 1835, the Indians were brought by the British to Mauritius, along with the Chinese, as cheap labour for the sugar cane plantations. Consequently, the government makes little effort to preserve historical sites and artefacts.

### The Portuguese & the Dutch

Arab traders knew of Mauritius as early as the 10th century. They called the uninhabited island Dinarobin, but did not settle it.

Nor did the Portuguese naval explorers settle Mauritius when they discovered it in the wake of Vasco da Gama's famous trip around the Cape of Good Hope in 1498, though they are credited with the first European landing. Instead, they continued on to the east coast of Africa, Indonesia and India to establish colonies.

Domingo Fernandez dropped anchor in Mauritius in 1511. He named the island Ilha do Cerne (Swan Island); perhaps this was the name of his ship or he might have been referring to the native dodo, which he took to be a sort of swan.

Rodrigues Island, 560 km to the north-east, takes its name from another navigator, Don Diego Rodrigues, who called by in 1528. Together with Réunion, the two islands were named the Mascarenes, after Portuguese admiral Don Pedro Mascarenhas. Apart from introducing pesky monkeys, rats and other animals, the Portuguese did little to Mauritius. That was left to the next wave of maritime supremos, the Dutch.

In 1598, Vice Admiral Wybrandt van Warwyck landed on the south-east coast of the island, claimed it for the Netherlands and named it Mauritius, after his ruler, Maurice, Prince of Orange and Count of Nassau. It was another 40 years before the Dutch decided to try settling the country, preferring to use it as a supply base for Batavia (Java). When they did settle in Mauritius, it was around their original landing spot. Settlement ruins can be seen opposite the church at Vieux Grand Port, near Mahébourg.

The colony never really flourished and the Dutch departed for good in 1710, leaving their mark behind. They are held to blame for the extinction of the dodo and the introduction of slaves from Africa, deer from Java, wild boar, tobacco and, above all, sugar cane. In 1642 they also sent Abel Tasman off from the island to discover Tasmania, Fiji and New Zealand.

## The French

Five years later Captain Guillaume Dufresne d'Arsal sailed across from Réunion, then called Bourbon, and claimed the island for France. It was renamed Île de France and given over to the Compagnie des Indes Orientales (French East India Company) to run as a trading base.

The French decided they would stay for good, and settlement began in 1721. Not until 1735 did things start moving under the governorship of Bertrand François Mahé de Labourdonnais, Mauritius' first hero. Under his leadership, port facilities were expanded, the first sugar mill and hospital were built and a road network was established. Also during his administration, Mauritius' best known historic event occurred – the *St Géran* tragedy.

In 1744, the *St Géran* was wrecked during a storm, off Île d'Ambre, near the north-east coast, whilst waiting to enter Port Louis to unload machinery for the new sugar mill. The event inspired Bernardin de St Pierre's romantic novel *Paul et Virginie*, an early best seller (see the Books & Bookshops section in the Mauritius – Facts for the Visitor chapter). A few years later, Labourdonnais went off to help fight the British in India and ended up in the Bastille, after falling out with his own side. He was released and his name eventually cleared.

As the English gained the upper hand in the Indian Ocean during the second half of the 18th century, the Compagnie des Indes Orientales collapsed and the sugar industry strengthened. Port Louis became a free trading base and a haven for corsairs – mercenary marines paid by a country to prey on the ships of its enemy. The most famous Franco-Mauritian corsair was Robert Surcouf. Freebooting English, American and French pirates, who had been operating so successfully out of Madagascar towards the end of the 17th and beginning of the 18th centuries, gave way to these licensed and semi-respectable pirates.

In 1789 the French colonialists in Mauritius recognised the revolution in France and got rid of their governor. But they refused to get rid of their slaves when the abolition of slavery was decreed in Paris in 1794.

## The British

In 1810, during the Napoleonic Wars, the British moved in on the corsairs and on Mauritius. At first, they were defeated at the Battle of Vieux Grand Port, the only French naval victory inscribed on the Arc de Triomphe in Paris. Later, they landed at Cap Malheureux on the north coast and took over the island.

The Treaty of Paris in 1814 gave Île de France, along with Rodrigues and the Seychelles, to the British. They changed its name back to Mauritius, but allowed the Franco-Mauritians to retain their language, religion, Napoleonic Code legal system and sugar cane plantations. In 1835, the slaves were freed and replaced or supplemented by imported labour from India and China.

The British opened up an international market for Mauritian sugar and it became the island's *raison d'être* for the next 150 years. Indian workers continued to be indentured in their thousands. The Franco-Mauritian families produced wealthy sugar barons, and indeed continue to do so to the present day. Through strength of numbers, the Indian workforce gradually achieved a greater say in the running of the country. The Indian political and spiritual leader, Mahatma Gandhi, visited Mauritius in 1901 to push for civil rights.

The island remained relatively unscathed by WW I and WW II. The greatest upheavals to the country and its one-crop economy were caused by cyclones, malaria epidemics (one in 1867 killed half the population of Port Louis), slumps and booms in the world

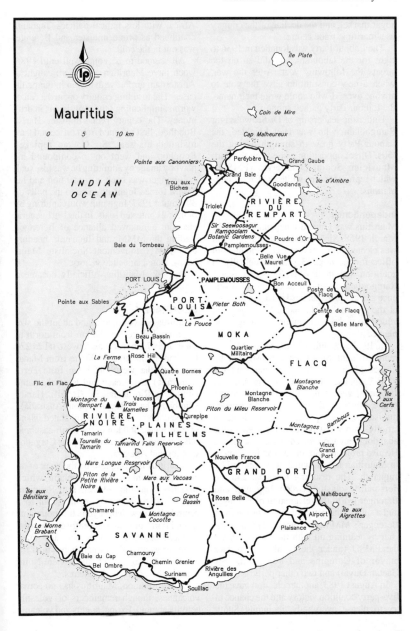

sugar market, and the decline of the country as a maritime trade centre.

The Labour Party was founded in 1936 to fight for the labourers, and did so on the streets the following year. After the war, when a new constitution gave the vote to anyone over 21 who could write their name, the Labour Party gained support.

Under the leadership of Dr Seewoosagur Ramgoolam, who was later knighted, the Labour Party grew in strength during the '50s. Direct opposition came from the Parti Mauricien Social Démocrate (PMSD), which represented the white and Créole populations.

### Independence
Mauritius was granted independence on 12 March 1968. Sir Seewoosagur Ramgoolam was elected prime minister and remained in office for the next 13 years, eventually in coalition with the PMSD. Sir Seewoosagur Ramgoolam continued to command reverence as a grand leader until his death in 1986, at the age of 86. His name has now been added to a host of public buildings and places.

In 1982 a coalition of the leftist Mouvement Militant Mauricien (MMM), led by Franco-Mauritian Paul Bérenger, and the Parti Socialiste Mauricien, led by Anerood Jugnauth, gained power. Jugnauth became prime minister. Bérenger became finance minister and perhaps surprisingly adopted a strictly monetarist policy which led to the abandonment of promised welfare measures. He also promoted South African investment in Mauritian hotels, which was opposed by Jugnauth. The resulting tensions, and the personality clash between Jugnauth and Bérenger led to the resignation of Bérenger and a split in the party. Jugnauth broke from Bérenger's MMM, but remained prime minister by teaming up with the Labour Party, the PMSD (under the flamboyant former mayor of Curepipe and Port Louis, Sir Gaetan Duval) and two other parties.

In August 1983, another election gave the five-party coalition victory and the chance to try to please everybody, including South Africa, with less radical policies. Jugnauth continued as prime minister and Bérenger was out in the cold.

All seemed to be going well until 1986, when three Mauritian MPs were caught at Amsterdam airport with heroin in their suitcases. The resulting enquiry opened a can of worms, implicating other politicians in drug money. The deputy prime minister, Harish Boodhoo, first resigned from office and later resigned his seat. Sir Gaetan replaced Boodhoo and went on to compound his playboy image by admitting he was bisexual.

Bérenger was back in contention and his MMM forced Jugnauth to go to the polls on 30 August 1987. Jugnauth won, capturing 39 of the 62 contested seats. In the 1991 general election, a renewed alliance of Bérenger, leading the MMM, and Jugnauth, heading the MSM (Mouvement Socialiste Mauricien), won a landslide victory.

In 1992, Mauritius officially became a republic.

### GEOGRAPHY
Mauritius is a volcanic island about the size of an English county, 58 km from north to south and 47 km from east to west. It lies 220 km from Réunion and 800 km from Madagascar to the west; 5854 km from Perth (Australia) to the east; and is on the same latitude as Rio de Janeiro (Brazil), Harare (Zimbabwe) and Rockhampton (Australia).

The country includes the inhabited island of Rodrigues, 560 km to the north-east, and other scattered coral atolls such as Cargados Carajos and Agalega.

Mauritius is thought to be the peak of an enormous sunken volcanic chain which stretches from the Seychelles to Réunion. The island rises steeply in the south to a central plateau which, beyond the mountains behind Port Louis, slopes gently down to the northern coast. The mountains are noted more for gaunt and unusual shapes than for height. The Piton de la Petite Rivière Noire is the highest peak at 828 metres.

Unlike Réunion, Mauritius has no active volcanoes, though remainders of volcanic activity abound. Extinct craters and volcanic lakes, such as the Trou aux Cerfs crater in Curepipe and the Grand Bassin holy lake, are good examples. Millions of lava boulders, further reminders of volcanic activity, cover the island. Hundreds of little pyramids of these rocks, which had to be gathered to clear the land for sugar cane, can be seen dotting the cane fields.

Mauritius is surrounded by a coral reef which provides several long stretches of white coral sand beaches. The reef is broken in many places. Between Souillac and Le Bouchon, on the southern coast, the sea crashes through the largest break in the reef and against the black cliffs, creating a rugged, wild coastline. There is a similar, though not so spectacular, break in the reef above Flic en Flac on the west coast.

## CLIMATE

The Mauritian climate is a mixed affair. Different regions of Mauritius are affected in different ways. Up on the plateau around Curepipe, temperatures average 5°C cooler than on the coast. It can be raining up there while it's clear around the coast, and vice versa. Similarly, east coast weather differs

from that of the west coast. The east coast is also much drier during January and February when the prevailing winds drive in from the east, hit the mountains, and dump rain on central and western Mauritius.

The hottest months are from January to April, when temperatures range from 25°C to 35°C. It's nice to get away from the northern hemisphere winter, but it can prove too hot and humid for some. This is also the cyclone season and although a direct hit only happens about once every 16 years, the island still suffers days of squally depression from the several cyclones that occur in the region each year. It's unlikely one will ruin your holiday.

There are no distinct monsoons. It can rain any and every day of the year. When it's not blowing from the north, the breeze comes from the south-east, courtesy of the regular trade winds.

The depths of a Mauritian 'winter' occur from July to September when temperatures average a chastening 24°C during the day and 16°C at night. This can be more pleasant. There is less rain and humidity, and less chance of frying yourself.

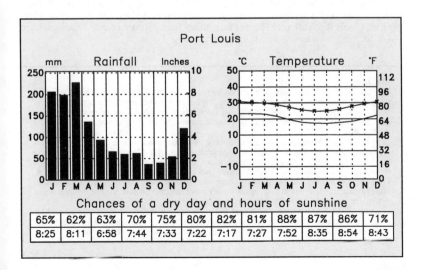

## FLORA & FAUNA

It's easy to think that as a result of the extinction of the dodo we are now sadder and wiser, but there's a lot of evidence to suggest that we are merely sadder and better informed.

*Last Chance to See* by Douglas Adams & Mark Carwardine

Together with the Seychelles and Madagascar, Mauritius is a haven for the botanist, biologist, zoologist, ornithologist and other '-ologists'. Mauritius is, or rather was, the home of the dodo. The funny, fat, flightless bird was wiped out not long after the island was first settled by the Dutch. The poor things were defenceless against humans and their pets or pests – dogs, monkeys, pigs and rats.

Several other species disappeared forever, including the black, flightless parrot, rails (small wading birds) and the giant Mauritian tortoise. Some unique, if less unusual, species survived. The same applies to the natural forests and vegetation, much of which was cleared or altered with the spread of sugar cane fields and the introduction of other plants and trees.

To experience most of what the island has to offer in the way of flora and fauna, the visitor must go to Sir Seewoosagur Ramgoolam and Curepipe botanical gardens, Casela Bird Park near Flic en Flac,

Domaine du Chasseur near Mahébourg, Le Val Nature Park, Île aux Aigrettes, Black River Gorges National Park, La Vanille Crocodile Farm near Souillac and, for stuffed replicas, to the Mauritius Institute in Port Louis. These places are dealt with in more detail in their respective area sections.

### Flora

Almost one third of the 900 plant species of Mauritius occur only on this island. Many of these indigenous plants have fared poorly in competition with introduced plants, especially guava and privet, and have been depleted by introduced animals, such as deer, pigs, and monkeys. General forest clearance and the establishment of crop monocultures have exacerbated the problem, so that Mauritius now possesses less than 1% of intact, original forest.

To research and conserve native species, the government Forestry Service together with the Mauritian Wildlife Appeal Fund (MWAF) and Royal Society of Arts and Sciences has set aside special vegetation plots which are protected from animal depredation and carefully weeded to remove the much faster growing introduced species. Rare species are propagated in government nurseries and then planted in these plots where they have a better chance of survival and

### Mangroves

The Collins English dictionary defines mangroves as 'Any tropical evergreen tree or shrub of the genus *Rhizophora*, having stiltlike intertwining aerial roots and forming dense thickets along coasts'. They are a much maligned species, the word that usually follows *mangrove* is *swamp* and the image is of something dark, muddy, smelly, full of insects and generally most unattractive.

In actual fact mangroves are an extremely interesting plant whose vital environmental importance has only been recognised comparatively recently. Mangroves are the advance troops, the first plants to reclaim land from the sea and they are able to do this because of their remarkable resistance to saltwater. Saltwater will kill most plants but mangroves thrive in it. They can either restrict its entry through their roots or expel excess salt through their leaves. Their remarkable adaptation to a hostile environment can also be seen in their extensive root system, which enables them to grown in unstable tidal mud.

Gradually mangroves create new land, but in the process they provide an environment for a host of other living things from oysters, crabs and snails to the mudskipper fishes that prefer to scamper around on top of mangrove mud rather than swim in water, like any normal fish. ■

regeneration. It is hoped that these areas will provide an added bonus by attracting and supporting rare Mauritian bird species, such as the echo parakeet, pink pigeon, and Mauritian cuckoo-shrike. Similar work is being done on Île aux Aigrettes, Round Island, and Rodrigues Island (for more details, see the respective chapters).

For a tropical island, Mauritius is not big on coconut palms. Instead, casuarinas fringe all the best beaches. These tall, slim trees look like limp-wristed pines, but although they cast needles galore, they are not members of the pine species at all. The casuarinas, which are also known as *filaos* from the Portuguese, act as useful wind-breaks and grow well in sandy soil. They may not be as visually appealing as palms but they are more aurally pleasing when you listen to the wind whistling through the branches.

Along with casuarinas, eucalyptus trees have been widely planted to make up for the decimation of the original forests. These included the tambalacoque tree, which is also known as the dodo tree and is not far from extinction itself. You'll find it, with the services of a guide, only in the forests south of Curepipe and Mare aux Vacoas. It's a tall tree with a silver trunk and a large, strange-looking, brown seed that is half smooth and half rough. Scientists are sceptical about the rumour that the dodo acted as a germinator, feeding on the tough seed which germinated easily after being passed through the bird's stomach.

Other impressive trees, which you don't have to go off the beaten track to see, are the giant Indian banyan and the brilliant red-flowering flamboyant.

Staying with shades of red, one flower you will see in abundance is anthurium, with its single, glossy petal and protruding yellow spadix. The flower, which at first sight you'd swear was synthetic, can last up to three weeks after being cut and is therefore a popular display plant. Now grown in commercial quantities for export, it is used to spruce up hotel and business rooms and public meeting places. The flower originated in South America and was introduced to Mauritius at the end of last century.

## Fauna

The first animal any visitor to Mauritius is likely to meet, unfortunately, is the domestic dog – although there's nothing domesticated about it.

Every family seems to have a mangy mongrel for 'security' purposes. *Chien méchant* (dangerous dog) is a common notice on house gates. Although the dogs' bark is generally worse than their bite, walking along some streets in the dark can be a nightmare. The dogs howl all night and have few redeeming qualities in the morning – you're just too tired to throttle one. From the roadside you may also catch glimpses of the mongoose, crossing from cane field to cane field, and Java deer, which were first imported by the Dutch for meat and are now hunted from June to September.

You must venture further into the wild, particularly around the Rivière Noire (Black River) gorges, to come in contact with wild pigs and bands of macaque monkeys. You'll see little else and there are no dangerous animals.

**Birdlife** The best known representative of Mauritian birdlife was the dodo, a large, plump, flightless dove which found its docility rewarded with extinction in the late 17th century. Although the dodo has since become a stereotype for extinction, few people realise that Mauritius still possesses several incredibly rare bird species in minute numbers which are as doomed as the dodo if the present efforts at conservation cannot be sustained.

The Mauritius kestrel suffered a massive decline in numbers as a result of habitat destruction, pesticide poisoning, and hunting. In 1974, the population of kestrels living in the wild was down to four birds. The Mauritius Kestrel Conservation Program, started in 1973, has used captive breeding followed by release and management of the birds in the wild to produce an amazing recovery. In 1992, the kestrel population had risen to 200 birds in the wild, including 35 breeding pairs.

The echo parakeet is the world's rarest parakeet. In 1992, its population was estimated at a mere 15 birds (including only four females). Since 1985, MWAF has been running a project to protect wild parakeets and boost their numbers through captive breeding.

The pink pigeon, the largest of all the pigeons and doves found on Mauritius, is another highly endangered species. The population is currently estimated at some 30 birds. Impediments to progress include poor nesting results due to predation from monkeys and rats, and what one might term a public relations problem – released birds ending up in local casseroles.

The native songbirds of Mauritius, such as the Mauritius cuckoo-shrike, Mauritius black bulbul, Mascarene paradise flycatcher, Mauritius fody, and Mauritius olive white-eye are also threatened. Many of these species are already down to a couple of hundred birds.

The predominant species include many introduced songbirds, such as the little red Madagascar fody, the Indian mynah with yellow beak and feet which make it look like it's just stepped out of a cartoon, the village Weaver, and the commonest bird on Mauritius – the Red-whiskered Bulbul.

**Marine Life** The rich tapestry of amazing fish and shells that you'll see around all the Indian Ocean islands is also found in Mauritius. Very recently, a survey conducted by MWAF showed that whales (finback, pilot, beaked, and sperm), dolphins (spinner and bottle-nosed), and turtles (green and hawksbill) are relatively common off the shores of Mauritius.

Game fishing is flourishing, but the subaqua set is not as well catered for, naturally or commercially, as it is in the Maldives or the Seychelles. For the tourist or casually interested person, there's a reasonable aquarium near Trou aux Biches, in the north-west.

A group of underwater sports enthusiasts and conservationists have formed the Mauritius Marine Conservation Society (MMCS) (☎ 6965368) and the associated Mauritius Underwater Group (MUG) to campaign against pollution and destruction of the coral reefs around Mauritius. Full details about MMCS and MUG are provided in the section on Useful Organisations in the Mauritius – Facts for the Visitor chapter.

A recent MMCS report called for marine biologists and fisheries experts to assess and evaluate the long term effects on the marine environment of the increasing population of Mauritius, the growth of industry, and the use of chemical fertilisers in agriculture.

In the last two decades some divers have been greatly concerned by the decline in the marine resources of the island and the widespread death of corals. Some of the causes already identified include indiscriminate fishing with spearguns, and the collection of shells. This has made coastal waters less attractive to tourist and resident divers and less productive as a source of food.

In the past, the frequent use of explosives to harvest fish was a wasteful and dangerous fishing method which destroyed many reef ecosystems. Damage is caused to corals by anchors and through removal by tourists and

Dodo

**Sex & Fish**

Nobody ever told reef fish those nice straightforward 'birds and the bees' stories – a high proportion of the fish you see around the Indian Ocean reefs are able to change their sex at some time in their life! Some of them are protandry – they start as males then switch to become females – others are protogyny – they start as females and switch to become males. Some of these fish are monandrous, that is they are all born one sex and only switch to the other sex later. Other species may be born either sex but some of them may later change sex.

The tiny angelfish is an example of protogyny. These fish normally live in small groups of four to seven which control a territory of several square metres. The group usually consists of one larger dominant male with a 'harem' of female fish, although there may sometimes be a smaller 'bachelor' male fish present. The dominant male guards the group's territory and warns off any intruding angelfish. At mating time the male mates with all the females in the group. If the dominant male dies the largest female changes sex and takes over. It appears to be the dominant male which prevents females from changing sex earlier. The male 'dominates' and harasses the larger females and somehow this affects their hormone balance and prevents them changing sex. As soon as the male is removed the largest and most aggressive female is able to switch sexes and start in on dominating her sisters!

The opposite situation can be observed in the familiar clown anemone fish. The small group which shelters around a protective anemone usually consists of a large adult female and a group of smaller males. The female mates with only one of the males and this mature male fish keeps all the other 'bachelor' anemone fish in line. If something happens to the female then the chief male switches sex and becomes the new female, while the most dominant and aggressive of the other males takes over as the new chief male.

Scientists have postulated a number of reasons for this strange state of affairs. Life on the reef is dangerous and very much dog eat dog. If changing sex were not possible and the sole male or female in the group died then the group could not reproduce. As it is there's just a quick change of sex on the part of one fish and life continues as normal! Competition is fierce and by staking out their own small territory and defending it against intruders the small groups of reef fish ensure their own survival. ■

local snorkelers. The wholesale removal of sea sand for building destroys an important lagoon ecosystem and causes erosion of beaches. The increasing use of the lagoons for recreation and tourism has considerably reduced the pristine areas of shoreline and coast.

The quality of the marine environment is further impaired by disturbance from motor boats, fishermen, divers, and others. Whales, dolphins and turtles are harassed and killed, and even the gazetted 'fishing reserves' are not respected. Increasing pollution of the coastal waters by river-borne refuse, sewerage outfalls and waste from fishing boats has also been noticed.

It is also an unfortunate fact that existing legislation which forbids the use of explosives, spearfishing, collecting of corals and shells, and fishing in some areas and in certain periods, appears difficult to enforce.

MMCS has issued a recommended code

of conduct to respect the lagoons and reefs of Mauritius:

1. take care not to remove or break any living corals
2. do not buy any shells, corals or preserved fish, turtles, etc from hawkers or tourist shops (even if the seller insists that the objects are not from Mauritius or that he/she has a permit)
3. do not litter the beaches and lagoons with plastic, paper, etc
4. commend hotel/lodgings management on any special consideration given to the beach, lagoon or reef, for example, conservation posters in reception, re-planting of coastal vegetation, etc.

A reader recently sent us the following comments on snorkelling and the condition of the coral:

From what I could gather from a local diving specialist, and also from my own experience, snorkeling within the reef (near Grand Baie and Trou aux Biches) is not that great.

The reason for this is that the coral has been

removed both by tourists and, presumably, by local traders, in order to make coral necklaces. Also guilty are some of the big hotels which have sent mechanical diggers into the sea to smash and remove coral in order to provide bathing areas for their residents – all the best swimming areas in Mauritius are off public beaches where hotels cannot be built.

## Information

The best source of information on Mauritian wildlife is the Mauritian Wildlife Appeal Fund (MWAF), which was founded in 1984 as a charity to protect and manage the rare birds, plants, reptiles and mammals of Mauritius. MWAF is vigorously supporting the creation of a national park; projects to restore populations of endangered bird species (Mauritus kestrel, pink pigeon, echo parakeet, Mauritius white eye and fody); programmes to restore and conserve endemic vegetation (Round Island and Île aux Aigrettes); and a survey of whales, dolphins and turtles around Mauritius.

The appeal fund is always in need of donations or sponsors; for example, the 'Sponsor a Kestrel Nestbox' scheme which provides safe nest sites (monkey proof and cyclone proof) for breeding kestrels. Sponsorship costs Rs 500 (US$40) to cover costs of material, labour and transport to the site; and sponsors receive information reports on their box plus an invitation to visit the MWAF Mauritius Conservation Programme. The Wildlife Supporters Club, a support group for MWAF, produces a newsletter three times a year, sells MWAF Christmas cards, and helps with projects. Enquiries about MWAF or the Wildlife Supporters Club should be made to the following address (enclose return postage): Mauritian Wildlife Appeal Fund (MWAF) (☎/fax 6836331), Public Relations Officer, Morcellement Carlos, Tamarin.

The Mauritius Marine Conservation Society and Marine Underwater Group (☎ 6965368), Railway Rd, Phoenix, are campaigning to stop the pollution and destruction of the coral reefs around Mauritius. Full details on MMCS and MUG are provided in the section on Useful Organisations in the Mauritius – Facts for the Visitor chapter.

**Books** You can read about Mauritian wildlife in naturalist Gerald Durrell's *Golden Bats & Pink Pigeons* (Collins, 1977). It's a funny and informative book. Durrell spends lots of time on Île Ronde (Round Island), off the north coast of Mauritius, where the country's only snakes (boas) live. The island must have been wrongly named for it is not round. The nearby Île aux Serpents (Serpent Island) has no snakes, but *is* round. This mix up must be the result of a cartographer's blunder.

Also highly recommended is *Last Chance to See* (1991) by Douglas Adams & Mark Carwardine. The authors manage to keep a fine sense of humour whilst wandering round the globe in search of species faced with imminent extinction. The chapter entitled 'Rare or Medium Rare' deals with Mauritius and includes a hilarious description of Mad Carl, an ornithologist specialising in kestrels, being amorously intercepted by Pink, a deranged kestrel.

## Conservation Note

We strongly urge you not to buy anything made out of turtle shell nor to buy or take any shells from the beach. Stocks of turtles and shells have been cleared in many areas, or are otherwise endangered. Governments are trying to do something about it, but please

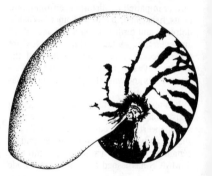

don't contribute to the problems by providing the incentive to continue the practices.

Despite the Mauritian government's ban on sales of shells, coral, and turtle shell, we saw an immense array of these items displayed by souvenir emporia, gift shops and beach vendors all over Mauritius. Some shells were even supplied with neat labels, such as 'rare', 'very rare', or 'live-collected'. When questioned about their sources, shopkeepers refer awkwardly to Thailand, Philippines, Réunion and the Indian Ocean. Whatever the true source of these items is, one very clear fact is that the purchase of rare and endangered species from any source directly contributes to their extinction.

Tourists who illegally possess or transport these items should also be aware that the items are liable to confiscation on leaving Mauritius, and to combined fines and confiscation by customs officials in most Western countries which have signed agreements on endangered species.

### National Parks

Since 1988, several international organisations have been working together with the government to set up the first national park in Mauritius. It is hoped that the park will extend over 4000 hectares to encompass the forests of the Gorges de la Rivière Noire (Black River Gorges) and the Bassin Blanc. Delicate and lengthy negotiations are still in progress with the private owners of part of this area, which is the last prime habitat for the highly endangered and unique fauna and flora of Mauritius. Given the fact that the island now possesses less than 1% of intact, original forest, it is clear why the establishment of this national park commands the highest priority.

Several maps of Mauritius show proposed 'nature reserves' which have not yet been officially delineated. Visitor access is (or will be) restricted in many of these reserves, most of which are tiny in size, since they enclose the last vestiges of rare species which are highly sensitive to disturbance. Although there has been talk of establishing a marine park off Baie aux Tortues (opposite the Maritim Hotel), at the time of writing no official pronouncement had been made.

### GOVERNMENT

Mauritius became a republic in March, 1992 and the role of the former governor general was changed to that of a president. The National Assembly consists of the speaker, 62 elected members, and eight additional members. The Cabinet has 25 ministers, including the prime minister. General elections are usually held every five years.

### ECONOMY

Despite its colourful politics, isolation and population problems, Mauritius achieved a minor economic miracle in the '80s and is now consolidating its economy in the face of world recession. Unemployment is still minimal, and the rate of inflation has been dramatically reduced from 42% in 1980 to around 5% at the time of writing. Exports have increased by 15% over the past few years.

The Export Processing Zone (EPZ), often described as the 'powerhouse of the Mauritian economy', was set up in 1970 to diversify the economy, which had become too dependent on the sugar industry. There are now approximately 600 export-oriented companies with over 100,000 employees. EPZ exports rose from Rs 1.3 billion in 1983 to nearly Rs 10 billion in 1991.

The average wage for a hotel worker is around US$110 per month; a secretary receives about US$170 per month. You will see beggars in the centre of Port Louis, but not to any great extent. There is a great deal of poverty, but it's at the subsistence level. Infant mortality, at 19.9 deaths per 1000, is the lowest in Africa.

### Sugar

Until recently, the Mauritian economy could be summed up in one word – sugar. It represented more than 90% of exports, covered most of the fertile land in the country and employed most of the people. Now, because of full employment, there is a shortage of labour.

The state of the nation depended solely on the sugar harvest and sales. Every so often, a bad cyclone would decimate the cane crop or a world drop in sugar prices would have bitter consequences.

A big sugar plantation ranges from 250 to 1000 hectares; a small one starts at 10 hectares. One hectare yields 75 tonnes or Rs 30,000 before costs. A cane field is productive for between five and 10 years before it must be cleared and replanted. The planter earns Rs 400 per tonne (Rs 200 after tax, labour and overheads). After cutting, the leaves can be used for fodder and thatching. There are 19 sugar mills in Mauritius, catering for the numerous plantations.

The cane work is mostly seasonal. The harvest is between June and September; all the cane cutting is done by hand. A worker is paid Rs 16 per tonne for cutting and Rs 20 per tonne for loading. A young man can do two tonnes a day, giving him Rs 72 (almost US$6). Off-season, 'task' workers on the sugar fields are paid Rs 43 for a 6.30 am to noon working day. The women get Rs 23 for the same period. If they're over 60 years old, the men earn Rs 25 to Rs 30 and the women earn Rs 20.

In each town or village you will see a SILWF building. This is the Sugar Industry Labour Welfare Fund centre, which acts as health clinic, family planning institute, and provides other social services. Health treatment is free, but there are no welfare payouts. Schemes are being considered to introduce mechanisation without causing unemployment.

## Other Crops

Since independence, the government has tried to wean the economy away from its dependence on sugar by introducing and encouraging other crops and industries.

Tea, although cultivated since the first settlements, has become the second crop to sugar. It is grown mostly around Curepipe on the central plateau and is used in blending. Tobacco, potatoes, tomatoes, corn and fruit are also being encouraged as alternative crops. The export of fruit and vegetables is still modest.

## Industries

Although surrounded by thousands of km of ocean, the Mauritian fishing industry has never been developed on a large scale. It remains primarily the domain of poor Créoles, leaving room for expansion.

The real successes since the early '70s have been the development of knitwear, textiles, footwear manufacturing and tourism. Pierre Cardin, Lacoste, Calvin Klein, Marks & Spencer and other famous brands are manufactured in Mauritius.

The clothing industry has now surpassed sugar as Mauritius' number one export. The amount of foreign investment in the industry has been remarkable. Hong Kong, due to revert to Chinese rule in 1997, has supplied almost all the foreign investment in textiles. Mauritius now ranks as the third largest exporter of woollen knitwear in the world. However, the rise of this industry has given the island some major pollution problems.

## Tourism

More than 30% of the 290,000 or so yearly visitors to Mauritius come from nearby Réunion. The flights between the countries are short and cheap, and the French franc goes a long way in Mauritius. The South Africans, French and Germans are the next most frequent visitors, followed by the Italians, British and Malagasy. Australia and Japan are vastly expanding markets. As of the late '70s, arrivals increased between 5000 and 10,000 each year. In 1990, tourism brought Mauritius more than Rs 3 billion.

There are currently some 65 upmarket beach hotels and around 75 budget hotels. New hotels spring up each year – at least 19 planning applications for beach hotels were made in 1992. In addition, several side industries supporting tourism have taken off – most notably model-boat building (see the Things to Buy section in the Mauritius – Facts for the Visitor chapter).

## POPULATION & PEOPLE

In 1990, Mauritius had an estimated population of 1.09 million. With more than 580 people per square km, it has one of the greatest population densities in the world.

Well over half the people are Hindus (both Tamil and non-Tamil), and approximately another 175,000 are Muslims; both these segments of the population are descended from the labourers who were brought to the island to work the cane fields. Only a few of the 25,000 Chinese or Sino-Mauritians came to the country as indentured labourers, most arrived as self-employed entrepreneurs. The remaining 340,000 people are mainly Créoles, descendants of African slaves, and the ever diminishing Franco-Mauritians, the original European settlers of the island.

Mauritius is often cited as an example of racial and religious harmony, and compared to most other countries it is. On the surface, there are few signs of intimidation or conflict. However, although there is no sign of racial conflict, the racial divisions are still apparent and adhered to, more so than in the Seychelles or Réunion. There is little inter-marriage or social mixing between the racial communities.

Because Hindus are a majority and Mauritius is a democracy, the Hindus always win control at the elections. People don't vote across religious lines. Naturally this causes more than a little resentment from the minority groups, particularly the Muslims. It simmers all the time without actually boiling over. Attempts are made to ensure it never does, with the smaller communities tending to be more than proportionally represented in government.

The Franco-Mauritians, who make up less than 2% of the population, often have wealth as a buffer. Generally, they live up on the cooler heights around Curepipe and have holiday homes on the coast. Since they own the sugar mills and run other big businesses, they can afford to live well in Mauritius or migrate to South Africa and France, as many did after independence.

The Chinese are involved mostly in commerce. Each village has one or two Chinese stores and there is a large Chinese quarter in Port Louis. They have the knack of mixing without getting involved.

The Créoles have their own pejorative or racist terminology for the others. They refer to the Muslims as *lascars*, the non-Tamil Hindus as *malabars*, and the Tamils as *madras*. The Chinese are simply the *chinois*.

Another small group you might come across are the 1300 Chagos islanders, the *ilois* as they are called in Mauritius, who are treated as outcasts. As inhabitants of the Chagos Islands of the British Indian Ocean Territory, they were evicted from their homes and resettled in Mauritius between 1965 and 1973 by the UK, when Diego García was leased to the Americans as a military base (see the Outer Islands chapter). The British paid UK£1.25 million in compensation directly to the Ilois in 1979, and moved them into housing estates in the northern districts of Port Louis.

The Mauritian government has adopted their cause and is seeking their repatriation to the Chagos Islands, as well as the removal of the US forces.

## EDUCATION

The government provides free education at 277 primary schools and 122 secondary schools. Although school is not compulsory, the attendance rate is around 90%. Further training is provided at special schools, technical institutes, handicraft training centres, and teacher training centres. Approximately 1300 students attend the University of Mauritius at Le Réduit which has recently expanded to include Schools of Law, Industrial Technology, Administration, and Agriculture.

## ARTS & CULTURE

All aspects of Indian culture are maintained and promoted, mainly by the Mahatma Gandhi Institute in Moka.

### Avoiding Offence

Although beachwear is fine for the beaches, you may cause offence or invite pestering if you dress skimpily elsewhere. A Swedish reader has commented that his Mauritian friends did not consider someone stripped to the waist or wearing shorts should be taken seriously; in fact, they used the 'foo-soo-koor' rule to judge such persons. According to this rule, such a person appearing in public must be either *fou* (mad), *saoul* (drunk) or *dans son cour* (inside a personal garden or backyard). Nude bathing is forbidden on Mauritius.

When visiting inside temples, you should usually remove your shoes. Ask if you are not sure.

## Dance

If you were to pick one art form to represent Mauritius, it would be the Créole *séga*. It was through this dance that the African slaves would let down their hair at the end of a hard day in the cane fields. Couples danced the séga around campfires on the beach to the accompaniment of drums. It was often a prelude to sex – a mating dance.

Because of the sand there could be no fancy footwork. So today, when dancing the séga, the feet never leave the ground and must shuffle back and forth. The rest of the body makes up for it and the result, when the fire is hot, can be extremely erotic. In the rhythm and beat of séga, you can see or hear connections with the Latin American salsa, the Caribbean calypso, and the African origins of the people.

Séga parties spontaneously combusting on the beaches are a thing of the past and you must now go to the big luxury hotels to see a well-choreographed show. There is usually one a week and you can slip in to watch if you are not a resident. Most hotels won't mind unless you are underdressed or in the company of local youths.

Smaller hotels also endeavour to put on a 'cultural show'. But the séga groups tend to be amateurs going through the motions for some extra money. There's nothing worse than a lifeless séga – especially when the participants feel obliged to ask you to join in.

Séga variations to Créole pop music are common in the discos and are sometimes more authentic than the hotel displays.

## Music

Western pop music is predominant and has given rise to Michael Jackson lookalikes in every hotel cabaret. But there are a number of good Créole groups and singers, such as Roger Clency and Jean Claude-Monique. For a séga group with politically radical lyrics, try Larmoni. Ras Natty Baby and Les Natty Rebels is the island's top group for seggae, a musical style which blends reggae and séga.

Ti-Frère, the most popular séga singer in the country, died in 1992. He is credited with reviving séga during the early 1950s, and his song 'Anita' has become a classic. In 1991, Radio France Internationale recorded a special Ti-Frère CD – highly recommended for séga fans.

A reader has recommended Power House Music Shop, 316 Royal Road, Rose Hill Arcade, Rose Hill as the best place on Mauritius to buy taped music.

## Sport

**Soccer** Soccer is the national sport, and the King George V Stadium in Curepipe is the main venue. Every town and village seems to have a sporting club based on soccer. Around Mahébourg, the clubs are all named after British soccer teams.

Basketball and volleyball are growing in popularity with young locals.

**Horse Racing** Mauritius has a busy horse racing programme over the winter season (May to October) at the Champ de Mars racecourse in Port Louis. The big race is the Derby, held at the end of August. Most of the jockeys are South African, with a few Australians. There are few Mauritian jockeys.

Entry into the stands costs Rs 60, but admission to the central area is usually free and you get a chance to mix with thousands of betting-crazy locals.

## Art

Unlike in the Seychelles, the works of Mauritius' artists are not widely displayed or available, which is a shame considering some of the beautiful landscapes you'd like to see painted.

There are plenty of 18th and 19th century prints of such scenes, but the originals must have gone back to France and Britain years ago. For contemporary paintings and sculpture, there is the Max Boullé Gallery at Rose Hill, and Port Louis Art Gallery at the corner of Malefille and Poudrière Sts.

The Naval Museum in Mahébourg has a selection of lithographs depicting local views and scenes from Bernadin de St Pierre's novel, *Paul et Virginie*. The statue of the famous couple in the small park outside Curepipe Town Hall and one of King Edward VII in the Champ de Mars, Port Louis, were both created by Mauritius' best known sculptor, Prosper d'Epinay.

The owner of the Colonial Coconut hotel at Grand Baie is very interested in colonial art and has some superb engravings and lithographs on display.

### Literature

Mauritius' most famous contribution to world literature to date, one which has become entangled in the island's history, is the romantic novel.

Those who want to read a 20th century Mauritian novel should read something by *the* Mauritian author, Malcom de Chazal, whose most famous work is probably *Petrusmok* (1951). Other works written by him include *Sens Plastique* (1948), *Sens Magique* (1956), *Poèmes* (1959) and *Sens Unique* (1974). Malcom de Chazal was known as quite a character. The Swedish author, Bengt Sjögren, met the author and later described him as an eccentric recluse who sat writing all day at the Hotel National in Port Louis, except for the walk that he took by the seaside every morning to cogitate and watch the mighty ocean. However, according to the locals, it was not de Chazal that contemplated the sea, it was the sea that contemplated him.

Other writers well known in Mauritius are Robert Edward Hart, Edouard Maunick, the Masson brothers (Loys & André) and Léoville L'Homme. The Mauritian humour-ist, Yvan Lagesse, has written a wry assessment of Mauritian life in *Comment vivre à l'île Maurice en 25 leçons* (How to live in Mauritius in 25 lessons).

Since the '70s, literature has also been published in Créole. Some examples are *Quand Montagne Prend Difé* by René Asgarally; *La Mare Mo Mémoire* (poems) by Ramesh Ramdoyal; and *La Fimé da Lizié* by Dev Virahsawmy.

Mark Twain, Joseph Conrad and Charles Baudelaire all visited the island. Joseph Conrad set a short story, 'A Smile of Fortune', in Mauritius, if you care to look for it in a collection of his works. His novel, *Twixt Land and Sea*, is based on a love story in Port Louis. Baudelaire's first poem, 'À une Dame Créole' was written in Pamplemousses.

Another adventure based around naval history is Patrick O'Brian's *The Mauritius Command* (Collins, 1977), about a Napoleonic swashbuckler. For more details about recommended titles and bookshops, refer to the section on Books & Maps in the Mauritius – Facts for the Visitor chapter.

### RELIGION

Mosques, churches and Hindu temples can be found within a stone's throw of each other in many parts of Mauritius. Thankfully, no one has been throwing stones – which, if it doesn't signify harmony, at least represents a commendable degree of tolerance of one religion for another.

Hinduism is the predominant faith, but as you might expect, it is more relaxed than in India. There is less evidence of a caste system even in matters such as marriage and employment.

Islam is also toned down. Although there seem to be as many mosques as temples, the prayer calls are not blasted out for all to hear. Visitors will first notice the Muslim presence when they go to a café and find there is no beer for sale.

The Sino-Mauritians are even less conspicuous in their worship. Many have turned to Roman Catholicism, but there are a few pagodas and Buddhist temples in Port Louis.

The Catholic church still seems to be active in Mauritius despite the comparatively low number of Christians. Hindus, being polytheistic, are wont to join in with Christian worship. Many Christians pray at the shrine of Père Laval, in the Ste Croix suburb of Port Louis. Père Jacques Laval (1803-64), a French missionary, is said to have converted more than 67,000 people to Christianity during his 23 years in Mauritius. Père Laval's shrine is described in the Port Louis chapter.

A Swedish traveller wrote to us about a type of native religion he encountered:

When having troubles of different kinds, the members of my host family went to see a person who was a cross between Hindu priest, doctor, and magician. He and his assistants carried out all sorts of ceremonies to cure their patients, who paid a fee of Rs 100. He seemed to have no problem finding customers. The 'surgery' was in the open air, with several benches and altars at an extremely picturesque site. I strongly recommend a visit.

To get to this place, take a taxi from Centre de Flacq to Queen Victoria. The taxi stops where this village ends, between two Chinese shops. From there you can see a brook which you cross via a small bridge. Follow the brook on its left bank for a few hundred metres until you see the place.

I also visited a similar practitioner in Bel Air, Flacq district. She was a bit different since she squatted in a dark tin shed. She cracked coconuts, set fire to meta tablets, made predictions with the help of playing cards, and read spells in an incomprehensible language. Her fee was also Rs 100, but she kept on for two hours, whereas the treatment by the man in Queen Victoria only lasted 20 minutes.

**Mikael Parkvall**

## LANGUAGE

When Mauritians have a community meeting, the people speak Créole, take minutes in English and discuss the outcome with government officials in French.

The official languages are English and French. English is used mainly in government and business literature. French is the spoken language in educated and cultural circles, and is used in newspapers and magazines.

Créole, the common bond, derives from French and has close similarities with the

Créole spoken elsewhere, even, it is said, in the French West Indies. Ironically, the Mauritian and the Seychelles Créoles are more comprehensible to French people than the patois of Réunion, a thoroughly French department.

### French

French is widely spoken and understood on Mauritius and in most parts of the Indian Ocean. Most visitors to Mauritius will find it useful to pick up a good French phrasebook, especially if they intend to visit Réunion or Madagascar as well.

For a list of useful words and phrases, refer to the Language section in the introductory Facts for the Visitor chapter.

### Créole

There are major differences between the pronunciation and usage of Créole and standard French. If you don't speak French in the first place, you're doubly disadvantaged. Editions de L'Océan Indien (EOI) book centres on Mauritius sell publications, such as *Parlez Créole (Guide Pratique pour Touristes)/Speak Créole (A Tourist Guide)*, *English-Créole Phrasebook*, and *Diksonyer Kreol/Anglé (Prototype Mauritian Créole/ English Dictionary)*. For more details on books and bookshops, refer to the section on Books & Maps in the Mauritius – Facts for the Visitor chapter.

Créole is a vibrant, direct language. For starters, you might want to try the following Créole phrases:

| How are you? | *Ki manière?* |
|---|---|
| Fine, thanks. | *Mon byen, mersi.* |
| I don't understand. | *Mo pas comprend.* |
| OK. | *Correc.* |
| Not OK. | *Pas correc.* |
| he, she, it | *li* |
| Do you have...? | *Ou éna...?* |
| I'd like... | *Mo oulé...* |
| I'm thirsty. | *Mo soif.* |
| Phoenix beer | *la bière zarnier* |

(literally 'spider beer' – the label looks like one)

Cheers!           *Tapeta!*
Great!            *Formidabe!*

## Language Trends

Mikael Parkvall, a Swedish traveller with an interest in language research, supplied the following comments on language trends in Mauritius:

From the 1983 census we learn that there are in the country about 36,000 speakers of French (these numbers indicate household languages) and 2000 anglophones. Créole is spoken by some 522,000, thus more than half the population. Among the oriental and Asian tongues, Chinese has 6000 speakers and Urdu 25,000. The Bhojpuri speakers number about 308,000. Tamil speakers 36,000 and speakers of Telugu and Marathi 15,000 and 12,000 respectively. These are the major languages, but 694 Mauritians also claim to speak another Indian language, such as Gujarathi, Bacha, Punjabi and Sindhi.

All Asian languages are losing speakers. English is fairly stable, whereas Créole becomes more and more popular all the time. The number of francophones has also declined, mostly due to emigration to South Africa. The census lists 19 languages currently used in Mauritius, nine of which are spoken by more than 1000 people. The major languages spoken on Mauritius (in order of popularity) include Créole, Bhojpuri, French, Tamil, Urdu, Telugu, Marathi, Hakka, English, Gujarati, Mandarin, and Cantonese. Languages spoken by less than 100 speakers include Polish (!), Punjabi, Sindhi, Bacha, Italian, German and Russian (some 20 speakers).

It is a myth that Hindi is spoken in Mauritius. Those who, according to the census, speak either Hindi or Bhojpuri are all Bhojpuri speakers. Bhojpuri is a sort of creole Hindi, and the relationship between these two languages is similar to that between French and Créole, the difference being that whereas French is spoken by at least some Mauritians, Hindi is spoken by none. Bhojpuri lacks prestige, and for all official purposes – as, for example, is the case with the Mauritius Broadcasting Corporation – Hindi is used. Thanks to the popularity of Indian films, however, even the least educated and illiterate Hindus understand Hindi. Although Bhojpuri is also spoken in India, this Indian version is unintelligible to Mauritians, partly due to the massive influence of French and Créole on Mauritian Bhojpuri. *All* the numerals, for example, are in French. It looks increasingly certain that Bhojpuri, and probably all the other Asian languages, will die out on Mauritius. Even in conservative villages, perhaps considered a 'bit behind the times', parents will rarely speak Bhojpuri to their children. Thus, the coming generations will probably be brought up entirely on Créole, with the additional usage of French and English.

# Facts for the Visitor

## VISAS & EMBASSIES

You don't need a visa to enter Mauritius if you are a citizen of the UK, Ireland, Australia, USA, Canada, New Zealand, or any western European country.

Unless you are with a holiday package group, you will be asked to show a confirmed air ticket out of the country and proof of sufficient finances on arrival. If you do not have an onward ticket, you may be invited to buy one, on the spot, from Air Mauritius.

Initial entry is granted for one to three months. Extensions for a further three months as a tourist are available on application.

### Embassies

Following are the addresses of some Mauritian high commissions and embassies around the world:

Australia
   Mauritius High Commission, 43 Hampton Circuit, Yarralumla, Canberra, ACT 2600 (☎ (06) 281 1203)
Belgium
   Mauritius Embassy, 68 Rue des Bollandistes, Etterbrek, 1040 Brussels (☎ (02) 733 9988)
Egypt
   Mauritius Embassy, 72 Abdel Moneim Riad St, Agouza, Cairo (☎ (02) 3464659)
France
   Mauritius Embassy, 68 Blvd de Courcelles, 75017 Paris (☎ (01) 42 27 30 19)
India
   Mauritius High Commission, 5 Kautilya Marg, Chanakyapuri, New Delhi 110021, (☎ (011) 301 1112/3)
Madagascar
   Mauritius Embassy, Ambataroka, Lot No VI 2113 (Bis), Antananarivo (☎ (02) 32157)
Pakistan
   Mauritius Embassy, House No 27, St No 26, Sector F-6/2, Islamabad (☎ (051) 823345, 823235)
UK
   Mauritius High Commission, 32-33 Elvaston Place, London SW7 (☎ (071) 581 0294/5)
USA
   Mauritius Embassy, Suite 134, Van Ness Centre, 4301 Connecticut Ave NW, Washington DC 20008 (☎ (202) 244 1491/2)

### Working Holidays

If you intend to work, the company concerned with employing you must apply to the Prime Minister's Office – Home Affairs Division (☎ 201 1015) for a work permit. You will still have to go through the visa extension procedure.

### Visa Extensions

To apply for an extension, you must go to the Passport Office (☎ 2081212) at the Line Barracks police station in Port Louis, next to the Victoria bus station.

Applications must be submitted with one form, two passport-size photos, your passport, an onward ticket and proof of finances. Two letters – one by the applicant explaining why he or she wants to stay longer and one by a local 'sponsor' (it can be someone providing accommodation) – are also necessary.

The process takes up to 15 days, but is free. Providing you can satisfy these demands there should be no further problems, but since the police are responsible for passport control and many Indian visitors overstay their entry permits, there are frequent 'get tough' periods.

### Foreign Embassies & Consulates

Rogers House, situated at 5 President John F Kennedy St, Port Louis, is home to most of the airlines and several of the diplomatic missions in Mauritius. It is also the headquarters of the Overseas Telecommunications Service.

The building contains the Australian High Commission (☎ 2081700), which also represents Australian interests in the Seychelles, Madagascar and the Comoros; the US Embassy & Information Office (☎ 208 2347); and the Finnish, Swedish and Italian consulates. Other embassies and consulates are:

British High Commission
    Ken Lee Building, 1st Floor, 20 Edith Cavell St, Port Louis (☎ 2089850)
French Embassy
    14, St George's St, Port Louis (☎ 2083755)
Indian High Commission & Cultural Centre
    Bank of Baroda Building, Sir William Newton St, Port Louis (☎ 2083775)
Madagascar Embassy
    Rue Guiot Pasceau, Floréal (☎ 6865015/6)
German Consulate
    32 Bis, St Georges St, Port Louis (☎ 2407425)

**Visas for Réunion, Madagascar & India**
Those travellers who require a visa for Réunion should apply in their own country. If you apply for one in Mauritius, the French Embassy must first contact the French embassy or consulate in your country. The process takes up to three weeks and costs 60 French francs. The visa section is open Monday to Friday from 8.30 am to noon. For details on Réunion representation in your country, see the Réunion – Facts for the Visitor chapter.

Madagascar visas are more readily available. The Madagascar Embassy is open Monday to Friday from 9 am to 4 pm. Visas take three days to process and cost Rs 120; or Rs 240 for a multiple entry visa. You must fill in four forms and supply four photographs.

Again, apply for Indian visas in your own country. The visa section is open Monday to Friday from 9.30 am to 12.30 pm. Visas are issued each day from 3.30 to 4.30 pm and take three days to process.

There is no representative of the Comoros in Mauritius.

## CUSTOMS
Airline passengers aged 16 years and over may import duty free goods: 250 cigarettes or 50 cigars or 250 grams of tobacco; one litre of spirits; two litres of wine, ale or beer; one quarter litre of eau de toilette; and a quantity of perfume not exceeding 10 centilitres.

Visitors may import Mauritian currency notes up to a maximum of Rs 700, and take out Rs 350. Duty-free items must be bought with foreign currency.

If you bring in plants or plant material you must have obtained a plant permit from the Ministry of Agriculture, Fisheries and Natural Resources (☎ 2011403, 2087859). An import permit (from the same ministry) and a sanitary certificate of country of origin is required for all imported animals and animal material.

If you have to deal with customs, the Customs & Excise Department (☎ 2409702) is in the IKS Building, Farquhar St, Port Louis.

## MONEY
The Mauritian unit of currency is the rupee (Rs), which is divided into 100 cents (c). There are coins of 1, 5, 10, 20, 25 and 50 cents; and Rs 1 and 5. The bank note denominations are 5, 10, 20, 50, 100, 200, 500, and 1000 rupees. There is no problem tendering old and battered notes.

All rates of exchange are set by the government and there is no difference from bank to bank. For the exchange of travellers' cheques they all charge a transaction fee of Rs 35. Some banks may also charge an additional Rs 2 per travellers' cheque. There is no black market.

Travellers' cheques bring a better rate than cash, and there are no problems with the major currencies. Personal cheques on the Eurocheque system can also be cashed, but there is a hefty commission.

Banking hours are Monday to Friday from 10 am to 2 pm and from 9.30 to 11.30 am on Saturdays. There are increasing numbers of foreign exchange counters, for example, in Grand Baie, Peréybère, Flic en Flac and Curepipe; and the banks at SSR Airport are open for the arrival and departure of international flights.

No restrictions apply on the amount of foreign currency you bring in and out of the country, providing you declare it and the amount taken out does not exceed the amount brought in. You are permitted to bring Rs 700 in and take up to Rs 350 out in local currency, but duty-free items must be bought with foreign currency.

### .ange Rates

| | | |
|---|---|---|
| 1 | = | Rs 16.7 |
| A.. 1 | = | Rs 11.2 |
| UK£1 | = | Rs 25.2 |
| DM1 | = | Rs 10.27 |
| Fr1 | = | Rs 3.06 |

1998  35 ₂kl

### Credit Cards

The following credit cards are widely accepted: VISA, MasterCard, American Express, and Diners Club. For cash advances on credit cards, the Mauritius Commercial Bank (MCB) handles MasterCard. Barclays, the other principal bank, deals with VISA. Other banks, including the State Commercial Bank and the Shanghai Banking Corporation, also give advances but tend to take longer to do so.

### Costs

Along with Madagascar, Mauritius is among the cheapest places in the Indian Ocean for visitors. However, the last few years have seen a rapid increase in prices for visitors, and there are official aspirations to turn the island into a luxury destination for affluent tourists. For the time being, if you keep to budget options you can get by in Mauritius on about US$25 per day for one person or US$45 for a couple.

The tourist bodies concentrate on promoting big, fancy beach hotels and tours that cater for the exclusive jet set, the honeymooners and other once-in-a-lifetime sprees, leaving the other end of the market to find its own level.

Independent tourist service operators that cater for individual travellers and day or weekend visitors are concentrated at Grand Baie, Peréybère, and Flic en Flac. Unlike in the Seychelles and Réunion, there are no set standards or regulations to follow. Private enterprise is given a free hand. Costs for travel, food and accommodation in the lower range of the market have remained low for several years. The beauty is, the longer you stay in one place, the cheaper the rate for the room or home – and you can see all of Mauritius by basing yourself in one place.

A decent single/double room in a *pension*, bungalow or small hotel will set you back around Rs 350/500, and a full meal about Rs 150 per person. Bus trips, of which the longest covers half the island, cost no more than Rs 10. There are no private beaches in Mauritius, so you are free to share the good hotel beaches and, at a reasonable cost in some cases, water-sports facilities.

Please note that prices given in this book for accommodation, restaurants and some other services are likely to have risen by about 15% from the time of writing.

### Tipping

Tipping is not compulsory. However, most of the upmarket hotels and restaurants will include a charge on the bill for government tax and service. In budget hotels and restaurants it's not necessary to tip, although there's nothing to stop you giving between 5% and 10% if the service was particularly good. In major tourist areas, such as Grand Baie, there's an annoying tendency for some waiters (usually those whose service is least appreciated) to try to automatically extract tips, for example, by not returning change. Airport porters expect a tip between Rs 5 and Rs 10. Taxi drivers don't receive tips; their prices are all-inclusive and often inflated anyway.

### Bargaining

Bargaining is very much part of life on Mauritius. Daily accommodation rates should drop by at least 30% if you stay for more than a week, and further discounts are usual for off-season or multiple occupancy. This means you can make substantial savings by basing yourself in one place.

Taxi rates should always be bargained to a sane level. For more details, refer to the section on taxis in the Mauritius – Getting Around chapter. You should also be able to negotiate discounts on car, motorbike or bicycle rental if you hire for more than a couple of days.

### Consumer Taxes

At the cheaper *pensions* or local cafés, there are no service charges or taxes on top of your bill. Restaurants and hotels in the middle to top end of the market add 15% government tax to the bill.

## WHEN TO GO
Apart from the Christmas and New Year period, Mauritius doesn't really have a high and low season. The situation varies throughout the year and is more dependent on outside factors, such as the Réunion holiday period, than on the weather. Consequently, factors other than the climate could determine the best time to visit.

Sporting and leisure considerations may play a part in when you choose to visit. December to March is best for diving, as the water is said to be clearer; June to August is best for surfing along the south coast; and September to March is best for big-game fishing, when the large predators feed closer to shore. There is no yacht-cruising around the region during the cyclone season (November to April).

## TOURIST OFFICES
### Local Tourist Offices
Independent European, Australian, Japanese and American travellers in Mauritius are not common. You'll find most shopkeepers, bus drivers, bar staff, etc very helpful without making a fuss. Police officers, in the tradition of the British bobby, sometimes fall over backwards to be of service.

Unfortunately, the same can't be said for the Mauritius Government Tourist Office (MGTO) (☎ 2011703) in Port Louis. Although it has a public counter, it appears the MGTO staff are not accustomed to helping visitors. There is little in the way of promotional literature, apart from a small information booklet on the country and lists of accommodation and coming events.

At SSR airport, the Mauritius Chamber of Commerce & Industry (MCCI) operates a free accommodation information service (☎ 6373635) which is helpful and can provide a limited amount of tourist literature.

Air Mauritius also seeks to promote tourism, but only limited information is available from local and overseas offices.

### Overseas Reps
According to the MGTO, overseas public relations and information offices for Mauritius are:

Australia
> Air Mauritius, Suite 1204, MLC Centre, level 12, 19-26 Martin Place, Sydney, NSW 2001 (☎ (02) 221 7300)
> Mauritius Tourist Information Bureau, 313 Abernethy Rd, Belmont 6104, Perth (☎ (09) 479 4283)

France
> Bureau d'Information de l'Île Maurice, 41 Rue Ybry, 92200 Neuilly – Cedex (☎ (01) 46 40 37 47)

Germany
> Mauritius Informationsbüro, Goethestrasse 22, D-6000 Frankfurt/Main 1 (☎ (069) 284348)
> Air Mauritius, Herzog Rudolf Strasse, 3, 8000 Munich 22 (☎ (089) 290 03930)

Italy
> Ufficio del Turismo delle Isole Mauritius, BMK SAS Publiche Relazioni, Foro Buonaparte 46, 20121 Milan (☎ (02) 865984, 879157)

Singapore
> Air Mauritius, 135 Cecil St, 04-02 LKN Bldg, Singapore 0106 (☎ 222 3033)

Switzerland
> Mauritius Tourist Information Service, Kirchenweg 5, CH-8032 Zurich (☎ (01) 383 8788)

UK
> MGTO London, 32/33 Elvaston Place, London, SW7 5NW (☎ (071) 584 3666)

USA
> Mauritius Tourist Information Service, 15 Penn Plaza, 415 Seventh Ave, New York, NY 10001 (☎ (212) 239 8367)

## USEFUL ORGANISATIONS
The best source of information on Mauritian wildlife is the Mauritian Wildlife Appeal Fund (MWAF) – more details about MWAF are included in the Flora & Fauna section in the Mauritius – Facts about the Country chapter. The Wildlife Supporters Club, a support group for MWAF, produces a newsletter three times a year, sells MWAF Christmas cards, and helps with projects. Enquiries about MWAF or the Wildlife Sup-

porters Club should be made to the following address (enclose return postage): Mauritian Wildlife Appeal Fund (MWAF) (☎/fax 6836331), Public Relations Officer, Morcellement Carlos, Tamarin.

The Mauritius Marine Conservation Society (☎ 6965368), Railway Rd, Phoenix, is campaigning to stop the pollution and destruction of the coral reefs around Mauritius. In conjunction with the Mauritius Underwater Group (MUG), a group of underwater sports enthusiasts and conservationists, the MMCS is working on the establishment of underwater trails in 'underwater gardens' and marine reserves. Efforts are being made to tackle reef degradation and control pollution and the effects of fertilizer application on land. In 1991, MMCS launched a successful pressure campaign to enact a new law against driftnetting, and published a booklet about the *Whales & Dolphins of Mauritius*.

The society is currently working on projects to build artificial reefs using appropriate materials; conducting surveys on the occurrence and status of whales and dolphins in Mauritius; making underwater videos of pristine and damaged reef areas for public viewing; and publishing articles on conservation and the marine environment in the MMCS newsletter, 'Diodon'.

MMCS and MUG share the Railway Rd premises, where they organise talks, films, etc which any visitors are welcome to attend. They're open Monday to Saturday from 8 am to 8 pm, and on Sundays and holidays from 8 am to noon. MUG holds a social evening every Tuesday at 8 pm – visitors are welcome.

If you wish to join MMCS, membership is available on payment of Rs 200 (or US$15) as an overseas member or Rs 100 (plus Rs 60 entrance fee) as an ordinary member.

Disabled travellers in the UK might like to contact the Royal Association for Disability & Rehabilitation, 25 Mortimer St, London W1N 8AB (% 071-242 3882). In the USA, a useful contact is the Society for the Advancement of Travel for the Handi-

capped, 26 Court St, Brooklyn, New York, NY 11242 (☎ 718-858 5483).

## BUSINESS HOURS & HOLIDAYS
### Business Hours

Office hours are between 9 am and 4 pm Monday to Friday. Most shops and cafés open at 8 am and close between 4 and 6 pm. On Saturdays, many close at noon. In Curepipe and Rose Hill, the shops are open an hour longer during the week, but close on Thursday and Saturday afternoons. Check restaurant times before arranging evening meals, as several close at 6 pm. (See Money and Post sections for bank and post office hours.)

### Fixed Public Holidays

These are as follows:

*New Year* – 1 & 2 January
*Independence/Republic Day* – 12 March (marked by speeches and displays at the Champ de Mars, Port Louis)
*Labour Day* – 1 May
*All Saints' Day* – 1 November
*Christmas Day* – 25 December

## CULTURAL EVENTS

With such a full range of beliefs and customs to accommodate, hardly a week goes by without some celebration. In that respect, it's a bonus for visitors. It can also be a hindrance, as there are more than the usual number of public holidays.

The following festivals are advertised in the newspapers and through the Mauritius Government Tourist Office (MGTO). There are also a few other minor Muslim and Buddhist festivals.

The MGTO produces a calendar of coming events every couple of months, but sometimes the events are over before the leaflet comes out. You can find out about the latest *cavadee* or *teemeedee* ceremonies by ringing the MGTO (☎ 2011703) in Port Louis.

### Hindu

**Cavadee** The cavadee is a wooden arch decorated with flowers and palm leaves, with pots of milk *(sambos)* suspended from each end of the base. Devotees carry the cavadee from the bank of a river to a temple in order to fulfil a vow in honour of Subramanya, the second son of the god Shiva, and to pay penance and cleanse their soul. Before the procession commences, skewers are threaded through the tongues and cheeks of devotees. Custom dictates that a reasonable pace must be maintained because the milk in the sambo must not have curdled by the time it reaches the temple.

The major Thaipoosam Cavadee takes place in January or February each year at most Hindu temples throughout the island. This is a public holiday. Small cavadees are scheduled once or twice during the rest of the year at selected temples.

**Maha Shivaratri** This celebration occurs over three days at the end of February or in mid-March, and is the largest and most important Hindu festival held outside India. One of the days over which it is held is a public holiday.

All the island's Hindus make the pilgrimage to the holy volcanic lake Grand Bassin (see description in the Central Mauritius chapter) in honour of the god Shiva. Many pilgrims, dressed in white, start walking in groups from their village a day or two beforehand, depending on how far they have to travel. They carry a *kanvar*, a light wooden frame or arch decorated with paper flowers, in the manner of a trade union banner. The majority of pilgrims, however, arrive in buses for a day trip. A constant stream of contract buses leaves from Bonne Terre (between Quatre Bornes and Vacoas). The queues are enormous but move quickly.

At the lake, some pilgrims perform *poojah* by making food sacrifices in the water or at various shrines, others bathe, and many take sacred water home. Events are much the same as those which take place on the banks of the Ganges in India.

On the return journey from the lake, the pilgrims who are walking or riding are given fruit and drinks by people in the villages they pass through.

**Teemeedee** This is a Hindu and Tamil fire walking ceremony in honour of various gods. The ceremonies occur throughout the year, but mostly in December and January. After fasting and bathing, the participants walk over red-hot embers scattered along the ground. The Hindu temples at Camp Diable, The Vale and Quatre Bornes are noted for this event. A feat along similar lines is sword climbing, seen mostly between April and June. The best demonstrations occur at Solitude, Triolet and Mt Choisy, in the northwest.

**Other Hindu Festivals** Hindus celebrate the victory of Rama over the evil deity Ravana during *Divali*, which falls in October or November. To mark the event, candles and lamps are lit around the home, and there is a public holiday.

During *Thai Pongal*, a Tamil thanksgiving in January or February, food is offered to the gods. It's also a public holiday. *Holi* is a riotous Hindu holiday in February or March.

### Chinese
**Chinese Spring Festival** The Chinese New Year falls around the end of January, or the beginning of February. On the eve of the event, homes are spring-cleaned and decked in red, the colour of happiness, and firecrackers are let off to ward off evil spirits. On the following day, wax cakes made of rice flour and honey are given to family and friends. No scissors or knives may be used. There is always a public holiday at this time.

### Muslim
Muslims celebrate *Id el Fitr* to mark the end of the fasting month of Ramadan, which is the ninth month of the lunar year. Id el Fitr day is always a public holiday.

### Christian
*Père Laval Feast Day*, on 9 September, is the anniversary of the Catholic priest's death. Pilgrims from around the world come to his shrine at Ste Croix to pray for miracle cures. For more details refer to the Port Louis chapter.

### Table of Muslim Holidays

| Hijra Year | New Year | Prophet's Birthday | Ramadan Begins | Id el-Fitr | Id el-Adha |
|---|---|---|---|---|---|
| 1414 | 21.06.93 | 30.08.93 | 12.02.94 | 15.03.94 | 21.05.94 |
| 1415 | 10.06.94 | 19.08.94 | 01.02.95 | 04.03.95 | 10.05.95 |
| 1416 | 31.05.95 | 09.08.95 | 22.01.96 | 22.02.96 | 29.04.96 |
| 1417 | 19.05.96 | 28.07.96 | 10.01.97 | 10.02.97 | 18.04.97 |
| 1418 | 09.05.97 | 18.07.97 | 31.12.97 | 31.01.98 | 08.04.98 |
| 1419 | 28.04.98 | 07.07.98 | 20.12.98 | 20.01.99 | 28.03.99 |
| 1420 | 17.04.99 | 26.06.99 | 09.12.99 | | |

## POST & TELECOMMUNICATIONS

### Post

The postal service is widespread, efficient and reliable. Even the tiniest village has its own post office. Because of the rare Mauritian Blue stamp, the little country is at least well known within world philatelic circles. (If you have a special interest in stamps see the Things to Buy section in this chapter.)

Post offices are open from 8 to 11.15 am and noon to 4 pm on weekdays and from 8 to 11.45 am on Saturdays.

**Postal Rates** Airmail letters are Rs 8 per 10 grams to Europe, the USA or Australia. Small/large postcards sent to the same destinations cost Rs 3/8. A one-kg parcel sent overseas by surface mail/airmail costs Rs 14/200.

### Telephone

In the last few years, the telephone service has been modernised so that most subscribers now have seven-digit numbers and international direct dialling (IDD) facilities. There are still a few hitches and glitches with wrong numbers, but the service is vastly improved.

**International Calls** International calls can be made from a private or business phone using IDD. Alternatively, you can use the Overseas Telecommunications Service (OTS) offices in Port Louis or in Cassis (24-hour operation). The rate for a call to Australia or Europe is Rs 72 for the first three minutes and Rs 24 for each subsequent minute. Charges for a similar call to the USA are Rs 84 and Rs 28 for each additional minute. These rates are reduced by about 25% from noon on Saturday until midnight on Sunday.

Some useful international dialling codes are: Mauritius 230; UK 44; USA 1; Australia 61; New Zealand 64; Réunion 262; Madagascar 261; Comoros 269; South Africa 27; and the Seychelles 248. For international enquiries dial 10 092.

**National Calls** The good news is that it is only Rs 1 for a local call anywhere on the island, and you have unlimited time after 6 pm. The bad news is that there are very few public phones and even fewer that work.

First check the local post office, then go to the police station. They are very helpful to visitors and do not charge for local calls. Failing that, shopkeepers and garages will let you use their phones for Rs 2 or Rs 3. There are no area codes for Mauritius. For directory enquiries dial 90.

### Fax, Telex & Telegraph

Private companies and hotels often allow clients or guests to use fax machines, and charge a small increment on the phone rates. Telex and telegraph services are available at the OTS offices in Port Louis.

## TIME

Daylight hours last from around 5.30 am to 7 pm in the summer and from 6 am to 6 pm in the winter.

Mauritius time is four hours (three hours during the European summer) ahead of Greenwich Mean Time (GMT) and Universal Time Coordinated (UTC), one hour ahead of Madagascar time and two hours ahead of South African time. So when it is noon in Mauritius it is 8 am in London; 3 am in New York and Toronto; midnight in San Francisco; 6 pm in Sydney or Melbourne; and 7 pm in New Zealand.

## ELECTRICITY

The power supply throughout the country is 220 volts. Continental two-pin plugs are the most common, but one reader noted square three-pins and round three-pins. If you need to link up with electricity on the island, play safe and take a travel plug. Port Louis has occasional blackouts, so it's not just the happy campers who need to pack a torch.

## LAUNDRY

Laundry services are widely available at guesthouses, bungalows and hotels.

## WEIGHTS & MEASURES

The metric system has now taken over from British standards, but be prepared for the occasional signpost in miles or grocer's sign in pounds.

## BOOKS & MAPS

For coverage of Mauritius' literary works and details of recommended authors, refer to the Literature section in the Mauritius – Facts about the Country chapter.

### History

Without a doubt, *the* historian of Mauritius and the Indian Ocean was Dr Auguste Toussaint who wrote books on the pirates in general, the Surcouf brothers in particular, and the history of Port Louis – *Port Louis: A Tropical City* (1973). He is best known for *The History of the Indian Ocean* (Routledge

& Kegan Paul, 1966). He died at his Forest Side home in February 1987.

For comparison, there is *A New History of Mauritius* (Macmillan, 1984) by John Addison & K Hazareesingh, *The Truth about Mauritius* by Basdeo Bissoondoyal and the *Historical Dictionary of Mauritius* by Lindsay Riviere (Scarecrow Press, London, 1982). For a discussion of the British presence, you might like to dip into *British Mauritius 1810-1948* by Dayachand Napal.

In *Prisoners in Paradise* (1985) the author Sheila Ward recounts the lives of five personalities who were imprisoned on Mauritius prior to Independence. The chosen characters cover an interesting historical and political span, including the British explorer Matthew Flinders; the Malagasy Prince, Ratsitatane; Ehelepola, the Kandyan chief from Sri Lanka; Reza Khan Pahlavi, the Shah of Iran; and Dr Stoyanovitch, a former prime minister of Yugoslavia.

For a more detailed account of Matthew Flinders, famed for his exploration of Australia, pick up a copy of *In the Grips of the Eagle: Matthew Flinders at Île de France* (Mahatma Gandhi Institute, 1988) by Huguette Ly-Tio Fane Pineo.

Another interesting roundup of visitors to the island is *They Came to Mauritius* (Oxford University Press) by Derek Hollingworth. It's out of print, but should be available through libraries.

### Créole Books

Mikael Parkvall, a Swedish traveller with an interest in language research, has written to say that those interested in learning Créole and obtaining books in Créole will discover that there is no Créole manual and very little literature available. He recommends the left-wing militant monthly, *Revi Lalit*, written in fairly easy language and published by Ledikasyon pu Travayer (Education for Workers). It's available from newsagents at the bus station in Curepipe.

A good source of books in Créole is the Toorawa Bookshop at 6 Queen St, Rose Hill. Ledikasyon pu Travayer at 153, Main Rd,

Grande Rivière Nord-Ouest, has reprinted Charles Baissac's 1888 Créole folk tale collection, *Sirandann Sanpek: Zistwar an Créole*, which includes parallel English translations; and has compiled a *Diksyoner Kreol-Anglé (Prototype Mauritian Créole-English Dictionary)*.

Another source is Editions de L'Océan Indien (EOI), a publishing company with several outlets on the island, which distributes several Créole titles, including Charles Baissac's *Le Patois Créole* and Goswami-Sewtohul's *Petit Dictionnaire Français-Créole*.

For more details about Créole language, refer to the Language section in the Facts about the Country chapter.

### Specialist Guides

Robert Marsh's *Mountains of Mauritius: A Climber's Guide* is now out of print, but several readers have been able to arrange (for a nominal charge) for photocopies to be made by staff at the Carnegie library in Curepipe where many of the rarer books on Mauritius can be found. This guide is a must for the more adventurous and can provide a unique perspective of the island, away from the beaches and tourist trails. Alexander Ward's *Climbing & Mountain Walking in Mauritius* (out of print) predates Marsh's book and is less comprehensive – a copy is held at the Carnegie library.

If you are interested in colonial and early Créole architecture, there is *Maisons Traditionelles de l'Île Maurice* by Jean-Louis Pagès (EOI, 1978). It will give you an idea of the best Créole houses in Mauritius.

Anyone interested in visiting Rodrigues should try to get hold of the French book *À la Découverte de Rodrigues* by Chantal Moreau (EOI, 1991), or *The Island of Rodrigues*, published in 1971 by Alfred North-Coombes with the help of the Mauritian Advertising Bureau. The latter is now out of print, but there are copies floating around.

### Tropical Flora & Fauna

For advanced reading on tropical fish, refer to either *A Field Guide to the Coral Reef Fish*

*of the Indian & West Pacific Oceans* by R H Carcasson (Collins, London, 1977) or *A Guide To Common Reef Fish of the Western Indian Ocean* by K R Bock (MacMillan, London, 1987). For a look at Mauritian birdlife, you could try *Birds of Mauritius* (1986) by Claude Michel.

For recommended books on Mauritian wildlife, see the Flora & Fauna section in the Mauritius – Facts about the Country chapter.

### Cookery

An enduring title is *a Taste of Mauritius* by Paul Jones & Barry Andrews (EOI, 1980), which portrays in mouthwatering colours what island cooking could be like. In reality, food like that is only available at the exclusive St Géran hotel, where the authors are, or were, manager and chef respectively.

### Bookshops

There are several bookshops *(librairies)* catering for the large residential area between Curepipe and Port Louis.

The best and most accessible for new books and those on Mauritius is the Librairie du Trèfle, in Royal St, Port Louis and in Les Arcades, beneath the Continental Hotel in Curepipe. New paperbacks from the UK cost between Rs 80 and Rs 150.

For a good selection of second-hand books to exchange or buy, go to the Librairie Bourbon, at 28 Rue Bourbon, in Port Louis. They have stacks of paperbacks in English.

A wide selection of books on Mauritius in French and English is available from Editions de l'Océan Indien (EOI) (☎ 4646761), at Stanley, Rose Hill (near the Buckingham cinema). They also have an outlet in Curepipe. The UK agent for EOI is Nautilus Publishing Company (☎ 081-767 2439), 2A Vant Rd, London SW17 8TJ – titles are available by mail order. The EOI agent in France is Librairie l'Harmattan (☎ (01) 43 54 79 10), 7, Rue de l'École, 75005 Paris.

Information on sources for Créole books is provided in this section under Créole Books.

Top:    Landing on Île aux Aigrettes, Mauritius (DS)
Bottom:    Salt collection at Tamarin, Mauritius (RW)

Top Left: Model boat shop in Mahébourg, Mauritius (RS)
Top Right: Victoria Regia water lillies, Sir Seewoosagur Ramgoolam Botanic Gardens, Pamplemousses, Mauritius (DS)
Bottom: Montagne du Rempart, seen from Tamarin Bay, Mauritius (RW)

## Libraries

The Mauritius Institute in Port Louis has a large library on the 1st floor behind the Natural History Museum. It is open from 9 am to 4 pm on all weekdays except Wednesday, and on Saturdays from 9 am to noon. It is closed all day Wednesday and Sunday. The only trouble is that you have to get the librarian to open up the bookcase doors when you want to look at a book. The most amenable is the Carnegie Library in Curepipe.

## Maps

The detailed map of Mauritius currently published by the French mapping agency, Institut Géographique Nationale (IGN), is clearly dated (the last revision appears to have been in 1977), but still very useful. MacMillan has recently published a map of Mauritius, including a small inset for Rodrigues Island, which is adequate for orientation, but less detailed than the IGN map.

Those wishing to go off the beaten track should call at the Ministry of Housing (☎ 2120580), in Edith Cavell St, Port Louis, to see if they can get copies of the detailed UK Military Survey maps. The Forestry Service (☎ 6754966), based at the Botanic Gardens in Curepipe, may also be able to help.

The Mauritius Government Tourist Office (☎ 2011703), at the Emmanuel Anquetil Building in Port Louis, supplies basic maps of the island and town plans of Curepipe and Port Louis in its brochures. A map of Rodrigues is available for Rs 25 in certain shops.

To study the earliest maps of Mauritius, go to the Naval Museum at Mahébourg.

In the UK, Stanfords, 12-14 Long Acre, London WC2E 9LP (☎ 071-836 1321) is an excellent source for maps of Mauritius and just about anywhere else in the world. A similarly extensive selection of mapping is available in the USA from Maplink, 25 E Mason St, Dept G, Santa Barbara, CA 93101 (☎ 805-9654402).

## MEDIA

### Newspapers & Magazines

The main daily papers are the morning *L'Express* and the afternoon *Le Mauricien*. Both are in French, with the occasional article in English. Either costs Rs 5, but they lack depth in hard news coverage of the island. They concentrate too much on political celebrities, meetings, proposals and developments. They're also short of international news, although they do carry the European soccer results.

The weekly *Mauritian Times* newspaper is mostly in English, but the Indian-flavoured feature content is too light and inconsequential for visitors. It's all right if you want to keep up with Bombay movie stars.

*Le Quatrième Pouvoir* is an independent satirical weekly. The cartoons are excellent but the commentary or captions are in French. *Le Militant Magazine* is the weekly voice of the MMM party. *Le Socialiste*, *The Sun*, *La Conscience*, and *The New Nation* cater for socialists. Right-wingers turn to *Le Rassembleur* or *La Vie Catholique*. *The Star* is aimed at a Muslim readership. For a read in Créole, pick up a copy of *Revi Lalit*.

Weekly magazines include *Cinq Plus*, *Cinq Plus Dimanche* and *Weekend Scope*. Coverage in these magazines concentrates on cinematic and political glitterati.

There are two good monthly magazines worth picking up if your knowledge of French is good enough. *La Gazette des Îles*, at Rs 15, contains articles on all aspects of Mauritian history and that of other islands in the Indian Ocean. It is a touch heavy for the average visitor, but a boon to students of the relevant subjects.

*Le Nouveau Virginie* deals with contemporary and controversial issues, without being sensationalist, and includes features on fashion, entertainment, food and personalities. It costs Rs 20.

A limited range of foreign newspapers and magazines is available in newsagents in the major tourist centres and major hotels.

There are also two useful publications produced in the UK. Both have news reports and advertisements. *Mauritius News* is published monthly and can be obtained by contacting Mauritius News (☎ 071-703 1071), PO Box 26, London SE17 1EG. *Mauritian International* is published quarterly and is available from Mauritian International (☎ 081-767 2439), Nautilus Publishing Company, 2A Vant Rd, London SW17 8TJ. Nautilus Publishing Company also stocks books about Mauritius which are available by mail order.

## TV & Radio

There are two channels on Mauritian TV. The Mauritius Broadcasting Corporation (MaBC) comes on each day in the evening, and covers important events live during the day. Most of the transmission is in French, with news breaks in English and Hindi. There are commercials and movies in English and French, but the programming is a bit erratic.

The alternative is the RFO station beamed across from Réunion. The presentation is a lot slicker, but it's all in French – even *Columbo* and *Les Deux Flics Miami (Miami Vice)*.

The daily papers publish the programme schedule of each TV station. In addition, *Télé 7 Jours*, the weekly Réunion magazine that is also available in Mauritius, gives the week's programmes along with other general interest magazine features.

MaBC operates a radio service which broadcasts in French, Créole, Hindi, and English (news reports at 8 am, 3 and 9 pm). With the right gear and decent reception, you can also tune in to the BBC World Service.

## FILM & PHOTOGRAPHY

There is a plentiful supply of film at a reasonable price around the island and there are several reputable processing outlets in Port Louis.

The main photographic shops in the centre of Port Louis are: Mimosa (Agfa), which also does passport pictures and photocopying; Kwon Pak Lin (Ilford), opposite Mimosa at the top of Sir William Newton St; Prophoto (Kodak), on Chaussée, opposite

the Company Gardens; and Scott & Co (Fuji), further along the same road into Barracks St.

Colour developing and printing takes one day and costs around Rs 15 for processing plus Rs 3.25 per print. So, for 24/36 exposures the final charge will be around Rs 93/132. The Fuji labs seem to have the more professional service.

Fujicolor print film costs about Rs 56/76 for 24/36 exposures. For slide film, prices are around Rs 98 for Fujichrome 100 (36 exposures); and Rs 184 for Velvia (36 exposures). For slide processing, Scott & Co takes three days and charges Rs 50 for processing plus Rs 150 if you have the slides mounted.

## HEALTH

For a rundown of possible health problems you may encounter in Mauritius, refer to the Health section in the introductory Facts for the Visitor chapter at the beginning of the book.

## Hospitals & Clinics in Mauritius

Should you get ill, the public health service is free to residents and visitors alike, but there may be a long wait for a consultation. The main hospitals are the Jeetoo (☎ 2123201), Volcy Pougnet St, Port Louis, the Princess Margaret Orthopaedic Hospital (☎ 4543031) in Candos, and the Sir Seewoosagur Ramgoolam National Hospital (☎ 2641661) at Pamplemousses.

A better and relatively inexpensive alternative is a private clinic. Two which have been recommended and are popular with the Franco-Mauritians and expatriate workers are the Clinique Darné (☎ 6862307), also known as the Medical & Surgical Centre, in Floréal, and the Clinique Mauricienne (☎ 4543061), between the university and the governor's residence in Le Réduit.

## WOMEN TRAVELLERS

Of the three countries covered in this book, Mauritius is the most difficult for solo women travellers, but it isn't nearly as bad as India or Latin America. Thanks to the popularity of Western videos, women of European origin may be expected to behave like the glamorous and morally questionable characters portrayed on the small screen.

In the eyes of some male Mauritians (particularly youths) who've had little contact with other facets of Western culture, female travellers who don't seem to be the property of any man may be regarded as either readily and willingly available – and consequently a candidate for romantic attention – or suspiciously disreputable and therefore worthy of contempt.

Having said that, things are unlikely to go beyond a bit of hissing or a few rude comments (although Deanna was once targeted by a glob of spit). Conservative dress seems to have little effect but it's still a good idea; don't wear shorts, sleeveless shirts or bathing costumes anywhere but in hotels or on the beach.

## DANGERS & ANNOYANCES

In case of emergency dial 999 and ask to be connected with the required service (police, fire, or ambulance).

### Security

For information on security in Mauritius, refer to the discussion under Dangers & Annoyances in the introductory Facts for the Visitor chapter.

### Drugs

Drug scandals involving politicians rocked all levels of Mauritian society a few years ago, so it would not be wise to declare or pursue an interest. You may be approached by the odd soul in Port Louis if you are in the wrong place at the wrong time but it is not a problem that should worry or attract any visitor.

### Exclusion from Beaches

There have been complaints from several readers about nonresidents being discouraged from entering hotel grounds and beach areas. The law is quite clear that there are no private beaches, but some hotels fence in land adjoining the beach and post guards at beaches. Although the ostensible aim of this

security is to keep undesirables out, it does seem as if hotels are assuming de facto ownership of 'their' beach and it is becoming increasingly common for foreign visitors who are nonresidents to be faced with bossy, gruff guards. The best approach is to calmly state that the beach is public property and you are legally entitled to use it.

One reader wrote with the following advice:

The approach to many beaches is inhibited by 'Private' or 'Keep Out' notices, as well as uniformed hotel security guards. Mauritians, however, are well aware of the law which states that the strip of beach between high and low tide is public property with free access, and the uniformed guards on beaches in front of the hotels will not interfere when you exercise this right. In fact, it's part of the Mauritian character that officials are generally unofficious, unaggressive and willing to concede if you stand your ground, but if it doesn't work every time, don't blame me!

### Shower Devices

In some of the budget accommodation on Mauritius the shower plumbing – often of Brazilian origin – can pose 'shocking' problems to the uninitiated. Some explanation and instruction for use may be helpful.

Hot, or tepid, showers are produced by a frightening and deadly-looking device that attaches to the shower head and electrically heats the water as it passes through. You may notice bare wires running into the shower head.

On the wall, you will find a lever that looks suspiciously like an ancient electrocutioner's switch. You have to flip the switch after the water is running (yes, really), so it's best to leave your shoes or flip-flops on and not get wet until this is done.

When the heater is activated, it will begin to emit an electrical humming sound and the lights in the room will dim or go out altogether. This is because the heater requires a great deal of electricity to operate effectively.

The temperature of the water can then be adjusted by increasing or decreasing the flow. A larger volume of water cannot be adequately heated in the time it takes to pass through the shower head, so a shower of a bearable temperature may become nothing but a pressureless drip.

When it's time to turn the water off, don't touch the controls until you've dried off and have your footwear on. This may be tricky, especially if the shower stall is small. Before turning the water off, flip the switch on the wall.

A hotel in Port Louis encapsulated instructions for this type of shower with a pithy notice: 'open the tap first, then you press the button, if not you may be electrocuted!'

## ACTIVITIES
### Hiking & Trekking
It seems that Mauritian tourism authorities haven't yet awakened to the attractions of walking, trekking or rambling around the island's interior, concentrating only on developing and promoting the beaches.

**Information** Don't bother asking the tourist office for information on hiking and trekking; you'll draw blank stares or, at best, amazement that you'd aspire to such physically taxing activities when there are plenty of beaches to lie around on! Readers have suggested that the Forestry Department at Curepipe is more helpful, although we found very little joy there; it probably depends greatly on whom you speak with.

Serious hikers and climbers will want to somehow locate a copy of the excellent book *Mountains of Mauritius: A Climber's Guide* (see the Books & Maps section in this chapter) by Robert Marsh. Marsh writes: 'Obviously the opportunities to enjoy the usual (but for many the unusual) activities of the beautiful seaside must not be missed, but as the locals know, there is a lot of pleasure to be found simply in walking, scrambling and climbing among the bush-clad hilly areas that add so much to the attractiveness of the country'.

The book, which due to the diminutive size of the Mauritian mountains is better suited to hikers and trekkers than to climbers, details 27 routes around and up such landmarks as Le Pouce (the thumb), Deux Mamelles (two breasts or udders), Pieter Both (the peak with an egg-shaped boulder balancing precariously on top), Lion Moun-

tain, Le Morne Brabant and Snail Rock. Marsh includes route maps with each and adds that, scenically, 'the most dramatic and spectacular' regions of Mauritius lie in the western half of the island.

The book also recommends a trek up to Le Piton Grand Bassin: 'It is a must on the itinerary of visitors, and the Piton, which is simply a high point on the rim of the crater in which the Bassin lies, will take only a few minutes easy scrambling to reach'.

Another particularly appealing little book which is unfortunately also out of print and hard to come by is *Climbing and Mountain Walking in Mauritius* (subtitled 'Particularly for those who would like to climb the Mauritius Mountains but who do not know the way') by Alexander Ward. This book provided the inspiration for Robert Marsh's book and Mr Ward is clearly on close terms with his subject matter. He speaks warmly of the mountains he climbs and describes and provides potential trekkers with a great deal of friendly motivation.

The biggest problem with both of these books is the age of the information. Quite a few things have changed since they were written; some of the trips on private property are now closed to the public while others have been rendered unappealing by growth and development. Copies of these books can be consulted at Carnegie Library in Curepipe.

**Maps** The 1990 IGN map shows most of the tracks and footpaths, although some are out-dated. The 'yellow roads' indicated are generally just rough vehicle tracks, some-times passable only to 4WD vehicles, and therefore may double as walking tracks. They're all easy enough to follow, but some smaller tracks (shown on the IGN map as dashed lines) are more difficult and some which are overgrown would require a great deal of bush-bashing to follow.

The IGN map will be adequate for most hikers but those in search of greater detail should apply to the Ministry of Housing. They produce excellent and detailed maps

suitable for serious off the beaten track walking.

**Getting Started** While we were updating this edition, with the help of several readers who'd written to tell us about their experi-ences walking in Mauritius, we spent a few days rambling in the bush. For us, the trips were the highlight of the island. Unfortu-nately, there were more possibilities than time would permit us to sample. If you do find an interesting route or re-discover an established one, we'd be interested in hearing how it went.

Most people will head for the *Réserve Forestière Macchabée* (Macchabée Forest Reserve), which is soon to become Black River Gorges National Park (see the map under Flora & Fauna in the Mauritius – Facts About the Country chapter). This mountain-ous area provides the bulk of the wild walks on the island. Although the map and infor-mation board at Le Pétrin clearly states that a Forestry Department permit is required by all hikers and trekkers in the Macchabée Forest Reserve, government conservation agencies had never heard of a permit system and the Forestry Department itself simply told us to 'come back later'. We're not really suggesting that you ignore the sign, but we didn't have permits (nor did the readers who've written to us about their walks) and nothing horrible happened.

Curepipe is the best base for trekkers and for stocking up before your walk, and Curepipe market has the best selection of fruit on the island, including Port Louis. Due to a dearth of public transport over mountain roads in the island's south-western corner, access to most trailheads will require private transport or a taxi ride. Taxi drivers are unused to maps, so when you're negotiating a price, pointing to a spot and asking for a price will not always work. It may help if you use a map to calculate the mileage and use this as a basis to coax a price from the driver.

For lowland walking, take into account the heat and humidity. If you prefer walking on the highland plateau, come prepared for rain at any time of year, especially from

October to March. Tropical downpours, frequently lasting for hours, will soak you to the skin. Even during the winter 'dry' season, the high plains trap clouds and moisture from the sea; it may be sunny in Curepipe and bucketing down on the Plaine Champagne. Since rainfall is most likely in the afternoon and public transport is more readily available along the coastal roads, your best option is to walk from inland *toward* the coast. This also provides the added benefit of net altitude loss!

**Suggested Routes** The following suggestions are just a few of many possibilities. Many thanks to readers Kitty Odell & Steve Shaw whose letter helped greatly with these descriptions.

*Le Pétrin to Grande Rivière Noire* This is a superb hike which traverses some of the finest and most scenic countryside on Mauritius. It begins at the junction of the Grand Bassin and Curepipe-Chamarel roads at Le Pétrin. The track is easy to follow through the Macchabée forest (by the time you read this, it may be known as the Black River Gorges National Park), with tiny pockets of indigenous vegetation dispersed through acacia and other introduced forest.

Stage one is an easy level walk which follows the forestry road west from Le Pétrin along the ridge through the forests. It affords splendid views into the Grande Rivière Noire and if it's been raining, there will be good views of waterfalls. The road ends at a picnic kiosk on a fantastic viewpoint.

The route then descends precipitously along a track indicated below the kiosk; it's exceptionally steep in parts and often slippery as soap, so it's not a good idea after heavy rain. After about one km, the worst of it is over and you emerge on a hunting road which is just passable for 4WD vehicles. This road is lined with deer blinds and during the hunting season (June to September) hikers should avoid the area altogether or seek local advice, wear bright clothing and exercise extreme caution in this area.

The road drops steeply to the river and the route becomes a flat easy stroll along the river valley, passing countless deer blinds and sections of forest hideously disfigured by clearing and wood cutting. Eventually, it issues into cane fields. Turn left at the T-junction and continue along the road strewn with sugar cane detritus to the coast road at Grande Rivière Noire (opposite the Pavillon de Jade Restaurant).

Much of the land along the lower part of this route is through private property but as far as we know, there's no problem if you just pass through and don't disturb anything.

Return to Curepipe by bus either via Souillac (change necessary at Baie du Cap) or via Quatre Bornes (change necessary). Reasonably fit walkers should allow four to five hours to do this spectacular walk.

*Le Pétrin to Tamarind Falls* This trip begins as for the trek from Le Pétrin to Grande Rivière Noire. Follow the forestry road for just over two km. Rather than taking the turn-off toward the picnic kiosk described in the Grande Rivière Noire route, take the right fork and continue for another 500 metres or so to a second fork in the road. To reach Tamarind Falls, you must follow the left fork (the right will lead you to the road which connects the Curepipe-Chamarel road with Mare Longue reservoir).

The route is easy throughout, with no steep or tricky bits, often following a scenic ridge. It's mostly forest along the way, with good views, then it descends into more open terrain near the reservoir. A detour at the end around the Seven Waterfalls of Tamarin is fun – there is a trail which drops down to the base of the falls, but people will have to explore for themselves to find it. If you have the energy, it's a wonderful finale to the walk.

Return to Curepipe by bus from the bus station in Henrietta. For this walk, allow three hours, more if you want to explore the falls area.

*Plaine Champagne to Bel Ombre (South Coast)* The trailhead for this walk is the Plaine Champagne viewpoint on the

Curepipe-Chamarel road which lies about two km past (ie toward Chamarel) the radio tower at the highest point on the road (744 metres). The trail (which is shown on the IGN map as a 'yellow' road) heads due south to Bel Ombre, passing en route a succession of wonderful views through some lovely mixed forests and plantations. The finish meanders along some rather confusing cane field tracks, but a reasonable sense of direction will get you to the coast road without too much difficulty. From Bel Ombre, there are buses to Souillac (change there for Curepipe) and to Tamarin via Baie du Cap. Allow about four hours for this fairly easy walk.

**Plaine Champagne to Bassin Blanc & Chemin Grenier** This walk begins about three km south of Le Pétrin along the road towards Plaine Champagne. Heading south, look for the spot where the road makes a sharp turn to the right and two trails branch off to the left. The left fork goes to Piton Savanne and the right goes to Mt Cocotte and Bassin Blanc.

Follow the track on the right. Although it's shown on the IGN map as a dotted line, it is actually paved for much of its length. The route is fairly open, passing through a variety of landscapes before emerging at Bassin Blanc, a classic crater lake surrounded by forest – a really idyllic spot. Although the IGN map shows a break in the route here, it does in fact continue to meet the yellow road which descends to Chamouny and Chemin Grenier. Return from Chemin Grenier to Curepipe via Souillac, where you'll have to change buses.

Allow two to three hours for this easy walk, plus several hours for the bus trip back to Curepipe.

If you want to make a longer day of it, get an early start and take a side trip to the summit of Montagne Cocotte. At the trailhead, also begin by taking the right fork. After about 1.2 km, there'll be a rough and boggy route taking off to the right. When this route crosses a stream, bear to the right and follow the clear path to the forested summit of Montagne Cocotte.

**Grand Case Noyale to Chamarel & the Terres de Couleur** Start at Grande Case Noyale and continue up the Chamarel road. Although this route is all on normal tarmac roads, there is little traffic, and it must surely rate as one of the most beautiful roads on the island. It's well worth the effort for the scenery and fabulous views of the mountains and the coast.

The IGN map also shows a much shorter walking route from La Gaulette on the west coast over the ridge to the Terres de Couleur but we haven't tried it. If you do have a go, let us know how it went.

Buses are scarce in these parts, so on the return trip, you may have to hitch. Traffic is sparse but drivers seem more inclined to stop than in more populated areas.

**Domaine du Chasseur & Les Montagnes Bambous (Bambous Mountains)** Your best chance of exploring these beautiful hills, some of which are crossed by inviting trails but almost free of roads, is to visit Domaine du Chasseur. This private estate has a hunting lodge, restaurant and rough 4WD tracks which double as walking tracks open to visitors. For Rs 50 admission, you receive a map of the easy-to-follow hunting trails. They are superb, if a little steep, and they offer magnificent views across forests and down to the coast. For further details, see under Domaine du Chasseur in the South Mauritius chapter.

**La Pouce** La Pouce, the prominent thumb-shaped peak which towers over Port Louis and Moka is an easy climb and makes a great introduction to walking in Mauritius. To reach the trailhead from Port Louis, follow St George St (which changes to Pandit Nehru St and then Mahatma Gandhi St), turn right into St Denis St and continue past Ste Anne chapel. The route is described in the following reader's letter :

We speak very little French, but by walking towards the hill through Port Louis wearing backpacks, and staring, puzzled, towards the hills, people regularly volunteered the necessary directions unbidden.

However, if you follow the roads in Port Louis at the base of Signal Hill, you will cross a dry creek bed, and with little prompting find yourself on a gentle grassy incline walking along a 4WD track.

Once you are abreast of the sheer granite escarpment on your right – watch to see when the conspicuous topknot on the escarpment is abreast of you – then take the first path leading sharply upwards to your right. The path is very narrow and the leaves deposit a lot of moisture on hikers and equipment if unprotected.

This narrow path opens onto a grassy plateau where the path becomes less distinct in places. Resist the great temptation to follow numerous goat tracks leading directly to the final granite cone. The true path circles behind the cone almost passing it, when it follows a cleft up the back side of the cone to the most magnificent view imaginable of Pieter Both, Port Louis, and the interior.

We had a rain squall catch us at the top, but there was a little shelf to leeward that provided reasonable protection in the whiteout conditions which brought swirling clouds, giving everchanging glimpses of the surrounding peaks. Very much like a Japanese painting.

We shared the peak with a school class, including very small children. Except for caution at the very summit of the cone, there is no danger in the climb, and we (not very fit 40-year olds) made the climb in 2½ very leisurely hours. We wore flip-flops and basketball shoes. The paths do get very slippery in the rain, so old clothes and the ability to sustain a few quick sitdowns are recommended.

For anyone even remotely inclined to hiking it would be a shame to miss the glorious views from the top.

**Barbara Dressler, UK**

*Railway Walking* A reader who has lived a fair slice of his life in Mauritius brought to our attention the possibility of hikes along Mauritius' system of defunct railways. Here's what he had to say:

The IGN map still shows bits of the old Mauritian railway system. Yes, Mauritius had a railway system. It stretched from Souillac and Mahébourg to Curepipe, down to Port Louis, swung north to Terre Rouge, Mapou, Poudre d'Or, and Rivière du Rempart; then curved east and south to Centre de Flacq; and terminated at Grande Rivière du Sud Est where you can still take the 'free' public ferry – a pirogue poled across the bay to the other side where you can either walk or take a bus back to Mahébourg.

The north-east section (Mapou to Grande Rivière du Sud Est) is easy to follow as the line is built up and the foundations are clearly visible. As you walk through farms and land covered by crops, the people

are very accommodating. Literally all the old bridges still exist and most of the post offices you see en route were the beautifully constructed railway stations.

Mountain climbing apart, this is a top trek and you do meet people. Yes, take a good water bottle. Even today, be prepared to be seen as a 'madman'!

**Ralph Watson, Australia**

### Hunting

During the hunting season (June to September), the Franco-Mauritian gentry take to their estates and blast the hides off 2500 Java deer each year. Sorry, hunting on estates is by invitation only.

An exception to this rule is Domaine du Chasseur (☎ 6319259), an estate on the south-east coast where visitors can hunt deer either by stalking or from miradors (observation posts). The owners have introduced controlled deer hunting as a means to contribute to the upkeep of the estate. The hunting area is quite separate from the rest of the estate (restaurant, accommodation, and hiking trails).

The basic hunting rate per person per day is Rs 3500. Hunters are accompanied by a hunting leader (Rs 1000 per day). There are further charges for each kill, ranging from Rs 5000 for a Daguet (one-year old male) to Rs 50,000 for a Gold Medal Super Trophy (big grandaddy of a deer over four years old). If a hunter wounds a deer and does not succeed in finding it after a search, a payment of Rs 1800 above the minimum rate is required. Any deer which are shot remain the property of the establishment, but the client may keep the trophy (head). Guns are provided on the premises and cartridges are sold at Rs 30 each. For an additional fee, taxidermy, freight and transfer can be arranged for trophies. More details about Domaine du Chasseur are provided in the South Mauritius chapter.

### Deep-Sea Fishing

October to March is the best time to catch record-size blue marlin. One of the world's top fishing spots is a couple of km off Le Morne. Here the bottom plunges 700 metres and the currents attract small fish pursued by huge predators. Marlin, sailfish, barracuda, wahoo, tuna, and shark are common.

All the big hotels run boats and there are several Mauritian clubs. Visitors can also hire cheaper local fishing boats if they're not too fussy about where they sling their hooks.

Minimum hire time is six hours and each boat can normally take five anglers. Expect to pay around Rs 6000 per boat when hiring from upmarket fishing centres or hotels, but local operators may drop to 50% of this price or less if approached directly.

The major big-game fishing organisations are:

Centre de Pêche de l'Île Maurice (☎ 6836552), Rivière Noire
Beachcomber Fishing Club (☎ 6836775), Le Morne
Black River Sportfishing Organisation (☎ 6836547), Rivière Noire
Organisation de Pêche du Nord (☎ 2616264), Trou aux Biches
La Pirogue Big Game Fishing (☎ 4538441), Flic en Flac
Sofitel Imperial Big Game Fishing (☎ 4538700), Wolmar
Sportfisher (☎ 2638358), Grand Baie

## Diving & Snorkelling

Mauritius is not really the place for a diving holiday. Diving around the island is not as deeply interesting as around the Seychelles and nothing like the Maldives. The exception would be on the outer isle of Cargados Carajos (also known as St Brandon), but that's a long way away and there are no organised trips there. Spear fishing and the collection of shells, coral, and fishes are prohibited.

Most of the large hotels either have centres to provide diving instruction or can arrange diving trips for guests. Ironically, the Mauritian Underwater Group (☎ 6965368) is based at Railway Rd, Phoenix, which is about as landlocked as you can get on the island. This is a good source for up-to-date information since it is also the headquarters for the Mauritius Marine Conservation Society, which is campaigning to stop the pollution and destruction of the coral reefs. For more

details, refer to the section on Flora & Fauna in the Facts about the Country chapter.

The best places to buy underwater equipment are Quay Stores (☎ 2121043), 3 John Kennedy St, Port Louis; and Gaz Industriels (☎ 2121453), Grande Rivière Nord-Ouest. The use of spearguns is illegal.

The best place for diving on Mauritius is off La Pirogue Hotel, near Flic en Flac on the west coast. Villas Caroline, at Flic en Flac itself, has a diving school and hires out equipment, as do the hotels at Le Morne. The main diving attraction off the coast at Flic en Flac is the cave known as the Cathedral. Other dive sites include Whale Rock, which can be reached from either Grand Baie or Trou aux Biches, and Roche Zozo, an underwater pinnacle of rock (accessible by boat only during the summer) off the south-east coast. The submerged crater near Île Ronde is a popular dive site accessible from tourist centres in the north, such as Grand Baie.

Snorkelling is a better proposition. There are over-the-side boat trips running from the major beach hotels and from Grand Baie beach. For those who don't want to get wet, there are fleets of glass-bottom boats. The

reef off Peréybère beach is said to be good for viewing.

## Surfing

A wave of Aussie and South African surfies built up in the '70s around Tamarin. A surfing movie called *The Forgotten Island of Santosha* was also made. But the wave crashed and wiped out all interest in surfing during the '80s. The increasing cost of air travel to Mauritius didn't help.

In the '90s, the low cost of self-catering accommodation at Tamarin and better air travel opportunities could bring another swell of enthusiasm, especially in the south-west part of the island. During our research, we saw various surfers fanning out from the airport. Tim Williams, of Durban, South Africa, has described some of the surfing spots around Tamarin as 'the perfect set up', with up to two metre waves.

Top of his list were Le Morne and One Eye's (named after the one-eyed owner of Le Morne estate), both off the beaches in front of the two hotels. It's uncertain whether these hotels will continue to permit access. Other good surfing locations are near the Baie du Cap; 'Lefts and Rights', which is further south by Îlot San Sancho; and one opposite the public gardens in Souillac.

The surfing season is from June to August. When the surf's not up, Tim talks of a good social scene 'eating eleven-spot crab soup, avocado and tuna rolls, and pawpaw for dessert, drinking beer and watching dogfights'.

## Other Water Sports

Other water sports, such as windsurfing, water-skiing, kayaking, pedalos, etc, are offered by the main beach hotels and often made available to nonresidents for a price.

## Golf

There are golf courses, mostly nine-hole affairs, at most of the major beach hotels, but they are designed more for the beach-bored holidaymaker than the enthusiast. The Brabant Hotel at Le Morne and the Belle Mare Plage hotel on the east coast might

appeal more to dedicated golfers since they both have 18-hole golf courses.

## Cycling

Surprisingly few visitors seem to realise that cycling is one of the best ways of seeing the island, even though it is cheap and easy to arrange.

Cycling enthusiasts may be interested to know that the Racing Club du Maurice has holiday villages with a bar and eats at Lafayette, near the St Géran Hotel, and at Centre de Flacq, on the east coast. They're for members only, but if you're passing...who knows. The headquarters (☎ 4549071) are in Trianon, Quatre Bornes.

## Horse Riding

Horse riding opportunities are limited to Domaine Les Pailles, an estate run as a tourist attraction, including its own riding centre, Les Écuries du Domaine (☎ 2124225).

## Weddings & Honeymoons

Well, these could be considered activities! Mauritius, in common with many other Indian Ocean islands, promotes itself as a romance centre. Many of the luxury hotels claim that at any one time up to half the guests are honeymooners, and most of these hotels have staff specially trained to make all nuptial arrangements.

Couples planning to marry on Mauritius must be resident on the island at least three working days before the ceremony. A visit to the relevant ministry in Port Louis is necessary before the wedding day. Mauritian law requires that divorced ladies must allow a minimum 300 day interval between divorce and new wedding date, or a pregnancy test taken locally must be negative. It seems divorced men can get rehitched quicker!

Most tour operators can arrange documentation for a nominal charge and provide optional extras such as videos, horse-drawn carriages, tropical cocktails, flower garlands, musical entertainers, cakes and photographers.

The relevant Mauritian authority for wedding technicalities is the Registrar of

Civil Status (☎ 2011727), Emmanuel Anquetil Building, 7th level, Port Louis.

## HIGHLIGHTS
The following suggestions are by no means exhaustive, but may provide indications of less obvious attractions than the island's beaches:

### Beaches
Pointe aux Roches (surf viewing); Flic en Flac (swimming); Bel Mare (swimming)

### Historical Settings
Balaclava; Eureka House

### Natural Scenery
Rivière Noire Gorges (hiking area); region between Benares and Rivière Dragon; Domaine du Chasseur; coastal area between Baie du Cap and Le Morne; and Chamarel Falls

### Gardens & Museums
Pamplemousses; Naval Museum (Mahébourg)

### Accommodation
Ranked high for charm is the upmarket Colonial Coconut Hotel close to Grand Baie. For a change from the beach, try Domaine du Chasseur in an elevated, forested setting in the interior of the island. In the middle price range, Hotel Les Bougainvilliers near Tamarin offers excellent value (and great breakfasts). Best value budget places include Pension Notre Dame and Pension Aquarelle in Mahébourg, and Jolicoeur Guesthouse in Peréybère.

### Restaurants
La Charette (Indian, Grand Baie); DSL Coffee House (Indian, Port Louis); Sea Breeze (Chinese fondue, Flic en Flac); Aquarelle (French, Mahébourg).

### Oddities
Market building resembling giant organ pipes (Curepipe); shop signs in Chinatown section (Port Louis).

## ACCOMMODATION
Mauritius offers the full range of accommodation from budget rooms to super luxury suites. The main categories are camping, *pensions de famille* (boarding houses), small Indian or Chinese-run hotels, bungalows or apartments, guesthouses and luxury beach hotels.

At the budget end of the market the most important thing to remember is: the more of you are there and the longer you stay, the cheaper the rates. It is possible to base yourself in one place and see all of Mauritius.

There are regular busy and quiet periods, but no separate high and low seasons. December, January, July and August are the busiest months, and some of the top hotels have a big hike in rates at this time. When it is quiet, most places will offer cheaper rates if prompted. The smarter guesthouses and beach hotels add a 15% government tax to the bill; the others tend not to. Half-board is commonly available and includes breakfast and dinner.

The most accurate and comprehensive source for accommodation and rates is the Mauritius Chamber of Commerce & Industry (MCCI), which operates a free accommodation service from a counter at SSR Airport to cater for unbooked visitors, and is open for each flight arrival. On telephone confirmation of a room booking, you pay the MCCI 20% of the daily rate and receive a voucher. This is deducted from your final bill by the hotel or guesthouse.

The Mauritius Government Tourist Office (MGTO) in Port Louis issues two biannual lists of accommodation tariffs: *Beach Hotel Tariffs* and *Tariffs: Budget Hotels, Bungalows & Boarding Houses*. You can obtain copies from MGTO offices abroad or at the MGTO office at the Emmanuel Anquetil Building on Sir Seewoosagur Ramgoolam St, Port Louis.

### Camping
There is little assistance offered to campers. By the same token, there are few hassles. There are no official camp sites and no restrictions, within reason, about where you

can camp on public land. Few shoestring travellers or outdoor enthusiasts bring a tent, but the opportunity to use one exists. The favoured sites are the public beaches such as Blue Bay near Mahébourg, Flic en Flac, Pointe des Puits near Belle Mare, Mon Choisy, and past Le Morne village in front of Baie du Cap estate on the south-west tip. Casuarina trees provide shade and shelter. There are public toilets on some beaches, but many are in a terrible state.

The main drawback, apart from the lack of facilities, is the lack of security. A good idea is to camp as close to the police station as possible, get them to keep an eye on your tent and leave your stuff with them when you're away for the day. The police on the island are generally very helpful. Several budget guesthouses, Aquarelle in Mahébourg is an example, now accept small numbers of campers and charge them a modest fee.

There are plenty of long stretches of quiet beach, but nowhere around the island is there a deserted beach. There are just too many people.

### Pensions de Famille

These budget boarding houses come in all sorts and sizes and cost between Rs 125 and Rs 250 per night for a single room.

Pensions are concentrated in Mahébourg and Curepipe, with one or two at Peréybère, Quatre Bornes and Rose Hill. There are none on the east coast and none to speak of in Port Louis. A few are small family affairs and offer meals. Others are loosely run by a young caretaker and rent out rooms on an hourly basis for the love trysts of frustrated local couples. Some are clean, some are grubby, but none are the absolute pits. All have communal toilets and showers. For this sort of price you can't afford to be fussy. Take an inner sheet sleeping bag if you intend staying in pensions or cheap hotels.

### Guesthouses

At an average of Rs 350 for a single and Rs 600 for a double per night, guesthouses provide intimate surroundings and service at a good hotel standard. Most are near the beach and the main centres are Flic en Flac and around Grand Baie.

### Hotels

**Cheap Hotels** Most of the cheap hotels are in Port Louis, with a couple in Curepipe. Most are run by Indian, Muslim or Chinese families.

Rates are equivalent to the pensions and meals, if available, are extra. Most rooms are clean, basic and have private bathrooms.

**Beach Hotels** Tucked away on the island's best beaches, a double room in a beach hotel can range from Rs 400 to Rs 8000 per night, including breakfast. Most of the top hotels are around Rs 2500 and the smaller ones Rs 800. These are fixed daily rates and the price drops if you book a fortnightly package. Given the large number of beach hotels competing for customers, you should have no qualms about shopping around for the best deals, and requesting discounts if you stay longer than a week.

The Sun group of hotels (St Géran, Le Touessrok, and La Pirogue) offers guests a special Suncard; and the Beachcomber group (Le Royal Palm; Brabant; Paradis; Shandrani; Le Mauricia, and Trou aux Biches) offers guests a similar deal with its Beachcomber Card.

The Suncard, which every guest receives on registration, entitles the holder to free transfers between St Géran and Le Touessrok hotels; free boat transfer to and from Île aux Cerfs; free use of many sports facilities, for example, tennis courts, squash, bowls, golf, sailing, canoeing, water-skiing, glass-bottom boats, and windsurfing; Rs 50 free casino chips; a discount at various shops and boutiques, and when paying for rental of certain sports facilities, such as scuba diving. It also lets holders interchange accommodation with other hotels in the group – subject to availability.

The Beachcomber Club card, which every guest receives on registration, entitles the holder to free use of many sports facilities, for example, tennis courts, squash, water-skiing, and windsurfing; Rs 50 free casino chips; and a discount when paying for rental of certain facilities for sports, such as scuba diving. It also lets holders interchange accommodation with other hotels in the group – subject to availability.

For advice on problems with hotel security guards and exclusion of nonresidents from public beaches, see the section on Dangers & Annoyances in this chapter.

**Urban Hotels** There are a few undistinguished urban hotels in and around Port Louis and Curepipe. They are probably used by travelling salespeople, visiting sports or cultural teams and people attending conferences, because we can't see that they have any advantage or attraction for travellers or tourists.

### Rental
**Bungalows & Apartments** There are bungalows and apartments around the coast, including seemingly hundreds of them in Grand Baie. You may have to go looking for others, as they are not listed with any organisation or agency. Most will have signs at the gate or nailed to a tree by the roadside saying *Bungalow à louer* or *Campement à louer* (Bungalow for rent), often with a telephone number. The Friday edition of the Mauritian newspaper, L'Express, has a page or two of *petites annonces* (classified advertisements) where you can usually find plenty of bungalows and apartments offered for rent in the columns entitled *à louer* (rental).

The units range from complete bungalows, with up to three bedrooms, for as little as Rs 350 per day, to small one and two-bedroom flats with a kitchenette and bathroom for Rs 200 and upwards. They are fully furnished and equipped with fridges. The more expensive ones will have a TV, washing machine and sometimes air-con.

For two to four people staying a fortnight or month, bungalows are the best bargains. The proprietor will reduce the daily rate if you stay a week or more. Many of the places rely on return visits by guests. You can write

with a deposit of the equivalent of US$50 and book in advance.

### FOOD
Despite the dominant Indian flavour of Mauritius, the country is sadly lacking in curry houses and Indian restaurants, probably because everyone cooks this type of food at home and so no-one has the urge to go out to eat it.

If you want lunch or dinner at a pension or guesthouse – and in some places there is no eating-out alternative – you must let the owner/manager know in advance so that sufficient supplies can be obtained. In most cases you cannot have meals without notice.

### Snacks & Fast Food
Mauritians are big on snacks and you can buy samosas, rotis, curries, curried rolls, meatballs, noodle specials, soups and a variety of other basic delicacies from street vendors in Port Louis, for between Rs 1 and Rs 10. Most smaller towns have a stall or two selling the same.

Fast food has arrived in Mauritius. There is a steadily increasing number of fast food outfits, including Kentucky Fried Chicken outlets in Curepipe and Centre du Flacq, and assorted similar places in Port Louis.

### Main Dishes
Most restaurants offer Créole, European and Chinese menus, and the speciality is usually seafood. However, the range of fish is not as large or varied as in the Seychelles.

At its best, Créole food is spiced up French cuisine that depends almost entirely on the sauce. It looks exciting and exotic in the tourist-oriented cookbooks, but you'll only come close to it in the best hotels and restaurants. At the other extreme, Créole cooking is basic fare, propped up with mountains of flavoured rice and designed to fill the belly rather than excite the tastebuds.

Except at the top end of the market, restaurants do not do justice to Mauritian Créole cooking which is best appreciated in the home; an invitation won't be long in coming once you've made friends with a Mauritian.

Common dishes are *rougaille*, a Mediterranean-type dish based on tomatoes, onions and garlic, which can contain any kind of meat or fish; *daube*, a Mediterranean type of octopus stew; and chicken curry. (See also the Food sections in the Facts for the Visitor chapters for Réunion and the Seychelles.)

The Chinese are the main caterers and are good at blurring the lines between the various cooking traditions. Indian food is best value at small cafés and street vendor outlets.

### Self-Catering

If you are camping or staying in a self-contained bungalow or apartment, self-catering is obviously the order of the stay.

Prices of tinned or packaged food (much of it imported from South Africa) and household goods are marked in most stores – the merchants tend not to surreptitiously increase prices for tourists.

The biggest and best markets for fruit and vegetables are in Port Louis, Curepipe and the bigger towns such as Mahébourg and Centre de Flacq. The self-catering accommodation areas around Flic en Flac and Grand Baie are served by well-stocked and relatively expensive supermarkets.

Fruits and vegetables are seasonal, and prices vary accordingly. Mauritius has the same variety as the other Indian Ocean islands, but seems to get more excited over lychees (July) and longans (February). To make sure you pay a fair price for your produce at the market, watch a local person buying the same, or check the rates of several sellers.

Heart of palm (for which the palm tree is sacrificed) is regarded as a rare delicacy. Unless you've got the money to be extravagant, it's not worth pining over. It's like tasteless coconut flesh and relies on vinaigrette or other dressings to give it flavour. In the Seychelles you are quite likely to get it served up without ceremony at a guesthouse, but not in Mauritius.

To buy fish, go to the fish-landing station in each coastal village and deal directly with the fishermen. In Grand Baie fish is about Rs 100 per kg.

### DRINKS

The price of all drink, be it cola, beer, rum or wine, purchased in bottles includes a deposit for the bottle. Remember to take along the empties when replenishing supplies.

### Nonalcoholic Drinks

**Tea & Coffee** Tea and coffee are hit-or-miss affairs. They're never Mauritian, as the local crop is used for blending. The tea is likely to be white and sweetened by condensed milk, unless you specify otherwise. The coffee fares a bit better. Instant coffee costs about the same as in the UK or Australia, but sugar and powdered milk are cheaper.

**Soft Drinks** Soft drinks are numerous and are consumed copiously by Mauritians. Pepsi Cola, affectionately referred to as the national drink of Mauritius, is by far the most popular soft drink. The islanders are also fond of locally and commercially made yoghurt drinks. One of the most popular of these is *lassi*, which is thick and sweet. Readers have also praised *alouda*, a syrupy brew of agar agar (china grass), milk and flavouring, which is sold on the streets – the alouda sold in the market in Port Louis is reported to be excellent.

If you don't trust the local water supply, there are plenty of bottles of imported mineral water.

### Alcohol

Beer and rum are potent, plentiful, and cheap but not nasty. Locally brewed Guinness is popular, at Rs 8 a bottle. Phoenix pilsner beer, which takes its name from the town where it's brewed, costs Rs 25 for a small bottle at the bar. At upmarket establishments or discos, the same bottle can cost between Rs 35 and Rs 50. In the local stores, most of which have liquor licences, you'll find less astounding prices: a small bottle for Rs 8 or a large one for Rs 15. If you look at the label, it's easy to see why the local nickname for the beer is *la bière zarnier* (spider beer).

There is a variety of rums. The best known is Green Island, but Power's No 1 and Anytime are the most popular brands with the Mauritians. A shot of the latter at a bar costs Rs 5, or you can buy a 750 ml bottle for Rs 50 at the store and get a Rs 5 refund on the bottle.

French wine is expensive and most Mauritians prefer South African wines, which start at Rs 80 to Rs 100 a bottle. The cheapest wines are Mauritian-bottled whites and reds for around Rs 30 over the shop counter. The origin could be a tankerload of table wine surplus from France or imported crystals watered down. It's just about palatable, though.

*Tapeta!* is Créole for 'Cheers'!

## ENTERTAINMENT
### Cinemas

Cinemas on Mauritius are fighting a losing battle with dozens of video rental shops which have sprung up in most villages and towns. Mauritians are big film buffs, but alas, not of good quality films. There are two categories – sex and violence.

In one cinema there'll be a double action feature in the Rambo-commando vein, while in the other you'll undoubtedly find a couple of erotic films. The limited choice is summed up by one reader who reported seeing one cinema advertising its week's programme as: *Police Assassin 5*; *Jungle Love* (an Indian romantic melodrama); *Death Warrant*; and *Voluptés Secrètes* (Voluptuous Secrets). Locals also report that for the five days following the release of a new Sylvester Stallone film, cinemas sell standing tickets!

All films are in French, but the soundtrack is terrible and the language is superfluous to the plot. It could be medieval Mongolian for all it matters or anyone cares.

### Theatres

The Mauritius Government Tourist Office news-sheet of coming events includes a programme of shows or plays at the theatres.

There are two theatres in Mauritius. One is next to Government House in Port Louis and the other, larger theatre is in Rose Hill. They are used mostly for local amateur productions, but host the occasional troupe from overseas. See the Port Louis chapter for details.

### Segá Dances, Discos & Jazz

The Mauritius Government Tourist Office in Port Louis publishes a news-sheet of coming events every two months, which includes a programme of dancing and ségá nights at the hotels and discos. For details about ségá, see the Culture & the Arts section in the Facts about the Country chapter. Most major hotels lay on at least one ségá night per week. Tickets to these events usually cost around Rs 250 to Rs 350 and include a buffet dinner.

Apart from the hotels, the main local jive shops are Sam's Disco at La Caverne in Royal Rd, Vacoas; Palladium, with bizarre architecture and an isolated setting, on the Port Louis-Quatre Bornes trunk road; Blue Mauritius at the Commercial Centre in Rose Hill; and Saxophone in Beau Bassin.

Grand Baie has several discos, including the Climax Club, and Dream On. At the latter, there's reported to be a predominance of ladies for hire.

Admission to discos usually costs at least Rs 100, and you'll rarely pay less than Rs 30 for a beer.

Finally, jazz fans might want to visit Le Jazz Club, part of Domaine Les Pailles (an estate run as a tourist attraction) where the island's top jazz musicians gather each Friday.

### Casinos

Roulette, blackjack, baccarat, and slot machines are some of the after-dinner diversions available for tourists at the casinos in the big beach hotels and the Casino de Maurice in the centre of Curepipe. The Chinese casino, L'Amicale, on Royal St in Port Louis, offers a whole range of Chinese gambling games.

## Spectator Sports

For details of the Mauritian sports and horse racing scene, refer to the Culture & the Arts section in the Facts about the Country chapter.

## THINGS TO BUY

Some prime buys for souvenirs are: model ships, model homes, clothing, Indian fabrics, footwear, stamps and rum. The best place to shop for them is Curepipe.

In the Flora & Fauna section in the Facts about the Country chapter, we have provided a Conservation section about items such as turtle shell, coral, and shells. Given the wide choice of other things to buy in Mauritius, there is no reason to purchase endangered species and thereby contribute to their extinction.

## Model Ships

It is unlikely you will come away from Mauritius without seeing or buying a model ship. Small scale shipbuilding has become big business during the past few years, after someone carved a model just for fun in 1968.

Magnificently intricate miniature replicas of *The Bounty, Victory, Endeavour, Cutty Sark, Golden Hind* and even the *Titanic* can be bought off the shelf or made to order from a range of small factories. Few of the famous ships made ever visited Mauritius, but there are models of vessels such as the *Confiance*, a 1792 corsair of 26 guns captained by the privateer Robert Surcouf, which featured in the island's history.

The models are made out of lintels (teak) or cheaper camphor wood, and larger ships take up to 400 hours to complete. The sails and rigging are dipped in tea to give them a weathered look. Shop around for price comparisons. Prices begin around Rs 900 for a small model of a 19th-century cutter, and average Rs 4500 for a 118-cm long model of the 18th-century French vessel *Superbe*.

Most visitors take the models aboard the plane as hand luggage. Sturdy, specially made boxes are usually supplied by the manufacturer. Air France and Air Mauritius reportedly charge freight rates for carrying a model in the cargo or luggage hold, but Singapore Airlines let it go free, as baggage. If your boat is boxed, Air Mauritius charges Rs 328 per kg with a six kg minimum.

Make sure you supervise the packing of the model you've chosen – it's not worth the disappointment of unpacking your box at home and finding you've got the wrong model. Also, get a bill of sale and a valid certificate which is recognised by European Community (EC) countries and other Western nations, to save paying duty on arrival home.

The Forest Side suburb of landlocked Curepipe seems to be the shipbuilding centre. Voiliers de L'Océan (☎ 6766986) on Celicourt Antelme St, off Royal Rd, employs about 20 people; the men work on the structure and the women do the rigging and sails. The director, Mr K Singh, will be glad to show you around the small factory without any pressure to buy. It is open each day, including Sundays, from 7.30 am to 5 pm.

Another outlet in Curepipe is La Société du Port (☎ 6766978) at 29 Rue Nicolas de Céré.

Model Ship: *Victory*

For more ships, go along Royal Rd towards Mahébourg and, at the sharp corner past the Forest Side post office, turn down the road to La Marie. About 750 metres away, on Gustave Colin St, is La Marine en Bois (☎ 6763503), which is bigger and more impersonal than Voiliers de L'Océan. It features a range of models in teak and camphor. Comajora (☎ 6761644) is about one km further down the street.

The biggest factory is Historic Marine (☎ 2839404), St Antoine Industrial Estate, Goodlands, in the north of the island. It is open Monday to Friday from 8 am to 5 pm and on Saturdays from 8 am to noon.

Several art and souvenir shops have models for sale, sometimes at reasonable prices. The Emporium d'Art, underneath the Lai Min restaurant in Royal St, Port Louis, is worth a look.

### Model Homes

The model-making industry has expanded to cover another historic feature – Créole and colonial homes and buildings.

For Rs 5500, you can buy an architect's replica of La Ville Bague, the 1740 home of Mauritius' great governor Mahé de Labourdonnais. Le Château de Bel Ombre, Maison Gimbeau in Forest Side and Le Relais Pointe Venus, the beautiful boarding house at Anse aux Anglais on the island of Rodrigues, are also reproduced.

There are also models of the 1820 theatre in Port Louis and the Royal College school in Curepipe. If you're interested, try contacting Maquettes de Maisons Traditionelles Mauriciennes, Seeneevassen Carpenen, Block 1A, Cité Atlee, in Forest Side.

### Clothing

Hardcore shoppers in search of bargain prices for swimwear, knitwear, sportswear, T-shirts, etc, head for the many shops in Rose Hill and Curepipe. The open-air market held on Saturdays in the centre of Quatre Bornes is also considered a good source of inexpensive clothing. One reader enthused about the low prices and high quality of the woollen and cotton goods and recommended a visit

to the Phoenix Factory Phoenix brewery in designer label goods ...

Since Mauritius has now clothing exporter, there are ba.... found in designer goods obtained ... from factory outlets. Prices tend to be high... in the fashion boutiques at beach hotels or in beach resorts such as Grand Baie. Many of the beach hotel boutiques run weekly fashion parades for the patrons.

### Indian Fabrics

The government-authorised Handloom House at the Bank of Baroda Building in Sir William Newton St, Port Louis, has a fair range of Indian garments and fabrics.

You can buy dresses, scarves and shirts. Cotton saris are around Rs 400 and kurtah shirts Rs 600. Silk fabric is around Rs 375 per metre.

### Footwear

You can buy good quality fashionable shoes or have them made for between Rs 150 and Rs 250. Try the shopping arcade beside Curepipe bus station.

If you buy flip-flops (thongs), chances are they will have red soles with blue straps. Look at the number of people wearing them. This particular brand is almost part of the national dress. Wear them in Réunion or Madagascar and people will know you've been to Mauritius.

### Stamps

Mauritius, like many island nations, prides itself on its colourful stamps and postal history. It was perhaps a stamp more than anything else which first brought the island to the notice of the rest of the world.

The Mauritian Blue, featuring Queen Victoria's head, was a 'Post Paid' stamp, but the engraver made it a 'Post Office' stamp by mistake. Quite a number were printed and posted before the error was discovered. The few that are left are now worth millions.

If you are at all interested in stamps, you must go to the Eureka colonial home at Moka to see Prakash Purmessur and his shop, the

Barnard Philatelic Boutique (Barnard s the engraver of the first stamp in auritius). Prakash's enthusiasm is infectious, and if you're not interested before you go in, you'll probably come out looking for a stamp album to stick your purchases in.

Without any pressure to buy, Prakash will show you the gems of his collection. These include the 'Post Paid' 1848, the second Mauritian stamp, worth around Rs 120,000. He only has reproductions of the Mauritian Blue 'Post Paid' and 'Post Office' stamps, but they're each worth Rs 15,000.

Sets of stamps depicting Mauritian birds for Rs 500 and marine life for Rs 350 are more affordable. A set of six, printed in 1968 to commemorate the bicentenary of the visit of *Paul et Virginie* author Bernardin de St Pierre to Mauritius, costs Rs 400. Only 1250 sets were issued.

Collectors can also buy other expensive philatelic printing mistakes such as the 5c stamp depicting not one paradise flycatcher, like the rest, but two (Rs 4000). Less glaring goofs and forgeries are cheaper.

Postcards and letters delivered in Mauritius, mostly as ship's mail as early as the mid-19th century, supplement stamp sales.

### Duty-Free

Mauritius is not a noted duty-free centre, and the sales are aimed at jet-setting residents rather than visitors.

Most stores will arrange duty-free sales, but the specialists are J Kalachand & Co, at 20 Lord Kitchener St, Port Louis. They only sell electrical and electronic goods, not alcohol, tobacco or cosmetics. Local cigarettes, which are called Matinee, cost Rs 16 for 20. There are no cigars or pipe tobaccos available locally. For duty-free jewellery, try any of the Poncini boutiques in the major tourist centres.

Duty-free prices aren't as low as in Singapore or Hong Kong. If you decide to buy, you must pay in foreign currency three days before departure and provide your ticket and passport. Delivery to the airport costs Rs 150 Monday to Friday between 9 am and 4 pm. Otherwise, you must pay an extra Rs 60 per hour to bring out a customs officer to clear the goods!

There are duty-free shops in the arrival and departure lounges at the airport. You can get spirits (including Mauritian rums), cigarettes and perfume at good rates, but only foreign currency is accepted.

### Handicrafts & Souvenirs

For those not going to Madagascar, there are a number of shops specialising in Malagasy handicrafts, including leather belts and bags, semiprecious-stone solitaire sets, and hats and baskets. There is a plethora of stalls in cramped aisles at the market in Port Louis pushing these products at browsing busloads of tourists.

In the souvenir shops is a range of objects featuring the coloured earths of Chamarel. They'll scream from anyone's mantelpiece. Not so distinctive, but just as earthy, are the dried-flower decorated stationery, bookmarks and picture frames from Aux Fantasies Florales at Peréybère, north of Grand Baie, and from the stall at the Eureka colonial house, Moka. These gifts don't go with the tropical image of the country, but are more representative of the actual flora.

The Societé des Petites Entreprises Specialisées (SPES) showroom on Labourdonnais Ave, Quatre Bornes, sells 'chunky African-style metal jewellery', coral jewellery, papier mâché animals, embroidery, pottery, paintings, baskets and carpets. The goods are made by a nonprofit organisation which employs disabled people.

At Cheshire Home Boutique, another charitable group, in Tamarin, the residents make baskets, clothes, shell boxes and other items.

# Getting There & Away

General information on travel options to and from the Indian Ocean are given in the introductory Getting There & Away chapter.

## AIR

Apart from the handful of people who sail in by yacht and those who arrive with the occasional cruise liner, all visitors to Mauritius fly into the country (you'll need to show the address of where you will be staying in Mauritius to the cutsoms official at the airport).

Expensive flights have always been the biggest deterrent to travellers. As with the Seychelles and the Maldives, the only way to cut the cost of flights is to take a package deal with hotel accommodation, or to include Mauritius in a round-the-world or other circular fare. Mauritius, following the Seychelles, is now beginning to offer better deals to Europe and the UK. Airlines generally apply low season tariffs between April and the end of June, and high season tariffs during July, August and December.

Watch out for being duped into losing a confirmed reservation. Prior to starting our trip from Europe, we received confirmation for a specific flight with Air Madagascar. When we double-checked by phoning the Air Madagascar office during our stay on Mauritius, the reservations clerk sweetly advised us that our flight had been annulled and our reservations wiped off the computer. A few days later, we started to make alternative arrangements for reservations and checked with the Air Madagascar office in Réunion. The sympathetic reservations clerk there quickly established that the original flight had never been annulled. We can only assume that we had simply been duped into ceding our reservations to passengers with more pressing needs.

### To/From the UK

*Mauritius News* and *Mauritian International* are two useful publications produced in the UK. Both have news reports and plenty of ads from travel agencies specialising in Mauritius. *Mauritius News* is published monthly and can be obtained by contacting Mauritius News (☎ 071-703 1071), PO Box 26, London SE17 1EG. *Mauritian International* is published quarterly and is available from Mauritian International (☎ 081-767 2439), Nautilus Publishing Company, 2A Vant Rd, London SW17 8TJ.

The Globetrotters Club (BCM Roving, London WC1N 3XX) publishes *Globe*, a newsletter for members which covers obscure destinations and can help find travelling companions.

Air France, Air Mauritius and British Airways operate flights from London. The cheapest fares, starting at around UK£700, usually require a minimum stay of 11 days and a maximum of four months.

### To/From Europe

Air Mauritius operates flights from Paris, Zürich, Rome and Munich each week. Air France has five flights from Paris, mostly including Réunion. Apart from holiday packages, look for bargain flights offered by Aéromaritime Charters, Nouvelles Frontières or Air France which will take you from Paris to Réunion; you could then take a cheap return flight to Mauritius from Réunion.

### To/From Asia

There are direct flights at least twice a week to connect Mauritius with Bombay, Kuala Lumpur, Singapore and Hong Kong.

### To/From Africa

You can fly to Mauritius direct from Johannesburg or Durban in South Africa, Harare (Zimbabwe), Antananarivo (Madagascar), Moroni (Comoros) or Nairobi (Kenya).

### To/From Australia

Air Mauritius currently operates direct flights to/from Perth and Sydney. Flights from Sydney cost around A$900 one way or

A$1600 return for excursion tickets (minimum stay of 14 days, maximum of three months); from Perth fares for similar excursion tickets are A$900 one way or A$1200 return. Interestingly, these excursion tickets are noticeably cheaper if bought ex Mauritius.

You can also fly from Australia to Mauritius via Singapore with Singapore Airlines. This will cost you A$2083 return.

Alternatively, you can fly to either Singapore or Kuala Lumpur and then take a connecting Air Mauritius flight on to Mauritius. The latter costs A$2100 from Sydney for a return excursion fare in the off season (all year except December and January). If you're doing just the Singapore-Mauritius leg the return fare will cost A$1979. You must stay in Mauritius between 14 and 90 days.

### To/From the USA

Air Mauritius low season return fares start around US$1900 from New York or US$2100 from San Francisco. If you're starting out from North America, it may prove more economical to go via South Africa, Hong Kong or Singapore than Europe. It's also worth checking out round-the-world and circular fares to take in destinations such as Madagascar, the Seychelles and Kenya.

### To/From Canada

Air Mauritius low season return fares from Toronto start from around US$1600.

### To/From Réunion

A return excursion fare (valid for one month) between Mauritius and Réunion costs approximately Rs 2290; the one-way fare is Rs 2184. The flight takes only 30 minutes and is popular with visitors from Réunion in search of a cheap holiday on Mauritius. This might explain why the same return excursion fare purchased in Réunion is 50% higher. Caveat emptor!

### SEA
### Passenger Ship To/From Réunion

The *Mauritius Pride* (for a description of this ship, see the Rodrigues chapter) has recently started operating between Mauritius and Réunion. Further details are provided in the Getting There & Away chapter for Réunion. For information contact Mauritius Shipping Corporation Ltd (☎ 2412550; fax 2425245), Nova Building, 1 Military Rd, Port Louis.

### Cargo Ships

Although there is still a fair amount of maritime trade to and from Mauritius, very few cargo ships take passengers. To enquire about sailings and bookings, contact the Shipping Division (☎ 2083241), Ireland Blyth Ltd, 1 Queen St, Port Louis.

### Cruise Liners

CTC Cruise Lines (☎ 071-930 5833; fax 071-839 2483), 1 Regent St, London SW1Y 4NN includes Mauritius on various cruise routes. Sunset Travel Holidays (☎ 071-498 9922; fax 071-978 1337), 306 Clapham Rd, London SW9 9AE offers cruises to Mauritius on the French vessel *Mermoz*.

### Yachts

Several yachts call at Mauritius during the non-cyclone season from June to November. They berth at Grand Baie or at Albion Dock in Port Louis.

On average, it takes a day to sail to Réunion and two days to return; five days to Madagascar and seven back; and 10 days to the Seychelles and two weeks back. Rodrigues, 560 km to the north-east, is a seven-day sail.

It is possible to hitch a ride on a yacht if you are willing to pay expenses and can crew, but the opportunities are rare. Check the notice board at Grand Baie Yacht Club. Alternatively, there is the remote chance of a charter, but it will be very expensive. There is no regular service, but try Blue Water Charters (☎ 2638015), based at the Veranda Bungalow Village in Grand Baie.

## TOURS

As a deterrent to mass tourism, Mauritius does not allow charter flights from abroad, however the package tour business is highly competitive. As a result, you can often find package tours (return flight, hotel, breakfast) being offered at bargain prices close to the cost of a return flight. The Mauritian Tourist Office can supply lists of tour operators.

Package holidays to Mauritius from the UK begin at about UK£800 per person (for seven nights in June on a twin-share, half-board basis). These tours can be extended to take in the Seychelles and Kenya, in which case the price increases to more than UK£2100 for 15 nights.

Various tour operators offer Australian holidaymakers several package deals. Most of these can be extended to take in the Seychelles, Zimbabwe and Kenya. Prices start at A$2200 for a week on a twin-share, half-board basis.

## LEAVING MAURITIUS

There is a Rs 100 airport tax on departure.

# Getting Around

## AIR

### Local Air Services

There are daily flights (except on Thursdays) to Rodrigues Island by Air Mauritius. The trip takes 1½ hours and costs Rs 4390 per person return (minimum stay five days, maximum stay 30 days). Mauritians can travel for half-price.

Air Mauritius also offers helicopter tours and charters from SSR (Sir Seewoosagur Ramgoolam) Airport and 22 major hotels. 'Helitours' cost Rs 3100 for a 15-minute flight, with a maximum of four passengers (Rs 775 per person). Extended tours last 20 minutes and cost Rs 3940 (Rs 985 per person). The tours take you over craters, waterfalls and mountains in the region of your hotel.

You can also hire the helicopters for Rs 3100 per 15 minutes or Rs 9980 per hour. Depending on the helicopter's operational base, repositioning flight time charges may also be required. Airport transfers can be arranged to all the top hotels. For information and reservations, contact Air Mauritius (☎ 2087700) or Helicopter Services Manager (☎ 4247174 – after office hours).

## BUS

The amazing bus system is one of the pleasures of travelling around the island. You brush shoulders with all sections of Mauritian society.

The buses are mostly single deck Ashok Leylands, Bedfords or Tatas in varying states of disrepair. There are five large bus companies: Corporation Nationale de Transport, Rose Hill Transport, United Bus Service, Triolet Bus Service and Mauritius Bus Transport, along with a score of individual operators.

To offset the bombed-out appearance of many of their vehicles, the private operators give the buses exotic, jet-set names such as 'Eiffel Tower', 'Arizona Express', 'Angel of Paradise', 'Sacred Arrow' and 'British Airways'!

A Swedish traveller sent us the following comments on bus travel:

Even the buses reflect the ethnic and religious mosaic of the country. In almost all buses, I saw stickers attached that showed all the gods and saints that protected the bus and its passengers, such as Jesus, Buddha, Vishnu, Sir Seewoosagur Ramgoolam, Krishna, Virgin Mary; and Donald Duck, Batman and Rambo.

**Mikael Parkvall**

No bus service covers the entire island. Rather, there are regional routes and services. The three main regions (north, centre and south) are served from major bus terminuses in Port Louis and Curepipe. If you want to go from Mahébourg to Grand Baie, for example, you must take two buses – from Mahébourg to Port Louis, and then from Port Louis to Grand Baie. Tamarin to Mahébourg involves two changes, one at Baie du Cap and the other at Souillac. The tourist office can supply a booklet, entitled *Mauritius – Information Guide*, which has a neat listing of bus operators, destinations, route numbers and departure points

There is never a long wait for a bus in the main towns. During the busy hours they run every 10 minutes. In more remote areas you may have to wait up to half an hour. Buses in urban areas start running at 5 am and stop between 6 and 8 pm; in rural regions, buses operate between 6.30 am and 6.30 pm. The only late night bus service operates until 11 pm between Port Louis and Curepipe and runs via Rose Hill, Quatre Bornes and Vacoas.

A trip shouldn't cost more than Rs 8 on a standard service or Rs 10 on an express service. There is generally no charge for luggage unless it is taking up a seat. Each bus has a conductor who is often indistinguishable from the passengers, until he asks you for money. They're good at changing large notes if you don't mind waiting until everyone else on the bus has paid. Check your change carefully. Keep your tickets, as inspectors frequently board to check them.

The buses are almost always packed, especially on the main routes, but with all the stops, turnover is quick. If you start the trip standing, you'll likely end up sitting. Chivalry is rarely practised, nor is the 'No Smoking' rule always observed.

The services appear to be fast because of the drivers' Niki Lauda impersonations, but the frequent stops slow things down. By standard service, it takes an hour from Mahébourg to Curepipe, an hour from Curepipe to Port Louis and an hour from Port Louis to Grand Baie. The exceptions are the express services which cost a bit more, but take half the time.

## TAXI

The biggest drawback to using Mauritian taxis is the ridiculous shenanigans required to negotiate a reasonable fare. Very few visitors, or locals for that matter, have a good word for the taxi drivers who can invent all sorts of fictitious reasons for absurd prices. It is common knowledge that a type of taxi clique exists which enforces a monopoly at the airport. Hopefully, a substantial drop in car rental charges and the continued improvement of an excellent bus system may soon combine to force taxi charges into line.

You *must* agree on the price before getting into the taxi, and make sure there is no doubt about it. If you arrange a daily rate and itinerary, it helps to get the details down in writing. Ignore sudden requests for extra petrol money en route. A Mauritian acquaintance regularly deals with major price disputes by referring the taxi driver to the local police station for all further discussion. If there is a genuine problem, the law will at least be present to adjudicate. If it's just a question of a blustering driver's attempt to extort more money, the driver usually loses interest and drives off in a thwarted huff.

There are, of course, some honest, knowledgeable, friendly taxi drivers around, but

they're not easily found. Many guesthouse managers/owners have attempted to mitigate their guest's constant frustration with rip-offs by making price arrangements with local taxi drivers. The quotes given under such arrangements, particularly those from small guesthouses, are often acceptable or at least form a sane basis for discussion. Once you've got a feel for the rates, you can venture into independent bargaining.

The fleet of venerable British Morris Minors and Morris Oxfords has been replaced by less appealing Japanese vehicles. Taxis are easily recognised on the road by their white registration plates with black figures; private cars have the opposite colour scheme for their registration plates. Although many taxis now have meters, it's rare for a driver to use one.

As a general rule, fares quoted by the taxi driver include payment for the return to base. A taxi operator, whose base of operation is at the airport or a hotel, may claim an additional fee of Rs 15 for every bag over 100 cm in width or length transported in the cab. To repeat a golden rule: when using a taxi at the airport or elsewhere on Mauritius, fix a price before you ride.

For around Rs 750 you can hire a taxi for a day tour of sights around the island. This allows you to tailor your tour to suit your interests and you can cut costs by forming a group – the price should *not* be calculated per person.

As a rough bargaining guide, here are some of the fares you can expect to pay for one-way trips:

| | |
|---|---|
| SSR Airport to Mahébourg | Rs 150 |
| SSR Airport to Curepipe | Rs 350 |
| SSR Airport to Tamarin or Port Louis | Rs 600 |
| SSR Airport to Grand Baie | Rs 400 |
| Trou aux Biches to Grand Baie | Rs 70 |
| Trou aux Biches to Port Louis | Rs 140 |
| Trou aux Biches to Curepipe | Rs 275 |
| Centre de Flacq to Port Louis | Rs 300 |

### Share Taxis

When individual fares are hard to come by, many cabs will cruise around their area supplementing the bus service.

For quick, short-haul trips, they pick up passengers waiting at the bus stops and charge the same fare as the bus. These are the 'share taxis' or 'taxi trains'. Mind you, if you flag down a share taxi you'll only be swapping a big sardine can for a small one. It's amazing how many people you can fit into a Morris Oxford! If you flag down an empty cab, you will probably have to pay the full fare.

## CAR & MOTORBIKE

Mauritian roads range from an excellent motorway to heavily potholed highways and minor roads. The semi-completed motorway system, which runs from SSR Airport to Port Louis and continues north to Pamplemousses, is due to be finished in the next couple of years.

Elsewhere the state of the highways and minor roads is inconsistent: a marvellous stretch of newly paved minor road will suddenly give way to a heavily patched and potholed major road. The danger comes from the drivers, particularly speeding Franco-Mauritians, not the roads. The heavy volume of buses is a hazard too, especially when they pick up speed and pass one another. Fortunately the frequency of townships and stops prevents the bus drivers getting completely carried away. Night driving should be avoided unless you enjoy an assault course of ill-lit oncoming vehicles, unfathomable potholes and weaving pedestrians. One car we rented had been thoughtfully supplied with super-tinted glass, so heavily tinted, in fact, that when dusk fell, it was impossible to see any of these potential obstructions properly without winding down the side window. It is also worth pointing out that the shock absorbers on many vehicles have long since given up the fight with the potholes.

There is not a great deal of scope for visitors to see Mauritius by motorbike, the most enjoyable area for this being around Grand Baie where motorbike rental is readily available. At present, there are relatively few machines on the island and hardly any over 70cc, which is a blessing, considering the number of people. The only bikes over 200cc have 'police' written on them.

## Road Rules & Safety

The speed limit is supposed to be 50 kp/h in the built-up areas or 65 kp/h on the open road. It doesn't matter. No-one bothers either way and there are plenty of accidents. Motorists seem to think they can save on electricity by not switching on or repairing their headlights and the police are better at people control than traffic control.

Traffic congestion is heavy in Port Louis, but the traffic is not fast-moving. There are many pedestrian zebra crossings, but drivers do not recognise them. Don't expect courtesy or drivers worried about their insurance – you'll get knocked over. One reader commented: 'Beware pedestrians! They are numerous, nonchalant, and not always sober'.

## Rental

In 1992, the government agreed to drop import tax on rental cars. The car rental agencies are now expected to make a corresponding cut in their prices. At the time of writing, the big name agencies such as Avis, Hertz and Europcar, as well as the smaller firms, were still charging extortionate rates for hiring vehicles – even the Mini Moke-type Reef Cubs, popular with hotel tourists. Drivers must be more than 23 years of age (some companies require a minimum age of 21), have held a driving licence for at least one year and payment must be made in advance. You don't need an international driving licence but you do need your ordinary one.

Most of the trade comes from visitors with a surplus of pocket money who decide to see the entire island in a day or are unable to find a private hire deal as outlined in the following section. A Reef Cub costs Rs 445 a day (or Rs 390 per day if taken over seven days) plus Rs 4.80 per km. Or you can have unlimited km for Rs 1095 a day (Rs 1000 per day if taken over a week). On top of that there is a collision damage waiver of Rs 110 per day, optional passenger insurance at Rs 100 per day, and a 15% surcharge on the total cost. In addition you pay for petrol (Rs 9 per litre) and Rs 50 plus mileage if you decide to have the car delivered or collected. Phew!

Top of the range is a Hyundai Stellar or Mitsubishi Galant for a basic Rs 1220 a day plus all the extras. You can also hire a chauffeur for Rs 400 a day or Rs 450 on Sundays and public holidays.

Grand Baie is the easiest place to rent motorbikes. Expect to provide a deposit of Rs 500, and to pay from Rs 150 to Rs 175 rental per day.

**Private Hire** A far better and cheaper alternative is private hire – all unofficial, of course. Legally speaking, you simply borrow a friend's car and slip him or her some money for the petrol and for presents for the kids.

There is no shortage of 'friends'. Ask small hotel and pension operators to put you in touch with someone. Donations range from Rs 250 to Rs 600 a day, depending on the state of the car and the friendliness of the car owner.

## BICYCLE

Definitely one of the best ways to see Mauritius is by bicycle. It is amazing how much ground you can cover in a day without killing yourself or getting saddle-sore. Around the coast roads, there are few hills. The inland roads are not particularly undulating either.

It's all in the mind. British people look at a map of Mauritius and subconsciously compare it to the UK, with the result that the distance from one Mauritian village to another takes on huge proportions. You don't fully understand the scale until you actually travel around the island and see that you're usually in the next place before you realise you've left the last one.

Practically all pensions, guesthouses, apartment operators and hotels, especially in the Grand Baie area, have bikes that they rent for a day or half-day. The cheapest rental deals start around Rs 40 per day. Rental models are usually mountain bikes. All should have a lock. Check the state of the bike before riding off into the sunset, as some are mighty uncomfortable.

## HITCHING

It's certainly worthwhile to try hitchhiking. If you're waiting for a bus, move along the road and try your luck. You should get a lift. Hitching is not recommended for lone females.

## BOAT

Many hold that some of the most beautiful parts of the island are only accessible from the sea. For advice on sailing around and from Mauritius, contact Hasib Hennes (☎ 2618395), director of Yacht Charters, Royal Rd, Grand Baie.

You can charter a yacht or join a sailing tour in Grand Baie, or go on a day trip along the coast for Rs 500, including drinks and BBQ (see the Grand Baie section in the North Mauritius chapter). Other popular sails are to Île Plate (Flat Island), Coin de Mire (Gunner's Quoin) and Baie du Tombeau (Tomb Bay).

To visit other, smaller islands dotted around the coastline, contact a local fisherman and make it worth his while to give up the day's catch. At Mahébourg, for instance, fishermen will take a group out for the day for about Rs 250 to Rs 350 per person, but not for less than Rs 700 overall.

Hotels and guesthouses run boat trips to the nearest islands. Île aux Cerfs, however, has a daily ferry service between 9 am and 5 pm, with crossings every 30 minutes. It costs Rs 25 per person return.

There are always the pirogues (small canoes) for getting across rivers and bays. Again, agree on a price before you shove off. You don't expect them to ferry you out of the goodness of their hearts, but some see you as the answer to all financial problems and maybe a month off work to boot.

The only way of getting to the outer isles of Cargados Carajos is by yacht, unless you know someone high up in the relevant ministry or with the administrators, Mauritius Fishing Development Ltd (☎ 2080299), 33 sectionsectionTer Volcy Pougnet, Port Louis. There are 52 small islands in the group, which lies 370 km north-east of Mauritius.

### Passenger Ships
The only passenger service is on the MV *Mauritius Pride*, which runs at least once a month to Rodrigues Island. The trip takes 24 hours and tourist class tickets cost Rs 750 one way or Rs 1500 return. A small number of 1st-class cabins are also available (Rs 1500 one way or Rs 3000 return), but should be booked several weeks in advance. Mauritians pay 50% less. For more details see the Getting There & Away section in the Rodrigues & Outer Islands chapter.

### LOCAL TRANSPORT
#### To/From the Airport
Mauritian taxis have no meters and you should agree on a price before the driver takes you first to your hotel and then to the cleaners! Refer to the taxi section in this chapter for more details and a table of sample fares from the airport.

A cheap alternative if you are backpacking or carrying little luggage is the public bus service. Ignore efforts by assorted taxi drivers to deny the existence of this service. Express buses travelling between Mahébourg and Port Louis stop at a small bus shelter just outside the entrance gates to the airport terminal once an hour, between 6 am and 6 pm. When leaving the terminal, walk straight across the car park to the bus stop – a distance of about 500 metres.

The terminal at SSR Airport has a restaurant and duty-free stores. The major banks

have offices open for the arrivals and departures of most international flights. With the vast majority of arrivals belonging to organised tour parties or package groups, the tourist board sees no need for a welcome or information counter. However, the Mauritius Chamber of Commerce & Industry runs a very helpful accommodation service for independent travellers (see the Accommodation section in the Mauritius – Facts for the Visitor chapter).

Readers have commented on the pushy porters at the airport who attempt to grab your bags or suitcases even when you do not require their services. A firm, polite refusal is enough to see them off.

### TOURS
The island's main tour operators book most of their custom through overseas travel agencies or through the hotels before the visitors' arrival. They do not go out of their way to attract passing trade, as many local tours are easy and cheap to organise individually. If you are pushed for time, but not money, the following tour operators may be worth contacting:

Mauritius Travel & Tourist Bureau (MTTB)
  Corner Royal St & Sir William Newton St, Port Louis (☎ 2082041)
Mauritours
  5 Venkatasananda St, Rose Hill (☎ 4541666)
  10 Sir William Newton St, Port Louis (☎ 2085241)
White Sand Tours
  La Chaussée, Port Louis (☎ 2126092 or 2123712)

There are also scores of smaller travel agencies, but they cater for Mauritians going overseas.

# Port Louis

Some pronounce it 'Por Lwee'; to others it is 'Port Loo-is'. The early Dutch settlers called it Noordt Wester Haven. Port Louis, the Mauritian capital, retains a fair bit of character and, if you have time, is worth a visit for a day or so. With a population of 142,000, it is a large city in proportion to the size of the island, but relatively small considering the total population of the country. During the day it bustles as a commercial centre. Nights are quiet and some might even say dead.

There is a distinct Muslim area around Muammar El Khadafi Square, and a Chinatown around Royal St. Many Franco-Mauritians working in the city live up on the plateau around Curepipe or Floréal and commute into Port Louis.

The once varied architecture of the city is being replaced by nondescript concrete structures; dust, noise, and clogged traffic are major features around the centre of town during the day.

## Orientation

The only disorienting thing about Port Louis is the street names. First, they are a mixture of English and French – even the government maps and literature mix up 'rues' and 'streets', 'routes' and 'roads'. Then there are similar-sounding names. Beware, there are three E Laurent Sts, all in the centre of town! There is Eugène Laurent, Edouard Laurent and Edgar Laurent.

On top of that there are renamed streets and streets which change names halfway along. For example, Desforges St (or Rue Desforges) has become Sir Seewoosagur Ramgoolam St, which some old maps have as Aldophe de Plevitz St, which is really what is now called Intendance St, which runs into Jules Koenig St, which becomes Sir John Pope Hennessy St...! Still with me?

Others have been changed for political or historical reasons, depending on who has fallen in or out of favour. New Moka St is now President John F Kennedy St, but so there are no hard feelings, Muammar El Khadafi Square is on the other side of the city centre.

Sir William Newton St is the main street. The centre point would be Government House, at the top of the Place d'Armes. The three bus stations surround the centre within easy walking distance.

You may not always be able to say exactly where you are, but you can't get lost. You can walk around Port Louis to see places of interest and do whatever business you have to do. Taxis or buses are not really necessary unless you want to get out to Ste Croix to see the tomb of Père Laval.

## Information

**Tourist Office** The Mauritius Government Tourist Office (MGTO; ☎ 2011703) is on the ground floor of the Emmanuel Anquetil Building in Sir Seewoosagur Ramgoolam St. It is open Monday to Friday from 9 am to 4 pm and from 9 am to noon on Saturdays.

Air Mauritius (☎ 087700), which acts as a major tourism promotion body, is at Rogers House, 5 President John F Kennedy St.

**Money** There is no shortage of banks in Port Louis centre, but you'll find none in the 'suburbs'. Half of Sir William Newton St seems to be taken up with main offices, with a few sub-branches within walking distance. The main Barclays Bank (☎ 2082685) and the main Mauritius Commercial Bank (MCB; ☎ 2082801) are on Queen St and Royal St respectively.

Banking hours are from 10 am to 2 pm on weekdays, and from 9.30 to 11.30 am on Saturdays.

**Post & Telecommunications** The Main Post Office in Port Louis is next to the harbour, at the bottom of Sir William Newton St. There is a poste restante service

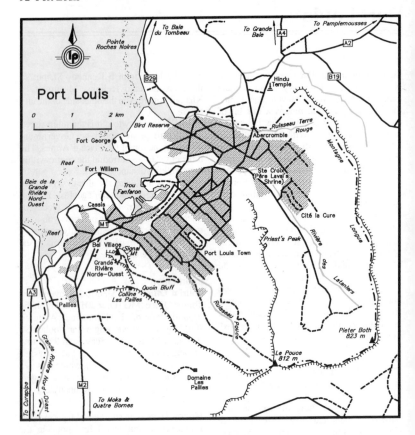

which holds letters for two months and registered mail for one month, without a charge.

There are other post offices in the centre of Port Louis: at the Victoria bus station, in the Emmanuel Anquetil Building and opposite the church at the end of Maillard St. They are all open Monday to Friday from 8 to 11.15 am and from noon to 4 pm, and on Saturdays from 8 to 11.45 am. The last 45 minutes before closing are for stamp sales only.

Now that international direct dialling is available from private phones, the service has improved considerably. If you do not have access to a private phone, you can make international calls through the Overseas Telecommunications Service (OTS) at Rogers House, 5 President John F Kennedy St. Telephone 2081036 for enquiries.

**Foreign Embassies & Consulates** Details are provided in the section on Foreign Embassies & Consulates in the Mauritius – Facts for the Visitor chapter.

**American Express** The American Express representative is the Mauritius Travel & Tourist Bureau or MTTB (☎ 2082041), close to the corner of Sir William Newton St and Royal St.

**Bookshops** The major bookshops in town are Librairie Bourbon and Librairie Natanda, both within a few metres of each other on Bourbon St; and Librairie du Trèfle on Royal St. These are the places to browse for a selection of local and foreign magazines, newspapers, books, and travel guides.

**Airline Offices** We'll take the risk and be repetitive. You must have a return or onward ticket before arriving in Mauritius, which you must reconfirm three days before use.

If you are allowed into the country under orders to buy an onward ticket, wish to change the one you have, or wish to take a side trip to Réunion, Madagascar, the Seychelles or Comoros, the best place to make flight arrangements and queries is at Rogers & Co Aviation (☎ 2086801), Rogers House, 5 President John F Kennedy St. They are efficient, recognised throughout the Indian Ocean and you have a better chance of a good deal through them than through the airlines.

Rogers House is also 'Airline House', the headquarters of Air France, Air Madagascar, SAA, Air India and Air Mauritius. Singapore Airlines (☎ 2087695) is next to the Cari Poulé restaurant at 5 Duke of Edinburgh Ave.

**Toilets** A reader wrote about the lack of adequate public toilets in Port Louis, but highly recommended Rogers House where the key to the excellent toilet is kept by the staff at the information desk.

**Dangers & Annoyances** Pickpockets, often operating by expertly slitting pockets or bags, are common in the market and on the buses. Port Louis seems quite dead at night, but locals warn about opportunistic theft and advise against roaming the streets late in the evening.

### Natural History Museum & Mauritius Institute
Most tourists visit the Museum and Institute, on Chausée St, to see the stuffed replica of the dodo, the 'abnormal member of a group of pigeons', which became extinct between 1681 and 1693. In 1989, the dodo exhibits underwent extensive repairs at the Royal Museum of Scotland in Edinburgh. The most pristine exhibit was returned to this institute in Mauritius three years later. The other exhibit has been loaned to the Jersey Wildlife Preservation Trust which sports a dodo as its emblem and has taken an active part in conservation work on Mauritius.

The dodo is the centrepiece, but there are stuffed representations of other extinct birds such as the Seychelles Dutch pigeon, the Bourbon crested starling, broad-billed and Mascarene parrots and the solitaire. The stuffing extends to specimens of other birds, animals and fish that are still with us.

If you want to read more about Mauritius, there is an excellent library upstairs at the back of the building. Sometimes the Institute, formerly the offices of the French East India Company, plays host to a commercial or artistic exhibition.

For more details on the exhibits, the Institute sells a *Guide to the Natural History Museum* for Rs 15. The Institute is open from 9 am to 4 pm on all weekdays except Wednesday, and on Saturdays from 9 am to noon. It is closed all day Wednesday and Sunday. Entrance is free.

### Jummah Mosque
Mauritius' main mosque is stuck in the middle of Chinatown! It was built in the 1850s and is very cloisterish. There is a sign just inside the heavy, carved wooden doors on Royal St inviting visitors every day, except Thursday and Friday, between 9.30 am and 12.30 pm.

### Champ de Mars Racecourse
Also known as the Hippodrome, the 'Field of Mars' was a military training ground until the Mauritian Turf Club was founded in 1812. The police and army still use it for the odd manoeuvre during the off season. The racing season is from May to October. There are two monuments – a statue of Edward VII, by the sculptor Prosper d'Epinay, and the

Malartic Tomb, an obelisk to a French governor. The latter was blown down by a cyclone in 1892 and re-erected the following year.

### Fort Adelaide

Fort Adelaide is also called the Citadel because it resembles a Moorish fortress, high on the crown of the hill. It is one of four forts in and around Port Louis that were built by the British in the first half of the 18th century. The other three, Fort George, Fort Victoria and Fort William, are in ruins or inaccessible. There is said to be a tunnel linking Fort Adelaide with Fort George, at the northern entrance to Port Louis harbour.

In August 1991, the fort was closed to the public.

### Signal Mt

Drive to the top of Signal Mt, via the Military Rd, for another splendid view of Port Louis and its surroundings. To get there, turn down Labourdonnais St before you reach the Champ de Mars. After about 800 metres, go left onto Rivet St. Military Rd is the third road on the right. Readers report that it is no longer possible to walk up from the Marie Reine de la Paix Gardens.

### Le Pouce

For details about the hike to this peak, refer to the Trekking section in the Mauritius – Facts for the Visitor chapter.

### Market

The city market, between Farquhar and Queen Sts, has suffered several fires in its long existence. Each time it springs back from the ashes livelier than ever.

The market is open Monday to Friday from 5 am to 5 pm and on Saturday from 5 am to noon. There is a meat section at the Farquhar St end and a large fruit and vegetable section, surrounded by little alleys of craft, souvenir, spice and plastic rubbish stalls. Food prices vary with season and availability. It's a good place to buy Malagasy goods such as leather bags and belts. The hustling is fierce, making it difficult to browse. Watch out for pickpocketing – see Dangers & Annoyances in this chapter.

### Père Laval's Shrine

This is the Lourdes of the Indian Ocean. To get there, take the Père Laval bus from Labourdonnais Square. For Rs 3, it goes directly to the shrine and church at Ste Croix, via Ramgoolam St, Plaine Verte and Abercrombie.

The shrine is separate from the church and is open for pilgrims every day from 6 am to 6 pm. Pilgrimage tours arrive mostly from Réunion, but also from South Africa, the UK, France and the Seychelles. You get a strange feeling when you look at the coloured plaster effigy of Père Laval on top of the tomb. Many pilgrims, including Hindus, touch the effigy and, in turn, touch their children. Miracle cures are said to have taken place. Candles and flowers are on sale to place on or near the shrine and there is a list of people to pray for.

To learn more about Père Jacques Laval, visit the shop and permanent exhibition of

Père Jacques Laval

his robe, mitre, letters and photographs. Opening hours are 8.30 am to 5 pm from Monday to Saturday, and 10 am to 4.30 pm on Saturdays. The church is an interesting example of modern architecture and design, with an unusual and effective use of mosaic and stained-glass windows.

## Other Churches & Cathedrals
Other notable places of worship are the St Louis Cathedral (1932) at the top of Sir William Newton St, the St James Cathedral (1828) at the top of Poudrière St, and the Holy Sacrament Church (1879) in Menagerie St, Cassis.

## Place d'Armes
A statue of Mahé de Labourdonnais stands near the quayside end of the avenue, which leads up to the colonial Government House. The avenue is lined with half-buried cannons chained together, which are supposed to symbolise peace.

## Company Gardens
Beginning on the Chaussée, next to the Mauritius Institute, this was once the vegetable patch of the French East India Company. It is now a meeting place and shady retreat for lovers, strollers and statues. The line of statues includes that of the poet Léoville L'Homme.

## Astrologers, Aquariums & Dragons
There are several aquariums and Chinese astrologers around the old centre of Port Louis; and around Rémy Ollier St there are a number of ladies' hairdressers with names like Dragon Rouge, Dragon Royal and Dragon Magique.

## Places to Stay
There is no problem finding a place to stay in the capital, unless you want something exclusive and luxurious. You'll find a surplus of small hotels scattered about the centre, but no Hiltons, Hyatts or Regents. Neither are there any pensions or boarding

houses. (There is still a sign for the 'Royal Pension de Famille' in Arsenal St, but this has closed.)

Because many of the hotels often appear empty, it is worth negotiating a cheaper rate, especially if you are staying a few days. Check to see if the price includes fan cooling, towels, toilet paper, soap and breakfast. The showers are rarely wonderful in these places. Instead of a hot spray, you'll get a cold dribble because the heater at the shower head is invariably broken.

If you arrive in Port Louis by bus from the south (Curepipe, Mahébourg, etc), you will see the *Tandoori Tourist Hotel & Restaurant* (☎ 2122131), on the corner of Victoria Square bus station and Jemmapes St. It's a bargain, although not a 'red hot' one. Owned by Mr Narrainen and managed by his son, Navin, the Tandoori has 17 basic, clean rooms of various sizes, most with a bathroom including shower, and some with air-con. Singles/doubles are Rs 175/250 per night, including a continental-style breakfast. A double with air-con costs Rs 350. For breakfast, you go down to the restaurant – see Places to Eat.

The worn and weary *City (Ambassador) Hotel* (☎ 2085340) on Sir Seewoosagur Ramgoolam St, next to the Mauritius Government Tourist Office, does not rate well. Singles/doubles are way overpriced at Rs 375/450, including breakfast and air-conditioning. Readers have commented on long nights spent battling armies of cockroaches (the size of which continue to be the stuff of nightmares) and the volume of early morning noise produced by the nearby mosque and building sites.

A bit better in style and standard is the *Bourbon Tourist Hotel* (☎ 2404407), at 36 Jummah Mosque St. It has 16 rooms and a cavernous bar, restaurant and balcony. Singles/doubles are Rs 350/400 plus tax, including air-con and breakfast. There should be a cheaper rate of Rs 300/350 for rooms without air-con. All rooms have a private shower and toilet.

Close to the Bourbon is the *Palais d'Or Hotel* (☎ 2425231) which has basic rooms.

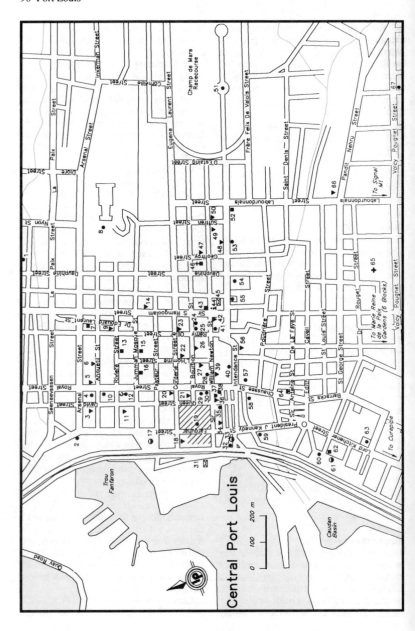

Central Port Louis

■  PLACES TO STAY

| 7 | Hotel Le Grand Carnot |
| 13 | Hotel Moderne |
| 15 | Bourbon Tourist Hotel |
| 16 | Palais D'Or Hotel |
| 43 | City (Ambassador) Hotel & Restaurant |
| 52 | Rossignol Hotel & Foong Teng Restaurant |
| 62 | Tandoori Hotel & Restaurant |

▼  PLACES TO EAT

| 3 | Kwang Chow Restaurant |
| 5 | Lai Min Restaurant |
| 6 | Poisson D'Or Restaurant |
| 9 | Foong Shing Restaurant |
| 11 | Merchant Navy Club |
| 14 | Providence Hotel Restaurant & Bakery, Toorawa Bookshop |
| 18 | Namaste Restaurant |
| 20 | Shamrock Restaurant |
| 21 | Chez Madeleine Restaurant |
| 22 | Paloma Restaurant |
| 23 | Briani Restaurant |
| 26 | Underground Restaurant |
| 27 | Dragon Palace Restaurant |
| 34 | Cari Poulé Restaurant |
| 36 | Snow White Restaurant |
| 39 | La Bonne Marmite Restaurant & Rocking Boat Bar |
| 42 | Taj Restaurant |
| 47 | DSL (Deva Saraswatee Laxmi) |
| 48 | National Hotel Restaurant |
| 49 | Chez Kayoum Snack Bar Coffee Shop/Restaurant |
| 50 | Jolie Madame Bar & Restaurant |
| 56 | Flore Mauricienne Restaurant |
| 64 | La Palmeraie Restaurant |
| 66 | Le Patrimoine Restaurant |

OTHER

| 1 | Muammar El Khadafi Square |
| 2 | Police Station |
| 4 | ONU Bar |
| 8 | Fort Adelaide (The Citadel) |
| 10 | L'Amicale Casino |
| 12 | Jummah Mosque |
| 17 | Immigration Square Bus Station |
| 19 | Market |
| 24 | Librairie Natanda |
| 25 | Librairie Bourbon |
| 28 | Indian High Commission |
| 29 | Librairie du Trèfle |
| 30 | Mauritius Commercial Bank |
| 31 | Main Post Office |
| 32 | Mahè de Labourdonnais Statue |
| 33 | Labourdonnais Bus Terminal |
| 35 | Barclays Bank |
| 37 | Mauritours |
| 38 | MTTB Travel (American Express) |
| 40 | Government House |
| 41 | Municipal Theatre |
| 44 | Tourist Office |
| 45 | Centre Post Office |
| 46 | St Louis Cathedral |
| 51 | King Edward VII Statue |
| 53 | Luna Park Cinema |
| 54 | Supreme Court |
| 55 | Police Station |
| 57 | Natural History Museum & Mauritius Institute |
| 58 | Local Handicraft Centre |
| 59 | Rogers House: OTS; US Embassy; Australian High Commission; Rogers Travel; Air Madagascar; Air Mauritius; Air France |
| 60 | Taxi Stand |
| 61 | Victoria Square Bus Station |
| 63 | Police Station |
| 65 | Jeetoo (Civil) Hospital |
| 67 | Chinese Pagoda |

Singles/doubles cost Rs 250/325, including breakfast.

A much safer bet and our recommendation is the *Hotel Le Grand Carnot* (☎ 2403054), at 17 Dr Edouard Laurent St. It is run by Mr Hossen, and you can see the effort he has made to welcome guests. The 16 rooms are very clean and each has an electric fan, shower and toilet. The phone in our room was a desk phone that had been inverted, attached to the wall, and cleverly adapted to stop the receiver falling off. Singles/doubles cost Rs 250/350, including breakfast. Possibly the best accommodation in town, the hotel is situated on a quiet street near the Flore Orientale Restaurant on Sir Seewoosagur Ramgoolam St.

The *Hotel Moderne* at 36 Rue Joseph

Rivière, is run by the owners of the Le Grand Carnot Hotel. There are seven double rooms with electric fan and communal showers and toilets. A double costs Rs 250, including breakfast.

Out towards the Champ de Mars racecourse, on Sir John Pope Hennessy St, the *Rossignol Hotel* (☎ 2121983) is currently under renovation. It provides 21 rooms with showers and toilets, for single/double Rs 200/300, including breakfast. Many of the rooms have private balconies. Prior to renovation, one reader wrote with a critical assessment of this hotel: 'it feels like you are sleeping and eating breakfast in the middle of the street'.

Much more exclusive is the *Husaini Guest House*, at the top end of Sir Seewoosagur Ramgoolam St on Muammar El Khadafi Square. There are only three bedrooms, it costs only Rs 45 per night, but you have to be Muslim. It is patronised mostly by Comoran and Malagasy Muslims suffering hard times back home.

## Places to Eat

Port Louis is spiced with restaurants, cafés and snack stalls. You can pay as little as Rs 10 or as much as Rs 150 for a meal and choose from Indian, Chinese, Créole or European cuisine, although sometimes it's difficult to determine which is which. (See the Food and Drink sections in the Mauritius – Facts for the Visitor chapter.)

The only drawback is that most places close in the evenings, proving that people who go out for meals at night don't live in Port Louis. Most of the hotels do dinners, but they are not the sort of places you go out to eat in. Remember that government tax is added to all meal bills in all restaurants.

## Places to Eat – budget end

There is no shortage of small, cheap eating establishments ranging from cosy cafés to huts and stalls. The fare is basic – rice and noodle dishes, curries and pastries. There are few outstanding ones, but at the same time there are few to be avoided. The choice will

more likely be determined by where you are staying and the friendliness of the nearest café proprietor.

One of the smartest snack bars is the grandly named *Taj* on Sir William Newton St. It has a good selection of Indian meals and savouries.

Across the road, in the Emmanuel Anquetil building, is the *Co-op Cafeteria*, a cheap but filling lunch venue, used by government employees working upstairs. The Mauritius Government Tourist Office is in the same building. You can get a big plate of fish and chips for Rs 15. But cafeteria is the word.

The samosas and other snacks at the *Providence 'Hotel' Bakery & Restaurant*, Sir Seewoosagur Ramgoolam St, attract queues of office workers at lunch time.

On Emmanuel Anquetil St, opposite the intersection with Léoville L'Homme St, is a nice little Chinese restaurant called *Poisson d'Or*. The meals cost around Rs 35. Another source of excellent and inexpensive Chinese food is *Foong Shing* restaurant on Remy Ollier St.

*Namaste*, near the corner of Farquhar and Louis Pasteur Sts, offers cheap curries and biryanis.

The *Merchant Navy Club*, at the bottom end of Joseph Rivière St near the Immigration Square bus station, is a private club, run by Norman and Dorothy Dean. This is one of the few places in Port Louis where you can enjoy a drink and a snack in peaceful surroundings away from the street. Temporary membership is open to visiting ship and yacht crews, but they also allow access to passing visitors. Snacks are served between 9 am and 10.30 pm. There is a billiards room, table tennis, Space Invaders, a small library and a bar. Toasted sandwiches are Rs 8; and coffee is Rs 3.50. Beer costs Rs 15 for a small bottle and Rs 25 for a large one. Soft drinks are Rs 7.

Another peaceful spot for a snack is the *Chez Kayoum Snack Bar* on Church St, where you can sit outside in a yard away from the street.

There are a number of rougher places –

cheap, without being too risky – on Jemmapes and Dumas Sts, leading down to the Victoria Square bus station.

'Junk food' hasn't grabbed hold of Port Louis yet, because it is well catered for with an indigenous version of fast food. But that hasn't stopped the outfits trying. *Chez Madeleine* on Bourbon St offers good lunch specials for Rs 40. Another takeaway is *Les Copains*, a Chinese shop opposite the Mauritius Institute museum on the Chaussée. You can get chicken, cheese or beef rolls for Rs 8.

If you're stuck for a snack at night, there are street stalls in Royal St, near L'Amicale Chinese casino.

The *National Hotel Restaurant*, opposite the Luna Park cinema, is in a converted colonial home behind wrought iron gates. The National once functioned as a hotel, but now only continues as a restaurant. It's worth a visit for its style and atmosphere: nothing much has changed since it was built in 1925. Lunch and dinner are available. The menu consists mostly of inexpensive Chinese dishes, but the venison steak is also reported to be good.

### Places to Eat – middle

*DSL (Deva Saraswatee Laxmi) Coffee Shop & Restaurant* (☎ 2120259), Geoffroy St, specialises in southern Indian food. We'd recommend it for quality, price, and its position beside St Louis Cathedral in a quieter part of town. DSL is on the first floor and diners can sit outside along the narrow balcony. Vegetarians have a wide choice of dishes. Main dishes start around Rs 35 or you can choose a special buffet meal for Rs 90 per person. One piece of advice: check the bill carefully. The restaurant is open daily, except Sundays, from 10 am to 4 pm.

The *Paloma* (☎ 2085861), on Léoville L'Homme St, near the corner with Bourbon St, is a Chinese-European restaurant with a balcony. The place mats are maps of Mauritius, so you can plan your tour of the island while you eat. Main dishes cost between Rs 40 and Rs 80. The octopus *daube* (braised stew) has been recom-

mended. The restaurant is open daily from 10 am to 8 pm, but closed on Sundays.

Similar in cuisine and price, but more centrally located and popular (especially with lunching office workers), is the *Snow White* (☎ 2083528), on the corner of Sir William Newton and Queen Sts. The restaurant is open daily from 10 am to 5 pm, but closed on Sundays. Nearby, the *Shamrock* (☎ 2125271), whose name, like the Snow White's, has absolutely nothing to do with the decor or the food, serves Europeanised Chinese food. Main dishes start around Rs 60. It's open daily from 10 am to 2.30 pm, and from 5.30 pm to 9.30 pm.

*Kwang Chow* (☎ 2409735), on the corner of Queen and Emmanuel Anquetil Sts, is a similar, cheaper alternative to the Lai Min (see Places to Eat – top end).

In the Victoria Square bus station is the *Tandoori* (☎ 2120031) restaurant which is part of the hotel of the same name described in the Places to Stay section. It is popular at lunch time and has a good atmosphere. The restaurant is open Monday to Saturday from 8 am to 5 pm. Main courses cost around Rs 75.

The *Underground Restaurant & Snack*, on Bourbon St between Léoville L'Homme and Rémy Ollier streets, serves a variety of dishes for between Rs 40 and Rs 75.

### Places to Eat – top end

The restaurant for diplomatic and business lunches is *La Flore Mauricienne* (☎ 212-6624), on Intendance St, near Parliament House. It specialises in French and Créole cuisine, but is only open weekdays for lunch from 11.30 am to 3.30 pm. Main dishes start at around Rs 125. Special daily dishes include couscous on Mondays and paella on Wednesdays. A café section upstairs, which is open on weekdays between 8.30 am and 4 pm, serves toasted sandwiches, cakes and instant coffee.

Another 'in' place is the *Cari Poulé* (☎ 21295), the best of the few Indian restaurants in Mauritius. You'll find it next to the Singapore Airlines office on Duke of Edinburgh Ave. Main dishes start from around

Rs 95. From Monday to Thursday, it opens between 11 am and 3 pm. On Friday and Saturday, opening hours are extended for dinner from 7 pm to midnight. It's closed on Sundays.

Once renowned for its Chinese cooking, *Lai Min* (☎ 2420042) on Royal St, seems to have allowed prices and service to slip upwards and downwards respectively. Set menus for a minimum of two people range from Rs 140 to Rs 275 per person. Individual dishes start at Rs 125. The Sunday special is dimsum served at noon. Lai Min is open daily from 11.30 am to 3 pm; and from 6.30 to 10 pm.

*La Palmeraie* (☎ 2122597), just off the Chaussée at 7 Sir C Antelne St, again, unfortunately, is only open for long lunches on weekdays. A set three-course meal is Rs 90. Steak dishes range between Rs 60 and Rs 90, fish from Rs 55 to Rs 75, and omelettes and pizzas from Rs 45 to Rs 65. It is run by Franco-Mauritians.

*La Bonne Marmite* (☎ 2122403) and the *Rocking Boat Pub*, opposite the Bank of Mauritius on Sir William Newton St, are in an attractive old building, formerly the oldest pharmacy in Mauritius. The restaurant serves Indian and Créole food. Diners are usually offered the fancy menu first, but there's also a cheaper list which includes steak and chips for Rs 55 or filling noodle or rice dishes at similar prices. The restaurant is only open for lunch and is closed on weekends.

*Le Patrimoine* (☎ 2120198) on Rue Labourdonnais specialises in Indian and Créole dishes. Set menus start at around Rs 75 and main dishes range in price from Rs 50 to Rs 125. It's open from 10 am to 10 pm, but closed on Monday.

### Entertainment

Port Louis may have been a lively port when the sugar ships took three weeks to load, but now that it's a 24-hour turnaround for the boats, the capital is dead after dusk. Only Chinatown has a bit of life and that's not an attraction in itself.

There's not a lot to do in Port Louis after dark. If you are not eating at one of the few Chinese restaurants which is open, there are the cinemas, a couple of street bars, and *L'Amicale Chinese Gaming House*. For advice on security at night, see the section on Dangers & Annoyances in this chapter.

**Street Bars** If you fancy meeting the locals in their watering holes, you could try the *ONU Bar* on Royal St, or *Jolie Madame Bar* on the corner of Suffren and Church Sts, both of which are unpretentious street bars (not recommended for unaccompanied women). Another option for a drink is the Merchant Navy Club – described under Places to Eat.

**Cinemas** The cinemas charge Rs 14 for a balcony seat and Rs 12 for the stalls. You can choose between the Luna Park, up towards the racecourse on Sir John Pope Hennessy St, and the Rex, which is next to the City (Ambassador) Hotel on Sir Seewoosagur Ramgoolam St.

**Gambling** If there is nightlife in Mauritius, *L'Amicale Chinese Gaming House* is it. For a start, it is open Monday to Saturday from 7 pm until 2 am and from noon until 2 am on Sundays, which is about eight hours longer than anything else. It is not plush as casinos go, but very plush as far as Chinese gambling joints go. Confirmed punters will be drawn

Chinese Buddhist Pagoda

to it like moths to a flame and may get burnt. But for canny spenders, it is worth visiting.

L'Amicale attracts a fair share of celebrities. A 'rogues gallery' of photographs in the entrance hall depicts, among others, Brigitte Bardot, Princess Stephanie of Monaco (in a skin-tight black leather suit), the former prime minister, Sir Seewoosagur Ramgoolam, and the younger playboy-politician Sir Gaetan Duval in a suit that makes him look like a tropical commissionaire or a deposed South American admiral. The gaming house doesn't welcome ordinary mortal sightseers with open arms, but neither does it shun them. As long as you are suitably dressed and look but don't disturb, they'll tolerate you in an inscrutable way.

A strong police presence makes sure there is no trouble. Signs ask you not to swear. There is a bar, but the drinks are quite expensive.

It is fascinating to watch the croupiers shuffling, stacking, dealing and tossing big five cent coins onto bets to weigh them down. The games differ from the Western versions and basically revolve around dice, dominoes and cards. Following is a brief description of some common Chinese gambling games you may see here.

*Fan Tan* is an ancient Chinese game practically unknown in the West. The dealer takes an inverted silver cup and plunges it into a pile of porcelain buttons, then moves the cup to one side. After all bets have been placed, the buttons are counted out in groups of four. The aim of the game is to bet on how many will remain after the last set of four has been taken out. You can bet on numbers one, two, three, four, as well as odd or even.

*Dai Siu* (Cantonese: 'big-small') is a very popular game, also known as *sik po* (dice treasure) or *cu sik* (guessing dice). The game is played with three dice which are placed in a covered glass container, then shaken. You bet that the total of the toss will be 'small' (from three to nine) or 'big' (10 to 18). Unless you bet directly on three of a kind, you lose on combinations where all three dice come up the same: 2-2-2, 3-3-3, etc.

*Pai Kao* is Chinese dominoes, and similar

to mahjong. One player takes the role of banker and the other players individually compare their hands against the banker. In return for providing the gambling facilities, the casino generally deducts a commission from the winnings rather than being directly involved in the game.

**Theatre** You may be lucky enough to catch one of the local productions at the Port Louis Municipal Theatre, behind Government House on the corner of Sir William Newton and Seewoosagur Ramgoolam Sts.

Plays in Créole by local amateur groups take place about once a month. One player-manager to watch out for is Soleman Nayeck. He's an excellent comic actor. A small entrance fee is charged, but the takings often go to a charity.

The theatre, in a style similar to that of the London theatres, has changed little since it was built in 1822. It seats about 600 on three levels, has an exquisitely painted dome ceiling with chandeliers and is often used for Hindu weddings. You won't see anything like it now – it takes you right back in time. Usually there is a caretaker at the back entrance who will be glad to show you around, take you backstage and put on the house and stage lights.

### Getting There & Away
**Bus** There are two major bus stations in Port Louis within easy walking distance of the city centre. Buses for the southern and western routes use the Victoria Square terminus, near Line Barracks; those for the northern and eastern routes are based at Immigration Square.

Buses running the shorter routes to the north of Port Louis, including Baie du Tombeau and Ste Croix (Père Laval's tomb), use the small Labourdonnais Square station.

Buses on the southern route to Pointe aux Sables leave from Dumas St, the short road which runs into Victoria Square.

**Airport Transport** There are no direct airport buses, but express bus services operating between Port Louis and Mahébourg run via the airport. They start running early in the morning, but stop early in the evening. Allow two hours for the journey, just to be safe. The fare is Rs 10.

Expect to pay around Rs 380 for a taxi ride from Port Louis to the airport.

### Getting Around

The centre of Port Louis, where you'll find most of the businesses and sites of interest, is easily covered on foot. The police are very helpful in giving directions.

**Taxi** In Port Louis the cabs have a printed list of tariffs that they are obliged to show you. In practise it may prove hard to fathom the correct charge. See the Mauritius – Getting Around chapter for more information on the trials and tribulations of dealing with taxi drivers. You should prepare for a bargaining session by asking an impartial local or your hotel staff for a rough idea of the going rate before taking a taxi. As a rough guide, expect to pay between Rs 20 and Rs 30 for a short hop across town.

# North Mauritius

The northern part of the island is divided into two districts: Pamplemousses in the west and Rivière du Rempart in the east.

The north-west coastline is practically all tourist development, for international visitors and local holidaymakers alike. In contrast, there is scant development on the north-east coast, probably because there are few beaches. In between, stretches a plain of sugar cane fields, which slopes gently down to the sea. There are no mountains.

Grand Baie is the holiday centre with a concentration of hotels, guesthouses, apartments, restaurants, shops, and a small but busy beach. Peréybère, a few km to the north, is similar but much smaller, quieter and cheaper.

Moving west around Pointe aux Canonniers, you'll find a 12 km stretch of terrific

beach on which several luxury hotels have sprung up. There are still some good, clean public beaches, the biggest of which is Mon Choisy.

When the coast road heads inland to join the Port Louis road, the area becomes quiet and private again. Just six km north of the capital is the Baie du Tombeau strip of down-market hotels and guesthouses. The beaches here are also smaller and dowdier. This is a popular weekend retreat for sports and social clubs.

The main attraction in the interior is the Sir Seewoosagur Ramgoolam Botanical Gardens at Pamplemousses. Elsewhere, there is little of specific fascination, but the area is worth travelling around for its beauty.

## BAIE DU TOMBEAU

'Tomb Bay', if you like (though nobody calls it that), was so named because it's a tomb for many ships. Pieter Both, a Dutch East Indies governor, went down with one in 1615. The distinctive mountain peak with the bobble on top, visible behind Port Louis, was named after him. It was predicted that the round boulder would topple off when British rule ended in Mauritius. So much for predictions.

The bay itself is sheltered within high cliffs. Access is possible for swimming, but in recent years there have been reports of serious pollution. An old pier acts as a good high diving point and is popular with local youths. At the mouth of the Rivière du Tombeau, the bay is the site of frequent searches by treasure hunters, convinced that pirates buried loot there. Not a single piece of eight has been found.

Route Royale, the coast road which stretches from Baie du Tombeau village down to Elizabethville, past the Dockers Flats and the New Goodwill rum distillery, is dotted with a number of small hotels and guesthouses. Most of the visitors are regulars from Réunion. The Trou aux Biches beach crowd doesn't stray this far.

## Information

Most of the hotels and some of the pensions run boat trips up and down the coast. Otherwise ask for Captain Neerunjun at Snack Le Goulet (see the Places to Stay section) about renting a boat. He also rents bicycles for Rs 75 per day.

## Places to Stay

*Corotel* (☎ 2472355) has singles/doubles with private balcony, electric fan, phone and shower for Rs 675/950, including breakfast. Other meals are also available if requested in advance.

*Le Cactus* (☎ 2472485) has double rooms with private shower and toilet for Rs 350. Breakfast is provided for an additional Rs 25. There's also a hotel bar and BBQ corner.

*Baie des Cocotiers* (☎ 2472442) is a complex of self-catering bungalows. Prices range from Rs 350 per night for single occupancy to Rs 1050 per night for occupancy by five persons. Meals are also available at the following prices per person: breakfast (Rs 40), lunch or dinner (Rs 120).

A few hundred metres down on the other side of the Route Royale is a large house called *Pension Cheval du Mer* (☎ 2638434); it's run by Mr Athion Laval. There are nine rooms and singles/doubles cost Rs 250/350, including breakfast. A meal costs Rs 100. Despite its size, there is a nice family feel to this pension. Mr Laval's Australian son-in-law, Frank White, is a former jockey and now trainer at the Turf club, Champ de Mars racecourse, in Port Louis. If you are interested, he may introduce you to the Mauritian racing scene.

Next in line is the *Arc-en-Ciel Hotel & Restaurant* (☎ 2472616/7), offering 20 air-conditioned rooms at various prices. Singles range between Rs 350 and Rs 575 per night, including breakfast. Doubles range between

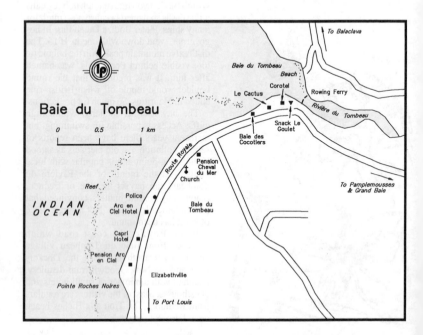

Rs 450 and Rs 675, including breakfast. Meals cost Rs 125. There is a tiny and untidy-looking beach out front and a disco.

*Le Capri* (☎ 2472533) is excellent value. Its eight rooms look open and clean. Singles/doubles/triples are Rs 220/400/480 with shower and toilet. Residents are allowed free admission to the Capricorne Disco, attached to the Capri, which bursts into life on Saturdays only.

After Elizabethville, the first lodging you'll come to is the *Pension Arc-en-Ciel* (☎ 2472592), not to be confused with the nearby hotel of the same name. The pension is not as inviting as the Capri, but the setup is similar. It offers the same seaside activities as most other hotels, plus weight training! If you want to lie down, a single/double room costs Rs 300/600 with toilet and air-con; and Rs 250/500 with toilet but without air-con. Breakfast is included; half board is an extra Rs 100. A supplement is charged in August, December and January. Outside, the owners have a monkey and a tortoise in a cage.

There are several private bungalows *(campements)* to let along and just off Route Royale. If you're confident of your French, try any of these telephone numbers: 4641391, 2122750, 6963786 and 2120524. Also enquire at Snack Le Goulet (see Places to Eat section) about a bungalow for Rs 225 per night.

### Places to Eat

There are no individual restaurants. (See the Places to Stay section for hotel restaurants.)

Overlooking Baie du Tombeau from the cliff top is *Snack Le Goulet*, which, as the name suggests, offers a range of snacks; it also has drinks and groceries.

### Getting There & Away

Baie du Tombeau is not on the bus route to Grand Baie or Trou aux Biches. Instead, you must take a bus from Labourdonnais bus station at the harbour end of Sir William Newton St, Port Louis. The buses turn around just past Snack Le Goulet.

## BALACLAVA & BAIE DE L'ARSENAL

The next bay north of Baie du Tombeau is the secluded but gorgeous Baie de L'Arsenal (also known as Baie aux Tortues). There you'll also find Balaclava, once one of the island's 'undiscovered' beauty spots, now rapidly being developed by hotel entrepreneurs. As it is tucked away from the public road in the grounds of the Hotel Maritim, it is still secluded. Nonresidents should ask at the security hut at the entrance to the hotel grounds for permission to visit the ruins complex. About 30 metres beyond the hut, a track on the right leads down to the ruined buildings of the French arsenal, flour mill and lime kiln, covered in vegetation and set among streams and waterfalls. The ensemble of buildings looks like an ancient water temple and garden. From here you can look across to the opposite riverbank which is marred by the sprawling outlines of a hotel building site.

By the way, the name Balaclava has no connection with the Crimean War. It is thought to be a Créole reference to the 'black lava' which once covered much of Mauritius.

### Places to Stay & Eat

*Maritim Hotel* (☎ 2615600) is a luxury hotel in a superb position with an excellent swimming and snorkelling beach, huge gardens, including walks through the ruined French arsenal, and the full gamut of facilities. Prices for half board per person range from Rs 2500 for a standard room to Rs 3000 for a superior room. Suites cost a whopping Rs 9000 for one or two persons, including breakfast. Curiously, the management claims that Baie aux Tortues (Turtle Bay) is the first Marine Park established by Mauritius, but the park does not appear to have been given official status yet. The hotel has two expensive restaurants, and a pool bar.

At Pointe aux Piments, on the coastline just north of Balaclava, the *Hyatt Hotel* (☎ 2615757) is scheduled to start operating by 1993. However, for a project that has been in progress for more than three years and has devoured some US$20 million, the only

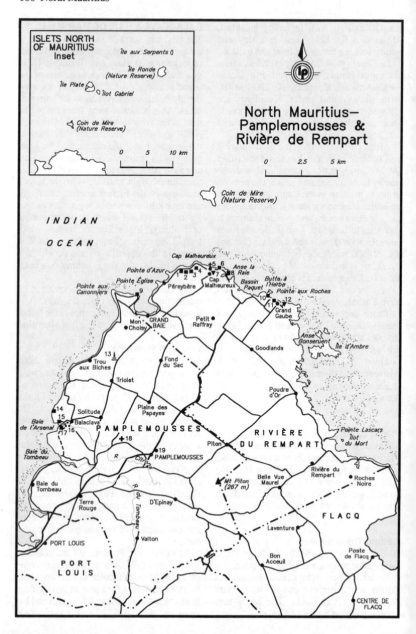

ISLETS NORTH
OF MAURITIUS
Inset

Île aux Serpents

Île Ronde
(Nature Reserve)

Île Plate    Îlot Gabriel

Coin de Mire
(Nature Reserve)

0     5     10 km

North Mauritius—
Pamplemousses &
Rivière de Rempart

0     2.5     5 km

Coin de Mire
(Nature Reserve)

INDIAN

OCEAN

Cap Malheureux

Pointe d'Azur

Pointe aux
Canonniers

Pointe Église

Péreybère

Anse la
Raie

Cap
Malheureux

Bassin
Paquet

Butte à
l'Herbe

Pointe aux Roches

Grand Gaube

Anse
Bonseurent

Île d'Ambre

Mon
Choisy

GRAND
BAIE

Petit
Raffray

Goodlands

Trou
aux Biches

Fond
du Sac

Triolet

Plaine des
Papayes

Poudre
d'Or

Baie
de l'Arsenal

Solitude

Balaclava

PAMPLEMOUSSES

Piton

RIVIÈRE
DU REMPART

Pointe Lascars
Îlot
du Mort

Baie du
Tombeau

PAMPLEMOUSSES

Mt Piton
(267 m)

Belle Vue
Maurel

Rivière du
Rempart

Roches
Noire

Baie du
Tombeau

Terre
Rouge

D'Epinay

Valton

Laventure

FLACQ

PORT LOUIS

PORT
LOUIS

Bon
Acceuil

Poste
de Flacq

CENTRE DE
FLACQ

results we could see (in 1992) were half-abandoned or half-finished walls and rusting ferroconcrete. Recent newspaper reports also indicate that the project may have been abandoned by the Franco-Japanese consortium in charge.

### Getting There & Away
From the south, Balaclava can be reached on the B41 road from Moulin à Poudre; from the north, there is a road zigzagging inland from Pointe aux Piments to Balaclava.

### TROU AUX BICHES
The name means 'hole of the does'. Trou aux Biches is the sister 'hole' of the Trou aux Cerfs (stags) in Curepipe, only here there is no actual hole to speak of. Instead there is a luxury resort, a golf course and a fine beach.

Trou aux Biches may be the Sunset Strip of Mauritius but it is still sedate. (As yet, there are no wild infestations of tourists in the Indian Ocean as you'll find in Bali, Majorca or Montego Bay.) There are still some good stretches with beaches not overlooked by hotels, but food and accommodation are more expensive in this area.

### Information
**Bank & Post Office** The bank and post office are at the Trou aux Biches Holiday Village. The MCB counter is open each day

from 10 am to 1 pm. The post office is open from 9 to 11 am and from noon to 4 pm.

### Things to See & Do
The best public beaches are at Mon Choisy, a nice little cove next to Le Corsaire restaurant and the main hotel reserves.

At the Aquarium Centre (☎ 2616187) there is a large and fascinating variety of marine creatures on view – it's fun trying to spot the well-disguised and deadly stone fish. The poor or nonexistent signs on the tanks are irritating. You don't know what half the creatures are and have to buy postcards in the shop to find out. The aquarium is open Monday to Saturday from 9 am to 5 pm; and from 9 am to 4 pm on Sunday. Admission costs Rs 50.

*Blue Water Diving Centre*, adjacent to Le Corsaire Restaurant, is run by Hugues Vitry

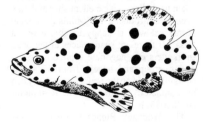

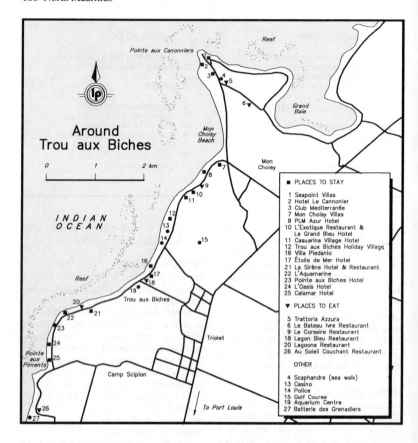

Around
Trou aux Biches

INDIAN
OCEAN

**■ PLACES TO STAY**

1 Seapoint Villas
2 Hotel Le Cannonier
3 Club Mediterranée
7 Mon Choisy Villas
8 PLM Azur Hotel
10 L'Exotique Restaurant &
   Le Grand Bleu Hotel
11 Casuarina Village Hotel
12 Trou aux Biches Holiday Village
16 Villa Piedanlo
17 Étoile de Mer Hotel
21 La Sirène Hotel & Restaurant
22 L'Aquamarine
23 Pointe aux Biches Hotel
24 L'Oasis Hotel
25 Calamar Hotel

**▼ PLACES TO EAT**

5 Trattoria Azzura
6 Le Bateau Ivre Restaurant
9 Le Corsaire Restaurant
18 Lagon Bleu Restaurant
20 Lagoona Restaurant
26 Au Soleil Couchant Restaurant

**OTHER**

4 Scaphandre (sea walk)
13 Casino
14 Police
15 Golf Course
19 Aquarium Centre
27 Batterie des Grenadiers

and his assistant Bruno. Several readers have recommended this outfit for diving and snorkelling trips. For Rs 350 per dive you are taken to shallow but excellent sites and may even be introduced to 'Monika', a tame moray eel who is happy to give divers a 'kiss'! If there are spare places in the boat, snorkellers can negotiate a price to join a diving group and benefit from the better snorkelling out on the reef. Hugues Vitry can be contacted at the Corsaire Restaurant (☎ 2616337).

The Trou aux Biches Holiday Village offers a range of sports and activities to nonresidents at a decent price. There is a nine-hole golf course across the main road, and a casino. Tennis enthusiasts can reserve a private court near Pointe aux Cannonniers between 7 am and 5.45 pm, by ringing 2618538 for a reservation. For snorkelling, the reef off the Holiday Village beach has plenty of colourful life. Glass-bottom boat trips cost around Rs 60 per hour.

Local hotels arrange excursions to Sir Seewoosagur Ramgoolam Botanical Gardens, Curepipe, Île aux Cerfs and the Aquarium Centre for between Rs 250 and Rs 400 per person.

## Places to Stay – bottom end

There is no budget accommodation in or near Trou aux Biches, only on the fringes of the area. Cheap guesthouses or bungalows are bunched along the coast road between Trou aux Biches and Pointe aux Piments.

*L'Oasis Hotel* (☎ 2615808) has small apartments with prices starting at a reasonable Rs 600 for a double.

*L'Aquamarine* (☎ 2616923) is signposted by three crudely painted signs at the gate informing you what it is called, not what it is. It has three double rooms for Rs 250 per night, including breakfast, and a two-bedroom bungalow with cooking facilities for Rs 400.

A few metres up the road is *La Sirène* (☎ 2616026), which is a hotel and restaurant. It is run by Mme Bakaoolah and looks promising. A single/double costs Rs 250/350, including breakfast. Half board costs an additional Rs 125 per person.

There are a few private bungalows for rent in the area.

## Places to Stay – middle

On the coast road between Trou aux Biches and Pointe aux Piments is *Pointe aux Biches Hotel* (☎ 2615901). This is a small complex of bungalows, each containing four studios with air-con, kitchen, shower, and terrace or balcony. Singles/doubles cost Rs 900/1200, including breakfast. Half board costs an extra Rs 300 per person per day.

Heading north past L'Alambik restaurant and the aquarium, you reach *Étoile de Mer Hotel* (☎ 2616178). The hotel offers rooms, studios, and suites – with half board only. The rates for single/double rooms are Rs 600/1000; Rs 900/1200 for a single/ double studio; and Rs 950/1450 for a single/double suite. A reader commented that this place is next to the road and very noisy; and the owners appear to be absent most of the time. Perhaps as a result, the staff show little interest in cleaning rooms or providing facilities.

*Villa Piedanlo* (☎ 2334614 or 2616189), run by Youssouf Goolmally, consists of bungalows with TV and air-con. Prices for two people range between R§ ▮ day.

Similar to the Étoile de Me▮, the *Casuarina Village Hotel* (☎ 2▮ with 50 large, 'Moorish-style' fully e▮ and self-catering family villas, as we air-con rooms. Facilities include a poo tennis court, boutique and bar. A self-catering bungalow with two bedrooms, fan, shower and toilet costs Rs 1190/1830/2025 for single/double/triple occupancy, including breakfast. A maximum of six persons can occupy this type of bungalow – the corresponding price is Rs 2100. Rooms with air-con, shower, toilet, and balcony cost Rs 1500/2100, including breakfast. Half board costs an additional Rs 285 per day.

*Le Grand Bleu Hotel* (☎ 2615812) has 20 rooms with kitchenette, air-con, toilet and shower. Single/double/triple rooms cost Rs 800/990/1035. Lunch or dinner is available at Rs 175 per person.

*Mon Choisy Villas* (☎ 2638771) has double rooms with air-con for Rs 800, including breakfast. Two-room studios are also available for Rs 1200. A supplement of Rs 75 per day is charged during peak season.

Further north, at Pointe aux Canonniers, is *Seapoint Villas*, a complex of self-catering beach bungalows (☎ 2638604/6964804). The 10 double-storey two-bedroom units on the beach can be occupied by a maximum of five people. The cost per night is from Rs 700/ 800/900 during low/peak/high season.

The *Calamar Hotel* (☎ 2615187/9), at Pointe aux Piments, has studios and bungalows that house up to five people for between Rs 1500 and Rs 1800, including breakfast. Full board costs an additional Rs 250 per person per day.

## Places to Stay – top end

The main resort in the area is the *Trou aux Biches Village Hotel* (☎ 2616562), a member of the Beachcomber chain of hotels. Daily rates for the 216 chalets, which depend on the period and location, range between Rs 3000 and Rs 5700 per night for a single, Rs 4400 and Rs 6800 for a double, and

450 and Rs 600 per
but better, is
61/53653/5),
quipped
as

& Résidence

24     Lakes Hotel cean
26     Ebrahim Flats
33     Les Palmiers Flats
37     La Canne à Sucre Flats
44     Peramal Restaurant &
       Guesthouse
48     Club Méditerranée
49     Le Canonnier Hotel
50     Sea Point Bungalows
51     Colonial Coconut Hotel

▼ PLACES TO EAT

3      Ristorante Beatrice
6      Café de Paris
11     Le Grillon Restaurant
18     Palais de Chine Restaurant
19     La Pagode Restaurant
20     Phil's Pub Restaurant &
       L'Assiette du Pêcheur

23     La Jonque Restaurant
29     Sakura Restaurant
30     Café Cactus
31     La Perle Noire Restaurant
34     La Mediterranée Restaurant
35     L'Esplanade Café & Restaurant
36     Chez Patty Pâtisserie
45     Le Capitaine
47     Trattoria Azzura

OTHER

4      Store 2000
5      Yacht Club
10     Hindu Temple
12     Caltex Petrol Station
14     Case Créole
16     Barclays Bank
21     GB Travel & Tours
22     Chinese Store
25     MCB Bank
27     Grand Baie Store
28     Éscale Nord/Eden Disco
32     School
38     Pharmacy
39     Mosque
40     Roman Catholic Church
41     Police & Telephone
42     Post Office
43     Papyrus Bookshop
46     Yacht Charters

Rs 7200 and Rs 10,600 for a family apartment. The price includes breakfast, dinner, government tax and all activities except deep-sea fishing, scuba diving and trimaran sailing.

The resort includes several restaurants, shops, a post office, bank, hairdresser, boathouse, coral reef, casino, golf course and the Beachcomber Club. The Beachcomber Card, which every guest receives on registration, is valid here – for more details refer to the Accommodation section in the Mauritius – Facts for the Visitor chapter.

The French-owned, dazzling white *PLM Azur* (☎ 2616070), has 88 air-conditioned rooms and two restaurants. You can get singles/doubles from around Rs 1050/1450 per day on a half-board basis. The hotel offers the usual shore and water sports, plus squash, and has a small beach between the piers.

*Club Méditerranée* (☎ 2638509) at Pointe aux Canonniers is worth mentioning, as it allows day visitors. For around Rs 500 you can have a day or night at the club with a meal and full run of the facilities and sports. Lunch is between 12.30 and 1.30 pm and you leave at 6 pm. Dinner is from 8.30 to 9.30 pm and there is a nightclub show and disco until 3 am.

Just beyond the Club Med is *Hotel Le Cannonier* (☎ 2637999), a five-star hotel with all the trimmings, including facilities for land sports and water sports. The beach bar, Le Navigateur, is transformed into an open-air discotheque at night. Prices for singles/doubles/triples start from around Rs 2800/4400/6000.

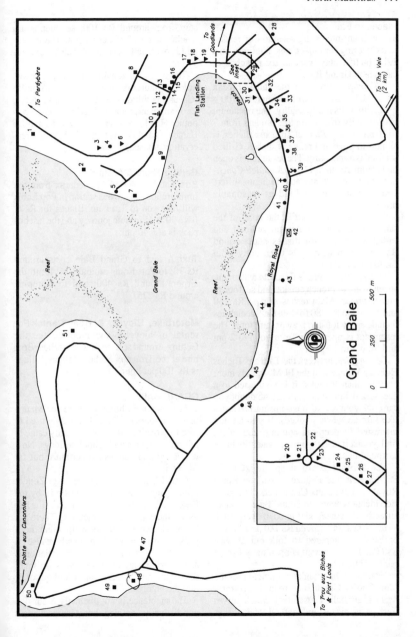

Grand Baie

## Places to Eat

There is an interesting selection of restaurants catering for most tastes, but those on a strict budget may want to try the cheaper eateries in Grand Baie.

*L'Exotique* serves Créole and European food. Main dishes start at around Rs 100 – beef with leeks is a speciality. The restaurant is open daily from noon to 2 pm and from 7 to 10 pm. *Lagon Bleu*, at Trou aux Biches, is similar in price and range of dishes. Grilled seafood is a speciality. The restaurant is open daily from 10 am to 11 pm. *Au Soleil Couchant*, south of Pointe aux Piments, offers Créole and Chinese food at reasonable prices.

*La Sirène Restaurant* in the hotel of the same name, concentrates on seafood and Indian dishes. Main dishes start around Rs 80. The restaurant is open daily from 11.30 am to 10 pm.

Opposite La Sirène is *Lagoona* restaurant, specialising in French cuisine and seafood at higher prices. Main dishes start at Rs 150 and extend to Rs 380 for lobster. Specialities include spiny lobster, prawns, and tuna. The restaurant is open daily from noon to 2 pm and from 7 to 10 pm.

*Le Corsaire*, between the Trou aux Biches Holiday Village and the PLM, sounds more exciting than it looks. It is connected to a deep-sea fishing enterprise, so no doubt you can cook your record-breaking marlin (tastes like salmon when smoked). If you are not interested in deep-sea angling, you might find yourself a fish out of water in these surroundings.

Yet another seafood specialist is *Le Bateau Ivre* (the Drunken Boat) on Route Royale at Pointe aux Canonniers. The roadside location nearer to Grand Baie is not so attractive, but the food is good, if overpriced. Main dishes start around Rs 180. For lobster or bass, be prepared to fork out at least Rs 600. The restaurant is open daily from 7 pm to midnight.

Nearby, at the roundabout junction of the Mon Choisy-Grand Baie road, is *Trattoria Azzura*, an Italian restaurant which serves fresh pasta, pizzas, and seafood. Main dishes start from around Rs 100; set menus are available at Rs 295 per person. The restaurant is open daily, except Monday, from 6 to 11 pm.

Top of the range would be the expensive hotel restaurants, including La Coquille (Casuarina Village – reservation obligatory); Le Frangipanier and le Navigator (Le Canonnier Hotel – reservation advised); and Le Barachois and Le Wahoo (PLM Azur – reservation advised).

## Getting There & Around

**Bus** The bus to Cap Malheureux from the Immigration Square bus station in Port Louis will take you to Trou aux Biches for Rs 6. It's a 30 to 45 minute journey and the last bus back is at 6.40 pm.

**Taxi** A taxi to Grand Baie costs around Rs 70; to Port Louis around Rs 140; to the airport around Rs 400; and to Curepipe around Rs 275.

**Motorbike, Bicycle & Boat Rental** For rental of bicycles and mopeds, see the Getting Around section for Grand Baie. Boat hire at the Trou aux Biches Holiday Village is Rs 100 per hour.

## GRAND BAIE

This is the main holiday centre for Mauritians and tourists alike. Grand Baie used to be a tiny fishing village which only came to life on weekends and school holidays. Now it is busy and congested, certainly but far from wild.

Grand Baie was called De Bogt Zonder Eyndt (Bay, or Bend, Without End), by the Dutch in the 17th century. Apart from the bay itself, there are few attractions. There's a better chance of mixing with other non-package visitors here than anywhere else on the island, as most of the accommodation is self-catering and in single units or small developments. You are not locked out of or into the hotel set.

The ambience is not distinctly Mauritian nor distinctly anything, but it is nonetheless relaxed. Practically everything in the town exists to cater for the visitors.

Grand Baie beach is a bit too close to the main street for comfort. The Royal Palm hotel has a good beach. The prime diving site in the area is the deep chasm at Whale Rock.

## Information
*Le Grand Baie News* is a bilingual (French/ English) free visitors' guide published monthly and available at most shops, hotels and bungalows. It has listings of hotels, bungalows, shops, restaurants, sports facilities and a host of other useful services.

**Money** The Mauritius Commercial Bank (MCB) has a foreign exchange counter open from Monday to Saturday and on public holidays from 8 am to 6 pm; opening hours on Sundays are from 9 am to 2 pm. The main MCB is opposite the main beach near the Grand Baie Store; it is open from 10 am to 2 pm on weekdays, and 9.30 to 11.30 am on Saturdays. Barclays Bank, further along the main street towards Peréybère on the same side as the MCB, has an exchange counter which is open the same hours as the MCB foreign exchange counter.

**Post & Telecommunications** The Post Office is opposite the police station, outside the main part of town. It is open Monday to Friday from 8 to 11.15 am and from noon to 4 pm, and on Saturdays from 8 to 11.45 am.

For domestic calls, you can use the phone in the post office. The public telephone is just past the post office, on the other side of the road and next to the police station. But don't rely on it working. For international calls it's best to try ringing from a hotel or local business.

**Travel Agencies** Grand Baie Travel & Tours (☎ 2638273), in the centre of Grand Baie, near the roundabout, runs tours of Mauritius, arranges airport transfers and rents accommodation, including bungalows at Trou aux Biches, Grand Baie and Cap Malheureux.

**Bookshop** Papyrus is a well-stocked bookshop which sells a wide range of local and foreign magazines and newspapers; travel guides; and stationery.

**Medical Services** The listings in *Le Grand Baie News* include contact details for doctors, dentists, and pharmacies.

**Dangers & Annoyances** The boom in tourism in the Grand Baie area has attracted petty thieves and burglars. The crimes are generally small scale stuff, but you should never leave valuables unattended.

Refer to the Dangers & Annoyances section in the Mauritius – Facts for the Visitor chapter for details about exclusion from beaches.

## Ruins
About two km south-east of Grand Baie, near The Vale village, are the ruins of a sugar mill belonging to the Daruty family. There are some splendid views from here across the cane fields and the pyramids of boulders. Enquire locally if you're interested in having a look around.

## Colonial Coconut Hotel
Primarily a hotel, this colonial edifice contains a most interesting display of paintings, aquatints, engravings (especially 'Company Art'), furniture (especially 'Export Art'), and old and intriguing books. The owner, a member of one of the island's oldest Franco-Mauritian families, is a keen traveller, colonial historian, and literary enthusiast. Refer to the Places to Stay section for more details.

## Coin de Mire & Île Plate
The two nearest islands off the northern tip of Mauritius, Coin de Mire and Île Plate, make good day trips.

Coin de Mire, four km off the coast, was so named because it resembles the wedge used to steady the aim of a cannon.

Further out is Île Plate, which has a lighthouse; it is the more popular island, offering easier landing and good snorkelling. There is a small army barracks here, as it is a training ground for the Special Mobile Force.

Most hotels and bungalow/flat owners will arrange boat trips to nearby Île Plate for around Rs 500 per person, often including food and drinks. Travellers have recommended trips on the *Moukila*, a small boat taking a maximum of seven people, which cost Rs 500 per person (including excellent grilled lunch) and can be booked at the Colonial Coconut Hotel. There are also a handful of yacht chartering operations which run day trips at Rs 800 (see the Yacht Cruises section).

### Île Ronde & Île aux Serpents

Île Ronde (Round Island) and Île aux Serpents (Snake Island) are about 24 km from Mauritius. Both are important nature reserves, but are difficult and dangerous to land on because of the sheer cliffs that drop into deep water.

Île aux Serpents, ironically, is round and has no snakes, but it is a renowned bird sanctuary.

The naturalist Gerald Durrell, in his book *Golden Bats & Pink Pigeons* (Collins, 1977), describes Île Ronde as a 'curious geological formation'. He wrote: 'The whole island was composed of tuff, and this soft stuff had been smoothed and sculpted by the wind and rain into pleats and scallops, so that the whole island was like a gigantic stone crinoline dropped on the surface of the sea with, here and there, standing up like jagged brocade, turrets, arches and flying buttresses carved by the elements'.

Île Ronde covers 151 hectares which scientists believe to be packed with the greatest number of endangered species in the world. Many of the plants, such as the Round Island hurricane palm (only two left on the island) and bottle palm are unique to the island. You can see transplanted Round Island bottle palms at the Le Réduit roundabout, near Moka.

The endemic fauna includes reptiles, such as the keel scale boa and burrowing boa

(possibly extinct); three types of skinks: Bojer's skink, Bouton's skink and Telfair's skink; and three types of gecko: Round Island gecko, ornate day gecko, and night gecko. Amongst the seabirds which breed on the island are wedge-tailed shearwaters, white-tailed tropic birds, and gadfly petrels.

Since 1984, Île Ronde has been managed as a nature reserve by the Mauritian government and MWAF. Although goats and rabbits were introduced here in the 19th century, rats never found their way onto the island. As a result, rare plant species once found on Mauritius, but long since wiped out by rats, have been discovered on the island. In 1986, the remaining goats and rabbits were eradicated. Scientists and volunteers make regular trips to the island to weed out introduced species, plant endemic species, and conduct surveys of reptiles and birds.

### Water Sports

There are glass-bottom boat trips for sightseeing on the reef. Snorkelling is leagues better out of the bay up at Peréybère, down at Trou aux Biches or around Île Plate.

For those who might fancy a walk underwater, Scaphandre (☎ 2637820) organises 'undersea walks' inside the reef, near Grand Baie. After donning lead boots and helmet (Jules Verne fans will enjoy this), you descend a ladder to a platform and stroll along the seabed to feed the fish. The price is Rs 600 per person. Bookings can be made either at the office (on the roundabout junction of the Mon Choisy-Grand Baie road) or at major hotels.

Most of the major hotels provide windsurfers, kayaks, etc, for the use of their guests.

### Yacht Cruises

You can charter a yacht or join a sailing tour in Grand Baie. Yacht Charters Ltd, Royal Rd (☎ 2618395), runs a range of tours and services with two yachts. You can rent one without crew for around Rs 3000 per day or charter one with crew for diving, fishing or cruising excursions. Deep-sea fishing costs Rs 600 per hour, with a minimum charter of six hours.

There are also cheaper trips along the coast for Rs 500 per person. The price includes drinks and a BBQ. Only day cruises are run in the cyclone season between December and April. Longer cruises are left to the rest of the year when gales are rare.

Yacht Sinhue Cruises (☎ 2637037) at Grand Baie also charges Rs 500 for a day trip, including drinks and a BBQ. They advertise in restaurants and hotels.

### Places to Stay – bottom end

There are no pensions in Grand Baie – you have to move on to Peréybère for one. However, every other building in town seems to be a bungalow or apartment to rent. There are some excellent deals around, especially if you arrive at a quiet time of the year with three friends in tow. All these places are fully furnished and have a shower, kitchen, small gas cooker and fridge. You'll be lucky, though, to get air-con at the lower end of the market. Many offer boat or fishing tours, and bicycles or mopeds for rent. The following are a few of the possibilities (see the map for locations).

*La Canne à Sucre* offers two flats with balconies; they're above a shop and cost Rs 300 per day. Contact Mr Kalam Joomen at home (☎ 2638822), or at La Pagode Restaurant (☎ 2638733). The flats have nothing to do with the shop below.

*Ebrahim Flats* rents six flats above a boutique. Single-room flats for one or two people are Rs 350 per day between February and July, or Rs 400 between August and January; two-room flats are Rs 500/600; and two three-bedroom flats are available at Rs 700 per day throughout the year. There is also a two-bed cottage and three-bed cottage on the beach for Rs 600 and Rs 700 per day. Contact Wah Moosa (☎ 038564). He also hires cars, mopeds and bicycles, and can arrange tours.

*Peramal Restaurant & Guest House* (☎ 2638771; fax 2638109) has several self-catering studios/apartments (two-bed and four-bed) ranging in price from Rs 250 to Rs 350; and a triple (up to six occupants) which costs Rs 450 per day.

*Résidence Cassamally* (☎/fax 2637521), also known as *La Résidence*, has one-bedroom, self-catering apartments for Rs 400 and two-bedroom versions for Rs 600.

*L'Esplanade Café & Restaurant* has two rooms to let for Rs 300 and Rs 400 per day. It's a nice restaurant but the rooms are very close to the eating and cooking action. Contact Charou Patrick (☎ 2638055).

*La Charrette* restaurant has a number of properties to let. A bedroom with a toilet and shower costs Rs 250 per night; a bedroom and kitchenette is Rs 300 per night; and a two-bedroom flat with a kitchen and lounge is Rs 400. Contact Mr Diva Narainen or Mrs Mala (☎ 2638976).

*Hotel La Terrasse* (☎ 2638992) has seven rooms for single/double Rs 300/400 per night, including breakfast; a one-bedroom apartment for Rs 500; and a two-bedroom apartment for Rs 600.

Readers have written to recommend contacting Mr Mansoor Khodabacus (☎ 263-8831). He offers clean, well-equipped, self-catering apartments in a good location in Grand Baie at Rs 300 per day.

### Places to Stay – middle

Apartments or bungalows to let in this range generally have better decor and facilities. Many are rented through the tour agency Grand Bay Travel & Tours, or GBTT (☎ 2638273, fax 2638274) and are more popular with elderly couples. There's also a continuing trend towards construction of mid-range hotels.

The *Colonial Coconut Hotel* (☎ 2638720; fax 2637116) at Pointe aux Canonniers is a real treat; one of the few remaining examples in the Indian Ocean of the traditional hotels which were once standard staging posts on the long passage to the East. The structure has been adapted and extended using traditional materials and designs, from a villa originally built by the owner's grandfather in 1920. The present owner, Louis Hein de Charmoy, is a passionate colonial historian and expert on the literary history of that era. He has maintained the ambience in the hotel interior with family furniture and artworks from the colonial past of Mauritius and the Far East.

On Wednesday evenings, the group 'Trio du Coconut' plays the traditional forms of séga. At the Mosquito bar you might like to try the 'sting' *(piqûre de moustique)* which is a powerful mixture of guava, mango, coconut, rum and gin! The management hazily recollects that nearly 50,000 of these have been consumed in the last decade or so! There's also an excellent restaurant serving Mauritian, Oriental, and French cuisine – the expresso coffee served is the genuine article.

Prices for single/double/triple rooms, including breakfast, start from around Rs 857/1128/1400 in the low season (February to October); and rise around 30% in the high season (November to January). Discounts are available for long stays, especially for writers. The Norwegian crime writer, Jon Michelet, stayed here to write his bestselling thriller, 'Le Coconut'.

*Sea Point Bungalows* (☎ 2638604) at Pointe aux Canonniers offers self-catering bungalows, for up to five people, at prices ranging from Rs 700 to Rs 900, per person per day, depending on the season.

*Villa Floralies* (☎ 2638269) is a three-storey block of units on a back road to Grand Gaube. Singles/doubles are Rs 325 per day. You can buy your own food and have it cooked for you. Price reductions are offered for long stays. Contact Mr Karamchand Jogee.

*Les Jacarandas* is another block of flats, shaded by palms. There are six, self-catering, two-bedroom units for Rs 600 per day. An extra bed costs Rs 50. Contact GBBT (☎ 2638771; fax 2638274) to make arrangements.

*Les Cocotiers* (☎ 2638771; fax 2638274) is an up-market development also let through GBTT. There are two self-catering, two-bedroom flats available for Rs 800 per day.

*Seaview* consists of two and three-bedroom flats for Rs 800/950. Contact GBTT to arrange rental.

*Les Palmiers* (☎ 2638464) is an attractive and congenial place with many repeat book-

ings. Robert Chan, the enthusiastic director, also rents three two-bedroom flats for single/double Rs 350/500 per day (including a cleaner!) and for Rs 600 for three or more people. Three studio flats have been added and are to let at similar rates. A continental-style breakfast is available on the small dining terrace for Rs 35. There is a bar, and a laundry service. Cars and bicycles are also available for hire.

Both *La Méditerranée* (☎ 2638019) and *Les Orchidées* (☎ 2638780) restaurants have rooms/units to let at prices starting from around Rs 350.

At the top end of the mid-range accommodation is *Verandah Hotel* (☎ 2638015; fax 2637369), also known as *Veranda Bungalow Village*, a beautifully laid-out complex near the yacht club. Each of the 35 self-catering bungalows has a verandah and houses two to five people. Tariffs range from Rs 2000 to Rs 2400, depending on the number of occupants. One-bedroom studios are also available at Rs 1400 per day; and single/double rooms cost Rs 1225/1660. There is a bar, restaurant and shop. Bicycle hire is a hefty Rs 20/80 per hour/day).

### Places to Stay – top end

The *Royal Palm* (☎ 2638353; fax 2638455), one of the Beachcomber group hotels, is considered one of the island's top hotels. Rates for single/double rooms start at Rs 4800/7200, including breakfast. The senior suite costs a cool Rs 19,500 – oh yes, including breakfast. Apart from all the usual topnotch facilities, guests are provided with a Beachcomber Card – for more details refer to the Accommodation section in the Mauritius – Facts for the Visitor chapter.

The British-owned *Merville* (☎ 2638621; fax 2638146) is marginally more affordable. Standard singles/doubles are Rs 2590/3890, including breakfast. Suites are available at Rs 5520/7180 for a single/double.

*Le Mauricia Hotel* (☎ 2637800; fax 2637888) competes in the lower bracket of the top range. Formerly known as the Pullman Hotel, it was taken over by the Beachcomber hotel group in 1992. No official rates were available while we were researching, but the Pullman rates used to be Rs 2450/3500 for singles/doubles. The Beachcomber Card, which every guest receives on registration, is valid here – for more details refer to the Accommodation section in the Mauritius – Facts for the Visitor chapter.

## Places to Eat

You are spoiled with choices in Grand Baie. Although Chinese places still dominate and are the least expensive, there is also an increasing number of competing restaurants offering different fare.

The big Chinese restaurants, *Palais de Chine*, *La Pagode* and *La Jonque*, all look alike and are all near each other on the main road. Their prices are around Rs 40 for fried rice, Rs 75 for meat dishes and Rs 200 for lobster. They are open daily from 11 am until at least 10.30 pm, but La Pagode and Palais de Chine close between 3 and 5 pm. Readers have recently commented that *Jade Garden* on the beach, opposite Sakura Restaurant, serves tiny, overpriced portions.

*La Charette* offers good Indian cuisine. Main dishes, such as tandoori, start from around Rs 45. It's open daily from 11.30 am to 11 pm.

For general European dishes, you can try *Café de Paris* or *Café Cactus*.

For Créole and French cuisine, two restaurants worth visiting are *La Mediterranée* (open daily from 11 am to 2.30 pm; and from 6.30 to 10.30 pm) and *Le Capitaine* (open daily from 10 am to midnight). Main dishes, such as curry chicken, start around Rs 65.

If you hanker after Italian food, and enjoy live entertainment in the evening, we can recommend *Ristorante Beatrice*, which is moderately priced and stays open daily from noon until 11 pm.

The *Sakura* Japanese restaurant (open daily from 6.30 to 10.30 pm; closed on Sunday) offers genuine Japanese food, but is overpriced.

*Phil's Pub* has drinks at the bar from 11 am to 1 pm and until 11 pm at night. Attached

to the pub is *L'Assiette du Pêcheur*, a specialist seafood restaurant with main dishes from around Rs 150. It's open daily from 11.30 am to 3 pm; and from 7 to 10.30 pm.

For croissants and cakes, try *Chez Patty Pâtisserie*, next to La Canne à Sucre Flats.

If cooking for yourself, the best places to shop in the town are *Grand Baie Store* and *Store 2000*.

## Entertainment

**Séga Dances & Discos** The Mauritius Government Tourist Office in Port Louis publishes a news-sheet of coming events every two months, which includes a programme of dancing and séga nights at the hotels and discos. Events are also covered in *Le Grand Baie News*, a publication described in the Information section for Grand Baie. For details about séga, see the Culture & the Arts section in the Mauritius – Facts about the Country chapter. Most major hotels lay on at least one séga night per week. Tickets to these events usually cost around Rs 250 to Rs 350 and include a buffet dinner.

Apart from the hotels, the main local jive shops and discos in Grand Baie include the Climax Club, and Dream On. At the latter, there's reported to be a predominance of ladies for hire.

Admission to discos usually costs at least Rs 100, and you'll rarely pay less than Rs 30 for a beer.

**Casino** For those with an urge to gamble, there's the casino at Trou aux Biches. See Trou aux Biches Village hotel under Trou aux Biches earlier in this chapter.

## Getting There & Away

**Bus** Buses run through Grand Baie en route from Port Louis to Cap Malheureux for Rs 8. They leave from Immigration Square bus station in Port Louis every half-hour. The trip goes via Triolet and Trou aux Biches and takes an hour to Grand Baie.

There are bus services between Grand Baie and Pamplemousses. The trip also costs Rs 8.

**Taxi** For taxi rides from Grand Baie, expect to pay Rs 70 to Trou aux Biches; Rs 150 to Port Louis; and Rs 400 to the airport. Since this is a major hotel centre, be prepared for taxi drivers to quote telephone number prices.

## Getting Around

**Car** Le Cap Car Hire (☎ 2637430), based in Cap Malheureux, may offer better deals than the Grand Baie companies. In Grand Baie, try Beach Car (☎ 2638759) which is open daily from 8.30 am to 4.30 pm; but closes at 11.30 am on Sundays and public holidays. Other companies include Grand Baie Contract Cars (☎ 2638564), Cassamally (☎ 263-7521), Location Mr Chetty (☎ 2638108), and the expensive, brand-name options, such as Avis (☎ 2637600) and Europcar (☎ 2637948). For the cheapest option, ask for an old mini, and expect to pay around Rs 700 for one day, less if you hire for several days.

Find out if the management of your hotel or guesthouse has a special discount agreement with a local company. Whichever company you choose, check all the surcharges before agreeing on a final price.

**Motorbike** Grand Baie has the largest number of moped rental companies on Mauritius, so it's a good place to hire a moped to scoot around the island. Most of the guesthouses and hotels can find you a moped to hire. We used Coastal Tour (☎ 2637595) and were impressed by their breakdown service. Within half an hour of phoning from Trou aux Biches to report a snapped throttle cable, the manager had appeared on the scene with a mechanic, replaced the cable, and bought us free consolation samosas from a passing vendor!

Rental charges hover around Rs 175 per day with insurance, but it should be easy to lower the price to Rs 150 per day if you are renting for more than one day. A deposit of Rs 500 per moped seems to be standard practice.

**Bicycle** Hotels and guesthouses can easily find you a bicycle to hire. Rates vary, but expect to pay around Rs 75 per day, less if you hire for several days.

## PERÉYBÈRE

Peréybère is a rapidly expanding resort a couple of km north of Grand Baie. It has a good beach, reef and a wide range of budget accommodation (mostly self-catering) and eating places.

### Things to See & Do

Beaches, snorkelling and windsurfing are all excellent off Peréybère. On the main public beach, the constant attentions of souvenir pedlars and people trying to sell you excursions can become wearisome. Topless bathing is definitely not the local norm, hence those women who do it can expect to be ogled and pestered with suggestive comments.

Snorkelling is best off the 'private' beaches. Turn down the track opposite the Stephan Boutique until you reach Pointe d'Azur. The beaches on either side are good bases for snorkelling expeditions. Another relatively secluded beach lies to the south of the Hibiscus Village Vacances. Masks, snorkels and flippers are sold in the supermarkets at Grand Baie, but it's not easy to find any for hire.

You can hire sailboards for Rs 35 per half-hour, but beware of the glass-bottom boat privateers.

Going north out of Peréybère, on the coast side of the road, is a sports complex, Currimjee Tennis (☎ 2638805), with tennis and squash courts.

### Places to Stay

*Jolicoeur Guest House* (☎ 2638202) is run by Welsh expatriate Arthur Hooper and his Mauritian wife, Marie. It is a rather ordinary, modern, two-storey house with seven rooms, but is clean and tidy and has a friendly, easy-going feel to it. Singles/doubles are Rs 250/300 per night, including breakfast. Jolicoeur is popular with travellers – a good place to meet and swap tales of Mauritius, Madagascar, and beyond. If you need to hire transport, Arthur has special agreements with local companies.

For a remote, rural, long-stay option in the centre of Mauritius, seven km from Le Val Nature Park, ask Arthur about renting his bungalow. It sleeps up to four persons and costs around Rs 575 per day, including use of a 50cc moped, gas, electricity and water.

*Casa Florida* (☎ 2637371; fax 4547336) is a complex of self-catering studios and two-bedroom apartments. Prices for the studios start around Rs 385/510 for singles/doubles. The apartments cost around Rs 730/765/800 for doubles/triples/quadruples.

Similarly priced is *Cases Fleuries* (☎ 263-8868), with four attractive studio apartments and a two-bedroom bungalow, owned by Mrs Seksun.

*Krissy's Apartments* (☎ 2638859) consists of one and two-bedroom, self-catering apartments which are priced at Rs 450/550 per day.

Nearby are the evocatively named *Fred Apartments* (☎ 2638830; fax 2638830). Fred is a German and his brochures and notices are all in German, but the present manager is called Günter. You don't have to be German to stay there, but if you're not, you may find yourself somewhat out of it. There are eight self-catering apartments at Rs 450 for one or two people and Rs 600 for three or four people. Fred's has a 'Bar und Klubraum' if you fancy a knees-up, and is known to run a séga dance or two.

There are eight *Peréybère Beach Apartments* (☎ 2638679), and each contains two bedrooms, a bathroom and a kitchen. The daily rate is Rs 350.

Opposite the Peréybère Beach Apartments is *Le Bénitier* boutique, which has a room to let for Rs 150 per night and a flat above the shop for Rs 250. Some travellers have complained about the noise at night.

On the main road, the *Étoile du Nord* (☎ 2638303) has 12 rooms with a shower and toilet for single/double Rs 225/275. There are bicycles and mopeds for hire; and

the manager can also arrange trips to Île Plate.

Next door, the *Sylvilla Pension* (☎ 263-8303) has standard rooms at Rs 225/275 per day for a single/double, including breakfast. Readers have griped about ants and warned about excessive street noise in the rooms next to the main road. There's also a restaurant here, and the manager arranges excursions.

Another option with balcony views of the beach and sea is the *Panorama Hotel & Restaurant* (☎ 2638641/2), a large, four-storey, white building with a spiral staircase. There are 34 rooms for single/double Rs 250/400.

Inland, towards the cane fields on Mt Oreb Lane, the *Malvilla* development (☎ 2638806) looks slightly incongruous. The four one-bedroom units cost Rs 250 per day, and the two two-bedroom units are Rs 300.

Moving north towards Cap Malheureux, you'll ride *Binos Villas* (☎ 2638320) which rents a two-bedroom flat for Rs 300 per day and a studio for Rs 200. Air-conditioning costs extra. Contact Rasheed to make arrangements.

Readers have recommended *Allamanda* (☎ 2638110 or 2638261), a block of 12 self-catering apartments about two km north of Peréybère near Cap Malheureux, which are basic, but clean and pleasant. The genial owner, Mr Sivayan Peramal, works as a policeman and also operates a taxi service. One-bedroom apartments (maximum two occupants) cost Rs 150 per night; and two-bedroom apartments (maximum four occupants) cost Rs 250 per night. The cleaners will do a reasonable load of laundry for Rs 50.

Other possibilities are: *Le Chatel-Relais Auberge du Petit Cerf* (☎ 2638908), with bungalows for Rs 275 per day; *Les Cinq Étoiles* (☎ 4542080), which has a bungalow for four at Rs 350 per day; *Gunness Rajaram* (☎ 2638717), with a three-bedroom flat for Rs 400 per day; and *Pension Sabina*, with a small apartment for Rs 175 per day.

*Hibiscus Village Vacances* (☎ 038554), on the shore heading out of Peréybère towards Grand Baie, is more expensive and exclusive. The beach on its doorstep is quite poor but the public Peréybère beach is close at hand. Single/double rooms are Rs 730/880, including breakfast; half board is Rs 870/1160. The hotel also has facilities, such as a scuba diving centre, sailboards, and bicycles. Special séga nights are held here once a week.

**Places to Eat**

Since much of the accommodation is self-catering, you'll have to do your major shopping errands in Grand Baie, for

| ■ PLACES TO STAY | | 19 | Jolicoeur Guesthouse |
|---|---|---|---|
| | | 20 | Mipan |
| 1 | Casa Florida | | |
| 4 | Malvilla | ▼ | PLACES TO EAT |
| 5 | Sabina | | |
| 6 | Sylvilla Pension | 7 | Cafétaria Peréybère |
| 8 | Étoile du Nord Apartments | 10 | La Sapienière Restaurant |
| 9 | Les Bougainvilliers | 15 | Restaurant Café Peréybère |
| 11 | Le Bénitier Boutique | | |
| 12 | Krissy's Apartments | | OTHER |
| 13 | Cases Fleuries Apartments | | |
| 14 | Hibiscus Village Vacances | 2 | Aux Fantasies Florales |
| 16 | Peréybère Beach Apartments | 3 | Stephan Boutique |
| 17 | Fred Apartments | 18 | Bureau de Change |

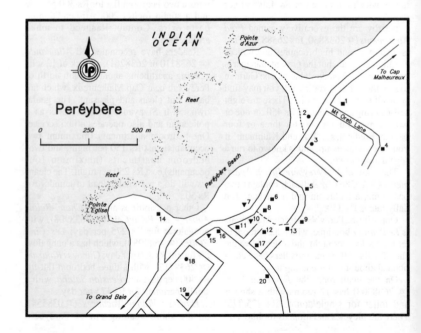

example, at the Grand Baie Store or Store 2000. The Chinese general store Stephan Boutique, in Peréybère, has a smaller selection and costs more. There are also two stores on the Cap Malheureux road, about one km north of the village.

Clustered around the bus park in the centre of Peréybère are three restaurants; there's little to choose between them. Meals are all Chinese-oriented and dishes cost around Rs 55. *Restaurant Café Peréybère* is said to have the edge, for food and value, on the *Cafétaria Peréybère* (don't be put off by the name). They also have a takeaway service. At the time of research, *La Sapinière* was closed for renovation and may now be the best of the lot. The management plans to hold séga dances on Fridays; the admission charge will be around Rs 200 per person, including dinner buffet.

There are also snack stalls and vans parked in front of the beach. A meal of beef or chicken noodles here costs Rs 15.

### Things to Buy
Aux Fantasies Florales has a shop and showroom in Peréybère displaying various pretty and practical products featuring dried flowers.

### Getting There & Around
Travelling to Peréybère is the same as for Grand Baie (see Grand Baie – Getting There & Away). If you want to hire a car, moped, or bicycle, find out if the management of your hotel or guesthouse has a special discount agreement with a local company. Most of these companies are happy to deliver and collect from your hotel or guesthouse. Taxi drivers tend to quote rapacious or ridiculous prices. If you know the price you want, bargain until you get it; otherwise save the bother and ask the advice of your hotel or guesthouse manager who can probably bring the driver's price quote down to earth.

### CAP MALHEUREUX
Cap Malheureux is a beautiful and peaceful village with a picturesque church, the Notre Dame Auxilia Trice, and a good view of the

Coin de Mire island. The most northerly tip of Mauritius, it was named the 'Cape of Misfortune' after several ships were wrecked in the area.

Grand Gaube, about six km east of Cap Malheureux, is a small fishing village with a decent beach.

### Places to Stay
**Cap Malheureux** Approximately two km west of Cap Malheureux, *Les Mascareignes Hotel* (☎ 2637373; fax 2637372) offers single/double rooms for Rs 390/650 and a self-catering apartment (maximum five persons) for Rs 1300.

Closer to Cap Malheureux is *Coin de Mire Village Hotel* (☎ 2637302; fax 2121361) which has studios (maximum two persons) at around Rs 700 and apartments (maximum four persons) at around 600. The Sultan's Luxury Suite houses a maximum of eight, and costs Rs 2500.

*La Maison* (☎ 2638974; fax 2637009), near the beach at Cap Malheureux, is a luxury residence for guests with exclusive tastes and thick wallets. Room prices start around Rs 5500. Facilities on offer include hire of a limousine and a yacht, complete with attendants.

An old favourite, especially with German tourists, is the *Kuxville* (☎ 2637913/263 8836), about 1.5 km east of Cap Malheureux village. The reception area is plastered with notices to guests. The eight bungalows, apartments or studios, with two to four beds each, have individual names such as 'Fritz', 'Olaf' and 'Elke'. Rates are given in Deutschmarks and must be paid in such or other foreign currency. They range from Rs 1160 (DM 110) per double for a night in studio 'Stefan', to Rs 1371 (DM 130) for the two-bedroom 'Fritz' bungalow. The price includes a maid/servant/cook. There is a small beach in front of the complex. Diving, fishing and sightseeing tours can be organised and a variety of vessels are available for hire.

There are also bungalows to rent between the post office and restaurant in Cap Malheureux.

*Marina Village Hotel* (☎ 2637651; fax 2637650) is just east of the Kuxville, at Anse La Raie. It consists of two-storey blocks with self-catering bungalows (maximum four persons). Prices start around Rs 1300 for ground floor units; and rise to around Rs 1500 for units on the 1st floor.

At the time of research, another hotel, *Hotel Paradasco*, was being constructed at Anse La Raie.

**Grand Gaube** The British-run *Island View Club Hotel* (☎ 2839544; fax 2839233) has single/double rooms for Rs 800/1500 on a half-board basis. Self-catering family suites are also available at around Rs 2000/3000 for a maximum of four/six persons. The hotel has 39 rooms in bungalows, a small beach and a freshwater swimming pool.

Nearby is *Le Grand Gaube Hotel* (☎ 2839350; fax 2839420), a luxury hotel with standard single/double/triple rooms at Rs 2200/3300/4100 for half-board. More expensive suites are also available. According to locals, construction of the hotel proved a delicate task because the site is part of an old cemetery.

**Places to Eat**
Les Mascareignes hotel has an attached restaurant which serves French, Chinese, and Créole food. Main dishes start at around Rs 75. It's open daily from noon to 3 pm and from 7.30 to 10 pm.

Opposite the church in Cap Malheureux is *Le Coin de Mire* restaurant and bar, specialising in Créole and Chinese food. It's a pleasant little place, open daily from 9.30 am to 10 pm, and charging Rs 55 for an average course. You can also buy fish from the village fishing station.

In Grand Gaube, *The Nomad* serves Middle Eastern, Italian and Créole dishes. Main dishes cost around Rs 55. The restaurant is closed on Sundays and Mondays. It is open from noon to 2.45 pm, and from 7 to 9.45 pm (10.30 pm on Saturday). Other more expensive options include the restaurants at the Island View Club (Créole buffet special

on Wednesday evening) and Le Grand Gaube hotels.

**Getting There & Around**
There are frequent buses running between Cap Malheureux or Grand Gaube and Port Louis (at the Immigration Square bus station) for Rs 8. A taxi to Port Louis will cost at least Rs 250, and Rs 450 to the airport.

Enquire at the Kuxville hotel about motorboat and canoe hire.

## GOODLANDS
Goodlands is a large town but isn't a place to stay. It's worth calling in to the large Historic Marine model boat-building factory at the St Antoine Industrial Estate (on the road to Poudre d'Or). It is open Monday to Friday from 8 am to 5 pm, and on Saturdays from 8 am to noon. (See the Things to Buy section in the Mauritius – Facts for the Visitor chapter.)

There is also an impressive Hindu temple in Goodlands, and several large colonial and Créole houses.

There are beaches around Poudre d'Or and about 10 km down the coast at Roches Noires. Roches Noires (Black Rocks) is so named because of the black lava rocks which fringe the shore.

## POUDRE D'OR
Whether the name, which means 'gold powder', refers to the sandy beaches or the treasure said to be buried near the church, we don't know, but this is the sort of place that is rich in history and character, if not in tourist developments.

**St Géran Monument**
It was off Poudre d'Or in 1744 that the famous *St Géran* was wrecked in a storm and sank, with many lives lost. The disaster inspired the love story *Paul et Virginie*, by Bernardin de St Pierre, later in the 18th century, and put Mauritius on the map as far as the French were concerned.

The *St Géran* was carrying machinery from France for the first sugar refinery on the island. A French diving expedition excavated the wreck in 1966 and the results of the expedition are on display at the Naval Museum in Mahébourg. A small, disappointing monument was erected on the shore near Poudre d'Or in 1944.

## Islands

Île d'Ambre and Île Bernache are within easy striking distance of Poudre d'Or, only 30 minutes by boat. Henri Samy can organise trips to the uninhabited islands for Rs 350 per day return or Rs 500, including overnight camping and meals. Enquire at the police station in Poudre d'Or, or call 2122334.

## Sunken Treasure

There are no signs and nothing in the tourist literature or any of the histories about the sunken treasure. Generally, either few people know about it or it was given up as a lost cause years ago, but the evidence is there, on the surface at least.

If you take a line about 200 metres due north from the steeple of Ste Philomène Church, you come to a deep hole at the river's edge. It is surrounded by reeds, often submerged and only accessible by pirogue. But it is there, it is deep and it is said to lead to a tunnel, perhaps connecting with another under the church or at the shore.

Somewhere inside is a treasure trove, possibly that of the infamous French pirate Olivier Levasseur, who was known as 'La Buse' (The Buzzard). La Buse's treasure has been the object of a long and controversial search at Bel Ombre in the Seychelles (see the Seychelles section). One theory is that people are looking in the wrong place, and that Poudre d'Or would be a better bet. See Roy Norvill's *Treasure Seekers' Treasury* (Hutchinson, London, 1978) for more about treasure seeking.

About 10 years ago, a French team of treasure hunting divers unofficially and unsuccessfully tried to excavate the hole. They found only a few coins.

I was told the story and shown the 'well' by Menon Prayag, a young sugar baron in the Rivière du Rempart district. His wealth today is a direct result of his great grandfather discovering buried treasure while working as a poor, immigrant labourer who had been brought over to work the cane fields. Thereafter, the Prayag family owned the cane fields and now runs garment factories and other businesses in the area. Menon has good reason not to scoff at the possibility of more treasure.

Happy hunting!

## Places to Eat

The *Coin du Nord*, a small café/bar next to the river on the road to Rivière du Rempart, serves meals.

## Getting There & Away

If you're coming from Port Louis (Immigration Square station) there is a regular bus service to Rivière du Rempart, or to Goodlands and Grand Gaube, via Pamplemousses. There do not appear to be any buses to Poudre d'Or itself.

## RIVIERE DU REMPART

There is little of interest in this town unless you can locate Menon Prayag (see the Poudre d'Or section) who lives there. He also owns the *Chemin de Fer* restaurant (☎ 4125571).

## PAMPLEMOUSSES

It is believed that the village of Pamplemousses, which means 'grapefruit', was named after the citrus plant, introduced into Mauritius from Java by the Dutch.

The Sir Seewoosagur Ramgoolam Botanical Gardens at Pamplemousses (also referred to as the Royal Botanic Gardens) were started by governor Mahé de Labourdonnais in 1735, as a vegetable garden for his Mon Plaisir Château. They were transformed by French horticulturalist Pierre Poivre (Peter Pepper!) in 1768. He imported plants from around the world in a bid to market spices. The gardens were neglected between 1810 and 1849, until a British horticulturalist, James Duncan, took over. He spruced things up and introduced the variety of palms seen today.

Pamplemousses provided a testing site for new sugar cane varieties and, in 1866 when a malaria epidemic hit Mauritius, the Sir Seewoosagur Ramgoolam Botanical Gardens acted as a nursery for the eucalyptus trees used to dry out marshes, the breeding sites of the mosquitoes.

Cyclones have periodically decimated the gardens. The last one to hit was in 1979.

## Sir Seewoosagur Ramgoolam Botanical Gardens

The gardens are hardly one of the wonders of the world, but they are a fascinating feature of Mauritius. If you are not botanically minded, you will be after a visit. If you are so minded, you won't want to leave. The gates (all the way from Crystal Palace in London) are open each day from 6 am to 6 pm and entry is free.

First some hints on how to get the most out of your visit. The best time to see the gardens is between December and April. It's a big place, so you'll need time and a decent map, such as the one in this book. Guidebooks are on sale for Rs 100, but they are not essential.

A notice warns you not to employ guides, though you'll probably be pestered by droves of fellows keen to show you a tree or two for an outrageous fee. If you want a proper guide, ignore them and find an official or one of the gardeners. Although some people may approach you, waving their Ministry of Agriculture ID card, there's no way to tell if they are genuine gardeners. If you find a likely guide, make absolutely certain you've got the fee and duration of the tour settled (preferably in writing!) *before* you start – and pay after the tour has been satisfactorily completed. As a rough guideline, expect to pay around Rs 50 as a fee for a small group or single visitor – ignore efforts to quadruple figures into absurdity.

The whole shenanigans with hustling guides can be a real pain, so much so, that some visitors simply take a guide to hold the others at bay. It also helps to say you've already had a tour, possess and have memorised the Pamplemousses guidebook,

or you can explain with imaginative detail that you are an independent believer in chaos and thus your politics dictate no use of guides (except written LP ones) whatsoever!

There are few flowers in the gardens; it is not a horticultural display. Having said that, one of the main features is the giant Victoria regia water lily, native to the Amazon region. The flowers at the centre of the huge trays open white one day and close red the next. Other star attractions include the 'decorative' golden bamboo and the vast variety of palms, which come in all shapes and sizes. Some of the more prominent are the talipot palms, which flower once after 40 to 60 years and then die, the stubby bottle palms, and the tall royal palms lining Poivre Ave, as well as the raffia, sugar, toddy, fever, fan and even sex palms.

Savour the smells – ginger, cinnamon, nutmeg, camphor, lemon, eucalyptus, sandalwood and others. Your guide (if you have

Water Hyacinths

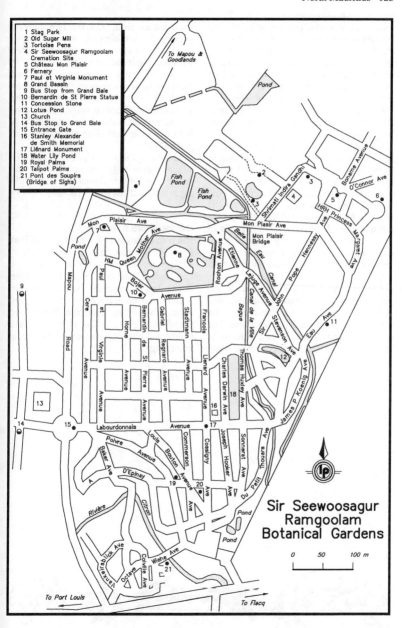

1 Stag Park
2 Old Sugar Mill
3 Tortoise Pens
4 Sir Seewoosagur Ramgoolam
  Cremation Site
5 Château Mon Plaisir
6 Fernery
7 Paul et Virginie Monument
8 Grand Bassin
9 Bus Stop from Grand Baie
10 Bernardin de St Pierre Statue
11 Concession Stone
12 Lotus Pond
13 Church
14 Bus Stop to Grand Baie
15 Entrance Gate
16 Stanley Alexander
   de Smith Memorial
17 Liénard Monument
18 Water Lily Pond
19 Royal Palms
20 Talipot Palms
21 Pont des Soupirs
   (Bridge of Sighs)

Sir Seewoosagur
Ramgoolam
Botanical Gardens

0    50    100 m

one) will know which ones to sniff. It's like walking through a department store trying on all the perfumes or aftershaves! Standing beside the more conventional mahogany, ebony and fig trees, you'll see the marmalade box tree, the chewing-gum tree, the fish poison tree and the sausage tree. There is a 200-year-old Buddha tree and, for Christians, the cross tree, whose leaves are shaped like a cross.

The gardens also play the roles of wildlife sanctuary, cemetery and art gallery. Sir Seewoosagur Ramgoolam, the first prime minister of Mauritius after independence, was cremated on a concrete block outside the château. His ashes were scattered on the Ganges. An enclosure with Java deer is near a pen of giant Aldabra tortoises. There is an old one with a noticeably chipped shell, damaged when a tourist threw a rock at it to make it move. He was fined Rs 500 and a fence was built around the pen.

Cars and bicycles are permitted in the gardens every day except Sundays and public holidays, but leave them at the gate if you want to see the most on your tour. You may have to pay someone Rs 5 or Rs 10 to keep an eye on the vehicle, in case some frustrated unofficial guide vents his anger on your tyres. Alternatively, you can hire a tandem. There is a sign saying that this deed wins you a 'gift and a diploma'!

You can't get away from Paul and Virginie, the lovers immortalised in Bernardin de St Pierre's novel. The stone on the avenue named after them was supposed to be the tomb of the fictional characters but it is in fact only the base of an old statue to the goddess Flora.

The Mon Plaisir Château is now for administration only and not open to the public. It is not the original palace; the 'old sugar mill' is also a reconstruction.

### Getting There & Away

Pamplemousses is 11 km north-east of Port Louis. To get there, take the Grand Gaube, Rivière du Rempart, Roches Noires or Centre de Flacq buses from Immigration Square bus station in Port Louis. There are infrequent direct buses from Peréybère and Grand Baie. From Trou aux Biches and Grand Baie, you can also go up to Grand Gaube and change, or down to Port Louis and change.

# Central Mauritius

The central plateau of the island is split between the Plaines Wilhelms district in the south and west and the Moka district in the north and east. Plaines Wilhelms is the main residential area of Mauritius, with a conglomeration of towns practically linked to each other from Port Louis down to Curepipe.

The Moka mountain range fringes the area to the north; the Black River range to the west. Quartier Militaire, at the centre of the Moka district and is perhaps, as the name suggests, the bleakest area in the island. South of Curepipe, around Mare aux Vacoas, the countryside is more appealing. The climate is cooler and less humid on the plateau and the way of life more European.

With the exception of Curepipe, there is little of interest for visitors in the towns, although there are some beautiful areas on the other side of the motorway, around Moka village.

## CUREPIPE

Curepipe and its environs owe their size and prominence to the malaria epidemic of 1867, which caused thousands of people to flee infested Port Louis for the healthier hill country.

It probably takes its name from a town in the south-west of France. For those who will not accept dull explanations, it could have been named by French soldiers who used the place as a rest and smoke stop where they could 'cure' (clean) their pipes on the way to or from the Quartier Militaire.

Curepipe has the flavour of an English market town. The Franco-Mauritians stay mostly in the suburbs around Curepipe, particularly Floréal, and come into Curepipe – by car, of course – to shop. The other locals come in by bus or walk under the shade of umbrellas. Umbrellas are a safe either-way bet any day, because it also rains frequently in Curepipe.

Curepipe is now the centre of the tea and

the model-ship building industries and the town is worth visiting if only to see the contrast with Port Louis. It also offers better shopping than the capital.

Of the 69,000 people in town, about 50,000 seem to be permanently milling around the bus station. That, in turn, leaves the rest of the town quiet and peaceful by comparison. Even without the people, the bus station at Jan Palach Square stands out from the rest of Curepipe. The administration building has an 'out of this world' or crashed spaceship design (another description was a 'tacky pipe organ').

### Orientation

The street-naming confusion is not as big a problem here as in Port Louis. The main confusion may arise over Royal Rd or Route Royale, the main drag from Port Louis, which runs through the centre of town, leading out south, towards Mahébourg. It is also called Plaines Wilhelms St on some maps and Port Louis Rd on others.

The wide road running past the bus station and casino, by the way, is not an attempt at a motorway. There used to be two roads with a railway line between them until the Mauritian railways were closed in 1964.

### Information

**Money** All the banks are on the Mahébourg Main Rd. The two main banks, the Mauritius Commercial Bank (MCB) and Barclays, are opposite each other at the western end of Châteauneuf St. Further along the main road, towards Mahébourg, is the Banque Nationale de Paris and the State Commercial Bank, and towards Port Louis is the Hong Kong & Shanghai Bank. Banking hours are 10 am to 2 pm on weekdays and 9.30 to 11.30 am on Saturdays.

The MCB also has a foreign exchange counter at its branch on Mahébourg Main Rd. It's open from 9 am to 5 pm Monday to Friday.

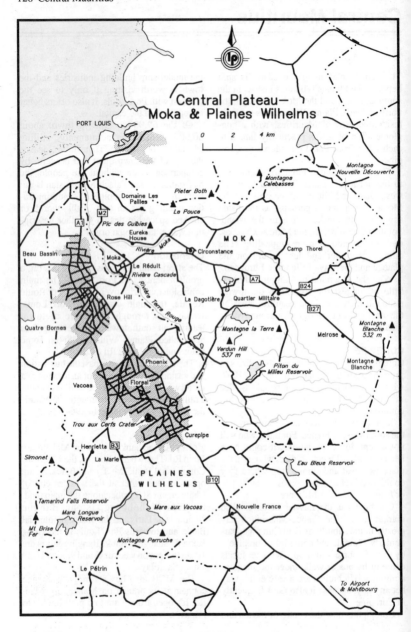

Central Plateau—
Moka & Plaines Wilhelms

Top Left: Chamarel coloured earths, Mauritius (DS)
Top Right: Sir Seewoosagur Ramgoolam Botanic Gardens, Pamplemousses,
Mauritius (DS)     Bottom Left: Île aux Aigrettes, Mauritius (DS)
Bottom Right: Chamarel Falls, Mauritius (DS)

Top: Poisson d'Or, Haute Gastronomie Chinoise, Port Louis, Mauritius (RS)
Bottom: Grand Baie, Mauritius (RS)

**Post** The main post office is behind the bus station at the entrance to the shopping arcade. It's open from 8 to 11.15 am and from noon to 4 pm on weekdays, and on Saturdays from 8 to 11.45 am.

**Bookshops** Allot Bookshop and Librairie du Trèfle, both in Les Arcades, beneath the Continental Hotel, have a good selection of books and magazines in French and English. Another source of books on Mauritius is Editions de L'Océan Indien (EOI), in the shopping arcade beside the bus station.

### Trou aux Cerfs
Possibly the main attraction of Curepipe for tourists, apart from the shopping, is the Trou aux Cerfs crater. It's been extinct for a long time and the crater floor is now heavily wooded, but the crater affords good views around the island. On a clear day, you're supposed to be able to see Réunion. A tarred road leads gently up to and around the rim. There are benches for rest and reflection, and a radar station for keeping an electronic eye on cyclone activity.

### Municipal Centre
Grouped together on Elizabeth Ave are the Hôtel de Ville (Town Hall), Carnegie Library, pond and gardens. The colonial-style town hall, built in 1902, has recently been restored. In the gardens is a bronze statue of the famous fictitious lovers Paul and Virginie, by Mauritian sculptor Prosper d'Epinay. The statue is to Curepipe and Mauritius what the Little Mermaid is to Copenhagen and Denmark. There are also statues of the French astronomer Abbé la Caille and poet Paul Jean Toulet.

### Botanic Gardens
The gardens are nowhere near as large or impressive as those of Pamplemousses, but they are well kept and informal, with little nature trails leading off from the main paths. There are no guides, on paper or on foot. It's a popular spot for picnics and lovers' trysts.

### Market
The permanent fruit and vegetable market under the cover of the bus station is open from early morning until 6 pm each weekday and Saturday, and until noon on Sunday. On Saturdays and Wednesdays there is a large outdoor market next to the bus depot that is open from 6 am to 6 pm.

### Places to Stay
Like Port Louis, Curepipe has no luxury hotels. The town's good selection of budget accommodation is not used much by tourists, who can easily see what Curepipe has to offer on a day trip.

The tourist board considers the small Chinese or Muslim-run boarding houses in Curepipe to be 'hotels'.

Paul & Virginie

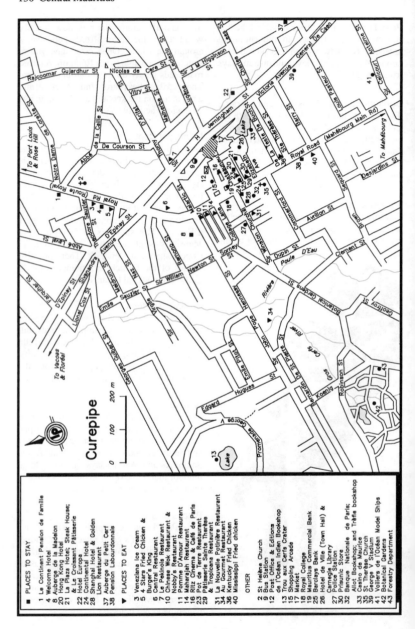

## Curepipe

■ PLACES TO STAY

1 Le Continent Pension de Famille
4 Welcome Hotel
8 Auberge de la Madelon
20 Hong Kong Hotel
21 La Plaza Hotel; Steak House;
   & Le Croissant Pâtisserie
22 Hotel Europa
24 Continental Hotel
28 Shanghai Hotel & Golden
   Lion Restaurant
37 Auberge du Petit Cerf
38 Pension Labourdonnais

▼ PLACES TO EAT

3 Veneziana Ice Cream
5 Stars Fried Chicken &
   Burger's King
6 Central Restaurant
7 Le Pekinois Restaurant
10 Chinese Wok Restaurant &
   Nobby's Restaurant
11 Pomme D'Amour Restaurant
14 Maharajah Restaurant
16 Ritz Cinema & Café de Paris
23 Pot de Terre Restaurant
29 Pâtisserie Sainte Thérèse
   & Tropicana Restaurant
31 La Nouvelle Potinière Restaurant
34 Au Gourmet Restaurant
36 Kentucky Fried Chicken
40 Mississippi Fried chicken

OTHER

2 St Hélène Church
9 Bus Station
12 Post Office & Editions
   de l'Océan Indien Bookshop
13 Trou aux Cerfs Crater
15 Shopping Arcade
17 Market
18 Royal College
19 Mauritius Commercial Bank
25 Barclays Bank
26 Hotel de Ville (Town Hall) &
   Carnegie Library
27 Police Station
30 Prisunic Store
32 Banque Nationale de Paris;
   Allot Bookshop; and Trèfle bookshop
33 Casino du Maurice
35 St Thérèse Church
39 George V Stadium
41 Voiliers de l'Océan Model Ships
42 Botanical Gardens
43 Forestry Department

### Places to Stay – bottom end

The best value among the options is the *Welcome Hotel* (☎ 6761469) on Royal Rd. It is a small, modern-looking block with eight clean and bright rooms, each with a shower. Singles/doubles are Rs 200/275, including breakfast. A triple costs Rs 300. It is managed by a friendly family.

Among the smaller pensions, *L'Auberge du Petit Cerf* (☎ 6762892), at 23 Anderson St, is by far the best. The owner, Mr Kiamtia Roland, speaks excellent English and chain-smokes Embassy. His home is a well-preserved old house with a surrounding verandah and nice garden. The seven rooms cost single/double Rs 160/240, including breakfast. Meals are Rs 80. Many former guests return in later years. There are rumours that Mr Roland, an interesting character who either ignores guests completely or regales them with tales, is seriously contemplating selling his house and moving away.

The *Hong Kong Hotel* (☎ 6765582) is sandwiched between the Prisunic supermarket, on Elizabeth Ave, and Châteauneuf St, in the heart of town. The entrance is opposite the big store. Singles/doubles are Rs 280/350 per night, including breakfast. The eight rooms each have a shower and toilet.

*Le Continent* (☎ 6766793), not to be confused with the Continental, is a large pension de famille at 184 Royal Rd. You'll recognise it by the big Pepsi signs painted on the side of the house. There is no sign of any family here, just a young student acting as porter-caretaker. The rooms are big and cheap, with a shower and toilet. Single/double rooms cost Rs 190/210. Nobody will bother you, but there is frequent to-ing and fro-ing by young couples seeking a quiet time together. Make sure you get clean bed linen.

Though its name may suggest character, *L'Auberge de la Madelon* (☎ 6762550) at 10 Sir John Pope Hennessy St appears somewhat cold and stablelike, with rooms in a line off a big corridor. Singles/doubles are Rs 180/250, including breakfast. Some rooms have a private shower and toilet. L'Auberge is next door to an excellent little café, La Bonne Bouffe.

Another suspect pension de famille is the *Labourdonnais* (☎ 6761634), past Ste Thérèse Church, at 270 Royal Rd (Mahébourg Main Rd). The seven basic and grubby rooms cost Rs 175 per night, including breakfast.

The *Europa* (☎ 6765084) is a soulless edifice opposite the casino, often used for conferences. Singles/doubles are Rs 200/300. Breakfast and other meals are extra.

### Places to Stay – middle

Next to La Nouvelle Potinière restaurant and the Continental Hotel, is the *Shanghai Hotel* (☎ 6761965). Singles/doubles are Rs 350/400, including breakfast in a room with all the ambience of an airplane hangar. You can get a meal in the Golden Lion restaurant which is connected with the hotel.

When we stayed, the Shanghai was in the throes of renovation, liberal coats of pink paint were being applied to its cavernous interior, and you almost needed a map to pick your way through the rubble, avoid falling down the inoperative lift shaft, and find your room. Opposite our room was a pigeon 'apartment' block where dozens of the wily birds had settled into the concrete matrix which looked remarkably like a pigeon hotel!

When we asked to make a local call, the receptionist estimated the cost at Rs 6. Then he changed his mind and lowered the price to Rs 4, but couldn't find change for a ten rupee note. Finally, we decided to put the call on our final bill, and were issued with a receipt for Rs 3!

In Floréal, you'll find the *Mandarin* (☎ 6965031; fax 6866858), a large hotel with close to 100 rooms. Singles/doubles/triples are Rs 298/363/463, including breakfast.

### Places to Stay – top end

The *Continental* (☎ 6753434; fax 6753437) is *the* hotel in Curepipe. A single/double in the 52-room hotel costs Rs 725/895, including breakfast. If you want a suite, you'll pay Rs 1250.

## Places to Eat – budget end

At the bus station there are eating stalls, such as the *Amigos Hotel*, which serve good chicken or beef biryani. Prisunic also has a variety of supermarket foods and takeaway snacks.

Where the Mahébourg Main Rd kinks, becomes Royal Rd and heads towards Port Louis, there is a bunch of small, cheap restaurants. Inexpensive fast food is easy to find in Curepipe at eateries with narrowly different names, such as Burger's King, Kentucky Fried Chicken, Mississipi Fried Chicken, 4 Stars Fried Chicken, etc. It's 'finger-lickin' good' as they say here in Mauritius.

## Places to Eat – middle & top end

*Nobby's Restaurant* (☎ 6761318), on Royal Rd, offers good European and Créole cuisine – main dishes start around Rs 90. For a splurge, try the steak, followed by a rum and passionfruit mousse. Nobby's is closed on Sunday and open on other days from noon to 2.30 pm and from 6.30 to 10.30 pm.

For lunch, a popular place with the locals is *La Bonne Bouffe*, next to L'Auberge de la Madelon, at the bottom of Sir John Pope Hennessy St. It is a little café, run by a friendly Indian family, which offers daube, curry or noodle dishes for around Rs 35.

*Le Pot de Terre* (☎ 6762204), in a small alley behind the Hong Kong Hotel and facing the Prisunic supermarket, is great for a cup of coffee and a cake. It also serves more expensive meals at prices around Rs 90. It's open from 7.30 am to 6 pm.

For a European dinner try one of the following: the *Tropicana* (☎ 6763286), next to the State Commercial Bank on the Mahébourg Main Rd, which is open until 11 pm; *La Nouvelle Potinière* (☎ 6762648), beside the Shanghai Hotel on Sir Winston Churchill St, which is open from 11 am to 2.30 pm and from 7 to 10 pm (closed on Sunday) – *Potin* is French for 'gossip'!; or *La Pomme d'Amour* (☎ 6764505) which is open daily from 11 am to 2 pm and from 7 to 9.30 pm.

For a real knockdown splurge, there's *Au Gourmet* (☎ 6761871), a pricey French res-

taurant housed in a renovated Créole home, La Sablonière, en route to the Botanic Gardens on Bernardin de St Pierre Ave.

You can't miss it if you head for the replica of the Eiffel Tower in the garden. It is tiny compared to the real one, but still stands far above the surrounding houses. The tower, built to commemorate the French Revolution, once stood outside the Port Louis Theatre. The Noël family bought it for the house at the end of the last century.

Au Gourmet is closed all day Sunday and Monday, and on public holidays. On other days it's open from noon to 2 pm; and from 7 to 10 pm. Main dishes start around Rs 150.

In the centre of town, *The Maharajah* (☎ 6762532) serves Indian and Chinese cuisine. Main dishes start from around Rs 80. Considering the price, the food was disappointing, and the intrusive service was hammered home when an attempt was made to present the bill with the 'discretionary' tip already tucked into the final amount. At the *Chinese Wok* (☎ 6761548), you can find standard Chinese fare at hefty prices.

## Entertainment

**Casino** The *Casino de Maurice* has an entrance fee, a minimum stake, poker slot machines and dress standards, but if it's not busy they'll let you in free to look around. It is open each weekday from 8 pm until the wee small hours and from 2 pm on Sundays.

## Things to Buy

Shopping hours in Curepipe are longer than in Port Louis. Shops are open from 9 am to 6 pm every day except Thursday and Saturday, when they close at noon. All shops are closed on Sundays.

There are several model-ship building workshops in the Forest Side suburb of Curepipe. A visit to at least one is worthwhile. (See the Things to Buy section in the Mauritius – Facts for the Visitor chapter.)

There are shopping arcades behind the bus station and underneath the Continental Hotel (Arcades Currimjee). The stores are very European in style; only a few specialise in Chinese and Indian goods. There are plenty of clothing and footwear shops. For more details about shopping in Curepipe, refer to the Things to Buy section in the Mauritius – Facts for the Visitor chapter.

## Getting There & Around

Curepipe is well linked by bus to Port Louis, Mahébourg, Tamarin, Centre de Flacq, Moka and surrounding towns such as Quatre Bornes. Most of the sights, such as the Trou aux Cerfs crater and the Botanic Gardens, are easy walks. Expect to pay around Rs 250 for a taxi ride from Curepipe to the airport.

There is little or no opportunity to rent motorbikes or bicycles in the town, unless you do so privately.

## AROUND CUREPIPE

The region to the south-west of Curepipe is a natural parkland and mini lake district, pleasant for drives and walks.

The largest lake on the island is the reservoir Mare aux Vacoas, flanked on the east, three km away, by Mare Longue and Tamarind Falls, accessible from the Tamarin road.

Near Henrietta, en route from Vacoas to the Mare aux Vacoas, is a stone cairn, a monument to the English navigator Matthew Flinders. He arrived in Mauritius from Australia on the leaky ship *Cumberland* in 1803, on his way back to Britain and his wife. The poor bloke didn't know France and Britain were at war and he was imprisoned for more than six years. He died, aged 40, a few years after his return to England. For an interesting read on the subject, take a look at *In the Grips of the Eagle: Matthew Flinders at Île de France (1803-1810)* (Mahatma Gandhi Institute, Moka, 1988) by Huguette Ly-Tio-Fane Pineo.

## Tamarind Falls

These falls are awkward to reach, but it's well worth the effort for a beautiful, deep, cool bathe at the bottom of the series of seven falls. You can see them from the Vacoas side, if you follow the signs from Henrietta.

From Curepipe or Quatre Bornes, take a bus to Henrietta, then walk to Tamarind Falls. For details about hiking to Tamarind Falls from the south, refer to the Activities section in the Mauritius – Facts for the Visitor chapter.

If you're coming from Tamarin, turn right about three km north of Tamarin, at the roundabout to Magenta and Yemen. A tarred, bumpy road through cane fields leads to the Magenta and Tamarind Falls turn-off. Continue past all the 'Private Estate', 'Permit Needed' and 'Prohibited Entry' signs, down towards the power station. Leave your car or bike and walk along the river up to the falls. The path is heavily overgrown and you must cross to the other side and boulder-hop the last 300 metres along the river bed to reach the top, but you will be richly rewarded.

A reader tells us that permits to visit the Falls may be necessary. You can get one from the CEB (Central Electricity Board) in Curepipe, situated opposite the church next to the Kentucky Fried Chicken.

## Plaine Champagne & Black River Gorges National Park

The beautiful highland area south-west of Curepipe, traversed by Mauritius' only mountain road, is like no other part of the island. The route climbs out of Curepipe and after about six km, reaches the dam wall of the large reservoir, Mare aux Vacoas. Surrounded by casuarina and coniferous trees, it more resembles a North American scene than one from the tropical Indian Ocean! Four km south along the road is the forestry station of Le Pétrin, which is the jumping off point for several hikes into the Macchabée Reserve (a hunting concession), soon to become Black River Gorges National Park.

At Le Pétrin, one road heads east two km to Grand Bassin – the sacred lake of the Hindus – while the main route climbs up onto Plaine Champagne, the rainiest part of Mauritius and the largest natural area on the island. The road's high point at 744 metres is marked by a radio tower. About three km beyond it is the Rivière Noire overlook, affording a spectacular view of waterfalls and 828 metre Piton de la Petite Rivière Noire, the highest point on Mauritius. In

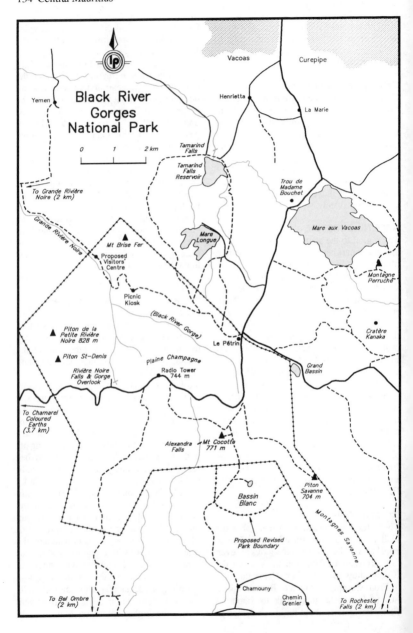

another 10 km, the road drops to the coast at Grande Case Noyale.

The best time to visit is during the flowering season between September and January. Look for the rare tambalacoque or dodo tree, the black ebony trees and the exotic birds that perch in them. You may also run into a band of monkeys, deer or wild pigs (see the Flora & Fauna section in the Mauritius – Facts about the Country chapter).

For further information about visiting these areas, see under National Parks (in the Flora & Fauna section of the Mauritius – Facts About the Country chapter); and Hiking & Trekking (in the Activities section of the Mauritius – Facts for the Visitor chapter).

## MOKA TOWN & AROUND

Bubbling brooks, waterfalls, valleys, towering mountains and some wonderful real estate make the area around the town of Moka extremely pleasant and picturesque.

Only 12 km south of Port Louis, Moka is also the centre of academia, with the University of Mauritius and the Mahatma Gandhi Institute.

### Le Réduit

This is *the* house in Mauritius – the governor's residence, now used by the military. Unfortunately, the house is open to the public only two days a year, in March and October.

Le Réduit, which means 'refuge', was built in 1778 by the French governor Barthélémy David, who succeeded Labourdonnais. It was from here, in 1874, that the English governor's wife, Lady Gomm, sent out invitations to her ball with the famous Mauritian Blue stamps, misprinted with 'Post Office' instead of 'Post Paid'. The few remaining stamps are now worth a fortune.

You can still walk around the gardens, sometimes under armed, although polite, escort. The grounds are open Monday to Friday from 9.30 am to noon.

There is a one km, forest-lined drive from the main gate and guard post down to the big colonial mansion. The countryside around

Le Réduit estate ... at the driveway e... down from the roac of the Rivière Casca

The two ravines w so dramatically are t their confluence – so e it sinks out of sight some 2000.

Across the road is an old chapel and overgrown cemetery, where a few former governors have been laid to rest. Along the road is a village overlooking a little bridge and waterfall. It could be a Constable painting, if it weren't for the tipped rubbish and motorway a few metres away.

To get to Le Réduit, take the St Pierre buses from Port Louis (Immigration Square station), Curepipe or Rose Hill and get off at the University of Mauritius. The gate to Le Réduit is only a few hundred metres away. If you're driving or cycling, follow the Port Louis-Curepipe motorway and turn west at the roundabout to the university.

### Eureka Créole House

Eureka stands about four km from Le Réduit, on the other side of the Port Louis-Curepipe motorway, just off the road to Moka.

This country house, lying under Montagne Ory, was restored and opened to the public in 1986 as a museum. It was built in the 1830s and purchased in 1856 by Eugène Leclézio, the first Mauritian Master of the Supreme Court. Like Le Réduit, and any of the properties around this area, it has terrific views across the river valley.

Entrance to Eureka is Rs 80 per person. It is open from 9.30 am to 5 pm every day, including holidays. A guided tour around and inside the house is free and optional. There is a music room, a Chinese room and a French East India Company room. Whether the rooms were always used as such or have just been created as showrooms for collections of Chinese and Indian household goods, is unclear. The top floor occasionally displays paintings by local artists. On the ground floor, note the colonial shower con-

ming the interior walls are some
que maps of Asia and Africa.

ou should take time to amble round the
gardens and enjoy the great views across the
gorge.

The courtyard behind the house is surrounded by stone cottages which were once
the staff quarters and kitchen. They have
been converted into tourist shops that sell
spices, shell jewellery, clothing, pressed-
flower products and stamps (see the Things
to Buy section in the Mauritius – Facts for
the Visitor chapter). Tea, coffee and snacks
are served on the verandah, but the prices are
steep.

To get to Eureka, take the same St Pierre
buses as for Le Réduit, but get off at Moka.
To get to Eureka from Moka, take the Port
Louis road, across the Barclay Bridge, past
the Moka Eye Hospital, and then follow the
road leading up to Le Pouce mountain.

## Domaine Les Pailles

Opened in 1991, Domaine Les Pailles
(☎ 2124225 or 2126003; fax 2124226) is an
elaborate cultural and heritage centre which
cost close to US$10 million to complete. The
facilities available here include rides in
horse-drawn carriages; a working replica of
a traditional ox-driven sugar mill; a rum
distillery producing the estate's own brew; a
spice garden; a natural spring; and a
children's play area.

A small cottage, *Le Lodge*, has been built
high in the surrounding hills. To hire Le
Lodge, reservations must be made in
advance. Access is provided by the same
ex-British Army Land Rovers which are
used to run visitors around on mini-safaris to
observe the local fauna and flora.

The Domaine has its own riding centre,
*Les Ecuries du Domaine*, with 42 horses
available for dressage and jumping; and for
riding in the foothills. Welsh ponies are provided for children to ride.

The centre also has two restaurants. *Le
Clos Saint Louis* is a luxury restaurant
(closed on Sunday) which caters to
businessfolk or visitors with plenty of money
to spend on their tastebuds. Main dishes start

around Rs 200. *La Cannelle Rouge* is a less
formal restaurant which offers a range of
quick meals, from pancakes to curries. Main
dishes start around Rs 90. It's open daily
from 10 am to 5 pm.

Jazz fans may be interested in *Le Jazz
Club des Ecuries du Domaine* (☎ 2081998)
which operates a weekly show here, featuring 'Mogoley and the Best Jazz Musicians
on Mauritius', every Friday evening at 9 pm.
Admission costs Rs 50 for club members,
and Rs 100 for non-members. Fast food is
available. You should phone to check performance details.

Admission to the Domaine costs Rs 100
for adults and Rs 50 for children under 12
years old. Prices for mini-tours start at
Rs 250 for adults, and Rs 125 for children.
Set lunch menus cost Rs 300 for adults and
Rs 150 for children.

To get to the Domaine, take any bus
running between Port Louis and Curepipe,
and ask to get off at Domaine Les Pailles (it's
clearly signposted). From the road it takes
less than half an hour on foot to the reception
centre. Alternatively, you can take a 10
minute taxi ride from Port Louis or Moka.

## Mahatma Gandhi Institute

Unless you are a researcher, have a special
interest in education, or especially want to
see a statue of Gandhi, the institute does not
merit a visit in itself. The campus is relatively
new and featureless, but the location is
impressive. You look across to a row of other
impressively located properties. If you're on
a tour of the university, Le Réduit, Moka and
Eureka, it's worth taking in the institute too.

The institute (☎ 4547001) is located in
Moka and you'll have no trouble finding it –
there's a special exit from the motorway. It's
open Monday to Friday from 9 am to
4.30 pm.

## The Moka Range

The Moka range contains a number of mod-
erate challenges for the energetic – namely
Le Pouce, Junction Peak, Pic des Guibies
and Snail Rock. All are relatively easy
ascents. The road to Le Pouce is signposted

off the Port Louis-Moka road near the turn-off to Eureka. Le Pouce and Snail Rock can be included on a cross-country trek from Moka to Port Louis. For more details get Robert V R Marsh's *Mountains of Mauritius* (see the Books & Bookshops section in the Mauritius – Facts for the Visitor chapter) or check with the Forestry Service (☎ 6754966) at the Botanic Gardens in Curepipe. See also our Hiking & Trekking section in the Mauritius – Facts for the Visitor chapter.

### Places to Stay

Curepipe and Port Louis would seem the best bet for accommodation, but there are some hotels and boarding houses in between the two large towns.

**Quatre Bornes** has more than its fair share of places to stay for some reason. Top of the tree is the *Gold Crest Hotel* (☎ 4545945; fax 4549599), opposite the town hall on St Jean Rd. It's neat with singles/doubles at Rs 1100/1440 per night, including half-board. A suite costs Rs 1365/1590 for a single/double. The hotel also has a smart bar and restaurant.

Nearby, on the same street, is the *Gavnor Hotel* (☎ 4641814). Singles/doubles are Rs 250/350 per night. There are no trimmings here. The *El Monaco* (☎ 4252608; fax 4251072), also on St Jean Rd, has singles/doubles/triples for Rs 300/350/450 including breakfast.

*The Riverside* (☎ 4644957; fax 4645553), on Royal Rd in the Belle Rose district of Quatre Bornes, has single/double/triple rooms at Rs 330/440/530, including breakfast.

*Garden House* (☎/fax 4649882), on the corner of Ollier and Stanley Aves, is in a spacious garden. Single/double rooms cost Rs 500/450. Meals are available on request. Transfers and sightseeing can also be arranged.

*La Charmeuse* (☎ 4547254; fax 2126056), at 93a Saint Jean Rd, has single/double rooms with shower and toilet for Rs 350/550, including breakfast.

*Le Gibier* (☎ 4246072), at 2 Stanley Ave,

offers rooms with a communal shower and toilet for single/double Rs 100/250, including breakfast.

*Maison R A P P* (☎ 4643371), at 16 Ave des Manguiers, Trianon, has four rooms with showers and toilets, and four without, for single/double Rs 180/245, including breakfast.

The *Victoria* (☎ 4245811), a pension de famille across from the bus park at 1 Ave Victoria, Quatre Bornes, has eight rooms with communal shower and toilet for single/double Rs 150/300, including breakfast.

*Labourdonnais Mon Plaisir* (☎ 4241197), 52A Impasse Stevenson, Quatre Bornes, has only two rooms with a communal shower and toilet for single/double Rs 125/175, including breakfast.

*Auberge de Quatre Bornes* (☎ 4242163), Trianon 2 Ave, Morcellement St Jean, has four rooms (two with shower and toilet) for single/double Rs 150/300, including breakfast.

**Rose Hill** In Rose Hill (pronounced 'Rozille' or 'Rozelle'), the *International* (☎ 4644290) has six rooms, each with shower and toilet, for single/double Rs 200/275. The general impression is rather dingy.

*Chez Roland* (☎ 4642651 at 52 Impasse Ambrose, offers a variety of rooms with shower, toilet and air-con; prices start at single/double Rs 250/325, including breakfast.

You could also try *Auberge de Rose Hill* (☎ 4641793), at 275 Royal Rd, which has single/double/triple rooms with shower and toilet for Rs 250/275/325, including breakfast; or *Pension de Famille Naheed* (☎ 464-6495), at 37 Boundary Rd, which has single/double rooms at Rs 100/150.

**Moka** *Le Carillon* (☎ 2082859), in St Pierre (Moka district), has 10 rooms with a communal shower and toilet for single/double Rs 150/225, including breakfast.

**Coromandel** About seven km south of Port Louis, on the climb up to Beau Bassin and

Rose Hill, is Coromandel, an industrial area with several garment factories. (One factory unit is actually the National Archives!)

The *Sunray Hotel* (☎ 2334777), is not out of place in these surroundings. Its cold, concrete exterior suggests business or imprisonment, not relaxation. It may be good for hosting conferences and putting up salespeople, but I can't imagine a tourist ever staying there. Just in case, singles/doubles are Rs 200/300.

### Places to Eat

There are several decent restaurants in Moka, frequented by the Franco-Mauritians in most cases, if not tourists. Specialities are either French or Chinese food and all are open for lunch and stay open until 10 pm.

The *Govinda* in St Jean Rd, Quatre Bornes, is a vegetarian restaurant which is closed on Tuesdays.

Two establishments, better known for fun than food, are the discos/nightclubs *Blue Mauritius* (☎ 4644097), Commercial Centre, Rose Hill, which is open for lunch and until 1 am every day except Thursday; and

*Mauritius By Night* (☎ 6966615), on Royal Rd, (or Ave John F Kennedy), Vacoas, which is open for dinner in its *Jade Garden* restaurant and for other pursuits from 9 pm each night.

The French restaurants in the area are *Nid d'Hirondelle* (☎ 4642713), on the corner of Royal and Monneron roads in Beau Bassin, which is closed on Mondays; and *Rolly's* (☎ 4548998), St Jean Rd, Quatre Bornes, which is a steak house. It's closed on Mondays.

Chinese alternatives include *Café Dragon Vert* (☎ 4244564), in La Louise, Quatre Bornes, which is closed on Mondays; *Chopsticks* (☎ 4247459), in St Jean Rd, Quatre Bornes, which serves lunches only; and the *Mandarin* (☎ 6964551), on Royal Rd, Vacoas. The *Green Dragon* (☎ 4547963), on the second floor of the Palladium discotheque, at Trianon, offers Chinese and European dishes. It's closed on Monday.

Finally, standard Chinese fare is also offered in Quatre Bornes by a restaurant with one of the best names in the business: *Restaurant Ah Fat*!

# The East Coast

The east coast of Mauritius was settled early in the 17th century by the Dutch, who cleared the ebony forests and introduced sugar cane.

The east coast district of Flacq is quieter than the Trou aux Biches or Flic en Flac areas on the west coast. Beaches are the major attraction and, as usual, big hotels have picked the prime stretches, but there is still enough sand and sea left to go around, particularly along Belle Mare beach and around Île aux Cerfs. The only trouble is the paucity of budget accommodation: it is difficult to find a moderately priced place to stay on a chance visit.

Inland, farmers place more emphasis on crop alternatives to sugar cane than anywhere else in Mauritius.

## ÎLE AUX CERFS

There are no stags *(cerfs)* remaining on this small island which now belongs to Le Touessrok Sun Hotel and attracts large numbers of holidaymakers on the east coast.

The ferry runs every half-hour between 9 am and 5 pm and costs Rs 25 per person return. Le Touessrok hotel residents travel for free – well, the room rates at the hotel aren't exactly peanuts. What you get when you step off the ferry is a sheltered, crowded beach and lagoon for water sports or sunbathing, restaurants and several souvenir stalls. You can walk only around the seaward half of the island, that is, clockwise from the landing site. That takes about half an hour and there are several isolated coves and bathing spots along the way. It doesn't take long to get away from the masses, but watch out for naturists and purple sea urchins. The west side of the island is impassable because of thick vegetation, and the water there is muddy anyway.

On the island is a boatshed where you can hire water skis, pedalos, sailboards, surfcats, Laser dinghies and canoes. Two-hour boat trips are offered to the Grande Rivière Sud-Est waterfall; and there's also a tour around Île aux Cerfs.

If you want to see stags, on the mainland there is a private stag park on the road between the St Géran and Belle Mare Plage hotels. There is no admittance, but you can watch the deer wading through the misty marshes in the early morning (great for pictures).

## BELLE MARE

This is a long, luscious, casuarina-fringed public beach. You can see it all from atop a reconstructed lime kiln, converted into a lookout tower. On the other side of the road stand the ruins of a sugar mill. There are more substantial sugar mill ruins behind Belle Mare village. This beach would make a good camping spot, but don't rely on the public toilets.

### Young Farmers Training College

Situated on the road from Belle Mare to Trou d'Eau Douce, the college is experimenting with alternatives to sugar cane. It also operates a craft shop at the roadside.

### TROU D'EAU DOUCE

The village takes its name, 'hole of sweet water' from a sea pool fed by a freshwater underground stream. Trou d'Eau Douce has lots of character, and steep lanes leading down to the harbour.

### CENTRE DE FLACQ & ENVIRONS

The only town on the east coast is Centre de Flacq. It's a pleasant, if busy, market town that does not cater for visitors.

### Hindu Temple

There is an attractive temple on a small island linked by a causeway to Poste de Flacq. It is a beautiful sight seen from the St Géran hotel across the bay. Provided they show respect, visitors are welcome.

## Flacq Union of Estates Limited (FUEL)

This sugar mill, a few km west of Centre de Flacq, is the largest on the island, and it's even reputed to be the second largest in the world! There are no formal tours of the facility, but one reader has written to say that his polite request was rewarded with a guided tour. Unfortunately the noise of the machines drowned the explanations, but he was allowed to taste the different types of sugar and sugar-like products that are extracted during the processing of cane into refined sugar.

## Carnaval Club

This is the Chinese casino and bar in Centre de Flacq. It's seedy and does not see many tourists, if any, but it's worth popping in to play the outsider and watch the old croupiers.

## PLACES TO STAY
### Poste Lafayette & Roches Noires

*Coral Beach Bungalows* (☎ 4239229) at Poste Lafayette has six self-catering studios with shower and toilet at Rs 360 per person, without breakfast. Breakfast costs an extra Rs 55. The studios are designed for two, but an additional bed can be provided at an additional cost of Rs 200. The stylish complex is in a great position right on the beach. It also has a swimming pool, a boat house; and the manager arranges excursions. A small restaurant is planned here to open in 1993.

At the time of research, locals reported that another hotel complex, *Plein Soleil*, would soon be functioning at Roches Noires.

### Belle Mare & Pointe de Flacq

*Le Surcouf Village Hotel* (☎ 4192800; fax 2121361) on Coastal Rd, Belle Mare, has apartments (up to six persons), studios (up to two persons), and luxury suites (up to eight persons). Prices for the apartments/studios/luxury suites, on half-board, start around Rs 840/900/3840 per person per day. For occupancy during the high season (November to mid April), add at least 15% to these prices – except for the luxury suites which have a fixed price all year.

On the Pointe de Flacq is the *Sandy Bay Hotel* (☎ 4132880; fax 4132054). Singles/double rooms here cost Rs 690/1200 on half-board.

*Les Flamboyants* (☎ 4132036; fax 2088328), just north of Belle Mare, was closed for renovation during 1992, but should have re-opened by the time you read this.

*Emeraude Beach Hotel* (☎ 4132107; fax 4132109) on Royal Rd, Belle Mare, offers rooms, on half-board only, at Rs 825/1350 for a single/double.

*Le Palmar* (☎ 4192041; fax 4192043) on Coastal Rd, Belle Mare, has rooms and studios. Prices for single/double rooms, on half-board, are Rs 1270/1890; for studios,

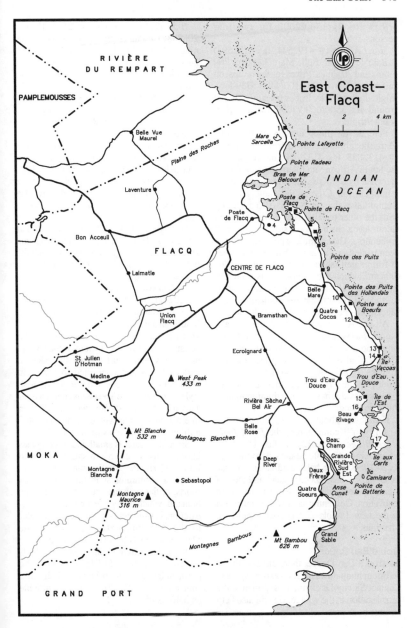

prices are Rs 1500/2000 for two/four persons.

*Hotel Ambre* (☎ 4192544; fax 4192594) at Baie de Palmar, Belle Mare, has over 200 rooms and 20 suites. Prices for the rooms, on half-board, start at Rs 3100/4400/5730 for a single/double/triple. Prices for suites start at around Rs 5500/6600/7700 for a single/double/triple.

Perched on the peninsula of the Belle Mare beach is *Le St Géran Sun Hotel* (☎ 4132825; fax 4132983), the flagship of the South African Sun International group. It is owned by Sol Krezner, who also owns the infamous Sun City in the 'homeland' of Bophuthatswana, in South Africa. Along with the other usual leisure facilities, the St Géran has a casino (for residents only) and golf course. The swimming pool has recently been tripled in size and enhanced with trees to form small islets for private dining. The Suncard, which every guest receives on registration, is valid here – for more details refer to the Accommodation section in the Mauritius – Facts for the Visitor chapter.

All the 163 rooms are available on half-board basis only. Prices for a basic single/double are Rs 5500/8400 per day. There are also 12 suites at prices ranging from Rs 10,000 to Rs 39,000. The beach gets muddy on the bay side, but there is a superb view across the bay to the Hindu temple at Poste de Flacq.

If you walk about one km south along the beach, you'll come across the *Hotel Belle Mare Plage* (☎ 4132515; fax 4132993), where single/double standard rooms are Rs 3400/5600 on a half-board basis. Like the St Géran, it has recently spent millions of rupees sprucing up its image with extensive renovation. Golf enthusiasts will be interested in the new 18-hole golf course, a rarity on Mauritius.

### Trou d'Eau Douce

At Trou d'Eau Douce, there are two three-bedroom bungalows for Rs 400 per day each. Contact Sidney Dardenn, a fisherman at the petrol station in the village. He will also help arrange boat trips.

*Blue Ocean Resorts* (☎ 2123243; fax 2087882) at Palmar Beach, Belle Mare, has nine self-catering bungalows (up to six persons) at Rs 400/600 during low season (May to September)/high season (October to April).

*Silver Beach Hotel* (☎ 4192600; fax 4192604) on Royal Rd, Trou d'Eau Douce, provides 30 rooms at Rs 900/1800 for a single/double.

*Résidence Valmarin* (☎ 2638771; fax 2638274) at Trou d'Eau Douce, provides four deluxe apartments, each with two bedrooms, for Rs 950 per person. No meals are included in the price, but guests do have use of the swimming pool, and the services of a maid.

*Le Tropical* (☎ 4192300; fax 4192302) at La Pelouse, Trou d'Eau Douce, has 48 rooms at Rs 1850/2900 for a single/double on half-board. Rates for room and breakfast are available on request.

*Le Touessrok Sun Hotel* (☎ 4192451; fax 4192025) is one of the most intriguing structures in Mauritius. It was designed by a Mauritian architect and built in 1978 around an islet and small lagoon, on the tip of a peninsula. To give each room a good view, the blocks were built around the islet on various levels and connected to the main hotel building by a covered bridge. Moorish style, they call it. Le Touessrok, named after a town in Brittany, is also owned by the Sun International group which spent some 400 million rupees on renovation in 1993.

Since the beach is small and poor, guests have free use of a ferry to shuttle across to Île aux Cerfs, the hotel's own island hideaway, for swimming, sunbathing, and water sports; or they can use the hotel pools. The Suncard, which every guest receives on registration, is valid here – for more details refer to the Accommodation section in the Mauritius – Facts for the Visitor chapter.

A standard single/double room on half-board costs Rs 4500/6700. For the presidential suite you'll have to shell out a cool Rs 17,350/25,000 for a single/double on half-board.

## PLACES TO EAT
### Trou d'Eau Douce & Île aux Cerfs
*Reflets de L'Est* on Route Royale, Trou d'Eau Douce, serves Chinese, Créole, and European food at reasonable prices. Main dishes start from Rs 40. It's open daily from 10 am to midnight. Just across the road is *Chez Tino* which offers similar cuisine and prices. It's open daily from 11 am to 3 pm and from 7 to 10 pm.

*Restaurant Sept*, at Sept Croisées, Trou d'Eau Douce, specialises in Indian cuisine and seafood dishes. Expect to pay from Rs 45 for a main dish. The restaurant is open daily from 11 am to 4 pm and from 6.30 to 11 pm.

The *Tropical Hotel* restaurant provides Créole and European cuisine at higher prices. Main dishes start from Rs 150, and gala dinners/buffets cost Rs 325/375. It's open daily from noon to 3 pm and from 7.30 to 9.30 pm.

Île aux Cerfs has two restaurants: *Paul et Virginie Restaurant* on the beach, and *La Chaumière*, on the hillside. Main courses at each cost around Rs 100. La Chaumière has an attractive, junglelike setting with thatched, individual wooden dining platforms, spread out among the treetops. The island restaurants are open daily from noon to 3 pm only.

### Belle Mare & Centre de Flacq
In Belle Mare village, behind what looks like the town hall but is in fact a private house guarded by dogs, is a busy, friendly café. *Belle Mare Plage Hotel* restaurant provides Créole and European dishes at steep prices. Main dishes start from Rs 120, and set menus are available for Rs 350. It's open daily from 12.30 to 3 pm and from 7.30 to 9.30 pm.

More affordable is *Le Kalao* pizzeria, inside the Emeraude Beach Hotel, where main dishes such as pizzas (cooked in wood-fired ovens) or seafood start around Rs 60. The restaurant is open daily from noon to 2 pm and from 7 to 9.30 pm.

Centre de Flacq has the usual array of shops and restaurants. The best value for food is *Le Pékinois* bar and restaurant, which is upstairs, opposite the bus park. If you're into self-catering, Centre de Flacq has a big open market on Sunday from early morning until 6 pm. There are also fish landing stations at Trou d'Eau Douce and Belle Mare.

*Chez Manuel* (☎ 4183599) in the hill village of St Julien, on the back road from Bon Accueil to Centre de Flacq, specialises in Chinese food. There is nothing out of the ordinary about its setting on the main street, but it has a reputation throughout the island for good food, such as oysters, sweet-and-sour seafood, and pork cooked in honey. Main dishes start around Rs 65, and set menus are available for Rs 100. It is open daily, except Sunday, from 11 am to 3 pm and from 6 to 9.30 pm.

*Symon's Restaurant*, at Pointe de Flacq, offers Chinese, Créole, and European food. Main dishes start around Rs 65. It's a clean, airy place open daily from 11.30 am to 10 pm.

*Restaurant Monaco*, in Poste de Flacq, has been recommended by locals for Créole food.

## GETTING THERE & AWAY
The bus from Port Louis (Immigration Square bus station) to Centre de Flacq costs Rs 7 and is a wild rollercoaster ride. Centre de Flacq is also linked by bus to Rose Hill (via the Quartier Militaire), to Curepipe, to Mahébourg (via Grand Sable on the coast), and to Grand Gaube in the north (via Rivière du Rempart and Poste Lafayette).

## GETTING AROUND
**Bus** There are local buses running between Centre de Flacq, Belle Mare and Trou d'Eau Douce.

There are no buses down to the ferry for Île aux Cerfs, a two-km walk from the main road, but most hotels, good guesthouses and tour operators offer day trips by boat or bus.

**Taxi** Taxis leave from Centre de Flacq and charge between Rs 55 and Rs 60 to go to the St Géran or Belle Mare Plage hotels, or the beach; and between Rs 70 and Rs 80 to Le Toucssrok or Île aux Cerfs.

# The West Coast

The Rivière Noire district has many attractions. The south-west coast is the centre for big-game fishing and, to a lesser extent, diving and surfing. It also boasts good, long beaches and the island's best nature reserve, the Macchabée Forest and Rivière Noire gorges.

In the north, most of the coastal plain is comprised of cane fields but in the south, where the Port Louis road hits the coast at Tamarin, the plateau drops steeply toward the sea. Along the way are a couple of detours to the contrasting beach resorts of Pointe aux Sables and Flic en Flac.

## POINTE AUX SABLES

If there were a red light area in Mauritius, Pointe aux Sables would be it. But the impression it gives is more a dirty orange.

Although there are beaches and a few hotels and cottages, it is a long way from being a Pattaya Beach (Thailand) or a Surfers Paradise (Australia). Dagenham (UK) would be a better comparison.

Pointe aux Sables is almost a mirror image of Baie du Tombeau on the north side of Port Louis, but its image is duller. Baie du Tombeau is seen as a class below Trou aux Biches and Grand Baie. Well, Pointe aux Sables is a class below that. It's not that bad; probably its reputation unfairly colours your actual impression.

There aren't many things to see around Pointe aux Sables. The beach at the point is popular with the locals on weekends and looks much better for swimming or relaxing than the public beach near Pointe aux Sables village.

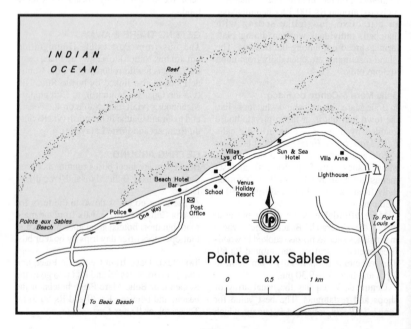

## Places to Stay

Like Baie du Tombeau, Pointe aux Sables is a popular holiday and weekend destination for Port Louis people, so the room standards and services are suited to them, rather than visitors from abroad. The first place you come to on the road from Port Louis is *Villa Anna* (no phone), which is supposed to be a pension de famille, but is actually two spartan, overpriced bungalows, without cooking facilities, for Rs 350 per night.

The best hotel, because it is the only hotel, is the *Sun & Sea* (☎ 2344494). Singles/ doubles with shower and toilet are Rs 225/ 390, including breakfast. Main dishes at the hotel restaurant start around Rs 60.

Past the scrubby public beach is the 'centre' of Pointe aux Sables, where you'll find the infamous Golden Moon Nightclub and the nearby *Venus Holiday Resort* (☎ 2344089). Both these places attract prostitutes and the resort also offers short-time rooms. There are a few bungalows and a restaurant in the resort complex.

Another possibility is the *Campements Lys d'Or* (☎ 6766068), near the public beach.

Be warned – the Beach Hotel is not a hotel. It is a bar where several ladies, made-up and dressed-up a bit too much for the midday sun, sit around at the tables. There are rooms, but they are not available on a nightly basis.

## Places to Eat

The same warning as above applies to the *Restaurant Golden* next to the nightclub. Eating is a secondary requirement at this spot.

The only other restaurant in Pointe aux Sables is at the *Sun & Sea* hotel (see the Places to Stay section).

There is a shop and snack bar near the beach at the point itself, where the coast road from Port Louis does a right turn and heads inland again.

## Getting There & Away

Buses for Pointe aux Sables leave from Dumas St, next to the Victoria Square bus station in Port Louis. The journey takes you through interesting districts of the capital, with such features as the 1866 Vagrant Depot.

## FLIC EN FLAC

The name Flic en Flac is thought to come from the old Dutch name, 'Fried Landt Flaak', or 'Free and Flat Land'. On older maps this was spelt as Fri-lan-Flac, subsequently adapted by the French into Flic en Flac. The Dutch word 'flaak' is the same as in 'Boere Vlakte' (Farmer's Plain) or 'Groote Vlakte' (Great Plain), and is the origin of the name Flacq, which is very common on Mauritius. Finally, to round off this musing on place names, a modern-day French slang interpretation of Flic en Flac would be 'policeman in strife'!

Flic en Flac, off the Port Louis-Tamarin road, lies at the bottom of a three km straight road running through cane fields. It is not as cute and carefree as its name suggests. Rather, it is an increasingly busy holiday village that lies and relies on a great stretch of beach, and caters for the middle range in the market rather than the budget level, which prefers Tamarin.

## Casela Bird Park

This bird park, between Tamarin and the turn-off down to Flic en Flac, is well landscaped and has good views across the Rivière du Rempart valley. It is expanding into a zoo. As well as parrots, pheasants and rare pink pigeons, there are leopards, tigers, lemurs, monkeys and deer. One of the giant tortoises is 150 years old. The park is open every day from 9 am to 6 pm and the entrance fee is Rs 40 for adults and Rs 10 for children. Between April and September the park closes at 5 pm. There is a shop and snack bar.

## Trois Cavernes

Unlike Casela Bird Park, this is not a tourist spot. In the cane fields, just south of the turn-off to Flic en Flac, are three caves – tunnels formed in the lava. A local character, Dr du Casse, used to throw parties in one of the caves. Now he is buried there.

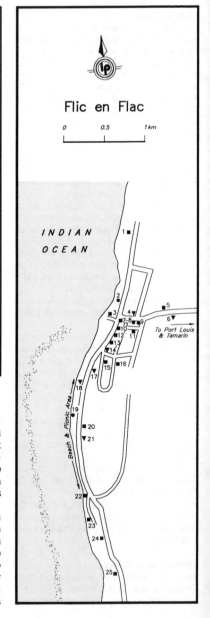

## Mountain-Climbing

Behind Casela Bird Park stands Mauritius' 'Pocket Matterhorn', the Montagne du Rempart. You can drive up to the base and park at Tamarin Pumping Station, just off the beginning of the road to Magenta. The climb is steep and difficult by Mauritian standards, although it should only take three hours up and two hours down.

Les Trois Mamelles, east of Montagne du Rempart, has three peaks to scale. The approach is better from Quatre Bornes than from Tamarin. Take the road from La Louise to Bassin. From there you need permission to go through cane fields and begin the climb. Refer to Robert Marsh's climber's guide *Mountains of Mauritius* (see the Books & Maps section in the Mauritius – Facts for the Visitor chapter).

### Diving Sites

The Cathedral cave, off Flic en Flac, is a favourite dive at a depth of 27 metres. There are diving schools at Villas Caroline, La Pirogue and Le Morne hotels.

### Places to Stay

Flic en Flac is well off for accommodation, with several bungalows to let as back-ups for some upmarket guesthouses and hotels. The luxury hotels are grouped at Wolmar, a small settlement lining the beach, about two km south of Flic en Flac.

**Flic en Flac** *Easy World Apartments* (☎/fax 4538557) provides self-catering apartments at Rs 400/600, including breakfast, for single/double occupancy.

*C & A Bungalows* (☎ 4257575) has self-catering apartments (up to four persons) and studios (up to two persons) for Rs 700/500.

There are several choices in the centre of Flic en Flac village. *The White Orchid* (☎ 4538430, 4538128), run by Linda Appadoo, offers several self-catering bungalows and apartments. Prices start around Rs 250 per person per day, and drop substantially if you stay more than a few days.

*Little Acorn* (☎ 4538431; fax 4538320), run by Mrs Mary Moutia, consists of self-catering apartments (up to two persons) and bungalows (up to four persons) which cost Rs 250/600 per day.

Close by is the dangerously named *Golden Showers* (☎ 4538438) which at the time of research appeared to be undergoing conversion. Behind it is the *Flic en Flac Hotel* (☎ 4538537; fax 4538374), formerly known as the Sun 'n Sea View Hotel, which has 14 rooms. Single/double rooms cost around Rs 600/750, including breakfast.

On the hill leading out of Flic en Flac are a number of bungalows for rent. To find out more, ring 4538204; or 6761103 or 6761053 after 5 pm.

The *Manisa* (☎ 4538558; fax 453 8562) has 40 rooms and five suites. Single/double

rooms cost Rs 1300/1600; and suites cost Rs 1800. All these prices are on half-board basis. The hotel has a swimming pool and its own restaurant, Le Flamboyant.

Tucked away on the northern edge of town, is *Klondike Hotel* (☎ 4538333; fax 4538337), a small 'village' composed of self-catering bungalows and studios. Half-board rates for the studios are Rs 1225/1815 for single/double occupancy. Rates for accommodation only in one-bedroom bungalows (maximum four persons) and two-bedroom bungalows (maximum six persons) are Rs 1330/1500. The swimming pool forms an ingenious optical illusion which seems to merge the pool and the sea.

*Villas Caroline* (☎ 4538411; fax 4538144), once an inexpensive option, has grown in reputation, size and, alas, price over the years. Right on the beach, it is known for good food and a good diving school. The group of 12 villas has been expanded by a 20-room complex. There are single/double rooms with air-con, shower and toilet for Rs 1180/1400, on half-board basis. Fully equipped, self-catering bungalows with air-con cost Rs 1540 for one to three people and Rs 1760 for up to five – no meals are included in this price.

**Wolmar** *Le Pearle Beach (Sunset) Hotel* (☎ 4538428; fax 4538405) offers single/triple rooms at Rs 1580/1880/2380 on a half-board basis, including air-con and private shower.

*Villas Sand 'n Dory* (☎ 4538420; fax 2085385) has self-catering apartments and rooms – all with air-con, telephone, shower and terrace. One-bedroom apartments cost Rs 900/1200 for single/double occupancy; two-bedroom apartments cost Rs 1700/2100 for occupancy by two/three/four persons, including breakfast. Single/double rooms cost Rs 750/1000, including breakfast. Half-board rates are an additional Rs 150 per person per day; or dinner can be taken separately for Rs 200.

*Sofitel Imperial Hotel* (☎ 4538700; fax 4538320) is a curious edifice. Built by Taiwanese investors, it looks more like a replica of the Forbidden City in Beijing than a luxury hotel in Mauritius. From the lobby a flight of stairs leads to the Ming Court Restaurant where the fancy embellishments would surely please an Empress. Japanese skills were used to create the garden which contains palm trees reportedly replanted in their exact original inclination and orientation. Full sports facilities are available, including clay tennis courts and a nine-hole golf course. Single/double rooms cost Rs 2410/3420, including breakfast. Also available are deluxe and presidential suites, which cost Rs 10,280 and Rs 15,230 respectively – oh yes, breakfast included.

Top of the luxury list is the Sun International group's *La Pirogue Sun Hotel & Casino* (☎ 4538441; fax 4538449). A pirogue is a dugout canoe, but the term is also loosely applied to small local fishing boats. The main building of the hotel has a white, concrete roof shaped like the sail on such a vessel. The Suncard, which every guest receives on registration, is valid here – for more details refer to Accommodation in the Mauritius – Facts for the Visitor chapter. The hotel casino is open to nonresidents.

Standard single/double rooms cost Rs 3050/4600 on half-board basis. Superior single/double rooms are also available on half-board basis for Rs 4450/6400.

### Places to Eat
*Sea Breeze* (☎ 4538413) is very popular with locals and tourists, who come to gorge on dishes such as Chinese fondue or glazed duck. Prices for main dishes range from Rs 40 to Rs 220. Reservations are recommended for special dishes. The restaurant is open daily, except Tuesday, from 11.30 am to 2.30 pm and from 6 to 10 pm.

Readers have written to recommend the Sea Breeze Chinese fondue at Rs 225 per person. Each person receives a plate piled high with lobster, crab, prawns, squid, chicken and beef, plus four bowls of leafy Chinese vegetables, a variety of sauces and a bowl of noodles – all uncooked. The idea is to cook the food yourself over a charcoal-fuelled steamer. Allow at least 2½ hours to munch your way through this splurge extraordinaire!

*Leslie Snack*, on the roadside just before the road hits the sea shore and Flic en Flac, is a small café with a big menu. Recent reports from readers indicate the quality is declining but the prices are rising.

*Villas Caroline* (see Places to Stay) has a good restaurant, but prices are high. The restaurant is open daily from noon to 2.30 pm and from 7.30 to 10 pm. *Klondike Hotel* (see Places to Stay) has similar food at similar prices.

Down at the start of the beach is the *Mer de Chine* restaurant, which serves unexciting Chinese, Créole and European food. It is open daily from 11 am to 3 pm and from 6 to 10 pm. Main courses start at Rs 45. Further down the road, in an annexe of the Manisa Hotel (see Places to Stay), is *Le Flamboyant Restaurant* which offers similar cuisine at similar prices.

Self-caterers will find supplies in the shopping centre opposite Leslie Snack.

### Getting There & Away
You cannot get to Flic en Flac directly by bus from Port Louis, Curepipe or Mahébourg. You have to catch the Wolmar bus from Quatre Bornes – Wolmar is at the opposite end of the beach to Flic en Flac.

### Getting Around
Most of the hotels and guesthouses can arrange bicycle hire. Alternatively, go to the supermarket in the shopping arcade – expect to pay around Rs 80 per day.

### TAMARIN
This is the surfing centre of Mauritius, although you can go for weeks without seeing a surfer. The character of the place is more laid-back than Flic en Flac and rougher around the edges. It has a good beach and is well situated for most of the other sights. The village is encircled by salt evaporation ponds.

See Activities in the Mauritius – Facts for the Visitor chapter for details about the best surf spots in the area.

## Shellorama Museum

On the road from Tamarin to Grande Rivière Noire at La Preneuse, the Shellorama Museum boasts the biggest private collection of shells in the Indian Ocean. If you are considering buying shells, please read the Conservation note regarding shells in the introductory Facts for the Visitor chapter. Given the wide choice of other things to buy in Mauritius, there is no reason to purchase endangered species and thereby contribute to their extinction.

## Tamarin Bay Beach

This is a small public beach with good views across the river estuary to Montagne du Rempart.

Two Australian travellers contributed the following humorous account of their stay in Tamarin:

The second week (at Laganes) brought to light the 'too close for comfort' theory as we were surrounded by a hysterical dog, an amorous couple, and a compulsive snorer – plus there must have been a full moon rendering the locals more 'animated' than usual (particularly at 2 am!), aided by consumption of the local 'Anytime' firewater.

To cap it off we had the misfortune to run into 'Dodgy Rodg' (Roger) from over the road who took us on a memorable boat trip to a nearby island where both he and Elvis (his offsider) spent the whole day getting blind drunk and finally got the boat stuck on the reef in the dark – with five Aussies swearing at them! It was a day we won't forget in a hurry, and has since been the source of many laughs!

## Places to Stay

For basic accommodation at budget prices, you should try *Edouard Lagane's Bungalows* (☎ 6836445), on the main road down to the beach and hotel. Mr Lagane, an elderly Franco-Mauritian, has eight self-catering apartments with fridges, gas stoves, solar-heated water and electric fans. It can be very friendly within the small complex of apartments or too close for comfort, depending on who you have for neighbours. But Mr Lagane and his wife live 'on site' and, aided by their son Jacques, give the place a familial feel.

Rates for the flats are negotiable, but should start at around Rs 150 for the top floor, Rs 175 for the middle floor, and Rs 200 for the ground floor. Readers have reported varied luck with reductions for stays over a week. Breakfast costs Rs 25, lunch or dinner is Rs 50, bicycle hire is Rs 80 per day, moped hire is Rs 200 per day, and surfboard hire is Rs 50.

*Saraja Guest House* on Anthurium Ave is run by the friendly Cooshne family. Two rooms are available (up to two persons per room): the top floor room costs Rs 250; the room on the ground floor costs Rs 200. Breakfast is not included in the price. There is no telephone yet, so you have to call in or write in advance.

As with Flic en Flac, there are several private houses in the village to let. On Church Ave, near Lagane's, *Mr R Sumbhoo* (☎ 6836734) rents out a two-bedroom bungalow with electric cooker, fridge and an Asian-style toilet for Rs 225 per night. The *Obaprix* Chinese store, on the main road running through Tamarin, has a two-bedroom bungalow to rent at Rs 4500 for four weeks. It has a big verandah, sitting room and a TV.

The *Tamarin Hotel* (☎ 6836581; fax 6836927) is right on the beach, but has been criticised by several travellers for offering poor value for money. Single/double rooms cost Rs 540/690 including breakfast and aircon. There are also two-bedroom bungalows for Rs 600 or three-bedroom bungalows for Rs 700 per night, without air-con and breakfast. The hotel rents out bicycles and surfboards.

## Places to Eat

There's not much of a choice in Tamarin itself, apart from the *Tamarin Hotel* and a few snack stalls. During our research, we heard there were vague plans for the Saraja Guest House to set up a restaurant.

About three km away, on the road to Grande Rivière Noire, is *La Bonne Chute* restaurant (see Places to Stay & Eat in Grande Rivière Noire). If you're self-catering, the three Chinese stores in Tamarin are useful and friendly towards visitors.

## Getting There & Around

The Quatre Bornes-Baie du Cap bus service covers Tamarin and Grande Rivière Noire. You have to change at Baie du Cap for Souillac and Mahébourg, and at Quatre Bornes for Curepipe and Port Louis. For the fastest route to Port Louis, a reader recommends taking the Quatre Bornes bus to Bambous, and then catching the Port Louis bus there. The fare on any leg is around Rs 8.

A taxi from the airport to Tamarin costs about Rs 380; from Tamarin to Quatre Bornes or La Pirogue Rs 130; to Port Louis Rs 225; and to Curepipe Rs 275. Rs 750 will get you a day tour anywhere.

Bicycles can be hired at Mr Lagane's or at the Tamarin Hotel (see Places to Stay). Local boats are available for hire for deep-sea fishing, snorkelling or cruising.

## GRANDE RIVIERE NOIRE & LE MORNE

If Tamarin is surf city, Grande Rivière Noire is the main centre for deep-sea fishing. For this reason, the town's two hotels go all out to attract a different type of visitor, one that mixes less comfortably with the Mauritians or their country.

Le Morne is the sheer rock mountain standing at the neck of the tap-shaped peninsula at the south-west corner of the island. This area is also dominated by two upmarket hotels.

## Martello Tower

An ancient lookout station for a French coastal battery on the coast road between Les Bougainvilliers and the Hotel Rivière Noire, the Martello tower stands with its cannons aimed at the sea.

## Chamarel

The spectacular waterfall and unusual 'coloured earths' of Chamarel are not actually in the village of Chamarel, but nearly four km further south. The 100 metre waterfall is halfway down an estate road, and can be appreciated from several good vantage points. It is difficult to walk down to the base of the cascade.

Further down the road is the area with seven differently coloured layers of earths which are intriguing but not mind-blowing. The blue, red, yellow and other colours appear to have been painted onto the smooth outcrop by the same chap who designed the Mauritius flag. It is believed that the colour bands are the result of the uneven cooling of molten rock. You can buy various trinkets with a test-tube creation of the various colours at the entrance gate.

To get to both these attractions, take the steep corkscrew road inland, at Grande Case Noyale, five km north of Le Morne. From here it's almost four km to the village of Chamarel. Keep to the right as you pass through the village and continue for two km until you come to a gate and a stall, the entrance to the estate road to the coloured earths and the waterfall. Here you pay an admission charge of Rs 10 per person. The waterfall is about 700 metres down this road; and the coloured earths are about one km further.

There are infrequent buses from Baie du Cap to Chamarel; or you can take the Baie du Cap bus from La Preneuse, get off at Case Noyale, and walk uphill about seven km to the coloured earths. From Quatre Bornes there's a bus service departing daily at noon for Chamarel.

If you are travelling by car or taxi, you can also get here via the scenic road which crosses Plaine Champagne.

All the major tour operators run excursions to Chamarel, usually including it with Grand Bassin and Trou aux Cerfs in Curepipe.

## Varangue sur Morne

According to information received from a reader just before this edition went to print, a restaurant and museum has been set up here in a breathtaking position by José Hitie, a timber specialist. The restaurant is built Swiss-chalet style from special wood and has its own spring water. The owner is currently setting up a museum of timber and woodworking tools. In the surrounding area he is also replanting endemic trees and plants

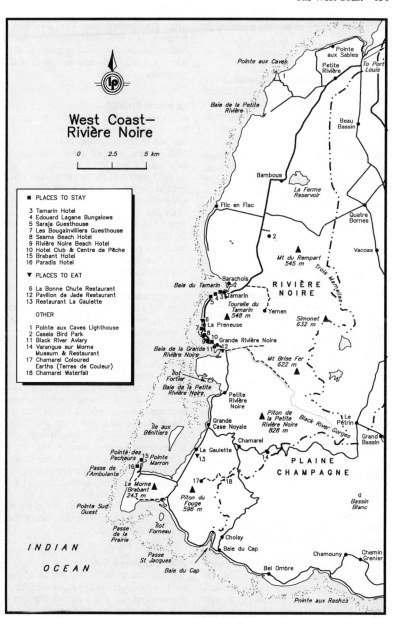

# West Coast—
# Rivière Noire

0      2.5      5 km

■ PLACES TO STAY

3  Tamarin Hotel
4  Edouard Lagane Bungalows
5  Saraja Guesthouse
7  Les Bougainvilliers Guesthouse
8  Seama Beach Hotel
9  Rivière Noire Beach Hotel
10 Hotel Club & Centre de Pêche
15 Brabant Hotel
16 Paradis Hotel

▼ PLACES TO EAT

6  La Bonne Chute Restaurant
12 Pavillon de Jade Restaurant
13 Restaurant La Gaulette

OTHER

1  Pointe aux Caves Lighthouse
2  Casela Bird Park
11 Black River Aviary
14 Varangue sur Morne
   Museum & Restaurant
17 Chamarel Coloured
   Earths (Terres de Couleur)
18 Chamarel Waterfall

and hopes thereby to provide a reserve for local fauna.

### Cécile Waterfall

Just after the Grand Bassin crossroads, on the way to Plaine Champagne and Chamarel, there is a viewing area overlooking Cécile Waterfall and the Savanne mountain range.

### Grand Bassin

This crater lake is a renowned pilgrimage site. Each year in February or March, most, if not all, of the island's Hindus come here for Maha Shivaratri celebrations on a pilgrimage to pay homage to the god Shiva who links the holy water of Grand Bassin to that of the Ganges:

According to legend, Shiva and his wife Parvati were circling the earth on a contraption made from flowers when they spied the dazzling beauty of an island and its encircling emerald sea. Shiva, who was carrying the Ganges River on his head to protect the world from floods, decided to land. After a bumpy descent, a couple of drops of water sprayed from his head and landed in a crater to form a natural lake. The Ganges expressed unhappiness about its water being left on an uninhabited island, but Shiva soothingly replied that dwellers from the banks of the Ganges would return one day to settle on the island and perform an annual pilgrimage, during which the water would be scooped out of the lake and presented as an offering.

There are temples on the rim of the crater and Hindus visit most days to make 'sacrifices'. The regular Vacoas to La Marie bus service is extended to Grand Bassin, via Mare aux Vacoas. Check with the National Transport Corporation (☎ 4262938) for departure times.

### Le Morne Peninsula

Formerly the site of the Dinarobin Hotel, the peninsula has been completely taken over by two hotels which effectively restrict access by charging an admission fee to nonresidents. The hotels' horse-riding club can arrange rides along the riding tracks inland. The sandy coastline continues, uninterrupted, for four km around the hammerhead,

after the Brabant and Paradis hotels' beaches. In 1992, locals reported that a Malaysian consortium was planning to build a hotel in multiple blocks across the tip of the peninsular.

### Le Morne Brabant

Reminiscent of the Rock of Gibraltar, Le Morne Brabant is very imposing. The cliffs are said to be unscalable, but, in the early 19th century, escaped slaves managed to hide out on top. The story says that the slaves, ignorant of the fact that slavery had been abolished, panicked when they saw a troop of soldiers making their way up the cliffs one day. Believing they were to be recaptured, the slaves flung themselves from the cliff tops. Thus the name: Le Morne, the 'mournful one'.

As you descend the road from Chamarel to the coast, the mountain to the north-west actually looks more mournful. The profile resembles an old lady's face with a bulbous nose and a beady eye. You need permission from the owner to climb Le Morne Brabant – ask around for him.

### Deep-Sea Fishing & Diving

At the Hotel Club & Centre de Pêche in Grande Rivière Noire a 13 metre fishing boat can be hired for a minimum of six hours at a minimum price of Rs 6000. The Brabant and Paradis hotels have four boats and charge similar prices. Also at Grande Rivière Noire is the private Bonanza angling club.

There are diving schools at the Rivière Noire, Brabant and Paradis hotels. (See also the Sports section in the Mauritius – Facts for the Visitor chapter.)

For less expensive fishing and diving options, have a chat with Francisco at Les Bougainvilliers hotel.

### Places to Stay & Eat

You can't camp on the beach at Le Morne, but if you carry on south-east for eight km to Baie du Cap you'll find a good site. This is one of the more peaceful beaches on the island. You can pitch your tent in front of the police station for safety.

## La Preneuse & Grande Rivière Noire To
find out about individual bungalows to let along the La Preneuse road, call 6964389.

Directly behind the telecommunications tower at La Preneuse is *Les Bougainvilliers Hotel* (☎ 6836525). Chris Poulos, the friendly septuagenarian owner, runs this charming house on the beach – a good value highlight on Mauritius. It is clean and hospitable, with a good restaurant, and has five double rooms for Rs 550, including perhaps the best value breakfast on the island. The upstairs rooms have balconies. Chris serves excellent food, such as curry chicken, and charges around Rs 75 for main dishes. The manager, Francisco, can organise excellent deals for car hire (from Rs 400 per day), fishing trips (Rs 2500 per day per boat for a maximum of four people), island excursions, and special discounts on model boats bought in the Curepipe workshops. Five minutes walk south of the hotel, along the beach, there's a deeper swimming area. Sadly, we've heard recent talk that the hotel might be changing hands soon. Advance reservations are advised: Les Bougainvilliers is very popular with repeat visitors.

Close by is *La Bonne Chute Restaurant* (☎ 6836552), beside the Caltex petrol station on the main road. It serves unexciting Créole and European food and main dishes start around Rs 100. Service is slack and the overpowering whiff from the petrol station doesn't exactly excite the appetite. The restaurant is open daily from noon to 3 pm and from 7 to 10 pm.

Opposite the public beach at La Preneuse is the recently opened *Seama Beach Hotel* (☎ 6836214) offering mid-range accommodation, and meals in its own *La Paille-en-Queue Restaurant*.

You don't really go to the *Hotel Club & Centre de Pêche* (☎ 6836522; fax 6836318) unless you are on a fishing holiday. The high season is determined by the deep-sea angling season from November to March. During low season, rates are reduced by up to 30%.

There is a beach, but because the hotel peninsula is in a sheltered bay and river estuary, the water is often like a warm bath – after somebody has had a wash! Singles/doubles during the high season are Rs 1595/1840 and Rs 1000/1210 during the low season, on a half-board basis. There is a daily Rs 200 supplement per person from 23 December to 2 January.

Rates for hiring a boat to go deep sea fishing start around Rs 5500 for a full day (nine hours) or Rs 4500 for a half day (six hours).

Not surprisingly, the hotel's restaurant specialises in seafood. Main dishes start from around Rs 90; special dishes include oysters, and seafood gratin. It's open daily from noon to 2 pm and from 7.30 to 9 pm.

The *Rivière Noire Hotel* (☎ 6836547; fax 6836768) next door is bigger. Rates range from Rs 750 to Rs 1300 for a single and Rs 1150 to Rs 1700 for a double on a half-board basis, depending on whether it is a room, studio or suite; whether it has air-conditioning or sea views; and whether it is high or low season. The hotel has diving as well as deep-sea fishing trips, and a separate disco called Maximus.

Just south of Grande Rivière Noire is *Pavillon de Jade*, a Chinese restaurant offering meals and takeaways at reasonable prices. It's open daily, except Mondays, from 11 am to 4 pm and from 6 to 10 pm.

## Le Morne About 12 km south of Grande
Rivière Noire, at Le Morne, are the two Beachcomber group hotels, the *Brabant* (☎ 6836775; fax 6836786) and the *Paradis* (☎ 6836775; fax 6836786). They are next to each other and are treated as one complex.

Nonresidents are kept at arm's length by guards at the driveway gatehouse. If you wish to enter to eat at the restaurants, an 'admission fee' of Rs 50 is charged, but this is graciously deducted from the bill if you dine at the hotels at night. During the day nonresidents still have to pay for the privilege of dining here – not exactly an incentive, to put it mildly.

The Brabant has less than half the capacity

of the Paradis. It is for more sedate holidays. The action takes place along the road at the Paradis, with the casino, discos and beach parties. In the middle, on the beach, is the *Blue Marlin Restaurant*. Guests can have dinner at either hotel. In addition to the usual free water sports, games and activities, the hotels have an 18-hole golf course, diving school, horse-riding school and deep-sea fishing centre, all of which you pay for. The Beachcomber Card, which every guest receives on registration, is valid here – for more details refer to the Accommodation section in the Mauritius – Facts for the Visitor chapter.

Standard single/double rooms at the Brabant are Rs 2850/4300 on a half-board basis. The Paradis charges Rs 3350/5000.

Five separate self-catering bungalows for Rs 2800 per day, each housing up to four people, provide an alternative. They stretch along a marvellous beach where camping is not allowed.

Just over three km before you reach the turn-off for the Paradis and Brabant hotels, you pass the inexpensive *Café La Gaulette*, in the village of La Gaulette. Here you can order Chinese or Créole main dishes at prices starting around Rs 45. It's open daily, except Monday, from 11 am to 3 pm and from 6.30 to 10.30 pm.

# South Mauritius

The southern region of Mauritius comprises the districts of Savanne and Grand Port, centred around the towns of Souillac and Mahébourg. The area differs little from the rest of the island, with mountains, forests, rivers, beaches, historic sites and plenty of sugar cane plantations. Its main attraction is the lack of tourism development.

## MAHÉBOURG

Mahébourg, named after the famous French governor Mahé de Labourdonnais but pronounced 'may burg', was once a busy port. Now it's a run-down commercial centre with a small fishing fleet.

But the town is a lot friendlier, has more character and is more relaxed than the tourist spiels would have you believe. It is also the nearest centre to the airport, and visitors may find themselves spending the first few days there. The bay is a picturesque backdrop for the town, with the sea changing from one intense colour to another at great speed.

### Naval Museum

The château housing the museum is on the outskirts of Mahébourg on the Curepipe road. It used to belong to the De Robillard family and played an important part in the island's history.

It was here in 1810 that the injured commanders of the French and English fleets were taken for treatment after the Battle of Grand Port. The story of the French naval victory is displayed in the museum, along with salvaged items from the British frigate *Magicienne*, which sank in the battle. Dives on the wreck in 1933 retrieved cannon, grapeshot and bottles.

A more famous wreck is that of the *St Géran*, sunk on 17 August 1744, off the north-east coast of Mauritius. The disaster inspired the love story *Paul et Virginie*, written shortly afterwards by Bernardin de St Pierre. Two maidens, who refused to undress and thus give themselves a chance of swimming to shore, went down with the ship. Bernardin de St Pierre was moved by this chaste sacrifice. The ship's bell was salvaged by French divers in 1966 and is on display at the museum.

A more recent sea disaster was the sinking of the British steamer *Trevessa*. She went down on 4 June 1923 in the middle of the Indian Ocean, 2576 km from Mauritius, on her way from Fremantle, Western Australia. Sixteen men survived at sea for 25 days in an open lifeboat which landed at Bel Ombre, near Le Morne, in the south-west of Mauritius. Exhibited at the museum is the last biscuit ration, a razor and the cigarette-tin lid used to measure out the water rations. There are further tributes to the men at the Merchant Navy Club in Port Louis (see the Port Louis chapter) and a monument at Bel Ombre. The survival is commemorated each year on Seafarers' Day (29 June), the day the lifeboat reached Mauritius.

The museum also contains a copy of a painting of Robert Surcouf, the 'King of the Corsairs', his pistol and the sword of one of his captives, Captain Rivington of the English ship *Kent*. The *Kent* was taken by Surcouf's *Confiance* on 7 October 1800 in the Bay of Bengal.

Other exhibits include lithographs of the lovers Paul and Virginie; the furniture of the former governor Mahé de Labourdonnais; early Dutch and Portuguese maps of Mauritius (one based on a visit by Abel Tasman in 1642); paintings of Prince Maurice of Orange (after whom the island is named), Pieter Both (the Dutch East Indies governor who drowned during a cyclone in 1615), Pierre Poivre (the botanist and creator of the Pamplemousses botanic gardens); and the death mask of poet-journalist Paul Jean Toulet (1867-1920).

The museum, set at the end of a tree-lined drive and surrounded by pleasant river walks, is open from 9 am to 4 pm. It is closed every

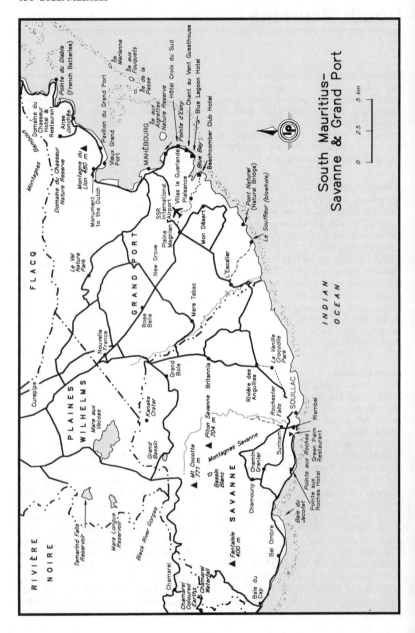

South Mauritius–
Savanne & Grand Port

Tuesday, Thursday, Sunday and public holiday. Admission is free.

## Assembly of God Church

This is not a significant building or religious group; there are probably several similar congregations throughout the island. A visit to one when there is a service in progress, and these are frequent, adds a great deal of colour, warmth and life to an otherwise ponderous round of 'sightseeing'. Worshippers belt out hymn after lively hymn in French, with plenty of 'hallelujahs', in time to a tambourine held by a boy standing next to the preacher. Hindus join in and nobody blinks an eye at visitors. The church in Mahébourg is near Rue des Flamands, on Rue de Maurice.

## Île aux Aigrettes

This island was established as a nature reserve in 1985. Many of the plant species found on the island's 25 hectares are very rare remnants of the coastal forests of Mauritius. As part of a MWAF project, approximately half of the island has been cleared of introduced species and native plants are being replanted. The ecosystem is also being restored with the eradication of rats and shrews, both of which are imported pests causing damage to rare plant species and currently preventing the reintroduction of endemic reptiles, such as snakes (Burrowing boa), skinks (Telfair's) and geckos (Gun-ther's).

The island serves as a convenient quarantine station for pink pigeons and Mauritius kestrels sent from overseas breeding schemes for eventual release in the wild. Guests at the nearby Croix du Sud Hotel on the mainland have become used to the sight of kestrels popping over from the island for a visit. When the kestrel project is further advanced, it may prove possible for a pair of the birds to take up permanent residence on the island.

MWAF plans to set up a visitor centre and nature trails so that limited numbers of tourist groups can visit and pay charges which will help to finance the project. For more details contact Mauritian Wildlife Appeal Fund

(MWAF, ☎/fax 6836331), Public Relations Officer, Morcellement Carlos, Tamarin. For an expanded discussion of Mauritius' wildlife, refer to the Flora & Fauna section in Mauritius – Facts about the Country chapter.

## Beaches

Blue Bay is the official public beach closest to Mahébourg. It gets busy on weekends. Good 'private' beaches stretch back to Mahébourg, past Pointe des Deux Cocos to Pointe D'Esny. Access is sometimes difficult from the road (through private property), but once you get to the beach, everything should be OK.

## Tours

Hotels and guesthouses can organise boat trips to Île aux Cerfs (described in the East Coast chapter) and other islands closer to Mahébourg. Their minimum rates for the day are usually around Rs 500 per person.

Should you charter a boat from Mahébourg, there are French fort ruins on Île de la Passe off Vieux Grand Port; a governor's summer residence on Île des Deux Cocos off Blue Bay; and the nature reserve on Île aux Aigrettes, described earlier in this chapter.

A reader wrote to recommend Gerard Etienne (☎ 6319514), a local fisherman who organises boat trips to Île aux Cerfs and other islands. Prices start around Rs 350 per person to Île aux Cerfs and include snorkelling, and a BBQ lunch on the beach. Lobster cook-outs are available on request. Trips to islands closer to Mahébourg cost slightly less.

## Places to Stay

**Mahébourg** Mahébourg caters well for independent travellers. Most travellers come from Réunion and stay in the several cheap boarding houses lining the beach front. The standards of these pensions de famille vary from year to year, depending on which has been the latest to do renovations or change managers. The pensions are very competitive, match each other's rates and organise boat trips with the local fishermen as well as other tours.

If you are particular about friendliness, cleanliness, peaceful atmosphere, and good value, the best choice by far is the *Pension Notre Dame* (☎ 6319582), next to the church at the top of the Rue du Souffleur. This residence, part of the convent, is run by the nuns at very reasonable prices – Rs 100/170 for a single/double room without breakfast; an additional Rs 50 per person if breakfast is required; and Rs 270/490 for half board. If you stay only one night, there may be a 25% surcharge on the price.

The eight rooms are small, but tidy. There is a washbasin in each room, but the shower and toilet are communal. The pension has a TV lounge, dining room and balcony for relaxing in the sun.

Readers have commented that early morning slumbers can be interrupted by yowling dogs, dawn calls to prayer from the nearby mosque, the church bells for the convent's 6 am service, and vociferous kids arriving for classes at the adjacent school.

There are 10 nuns, and as you would expect, they are very kind. Most come from France to teach, but the order does have members from other countries. The pension closes occasionally during the year for the nuns to attend 'retreats'. Phone ahead to check if the pension is open, and since it's a popular place to stay, advance reservations are recommended.

The other boarding houses are in a line along the former railway line, now called Rue Swami Sivananda. They are all close to the sea, though you can't swim here. Readers have warned about prostitution at the *Sea Breeze* and *Monte Carlo* pensions and advise guests not to leave valuables unattended.

The first, nearest to the Blue Bay road, is the *Pension St Tropez* (☎ 6319646), which is run by Ashok Beejadhur. Several readers have warned that the standards here are dodgy: showers that rarely function, cupboards full of black beetles, and lack of cleanliness. The house is right on the water's edge and has five rooms with communal shower and toilet for single/double Rs 175/220, including breakfast. One-bedroom and two-bedroom bungalows are also available for Rs 300/500.

Directly next door to St Tropez – and much better value – is the bigger, two-storey *Aquarelle* (☎ 6319479) with its own restaurant, Chez Jacqueline. Rates are Rs 180/280 including breakfast for single/double rooms with common toilet and bathroom; and Rs 400 for a one-bedroom bungalow, including breakfast. Half-board rates are an additional Rs 120 per person. Rooms 1 and

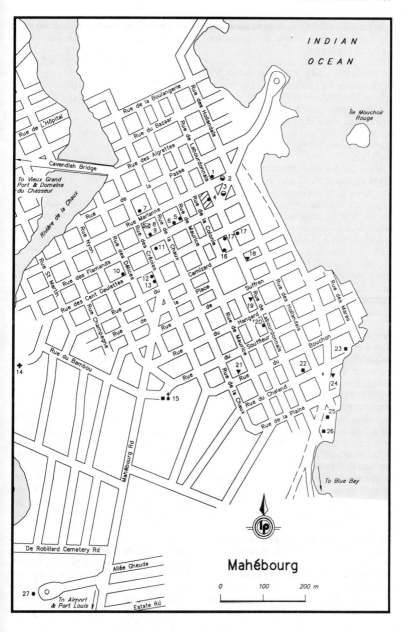

INDIAN

OCEAN

Île Mouchoir
Rouge

Rue de la Boulangerie

Rue du Bazaar

Rue des Aigrettes

Rue des Hollandais

Rue de Labourdonnais

Rue de L'Hôpital

Rue de la Chaux

Cavendish Bridge

To Vieux Grand
Port & Domaine
du Chasseur

Rivière de la Chaux

Passe

la

de

Rue

Rue Nyon

Rue St Martin

Rue des Flamands

Rue des Cent Gaulettes

Rue Champagne

Rue des Délices

Rue Marianne

Rue des Créoles

Rue des Créoles

Rue de la Colonie

Rue de Maurice

Rue du Souffleur

Rue de la Chaux

Camizard

Place

de

Suffren

Hangard

Rue de Labourdonnais

Rue des Hollandais

Rue des Mares

Bouchon

Rue du Bambou

Mahébourg Rd

Rue de la Plaine

Rue du Chaland

To Blue Bay

De Robillard Cemetery Rd

Allée Gheude

To Airport
& Port Louis

Estate Rd

Mahébourg

0          100          200 m

1
2
3
4
5
6
7
8
9
10
11
12
13
14
15
16
17
18
19
20
21
22
23
24
25
26
27

2 are recommended for their views across the bay. Camping is also permitted in the garden for Rs 25 per person.

Next in line is the *Auberge Sea Fever* (☎ 6319218), which has seven rooms for single/double Rs 130/250, including breakfast, and Rs 180/Rs 340 for half board.

*Monte Carlo Guest House* (☎ 6319514) is an elevated white and red Créole house. It can get cramped and noisy here at times. Singles/doubles cost Rs 150/200, including breakfast.

*Hotel Les Aigrettes* (☎/fax 6319094), formerly known as Hotel Blue Bay, is a smart complex which was renovated in 1991 and now offers 19 clean, airy self-catering apartments. Prices start at Rs 450/650 for single/double occupancy. The smaller apartments can take a maximum of two persons, the larger ones will take up to four. Long-stay discounts can also be negotiated. A restaurant is planned for residents only; and guests have the use of the recreation room in the annexe, a striking piece of architecture built to resemble a castle.

**Around Mahébourg** On the Mahébourg-Blue Bay road, at Pointe Jérôme, is *La Croix du Sud* (☎ 6319505; fax 6319603), a bungalow resort with a lush garden landscape at its centre. For short stays (up to three nights) between May and October, a single/double/triple room costs Rs 1230/1680/2000, including breakfast, or Rs 1470/2160/2720 on a half-board basis. If you stay longer, prices are reduced by around 10%. During the high season, November to April, prices are increased by around 15%.

The hotel offers facilities for a wide range of land sports and water sports, including free glass-bottom boat excursions. Bikes can be hired for Rs 50/150 per hour/day. Trips are also arranged to Île aux Cerfs, and there are plans to take small groups to visit Île aux Aigrettes, the nature reserve island opposite the hotel.

On the hotel beach you may meet pedlars selling trinkets made from corals, shells, etc. Please do not buy these items since this only hastens the destruction of the marine environment – for more details refer to the Flora & Fauna section in the Mauritius – Facts about the Country chapter.

Nightly entertainment is provided by the Hotline group, and Wednesday is séga night. The hotel restaurant, Les Aigrettes, offers special dinner buffet menus (for details, see Places to Eat).

About four km from Mahébourg on the same road, is the pension de famille *Chante au Vent* (☎ 6319614). A single/double room is Rs 450/550, including breakfast. It is a cut above the Mahébourg boarding houses and right on the beach.

*Chante Mer* (☎ 6319688) is another attractive pension de famille with single/double rooms with private shower and toilet at around Rs 750/950 including breakfast. A family room for two adults and one child costs Rs 1200 including breakfast. Meals are available on request.

*Villa Le Guerlande* (☎ 6319225) is a small complex of self-catering bungalows in a pleasant garden setting. A two-bedroom bung-alow with kitchen, terrace and sea view costs Rs 880/980/1080 for double/triple/quadruple occupancy – single price is the same as the double. Evening meals are available for Rs 180 per person. Windsurfers are available for the use of guests.

*Clement Dalé* (☎ 63119891) has a nice three-bedroom bungalow to rent near Blue Bay for Rs 550 per day.

The *Blue Lagoon Beach Hotel* (☎ 631-9529; fax 6319045), some six km south of Mahébourg at Blue Bay, is an attractive hotel with a fine beach. It is very popular with Réunionnais and South African visitors. Single/double rooms cost Rs 845/1260, including breakfast. Half board is an extra Rs 550. During high season, prices are increased by around 20%.

**Plaine Magnien & SSR Airport** There is a contrasting choice of hotels close to SSR Airport. In one direction, two km away, is the small town of Plaine Magnien. The *Tourist Rendezvous* (☎ 6373516) is above the petrol station in the centre of town. Single/double

Top: Créole home, Mahébourg, Mauritius (DS)
Bottom Left: View from Domaine du Chasseur, Mauritius (DS)
Bottom Right: Sir Seewoosagur Ramgoolam Botanic Gardens, Pamplemousses,
Mauritius (DS)

Top: Church at Cap Malheureux, Mauritius (RW)
Bottom: Sailboat in Blue Bay near Mahébourg, Mauritius (RS)

rooms with a shower and toilet cost Rs 250/300, including breakfast.

Almost six km in the other direction is the *Shandrani Hotel* (☎ 6319301; fax 6319313), which is a member of the Beachcomber Hotel group. It is actually on the other side of Blue Bay from the Blue Lagoon Beach Hotel. Single/double/triple rooms start at Rs 3000/4400/5800 on a half-board basis. Suites are also available for Rs 10,000 on a half-board basis. The Shandrani has all the sport and leisure activities of other luxury beach hotels, including diving, big-game fishing and horse riding. The Beachcomber Card, which every guest receives on registration, is valid here – for more details refer to the Accommodation section in the Mauritius – Facts for the Visitor chapter.

### Places to Eat

*Chez Jacqueline* restaurant is part of pension Aquarelle and probably the best place to eat in Mahébourg. It serves French and Créole cuisine with main dishes starting from around Rs 45.

Close by is *Le Vacancier* restaurant which was a popular eatery until 1992, when it was reduced to half its size by a fire. The current menu is restricted, but it's inexpensive. Le Vacancier is open daily from 10 am to 11 pm.

There are several local café/bars in Mahébourg. The *Monte Carlo*, at the corner of Rue du Bouchon and Rue de Maurice, has nothing to do with the Monte Carlo Guest House. In fact, the owner is the brother-in-law of Ashok Beejadhur, from the St Tropez pension. The bar is a lively, friendly place with a fascinating range of local characters. You can choose from a variety of cold curries (fish, octopus, cuttle fish, chicken) with rice for Rs 35.

For fast food, try *Chick Magic Snack Bar* or *Recréation Café*, on Rue de Labourdonnais.

On the Rue des Flamands, opposite the Odéon cinema, there are two good patisseries. The best is the *Rialto*, with a large selection of cakes, biscuits and savouries. The *Nouvelle Moderne* is not so appetising.

The Croix du Sud and Blue Lagoon Beach hotels (see the Places to Stay section) are popular bicycle destinations for a late breakfast or lunch. The Croix du Sud restaurant, *Les Aigrettes*, offers special dinner buffet menus four times a week: Monday (Chinese); Wednesday (BBQ); Friday (Indian); and Saturday (gastronomy). A buffet lunch (Créole) is available on Sunday.

### Entertainment

Mahébourg differs little from Curepipe or Port Louis for nightlife. A good night out requires a six km trip out to the Blue Lagoon Beach Hotel in Blue Bay, or even further afield to the plusher Shandrani Hotel, near the airport.

Otherwise there are two cinemas, the Odéon and the Mahé, both near the bus park, or the Star Light Chinese Gaming House & Bar, at the corner of the Rue des Flamands and the main drag, Rue des Créoles.

### Getting There & Away

**Taxi** A taxi from SSR Airport to Mahébourg costs between Rs 75 and Rs 100. For tips on dealing with taxi drivers on arrival, see the Mauritius – Getting Around chapter.

A reader wrote to recommend Premdath Jhugroo (taxi No. 9887) as a taxi driver providing fair deals. His nickname is 'Babu' and he can be contacted through Pension Notre Dame.

**Bus** The quickest way to get to Port Louis and continue, for example, from there to Grand Baie, is to take the express service which leaves about once an hour during the day. It costs a bit more, but takes half the time of the standard services which can take up to two hours to reach Port Louis.

On a much less frequent basis, buses run in the other direction to Centre de Flacq, via Vieux Grand Port and Grand Sable, and to Souillac, via Rivière des Anguilles.

### Getting Around

**Car & Motorbike** J. H. Arnulphy Car Hire (☎ 6319806; fax 6319991) charges reasonable rates. Prices start around Rs 800 for one day including unlimited mileage, and drop progressively if you hire for longer – ask for an appropriate discount. You will also have to pay a deposit or collision damage waiver of Rs 3000, insurance, and tax. Delivery or collection at the airport costs an additional Rs 50. Arnulphy also provides a fax service and arranges group tours by boat or minibus.

It is sometimes possible to hire a moped at the Notre Dame Store opposite the Pension Notre Dame. Expect to pay around Rs 160 per day.

**Bicycle** Bicycles are readily available for hire from Arnulphy Car Hire, Le Chrysanthème shop, and local pensions or hotels for between Rs 50 and Rs 75 per day. Blue Bay is a leisurely excursion by bicycle.

### AROUND MAHÉBOURG
### Domaine du Chasseur

If you feel like a break from beach life, a visit to this large estate on the south-east coast is highly recommended. Domaine du Chasseur (☎ 6319259; fax 2080076) covers some 900 hectares of forested slopes. Visitors have a choice of activities, including hiking, bird-watching, and accompanied mini-safaris. For details about hunting in Domaine du Chasseur, see the Activities section in the Mauritius – Facts for the Visitor chapter.

The forest contains many different species of trees, such as ebony, cinnamon, eucalyptus, and traveller's palm. Various types of wildlife roam here: Javanese deer, boar, monkeys, and many endemic species of birds, including a pair of Mauritian kestrels – one of the world's rarest birds of prey. You can watch the kestrels being fed white mice daily at 3 pm in the car park near the reception kiosk. Hikers are charged Rs 50 for admission and provided with a sketch map of the estate and a guided tour in French or English. There is no compulsion to take the guided tour. Guests staying at the bungalows or eating at the restaurant are excused from the admission charge.

There are some 28 km of rough tracks available for hiking, the most popular route is a one-hour return climb to the helicopter landing pad and excellent viewpoint.

Accommodation is provided on the hillside in six bungalows, all named after birds, and surrounded by trees – a great spot if you fancy a splurge away from the beach. For the pick of the views, reserve the Bengali bungalow. Rates for single/double occupancy are Rs 1150/1700; and an additional bed costs Rs 350.

The restaurant is ranged along the hillside in the form of individual tables protected by thatched pagodas and linked by walkways. It's an original idea with fine views, and the cuisine is worth a splurge. Specialities include venison and boar from the estate, and fresh seafood. Gourmets will appreciate the wine cellar and fine old spirits. Expect to pay at least Rs 300 per person for a three-course meal plus a couple of beers.

**Getting There** Domaine du Chasseur is at Anse Jonchée, close to the village of Vieux Grand Port. From the main road, it's a three km drive (or walk), passing through flat cane fields then climbing steeply along an increasingly rough track, to the restaurant and bungalows, and the trailhead for hikes into the forest. If you phone ahead, it is usually possible to arrange to be picked up at the main road where there are frequent bus connections between Mahébourg and Centre de Flacq. From Mahébourg it's about 20 minutes by taxi, expect to pay around Rs 100 one way.

### Vieux Grand Port

About seven km north of Mahébourg, Vieux Grand Port has great historical significance for Mauritians, but unfortunately few historical remains for visitors.

The Dutch made Vieux Grand Port their base and called it Fort Frederick Henrik. About four km from Mahébourg, on the banks of a river, is a monument commemorating the first landing by Dutch sailors, which took place on 9 September 1598 under the command of Wysbrand Van Warwick. The monument was erected in 1948 by the Mauritius Historical Society.

Beside the new church on the roadside at the northern end of Vieux Grand Port are the ruins of a Dutch settlement, although many believe they are French ruins.

Unfortunately we also have to report that the Salle d'Armes, once an attractive little maze between the coral rocks beside the sea, has been turned into a quarry. There's nothing left now, just a pile of rubble where there was once said to be an old duelling ground with a great 'buccaneer' atmosphere.

Vieux Grand Port was also the site of the only French naval victory to be inscribed on the Arc de Triomphe in Paris. The relics of the 1810 battle with the English are on display at the Naval Museum in Mahébourg.

The area is historically important for the sugar industry. The Ferney sugar estate, five km from Mahébourg, is one of the oldest in Mauritius. Nearby is a monument commemorating the introduction of sugar cane by the Dutch in 1639.

### Pointe du Diable

'Devil's Point', eight km north of Vieux Grand Port, was once the site of a French coastal battery. The cannons remain.

### Lion Mt

Overlooking Vieux Grand Port is Lion Mt, so named because it resembles a crouching lion. There are two routes up – one via the road opposite the church in the town and through the cemetery; and the other via the police station. Both lead through sugar cane fields on the footslopes. The climb is relatively easy although steep, but can be dangerous because it becomes slippery when wet. Allow five hours for the ascent and return.

### Le Val Nature Park

The road into Le Val is at Union Park village, about halfway on the Mahébourg-Curepipe road. Cluny village, the gateway to Le Val Nature Park in the valley of the Rivière des Créoles, is about seven km down the road.

Many of the amazing anthurium flowers are grown at Le Val in shade houses. There are also water fields full of watercress, which

complements many Créole meals, and attempts at prawn farming. Other facilities include a small aquarium and a deer park. Le Val is open Monday to Friday from 9 am to 5 pm. Admission costs Rs 15.

There is a bus service from Curepipe to Rose Belle, via Cluny.

### Le Souffleur

The reef which nearly surrounds Mauritius has a major break in it on the south-east coast. Instead of beach and calm lagoon, the sea rushes up against lava rocks and cliffs, carving out a variety of stacks and other coastline sculptures, the best known of which is Le Souffleur blowhole. It doesn't blow like a whale every day because it depends on the sea conditions. In fact, erosion is rapidly diminishing its grandeur, but even when Le Souffleur is dormant, there is still a knee-trembling power rumbling away below. Don't go too near the hole.

If you walk for about 20 minutes along the cliffs east from Le Souffleur, you'll come to a spectacular natural bridge formed when the roof of a sea cave collapsed.

To get there, take the Plaine Magnien-Souillac road (or bus from Mahébourg to Souillac). About six km from Plaine Magnien, as you enter the village of L'Escalier, is the entry to the Savanne sugar mill. Follow the signs for some two km to Le Souffleur, through the mill grounds and the cane fields. The blowhole is at the end of the biggest promontory, joined to the shore and car park by landfill. Cars and bicycles can go all the way down, but you must first get a free permit from the factory office or the estate office. You can visit Le Souffleur Monday to Friday from 7 am to 4 pm and on Saturday from 7 am to noon.

By the way, there is a nice little patisserie in the village just before the road down to L'Escalier beach.

### SOUILLAC

Named after the Vicomte de Souillac, the island's French governor from 1779 to 1787, Souillac, like Mahébourg, is of little interest in itself. It is not particularly welcoming or helpful to visitors, probably because it is not used to getting them. Souillac seems a place that Mauritians like to visit. Gris Gris and Robert-Edward Hart's house are popular school outings.

### Robert-Edward Hart Museum

Robert-Edward Hart (1891-1954) was a renowned Mauritian poet, appreciated by the French and English alike. He wrote in French and translations of his poetry are hard to find. He lived out the last 13 years of his life at Le Nef, a coral beach cottage about 500 metres east along the shore from the Souillac bus park. It was taken over by the Mauritius Institute and opened to the public in 1967. The bedroom and kitchen have been maintained.

On display are copies and originals of Hart's letters, plays, speeches and poetry, as well as his spectacles, pith helmet and fiddle. One speech, on love and marriage, was delivered at the Curepipe Hotel in November 1914, for the benefit of English and French war victims. The house is open from 9 am to 4 pm each day except Tuesday, Friday and on public holidays; entry is free.

### Gris Gris

Continue along the road past Le Nef and the Hart museum and you come to a grassy cliff top, which affords a view of the black rocky coastline where the reef is broken, and a path down to Gris Gris beach. It is a popular spot for shell collecting but a big wooden warning sign shaped like a dodo warns of the dangers of swimming here. 'Gris Gris' is said to mean 'sorcery' or 'black magic'.

### La Roche qui Pleure

'The rock that cries' is a little further east along the coast from Gris Gris and resembles a crying man. In fact it looks like the profile of the poet Robert-Edward Hart. Two pictures in the Hart museum show the comparison in case you can't find the actual rock.

### Telfair Gardens

More like a small municipal park than actual gardens, the Telfair Gardens are hardly an outstanding sight. But they are conveniently opposite the bus park in Souillac, on the road to the Robert-Edward Hart house and Gris Gris. The gardens were named after Sir Charles Telfair, secretary to the first English governor, sugar baron and superintendent of Pamplemousses Gardens. You get a good view across the bay from Telfair to the graveyard at Cemetery Point, where Hart is buried.

As in Gris Gris, there is a concrete slab informing you that swimming is hazardous because of dangerous currents off the rocks at the foot of the park.

### Rochester Falls

A five km walk from Souillac, past the Terracine sugar mill and through the cane fields along a well-marked route, brings you to this gushing little number. The falls are not so much high as wide, a sort of pocket-sized Niagara. A car can just about make it along the potholed cane field tracks; this is something a new taxi won't risk, but an old one might, for around Rs 120 return from Souillac.

### La Vanille Crocodile Park

This small zoo and 'handbag factory' is two km south of the hill town of Rivière des Anguilles on the road to Britannia. You'll see a sign for the farm. Nile crocodiles were imported here from Madagascar in 1985 and have been joined by giant tortoises, monkeys, deer, bats, giant land crabs, lizards and other wildlife. It's a pleasant spot to ramble through thick, steamy forest and enjoy the local fauna and flora. There is a snack bar and restaurant. The park is open daily from 9.30 am to 5 pm. Admission costs Rs 30/15 for an adult/child during the week, and Rs 25/12 at weekends.

### Beaches

Reef-protected beaches at Riambel and further west at Pointe aux Roches provide good swimming. Wild and windswept Gris Gris is far too dangerous.

## Baie du Cap

In spite of a great variety in coastal scenery, including some marvellous stretches of casuarina-lined beaches at La Prairie, west of the bay, this area has not been developed. Years ago surfers discovered the good waves around Macondé Point, on the other side of the bay.

## Baie du Jacotet

It is said there is a buried treasure on Îlot Sancho, a stone's throw from the shore – under the old cannon perhaps? There is also a good surfing spot nearby. And by Bel Ombre stands a monument to the survivors of the *Trevessa*, at the place where the lifeboat landed after 25 days at sea (see the Naval Museum section under Mahébourg).

## Places to Stay

There's only one place to stay in Souillac, the *Villas Pointe aux Roches* (☎/fax 6262507), which is about four km west of Souillac, past Riambel on the coast road. The villas are 27 plain white boxes set among palm trees facing a fantastic beach. The bar charges exorbitant prices, but it's a great place to watch the surf thundering onto the rocks. Single/double rooms cost Rs 800/900 including breakfast; the equivalent half-board rates are Rs 966/1242. The complex includes a restaurant.

## Places to Eat

Choices in Souillac are slim. There is a local café next to the bus park, which serves cheap noodle dishes. The *Green Palm Restaurant*, three km west of Villas Pointe aux Roches on the coast road, serves Indian, Chinese and European cuisine.

## Getting There & Around

Souillac and Rivière des Anguilles are on the Baie du Cap-Mahébourg bus route. There are also regular buses to and from Curepipe, via Rivière des Anguilles.

There is a bus service running direct between Curepipe, Souillac and Pointe aux Roches three times a day. Departures from Curepipe are at 6 and 11 am, and 2.30 pm; and from Pointe aux Roches at 7.40 am, 12.15 and 4.15 pm. A taxi from Souillac to Villas Pointe aux Roches costs Rs 45.

# Rodrigues & the Outer Islands

## RODRIGUES

Rodrigues is a volcanic island, 18 km long by eight km wide, with 37,000 people. It's surrounded by a coral reef and is similar to Mauritius in vegetation, mountains, beaches and climate.

Compared to Mauritius, Rodrigues is more vulnerable during the November to May cyclone season. The most recent cyclone, Bella, raged past the island in January 1991, when wind speeds in excess of 200 kp/h were recorded. The wettest months are February and March.

The population grew rapidly early in this century, but has now stabilised at about 37,000. One of the island's major problems is the strain that such a relatively large population puts on land resources. In contrast to Mauritius, the people are more African than Indian in origin and most are Roman Catholics. Many liberated slaves settled in Rodrigues.

The economic mainstays for the islanders are fishing, subsistence agriculture, handicrafts, an infant tourism industry, and subsidised imports from Mauritius.

For the time being Rodrigues remains unspoiled, but it is receiving increasing attention from Mauritian tour operators keen to promote something different. You should take with you supplies of any special items, such as prescription medicines or films. The extra cost of transport is reflected in the prices of goods imported from Mauritius. As presents for the friendly or helpful locals, you might want to bring some fruit and copies of the latest magazines.

### History

The Portuguese had the honour of discovering Rodrigues (for Europe) and naming it after one of their intrepid seamen, but it was the Dutch who first set foot on the island, albeit very briefly, in September 1601.

The Frenchman, François Leguat, and a small band of Huguenot companions sailed away from religious persecution in France and arrived here in 1691. Leguat enjoyed his paradisiacal existence on the island, but the lack of female company was an impediment to perfection. The island's fauna and flora was a source of wonder and comestibles – survival rather than conservation was top priority in those days. Leguat's journal, entitled *Voyage et Aventure de François Leguat en Deux Îles Désertes des Indes Orientales*, provides a vivid account of the group's two-year stay, and was a publishing success in Europe.

Subsequent visitors to Rodrigues set about ruthlessly removing the island's thousands of giant tortoises which were a prized source of nourishment. Rodrigues also had a big flightless bird, the solitaire, which went the same way as the dodo and just as quickly.

The French returned early in the 18th century for another attempt at colonisation, but had abandoned Rodrigues by the end of the century. In 1809, the British landed on the island and used it as a provisional base from which to attack and capture Mauritius.

Until it gained independence with Mauritius in 1968, Rodrigues had an uneventful history. There is now a Ministry of Rodrigues in the Mauritian government which appoints an Island Secretary to look after the island's affairs. There are two political parties on Rodrigues: *Organisation du Peuple Rodriguais (OPR)*, the dominant party, led by Serge Clair; and *Rassemblement du Peuple Rodriguais (RPR)*, headed by France Felicite.

### Culture

The islanders are known for their versions of old colonial ballroom and country dances such as the scottische, waltz and mazurka. The Créoles know them as the *kotis*, *laval* and *mazok*. They also have a more African version of the séga, known as *séga tambour*.

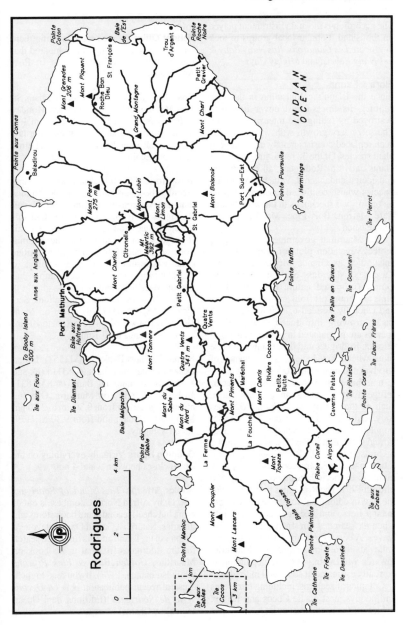

Rodrigues

The accordion is the main instrument played on the island. Popular local groups to look out for are *Les Camarons*, *Ras Natty Baby & Les Natty Rebels*, and *Mighty Guys*.

## Flora & Fauna

Since the island's colonisation in the 17th century, its thick forest cover has been destroyed by felling and intensive grazing. The secondary growth with which this has been replaced consists mostly of introduced plant species. Of the 38 remaining species of plants native to Rodrigues, all but two are considered endangered, vulnerable, or rare. Species whose continued existence depend on one or two specimens in the wild include Café Marron, Bois Pipe, Mandrinette and Bois Pasner.

The Mauritian government is acting to protect vegetation plots of critical importance, such as Grande Montagne, Pigeon, Cascades, Mourouk, St Louis, and Anse Quitor (proposed nature reserve). These plots are fenced off from animal depredation and carefully weeded to remove the much faster growing introduced species. Rare species are propagated in government nurseries on Rodrigues and then planted in these plots where they have a better chance of survival and regeneration.

It is hoped that these areas will act as refuges for the island's rare endemic fauna, such as the Rodrigues warbler, Rodrigues fody, and Rodrigues fruit bat. The warbler population has made a shaky recovery from virtual extinction in the '60s to an estimated 50 birds in 1991. The Rodrigues fody population has also increased from very low numbers in the '60s to approximately 400 birds in 1991. The Rodrigues fruit bat spends the day in communal roosts, usually in old mango trees, and becomes active at night when it searches for fruits, flowers and leaves. A common haunt for the bats is the valley about four km south of Port Mathurin, towards Mt Lubin. The bat population is currently estimated at some 900 individuals.

Colonies of seabirds, including fairy terns and noddys, nest on Île Cocos and Île aux Sables off the north-west coast.

## Information

**Tourist Office** At the time of writing there was no tourist office, but it is rumoured that one will be established soon in Port Mathurin.

**Post** The main post office is on Mann St, Port Mathurin. Opening hours are Monday to Friday from 8 to 11.30 am and from 1 to 4 pm; and from 8 am to noon on Saturday. There are also small post offices at La Ferme and Mont Lubin.

**Telephone** The telephone service has recently been upgraded – all Rodrigues numbers now consist of seven digits. To call Rodrigues from Mauritius, dial 00095 followed by the Rodrigues number. To call Rodrigues from abroad, dial the international access code followed by the Mauritius country code and the Rodrigues number. To call Mauritius from Rodrigues, simply dial the full Mauritius number.

The Overseas Telecommunications Services (OTS) (☎ 8311724) office on Mont Vénus is open weekdays from 8 am to 10 pm, and on weekends until 1 pm.

**Banks** Barclays Bank (☎ 8311553), Indian Ocean International Bank (☎ 8311591), and Mauritius Commercial Bank (☎ 8311831) all have offices in Port Mathurin. Opening hours are generally from 9.30 am to 2.30 pm Monday to Friday; and from 9.30 to 11.30 am on Saturday.

**Opening Hours** Virtually everything on the island closes between 3 and 4 pm.

**Books & Maps** *The Island of Rodrigues* (1971), by Alfred North-Coombes, is out of print, but check second-hand book stores and libraries. Naturalist Gerald Durrell devotes a chapter to the island and his fun-filled search for the Rodrigues fruit bat in his book on Mauritius, *Golden Bats & Pink Pigeons* (Collins/Fontana, 1977). If you read French, a useful recent publication is *À La Decouverte de Rodrigues* (Éditions de l'Océan Indien) by Chantal Moreau.

The most useful road and features map is in French, published by Institut Géographique Nationale (IGN), and costs Rs 25. It's available from bookshops, including Maxime Wong General Merchants on Jenner St, Port Mathurin; and the Librairie du Trèfle in Port Louis and Curepipe. Maxime Wong General Merchants is also the place to look for postcards. MacMillan has recently published a map of Mauritius, including a small inset for Rodrigues Island, which is adequate for orientation.

Hikers requiring more detailed information should contact the Ministry for Rodrigues at Fon Sing building, Fifth Floor, Edith Cavell St, Port Louis, or visit the Ministry's office (☎ 8311590) on Jenner St, Port Mathurin, Rodrigues.

**Tours** HenriTours (☎ 8311823; fax 8311697) on Mann St, Port Mathurin appears to have a firm grip on the market for guided tours. One

reader commented: 'Henri regards himself as a bit of an action man, note the Rambo poster in the office and the walls covered with photos of Henri pursuing manly activities'. The company offers tours of the island by boat or minibus ranging from three to six days, including excellent meals. Diving trips and excursions to nearby islands, such as Île Cocos and Île aux Sables can also be arranged.

Most of the hotels and guesthouses can also arrange tours and transport for guests.

**Dangers & Annoyances** Drinking water is generally neither chlorinated nor filtrated. Bottled water is available from shops.

**Port Mathurin**
As the administrative, commercial and industrial hub of the island, Port Mathurin is a natural base for visitors. An adjacent section of town, known as Camp du Roi, is

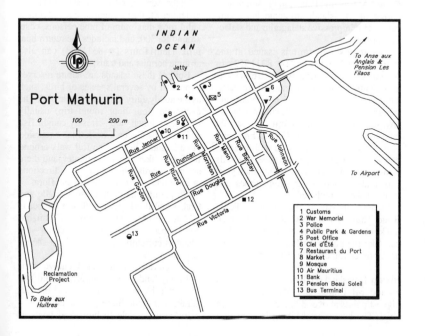

Port Mathurin

INDIAN OCEAN

Jetty

To Anse aux Anglais & Pension Les Filaos

To Airport

To Baie aux Huitres

Reclamation Project

0  100  200 m

Rue Jenner
Rue Gordon
Rue Ricard
Rue Duncan
Rue Morrison
Rue Mann
Rue Barclay
Rue Johnson
Rue Douglas
Rue Victoria

1 Customs
2 War Memorial
3 Police
4 Public Park & Gardens
5 Post Office
6 Ciel d'Été
7 Restaurant du Port
8 Market
9 Mosque
10 Air Mauritius
11 Bank
12 Pension Beau Soleil
13 Bus Terminal

being developed as an administrative, commercial, and industrial complex. Current construction projects here include a new court house, fire station, police station, public library, and offices for banks, trading companies, and social services.

## Around the Island

**Beaches** Pointe Coton, on the east coast, has the best beach on the island. There are other nice beaches at St François, Trou d'Argent, Petit Gravier, and Port Sud-Est.

**Diving** There are several good scuba-diving locations around Rodrigues, but unfortunately there is no diving school or public-use compressor on the island, and you need a boat. The best dives are off Pointe Coton and Pointe Roche Noire, on the east coast, and off Pointe Palmiste, on the west. Baladirou, at Pointe aux Cornes, is also popular for diving. HenriTours can organise diving trips.

**Caves** At Caverne Patate, in the south-west corner of the island, are some interesting caves with impressive stalagmite and stalactite formations.

The requisite permit is issued at the Administrative Office (☎ 8311512) in Jenner St, Port Mathurin. A guided tour starts at the entrance to the caves at 10 am daily. The permit charge is Rs 25 per person and you should arrive at the cave entrance on the day specified on your permit. You should take your own torch. *Goni* (jute sacking) and *pétrole* (petrol) are also sold at stalls near the entrance. The guide may use these materials to make flaming torches to illuminate your way underground. Wear strong shoes and take a jacket or pullover.

To get to the caves, take the road to Petite Butte. The cave warden's hut is down a small track, close to the Centre Communal. You can take the bus to La Fouche and ask the driver to let you off at the right spot.

**Hiking** The island is hilly and hiking is good around Mt Limon and Mt Malartic, the highest points at over 390 metres above sea level. The best coastal hiking is from Port

Mathurin, around the east end of the island, to Port Sud-Est.

A reader has also recommended a good, long hike along the coastal road under construction from La Ferme to Port Mathurin via Baie aux Huîtres. Starting from La Ferme, walk back along the road and take the first road to the right after the women's centre. From there follow the road.

This coastal road will eventually be extended around this end of the island to connect the airport in the south-west with Port Mathurin in the north.

## Offshore Islands

There are many small islands dotted around Rodrigues. The four islands most commonly visited are Île Cocos, Île aux Sables, Île aux Crabes and Île Hermitage.

The permits required to visit Île Cocos, barely one km in length, and its even smaller neighbour, Île aux Sables, can be obtained from the Administrative Office (☎ 8311512) in Jenner St, Port Mathurin. Each permit is valid for a maximum of nine persons, costs around Rs 300, and includes the return boat fare. HenriTours (☎ 8311823) can also arrange permits and transport.

Both of these islands are nature reserves populated by several species of birds, such as the noddy, fairy tern, and frigate bird. The excursion (four hour round trip) usually includes a lunch stop – freshly caught fish grilled on Île Cocos. Check if the excursion price includes lunch. The full walk around Île Cocos takes about 45 minutes, and there are two guards who can provide directions or information about the fauna and flora.

No permits are required to visit Île aux Crabes and Île Hermitage. Île aux Crabes is a 20 minute boat ride from Pointe Corail, but don't expect much in the way of crabs – the island is currently being used for a sheep-farming project!

Île Hermitage, a tiny island renowned for its beauty (and possibly hidden treasure), is accessible by boat from Port Sud-Est (25 minutes) or Petite Butte (90 minutes).

It's also possible to hire local boats at

Rivière Cocos for trips to Île Gombrani or Île Paille-en-Queue.

## Places to Stay
**Camping** If you have a tent, you can camp just about anywhere on the island and local people are friendly and eager for conversation.

**Hotels** The best known abode in Rodrigues is the 11-room *Hotel Relais Pointe Vénus* (☎ 8311577), near the Overseas Telecommunications Services station on a hilltop between Port Mathurin and Anse aux Anglais. This is a wonderful, dilapidated, colonial house, built in 1870, with a surrounding verandah and great views. 'It resembled nothing so much as an exaggerated film set for a Somerset Maugham story...', wrote Gerald Durrell. Singles/doubles are Rs 240/350, including breakfast.

The *Cotton Bay Hotel* (☎ 8313000; fax 8313003) at Pointe Coton is a new luxury hotel beside an excellent beach. There are three types of room: standard single/double rooms cost Rs 2230/3240; superior single/double rooms cost Rs 2420/3600; and deluxe single/double rooms cost Rs 3460/5700. All these prices include half-board.

**Pensions de Famille** At Anse aux Anglais, two km east of Port Mathurin, is the six-room *Pension Les Filaos* (☎ 8311644), which charges single/double Rs 200/350 per night, including breakfast; half-board costs an additional Rs 60 per person. The staff organises 4WD tours of the island and fishing trips, and there's a video for stormy nights.

In Jenner St, Port Mathurin, *Pension Ciel d'Eté* (☎ 8311587), has four rooms. Singles/doubles are Rs 175/350, including breakfast. Half-board is available by prior arrangement. The pension also has two-bedroom bungalows (maximum of four persons) which cost Rs 175 per person.

*Pension Beau Soleil* (☎ 8311673; fax 8311916) on Victoria St has 18 rooms. Prices start around Rs 255/350, including break-

fast; Rs 330/500 for half board; and Rs 400/600 for full board.

We have recently heard of two new pensions in Port Mathurin, *Kam John* and *Ebony Guest House* (☎ 8311540); and a religious order is now offering accommodation in a converted monastery, *La Roseraie*. There are also plans to start a *table d'hôte* (local B&B) scheme in the Port Mathurin area.

## Places to Eat
For good seafood dishes, try *Lagon Bleu Restaurant*. It's attached to HenriTours on Mann St and is run by Henri's wife. Other restaurants in town include *Ebony Restaurant* and *Restaurant du Port*.

## Things to Buy
Handicrafts, especially many styles of baskets and hats made from all sorts of materials are available at shops in Port Mathurin; at the Centre des Femmes in Mont Lubin; and at Emeraude in Petit Gabriel. In the island's markets you might like to buy handicrafts, spices, limes, jams, local honey (Rs 40 a jar), local ham, and dried octopus and squid. The main market of the week in Port Mathurin is held very early on Saturday morning between 6 and 8 am.

## Getting There & Away
**Air** Air Mauritius operates flights to Rodrigues daily, except on Thursday. The one-way flight takes 1½ hours. The return fare is Rs 4390 (ticket valid for a minimum stay of five days; maximum stay of one month), but Mauritian residents travel half-price. The fare for a ticket valid for one year is Rs 4880.

The main Air Mauritius office on Rodrigues is in the ADS Building, Ricard St, Port Mathurin (☎ 8311632). There is also an office (☎ 8311301) at Plaine Corail airport.

**Boat** The good ship *MV Mauritius*, a romantic and nostalgic freighter which used to provide a passenger service between Mauritius and Rodrigues, was taken out of service in 1991.

The new ship, *Mauritius Pride*, does the trip from Mauritius to Port Mathurin in 24 hours and the return trip takes 27 hours. The following prices reflect the 50% surcharge for non-Mauritians.

Tourist class (comfortable aircraft ferry seats) costs Rs 750/1500 one way/return, including three basic meals. It's all kept spotlessly clean and passenger facilities include air-con, radio, TV, and toilets.

First class consists of six double cabins which cost Rs 1500/3000 (per person) one way/return. Readers have raved about the 1st-class lounge and the meals served in the restaurant. It's also possible to keep your cabin on a B&B basis (Rs 400 per day) during the ship's five-day stopover in Port Mathurin harbour. This allows you to explore the island by day and return to the ship at night.

The *Mauritius Pride* sails twice a month – advance reservations are recommended. For information contact Mauritius Shipping Corporation Ltd (☎ 2412550; fax 242 5245), Nova Building, 1 Military Rd, Port Louis. For information on Rodrigues, contact Marine Services (☎ 8311595) in Port Mathurin.

**Yacht** Due to prevailing winds, Rodrigues is difficult to reach by yacht from Mauritius. The trip takes up to a week, but the journey back is much easier and quicker.

### Getting Around

The road system on Rodrigues is being improved and expanded. There are now numerous asphalted roads, but 4WD vehicles or jeeps are still essential for negotiating the many unpaved tracks through the steep terrain.

**To/From the Airport** Flights arrive at Corail airfield in Rodrigues. The 'Supercopter' bus service to Port Mathurin operates for flight arrivals and departures only and takes 35 minutes. The price for a one-way ticket is an astounding Rs 75.

**Car Rental** Ask your hotel or pension manager about car hire or contact Mr Cassam Vallymamode (☎ 8311537). Mini-mokes are available for around Rs 750 per day.

**Motorbike** Most hotels or pensions can arrange moped hire for around Rs 175 per day.

---

### Octopus & Squid

It scarcely seems credible that *cephalopods*, the tentacled octopus and squid, should be related to oysters, clams, cowries and cone shells, yet all are molluscs. The eight-tentacled octopus usually shelters in a cavity or cave in the coral, coming out to grab unwary fish or crustaceans which it kills with an often venomous bite from its beak-like jaws.

Squid are rather like a longer, streamlined version of an octopus. Like an octopus they move by a form of jet propulsion, squirting out the water which is taken over their gills. They can move at remarkable speed and catch their prey, usually small fish and crustaceans, by shooting out two long tentacles. Like octopus they are also masters of disguise, able to change their colour by squeezing or flattening out cells which contain coloured material.

Cuttlefish are like a larger squid and along with speed and the ability to change colour they are also able to perform a type of animal smokescreen trick. When threatened they turn a dark colour then shoot out a blob of dark ink which takes a cuttlefish-like shape. The real cuttlefish then rapidly turns a lighter colour and shoots away, leaving the predator to grab at its ghost! The familiar cuttlebone found washed up on beaches is a cuttlefish's internal skeleton. It is made up of thin layers and by filling the space between layers with gas the cuttlefish uses it as a flotation device.

Octopus and squid have evolved from earlier *cephalopods* which had shells. The chambered nautilus is the best known and most spectacular survivor of these creatures. The large brown and white nautilus shell is divided into chambers and the tentacled creature can vary its buoyancy by changing the amount of gas and liquid in individual chambers. ■

**Bus & Camionette** There are now several private bus lines which operate standard buses and camionettes (small pick-up trucks) from the bus station *(gare routière)* in Port Mathurin. Fares depend somewhat on the driver so ask the locals what they are paying. When travelling on a camionette, you may have to pay extra for your backpack.

At present there are bus routes from Port Mathurin to Baie aux Huîtres (3 Rs); La Ferme via Mont Lubin (4 Rs); Pointe Coton (Rs 30); and Grand Baie (Rs 3). Schedules are irregular.

## OUTER ISLANDS
Four other islands or island groups in the Indian Ocean are claimed by Mauritius.

### Cargados Carajos (St Brandon)
This 22-island atoll, 370 km north-east of Mauritius is, like the Maldives, a diving paradise. Unfortunately it is only accessible by yacht or fishing boat. Fishermen ply the waters and camp on Albatross (in the north) and Coco (in the south), and maintain a base at Raphael (in the central part), but there is no permanent settlement. Mauritius Fishing Development Ltd (Raphael Fishing Company) (☎ 2080299), 33 Ter Volcy Pougnet, Port Louis, are the people to see.

### Agalega
There are more than 300 people involved in the copra industry on this 70 sq km island, 1100 km north of Mauritius, en route to the Seychelles. An old airstrip exists, and there are plans to repair it and open the island to tourists. For further information, contact the Outer Islands Development Corporation (☎ 2422275), Jade House, Jummah Mosque St, Port Louis.

### Tromelin
This island is claimed by both Mauritius and France. Rather than let the dispute upset relations, both have agreed not to pursue a claim in any way, so no-one lives there.

### Chagos Archipelago
The Chagos Archipelago was formerly administered from Mauritius. Then, a few years before independence in 1968, the British annexed the island under the British Indian Ocean Territory and leased the main island, Diego García, to the USA as a military base for its Rapid Deployment Force. The Chagos islanders were moved to Mauritius and given financial compensation for the upheaval. This issue is discussed in more detail under Population & People in the Mauritius – Facts about the Country chapter.

# Réunion

# Facts about the Island

The island of Réunion is so sheer and lush, it looks as if it has risen dripping wet from the sea. It is often compared to Hawaii, as they share spectacular landscapes, volcanic activity and a pleasant not-too-stifling climate, but the similarities stop there.

Réunion is completely and emphatically French. A French overseas *département* with mostly proud ties to its European heart: the baguette is a national institution, instant coffee is considered an abomination and English-speaking visitors will need at least a few words of French. A well-kept secret, few people outside *le Métropole* (mainland France, that is) know of Réunion and even fewer know of its natural and scenic wonders. The island's lack of world-class beaches probably has a lot to do with its avoiding an international tourism invasion, but whatever Réunion lacks at sea level, it more than makes up for in its spectacular mountain country. In fact, Réunion leaves Mauritius looking flat and plain by comparison!

Tourism authorities have recognised that Réunion is a trekker's paradise, and provide well for the walker and backpacker by maintaining footpaths and mountain huts. If you loved Nepal or New Zealand you'll also love Réunion, which provides similar quality hiking and trekking but with an exotic tropical twist.

You can also live in style, as the Réunionnais enjoy a comfortable subtropical climate as well as most of the luxuries of metropolitan France. Unfortunately, this means prices can tower with the peaks, so a respectable budget is requisite. It would be financial suicide to arrive in Réunion on a shoestring – real 'wing and a prayer' stuff – and you may risk being repatriated as *un misérable*!

Réunion has a useful tourist service which helps potential visitors plan trips, and the advance effort is well worth it. It is possible to experience much of Réunion's appeal on a medium range budget if you know about cheaper alternatives and book ahead; the French themselves are quick to take advantage of good deals. Work out an itinerary first, make your bookings and let the options present themselves within that framework.

## HISTORY

The island of Réunion has a history similar to that of Mauritius and was visited, but not settled, by early Malay, Arab and European mariners. The archipelago, comprised of Mauritius, Rodrigues and Réunion, was christened the Mascarenes by Portuguese navigator Pedro de Mascarenhas, following its European discovery in 1512. Some historians maintain that Réunion had first been named Santa Apolónia after the day in 1507 on which it was sighted by Tristan da Cunha's fleet returning from India. After these initial sightings, the island moved through a succession of names given by Dutch, English and French explorers who claimed to be the first to spot it.

### 1600 to 1800

In 1642 the French took the initiative of settling the island, which at the time was called Mascarin, when La Compagnie des Indes Orientales (the French East India Company) sent its ship, the *St-Louis*. No-one actually settled on Réunion until four years later, when the French governor of Fort Dauphin in southern Madagascar banished a dozen mutineers to the island. The mutineers landed at what is now St-Paul and lived in a cave for three years. In fact, this Grotte des Premiers Français still exists and is open to visitors.

On the basis of enthusiastic reports from the mutineers, in 1649 the island was officially claimed by the King of France and renamed Île Bourbon, after Colbert Bourbon, the founder of the French East India Company.

However appealing it seemed, there was no great rush to populate and develop the

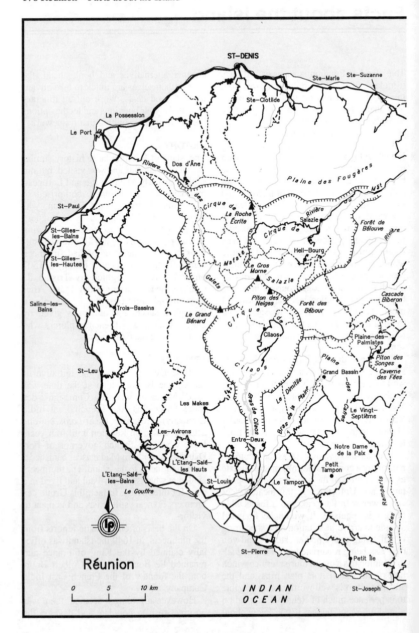

Réunion

0     5     10 km

INDIAN
OCEAN

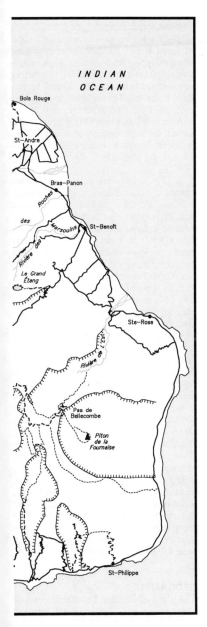

INDIAN
OCEAN

Bois Rouge

St–Andre

Bras–Panon

Roches

des

Marsouins

St–Benoît

Rivière des

Le Grand
Étang

Ste–Rose

Rivière de

Rivière

Pas de
Bellecombe

Piton
de la
Fournaise

St–Philippe

island and, from around 1685, Indian Ocean pirates began using Île Bourbon as a trading base. The 260 settlers benefited from these illicit dealings until the French government and the French East India Company clamped down on them and took control at the beginning of the 18th century.

Until 1715, the French East India Company was content to provide only for their own needs and those of passing ships, but then coffee was introduced, and between 1715 and 1730 it became the island's main cash crop. The island's economy changed dramatically. As coffee required intensive labour, African slaves were introduced despite French East India Company rules forbidding the use of slave labour. During this period, grains, spices and cotton were also brought in as cash crops.

Like Mauritius, Réunion came of age under the governorship of the remarkable Mahé de Labourdonnais who served from 1735 to 1746. However, Labourdonnais treated Île de France (Mauritius) as the favoured of the sibling islands and Île Bourbon was left in a Cinderella role.

As a result of poor management and the rivalry between France and Britain during the 18th century, as well as the collapse of the French East India Company, the government of the island passed directly to the French crown in 1764. After the French Revolution, it came under the jurisdiction of the Colonial Assembly. It was at this time that the island's name was changed to La Réunion (which means 'the meeting') but for reasons known only to the Colonial Assembly. Certainly the slaves were not officially meeting with anyone; nor did the name find favour with slave owners, who a short time later decided to rename it Île Bonaparte after you-know-who.

In the late 18th century, there were a number of slave revolts and those who managed to escape made their way to the interior. They organised themselves into villages run by democratically elected chiefs and fought to preserve their independence from colonial authorities.

While the Mascarenes remained French

colonies, Réunion had the function of providing the islands with food products while Mauritius made the profits exporting sugar cane.

## 1800 Onwards

The heretofore productive coffee plantations were destroyed by cyclones very early in the 19th century, and in 1810, during the Napoleonic Wars, Bonaparte lost the island to the *habits rouges* (redcoats). On 9 July, Britain took possession of Réunion but five years later, under the Treaty of Paris, the spoil was returned to the French as Île Bourbon. The British, however, retained their grip on Rodrigues, Mauritius and the Seychelles.

Under British rule, sugar cane was introduced to Réunion and quickly supplanted food production as the primary crop. It resulted in the dispossession of many small farmers who were forced to sell out to those with capital to invest in the new monoculture. The supplanted farmers migrated to the interior to find land and carry on with their agricultural activities. During this period, the Desbassyns brothers rose to success as the island's foremost sugar barons. The vanilla industry, introduced in 1819, also grew rapidly.

In 1848, the Second Republic was proclaimed in France, slavery was abolished, and Île Bourbon again became La Réunion. At the time, the island had a population of over 100,000, mostly freed slaves. Like Mauritius, Réunion immediately experienced a labour crisis and like the British in Mauritius, the French 'solved' the problem by importing contract labourers from India, most of them Hindus, to work the sugar cane. In 1865, around 75,000 immigrants arrived on the island and they remain largely distinct from the Muslim Indians who arrived in the early years of the 20th century.

The golden age of trade and development in Réunion lasted until 1870, with the country flourishing on the trade route between Europe, India and the Far East. However, competition from Cuba and the European sugar beet industry, combined

with the opening of the Suez Canal (which short-circuited the journey around the Cape of Good Hope), resulted in an economic slump; shipping decreased, the sugar industry declined and land and capital was further concentrated in the hands of a small French elite. Some small planters brightened their prospects by turning to geranium oil.

After WW I, in which 14,000 Réunionnais served, the sugar industry regained a bit of momentum but it again suffered badly through the blockade of the island during WW II.

In 1936, a left-wing political group, the Comité d'Action Démocratique et Sociale, was founded on a platform of integration with France, but after the island eventually became a *Département Français d'Outre Mer* (DOM) in 1946, they changed their minds, hoping instead for self-government (with continuing infusions of capital assistance from France). The conservatives who initially opposed integration with France for fear of losing their privileges as colonists also did an about-face when they realised that the alternative to French integration would probably be a corrupt and chaotic independence.

Despite all the second thoughts, the island now falls under the jurisdiction of the French Minister for DOM-TOM. There have been feeble independence movements from time to time but, unlike those in France's Pacific territories, they have never amounted to anything. Even the Communist Party on the island seeks autonomy rather than independence and until recently, Réunion seemed satisfied to remain totally French.

In February, 1991, however, anti-goverment riots in St-Denis left 10 people dead, and a reactionary visit by the French prime minister Michel Rocard in mid-March drew jeers from the crowds. By 1993, things appeared to have calmed down but there were still undercurrents of discontent.

### GEOGRAPHY

The island of Réunion lies 800 km east of Madagascar and 220 km south-west of

Mauritius. Just in case anyone was in doubt about its origins, its active volcano, Piton de la Fournaise, erupted in 1986, spewing lava into the sea and adding another few square metres to the island. In September 1992, it erupted again, but this time the lava stream stopped well short of the coast. Before the minor lava extension, the island was 2512 sq km in area with a circumference of 207 km, a bit larger than Mauritius, but with half the population.

There are two major mountain zones on Réunion; the older covers two-thirds of the island's western half. The highest peak is Piton des Neiges at 3069 metres, an alpine-class peak which occasionally sports a crown of snow. Surrounding it are the three immense and splendid amphitheatres: the cirques of Cilaos, Mafate and Salazie. These long, wide, deep hollows are sheer-walled canyons filled with convoluted peaks and valleys, the eroded remnants of the ancient volcanic shield which surrounded Piton des Neiges.

The smaller mountain zone lies in the south-east and hasn't yet finished evolving, with several extinct volcanoes and one that is still very much alive, the previously mentioned Piton de la Fournaise. This rumbling peak still pops its cork relatively frequently in spectacular fashion, and between eruptions quietly steams and hisses away. No one lives in the shadow of the volcano, where lava flowing down to the shore has left a spectacularly jumbled slope of cooled black volcanic rock. It's undoubtedly the island's most popular and intriguing attraction.

Between these two major mountainous zones are the high plains and the valley plains, and all the central uplands are ringed by a coastal plain of varying width. Numerous rivers wind their way down from the Piton des Neiges range, down through the cirques, cutting deeply into the coastal plains.

## Volcano Glossary

The following list of geological terms commonly used in discussions about volcanoes may be useful during visits to Piton de la Fournaise:

*aa* – sharp, rough and chunky lava from gaseous and explosive magma

*basalt* – a rock material that flows smoothly in lava form

*bombs* – chunks of volcanic ejecta that are cooled and solidified in mid-flight

*caldera* – the often immense depression formed by the collapse of a volcanic cone into its magma chamber

*dyke* – a vertical intrusion of igneous material up through cracks in horizontal rock layers

*fissure* – a break or fracture in the earth's crust where vulcanism may occur

*graben* – a valley formed by spreading and subsidence of surface material

*hornitos* – small vertical tubes produced in lava by a strong ejection of gases from beneath

*laccolith* – a mushroom-shaped dome of igneous material that has flowed upward through rock layers and then spread out horizontally, often causing hills to appear on the surface

*lava* – flowing molten rock, the name for magma after it has been ejected from a volcano

*lava cave* or *lava tube* – a tunnel or cavern caused by a lava stream flowing beneath an already solidified surface

*magma* – molten rock before it reaches the surface and becomes lava

*magma chamber* – a cavity in the rock which contains magma

*obsidian* – naturally formed volcanic glass

*pahoehoe* – ropy, smooth-flowing lava derived from non-gaseous magma.

*pillow lava* – lava formed in underwater or subglacial eruptions. It is squeezed out like toothpaste in pillow-like bulbs and solidifies immediately.

*plug* – material that has solidified in volcanic vents and is revealed by erosion

*pseudocraters* – small craters formed by steam explosions when molten material flows into a body of water

*pumice* – solidified lava froth. Pumice is so light and porous it will float on water.

*rhyolite* – light-coloured acid lava solidified into beautifully variegated rock

*scoria* – porous and glassy black or red volcanic gravel formed in fountain-like eruptions

*shield volcano* – flattish cones of oozing pahoehoe lava. Réunion's Piton de la Fournaise is a shield volcano.

*sill* – a finger or vein of molten material that squeezes between existing rock layers and solidifies

*tephra* – a collective term for all types of materials ejected from a volcano and transported through the air

## GOVERNMENT

In 1946 Réunion became a *Département Français d'Outre Mer* (DOM). It became, and remains, party to the French economy. Other DOMs are Guadeloupe, Martinique and French Guiana. The TOMs *(Territoires d'Outre Mer)* are New Caledonia, Wallis & Futuna and French Polynesia. You will often see or hear the expression DOM-TOM (which may refer as well to the two Colectivités Territoriales of Mayotte in the Comoros and St-Pierre & Miquelon off the coast of Newfoundland). In 1986, France was admitted to the IOC (Indian Ocean Commission) because of its sovereignty over Réunion (and Mayotte).

Government affairs in Réunion are the responsibility of the French Minister for DOM-TOM. The département is administered by a prefect and an elected council, and is represented in the French National Assembly by three deputies, and in the French Senate by two councillors.

## CLIMATE

Réunion not only cops it from the volcano now and again, it also gets a lashing from cyclones. A major recent one was Cyclone Clotilde, which crashed into the island on Black Friday (13 February, 1987 – a memorable Friday the 13th), causing millions of dollars' damage to crops, roads and buildings.

Because of the high mountains, the island's climate varies more than that of Mauritius. However, it still experiences only two distinct seasons: the hot, rainy (cyclonic!) summer from October to March and the cool, dry winter from April to September. The windward east coast is considerably wetter than the dry, brown west coast, but the wettest region is the heights above the east coast – the Takamaka region, the Plaine-des-Palmistes and the northern and eastern slopes of Piton de la Fournaise.

Temperatures on the coast average 21°C during winter and 28°C during summer. In the mountains, they drop to a 12°C winter average and an 18°C summer average. The south-east trade winds blow all year round and can make tramping around the volcano or up the Piton des Neiges uncomfortably cold in winter.

Mist and clouds surround the higher peaks and plains much of the time. They lift, drop and swirl spasmodically during the day. The

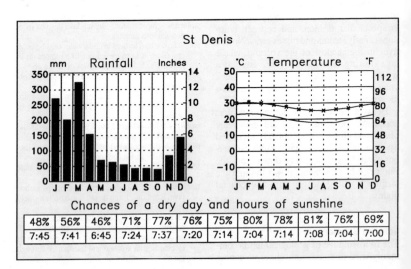

best time for viewing the landscape is at first light, before the clouds begin to build and the sun sets everything steaming.

## FLORA & FAUNA
### Flora

Parts of Réunion are like a grand botanical garden. Between the coast and the alpine peaks one finds palms, screw pines (also known as pandanus or *vacoas)*, casuarinas *(filaos)*, vanilla, spices, other tropical fruit and vegetable crops, rainforest and alpine flora. More than half the cultivable land area of Réunion is planted in sugar cane, on slopes up to about 800 metres above sea level.

Away from cultivated areas, especially on the east coast, the vegetation is lush and thick. Unlike the natural forests of Mauritius, which were done over by the defoliating Dutch, many of the forest species and environments of Réunion have survived to the present day. You won't find any of the large and grand rainforest trees which were once present; perhaps the best remaining example of the natural vegetation cover is found in the Forêt de Bélouve east of the Cirque de Salazie.

At the other extreme, the lava fields around the volcano exhibit a barren, moon-like face of the island. Here the various stages of vegetation growth, from a bare new lava base, are evident. The first plant to appear on lava is one the French call *branle vert*. Its leaves contain a combustible oil. Much later in the growth cycle come tamarind and other acacia trees.

There is a large and active forestry division, the Office National des Forêts (ONF), which is more concerned with preserving than chopping the forests. Afforestation has concentrated primarily on Japanese crypto-merias, tamarinds, coloured woods, casuarinas and cabbage palms.

Like any tropical island, Réunion has a wealth of flowering species – orchids, hibiscus, bougainvillea – and flowering trees or bushes, such as the flamboyant, frangipani, jacaranda, grevillea, acacia and mimosa.

### Fauna
**Birds** Since the arrival of humans, the flora on Réunion has fared much better than the wildlife. Like Mauritius, Réunion had dodos and giant tortoises which quickly disappeared. Another extinct wonder was the crested bourbon bird; if you want to see what it looked like, have a look at the model in the Natural History Museum in the Jardin de l'Etat in St-Denis.

The rarest bird on the island now is the *merle blanc* or cuckoo shrike (Coracina newtoni). The Créoles call it *tuit tuit*, for obvious reasons. The best chance of seeing it is on the Plaine des Chicots, directly south of St-Denis near the foot of La Roche Écrite. It is exclusive to the island, but there is a closely related species on Mauritius. Bulbuls, which resemble blackbirds and are locally known as *merles*, are more common.

The *vierge* or Mascarene paradise fly-catcher is a pretty little bird with a violet head, a small crest and a long, flowing red tail. Créoles believe the bird has seen the Virgin Mary. Other unique birds native to the highlands include the *tec-tec* or Réunion stonechat – the Créole name is onomato-poeic – and the *papangue* or Réunion harrier, a protected hawk-like bird which begins life as a little brown job and turns black and

---

### Sea Cucumbers or Bêche-de-Mer
The sea cucumber, or bêche-de-mer, is another variety of echinoderm. They are typically cucumber-like in shape but with a soft, leathery feel. There are a variety of types including *Holothuria*, *Stichopus* and *Thelonota*. You can see them scattered across shallow reef flats where they feed either on plankton or by filtering sand. Their mouth is at one end, their anus at the other and some varieties will, when alarmed, expel long sticky threads from their anus as a defence mechanism. Sea cucumbers are quite harmless. ∎

white as it grows older. Falcons and swallows are also seen.

Mynahs, introduced at the end of the 18th century to keep the grasshoppers under control, are common, as are the small, red cardinal-like birds known as *fodies*. The best known sea bird is the white *paille-en-queue* (Phaeton lepturus) or white-tailed tropicbird, which sports two long tail plumes. Other sea birds include the shearwaters and visiting albatross. Common game birds include moorhens (which may be observed around the ponds near St-Paul, Bois Rouge and Gol) and introduced quails, francolins and partridges.

Birdwatchers may want to hunt up a copy of the field guide *Oiseaux de la Réunion* (Nicholas Barré & Armand Barau, Imprimerie des Arts Graphiques Modernes, St-Denis). The text is in French but there are accurate colour illustrations of all species present on the island, identified by their Latin, English, French and Réunionnais names.

**Other Animals** During the rainy season, Réunion's roads are paved in squashed frogs; the silhouette of a flattened frog would be one of my symbols for the island. There are also tenrecs, introduced from Madagascar, which resemble hedgehogs. They are few in number and don't seem to find the roads as much of a challenge as their British counterparts.

There are a few other land creatures – some lonely deer (introduced for hunters), a hare or two (also introduced) and a few chameleons *(endormi)* – but you'd be very lucky to spot any of them. On the bright side, there are no poisonous or toothy nasties of any description.

Although land turtles were numerous on Réunion when the island was first settled, the first colonists and their animals made short work of them. Due to the hunting of sea turtles for their meat and for their shell, which is used in jewellery and other ornaments, their numbers are decreasing dramatically throughout the Indian Ocean region and worldwide. Sea turtles are farmed

in Réunion near St-Leu at the south-west end of the island.

**Insects & Spiders** The mosquitoes that plague Réunion's rainy season are nasty. Oddly enough, they seem to be at their worst in the capital, St-Denis. The higher into the hills you go, the less evident the whining little bloodsuckers become.

The most interesting creepy crawlers are the giant millipedes – some as long as a human foot – which loll around beneath rocks in more humid areas.

**Fish** Réunion, without beach fronts and reef lagoons, lacks optimum diving and snorkelling, but both activities are well catered for around St-Gilles-les-Bains. For the best view of Indian Ocean fish, go to the aquarium at the Natural History Museum in St-Denis.

The rivers contain rainbow trout (introduced) and a sort of small fry called *bichiques* – delicious when cooked in a Créole curry.

## ECONOMY

Réunion imports more than 60% of what it needs from the *Métropole* (France). In turn, France buys almost the same percentage of Réunion's products. But the island's imports are increasing at a much faster rate than its exports, and the inflation rate on the island is higher than in the métropole.

France spends an estimated 10% of its social security budget on the 1.2% of the population living in the Départements d'Outre Mer and Territoires d'Outre Mer (DOM-TOM), of which Réunion is one. The island's initially shocking official unemployment rate of 36%, however, is misleading: the majority of Réunion's unemployment is voluntary and workers are frequently imported from the métropole to satisfy the demand for both professional and unskilled labour.

The basis of the island's economy is agriculture, which, in turn, is based on the sugar cane that covers 65% of the arable land and accounts for 80% of the agricultural revenue.

Sugar has a guaranteed market and fixed prices within the EC. From the molasses, rum and cane spirit are produced, but these are not widely available outside France. There are several sugar factories which offer tours to visitors during the cutting season in July.

Réunion is the world's largest producer of geranium oil, but don't expect to see acres of beautiful flowers as in Holland. The oil, used as a fixative in perfumes, is drawn from the leaves of the plants. It is still a cottage industry, concentrated mainly around Maïdo and Le Tampon, and most producers use a crude, but effective, home-made still to extract the oil.

Oil from vétiver (an Asian grass) roots is also produced, though on a much smaller scale (around 15 tonnes annually), in the foothills near St-Pierre and St-Joseph. There were also once large plantations of ylang-ylang, a bush whose yellow flowers yield an overpowering essence, but this industry died out during the 1970s. (Madagascar and the Comoros still produce large quantities of ylang-ylang.)

The cultivation of vanilla, which is concentrated on the east coast between Ste-Suzanne and St-Philippe, has been a limited but stable earner since the last century; the island currently exports around 100 tonnes of vanilla annually. Tobacco has recently made a comeback (the local Amarello brand is black) and popular spice crops include black pepper, cloves and cinnamon. Maize, potatoes, lentils, beans, garlic, onions and such warm weather fruits as lychees, mandarins, oranges, bananas, lemons, papayas and mangoes are also produced in significant amounts.

Livestock-wise, pig breeding satisfies local consumption and poultry farms keep the populace in eggs and the ubiquitous *cari poulet* (chicken curry). At St-Leu, there's a marine turtle farm which keeps around 6000 turtles for their meat and shell.

With few good harbours, the fishing industry is small and restricted; however, Réunion oversees fish factories on the sub-Antarctic French islands of St-Paul and Amsterdam more than 3000 km to the south-east.

The island has no mineral resources to speak of so there's little industry apart from construction, sugar refining and food and drink processing.

## Tourism

One of the biggest drawbacks to the development of Réunion as an international tourism destination is the tropical paradise image of nearby Mauritius, which is cheaper and has much better beaches. The French, not surprisingly, are by far the most numerous visitors to Réunion, with more than 40,000 annually taking advantage of special air fares from the métropole.

A few thousand Swiss tourists (primarily French-speaking) and quite a few shopping-happy Mauritians also arrive each year. Other nationalities number in the hundreds; on our research trip, we didn't encounter a single native English speaker and in fact, the only non-French travellers we met were in a German trekking group in the Cirque de Mafate.

## POPULATION & PEOPLE

Réunion has a larger land area than Mauritius, but its population of 620,000 is about half that of its neighbour. Because the birthrate has been quite high for the past 25 years, the population is weighted in favour of youth, with 40% of the population under 20 years of age. The population is expected to grow to 700,000 by the turn of the century.

Réunion has the same population mix of Europeans, Indians, Muslims, Chinese and Créoles as Mauritius, but in different proportions. The Indians *(malabars)* comprise about 20% of the population and the Chinese 3% and Muslims *(z'arabes)* 1%. In Mauritius, the British and the Franco-Mauritians did not intermarry with freed African slaves but the Réunion French did not discriminate, and today the Créoles are the largest ethnic group, comprising 40% of the population.

Most of the French who did the mixing – the original settlers – were Bretons and

Normans with distinctly Celtic features, and at the village of Palmiste Rouge, near Cilaos, the Créole inhabitants retain the red *(rouge)* hair of their ancestors. The Créoles themselves range in colour from black through every copper or bronze tint to Parisian porcelain. The main division amongst Créoles is between country and city folk; some mountain people even resemble the Cajuns of Louisiana.

After the Créoles, white Europeans (ie, French) make up the largest group. They are involved in the island's administration and business, generally come from France and are called *z'oreilles* (the ears) by the Créoles, who imagine them to be straining to hear what's being said about them in the local *patois*. Other visitors, unless they're a coloured brother or sister, are treated in a not-too-serious manner as z'oreilles.

## ARTS & CULTURE

One of the great pleasures of visiting Réunion is getting a taste of Créole-flavoured French culture, or French-flavoured Créole culture. For news of cultural activities on the island contact the Office Départemental de la Culture (☎ 41 11 41), based at the Jardin de l'Etat in St-Denis. It publishes a free monthly newsletter, *Trajectoires*, available at tourist and travel offices, giving details of forthcoming theatre, jazz and classical music performances, exhibitions, cinema, conferences and photography events, many of which have youth and student rates. They also have a recorded information line (☎ 21 44 61) and act as a central body for ticket reservations (☎ 21 16 94).

### Dance

It is interesting to see how the *séga* (traditional dance) differs here from the Mauritian, Seychellois and Malagasy versions. There are more variations in Réunion because the slaves adopted and adapted the dances of the white settlers, particularly the quadrille, to their own African rhythms. The séga is now danced by everyone in the manner of a shuffling rock step.

The more traditional slaves' dance in Réunion is called the *maloya*, a slower, more reflective rhythm, similar to the New Orleans blues. A séga or maloya performance is often accompanied by melancholy ballads or *romances*. Séga and maloya music, as well as other Créole sounds, are available on cassette for F80 or on vinyl for F95.

Instruments used by the band range from traditional home-made percussion pieces, such as the hide-covered *houleur* drum and the maraca-like *caïambe*, to the accordion and modern band instruments.

Some of the best exponents of ségas and maloyas belong to the Group Créolie, which is under the direction of Gerard Pillant. They are resident at the Novotel Hotel (☎ 24 44 44) in St-Gilles-les-Bains. If you can't make it to one of the hotel or other scheduled performances, you may catch them rehearsing behind the hotel near the beach. Etincelles Pannonaises, from Bras-Panon in the north-east, is another big group, with 25 members. Stéphanie, from the same town, has 18 members.

### Music

Réunion mixes the African rhythms of reggae, séga and maloya with the best of French, British and American rock and folk music. As for Créole-flavoured modern sounds, the Réunionnais leave that to their tropical cousins in Martinique and Guadeloupe (these are also popular listening in Réunion, especially the French-Caribbean disco groups Kassav and Zouk Machine). Compagnie Créole, now based in Paris, has won a greater middle-of-the-road success. A new local favourite is rastaman Michel Fock, known professionally as Ti-Fock, who adds a synthesized touch to traditional maloya and séga rhythms.

It's all catchy stuff, and you'll hear it in bars, discos and vehicles throughout the Indian Ocean. A good selection of séga, maloya and jazz recordings is available at Megatop (☎ 41 00 41) at the corner of Alexis de Villeneuve and Jean Chatel in St-Denis.

St-Louis is a relatively quiet, dull town for visitors, but it boasts three good folk groups

– Pangar, Lèv la Têt and Jeunesse Komèla. At St-Gilles-les-Bains, several hotels and restaurants offer folk soirées with music and dancing.

## Art

If there is a distinctive Créole sculpture or painting style in the Indian Ocean, it's easy to miss. The tone favoured by local artists seems to be European. It doesn't always work but it can be interesting: it's either too bright and gaudy, too ordered and dull, or too much like Gauguin!

There are at least 15 professional artists living and working in Réunion. Among them is Philippe Turpin of Cilaos who etches onto copper and then rolls the prints off the inky plates. But the effect, like the technique, has little to do with Créole tradition. Instead, he captures the wonder of Réunion in a fantastical, almost medieval way; his renditions of the cirques resemble illustrations of fairy kingdoms. His prices are fantastic too, but the work is worth the money if you have it. Turpin's studio in the mountain spa village of Cilaos is open to the public.

Another artist who welcomes visitors (and sales) is Bruno Czaja, whose studio is on the south-west coast road near Les Avirons. A former student of the Leonardo Da Vinci Academy in Italy, Czaja claims to have discovered a new style of painting, which is effective in capturing lava effects.

The work of other artists and artesans can be seen at Galerie Artisanale at the Centre Euromarché between St-Denis and the airport or at the Boutique Artisanale de L'Association Lacaze (beside Maison de la Montagne) on Place Sarda Garriga in St-Denis; at Galerie Cote Cour in St-Gilles-les-Bains; and at Galerie Vincent, on Chemin Archambaud between Le-Tampon and St-Pierre.

For those interested in sculpture there are a couple artists of note in St-Louis: Karl Payet, 20 Impasse des Qautais, Cité Luce Fontaine, La Rivière; and Gilbert Clain, 184 Route de Cilaos, La Rivière. In St-Joseph, there's Claude Berlie Caillat, 62 rue Marius et Ary Leblond. Nearer to St-Denis, in La Montagne, is Eric Pontgerard, 18 Chemin de la Boucle, Route de la Montagne.

Woodworking, including 'East India Company' furniture and miniature replicas of Créole architecture homes, is on display and sale at the Centre Artisanal du Bois in Rivière St-Louis.

If you'd like to see a bit of transplanted European art, visit the Museum Léon Dierx at the top of the Rue de Paris in St-Denis. It contains paintings by well-known artists, including works by Gauguin, Renoir and Picasso.

## Architecture

The distinctive 18th century Créole architecture of Réunion is evident in both the *grands villas créoles* (homes of wealthy planters and other *colons)* and the *tit' cases créoles*, the homes of the common folk.

The style which is marked primarily by the lovely *varangues* (immense open verandahs) fringed with delicate, lace-like *lambrequins* or *dentelles* (rows of carved wooden cutout borders above roofs, windows and overhangs) is at risk of being undermined by modern European square block architecture. The cost and the effort involved in designing, creating and maintaining the traditional look is generally no longer considered cost effective. However, there is now an organised government entity, the *Conseil Departemental d'Architecture*, which exists to ensure the preservation of remaining examples.

## Theatre

The island has several excellent professional theatre groups. Théâtre Vollard is the most established. The group works out of the 300-seat theatre at 23 rue Léopold Rambaud in St-Denis. Other professional troupes include Théâtre Talipot and the newly established Théâtre Dallon.

Of the companies, Vollard is the most conventional and Talipot the more progressive and experimental. Both base the classic or avant-garde forms of Western theatre on Créole traditions. Their island tours usually cover the main theatres: Fourçade at Grand

Marché, Vollard at rue Léopold Rambaud, the Salle François Truffaut at Jardin de L'Etat and L'Espace Culturel de Champ-Fleuri, all in St-Denis; the theatre in Le Tampon; and the Théâtre de Plein Air amphitheatre outside St-Gilles-les-Bains. Often the groups take productions overseas to Madagascar, Mauritius and Mayotte.

## SPORTS

The affluent European life style leads to many sporting as well as cultural distractions. There is nothing particularly Réunionnais about the main Créole pastimes on the island: soccer, volleyball and handball are all popular, judging by the extent given to the local leagues in the press. *Pétanque* or *boules*, a game in which metal balls are thrown to land as near as possible to a target ball, is another favourite. Boxing, cycling, martial arts, athletics, hockey and even rugby are also popular. The surrounding Indian Ocean countries provide the competition on an international basis.

Then there's cockfighting. It is not outlawed, but neither is it widespread or promoted. It takes place in St-Pierre every Monday after 5 pm at 182 Rue du Four à Chaux. There's an entry fee of a few francs. Call Mme Vayaboury (☎ 25 00 42) for details.

## RELIGION
### Catholicism

The Catholic faith dominates the island's religious character. It is visible in the shrines along every highway and byway, in caves and at cliff tops (many of these were constructed for family members killed in accidents on those sites), and in the many saint's days and holidays. St-Denis, the capital, shuts down on Sunday, when half the city goes to *the* beach – Boucan Canot!

**St-Expédit** Oddly enough, one popular saint in Réunion is St-Expédit, whose origin is attributed to a box of *un*attributed religious relics and icons shipped from Rome to a new chapel in Paris. Legend has it that the nuns who received the box saw the Italian word *espedito* (expedited) on the box and guess what...the new chapel was christened La Chapelle de St-Expédit!

The idea was brought to Réunion in 1931 when a local woman erected a statue to the 'saint' in l'Église de la Délivrance as a *remerciement* (thanks offering) for answering her prayer to return to Réunion. Another version has it that Réunion had requested that the Vatican send the relics of a powerful saint who could be used as the island's patron, and the box bore the word *expédit*. Either way, it's bizarre.

Over the years, it was somehow twisted into a rather sinister voodoo cult. Shrines to St-Expédit, which are normally covered in brilliant red paint representing blood, abound around the southern end of the island and are used primarily for wishing ill on others. Beheaded statues (which are common) are normally the result of either unanswered petitions or the fears of paranoid potential victims.

### Other Religions

Hindus and Muslims are permitted to follow their respective religions freely and most large towns have both a mosque and a temple. Traditional Hindu rites such as *pandialé* or *teemeedee*, which includes fire walking, and *cavadee*, which includes the practice of piercing one's cheeks with silver needles, take place regularly. (For further information on these rites, see under Cultural Events in the Mauritius – Facts for the Visitor chapter.) Interestingly, a great deal of syncretism with Catholicism has evolved over the years – and vice versa. In fact, many of the Malabar-Réunionnais participate in Catholic rites and rituals as well as those of the Indian community.

Apart from celebration of Chinese New Year, the well-dispersed Sino-Réunionnais community is not too conspicuous in its traditional or religious practices.

## LANGUAGE

French is the official language, but Créole is the most widely spoken. Few people speak

English. Réunion Créole is even beyond understanding by the French – deliberately so, I suspect, on the Créoles' part. A word which means one thing in French can mean something completely different in Créole. And where a word does have the same meaning, Créoles pronounce it differently.

The Créoles have quite a number of *bons mots* and charming idioms, which are often the result of Hindi, Arab and Malagasy influences or misinterpretations of the original French word. *Bonbon la fesse* (bum toffee) is a suppository, *conserves* (preserves) are sunglasses, *bazaar* is the market and *coeur* *d'amant* (lover's heart) is a cardamom seed. *Coco* is your head, *caze* is a house, *marmaille* is a child, *baba* is a baby, *band* means family, *le fait noir* means night, and, if the stars are out, *mi aime jou* means 'I love you'.

Two basic rules of Créole speech are not to pronounce 'r', or to do so lightly, and to turn the soft 'j' or 'ch' sounds of French into 'z' or 's', as in *manzay* for *manger* (to eat), *zamais* for *jamais* (never), and *sontay* for *chanter* (to sing).

You'll find French-Créole dictionaries for sale in Réunion, but none for English speakers.

# Facts for the Visitor

## VISAS & EMBASSIES

The visa requirements for entry to Réunion are the same as for France. Citizens of the USA, Canada, New Zealand, most European countries and a handful of other countries may enter France for up to three months without a visa. Australians, on the other hand, must have visas which are normally valid for stays of up to three months. Technically, all visitors must produce a return or onward ticket – or they may be asked to leave money to cover the cost of one. However, on our several visits, we've never been asked for tickets.

Visa applications should be made to the French Embassy or Consulate nearest your home address. In the Indian Ocean region, there are French Embassies in Mauritius, Madagascar, Comoros and the Seychelles but at any of these, there can be long waits – sometimes for several weeks.

### French Embassies & Consulates

Australia
>   French Embassy, 6 Perth Ave, Yarralumla, Canberra, ACT 2600 (☎ (062) 270 5111)

Canada
>   French Embassy, 42 Sussex Drive, Ottawa, Ontario K1M 2C9 (☎ (613) 232 1795)

Germany
>   Französische Botschaft, Rheinstrasse 52, 5300 Bonn (☎ (0228) 362031)

New Zealand
>   French Embassy, Robert Jones House, 1-3 Willeston St, Wellington (☎ (04) 720 200)

UK
>   French Embassy, 58 Knightsbridge, London SW1X (☎ (071) 235 8080)

USA
>   French Embassy, 4645 Reservoir Rd NW, Washington, DC 20007 (☎ (202) 298 4000)

### Foreign Consulates in Réunion

The Malagasy Consulate (☎ 21 05 21), is a 2nd-floor office at 77 Rue Juliette Dodu in St-Denis, a block up the street from the Air Madagascar office. It is open Monday to Friday from 8.30 to 11.30 am. On receipt of F150, four identical application forms and four passport photos, the consulate will issue a 90-day visa within 48 hours.

If you want to visit South Africa, nationals of all countries, except the UK, Germany and Switzerland, need a visa. The South African Consulate (☎ 21 50 05) is in the Compagnie des Indes Orientales building at 18 Rue de la Compagnie, near the Avenue de la Victoire, and is open Monday to Friday from 8.30 am to 4 pm. You will need only one application form and photo. There's no charge for a visa valid for up to three months. Although it's no longer such a major issue, ask for the visa on a separate paper rather than stamped in your passport; in theory, this prevents problems when entering countries with a less than rosy view of South Africa.

The British honorary consul, R Gault (☎ 21 06 19), is at 2 Rue de la Digue in St-Denis. The German consul is at 18 Rue Papangue, 97490 St-Clotilde (☎ 28 13 02).

Photography shops will do passport/visa pictures, but it's cheaper to go to an automatic photo booth; there's one near the Prefecture on Avenue de la Victoire and another at the corner of Rue Marechal Leclerc and Felix Guyon, both in St-Denis.

## MONEY

### Currency

The French franc is the unit of currency and the more francs you have, the happier you'll feel about staying in Réunion. They can go quickly and in bulk if you are not prepared. Franc notes come in denominations of 500, 200, 100, 50 and 20; franc coins in 10, five, two and one. There are 100 centimes in a franc; centime coins come in denominations of 50, 20, 10, five and one.

### Exchange Rates

At the time of publication, the exchange rate for the franc was:

| US$1 | = | F5.45 |
|------|---|-------|
| A$1 | = | F3.66 |
| UK£1 | = | F8.25 |
| C$1 | = | F4.28 |
| NZ$1 | = | F2.94 |
| DM1 | = | F3.36 |

## Changing Money

The main banks are Banque de la Réunion (BR), Crédit Agricole (CA) and Banque Française Commerciale (BFC). There's technically no problem changing foreign currency in Réunion – all banks offer exchange facilities – but low official exchange rates and punitive commissions (normally 3% to 5%) on changing foreign currency travellers' cheques make it sensible to carry French francs – or at least French franc travellers' cheques – for your stay in Réunion. Eurocheques may be cashed at Crédit Agricole.

Be warned that the Crédit Agricole branch at Gillot Airport is only open from 10.30 am to 7 pm, except on Sunday, when it opens at 1 pm. If you're arriving at an odd hour, be sure to have some French francs.

The American Express agency in Réunion is Bourbon Voyages (☎ 21 68 18) at 14 Rue Rontaunay in St-Denis but they don't change money or travellers' cheques. In a pinch, try the main hotels, including the Méridien, Ascotel, Bourbon or Central, all of which will exchange currency but always at a real premium.

Probably the most widely accepted credit card is VISA. At the time of writing, only French-issued cards may be used in the banks' magic money machines. However, very recent reports indicate that this is changing and international VISA and MasterCard charge cards may now be used in bank and post office cash dispensers. The new cash dispenser booths being set up by Crédit Agricole Banks are called *gabiers*, a new word derived from *guichet automatique bancaire*.

It is also possible to make cash draws on VISA cards over the counter at Crédit Agricole on Rue Felix Guyon in St-Denis. Some form of identification, preferably a passport, will be necessary for the transaction.

## Costs

For information on costs in Réunion, see the Costs section in the introductory Facts for the Visitor chapter.

## Tipping

Most restaurants include service charges in their prices and surprisingly don't encourage additional tipping, but those which advertise *service non compris* on their menus definitely expect something. Also surprisingly, neither do taxi drivers seem to expect tips. Naturally, a *pourboire* would be accepted, but with prices so high anyway, few people seem inclined to increase the pain of it all.

## WHEN TO GO

Climate should be your first consideration if you want to experience Réunion at its best. Unless you have webbed feet, there's no point in setting out to explore the cirques on foot if all you can expect weather-wise is swirling mist, pouring rain and slippery slide walking tracks. The only time to seriously consider trekking through Réunion's spectacular mountain country is during the dry season from April to October. For more specific information, read the discussion under Climate in the Réunion – Facts about the Island chapter.

The down side of climate-related trip planning is that everyone else has the same idea. April, May and the French school holidays from late July to early September are the busiest times to visit, and in August you risk being left high and dry without accommodation unless you book in advance. This is also high trekking season and the mountain gîtes are packed out, so if you dare brave the crowds, you may want to pack a tent. Even non-walkers will have problems, having to battle it out at the beach resorts or manoeuvering through the heavy traffic. And just try to get a bunk at the vehicle-accessible Gîte du Volcan in August!

The Christmas/New Year holidays also attract crowds which fill hotels and pensions.

However, the northern winter holidays fall in the middle of Réunion's hot rainy season so there isn't much of a demand on mountain gîtes.

The quietest times are during cyclone-prone February and March. The seasons normally change in April and that isn't too bad for a visit but for maximum spatial and climatic enjoyment, May and June are probably the best months of all.

One reader, however, recommends visiting between late September and mid-October:

The climate was beautiful – the coast had warm days with bright sun every morning and usually a bit of cloud cover in the afternoon and the occasional windy day. In the evenings you could eat outside (in long trousers rather than shorts, though). Up in the mountains, the mornings were sunny and if you climbed above the clouds the afternoons were, too. (Climbing the volcano we got bad sunburn on the few square inches of skin we forgot to smear with sun cream.) It was perfect hiking weather. Evening were pleasantly cool and there were no mozzies!

Furthermore, flights were cheap; hotels weren't all full and some had reduced off-season rates; it was dry but most of the waterfalls were still doing their stuff; and the coast wasn't swamped with tourists. The only drawback is that some places may be closed – it's best to ring restaurants to make sure they're open, especially if you must travel some way to get there.

## TOURIST OFFICES
### Local Tourist Offices

To compensate for its high costs, Réunion has excellent tourist information resources and with the funding of the French government behind them, services are generally as good as you may expect.

For sources of trekking information, refer to the discussion of Trekking in the Activities section later in this chapter. Ordinary tourist queries should be taken to the main Syndicat d'Initiative (☎ 41 83 00) in St-Denis at 48 Rue Ste-Marie. It has an efficient staff, a couple of whom speak English, and they also operate a terrific information and welcome counter at Gillot airport to meet international flights. They'll offer plenty of advice and information and provide myriad maps, brochures and advertising.

The branch offices at St-Pierre, Bras Panon, Plaine-des-Palmistes, St-Benoît, St-Gilles-les-Bains, Salazie, St-André and Cilaos are also helpful, but many are staffed by only one person and seem to be open sporadic hours. I attempted to visit the Syndicat d'Inititive at Plaine-des-Palmistes in the high tourist season (August) at various posted opening hours and never found it open.

Addresses of Syndicats d'Initiative and tourist offices, heading clockwise around the island from St-Denis, are:

Syndicat d'Initiative de St-Denis, 48 Rue Ste-Marie, 97400 St-Denis (☎ 41 83 00)
Office Municipal du Tourisme de St-André, 68 Centre Commercial, Rue de la Gare, 97440 St-André (☎ 46 91 63)
Syndicat d'Initiative de Salazie, Mairie Annexe, Rue Georges Pompidou, 97433 Salazie (☎ 47 50 14)
Syndicat d'Initiative de Bras-Panon, 21 Route Nationale, 97412 Bras Panon (☎ 51 50 62)
Syndicat d'Initiative Région Est, 44 Rue Amiral Bouvet, 97470 St-Benoît (☎ 50 10 65)
Syndicat d'Initiative de la Plaine-des-Palmistes, Place de la Mairie, 97431 Plaine-des-Palmistes (☎ 51 32 57)
Office Municipal du Tourisme de St-Philippe, Place de la Mairie, 69 Rue Leconte de Lisle, 97442 St-Philippe (☎ 37 10 43)
Syndicat d'Initiative de St-Pierre, 27 Rue Archambaud, 97410 St-Pierre (☎ 25 02 36)
Syndicat d'Initiative de Cilaos, 2 Rue Victor Mac Auliffe, 97413 Cilaos (☎ 31 78 03)
Syndicat d'Initiative de l'Entre-Deux, 9 Rue Fortuné Hoareau, 97414 Entre-Deux (☎ 39 62 99)
Syndicat d'Initiative de l'Étang-Salé, Ancienne gare du chemin de fer, Rue Octave Bénard, 97427 Étang-Salé (☎ 26 67 32)
Syndicat d'Initiative de l'Ouest, Galerie Amandine, 97434 St-Gilles-les-Bains (☎ 24 57 47)
Syndicat d'Initiative de La Possession, 3 Rue Nelson Mandela, 97419 La Possession (☎ 44 73 66)

The Comité du Tourisme de la Réunion publishes a monthly magazine called *RUN* (RUN is the airport code for St-Denis) which outlines current happenings of interest to tourists and contains articles about various aspects of the island. In addition, twice annually, they publish *RUN – le guide*, a directory of hotels, restaurants, night clubs, travel agencies and other addresses of tourist interest. A new large format publication which may or may not endure is *Escapades*, which bills itself as *Le Magazine Touristique de la Réunion*. It contains a variety of articles about island culture, attractions and leisure activities as well as advertising for tourist-related establishments.

All three publications are available free at Syndicats d'Initiative around the island, however they are in French only. If you want to obtain a copy before you arrive in Réunion, contact the Comité du Tourisme de la Réunion (☎ 21 00 41) at Résidence Vétyver, 23 Rue Tourette, 97482 St-Denis.

For information on accommodation in rural gîtes, contact the Relais Départemental des Gîtes Ruraux (☎ 20 31 90; fax 21 83 36), Résidence Ste-Anne, 18 Rue de Ste-Anne, 87400 St-Denis.

### Overseas Reps

For advance information and details on coming events and major changes on the island, you could try contacting Réunion's tourism representatives abroad. The French one is the best bet as the other offices are unlikely to keep much information on Réunion. The representatives are:

**Australia**
French Tourist Bureau, Kindersley House, 33 Bligh St, Sydney, NSW 2000 (☎ (02) 231 5244)
**France**
Conseil Général de la Réunion, 3 Rue du Faubourg St-Honoré, 75008 Paris (☎ (1) 42 66 33 80)
Comité du Tourisme de la Réunion, 90 Rue de la Boétie, 75008, Paris (☎ (1) 40 75 02 79)
**South Africa**
French Tourist Office, 9 Summit Rd, Dunkeld West 2196 (P O Box 41022, Craighall 2024), Johannesburg (☎ (011) 880 80 62)
**UK**
French Tourist Bureau, 178 Piccadilly, London W1V 0AL (☎ 493 6594)
**USA**
French Tourist Bureau, 610 Fifth Ave, New York, NY 10020 (☎ (900) 990 0040 – NB: this is a pay-for-service number)

### Foreign Tourist Offices

Madagascar is the only Indian Ocean country with representatives in Réunion, namely Air Madagascar and the consulate, but don't expect miracles information-wise.

Mauritius is represented by Air Mauritius (☎ 41 33 00) at 3 Rue de la Victoire, St-Denis. And only the Réunion Air Service, 9 Rue du Mât-de-Pavillon, St-Denis, has any information on Mayotte and the Comoros – and Mayotte is a French territory!

### BUSINESS HOURS & HOLIDAYS

Lunches are long, relaxed affairs in Réunion; shops and businesses are generally open from 9 am to noon and from 2.30 to 6 pm. Most shops are closed on Saturday afternoons and some are closed on Monday mornings. On Sunday, the streets are almost eerily silent.

The main banks, Banque de la Réunion (BR), Crédit Agricole (CA) and Banque Française Commerciale (BFC), are open Monday to Friday from 8 am to 4 pm, all with branches in each major town. The CA branch at Gillot airport is open each day from 10.30 am to 7 pm, except on Sunday, when it opens at 1 pm.

ILE de la REUNION

RF

Réunion Coat of Arms

## Holidays

Public holidays in Réunion include:

*New Year's Day* – 1 January
*Labour Day* – 1 May
*Victory Day 1945* – 8 May
*Ascension* – May
*Bastille Day* – 14 July
*Assumption* – 15 August
*All Saints' Day* – 1 November
*Armistice Day* – 11 November
*Christmas Day* – 25 December

## CULTURAL EVENTS

Major festivals in Réunion involve exhibitions with sales, competitions, sports events, music, dancing, and various other activities. For exact details contact any of the Syndicats d'Initiative (Tourist Offices) or the *Mairie* (Town Hall) in the respective towns. The Indian community is principally made up of Tamil Hindus and in November, December, January, March, April and July they hold some amazing rites, including cavadees and fire-walking ceremonies. The Hindu temple in St-André is the most popular location for these events. Again, the Syndicats d'Initiative will have details; alternatively, ask them to ring Mr Samourgompoullé (☎ 21 99 69).

Towns and villages across the island take turns at celebrating over a week or weekend; the excuse is to honour their primary product, which can be anything from chouchou to sugar cane. One British couple attended several of these festivals and made the following assessment:

Don't expect a lot of local colour at most of these events. You'll hear more amplified rap, reggae and rock than any indigenous music. There's usually a beauty contest in which the girls are white, or made up to look as pale as possible, and the feted produce is most apparent in its relative absence!

**Ginette & Peter Scott**

*Fête du Miel Vert* (honey)
Le-Tampon, one week in mid-January
*Fête du Vacoa* (rope made from the screw pine fronds)
St-Benoît, April
*Fête du Chou Chou*
Hell-Bourg, first weekend in May
*Fête de la Vanille* (vanilla)
Bras-Panon, 10 days in mid-May

*Fête des Goyaviers* (guava trees)
Plaine-des-Palmistes, a weekend in June
*Fête de la Canne* (sugar cane)
Ste-Rose, end of July
*Fête de St-Paul*
St-Paul, two weeks in July
*Foire du Bois* (wood)
Rivière-St-Louis, 10 days at the beginning of August
*Fête du Safran* (saffron)
St-Joseph, 10 days in August
*Exposition des Fleurs* (flower show)
Le Tampon, end of September or beginning of October
*Fête de la Rose* (roses)
St-Benoît, five days in November
*Fête des Lentilles* (lentils)
Cilaos, a weekend in November
*Fête des Mangoustans* (mangosteens)
St-Benoît, November
*Foire de St-Pierre*
St-Pierre, 10 days at the beginning of December
*Fête des Letchis* (lychees)
St-Denis, one week in mid-December
*Fête de l'Ail* (garlic)
Petite-Île, a weekend in December

## POST & TELECOMMUNICATIONS

Post offices (known as *La Poste* or PTTs) are open Monday to Friday from 7.30 am to 6 pm, and on Saturdays from 8 am to noon. Many close for lunch between noon and 2 pm; those that do remain open through the lunch hour can get extremely crowded.

Since French post offices normally offer a vast array of services – from banking to gas and telephone bill collection – queues can be very long and slow. Fortunately, there's normally a special desk or window for those poor souls who only want a couple of postcard stamps.

The central PTT is in St-Denis, at the corner of Rue du Maréchal Leclerc and Rue Juliette Dodu.

### Sending Mail

Airmail letters under 20 grams to anywhere within France (including the métropole and DOM-TOM) costs F2.50. For every additional 10 grams, there's a surcharge of F30 for the métropole and F70 for DOM-TOM.

To anywhere else in the EC, Austria, Liechtenstein or Switzerland, letters up to 20 grams go for F2.50. To the rest of the world, they're F3.40. For letters weighing 20 to 50 grams, postage costs F4 to the EC, F5.50 to francophone Africa and F6 to anywhere else.

For packages, SAL (Surface Air-Lifted) is available at a considerable discount over regular airmail and we've found it to be quite reliable.

### Receiving Mail

Poste restante is at the main post office on Rue Juliette Dodu at the Boîtes de Commerce door. To avoid confusion, post should probably be addressed according to French tradition – with the surname first followed by the given name. If you want things to run even more smoothly, tell potential correspondents to capitalise or underline the surname. Poste restante charges F2.20 tax per letter collected; if you're expecting a bag of mail, get an address!

### Telephones

The Réunion telephone and telex system is efficient. There are 500 public telephones scattered around the island and you can directly dial international numbers on them. However, very few coin phones remain in Réunion; most public telephones accept only Télécartes (telephone cards). Telephone cards with 50 or 120 impulses are available at post offices and shops for F35 and F85 respectively.

Local calls cost F1 and calls to other locations in Réunion cost F1 per minute. Calls to Australia are F23.10 per minute and to the UK, Canada or USA, they cost F18.50. Calls to other locations in France range from F3.85 to F11 (peak) per minute. British Telecom charge card holders may charge calls from Réunion by dialling 19-0044 (pay phones need a F1 coin or a Télécarte).

To phone Réunion from abroad, dial the international access code followed by the Réunion code (262) and the number desired.

In St-Denis, the emergency number for police is (☎ 21 00 17). The ambulance is at (☎ 20 10 10) in St-Denis and (☎ 25 16 16) in St-Pierre.

### TIME

Réunion is four hours ahead of GMT (Greenwich Mean Time) and UTC (Universal Time Coordinated), making it four hours ahead of London in the northern winter and three hours ahead from April to October. It is two hours ahead of Johannesburg year round, and in the winter, is nine hours ahead of New York and Toronto, 12 hours ahead of San Francisco and Vancouver and four hours behind Perth, Australia.

### ELECTRICITY

The current in Réunion is 220 volts. Outlets take continental two-pin plugs, so British and non-European visitors should use an adaptor for electric appliances.

### BOOKS & MAPS

There is a fine selection of books on Réunion but they're mostly in French. If you want the best guidebook in English (and practically the only guidebook in English!), you're looking at it!

### General

If you're looking for a French treatise on the island, the best choice is Catherine Lavaux's *La Réunion: Du Battant des Lames au Sommet des Montagnes* (Editions Cormorans, Paris, 1975). The hardcover volume of this highly recommended travelogue and history will set you back a whopping F300. In the paperback *Que Sais-Je* series, there's a general interest history book on Réunion by André Scherer (PUF, Paris, 1973).

Taking the emphasis off the French text, with good colour plates of the island, are the F200 books by Folco, Salvat & Robert: *La Réunion* has photos from ground level, and *La Réunion – Vue du Ciel* contains magnificent aerial shots. For a cheaper, colourful alternative and an accompanying English translation of the text, there's *L'Île de la Réunion* by Claude Huc (Editions Delroisse, Boulogne) for around F160.

For pre-trip reading, you can look out for *Blue Africa* by Australian Colin Simpson

(1981), writing about his organised tour through Africa. It has a chapter on Réunion.

## Fiction

The market for historical romances seems to have been cornered by one Daniel Vauxelaire, whose books are in French. In *Blue Africa*, however, Colin Simpson refers to one called *Island of Fire* by fellow Australian writer Helga Mayne. Set among slaves and Napoleonic officers, it sounds like a variation on *Mandingo*.

## Travel Guides

In English, the only locally available guide is the translation of Albert Trotet's locally published booklet *Tourist Guide to Réunion Island* (1979) at F55. Especially if you're interested in architecture, it's well worth the investment. However, there are few English copies still available and you may have to resort to the French version, *Guide Touristique de la Réunion*.

The only other English language option is *Visitor's Guide to Mauritius, Rodrigues & Réunion* by Katerina & Eric Roberts (Moorland, UK, 1992) but it's more like an expanded tourist office brochure than a practical guide and Réunion gets only 24 pages.

There are several standard French guides: the colourful *La Réunion Aujourd'hui* by Hureau & Bruyère (Les Editions Jeune Afrique, Paris, 1990); the detailed *Le Guide Pratique* by Serge Hoarau (Mercure Océan Indien, St-Pierre, 1986) for F50; the very general *à la Réunion, à l'Île Maurice, aux Seychelles* (Guide Hachette, Paris, 1989); and the oddly organised *Îles de l'Ocean Indien: Réunion, Maurice, Les Seychelles* by Jean-Pierre Jardel (Guide Arthaud, Paris, 1990). In addition, there's another expanded tourist brochure sort of book entitled *Evasions Réunion*, edited by Agostina Calderon (Editions Evasions, St-Denis). The photos are nice and it includes a large map.

A new hardback book, called *Bonjour Réunion*, part of the French *Bonjour* series, is a very good source of basic background material on the island and is full of nice colour photos. It purports to be a travel guide

*pour voyageurs curieux*, but the very limited practical information is next to useless.

Of several German language guides available, the best seems to be *Richtig Reisen – Réunion* by Dirk & Henriette Althoff (DuMont Buchverlag, Köln, 1991).

For hikers there is a series of five booklets by Mayer & Vaxelaire called *Suivez Le Guide* for F55 each, which cover different regions of the island. They were published in 1979, but the trekking circuit has changed little. For more concise information on treks in Réunion, pick up the useful (but confusingly formatted!) *Île de la Réunion – GR R1 et GR R2*. They're available at Maison de la Montagne in St-Denis. Another walking book available in some shops is *50 Itineraires de Promenades Pedestres à la Réunion*.

Another excellent hiking guide is the *Topoguide*, a meticulously detailed description of Réunion's hiking routes complete with interesting background information on the history, flora, fauna and geology along the way. It also includes particulars on all the gîtes and chambres d'hôtes in Réunion's backcountry. It's available from the Office Nationale des Forêts (☎ 20 10 59), Colline de la Providence, St-Denis, and at major St-Denis bookshops.

## Miscellaneous

Réunion is a fascinating place for the magically minded. Créole beliefs and potions have spawned a number of books on voodoostyle sorcery. For the serious student there is a four-book set entitled *Vertus et Secrets des Plantes Médicinales des Tropiques et de la Réunion* by Dr Robert Zamore & Ary Ebroin. You will have to conjure up F2400 for it though.

The treasure hunter extraordinaire of the island is a character called Bibique. He has written a book called *Sur la Piste des Frères de la Côte* (Editions de la Réunion Insolite, St-Denis, 1984), which is about the Indian Ocean pirates and their booty.

The bible of Créole cookery is *Les Délices de la Cuisine Créole*. It costs around F3000 for the six-volume set, but it's the *crème de la crème* of cookbooks. Some of the table d'hôte owners have copies.

## Bookshops & Libraries

Remember that a bookshop is *une librairie*. The word for library is *bibliothèque*.

If you want to do a lot of reading in English, you'd better bring along some paperbacks. The best chances of finding English language reading material is at the Librairie de la Réunion on Avenue de la Victoire in St-Denis, which supplies the university across the street. The cheapest I could find was a Penguin edition of *Hard Times* by Charles Dickens for F45!

The Syndicat d'Initiative on Rue Ste-Marie, St-Denis, also has a range of books for sale. For the latest in Gallic publishing there are numerous bookshops on the Rue Juliette Dodu, also in St-Denis.

The central library is beside the bus station in St-Denis. It's open from Monday to Friday, but the books are for reference only. The departmental borrowing library is at the corner of Rue Roland Garros and Rue Jean Chatel.

## Maps

Syndicats d'Initiative distribute several maps of the island, including the fairly good *Excursion Carte Touristique*. You can also pick up town plans from the appropriate Syndicats d'Initiative.

Most island maps include at least some of the hiking trails and mountain gîtes. For all purposes, the IGN (Institut Géographique National) 512 map of the island, available for F50, is the best and most detailed. Although it's fairly accurate, one potentially dangerous oversight is the casual placing of the gîtes. For the most part they are marked in the vicinity of where they should be rather than the exact location. When you are trying to find a gîte at the end of a long walk, sweaty, sore and starving, and you take a wrong turn in the track, the IGN map will only be saved from the fire by its other attributes.

Far and away the best hiking maps are the new TOP25 1:25,000 series produced by IGN. They cover the island in six sheets, using beautiful relief shading and showing vegetation cover. Contour lines are at 10 metre intervals. These maps replace the old Carte Topographique 1:25,000 series which took nine sheets to cover the island and four sheets for the cirques; with the new series, you need to purchase only two sheets (4402RT and 4405RT) for most cirque hiking. Piton de la Fournaise is now covered in one sheet (4406RT) as opposed to two previously. The maps cost F60 per sheet and may be ordered from Institut Géographique National, 107 Rue de la Boétie, 75008 Paris, France.

## MEDIA
### Newspapers & Magazines

There are three daily morning papers published in St-Denis and sold around the island.

There are two popular daily newspapers: the conservative *Le Journal de l'Île de la Réunion (JIR)* and the more liberal *Le Quotidien*. Both carry sections on local, métropole, Indian Ocean and world news. They're both good for features and excellent for up-to-date information and views on the Comoros, Madagascar and Mauritius. The *JIR* also has a large Sunday edition. Free classified advertising is available in the Quotidien on Friday and the Journal de l'Île de la Réunion on Tuesday.

The communist daily *Témoignages* presents all these items as well, but from a different perspective. The only English language newspaper available is *The European* which is sold at Gillot airport and at large bookshops in St-Denis.

There is a weekly magazine, *Télé 7 Jours*, which not only carries the week's radio and TV programme lists, but also offers general interest articles.

A magazine of interest to visitors will be bi-monthly *Plein Sud* which is published in Réunion but focuses on the history, oddities, culture and (especially) leisure activities throughout the entire Indian Ocean region. A year's subscription costs F120; contact Plein Sud Magazine, BP 1383, 97403 St-Denis.

## Radio & TV

There are two government (RFO) radio stations and scores of 'free' stations with names like Radio Scooter, Radio Arc-en-Ciel and Radio Dominique; these cover the island and satisfy a range of creeds and tastes.

TV viewers have the choice of two government (RFO) channels as well as the independent Free-Dom station, with its more risqué pop and film videos. Most of the programming on the RFOs is produced and shown in the métropole first. Nobody finds much of it very stimulating; there are a variety of political discussions and quiz programs (how about *Des Chiffres et des Lettres* – 'Numbers and Letters'?) but the worst is undoubtedly the nauseating kiddie talent competition which appears to be on every evening.

## FILM & PHOTOGRAPHY

There's plenty of scope for spectacular photography on Réunion. The volcano may not perform on cue, but several photographers have caught it in the act and have colour shots of the eruption on display or for sale. Serge Gélabert, 85 Rue Juliette Dodu, St-Denis, is recommended.

Stocks of film are plentiful and fresh, but more expensive than in Europe. A 36-exposure colour print film costs around F56; processing is also expensive at F4 per print and an additional F18 per roll. Slide processing and mounting costs F46 per 36-exposure roll. Try Galeries Photo Cine at 12 Rue Victor Mac Auliffe.

For further information on photography in this part of the world, see Film & Photography in the introductory Facts for the Visitor chapter.

## HEALTH

For general travel health information, refer to the Health section in the introductory Facts for the Visitor chapter.

## Vaccinations

Vaccination certificates for cholera and yellow fever are required of travellers arriving from an infected area.

## Travel Insurance

EC nationals will enjoy to a certain extent the benefits of reciprocal agreements between member countries. Other nationals are advised to carry medical/travel insurance.

## Water

Tap water is safe to drink everywhere on the island.

## Health Precautions

Although there are mosquitoes on the island, there is no malaria. However, authorities ask that visitors 'take some form of antimalarial treatment before they fall ill' if they're coming from Mauritius, Madagascar or another area where malaria is endemic. For further details, refer to the discussion under Health in the introductory Facts for the Visitor chapter.

The greatest health threat in Réunion will probably be spraining, blistering, twisting or breaking something while hiking. If the worst does happen, the best medical care is at hand. Réunion has a large, 21-hospital health service, more than 800 doctors, 180 chemists and the best equipment and emergency services in the Indian Ocean. Even remote areas are covered and l'Hôpital Fred Isautier, at St-Pierre, is the biggest hospital on the island and has the only CAT scanner in the Indian Ocean region!

If you have any queries about health precautions upon arrival or departure, the Frontier Health Authority at Gillot airport is open daily from 7.30 am to 8 pm.

## WOMEN TRAVELLERS

Since most visitors to Réunion are French couples or families, and because most z'oreille residents and métro French visitors have or hire vehicles, light-skinned women walking alone will invariably elicit some sort of response from youngish local men. The most common will simply be a less than polite comment in passing. It gets annoying but there's none of the rude hissing and spitting you get in Mauritius, and physical aggression is very rare. Nevertheless, it's definitely not a good idea for women to hitch alone or walk alone after dark in St-Denis or any of the beach areas along the west coast (Boucan Canot, St-Gilles-les-Bains, Hermitage-les-Bains, etc).

## WORK

EC citizens have the right to live and work in Réunion for up to three months. For longer, you need an employer to fill out forms or provide a guarantee of means for at least one year. This will enable you to apply at Immigration for a Carte de Séjour which will allow you to remain in France for five years. You must also provide an E2 form and a birth certificate.

The going rate for private English lessons by a native English speaker is F100/hour. If you have a telephone, you can advertise your services free in the *Quotidien* on Friday and the *Journal de l'Île de la Réunion* on Tuesday.

For formal English-related employment, try the Chambre de Commerce et de l'Industrie. Alternatively, you may be able to find work at the Université de la Réunion as a *repetiteur* (apply to the Faculté d'Anglais at the university) or as a *maître auxiliare* (apply at the Rectorat in St-Denis).

## TREKKING

For most visitors, trekking is the highlight of Réunion. If you want tropical beaches, go to Mauritius, the Seychelles or the Maldives. In Réunion, what little beach there is should be treated as a relaxing reward at the end of a week or fortnight of mountain trekking.

Trekking in Réunion ranges from an afternoon stroll to a week-long expedition. Going as you please is fine as long as you know where you want to end up. Last-minute decisions severely reduce your options, mainly because of the vagaries of accommodation and food. For information on mountain gîte accommodation and meals, see under Accommodation later in this chapter.

Your options are already restricted by other factors. There are only 10 gîtes and you're restricted to a stay of only two consecutive nights (maximum) in each. Demand soars on weekends and during the French holidays in July and August. When the mists and rain fall, the going gets tough and the views disappear behind a bank of cloud and mist, so advance planning and booking are important. Gîte reservations must be made in advance through Maison de la Montagne in St-Denis or Cilaos.

Also, if you have a vehicle and want to do a traverse route, you'll need to find someone to shuttle it to the other end of your route or somehow make your way back to your starting point. There's a vehicle shuttle service, Chauffeur Relais (☎ 23 00 82 day, 28 41 26 evening) operated by M Robert Elion at # 14, 3 Rue Th Cadet, Moufia, Ste-Clotilde.

You can combine trekking with camping – although that means heavier backpacks – and staying at hotels and chambres d'hôte between treks to break up the spartan living with good home cooking and other comforts.

### Information

For information on hiking, trekking and other outdoor sports, as well as bookings for most mountain gîtes, you must visit one of the two offices of Maison de la Montagne. They can also provide guides and organise tours for *randonneurs* (walkers). The main office (☎ 21 75 84) is at 10 Place Sarda Garriga (near Le Barachois) in St-Denis. They're open Monday to Thursday from 9 am to 5.30 pm, Friday from 9 am to 4.30 pm and Saturday from 9 am to 4 pm. In Cilaos, they're at 2 Rue Mac Auliffe (☎ 31 71 71).

They're quite reliable for making arrangements, but they aren't all that clued up about routes and making route suggestions, so it's a good idea to have your route planned beforehand, or work out an itinerary using the large and incredible model of the island in the St-Denis office.

Several French language guides contain brief sections on the *sentiers* (the footpaths) and the English language guide, Albert Trotet's little yellow *Tourist Guide to Réunion Island*, offers some suggestions (but without practical details). Much more detailed is *50 Itineraires de Promenades Pedestres à la Réunion* which describes 50 day walks and longer trips on the island. It's available in some bookshops in St-Denis.

The *Suivez Le Guide* trekking series by Mayer & Vaxelaire concentrate on five separate regions of the island. They're available for F55 each at Maison de la Montagne in St-Denis. If you want the whole enchilada in one volume, pick up a copy of the government-published *Île de la Réunion – GR R1 & GR R2*; it covers the two Grandes Randonées (grandes randonées are a system of French long-distance trekking routes) as well as access tracks and numerous other hiking and trekking possibilities. It's available at Maison de la Montagne in St-Denis and at the Prisunic bookshop on Rue Marechal Leclerc, also in St-Denis.

Another very good source of outdoors information is the ONF or Office National des Forêts (☎ 20 10 59), Colline de la Providence, St-Denis, which looks after most of the paths and tracks. They sell the excellent metre-by-metre *Topoguide*, a detailed French language guide to the major and minor walking tracks and their variations, with notes on the wildlife, vegetation and sites of interest along the way. They also produce those clear and detailed route maps posted at strategic points along the routes. Unfortunately, these maps aren't for sale. The tracks are generally well signposted, with signs giving distances and the time required to cover them.

The ONF is located well outside the centre, on Colline de la Providence. To get within reasonable walking distance, take bus No 23 from the Gare Routière or from the Hôpital d'Enfants south of the Jardin de l'État, and get off at the Doret bus stop. From there, the route up the hill is rather complicated, so you'll probably have to ask directions.

The IGN 1:100,000 map of Réunion won't really suffice for trekkers, although we've had letters from people who've relied on it successfully. Keep in mind, however, that the positioning of the gîtes isn't always

accurate and many routes are missing or are ambiguously marked. For further information on maps, see the Books & Maps section in this chapter.

Most of the trekking routes are in the interior but there are a couple of walks near the coast. For specific route suggestions and descriptions, refer to individual chapters.

Clubs and groups which will provide further information, suggest routes, offer guided treks and hire equipment include the following:

Association Réunionnaise d'Excursion et de Randonée, St-Denis (☎ 28 21 57)

Compagnie des Guides de la Réunion, Maison de la Montagne, 2 Rue Mac Auliffe, Cilaos (☎ 31 71 71)

Compagnie des Guides de la Réunion, Maison de la Montagne, 10 Place Sarda Garriga, 97400 St-Denis (☎ 21 75 84)

Écologie Réunion, 1 Lotissement Payet, Gillot, Ste-Marie (☎ 29 21 38)

Les Randonneurs du Week-end, Le-Tampon (☎ 27 00 04)

SREPEN, 4 Rue Jacob, St-Denis (☎ 20 30 30)

### Equipment

Along with the 'splattered frog', another motif for Réunion could be the *sac à dos* (backpack). This is one of the few places in the world where people don't turn their noses up at down-at-heel travellers lumping around with rucksacks. They just assume you've come down from Piton des Neiges or La Roche Écrite! (Perhaps they also assume you must be well-heeled to come to Réunion in the first place.)

The logistics of backpacking (tramping, trekking, bushwalking, hillwalking, etc) are beyond the scope of this book but hopefully the following discussion of what to bring will be useful in your preparations.

In the interest of comfort and safety, a good pair of walking boots is probably the best footwear but is not essential and if you find that hiking boots turn your feet to mince meat, a good pair of trainers (tennis shoes, sandshoes) with lots of tread should work just fine. Unless you want to pay a bundle for a good pair on the island, bring your footwear from home.

Good warm woollen socks will also be useful, especially if you're visiting in July or August. You'll also need some sort of waterproof poncho or jacket. Rob Willox found that his army-style plastic poncho-cape was a lifesaver, as it covered his rucksack as well. They're not particularly fashionable, but they're light, cheap and fold into a tiny bundle. Except in the coolest weather, in heavily forested areas and around dawn or dusk, shorts are the only way to go. If you're trekking in the cirques, carry a warm jumper at any time of year.

Other important items to bring are a torch, a waterproof, see-through map case, a compass, loo paper, a knife and spoon and at least a one litre water container; most of the time it's hot and humid during the day and you'll sweat buckets. Don't worry about trying to carry all the water you'll need – there's water, water everywhere – but you should carry some sort of purification tablets (see the Health section in the introductory Facts for the Visitor chapter at the beginning of the book).

Food is another matter and if you haven't reserved meals at the gîtes, you'll need to carry at least some staples. If you're staying in the gîtes, you'll have access to their cooking facilities, but bring your own cutlery. Rice, noodles, dried soups, tinned meat and sardines, biscuits and other lightweight items are naturally the best choices. Don't forget to bring lots of chocolate bars for instant energy, and coffee or tea. Most villages in the cirques have shops but their stores are normally very basic and in the case of Mafate, must be flown in by helicopter and are therefore very expensive. If you're camping, you'll have to either carry a portable stove or bring only items which don't need to be heated; unfortunately, they won't be very satisfying after a long day of hard walking!

To hire equipment, contact one of the organisations listed under Information earlier in this section. Alternatively, camping, sport and other outdoor equipment may be hired from *Altimarines* (☎ 41 62 61), 21 Rue Monthyon, 97400 St-Denis.

### Routes

There are basically two kinds of footpaths: the forest tracks known as routes forestières (RF1, etc) and the *sentiers* (paths). Many of the latter are linked into a clearly signposted and well-maintained 80-km route that touches on all three cirques. This circuit is known as the GR R1 (Grande Randonnée Route 1). It has been recently joined by the GR R2 which crosses the island from the Cirque de Mafate to Piton de la Fournaise. These extremely well maintained major routes are backed up by numerous feeder routes and other subsidiary routes of varying popularity and state of repair.

The system operates along the same lines as the GR system in Metropolitan France. Arrows and blobs of paint mark the route, without imposing too much on the landscape. Two parallel horizontal bands, white on top and red on the bottom, indicate a Grande Randonée route. Yellow on the top and red on the bottom signifies a variation on the main route. These same signs with an arrow beneath them indicate a change in the direction of the main or subsidiary routes.

A word of warning, however: unless you're not carrying a pack or have shock-corded legs, don't pay much attention to the estimated hiking times posted on GR system signs. We're both fairly strong walkers, yet nearly always found ourselves doubling the posted times.

With most hikes of a day or more, it's vital to get an early start. Not only does it give you sufficient time for rest and meal breaks and prevent mad, last-minute dashes to gîtes, it also allows good views of the surroundings; normally, around 9 am, the mists rise in the valleys and the clouds close around the mountain peaks. Clear sunrises and sunsets over the cirques and volcano should not be missed.

### Emergencies

The biggest dangers are from stumbling on rocks or slipping on mud and breaking or spraining a limb; hiking boots will add extra protection. Although the routes are maintained regularly, wet weather can cause ankle-grabbing mud so watch your footing. If you suffer from vertigo, choose your route carefully; many tracks in the Cirque de Mafate are literally carved from sheer precipices. For optimum balance, pack your heaviest items near the bottom of your rucksack.

A few other guidelines include: be fit and healthy; carry a good map (see under Books & Maps in the Réunion – Facts for the Visitor chapter); always let someone know your route and timetable; know what to do in case of bad weather, accident or loss of way; and carry insurance which will cover trekking accidents!

In case of accidents there is a representative of the Office National des Forêts (ONF) at every gîte, often the *gardien* (caretaker) who knows how to contact the helicopter rescue service.

## ACTIVITIES

In true French style, the recreational emphasis in Réunion is on sweat, adventure, pushing beyond conventional limits and all that. Whether or not anyone actually breaks new ground, however, seems to be immaterial as long as some suffering is involved! There are established clubs for just about every sort of activity you can imagine: flying, parachuting, sailboarding, hanggliding, hunting, equitation, mountain biking, motor sports, diving, deep-sea fishing, sailing, water-skiing and numerous competitive sports.

What's On enquiries should be directed toward the Syndicats d'Initiative or the Office Départemental de la Culture (☎ 41 11 41) at the Jardin de l'Etat in St-Denis. The latter publishes a free monthly brochure outlining cultural activities. The local press will also have details on events. Another good source of information is the RUN magazine, available free from Syndicats d'Initiative around the island (see under Tourist Offices earlier in this chapter).

## Water Sports

Water sports associations are clustered around the waterfront at St-Gilles-les-Bains (and are springing up in neighbouring communities), which is the holiday and leisure centre of Réunion.

There are several surfing clubs and schools, but the only surf spots are around St-Gilles-les-Bains. The best is said to be a reef break near the Club Med, but it is dangerous. Another good location is at Ravine des Colimaçons, near the Le Corail turtle farm in St-Leu. The most popular spot and surfing centre is Roches Noires beach at St-Gilles-les-Bains itself. For information on diving in the Indian Ocean, refer to the Activities section in the introductory Facts for the Visitor chapter at the beginning of the book.

Deep-sea fishing from St-Gilles-les-Bains costs F800 to F1500 per half day for two to four people. Contact any of the numerous fishing charters in and around St-Gilles-les-Bains: Centre de Peche Europa (☎ 24 43 79), Marlin Club de la Réunion (☎ 55 63 16), Réunion Fishing Club (☎ 24 36 10), Blue Marlin (☎ 22 54 47), Etoile du Sud (☎ 27 48 33), Le Zanatany (☎ 43 65 42), Tilani (☎ 24 02 05) and Sindbad (☎ 24 56 54).

The following clubs and organisations can help with information, hire equipment and organise marine recreation for visitors:

### Diving

Au Gloria Maris, M Florès, St-Gilles-les-Bains (☎ 24 41 42)

Bourbon Marine, St-Gilles-les-Bains (☎ 24 45 05)

Corail Club de Plongée, Zone portuaire, St-Gilles-les-Bains (☎ 24 37 25)

Comité Régional des Etudes et Sports Sous-Marins, Président Masanneli, Maison Régionale des Sports, St-Denis (☎ 20 09 79)

Club de Plongée du Grand Bleu, St-Gilles-les-Bains, Zone portuaire (☎ 24 33 94)

Club Subaquatique Réunionnais, Centre International de Plongée, BP 466, St-Denis (☎ 24 34 11)

École de Plongée et Exploration GEO, M Donatien, St-Gilles-les-Bains (☎ 24 56 03)

M Philippe Toussaint, St-Gilles-les-Bains (☎ 21 47 40)

## Canoeing, Kayaking, Sailboarding & Waterskiing

Club Nautique de Bourbon, 2 Rue des Brisants, 97434 St-Gilles-les-Bains (☎ 24 40 93)

Club Nautique de l'Est, Case de la Rivière-des-Roches, St-Benoît (☎ 50 32 06)

Coconuts, Plage des Roches-Noires, St-Gilles-les-Bains

Ligue de Voile Réunion, Maison Régionale des Sports, Route de la Digue, Ste-Clotilde (☎ 20 09 79)

Ski Nautique Club de St-Paul, 1 Rue de la Croix, l'Étang-St-Paul (☎ 45 42 87)

Société Nautique de St-Paul, 78 Route de la Baie, 97460 St-Paul (☎ 22 56 46)

Société Nautique de St-Pierre, BP 123, 97453 St-Pierre (☎ 25 04 03)

## Surfing

Aloha Surf Club, Patrick Flores Teyssedre, Boucan-Canot (☎ 24 47 71)

Boucan Surf Club, 106 Allée des Topazes, 97400 Bellepierre, St-Denis (☎ 21 23 79)

Ligue Réunionnaise de Surf, Maison Régionale des Sports, St-Denis (☎ 21 23 79)

Sud Surf Club, 16 Rue R-Payet, 97427 Étang-Salé-les-Bains (☎ 25 34 28)

## Mountain Biking

Recently, Réunion has seen an explosion of interest in the *velo tout terrain* (VTT) or mountain bike and several *stations VTT* have sprung up to provide information, hire bikes and organise backcountry tours. If you're interested, contact one of the following:

VTT Evasion, Mare Longue, 12 Chemin Ceinture, 97442 St-Philippe (☎ 37 06 72)

Parc du Maïdo, 350 Route du Maïdo, 97423 Le Guillaume (☎ 32 41 81)

Cilaos Fun, Place de l'Église, 97413 Cilaos (☎ 31 76 99)

## Tours

There are a number of sugar factories which offer tours to visitors. Guided tours may be arranged through the Syndicat d'Initiative in St-Denis.

## Other Activities

The Golf Club de Bourbon (☎ 26 33 39) plays a nine-hole course at L'Étang-Salé-les-Bains in the south-west.

In Hermitage les Bains, just south of St-Gilles-les-Bains, the Club Saïn Gym (☎ 24 56 42) offers squash, weight training, yoga and aerobics among other sweaty diversions. You can subscribe for a month at F600. A game of squash is F60 per person for 45 minutes.

Other clubs and recreational organisations open to visitors include the following:

## Parapente, Parachuting, Abseiling & Rock Climbing

Aventures Ocean Indien, Souris-Blanche, Trois-Bassins (☎ 24 13 42)

Compagnie des Guides de la Réunion, Maison de la Montagne, 2 Rue Mac Auliffe, Cilaos (☎ 31 71 71)

Parapente Réunion, 2 Rue A-Bègue, Chaloupe-St-Leu (☎ 54 80 69)

Centre École de Parachutisme de la Réunion, BP 85, 97453 St-Pierre (☎ 25 54 41)

## Horse Riding

Ligue Equestre, Distillerie Chatel, CD 44, Le Chaudron (☎ 28 01 90)

Club Hippique de la Réunion, Ste-Marie (☎ 28 23 30)

Club Hippique de l'Est, Chemin de la Rivière-du-Mât, Bras-Panon (☎ 51 50 49)

La Diligence, Vingt-Septième, Bourg-Murat, Plaine-des-Cafres (☎ 59 10 10)

Société Hippique Rurale du Tampon, Chemin de Bérive, Le-Tampon (☎ 27 03 07)

Centre Equestre de l'Hermitage, Hermitage-les-Bains (☎ 24 47 73)

## HIGHLIGHTS

The west coast beaches, the high plains and the rugged south-east coast are all nice but they pale in comparison to the volcano and the high rugged cirques of Cilaos, Salazie and Mafate. No visitor to the island should miss them, even if that only means visiting one of the villages (Cilaos, Salazie or Hell-Bourg) or driving to one of the several lookout points along the rim of Piton de la Fournaise or the Cirque de Mafate. If you want to heap on yet more superlatives, climb the volcano and peer into the daunting Cratère Dolomieu or spend a few days trekking through the jumbled peaks and valleys of the Cirque de Mafate.

The best beaches are all on the west coast. The tourist beaches include St-Gilles-les-

Bains, Saline-les-Bains, Hermitage-les-Bains and Étang-Salé-les-Bains. *The* beach as far as locals are concerned is Boucan Canot.

## ACCOMMODATION

Advance preparation in choosing and booking accommodation is a very good idea because of the high cost and equally high demand, especially during French holidays: late July to early September. You won't be able to see, let alone appreciate, the beauty of the island if a good percentage of your time is taken up in search of a place to stay. That doesn't mean there isn't a range of accommodation, but things do fill up and some places are permanently packed out.

### Camping

Camping is possible either in the wild or at several organised camping and caravan sites. It is the cheapest official accommodation alternative and fees range from F13 to F40 per person per day.

There are community camping and caravan sites at Hermitage-les-Bains (☎ 23 74 12, open August only), Cilaos (☎ 31 77 41, open year round), St-Leu (☎ 34 80 03, open August only), Colorado (☎ 23 74 12, year round), Grande Anse (☎ 56 81 03, school holidays only) and Rivière-des-Roches (☎ 51 58 59, year round). All the sites have full facilities but, additionally, Colorado has bungalows for rent, and the Cilaos site has a bar and restaurant. Also in Cilaos, there's a forestry camp site which may be used free of charge with permission from the Office National des Forêts, Rue du Père-Boiteau, Cilaos (☎ 31 71 40).These public camp sites aren't particularly well policed, and robbery and vandalism are real problems, especially at Hermitage-les-Bains. Campers at any of the official sites are required to clear out at the announcement of a cyclone warning.

Another option is the *Camping à la Ferme* (an organisation of privately owned French camp sites) of Mme Lucette Ahrel (☎ 51 36 26) at 37 Rue Pignolet, Chemin de la Petite-Plaine in Plaine-des-Palmistes. She charges

F10 per day for the site and F6 per person. Meals are available for F70 each.

If you're heading for the cirques in August, you may want to carry a tent and forego the urban life in the gîtes. There are also emergency shelters along some of the main trekking paths, but they provide only a roof.

**Camper Vans & Motor Homes** These are worth considering if you're hopeless at putting up tents or prefer the self-contained approach to camping and travelling. Rando-Car (☎ 31 41 89), 100 Route du Maïdo, 97423 Le Guillaume, specialises in camper van rental and Tropical Loisirs (☎ 41 48 34) in St-Denis hires camper vans and mini motor homes.

### Youth Hostels

Réunion now has three *auberges de jeunesse* (youth hostels) – at Bernica, Entre-Deux and Hell-Bourg. In Cilaos, the Auberge de Hameau operates as an unofficial youth hostel. They're operated by the Féderation Réunionnaise des Auberges de Jeunesse, which is an affiliate of the French Youth Hostel Association (Ligue Française des Auberge de Jeunesse).

Officially, the hostels are only open to IYHF card holders. Others may be required to purchase a French Youth Hostel association membership or an international guest card for F100; you'll also need one passport photo and a photocopy of your passport details.

For lodging, guests over 18 years of age pay F60 per night and an additional F10 for breakfast. Evening meals are available for F45. Reservations may be made through the Féderation Réunionnaise des Auberges de Jeunesse (☎ 45 53 51; fax 45 61 07), S/C Arts & Traditions, BP 12731, Rue de la Caverne, 97863 St-Paul.

### Gîtes de Montagne

Mountain gîtes are basic mountain cabins or lodges, operated by the government through Maison de la Montagne. It is possible to organise a walking holiday using the gîtes only, as there are 11 distributed around the interior of the island. Cirque de Mafate, inaccessible by road, has five of them: at Îlet à Bourse, La Nouvelle, Roche Plate, Grande Place and Marla. Plaine d'Affouches and La Roche Écrite are two others en route between St-Denis and the Cirque de Salazie. Bélouve and Piton des Neiges gîtes are between Salazie and Cilaos cirques, and Volcan is accessible by road, en route to the volcano at Pas de Bellecombe. Basse-Vallée is in the south-eastern part of the island.

The gîtes in Réunion are generally in better condition than their counterparts in metropolitan France and, thanks to recently installed solar panels, they all have electricity. None, however, gets as cushy as providing warm showers.

Any hopes of using a gîte as an inexpensive base will be short-circuited by the rule that trekkers may only remain for two consecutive nights. Hikers under 18 years of age can stay at the gîte only as part of an organised group under the supervision of an adult.

The gîtes must be booked and paid for in advance and gîte reservations are not refundable, unless a cyclone or a cyclone alert prevents your arrival. A night in each without food costs F50 per person and must be booked through Maison de la Montagne: the main office (☎ 21 75 84) is at 10 Place Sarda Garriga in St-Denis. In Cilaos, they're at 2 Rue Mac Auliffe (☎ 31 71 71).

If you'd rather not carry food for an evening meal, you can arrange to have meals prepared by the caretaker or local people, but this must be booked in advance by phoning the gardien *after* you've booked and paid for your reservation. Meals are not generally available on Sunday. Breakfasts are also available in some gîtes for F20 but they consist of only biscuits, preserves and coffee, and aren't worth the money.

Sleeping arrangements are mostly bunk beds in rooms sleeping four to eight people. There are two blankets and a mattress cover per bed. The blankets are often dusty, so bring a sleep-sheet or sleeping bag, toilet paper and a torch. It also gets quite chilly at night, so warm clothing will be in order. Cooking is done mostly by a wood-fired stove but some kitchens are so filthy, you probably won't bother.

On arrival and departure you must 'book' in and out with the gardien who will collect your *caution* of F100 per group. He or she returns it to you when you leave, if satisfied you have left the gîte in good order. If not, the caretaker keeps the cash. In theory, you're not meant to occupy a gîte before 3 pm or remain past 10 am. The telephone numbers are:

| | |
|---|---|
| Basse Vallée | ☎ 37 00 75 |
| Bélouve | ☎ 41 21 23 |
| Grand Place | ☎ 43 85 42 |
| Îlet à Bourse | ☎ 43 43 93 |
| Marla | ☎ 43 78 31 |
| La Nouvelle | ☎ 43 49 63 |
| Piton des Neiges | ☎ 51 15 26 |
| Roche Écrite | ☎ 21 75 96 |
| Roche Plate | ☎ 59 13 94 |
| Volcan | ☎ 21 28 96 |

### Bivouac Gîtes

These very basic huts, simply a roof under which to crash in a sleeping bag, may be used free of charge. They're found in several locations in the Cirque de Mafate: Trois Roches, Maison Leclos, Mafate (between Grand Place and La Nouvelle) and in several other sites near villages. They normally have bed frames and a basic loo but no other amenities and are often filled with trail maintenance crews or partying male teenagers from the lowlands. Lone women should give them a miss.

### Gîtes d'Étape

The privately owned gîtes d'étape, five of which – two at Aurère, two at La Nouvelle and one at Grand-Place-les-Hauts – are in roadless areas of the Cirque de Mafate function much the same as the gîtes de montagne. They charge about the same but they generally aren't as tidy or well kept. Accommodation is in dormitories, and some of them offer common cooking facilities.

## Gîtes Ruraux

These are private houses and lodges which families and groups can rent for self-catering holidays. There are over 50 gîtes ruraux in Réunion, mainly in the southern half of the island and around Plaine-des-Palmistes and Plaine-des-Cafres. There are none in St-Denis (the nearest is at Le Brûlé) or on the coast, but several are within striking distance – mainly in the St-Paul and St-Leu areas.

There is a wide selection of gîtes, with facilities for lodging up to 12 people. Most have fridges and hot water, and bed sheets are available in some cases. If there are vacancies, some gîtes will allow overnight guests, but they're normally only let by the week or weekend. Costs vary from F800 to F2500 per week and F500 to F1100 for a weekend. A security bond equivalent to one week's rent is required in advance.

You may book the gîtes by phoning the proprietors directly or contacting the Relais Départemental des Gîtes Ruraux (☎ 20 31 90; fax 21 84 47), Résidence Ste-Anne, 97400 St-Denis. They publish a yellow booklet entitled *Vacances en Gîtes de France* containing photos and full details on each gîte.

## Chambres d'Hôte

These small and personal B&B establishments are normally set in places convenient to places of interest to tourists. There are more than 30 on the island and they provide a pleasant introduction to Créole life. All are family-run, but some treat guests more like a member of the family than others. Bed and breakfast rates are set at F80 to F120 per person or F106 to F150 for a double room. Huge traditional meals cost from F70 and must be reserved in advance. You can reserve a room by telephoning the proprietor or by booking through the Relais Départemental des Gîtes Ruraux (see Gîtes Ruraux) or Maison de la Montagne in St-Denis or Cilaos (see Gîtes de Montagne).

## Pensions de Famille

Pensions de Famille are the only budget alternative to hotels in St-Denis, where there are no gîtes or chambres d'hôte. There are few vacancies for visitors because so many rooms are taken on a long-term basis by students, foreigners looking for work and contract tradespeople. There are 11 pensions in the capital and a few more in St-Pierre, St-Andre, Le Tampon, St-Louis. They vary from the shoddy doss house to well-run guesthouses, and rates range from F90 to F160 per night for a double room, including breakfast. Evening meals cost around F60 per person.

## Hotels

Réunion isn't flush with hotels so getting a room can often be difficult. Primarily, they're found in St-Denis and around the beach resorts of the west coast, especially St-Gilles-les-Bains. Of the 65 hotels on the island, only the Méridien St-Denis and the Alliance Créolia in St-Denis and the Grand Hotel des Mascareignes in St-Gilles-les-Bains are in the four-star class. There are 16 three-star hotels and 13 are two-star. There are two one-star establishments, one classed *grand confort*, and lots of no-star or unclassed hotels.

Hotel prices begin at around F110/140 a single/double in an unclassed hotel, including a basic continental breakfast, while four-star options will set you back as much as F760/820 for a single/double room. Several of the one-star and two-star hotels offer fairly good value, including the Hôtel Les Mascareignes in St-Denis (F165/190 single/double) and the Hôtel Les Orchidées in Le Tampon (F200/250 single/double). Like the pensions, however, they're often booked out by business people.

## VVF Holiday Villages

The three VVFs (Villages Vacances Familles) which, like the rural gîtes, are a French holiday institution, are relatively quiet, low key and nothing like a Butlins camp. In order to stay, you must first join the VVF organisation, which costs F100 per family.

There are VVF's at St-Leu, St-Gilles-les-Bains and Cilaos. Rates begin at F200 a double on weekdays and F350 a double on

**Sea Urchins**
The spiny sea urchins are another member of the *echinoderm* group which includes starfish and sea cucumbers. With a ball-like body covered in spines it is the sea urchin which gives the group its name, Greek for spiny *(echino)* and skin *(derm)*. The spines can vary considerably from the short blunt spines of the slate-pencil urchin to the long, sharp black spines of *Diadema* urchins. These spines will easily penetrate skin if the urchin is stepped on or handled and once broken off they are very hard to remove and can cause infections.

When an urchin dies the spines fall off and the circular 'sea egg' which remains makes a fine if fragile ornament. It's easy to see the five-armed star pattern on the casing which shows the urchin's relation to starfish. The sea urchin's mouth at the bottom is a complex structure known as Aristotle's lantern and with this the urchin grazes as it crawls across the sea bottom. Despite the formidable protection of its spines urchins hide away during daylight and come out to feed at night. Spines or not, some triggerfish will eat sea urchins and it is a popular ingredient in Créole cooking. ∎

Saturday and Sunday, all with meals. You can opt for a 'studio' unit with two or four beds, or a six to 20-bed bungalow. The price increases for the weekends. Reservations for any of the three should be made through the VVF de St-Gilles (☎ 24 04 64), BP 20, Les Filaos, 97434 St-Gilles-les-Bains.

Note that the 'Grand Confort' Le Récif Village, in St-Gilles-Les-Bains, isn't part of the VVF chain.

### University
During school holidays in July and August, you may be able to find single room accommodation at the university halls in Ste-Clotilde. Rooms cost around F50 per night or F800 per month. Contact La Directrice – CROUS, Rue Hippolyte Foucque, 97490 Ste-Clotilde.

### FOOD
As in France proper, much time and effort in Réunion is devoted to growing, preparing and enjoying food. What's more, the Réunionnais have many culinary traditions to choose from: French, Indian, Chinese and Créole; and many recipes contain elements of several cuisines.

Most imaginable fruits and vegetables, as well as a few unknown in Europe and elsewhere, are served up. Among the latter, two stand out – the *tomate d'arbuste*, the sweet tree tomato New Zealanders call tamarillo, and the pear-shaped, green vegetable called

*chou chou*, which was introduced from Brazil; in Australia it's called a choko and in Europe, a crystophène.

Other common ingredients in Créole dishes are some sort of *graines*, which may be red or white beans *(haricots)*, lentils *(lentilles)* or peas *(petits pois)*, invariably served as a creamy side dish along with *rougail* (spicy hot tomato and vegetable chutney) and *brèdes*, digestive greens which resemble spinach.

Réunion is not a vegetarian's paradise. In the highlands, chicken and meat (primarily beef, goat or pork) are central to practically every dish. On the coast, there is the additional choice of fish or crustaceans.

More often than not, the meat or fish available is cooked in a mild Indian curry and served on a rice base; specialities include sea urchin curry *(cari z'ourite)*, octopus curry *(cari poulpe)*, jackfruit curry *(cari p'tit jacques)* and smoked pork curry *(cari boucané)*. Heart of palm and vanilla figure in many recipes. Arabic influences are evident in the addition of cloves, cinnamon and nutmeg in some recipes, while the Swahili contribution is coconut cream. The Chinese have contributed ginger.

If you want to spice up the meal, there is often a bowl of *piments* (chillies). Beware, you need only a smidgen of this stuff. A teaspoonful may cauterise your insides!

Good home cooking wouldn't be the same without the cakes. They're not the fancy fruit, cream and pastry delicacies of the patisserie, but sweet and heavy puddings made out of sweet potatoes, chou chou, cassava or rice.

## Eating Out

There is a dearth of budget eating houses in Réunion and unless you can subsist on snacks (tiny samosas and meatballs are sold on the streets for F1 to F2 each), you won't find much for less than F20. There are a few Chinese-Créole restaurants or cafés where a reasonably filling meal costs between F30 and F40. Thereafter, set-menu lunches offered by most restaurants for between F45 and F75 are the best value.

The *Guide des Piments Bleus* (Blue Chilli Guide) provides the most objective assessment of the best restaurants in terms of price (average top of F200 a meal) and quality. A restaurant which has three chillies, such as Le Landais in St-Gilles-les-Bains or Le Labourdonnais in St-Denis, is tops.

Most restaurants take Sunday, Monday or Tuesday as a day off.

**Tables d'Hôte** Most chambres d'hôte are *tables d'hôte* as well, but many establishments have only table d'hôte. These places dish up three to four-course treats accompanied by wine, punch or rum for around F60 per person. The Créole cuisine you'll find in the tables d'hôte (the cheapest places to eat) is rich and filling, though it rarely gets too daring; these set meals normally contain meat (vegetarians be warned) and about 80% of the time you'll wind up with cari poulet. If

you like variety, you'll occasionally have to splash out on a restaurant.

There are quite a few tables d'hôte in the Cirque de Salazie, the Plaine-des-Cafres and the Plaine-des-Palmistes. Some cater for clubs and other large parties. To reserve, just telephone or get the tourist office to book for you.

**Vegetarian Meals** Reader Stephen Clarke has written to provide a few ideas for vegetarians:

A tip for vegetarians is to stick to starters. In most restaurants serving French food, they'll have salads; for example, mixed salads or *crudités* (although they may contain tuna so you'll have to ask). In the mountains, you might be lucky enough to get *chèvre chaud*, local goat's milk cheese on toast with a bed of green salad. In Créole restaurants they'll have *gratin de chou chou* or *salade de palmiste*, and they'll always be happy to serve up rice with rougaille and *grains* (either beans or lentils).

## Self-Catering

When camping, trekking from gîte to gîte or renting a bungalow, the cheapest places to get provisions are the supermarkets and department stores such as Score and Prisunic. Here, you'll find the same cheap and nasty pre-packaged and instant food items you probably carry on outdoors trips at home. For fruit and vegetables, the markets are better value.

Local cheeses are available at some supermarkets and from the smaller grocers in the highland areas. The fresh goat's cheeses are very good and baguettes are available everywhere, as are pre-made baguette sandwiches. One Créole variation is the *sandwich aux achards de légumes*, a sort of pickled vegetable sandwich. Then there are the small snacks and titbits which are available in shops and street stalls all around the island. Small chicken, fish or beef samosas cost F1 to F2 each. Or you can try *bon bon piments*, spicy meat fritters, and *bouchons*, Chinese-style meat dumplings which cost around F2 and are served with soy or pepper sauce.

Slate Pencil Urchin

## DRINKS
### Coffee
A cup of coffee generally costs between F4 and F6. If you want it with milk *(café au lait)*, it goes from F6 to F10.

### Alcohol
**Fruit Brews** The variety of home-made rums and punches available in Réunion is astounding. The cheapest seems to be a blend of cheap *charette* rum, sugar and fruit juice. It's quite rough, and discriminating palates will want to move a bit upmarket.

A lot better is *punch créole*, a mixture of rum, fruit juice, cane syrup and a blend of herbs and berries. Every table or chambre d'hôte landlady prides herself on her brew. Choose from a mixed-fruit and mixed-spice *rhum d'arrangé* or a single-fruit brew of banana, vanilla, lychee (rhum rose) or pineapple. You'll normally have the opportunity to taste several. Commercially produced varieties are available in most stores and in bars or restaurants. Isautier of St-Pierre and Chatel of Ste-Clotilde are the main distillers.

**Wine** True to French tradition, most meals are accompanied by wine. The full French selection is available from about F18 a bottle for Vin Royal (a table wine). There are also Italian and Spanish table wines for around F25. The spa resort of Cilaos has its own concoction, more like a sherry than a wine.

**Beer** The local brew is Bière Bourbon (known as *Dodo*, thanks to the picture on the label); not a bad drop at all at F8 to F10. There is also a range of imported beers which includes such surprises as Heineken Malt from Holland and Tennants Stout from Scotland. A 150 ml bottle of imported beer costs around F10 over the counter and up to F15 in cafés and restaurants.

## ENTERTAINMENT
For the relatively wealthy, the Méridien (St-Denis), Novotel (St-Gilles-les-Bains) and Hotel Sterne (St-Pierre) hotels have casinos. For the restless rest, there are discos dotted around the island – see Entertainment sec-

tions under individual towns for further information. For info on theatre, see under Arts & Culture in the Réunion – Facts about the Island chapter.

There are cinemas in most population centres around the island and films are screened in Réunion shortly after their release in metropolitan France.

## THINGS TO BUY
The Syndicats d'Initiative, particularly the main one in St-Denis, market a selection of local handicrafts. Otherwise, as with agricultural products, each town and surrounding region is known for a special craft. This regional variation was re-established during WW II when supplies were blocked and the islanders had to make their own clothes, furniture and utensils as well as grow their own food. Times were hard, but the crafts taken up are now paying dividends.

The tourist and craft shops also sell a variety of art prints, lithographs and poster reproductions ranging in price from F50 to F150. The engravings of well-known artist Philippe Turpin, however, are not for sale in the shops. (See the Arts & Culture section in the Réunion – Facts about the Island chapter.) Unfortunately, there isn't a wide selection of spectacular postcards available; the postcard photography market appears to have been cornered by a character called Noor Akhoun who seems to believe that Réunion looks better through an orange filter.

There's also a granny's cupboard full of concoctions made from the various fruits, spices and herbs available. They can be bought in their natural state of preservation, or as jams, compotes, pâtés, sweets, rums, punches and liqueurs. A one-litre bottle of dark or white rum is F35, Rhum Vieux is F50 for a 700 ml bottle and Planter's Punch is as low as F20 for 700 ml.

Several shops, particularly in St-Gilles-les-Bains, specialise in fashionable tropical wear, beachwear and accessories. In St-Denis try Prophoto Tropica at 9 Rue Charles Gounod. Mind you, you'll see very few good

T-shirt designs in Réunion and T-shirts are expensive, often upwards of F60.

Réunion is not a patch on Mauritius when it comes to miniature ship replicas. The main builder is Vincent Donnadieu. His shop, Marine en Bois (☎ 29 27 44), can be found at the aptly named 9 Route des Artisans, Zac Patates à Durand, Chemin Finette II, Ste-Clotilde. The work is as intricate as the address.

Some other less localised crafts include wicker and bamboo work, hat making and stone carving. The following is a rundown of some villages and their specialities:

Cilaos
The nuns in Cilaos have been doing embroidery since the beginning of the century, when a doctor's daughter, Angèle MacAuliffe, introduced the craft. There are now 120 embroiderers and an embroidery school at Cilaos. The needlework includes everything from table mats to huge tablecloths at prices ranging from F60 to F4000. For the widest selection, visit the Maison de la Broderie (☎ 31 77 48).

Vétiver grass, the roots of which produce an essence used in perfumes, is woven into smaller items such as purses, hats and corn-dolly-style mascots. Cilaos also makes its own distinctive sweet wine for around F35 per bottle.

Entre-Deux
North-west of Le Tampon is Entre-Deux, which is known for slippers and *babouches* (scarves), woven out of *chocas* fibre.

St-Philippe & St-André
In the St-Philippe and St-André areas, the fronds of the screw pine (pandanus) are made into mats, baskets and handbags of all sizes, including the traditional *tante* lunch box. St-André also produces colourful patchwork quilts and mats known as *tapis mendiants* (beggars' mats), which cost between F1500 and F3000. Quilt bags are available for around F130.

L'Étang-Salé-les-Hauts
Artesans here turn out cane chairs made of lilac and casuarina wood.

Ste-Suzanne
This small seaside town is known for its bamboo work, primarily baskets and fanciful bird cages.

Rivière-St-Louis
Tamarind, olive and camphor wood is made into period furniture like that originally introduced by the French East India Company. For the best selection, visit the Centre Artisanal du Bois (☎ 39 06 12) in Rivière-St-Louis.

La Possession
Créole rag dolls hail from this otherwise unremarkable town west of St-Denis. Prices range from F100 to F200.

# Getting There & Away

## AIR

There are flights between Réunion and Mauritius, the Seychelles, Comoros, Mayotte, Madagascar (Antananarivo or Tamatave), South Africa (Johannesburg), Kenya (Nairobi), Djibouti, the United Arab Emirates (Abu Dhabi), Saudi Arabia (Jeddah) and, of course, metropolitan France.

### To/From France

Air France operates nine to 12 flights weekly between the métropole and Gillot airport. Some of these routes are either shared with Air Mauritius or Air Madagascar; or are on planes chartered from these airlines. Air France also operates flights between St-Denis and Lyon, Bordeaux and Marseille.

Air France splits the year into green, orange and red rating periods. The green period is the cheapest (F5580 return) and includes most of March, May, June and October. Red is the peak period, also the most expensive (F10,590 return), and falls during the French holidays in July-August and December-January. The month of April, the first half of February and the second half of November are in the orange period, which falls in the middle price range (F7410 return). You can fly out in one period and return in any other period with relevant fare adjustments up or down.

The major problem with the Air France Paris to Réunion flight is the length of time it takes – 13 to 16 hours – due to the number of stops they normally make en route: Antananarivo, Mauritius, the Seychelles, Djibouti, Jeddah, Abu Dhabi and so on.

Air France now has a great deal of competition on this route. Aéromaritimes runs charter flights once a week on Monday in either direction and the fare works out to around F5000. Minerve, a private charter company, has also taken up the challenge. Another option – and an excellent one – is to fly Air Outre Mer (AOM), which has seven

flights weekly from Orly airport. The trip takes only 11 hours. The service is excellent and low season fares begin at F5300 return, while the least expensive high season fare is F9900. Corsair also flies from Orly but has only two flights weekly, departing on Sunday at 8 pm (two stops) and on Tuesday at 2.30 pm (one stop). Fares begin at a very reasonable F4470. The final and cheapest option is with Air Liberté, which departs from Orly twice weekly: Tuesday at 3.15 pm and Wednesday at 4 pm. There's normally one stop en route and the trip takes only 12 hours. Fares begin at F3990 return.

Any of these airlines may be contacted through the tour operator Nouvelles Frontières (☎ 42 73 10 64), 87 Blvd de Grenelle, Paris 75738; in Réunion they're at 92 Rue Alexis Villeneuve, St-Denis (☎ 21 54 54). They also have an office in the UK: Nouvelles Frontières (☎ (071) 629-7772), 11 Blenheim St, London W1. Either of these sell low-season tickets between Paris and St-Denis on Corsair starting at just F4470 in low season.

All airlines flying between Metropolitan France and Réunion offer discounts for students and travellers over 60 years of age.

### To/From Indian Ocean Countries

Another option for reaching Réunion is via Mauritius; Air Mauritius and Air France have several flights daily between the two islands. Refer to the Mauritius – Getting There & Away chapter for details.

A return excursion fare (valid for one month) between Mauritius and Réunion costs approximately F1200 (only Mauritian Rs 2290 if you're coming the other way). The flight takes just 30 minutes and is popular with visitors from Réunion in search of a cheap shopping holiday on Mauritius. This might explain why the same return excursion fare purchased in Réunion is 50% higher.

Average return fares to other destinations

include: Antananarivo, Madagascar F2275; Tamatave, Madagascar (Air Austral) F2320; the Seychelles F5390; Moroni, Comoros F4500; and Mayotte (Air Austral) F2700.

In many respects, particularly if you'd like a stop in the Seychelles, it's worth considering 'interlining', ie flying from A to Z with as many stopovers as you want going one direction, rather than buying individual tickets. And always do it through a knowledgeable travel agent and not the airlines. That way, the fare may be calculated on a mileage basis rather than the sum of your journey's parts.

### Arriving in Réunion

Customs and immigration procedures on arrival in Réunion are the same as in France. Gillot airport is a spacious, modern and well-designed complex, about 11 km east of St-Denis. It has a bank, post office, tourist counter, restaurant and café, as well as shops, car hire desks and luggage lockers. The bank opens at 10.30 am (1 pm on Sunday) and closes at 7 pm, and the tourist counter is staffed, usually from noon to 8 pm, in order to meet all flights from France. The small/large 24-hour lockers cost F3/10.

When you arrive at Gillot airport, you'll have to pay a deposit of F10 for a baggage trolley, so have the change on hand. Once you've finished with the trolley, return it yourself to the trolley lineup just outside the door of the terminal; when you plug in the little key to attach it to the other trolleys, your F10 will pop out. Don't be intimidated by people demanding to return the trolley for you!

### Airline Offices

The addresses of airlines represented in Réunion are:

Air Austral
    Rue de Nice, 97400 St-Denis (☎ 20 20 20; fax 21 06 72)
Air France
    7 Ave de la Victoire, St-Denis (☎ 40 38 38)
    7 Rue Archambaud, St-Pierre (☎ 25 65 63)
Air Madagascar
    2 Rue Victor Mac Auliffe, St Denis (☎ 21 05 21)

Air Mauritius
    Angle Rue Alexis de Villeneuve & Rue C Gounod, St Denis (☎ 20 25 00)
Air Outre Mer (AOM)
    77 Rue Roland Garros, 97400 St-Denis (☎ 21 53 00; fax 20 07 16)
Corsair
    Aéroport de Gillot, Ste-Marie (☎ 48 82 48)
Nouvelles Frontières
    92 Rue Alexis de Villeneuve, St-Denis (☎ 21 54 54)
Minerve
    Aéroport de Gillot, Ste-Marie (☎ 29 23 13)
Jet Ocean Indien
    26 Rue Labourdonnais, 97400 St-Denis (☎ 21 47 21; fax 41 49 37)

### BOAT

The water transport situation is much the same in Réunion as in Mauritius. There is now little chance, with the recent 'no passengers' policy, of a berth on a ship of the Compagnie Générale Maritime. Besides that, cruise liners mostly give Réunion a miss in favour of the Seychelles or Mauritius. The three main shipping companies are based in Le Port.

One very new development which was passed on to us by a reader is the ferry which runs between Mauritius and Réunion. The *Mauritius Pride* sails between the Mauritian capital, Port Louis, and Le Port in Réunion. The return fare is F850 per person and the trip takes 12 hours, departing every second day at 5.30 pm from both Port Louis and Le Port, except during the boat's monthly sailing between Mauritius and Rodrigues. There are no cabins but blankets are provided and since the boat is rarely full, you can occupy several seats. Videos are shown and evening meals are served at 7 pm. For further information and a contact address, see the Mauritius – Getting There & Away chapter.

### Yacht

There are a number of long-distance yacht charters. Ylang-Ylang (☎ 24 41 18), 48 Rue Général du Gaulle in St-Gilles-les-Bains, runs return cruises to Mauritius lasting seven, 12 and 14 days. These are mainly for divers, and your chances of booking a one-way berth back to Réunion are remote. The Mauritius cruises cost from F4000 to F8000 per person. Claire-Caroline Croisières (☎ 46 25 74), 402 Menciol, Bras des Chevrettes in St André, will go anywhere – Madagascar, Mauritius, Mayotte – but only on demand and if a group of people makes it worthwhile.

Otherwise they concentrate on diving trips around the island.

## LEAVING REUNION

The airport duty-free shop is well stocked; a one-litre bottle of blended whisky costs around F75. There's no departure tax.

# Getting Around

## AIR

When you're walking around the volcano or the cirques it can resemble a scene from *Apocalypse Now*; the sky buzzes with noisy squadrons of helicopters on sightseeing forays.

Several companies are cashing in on the appeal of Réunion seen from above. Air Réunion International (☎ 29 78 78) at the old Gillot airport terminal offers a variety of helicopter and light aircraft tours of the island. The tours depart from Gillot Airport or St-Gilles-les-Bains airstrip. The price starts at around F750 per person for a 25 minute overview of Cirque de Salazie and the Cirque de Mafate, and climb to F1180 for 50 minutes for a sweep over all three cirques and the volcano. Other companies include Heililagon (☎ 55 55 55) at L'Eperon just outside St-Gilles-les-Bains, and L'Orion Transports Aeriens (☎ 35 19 00) at St-Pierre.

These aerial sightseeing trips are extremely popular and almost any travel agency on the island will make arrangements for you. It will be a bit less expensive if you can make up a party of five for a light plane trip, although planes don't really have the sightseeing flexibility you'll get with a helicopter. You may also enquire at the Aero Club Roland Garros (☎ 28 45 85) at the old Gillot air terminal for better private deals – even as little as F250 per person for a one to 1½ hour trip with a minimum of three people.

Another possibility is to thoroughly expose yourself to the elements in an ultralight aircraft. This is probably the ultimate airborne sensation in Réunion because the view is 360°. A grand circuit over Mafate and Cilaos will cost F800 per person. A buzz over all three cirques as well as the Hautes Plaines and the west coast costs F900. For further information, contact Felix ULM Service (☎ 45 58 38; fax 45 63 08), 4 Épices-Cambaie, 97460 Le Port.

## BUS

The Réunion bus service Alizés, comprised of a number of formerly private lines, covers most parts of the island with several main routes. There are quite a few variations on these routes – for example, some buses cover only part of a particular route – so enquire before making firm plans. For bus information, phone (☎ 21 25 21) in St-Denis.

St-Denis to St-Pierre
 This bus travels via Le Port, St-Paul, St-Gilles-les-Bains, St-Leu, St-Louis and Pierrefond. South of St-Gilles-les-Bains, there is an option of two routes: *par les bas* (the low road) and *par les hauts* (the high road). The former is much quicker but the latter is useful if you want to reach La Possession, Rivière des Galets or Trois-Bassins. Buses leave approximately every half hour from either end. If you're headed for Cilaos, change at St-Louis to the Cilaos bus. The fare between St-Denis and St-Pierre is F36.50. To St-Louis is F33.70.

St-Denis to St-Benoît
 This bus travels via Rivière des Pluies, Ste-Marie, Ste-Suzanne, Cambuston, St-André and Bras-Panon. Get off at the terminal in St-André to catch a bus to Salazie, Hell-bourg or Grand Îlet. On weekdays, buses leave every 15 minutes to every half hour from either end. The fare from St-Denis to St-Benoît is F18. To St-André is F11.20.

St-Pierre to St-Benoît
 The coastal bus travels via Grand Bois, Petite Île, St-Joseph, Vincendo, St-Philippe, Tremblet, Bois-Blanc, Ste-Rose and Ste-Anne (four buses daily). Alternatively, you can take the high road via Le-Tampon, Plaine-des-Cafres and Plaine-des-Palmistes (three buses daily). The fare for the entire trip along either route is F39.50.

St-André to the Cirque de Salazie
 There are four buses daily between St-André and Salazie/Hell-bourg; two of these continue from Hell-bourg on to Îlet à Vidot. There is another bus which runs twice daily between St-André and Grand Îlet/Le Bélier. The fares to or from St-André are: Salazie (F8.40), Hell-bourg (F14), Grand Îlet (F19.70), Le Bélier (F22.50).

St-Pierre or St-Louis to the Cirque de Cilaos
 This route runs via La Rivière, Petit Serré, Pavillon, Peter Both and Palmiste Rouge. There are eight buses each way on weekdays and Sat-

urdays and only four on Sunday (the Sunday routes don't include St-Pierre and only go as far as St-Louis). One or two of these continue to Îlet à Cordes, useful for reaching the Col du Taïbit trailhead, and quite a few connect Cilaos with the village of Bras Sec. The fare from St-Louis to Cilaos, Îlet à Cordes or Bras Sec is F22.50.

Fares work out at around F0.50 per km and the last buses run between 7 and 8 pm. Timetables are available from the Syndicat d'Initiative or the *gare routière* (main bus station) in St-Denis.

Public buses in Réunion are luxurious Mercedes, Renault or Volvo touring coaches, complete with stereo radio and cassette players. Although there's a conductor, there is no bell to stop the bus; when approaching your stop you must yell *dévant!* (ahead!) or clap your hands! Sometimes the radio is so loud that you also have to shout or whistle.

### TAXI

Taxis operate in the towns on the normal hire-on-demand basis. In country areas, where there are no buses, they operate on a scheduled *taxi-collectif* timetable.

Regular taxi fares start with F10 on the metre and an F10 surcharge at night. For example, by day, the fare from Jardin de l'Etat to the Hotel Le Méridien in St-Denis will be around F35. Fares from St-Denis are: F100 to Gillot airport; F250 to Boucan Canot beach; and at least F1000 to Cilaos or on a circuit of the island.

It's also possible to hire a taxi and driver for a day tour around the island. You'll pay around F400 per person for the day. Book in advance through one of the island tour agencies in St-Denis (Ségatours, Reucir Voyages, Bourbon Voyages, etc) or through the Syndicat d'Initiative. Readers have recommended a driver called Jean-Michel (☎ 43 05 10 or 53 43 08) who is quite friendly and speaks a little English.

Taxi-collectifs are usually Peugeot station wagons, seating up to eight people, which run from the main towns out to the surrounding villages. The timetables are posted at the taxi stands. Alternatively, ask local shop-keepers, or chambre and table d'hôte owners. The taxi-collectifs circulate from around 7 am to 6 pm (although there's a later one between Cilaos and St-Louis) and they cost about the same as buses.

### BOAT

Yacht and catamaran charter companies run cruises around the island and further afield, mainly for diving and fishing expeditions. See under Boat in the Réunion – Getting There & Away chapter and under Activities in the Réunion – Facts for the Visitor chapter for further details.

If you prefer to hire a boat and buzz around on your own, small motorboats are available for as little as F1300 for a half day or F6400 per week. Larger boats rigged for deep sea fishing may be hired for F3000 per day or F15,000 per week. Contact *Abysses* (☎ 41 22 90; fax 21 65 59) at the Port de Plaisance de la Pointe des Galets in Le Port.

### CAR

As with the rest of France, Réunion keeps to the right. Foreign drivers need only their driving licence from home and not an international driving licence. The road system on the island is excellent and it's well signposted. Route Nationale 1, the main road around the island, approaches motorway standards in parts.

La Corniche, built in 1963 along the sheer cliff face between St-Denis and La Possession, is said to be one of the world's most expensive stretches of road. As the road follows the old railway line through tunnels, it passes a network of artificial caves and shelters used for seismic tests.

Heading into the mountains via the cirque roads – especially the route into Cilaos – is a magnificent experience. The superbly engineered roads snake through hairpin bends, up steep slopes and along sheer drops, surrounded all the while by glorious – and distracting – scenery. Adding to the challenge are those local motorists who enjoy asserting their confidence on the road: small Peugeots, Renaults and Citröens cither zoom past at dizzying speeds or intimidate cautious drivers into clearing out of the way. Anyone who's driven in France will have some idea; try to keep a cool head.

## Car Rental

In French, 'car hire' is *location de voitures* and as you may imagine, there are quite a few firms specialising in providing wheels for visitors. Most companies stipulate that the driver must be at least 21 to 23 years of age, have held a driving licence for at least a year, have a passport or other piece of identity and hire the vehicle for at least one or two days. If your personal auto insurance isn't valid in Réunion, you'll also need to purchase CDW (collision damage waiver) insurance. Even with the insurance, you may be personally responsible for up to F4000 accidental damage to the vehicle; read the small print carefully.

With the main firms, prices and regulations don't vary much. If you don't have a credit card, you'll have to pay a cash deposit of around F3000. In some cases, the total hire cost is payable in advance.

The least expensive model, normally a Fiat Panda, Peugeot 106 or Renault 4, costs around F80 to F90 (all taxes included) per day plus F1 per km driven. Some companies offer an unlimited km scheme which costs around F190 per day for a rental of one to five days, and around F155 per day for two weeks. Rental charges are also subject to 7.5% value added tax. The additional insurance charges will cost up to F50 per day and if you're receiving or dropping the vehicle at anywhere but the main rental office, there'll be delivery/collection charges as well. In addition, the hirer pays for petrol, which costs around F4.50 per litre for 'Super' grade.

The good news is that there are less expensive options. In most towns, there are smaller car hire agencies (sometimes attached to a local garage) which charge 25-30% less than the major firms. Some major and minor firms include (those marked with an asterisk have a desk at Gillot airport):

Au Bas Prix
    35 Rue Suffren, 97460 St-Paul (☎ 45 43 36; fax 22 54 27)
ADA
    9 Boulevard Doret, 97400 St-Denis (☎ 21 59 01; fax 21 23 18)
Boucan Auto Location
    41 Rue d'Armagnac, Lot Armagnac 1, Route du Théâtre, 97434 St-Gilles (☎ 24 38 50)
Budget*
    18 Rue Stanislas Guimart, 97490 St-Denis (☎ 29 60 00)
Citer Foucque*
    69 Boulevard du Chaudron, 97490 Ste-Clotilde (☎ 28 15 11; fax 28 09 42)
    Rue Général de Gaulle, 97434 St-Gilles-les-Bains (☎ 24 35 00)
    154 Boulevard Hubert de Lisle, 97410 St-Pierre (☎ 25 16 32)
ERL*
    14 Rue Léopold Rambaud, 97490 Ste-Clotilde (☎ 21 66 81)
    240 Rue du Général de Gaulle, 97434 St-Gilles-les-Bains (☎ 24 02 25; fax 24 06 02)
Eurodollar*
    2 Rue Neuve, 97400 St-Denis (☎ 21 43 50; 21 54 64)
Europcar/Inter Rent*
    1 Boulevard Doret, 97400 St-Denis (☎ 21 81 01)
    Coralia Novotel, Les Filaos, 97434 St-Gilles-les-Bains (☎ 24 51 15)
GIS
    180 Avenue du Général de Gaulle, 97434 St-Gilles-les-Bains (☎ 24 09 73)
L'Île en Moto
    216 Avenue du Général de Gaulle, 97434 St-Gilles-les-Bains (☎ 24 05 63)
Oeüropa*
    62 Rue de Nice, 97400 St-Denis (☎ 48 80 71)
RFS
    44 Rue Labourdonnais, 97400 St-Denis (☎ 20 09 62; fax 41 63 55)

## Camper Van Rental

Camper vans can be rented for around F4500 per week with unlimited km, or F400 per day plus F3 per km. Contact Rando-Car (☎ 32 41 89), 100 Route du Maïdo, 97423 Le Guillaume or Tropical Loisirs (☎ 41 48 34), 97400 St-Denis.

## MOTORBIKE

Although mopeds, Vespa scooters and motorbikes will be useful for getting around in a small area (ie St-Gilles-les-Bains), those who would use them as a means of long distance transport will largely share the concerns of cyclists: the amount and speed of traffic, and the steep and winding nature of mountain roads. Although both the coastal and highland roads are in good condition, beginner bikers should think twice – and have a good insurance policy – before attempting them.

There are a couple of rental firms which hire out scooters and motorbikes. See Getting Around under St-Gilles-les-Bains for details.

## BICYCLE

Due to the traffic, the haste of most motorists and the steep and precarious nature of the mountain roads, those considering cycling as a form of transport in Réunion should be prepared for some hair-raising and potentially dangerous situations.

The coastal roads are too busy for casual cycling and the cirque roads are too steep, but the back roads and rugged terrain of the interior are ideally suited to mountain bikes. Mountain bikes may be hired from the three *stations de VTT* (rates given are for one hour/half day/full day): Cilaos Fun in Cilaos (F30/70/100), Parc du Maïdo on the Route du Maïdo (F30/70/120) and VTT Évasion at St-Philippe (F30/60/100).

Conventional bikes may be hired from Locacycles (see the Motorbike section) in St-Gilles-les-Bains for full/half day F80/50, plus a F200 deposit.

## HITCHING

Getting a lift in Réunion is subject to pretty much the same quirks of luck and fate that one experiences hitching anywhere. Your chances may be better if you're away from the tourist beats, where curious local people will help you, especially if you're sporting colours other than those of France. If you're tramping around the cirques in the rain, you'll probably be passed by carloads of other less sympathetic tourists. Hitching on the main roads can be more difficult, primarily because vehicles travel so fast, it's difficult (and dangerous) to stop in a hurry.

The standard advice not to hitch at night applies in Réunion, too. Furthermore, women shouldn't hitch alone and even several women together shouldn't accept lifts from only men; ascertain there are women and/or children in the vehicle before climbing in.

Here are a couple of readers' opinions on hitching:

If you're going to the beach, hitching is much quicker than the bus and it is often quicker even if you're not! Most people who pick you up are local, although Mauritians do oblige. It's a great way to meet people – I was forever being invited out to meals, to parties and such like. People in Réunion are very friendly and like to make you welcome.

**Gillian Chambers**

I dispute that hitching is subject to the same chances as in the US or Europe and that you are better off away from the beaten tracks. Hitching in Réunion is easier than almost anywhere I have ever been and the main road (RN1) is as good as any other!

**Mike Steane**

## LOCAL TRANSPORT
### Airport Transport

A taxi between St-Denis and Gillot airport costs F100 by day and F150 after dark. There's no regular bus service to or from the airport. To catch the public bus into St-Denis, walk straight across the airport car park and under the motorway flyover, then continue along the road leading up the hill. The bus stop is several hundred metres away on the right. The bus to catch is coming from St-Benoît (or Ste-Marie) and charges F6 to St-Denis. The first bus passes at around 6.15 am and the last at 6.45 pm.

The local Chamber of Commerce & Industry runs a minibus from the Hôtel Le Méridien to the airport two hours before flight departures to France. It returns to St-Denis shortly after a flight has landed. The trip costs F24 per person. For information, phone Le Méridien (☎ 21 80 20).

## TOURS

If you're visiting on a brief stopover (such as a day tour from Mauritius) or if you prefer to leave the organisation to someone else, you may want to approach the private tour agencies. Their offerings range from bus-based sightseeing tours to more adventurous and offbeat options. Some possibilities include:

**Bourbon Voyages**
14 Rue Rontaunay, 97400 St-Denis (☎ 21 68 18). Bourbon Voyages is the American Express affiliate and has offices in St-Benoît, St-Paul, St-Pierre, St-Louis and Le-Tampon. Unfortunately, they are also the most expensive, charging F330 to F400 per person for a day tour to one of the cirques or the volcano.

**Comète Voyages**
Angle de la (corner of) Rue Jules-Auber & Rue Moulin à Vent, 97400 St-Denis (☎ 21 31 00) Offers day tours to the major sites, helicopter trips and multi-day circuits.

**L'Orion Voyages**
22 Résidence Bénédicte, 97434 St-Gilles-les-Bains (☎ 24 64 24) Offers bus and helicopter tours of the island.

**Mascareignes Évasion**
Ste-Clotilde (☎ 48 67 55) This company offers bus and helicopter tours to the cirques, volcano and around the island.

**Nouvelles Frontières**
92 Rue Alexis de Villeneuve, 97400 St-Denis (☎ 21 54 54) The standard cirque or volcano tour will cost from F230 to F320.

**Reucir Voyages**
74 Rue Juliette Dodu, 97400 St-Denis (☎ 41 55 66) They charge F295 to F300 for a cirque or volcano tour but lunch is not included.

**Ségatours**
35 Rue Ste-Anne, 97400 St-Denis (☎ 20 37 30) They charge F250 to F300 for cirque or volcano tours, but readers haven't been impressed with their services; one wrote to report that too much time was wasted pausing for meals and that the tour returned to St-Denis nearly two hours earlier than indicated.

# St-Denis

St-Denis (pronounced 'san-de-NEE') is an attractive, clean and expensive capital city. Even visitors with a good supply of cash may feel a bit alien unless they have local friends to introduce them around the café set or some other clique. Perhaps that's why most tourists don't remain longer than it takes to book mountain gîtes and arrive or depart from the island.

St-Denis is known to some as the Paris of the Indian Ocean but unlike Paris, you won't find loads of down-at-heel student travellers struggling to survive on a slim budget. In their place are legions of hopeful workers from Madagascar, Mauritius, the African mainland and the EC – some legal and some not – searching for lucrative employment in the Indian Ocean's extension of the developed world.

St-Denis was founded in 1668 by the governor Regnault. Its name was taken from the Rivière St-Denis, on whose banks it was built (the river was named for a ship which ran aground there in 1667). In 1738, the capital was shifted to St-Denis from St-Paul by the governor Mahé de Labourdonnais. Numerous attempts at constructing a harbour near Le Barachois were foiled by a succession of cyclones.

Today, the population of St-Denis and its suburbs is only about 125,000, of whom about 40,000 live in the centre. Unlike the Mauritian capital of Port Louis, the city feels small and uncrowded.

## Orientation

The main shopping area is strung along Rue du Maréchal Leclerc and several blocks north of it. Where Rue du Maréchal Leclerc turns the corner at Rue Charles Gounod and heads eastward out of town, the shops head down-market; here one finds small shops and stalls selling inexpensive clothing and other goods.

The chic area of town is Le Barachois, St-Denis' promenade venue, which lies at the western end of the waterfront. Here are the upmarket bars and sidewalk cafés as well as the Hôtel Le Méridien, St-Denis' ritziest place to stay.

## Information

**Tourist Office** Tourist queries should be taken to the Syndicat d'Initiative de St-Denis (☎ 41 83 00), 48 Rue Ste-Marie. Several of the staff speak English and they can provide plenty of information, maps, brochures and advertising. There's a subsidiary branch at Gillot airport which is open for the arrival of international flights.

For trekking information and bookings, go to Maison de la Montagne (☎ 21 75 84) is at 10 Place Sarda Garriga (near Le Barachois). You can plan your itinerary using the large model of the island in their office.

If you're looking for information on any forthcoming events, make enquiries at the Syndicat d'Initiative or the Office Départemental de la Culture (☎ 41 11 41) at the Jardin de l'Etat.

**Money** The main banks are Banque de la Réunion (BR), Crédit Agricole (CA) and Banque Française Commerciale (BFC) and all will change money. They're open Monday to Friday from 8 am to 4 pm. The Crédit Agricole branch at Gillot Airport is open from 10.30 am to 7 pm, except on Sunday, when it opens at 1 pm.

The American Express agency is Bourbon Voyages (☎ 21 68 18) at 14 Rue Rontaunay but they don't change money or travellers' cheques. In an emergency, try one of the main hotels.

**Post & Telecommunications** The main post office at the corner of Rue du Maréchal Leclerc and Rue Juliette Dodu is open Monday to Friday from 7.30 am to 6 pm, and on Saturdays from 8 am to noon. Poste

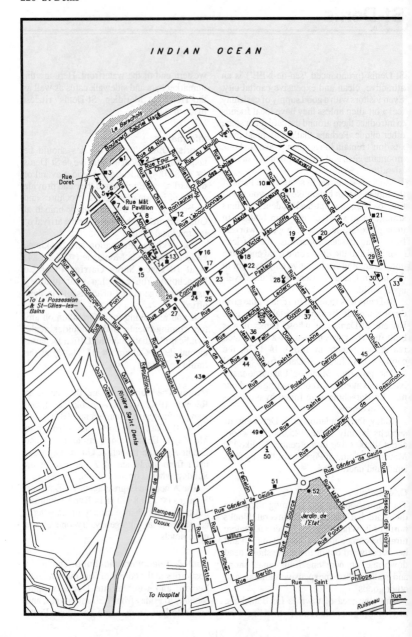

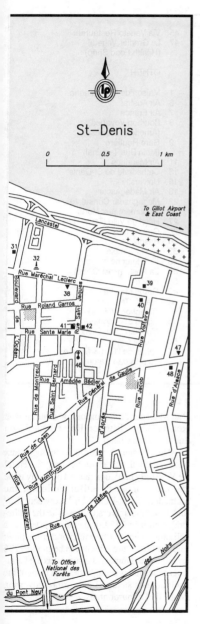

St–Denis

0        0.5        1 km

To Gillot Airport
& East Coast

Lancastel

31
32
Rue Maréchal Leclerc
38
Rue Roland Garros
Rue Santé Marie
39
40
41    42
47
46
Rue de Montreuil
Rue Saint Bernard
Rue Amédée Bédier
Rue Général de Gaulle
Rue Jacob
Rue d'Apres
Rue d'Alsace
48
Rue de Caen
Rue Monthyon
Rue Mazarin
Rue Bois de Nèfles
Rue des Noirs

To Office
National des
Forêts

Du Pont Neuf

restante is on Rue Juliette Dodu at the Boîtes de Commerce door of the main post office.

There are very few coin phones in St-Denis. Purchase Télécartes with 50 or 120 impulses at post offices and shops.

**Laundry** There's a one-hour dry cleaning service and automatic laundrette, *Pressing Arc en Ciel*, at the Euromarché centre between St-Denis and Aéroport de Gillot. The machines cost F25 to wash up to seven kg and F2 per five minutes to dry. It's a few km out of town; take the St-Benoît bus and ask the driver to drop you at the stop nearest Euromarché.

**Foreign Consulates** Since Réunion isn't an independent country, St-Denis lacks the usual complement of embassies and consulates befitting a capital city. The Malagasy Consulate (☎ 21 05 21), is a 2nd-floor office at 77 Rue Juliette Dodu. It's open Monday to Friday from 8.30 to 11.30 am.

The South African Consulate (☎ 21 50 05) is in the Compagnie des Indes Orientales building at 18 Rue de la Compagnie, near the Ave de la Victoire. It's open Monday to Friday, 8.30 am to 4 pm.

**Bookshops** The best stocked bookshop in St-Denis is the Librairie de la Réunion on Avenue de la Victoire. It supplies the university across the street, so it carries a range of English language titles.

The Syndicat d'Initiative also has a range of books for sale. For souvenir books and the latest French publications, there are numerous bookshops on the Rue Juliette Dodu.

**Emergency** The emergency number for police is (☎ 21 00 17). The ambulance is at (☎ 20 10 10).

**Créole Houses & Interesting Buildings**
There is a variety of impressive Créole mansions and houses throughout old town; the larger ones are mainly strung out along Rue

■  PLACES TO STAY

 3  Hôtel Le Méridien
10  Ascotel Hotel & Le Verger
    Restaurant
20  Hôtel Les Mascareignes
21  Pension Le Vieux Carthage
24  Hôtel Central
31  Hôtel de l'Océan
37  Hôtel-Pension La Palmeraie
    & Restaurant
39  Pension des Îles
40  Pension du Centre
41  Pension Touristique Aïcha
42  Pension Au Bon Refuge
48  Pension Salim (Chez Jaky)
51  Pension de Mme Roche

▼  PLACES TO EAT

 2  La Provençal, Piano Bar
    & Las Mimosas
 4  Le Roland Garros Restaurant
 5  Le Ralleye PMU
12  Royal Snack
14  Snack Soui-Mine
16  Le Massalé Restaurant
17  l'Igloo Glacerie
19  Restaurant l'Oriental
23  Deutsche Stube
25  Arts Malgache & Cesar Pizzeria
29  Snack l'Oriental
34  Kim Son Restaurant
38  Pavillon d'Or Restaurant

45  Via Veneto Restaurant
47  Le Grenier Vegetal
    (Health Food Shop)

OTHER

 1  Maison de la Montagne
 6  Air Austral
 7  Air France
 8  Bourbon Voyages
    (American Express)
 9  Gare Routière
    (Main Bus Terminal)
11  Air Mauritius
13  Cathédrale de St-Denis
15  University
18  Air Madagascar
22  Madagascar Consulate
26  Monument aux Morts
27  Hôtel de Ville (Town Hall)
28  Grande Mosqueé
30  Prisunic
32  Hindu Temple
33  Petit Marché
35  La Poste (Post Office)
36  Police
43  Grand Marché
44  France Telecom
    (Telephone Office)
46  Église St-Jacques
49  Museum Léon Dierx
50  Tourist Office
52  Jardin de l'Etat & Musée
    de l'Histoire Naturelle

de Paris between Rue Pasteur and Rue
Roland Garros. They include the family
home of former French Prime Minister under
Giscard d'Estaing, Raymond Barre, which is
near the corner of Rue de Paris and Rue
Maréchal Leclerc.

Smaller places are just as charming, and
since the grounds are generally more
compact, you'll get a better look at the characteristic verandas and intricate lambrequins
(ornamental window and door borders). The
best advice is to wander and see what you
discover. Good places to begin include along
Rue Alexis de Villeneuve between Rue Juliette Dodu and Rue Jean Chatel; along Rue
Juliette Dodu just south of Rue Alexis de
Villeneuve; along Juliette Dodu just south of

Rue Manager de Beaumont; and along Rue
Roland Garros between Rue Juliette Dodu
and Rue Jean Chatel.

Also of interest are the Monument aux
Morts, the tall victory monument; the Hôtel
de Ville (city hall), considered by many to be
the city's most beautiful building; the
Cathédrale de St-Denis, built between 1829
and 1832; the university, opposite the cathedral – built in 1759, it has also served as a
religious school, a barracks and a hospital;
and the Préfecture which was begun in 1735
by Governor Dumas, and served as the Compagnie des Indes headquarters. In front of the
building is a statue of the former governor,
Mahé de Labourdonnais.

## Museum Léon Dierx

More an art gallery than a museum, the Museum Léon Dierx is housed in the former bishops' palace, constructed in 1845, and situated on Rue de Paris, near Rue Sainte Marie. Most of the paintings, by both French and Réunionnais artists, date from the turn of the last century. The collection was donated by art dealer Ambroise Vollard and includes a lithograph by Renoir, a bronze by Picasso and works by Chagall, Cézanne, Delacroix, Degas, Matisse and Gauguin. The museum is named after the Réunionnais poet and painter Léon Dierx (1858-1912). It's open daily except Tuesday from 10 am to 5 pm. Admission is free.

## Jardin de l'Etat & Natural History Museum

The Jardin de l'Etat was originally established beside the river by the East India Company in 1764. In 1773, after several floods, it was relocated and named the Jardin du Roi. For many years it served as a repository for the plants and crops destined for distribution to local planters. In 1834, the Palais Législatif was constructed and 20 years later, Mayor Gustave Manes installed in it the Natural History Museum, and renamed the garden Jardin Colonial. The name wasn't changed to Jardin de l'Etat until Réunion became a full French département in 1948.

The gardens are quiet and well kept, featuring numerous perfume plants, tropical oddities from around the world and lots of orchids. You may also want to take a look at the monuments to the botanist Pierre Poivre, who was based on Mauritius (Île de France) and to agronomist Joseph Hubert from St-Benoît who brought many useful agricultural specimens – including cloves, mangosteen, lychees, jamalac and breadfruit – to Réunion.

While the museum isn't spectacular, it does contain stuffed specimens of the island's former fauna, including dugongs, giant tortoises, the crested bourbon bird and even a rare coelacanthe caught off the

Comoros islands. There's also an aquarium which is worth a visit. The museum is open weekdays from 10 am to 4 pm. Entry is free.

## Le Barachois

This seafront park, lined by cannons facing out to sea, is the main promenade venue in St-Denis. The park has *boules* matches, cafés and a monument to the French aviator Roland Garros, the first pilot to cross the Mediterranean and the inventor who worked out a way of timing machine-gun fire so it could be directed through a turning propeller. In 1988, Réunion commemorated the centenary of Garros' birth in St-Denis.

Nearby is Place Sarda Garriga, with its quiet park. It was named after the governor who abolished slavery in Réunion on 20 December, 1848.

## Hindu Temple

The small but wildly colourful Hindu temple stands out among the shops east of the centre along Rue du Maréchal Leclerc, opposite Rue de Montreuil. When we were there, it was undergoing renovation and covered with scaffolding. Hopefully, you'll have better luck getting a photo.

## La Montagne & Le Brûlé

These hill districts behind St-Denis offer great views over the town and are starting points for treks to Plaine d'Affouches, La Roche Écrite and even over the mountains into the Cirque de Salazie. Access to these areas is by taxi or bus up the steep winding roads; to reach Le Brûlé at 800 metres, take bus 23 from the Gare Routière. For La Montagne, take bus Nos 21 or 22.

From Le Brûlé, there are some pleasant walks along the Route Forestière de la Roche Écrite. One of the nicest is to the waterfall Cascade Maniquet about four km from the village.

Another possibility is Bassin du Diable, a wild and isolated valley accessible from upper Bellepierre, the first village downhill from Le Brûlé. The track turns off to the right (headed uphill) at a small reservoir. The valley lies about 4.5 km along this track, which traverses the slopes above the eastern side of the Rivière St-Denis.

## La Roche Écrite

Like the higher Piton des Neiges, this 2277 metre peak is often obscured in clouds. Although it isn't technically *in* the Cirque de Mafate, it does offer a spectacular view of the lower cirque. Dawn is the best time to see it. There is a choice of four routes to reach the peak:

- Along RF1 from Le Brûlé village above St Denis to the Plaine des Chicots gîte at Caverne Basse (three hours), then to Caverne des Soldats, through huge slabs of lava and limestone, and the summit (1½ hours).
- From Le Quinzième hamlet on the La Montagne road by footpath (at least four hours) or GR R2 *variante* from the kiosk overlooking the upper Rivière St Denis to the Plaine d'Affouches (two hours) and on to join the Le Brûlé route at the Plaine des Chicots gîte at Caverne Basse (two hours). From there, it's at least 1½ hours to the summit.
- From Grand Îlet along the road to Mare à Martin. The path winds precariously up the side of the mountain, making it a steep and difficult climb that is only for the fit. Allow at least two hours for the ascent.
- From Dos d'Ane east along the Cirque rim to the Plaine des Chicots gîte (about three hours) to meet up with the previously described routes.

## Places to Stay – bottom end

As already warned, there is high local demand throughout the year for budget accommodation in St-Denis, so advance booking is recommended. Most establishments require at least partial advance payment. There are no chambres d'hôte in St-Denis and there are few rooms available for less than F100 per night.

**Pensions de Famille** The pensions de famille come in all shapes and conditions. One of the strictest and best run is the *Pension de Mme Roche* (☎ 41 31 30) at 34 Rue du Général de Gaulle, which has a selection of rooms, some with washbasins. The house is a mixture of old and new but showers and toilets are communal. Single/double rooms with breakfast cost

F125/200 and large evening meals are a very reasonable F35. Mme Roche's is very popular with students and contract workers; monthly rates are F1800 per person in a four-bed dorm or F2300 to F2700 in a private room.

*Pension du Centre* (☎ 41 73 02 or 41 19 43), 272 Rue du Maréchal Leclerc, is more like a hostel or unclassed hotel, hidden at the end of an alley between Rue Voltaire and a paved laneway. It serves primarily as an option for long-term contract workers and is a bit grubby, but the owner, M Nassor is an extremely friendly character. If you phone from the airport, they'll pick you up for a very reasonable fee.

There are nine individual rooms that cost F80 per night and two, six-bed communal rooms at F60 per person per night. Private rooms cost from F120 to F160; some have balconies. All rooms include breakfast but there are no other meals. Opposite is the *Pension des Îles* which charges the same prices and is an option if the Pension du Centre is full.

Another option is *Pension Au Bon Refuge* (☎ 41 73 29) at 13 Rue St-Jacques, but I was less than impressed with their attitude; when I asked about accommodation, they led me to a room occupied by an elderly man and said if I wanted to stay, they'd throw him out (I continued my search elsewhere!). At any rate, it tries to cater for travellers and has an interesting setup with eight individual rooms, some mere cubbyholes, and four communal rooms. The communal showers and toilets aren't exactly sparkling clean. This 'refuge' charges F100/150 a single/ double and F50 per person for a dormitory room. For longer stays, you'll pay F90/120 a single/double and F40 for a dorm room. Breakfast costs F15 and a set meal costs F45. There is also a separate restaurant-style dining room.

A nicer option is the *Pension Touristique Aïcha* (☎ 20 37 02) at 24 Rue St-Jacques, opposite Au Bon Refuge. It charges F100/150 a single/double and F25 for breakfast. Delicious Indian meals cost F70.

On a more cramped, seedier scale are the

Top Left:   Church, Ste-Anne, Réunion (DS)
op Right:  Swinging footbridge, Ravine Bruneull, Cirque de Mafate, Réunion (DS)
   Bottom:  La Nouvelle, Cirque de Mafate, Réunion (DS)

Top: Waterfall on the Ravine St Gillies, Réunion (RW)
Bottom: Helicopter at Bord à Martin, Réunion (RS)

malabar (Indian-run) pensions which are popular with itinerant and contract workers. One such place is *Pension Jaky* aka *Pension Salim* (☎ 20 05 67) at 148 Rue du Général de Gaulle, warmly recommended by a reader:

I helped a local lady by carrying her luggage off the aeroplane and benefited from the occasion by asking her to give me some advice. She and her sister turned out to be helpful characters and they led me to a Hindu-owned pension in St-Denis called Pension Jaky.

The owner, Jaky himself, had placed signs in the reception saying something like 'The guests are kindly asked not to consume alcohol or to eat pork in this establishment' (although normally Hindus are allowed to drink alcohol, aren't they?). The first thing that caught my eye was a couple of Malagasy (for some reason, all of Jaky's guests are from Madagascar) sitting on the stairs drinking rum and eating pork. The answer to my obvious question was '*Mais t'sais, le patron, il est bien tolérant*' (But ya know, the owner, he's very tolerant).

And now for the interesting part: Jaky charges only F35 for a bed if you agree to share the room with Malagasy teenagers (who are polite and extremely friendly – I got along well with them and even accompanied them on a trip to St-Louis selling handicrafts). There are toilets and a shower but otherwise, the hygienic standard of this place is about as high as you might expect for F35. And Jaky always seems to have a spare bed.

**Mikael Parkvall**

Another cheap place is *Pension Roger* (☎ 41 24 38) at 22 Rue Mazagran (a couple of blocks east of the Jardin de l'Etat) which costs F45 per person in dormitory rooms.

*Pension Calixte* (☎ 21 26 90) – also known as *Pension Butor* – at 6 Rue du Butor, has five dormitories, each accommodating four guests. It's a cheap option at F40 per person but it's very busy and dirty (one reader used the adjectives 'sleazy', 'seedy' and 'noisy'!) so don't expect much. As with much of the bottom end accommodation in St-Denis, most of the guests are long-term workers from France, Madagascar and Mauritius. It lies near the canal known as Ravine du Butor at the eastern end of Rue du Maréchal Leclerc, a 30 minute walk from the centre. It's accessible by city bus numbers 6 and 8 which stop nearby; get off at the

Marcade stop. If you're a night owl, it's worth noting that the gate is locked at 9.30 pm.

Alternatively, there's a more upmarket place, *Pension Amanda* (☎ 20 80 76) at 20 Rue Amédée Bédier (behind the church of St-Jacques), which charges F120/150 a single/double. Breakfast costs an additional F20.

The well-managed *Pension le Vieux Carthage* (☎ 20 24 18) at 13 Rue des Limites, is popular with visitors. There's a shop attached, as well as a lively bar and small restaurant out the front where you'll get a good value plat du jour for around F35. Rates are F150/200 a single/double. Breakfast costs F25 extra (readers reckon it isn't worth the money). For the same price, you can stay in an individual room at *Auberge Beau Soleil* (☎ 21 67 10; fax 21 62 11) at 93 Rue d'Après south of Rue du Général de Gaulle. They also have dormitory rooms for F75 per person. Evening meals cost F45 and breakfast is F15.

A night at *Pension Jacqueline Balnaik* (☎ 20 29 11), 30 Rue du Général de Gaulle, costs F100 per person, including breakfast, in an individual or dormitory room. Monthly rates are F2500 per person in an individual room with evening meals. It's nearly always full of long-term visitors so you may have trouble finding a bed.

At 107 Rue du Général de Gaulle is *Bungalow Chez Jean* (☎ 41 06 82) which charges F700 per week for a double. *Pension Le Palmier* (☎ 20 00 95), near the church of St-Jacques at 16 Rue St-Bernard, costs F100/120 a single/double in an individual room or F40 per person in the dormitory.

In the foothills east of town at 12 Ave Desbassyns in Ste-Clotilde is the *Villa les Bougainvilliers* (☎ 29 12 96; fax 29 63 77) which charges F150 per person per night. The monthly rate is F1900. There are also several more elaborate schemes for tourists, including the following package: 15 nights, demi-pension (breakfast and dinner) and three guided day hikes for F4125/6300 a single/double. Also in Ste-Clotilde at 26 Allée de l'Ancienne Poste is the *Pension Les Anthuriums* (☎ 28 19 44). They charge F120/

200 a single/double, breakfast included, with a minimum stay of three nights.

Up in La Montagne is *Le Home Fleuri de Cendrillon* (☎ 23 63 28). The minimum stay in this family home is three nights and single/double rooms with bath cost F120/200. There are discounts for longer stays. La Montagne is reached on bus No 21 from the gare routière in St-Denis.

Also in the mountain area is an unchecked option, *Domaine de la Prévalée* (☎ 23 02 32), at 17 Chemin Cimetière in Le Brûlé. It's owned by Jean-Paul and Jacqueline Lepée. If you wind up there somehow, let us know how it was!

**Hotels** For not much more than the pensions, you can stay in the *Hôtel des Mascareignes* (☎ 21 15 28), 3 Rue Lafférière, a calm place on a quiet back street in the centre. Classed as third class, it has 12 fully equipped rooms. Singles cost F220/165 with/without bath and doubles are F220/260, all rooms including breakfast.

*Hôtel-Pension La Palmeraie* (☎ 41 23 47), a renovated pension at 56 Rue Félix Guyon, is also fairly inexpensive. It has eight rooms and charges F170/200 a single/double. Breakfast costs an extra F15.

**Gîtes** The only true gîtes in the St-Denis area are those of Mme Sylvaine Robert (☎ 23 00 15) at 105 Route des Azelées up in Le Brûlé. This is a good point of departure for walking trips to the Plaine d'Affouches and La Roche Écrite. The smaller of these self-contained units holds three guests and rents for F1000 per week. The larger, which accommodates five people, rents for F1400 per week.

Alternatively, you can stay at the *Zone de Loisirs du Colorado* (☎ 23 74 12) or Colorado Leisure Area, where there are 10 tiny *cabanes* (cabins) renting for F20 per night. They're extremely basic but are an option if everything else is booked out. It lies within a half-hour walk of La Montagne village; from the Gare Routière in St-Denis, take bus No 21 and get off at the Bougainvilliers stop. From there, continue walking, bearing left at the fork. Shortly after the fork, there's a sign pointing uphill toward Colorado; from this point, it's a two km walk.

**Gîte de Montagne** High above St-Denis near the base of La Roche Écrite lies the Plaine des Chicots gîte (☎ 21 75 84). The only access is on foot; for information, see under La Roche Écrite earlier in this chapter. A bunk costs F50 per person and should be booked through Maison de la Montagne.

**Places to Stay – middle**
There are three two-star hotels, the biggest and most central of which is the appropriately named *Hôtel Central* (☎ 21 18 08), at 37 Rue de la Compagnie. Single/double rooms cost F315/349, including breakfast.

The *Hôtel Astoria* (☎ 20 05 58), a no-star hotel at 16 Rue Juliette Dodu has 17 rooms; they charge F250/370 a single/double.

Near the Jardin de l'Etat at 5 Ruelle Boulot is *La Marianne* (☎ 21 80 80; fax 21 85 00), a new 24-room hotel charging F240/300 a single/double, with kitchenette available.

The *Hôtel de l'Océan* (☎ 41 43 08), 10 Blvd de l'Océan (near Rue du Maréchal Leclerc toward the sea), is a spanking new, clean edifice with a decidedly air-conditioned and hermetically sealed atmosphere rather than a warm and homely feeling. Singles/doubles cost F210/280.

**Places to Stay – top end**
The four-star *Hôtel Le Méridien* (☎ 21 80 20), 2 Rue Doret at Le Barachois, is Réunion's Sheraton-class offering and is a third dearer than anything else. Singles/doubles cost F760/820 and an additional F70 for breakfast! It has a casino and a classy disco, La Locomotive, as well as a piano bar, snack bar and restaurant.

A newish hotel, the three-star *Ascotel* (☎ 41 82 82), is at 20 Rue Charles Gounod. It has 52 rooms at F460/560 a single/double. It's well located near the gare routière and about a 10 minute walk from Le Barachois. Both of its restaurants, *Le Pont du Ciel*, which specialises in Chinese cuisine, and the buffet restaurant *Le Verger* are quite good.

Approximately one km due south of the town centre on the Rampes de St-François foothills, is the 197-room *Hôtel Le Bourbon* (☎ 21 27 24). Compared to Le Méridien, the three-star Bourbon is reasonably priced, at F520/590 a single/double. It has a pool, changes money, organises big-game fishing trips and provides vegetarian meals.

Then there's the four-star *Hôtel Alliance Créolia* (☎ 30 43 43; fax 30 18 18) at 14 Rue du Stade in the Montgaillard neighbourhood south-east of town. It has a large swimming pool, sauna, sports centre, and tennis courts as well as a restaurant serving Créole dishes. The least expensive single/double rooms cost 650/700. To get there, take bus No 4 from the centre and get off at Montgaillard.

## Places to Eat – bottom end

Thanks to the French passion for *la gastronomie*, there's a beaut or cute restaurant around every corner in St-Denis. Unfortunately for budget travellers, they're mostly quite pricey. At lunchtime, you may be able to get a reasonable *plat du jour* or *menu du jour* (set meal) for between F40 and F70, but to experience haute cuisine in Réunion, you'll have to bid *adieu* to a pile of francs.

You may also want to check the 'Restaurants' classified page in the daily papers for menus and special offers. Most cafés, bars and restaurants have a menu and price list on display, which saves embarrassing questions like *Combien?* Those pensions which serve meals are worth a try, providing you book in advance. Mme Roche may not welcome nonresident guests, but the pension Au Bon Refuge does and Pension le Vieux Carthage has an excellent restaurant which is open to anyone.

If you call F20 cheap for a revolting imitation of an American hamburger, then *Mac Burger* on Rue Jules Auber, around the corner from the Grande Mosquée on Rue du Maréchal Leclerc, is the place. They also sell flat Coke for F5. Much better are the small snack bars around Place Sarda Garriga at Le Barachois which sell samosas and sandwiches for people on the run.

Good value for weekday lunches is at *Snack Soui-Mine* at the corner of Rue Labourdonnais and Ave de la Victoire. It is very popular with office workers and there can be queues at 12.30 pm, but they soon disappear. The set menu costs F27 and consists of meat or fish with *daubes* (stews), rice and *graines* (usually beans).

For a warm welcome and good food at reasonable cost, a reader recommends the *Pause Café* on Avenue de la Victoire opposite the university. The menu isn't vast but there is a wide selection of freshly squeezed fruit juices and it's very homely. The friendly staff don't hurry you – just the opposite, in fact, with newspapers and magazines to keep you occupied! Also highly recommended, especially for its Créole-style grilled fish, is the *Vieux Portail* on Boulevard Doret.

On Rue du Général de Gaulle opposite the Jardin de l'Etat, is a small and unpretentious Sino-Créole café/restaurant, the *Snack du Jardin*. It's open daily for lunch and dinner and does takeaways. A big portion of *sauté mine* (fried noodles) is F25, chop suey is F15 and *riz cantonnais* (fried rice) costs F18. Bourbon beer costs F7 and soft drinks are F4. The Jardin also has delicious ice cream at F4; try the Créole rum and raisin.

One of the best places for ice cream in St-Denis is *La Sorbetière* on Rue Jean Chatel, which also does breakfasts and snacks. Even better is the extremely popular lunchtime and Sunday afternoon venue *L'Igloo Glacerie* at 67 Rue Jean Chatel, which makes its own ice cream and serves good plats du jour for only F45. The elaborate *tarte du jour* (quiche of the day) costs F42 while other quiche concoctions are F38. After, there's the 20-page ice cream menu! The place is made even more interesting by the trompe l'oeil on the inside walls; with Antarctic and tropical themes superimposed, it can make you feel hot and cold simultaneously!

The *Royal Snack*, near the police station at 143 Rue Jean Chatel, is a good meeting place and is open from 7 am to 2 am. It's also popular at lunchtime with a reasonable three-course set menu for around F60.

For reasonable and authentic Indian snacks, takeaways and meals, go to *Le Massalé* near the corner of Rue Alexis de Villeneuve and Rue Jean Chatel. They also have a variety of wonderful samosas – chicken, fish, prawn, etc – but they're rather expensive at F2 a shot.

A reader has recommended *Le Vieux Carré* at Ste-Clotilde which serves delicious cheap meals for F25. It's on the main road east out of St-Denis just beyond La Case du Chaudron. It's closed on Sunday and Monday.

For self-catering, the Prisunic and Score supermarkets are probably the easiest options, although the markets are considerably more economical for fresh fruits and vegetables. There's also a whole food shop, *Le Grenier Vegetal*, on Rue du Général de Gaulle.

For a good lunchtime menu, Scottish reader Stephen Clarke recommends the friendly *Le Cascroute* on Rue Juliette Dodu, where you can get a tasty set menu lunch for just F37.

### Places to Eat – middle & top end

At the bottom of Ave de la Victoire, near Le Barachois, is the weird *Le Rallye PMU* café/bar/brasserie. Its interior décor is certainly memorable with odd neon art flashing unnatural colours on the walls and a video juke box screeching, whining and clattering away. When I was there, the emphasis seemed to be on avant-garde alternative French pop music. They make good snack meals – pizzas, salads, quiche, soup and the like – and serve typically corpulent coffee.

You'll find a similar menu around the corner in the quieter, more upmarket *Café Roland Garros*. It's busy and offers terrace seating where you can put away a few Bourbons, read tasteful novels and just observe the passing scene. (Those in search of reading material will find French magazines and newspapers from all over Europe in the newsagents attached to Le Rallye PMU.) Women should check out the bizarre 'permutating' loo!

The Chinese specialists are at *Le Pavillon d'Or* (☎ 21 49 86), at 224 Rue du Maréchal Leclerc and the food is expensive but extremely good. The café downstairs serves inexpensive meals at lunchtime, but is closed on Sunday. Another good Chinese option is *Restaurant l'Oriental* on Rue Pasteur near Rue Charles Gounod.

African and Caribbean cuisine is available at *La Bambara* (☎ 41 04 51) at 160 Rue Monthyon. It's open from early morning until 2 am daily except Monday. Surprisingly, St-Denis even has a German restaurant, *Deutsche Stube* (☎ 21 14 26), at Rue de la Compagnie 34. It's closed on Sundays.

I confess, however, that my favourite St-Denis restaurant is *Kim Son* (☎ 21 75 00), a small and friendly place opposite the Grand Marché at 13 Rue du Maréchal Leclerc. It's upper mid-range price-wise, but is super for a splurge meal. Try *nems* if you're after delicious Vietnamese spring rolls with mint and fish sauce; *rouleaux de printemps* are something entirely different and are available only at Friday lunch.

Another very good option is the cosy and casual *Via Veneto* (☎ 21 92 71) Italian restaurant at the corner of Rue Ste-Marie and Rue Jules Auber. Prices aren't too bad and they're open on Sunday evening, a real oddity for St-Denis.

*Le Reflet des Îles* (☎ 21 73 82) at 27 Rue de l'Est near the corner of Rue Pasteur is heartily recommended for Créole dishes. It's open for lunch and dinner daily except Sunday. Some others worth trying are *Le Pasteur* (☎ 21 92 05) at 49 Rue Pasteur; for Indian meals, *Les Délices de L'Orient* (☎ 41 44 20) at 59 Rue Juliette Dodu; and *Chez Antoine* (☎ 21 60 13) at 28 Rue de l'Est.

The top French restaurants are *Le Labourdonnais* (☎ 21 44 26) at 14 Rue l'Amiral Lacaze, and *Chez Piat* (☎ 21 45 76), at 60 Rue Pasteur, which is closed on Sundays and Mondays. If you want to pretend you're in Paris or you'd just like to appear chic for an evening, opt for a financial blowout on nouvelle cuisine at *Restaurant à la Girandole* (☎ 21 31 60) at Rue Jean Chatel

173. Plan on spending F500 to F600 for a meal for two with wine. It's closed on Sundays.

## Entertainment

**Nightlife** Little of Paris has rubbed off on St-Denis as far as nightlife goes but there are a few discos. The best and most chic is *Le Kabar* (☎ 30 43 43) at the Hôtel Alliance Créolia, which is open Tuesday to Saturday from 10.30 pm to dawn. Among the others are *Le First* (☎ 41 68 25) at 8 Ave de la Victoire (closed Sunday and Monday), *Le Jardin des Délices* (☎ 30 31 91) on Boulevard de la Providence (open Friday and Saturday only) and *La Plantation* at 24 Rue Pasteur (closed Sunday).

The Le Méridien also has a casino which is open daily except Sunday from 9 pm to 3 am.

*Le Shaker* at 20 Rue de Nice runs good piano jazz sessions with the house ensemble and various guest performers. There are also performances nightly except Sunday at the pub *La Distillerie* in the Hôtel Le Méridien. Other pubs of note include *Le Guetali* at Hôtel Alliance Créolia, *Le Pub Alexander* at 108 Rue Pasteur (open nightly except Sunday from 5 pm), *Le Rallye PMU* at Le Barachois (open daily from 7 am to midnight) and *Le Ti-Bird* on Rue Léopold Rambaud east of the centre (open Friday and Saturday nights and whenever there are performances at the nearby Théatre Vollard).

**Cinemas** St-Denis has two main cinemas, the Ritz on Rue Juliette Dodu with three screens and the Plaza on Rue Pasteur with two screens. The Plaza sometimes shows English-language films with subtitles.

**Theatre** Performers of French renown stage performances in Réunion and there are frequent festivals and spectacles, normally with two or three plays per performance. Details of what's on can be found in the daily newspapers, the free brochure from the l'Office Départemental de la Culture (☎ 41 11 41) at the Jardin de l'Etat. Another good source of information is the *RUN* magazine, available free from the Syndicat d'Initiative.

## Getting There & Away

The gare routière complex near the corner of Rue Labourdonnais and Rue Joffre contains both the city and long-distance bus terminals. See the Bus section in the Réunion – Getting Around chapter for details on buses to and from St-Denis.

## Getting Around

**To/From the Airport** Taxis between St-Denis and Gillot airport cost F100 by day and at night, the price goes up to F150. There is an airport bus which costs F18 but it only stops at the Gare Routière and the Hôtel Le Méridien in St-Denis. Going the opposite direction, it departs from the Hôtel Le Méridien two hours before flight departures to France.

To get the regular bus into St-Denis, you need to cross the airport car park, walk under the motorway flyover and follow the road uphill. It's about 300 metres from there to the bus stop. The bus you're looking for is St-Benoît to St-Denis and it will cost around F6 into town. To reach the airport, take any St-Benoît bus from the Gare Routière or along Rue du Maréchal Leclerc.

**Bus** St-Denis is small and getting around on foot is a breeze, but there is nevertheless a good city bus service. It's operated by Réseau Transports Dionysien (RTD) and goes just about everywhere in town. The city is divided into two zones – 1 and 2. Zone 1 tickets cost F5 each or F21 for a book of five tickets from RTD kiosks. On the bus, single tickets cost F7. Weekly and monthly passes are available and reduced fares are offered to students and children. Hang onto your ticket after boarding since random checks are common. The city bus terminal lies near the corner of Rue Labourdonnais and Rue Joffre just south-east of the long-distance terminal.

Bus stops are well marked; work out the bus routes by trial and error or rely on locals to help sort you out. Alternatively, you can buy Albert Trotet's F25 *Plan de l'Agglomération et du Reseau d'Autobus de St-Denis* which shows all city bus routes. It's available at the Prisunic bookshop.

**Taxi** Taxis around town are generally expensive and you won't get by paying less than F30 for even a hop of a couple of blocks. A trip across town will set you back at least F60.

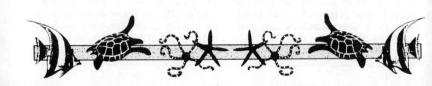

# Around the Coast

There are surprising differences in atmosphere between the 15 or so main communities around the coast of Réunion. Some are quiet and insulated, others seem industrious and still others turn a vivacious and outgoing face on the world. For example, most people find St-Pierre lively and pleasant, but St-Benoît grimy and uninteresting. St-Philippe is a much nicer place than St-Joseph and Ste-Suzanne is preferable to Ste-Marie. Keep in mind, however, that these are personal opinions and you may find the opposite to be true – and that even the most agreeable of towns will appear dead and dull on Saturday afternoon and Sunday.

For short-term visitors, the holiday and accommodation centre stretches from Boucan Canot just north of St-Gilles-les-

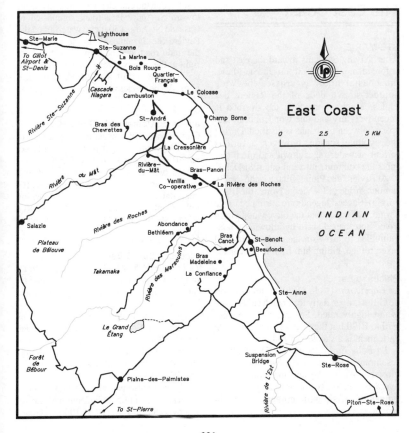

East Coast

Bains south to Étang-Salé-les-Bains. This area contains all of Réunion's paltry 30 km of beaches. The south-eastern end of the island, however, is the emptiest, most remote and least developed region. It lies under the shadow of the volcano and in the path of lava flows. In places along back roads, you can still see bullock carts in use.

While the west coast is lined with casuarina trees *(filaos)*, the east coast is fringed by screw pines *(vacoas)*. The fibre from its fronds is made into rope and you'll see strands of it left to dry on the roadside.

# The East Coast

## STE-MARIE

After leaving St-Denis toward the east and before reaching Gillot airport and Ste-Marie, the coastal highway crosses the wide boulder-strewn beds of the Rivière des Pluies. Much of the time the riverbed is deceptively dry and one wonders if all that space between the banks is justified. During the cyclone season, however, a furious torrent of water rages down and often disrupts the commute into and out of St-Denis.

At Rivière des Pluies village is the locally famous shrine of La Vierge Noire (the Black Virgin). Several legends are attributed to the shrine; one states that the olive wood virgin saved an escaped slave by allowing a bougainvillea to grow on the rock where he'd taken refuge, hiding him from his pursuers.

### Places to Eat

*Le Capricorne* (☎ 48 81 70) at the Aéroport de Gillot is open daily for French cuisine, but is not highly rated. Set menus range from F70 to F120 but the price of an average à la carte meal is a shocking F150.

*La Belle Étoile* (☎ 53 40 78), a Chinese restaurant at Ravine des Chèvres-les-Bas, is closed on Wednesday and Sunday nights. An average meal costs F60 and the *poisson au gingembre* (fish with ginger) is recommended.

## STE-SUZANNE

Ste-Suzanne, one of the prettiest towns on the Réunion coast, was the site of the first population on the island; in 1646, 12 mutineers exiled by the Governor Pronis from Fort Dauphin in Madagascar settled for three years at the site of present-day Quartier Français. The area is now a main sugar-producing centre, which will be obvious as you approach from any direction. The most imposing and beautiful structure at Ste-Suzanne is the classic lighthouse perched on the rocks near the western end of town.

### Cascade Niagara

Just beyond the church on the highway south toward St-André is a track signposted to Cascade Niagara, a 30 metre waterfall on the Rivière Ste-Suzanne. From the turning off the main road, go about two km then bear right at the next two road junctions to wind up at the waterfall and attendant tropical pool. At the weekends, it's a popular picnic site.

### Jardin du Domaine du Grand Hazier

Garden fans will especially enjoy a visit to this 18th century sugar planter's residence, an official French historical monument, whose two hectare garden is planted in a variety of tropical flowers and fruit trees. It's open daily for guided tours by reservation only. Contact M Chassagne (☎ 52 32 81), 97441 Ste-Suzanne. The tours cost F35 per person.

### Places to Stay & Eat

*Le Bocage* (☎ 52 22 72) is a good restaurant (and is indeed the only restaurant) in Ste-Suzanne. It's closed on Sunday nights and Mondays.

The only chambre d'hôte is that of *Mme Caladama* (☎ 46 11 43) at Rue Raymond Vergés 58 in Quartier Français. She has three rooms with private bath, and two double rooms with shared facilities. Singles/doubles cost F100/130.

There are also two gîtes de France: *Mme Gauvin* (☎ 42 11 05) at 8 Chemin Maturine, Bellevue, and *M Payet* (☎ 46 10 78) at Quartier Français. The former charges F1270 per week for six people and the latter costs F1450 per week for seven people.

## ST-ANDRÉ

This town of over 30,000 people contains one of the largest Indian communities in Réunion thanks to a policy of importing cheap labour to work in the sugar cane fields after slavery was abolished in 1848. Today, St-André has two *Tamoul* (Tamil) temples, one known as *Le Colosse* near the coast north-east of town. The other, the Kali Temple with its monumental gateway, the Gopuram, is right in the centre on Avenue de l'Île de France. The latter is open to visitors (shoes must be removed before entering).

In the church square and bus park, the cemetery and the town hall, there are large *ficus nitida* trees; these are known as *élastiques* by the Créoles, due to the elastic, rubberlike gum in their bark. Also, take a look at the Maison Valliamé, a classic Créole mansion on the main street.

### Information

The local Syndicat d'Initiative is known as Office Municipal du Tourisme de St-André (☎ 46 91 63). It's found at 68 Centre Commercial, Rue de la Gare, 97440 St-André, not far from the bus terminal.

### La Maison de la Vanille

At 466 Rue de la Gare in the centre, this old Créole mansion is open to the public Tuesday to Sunday from 8.30 am to noon and 2 to 5.30 pm. It's set amid lawns, gardens and vanilla plantations and visitors can learn the elaborate process of hand pollination necessary to coax the vanilla orchid to produce those gloriously aromatic beans we know and love. Guided tours are available upon advance request (☎ 46 00 14).

### Champ-Borne

If you are staying awhile in St-André, a trip to Champ-Borne on the coast is worthwhile. This place has borne the brunt of several cyclones and storms; in 1962, a tidal wave caused by Cyclone Jenny swept over the area and destroyed the local church. The remains still stand. Two shipwrecks dating to the turn of the last century lie just offshore.

### Sugar Refinery

North of town at Bois Rouge, also on the coast, is a sugar refinery. Guided tours may be arranged through the Syndicat d'Initiative in St-Denis or the refinery itself (☎ 41 36 94).

### Festivals

Tamil fire-walking ceremonies are normally held in January, while the Cavadee celebration takes place in February or March. Contact the Syndicat d'Initiative in St-André for specific dates.

### Places to Stay

A nice inexpensive option is the pension de famille *Pluies d'Or* (☎ 46 18 16) at 3 Allée des Sapoties in La Cressonnière. It's a F25 taxi ride or a 15 minute walk from the bus terminal. Single/double rooms cost F90/170. Evening meals are an additional F60.

The chambre d'hôte of *Georges de Palmas* (☎ 47 00 07) is at 174 Bras des Chevrettes and charges F95/120 a single/double. *Mme Gaston Cadet* (☎ 46 56 37) at 96 Rue du Stade has four rooms to let for the same price. She also runs a table d'hôte.

### Places to Eat

*Le Ficus Nitida* (☎ 46 01 41) at 2 Pont Minot, gets its name from the élastique tree. The cuisine at this restaurant stretches from French to Italian to Chinese and Créole. The bill stretches from F50 to F100 per person. It's closed Monday and Tuesday evenings.

For lunches, try the cheaper *Chez Sully*, 50 metres up the street on the opposite side. It offers a choice of four menus under F45, which include a small entrée, main course and dessert. There are also takeaway food and drink stalls in the church/bus square and a couple of nice snack bars along Rue de la Gare. The *Pluies d'Or* described under places to stay also has a small restaurant which specialises in home-cooked Créole cuisine.

In Champ-Borne, at the Place de la Mairie (Town Hall Square), is the restaurant *Le Beau Rivage* (☎ 46 08 66) which specialises in Chinese and Créole cuisine. It's closed on Sunday and Monday evenings.

### Entertainment
The swimming pool near the centre of St-André (the Piscine bus stop) costs F4 for two hours.

### Getting There & Away
All the buses between St-Denis and St-Benoît pass through St-André. Those travelling to the Cirque de Salazie from St-Denis by bus will have to change buses at St-André, a large agricultural (notably tobacco) and commercial centre. The drive up the valley of the Rivière du Mât to the cirque is astounding.

### BRAS-PANON
Bras-Panon, with a population of 8500, is Réunion's vanilla capital, so most visitors are interested in the government-run Co-opérative de Vanille which was begun in 1968. Vanilla was first introduced in Réunion (the orchid is a native of Mexico) in 1819. However, lacking the Mexican insect responsible for pollination of the orchid (which in turn causes the fertilisation of the plant and the production of vanilla beans), it's necessary to pollinate by hand. The process was discovered in 1841 by Créole slave Edmond Albius and it's still in use today.

### Information
The Co-opérative de Vanille also houses a Syndicat d'Initiative (☎ 51 50 62), which, among other things, can provide details about nice walks in the area.

### Co-Opérative de Vanille
If you want to learn all there is to know about Réunion's famous *vanille Bourbon* and vanilla production in general, watch a video film of the vanilla production process and pick up a few samples, the factory and sales and exhibition shops are open Monday to Friday from 8 to 11 am and 2 to 4 pm.

### Riviére des Roches & Cascade de la Paix
A pleasant walk follows along the Rivière des Roches to the waterfalls at Bassin de la Paix. If you want to have a go, head south on the main road past the Rivière des Roches and turn right at the first opportunity. Then turn right again and follow the road up the valley. After 4.5 km, you'll reach a house from which a rough track descends to the lovely 10 metre high falls.

### Places to Stay
One accommodation option is the *Gîte de Bethléem* up on the hills about equidistant from Bras-Panon and St-Benoît. It will accommodate up to 15 people and costs F50 per person per day. Bookings should be made through the Syndicat d'Initiative in either Bras-Panon (☎ 51 50 62) or St-Benoît (☎ 51 50 62).

There's also a municipal camp site (☎ 51 58 59) near the river at Rivière des Roches village. It's open year round.

### Places to Eat
*Le Bec Fin* (☎ 51 52 24), on the main road, and *Chez Nicolas*, (☎ 51 50 70) on Chemin Crépu, provide two reasonable Créole options. The former is closed on Wednesdays and the latter on Sunday evenings, Monday and Tuesday.

### ST-BENOÎT
St-Benoît is another agricultural and fishing centre. It specialises in rice, spices, lychees, coffee, maize and sugar and also in the spratlike delicacy *bichiques* (small fry of various species) which are caught at the mouth of the Rivière des Marsouins, which runs through the decidedly uninteresting centre of town.

## Information
The Syndicat d'Initiative de St-Benôit (☎ 51 50 62) is at 21 Route Nationale in the centre.

## L'Habitation du Cratère
Orchid afficionados won't want to miss this orchid cultivation centre which claims to have 30,000 plants, representing 1600 different species. It's located on Route Départemental 54 about seven km from St-Benôit. Visits must be arranged through the Syndicat d'Initiative in town.

## La Confiance
About six km from St-Benôit along the road toward Plaine-des-Palmistes is the village of La Confiance. It's the site of Le Domaine de la Confiance (☎ 50 90 72), a grand 18th century Créole mansion. It's considered a protected historical monument and is attended by a garden of lush tropical vegetation and a ruined sugar mill. The owner, Mlle Nicole Carrère runs a table d'hôte, open daily except Sunday, which is open to garden visitors by reservation only.

Catherine Lavaux says in her celebrated book on the island: 'If you have only one day to tour the island, go very early in the morning to the volcano then return to wait for your plane at La Confiance. You will have two unforgettable impressions and the desire to return'. Well, I wouldn't go so far as to agree with her (maybe it was something in the water), but it is a pleasant village.

## Sugar Refinery
Just south of St-Benôit, at Beaufonds, is another of Réunion's five sugar refineries. It was once open to the public, but during our visit they weren't conducting tours. That may change, however, so if you're interested, ring the refinery (☎ 50 34 34) or contact the Syndicat d'Initiative.

## Grand Étang
Twelve km from St-Benôit along the road toward Plaine des Palmistes, before the L'Echo lookout point, is the turning onto a six km road/track to Grand Étang, the 'big pond'. This mysterious-looking lake lies at the bottom of a vertical ridge separating it from the Rivière des Marsouins valley. It's an awesome spot.

## Takamaka
The 15 km drive (or walk, if you're very energetic) up the Rivière des Marsouins to Takamaka ends in glorious views of the Cascade de l'Arc en Ciel waterfall and an immense (for Réunion, anyway) hydro-electric complex. From the end of the road, there's a track that carries on to the Forêt de Bébour and eventually to Piton des Neiges and the three cirques.

## Places to Stay
The *Hôtel Le Bouvet* (☎ 50 14 96) is a small, unclassified hotel near the sea at 75 Route Nationale. Singles/double rooms cost F150/200.

Near the school on Route de Cambourg, at 20 Chemin de Ceinture, is the chambre d'hôte of *Mme Marguerite Derand* (☎ 50 90 76). She charges F110 for a single or double room. Meals cost F70.

## Places to Eat
For meals, try the *Café de Chine* (☎ 50 12 47) at the Place du Marché. It is closed on Tuesdays. There's also a restaurant at the Hôtel Bouvet (☎ 50 14 960) which specialises in Créole and French cuisine. It's closed on Thursdays and Sunday nights.

## Getting There & Away
From St-Benôit, there's a scenic road that cuts across the island to St-Pierre and St-Louis, via the Plaine-des-Palmistes and Le-Tampon. Alternatively, you can continue south along the scenic coastal road through Ste-Anne, Ste-Rose, St-Philippe and St-Joseph to reach St-Pierre. This is the way to go if you want to see Le Grand Brûlé, the eerie landscape created by lava from Piton de la Fournaise on its route to the sea.

There are three buses daily to St-Pierre via the high road and four buses via the coastal road. The fare for either route is F39.50. Buses to and from St-Denis leave approximately every 15 minutes.

## STE-ANNE

The village of Ste-Anne, about eight km south along the coast road from St-Benoît, is noted for its unusual church. Its cornerstone was laid in 1857 but the ornamental baroque-style stonework inside and out was intricately carved under the direction of one man, Father Daubemberger from Alsace, beginning in the 1920s. The style, ornately covered in fruits and flowers, is reminiscent of the renowned Mestizo architecture of the Andes in South America. 'Père Daubem' died in 1948; he was laid to rest inside the church itself. Next door is a handicrafts centre which sells furniture and other items made by disabled people.

## STE-ROSE

The small fishing community of Ste-Rose has its harbour at the inlet of La Marine, where there's a monument (a lava pyramid, in fact) to the young English commander Corbett, defeated and killed in an 1809 battle against the French commander, Bouvet.

Between Ste-Anne and Ste-Rose is a lovely old Pont d'Anglais suspension bridge over the Rivière de l'Est, now bypassed by the main highway. It's open to pedestrians, however, and there are nice picnic spots at the southern end. It claims to have been the longest suspension bridge in the world at the time of its construction in 1894.

### Notre Dame de la Lave

There's another famous church, Notre Dame de Lave, at Piton Ste-Rose, 4.5 km south of town. The lava flow from a 1977 eruption went through the village, split when it came to the church and reformed again on the other side. Many see the escape as a miracle of divine intervention. (There could be something to this; I've encountered similarly lava-resistant shrines in Western Samoa and Iceland, as well!) Just as miraculously, there was no loss of life during the eruption. A wooden log 'washed up' by the lava and found at the door of the church is now a memorial beside it. The road cuts through the solidified lava flow.

### L'Anse des Cascades

About three km south of Piton Ste-Rose, turn off toward the sea from the main road to reach L'Anse des Cascades. In this little fishing port, the water from the hills drops dramatically into the sea. It's worth a look, especially after rains.

### La Vierge au Parasol

From Bois Blanc, the road continues south along the coast, then climbs and drops dramatically into the six km wide volcanic ravine known as Le Grand Brûlé. Just inside the ravine, beside the road, is the shrine, La Vierge au Parasol. Yes, the Virgin Mary is holding a parasol. The brolly is not for pro-

Virgin with Umbrella

tection against the sun or rain. It was set up by a Bois-Blanc planter at the turn of the century in the hope of protecting his vanilla beans from volcanic hellfire and brimstone.

Watch out also in this area for the red shrines dedicated to St-Expédit.

### Places to Stay & Eat

At Piton Ste-Rose is a small Créole restaurant, *L'Anse des Cascades* (☎ 47 20 42). It's open for lunch only, from noon to 2 pm, and is closed on Wednesdays. It opens in the evening only if there's sufficient demand, so phone in advance if you're interested. *Les Deux Pitons* (☎ 47 23 16), also in Piton-Ste-Rose, is open daily for lunch and dinner and serves Chinese, Créole and French cuisine.

On the main road, *Mme Adam de Villiers* (☎ 47 21 33) runs a two room chambre d'hôte; single or double occupancy costs F150. Her imaginative meals are recommended but expensive at F80 per person.

### Entertainment

Ste-Rose has a disco, Rose d'Zil, at the hamlet of Ravine Glissante about 1.5 km south of town.

### Getting There & Away

There are around 10 buses daily between St-Benoît and Ste-Rose.

# The South Coast

### THE SOUTH-EAST CORNER

Along the route from Ste-Rose to St-Phillipe, the Route Nationale crosses the deserted Le Grand Brûlé, the immense ravine formed by the main lava flow from the volcano, and the steep slopes of Les Grandes Pentes, the conduits for lava flows ancient and modern.

The last flow which reached the sea down this route was in 1976. In March 1986, the lava took a more southerly route and crossed the main road between Pointe du Tremblet and Pointe de la Table at Takamaka and Tremblet villages. This eruption added over 30 hectares to the island's area, but more than 450 people had to be evacuated and several homes were lost. In the 1992 eruptions, the lava slowed and cooled half-way down the slope and never threatened the road.

As one rounds the south-eastern corner from Le Grand Brûlé, the rugged lava coastline opens up a bit and the coastal plain widens, accommodating agricultural activities as well as the village of St-Philippe and, further along, the town of St-Joseph. There are a couple of viable beaches in the area which provide relatively uncrowded alternatives to the popular west coast beaches.

### Information

At the Office du Tourisme de St-Philippe (☎ 37 10 43), Place de la Mairie, 69 Rue Leconte de Lisle, 97442 St-Philippe, you can pick up information on the entire south-eastern coast of the island.

### Interpretive Centre & Les Sentinelles

On the roadside near the southern end of the Grand Brûlé, there's an interpretive centre with pictures and descriptions of what's going on there.

Just north of the interpretive centre is a turning inland marked *Symboise pour Volcan et Oiseaux*. Follow this road about one km to the parking lot, from which it's a 100 metre walk to the edge of the 1976 lava flow and a garden of bizarre sculptures known as *Les Sentinelles*. They were created by the Réunionnais sculptor Monsieur Mayo.

### Volcano Climb

After the road makes its dramatic exit from the ravine near Tremblet, there's a GR R2 trailhead from which the extremely energetic can climb to the summit of the volcano, Piton de la Fournaise. It's a steep, rugged and normally wet walk and is considered one of Réunion's most challenging, so don't take it lightly. Reader Frederic Belton of the USA writes 'For any real masochistic trekkers looking for tough walks, I will heartily recommend the route up the volcano from le Tremblet via Nez Coupé du Tremblet...'

Plan on two to three days to reach the gîte at Pas de Bellecombe. An alternative route takes off from the village of Takamaka (not to be confused with the Takamaka region further north) and joins the Tremblet route at the Abri du Tremblet bivouac gîte. For more information on visiting the volcano, see under Piton de la Fournaise in the Interior chapter.

### Les Puits

Along the coast on either side of the village of St-Philippe is a series of four mysterious *puits* (wells), artificially dug into the lava rock; three of them are named after the French, English and Arabs, and the fourth is called Puits du Tremblet. The purpose of the wells and who created them is unknown. Some far-fetched theories even attribute them to the Egyptians!

A reader writes:

The Puits Arabe itself is actually a pretty dull and scruffy thing but someone somewhere wants to attract visitors there. The 1986 eruption of Piton de la Fournaise sent a lava flow only metres from the Puits Arabe and now, if you drive down the track to the car park (equipped with loos and picnic benches) there's a fascinating walk mapped out on notice boards. The marked trail takes you along the new cliff (with the waves lashing away just below you), pointing out the various lava formations and the old 18th century lava cliff (now about 50 metres inland), and then takes you up to where the lava flows wiped out the main road. It's an excellent hour's entertainment!

**Stephen Clarke**

Puits du Tremblet is accessible from the road via a short walking track just south of Le Grand Brûlé. The most interesting are the Puits des Anglais at Le-Baril, four km west of St-Philippe, and the Puits Arabes, five km in the opposite direction. The road to the sea at Basse-Vallée takes you to Cap Méchant and the Puits des Français, providing a good view of the sea crashing against the black lava cliffs and rocks.

### Notre Dame de la Paix

Near St-Philippe and on the other side of the road, is another curiosity. A cave in the rock face by the road contains an altar and several rows of pews. This church cavern is called Notre Dame de la Paix.

### Forest Walks

There are several forest walks *(Sentiers Forestiéres)*, zigging and zagging into the hills from Mare Longue, Le-Baril, Basse Vallée and Langevin; the last two lead to tracks which eventually wind up at the Plaine des Sables and the volcano.

The Langevin track ascends the Rivière au Langevin to meet up with the volcano road on the Plaine des Sables, passing lots of waterfalls and inviting pools along the way. It's a manageable 10 km walk upstream to the waterfall, Cascade de la Grande Ravine, and the trout-laden waters of Grand Galet (you can also get there in a vehicle).

The Basse Vallée track ascends the hopefully named Vallée Heureuse (Lucky Valley) to connect with the Tremblet/Takamaka routes of the GR R2 from the east coast. See under Places to Stay for info on the Basse-Vallée gîte de montagne.

The track from Mare Longue is especially interesting; known as a Sentier Botanique (Botanical Path), it features a variety of rare plants. There's also a formal three hectare garden, open for only a few years now, which is planted in perfume-yielding plants, fruit trees, orchids and spices. It's open daily year round from 8.30 am to 12.30 pm and 2.30 to 5 pm. Entry is F30 per person and guided tours may be arranged through the Office du Tourisme de St-Philippe (☎ 37 10 43).

### Places to Stay

The village of Le-Baril is the base normally used by visitors. This is owing partly to its superb location above a stunning black lava coast and partly to the fact that there's no other place to stay in the area. The *Hôtel Le-Baril* (☎ 37 01 04) is a small, one-star hotel & restaurant set above the rocky shoreline among pandanus trees. One of the nine rooms costs F200/250 single/double. Breakfast is an additional F20. The hotel also has a swimming pool.

There are no pensions de famille, table d'hôtes or chambre d'hôtes in the entire south-east corner of the island but about eight km above the hamlet of Basse-Vallée, along the Route Forestière de Basse-Vallée or the GR R2 variante, is a gîte de montagne, known conveniently as *Basse-Vallée* (☎ 37 00 75). It costs F50 per person per night and should be booked through the Maison de la Montagne in St-Denis.

### Places to Eat

The *Hôtel Le-Baril* has a restaurant specialising in Chinese food. *Le Cap Méchant* (☎ 37 00 61) at the cape of the same name in Basse-Vallée offers excellent and renowned Créole cuisine. Also at Basse Vallée is *L'Étoile de Mer* (☎ 37 04 60) which serves both Créole and Chinese specialities. In St-Philippe itself, there's another Créole restaurant, *La Canot* (☎ 37 00 36). All of these are open daily for lunch and dinner.

### Getting There & Away

St-Philippe lies on the coastal bus route between St-Benoît and St-Pierre; there are four buses daily in either direction.

## ST-JOSEPH

St-Joseph, at the mouth of the magnificent valley of the Rivière des Remparts, is a rather dull town. The area (especially the nearby village of Vincendo) is known primarily for its production of baskets and bags from the fronds of the vacoa (pandanus or screw pine).

East of St-Joseph, it's possible to swim at the black-sand beach of La Marine de Vincendo, the old port for the village of the same name. The fishing community has since moved along to Langevin's harbour. The shady avenue leading to the coast is lined with vacoas.

### Rivière des Remparts

The best view over the Rivière des Remparts valley is from the head of the valley at Nez de Boeuf, over 30 km north of St-Joseph on the road to the volcano (see the Interior chapter for more information). Other good views are available from lookout points near Notre-Dame-de-la-Paix village, accessible only via the town of Le-Tampon.

From St-Joseph, there's a walking track which gently ascends the river valley for an incredible 30 km, then arduously scales the valley headwall to meet the volcano road at Nez de Boeuf. It's probably better, and much more easily done in the opposite direction as a means of returning from the volcano to the coast. Along the route at Roche Plate hamlet, there's a remote table d'hôte operated by Mme Begue (☎ 59 13 94).

By vehicle (or bus from St-Joseph), it's also possible to ascend for 22 km along the eastern rim of the valley, through plantations of tea and geraniums to the village of Grand Coudé. Along the route there are several scenic lookouts over the Rivière des Remparts.

### Manapany-les-Bains

The main attraction in this area is Manapany-les-Bains, with a safe natural swimming pool between the rocks and Le Manapany, one of Réunion's most acclaimed restaurants.

Just west of the village is the spectacular Ravine Manapany. Here the road crosses a dramatic gorge and there's a steep pedestrian track leading down to the river mouth. Still further west, seaward from the village of Petite-Île, is the attractive white-sand beach at Grande Anse. This was once a favourite bathing spot but there are now large placards announcing that swimming is forbidden. However, if you're desperate to get wet, there is a protected bathing pool. Within sight is Petite-Île, Réunion's only offshore island, which serves as a sea bird nesting site.

### Le-Goyave to Petite-Île

This circuit trip along wildly twisting roads through the gentle and fertile heights from Le-Goyave, through Les-Lianes and Manapany-les-Hauts to Petite-Île, will introduce you to sugar cane, vétiver, garlic and geraniums, among other produce. There are also superb views up toward the higher heights and down toward the sea far below. It's best in a private vehicle, naturally, but there are small short-haul buses from the Gare Routière in St-Joseph which do the route.

## Grand-Bois Sugar Refinery
Near Grande-Anse on the road towards St-Pierre is the Grand-Bois sugar refinery (☎ 25 15 77). Guided tours can be arranged by phoning directly.

## Places to Stay
There are quite a few gîtes de France and chambres d'hôte in the area. On Boulevard de l'Ocean at Manapany-les-Bains, *M Jean-Paul Grondin* (☎ 56 51 66) has three gîtes accommodating from three to nine people each. Prices range from F900 to F1120 per week. Over 20 km inland at Grand-Coudé, *Jean-Pierre Chan-Shit-Sang* (☎ 56 14 44) operates a gîte and chambre d'hôte. For the former, he charges F790 per weekend. The latter has four rooms and costs from F130 to F150 a single or double. Meals cost F80 extra.

Another option is the rather remote chambre d'hôte of *Mme Turpin* (☎ 37 27 03) at Le-Crête, eight km inland from Vincendo. Single/double accommodation costs F90/120 and meals cost F75 extra.

If the chambre d'hôtes are full, as a last resort, try the *Restaurant Dodo* which rents very basic insect-infested rooms for F180 a double. One reader said that when they were there, the noise was insufferable and all the other clientele were drunk. Perhaps you'd prefer the seaside camp site at *Grande-Anse* (☎ 56 81 03) which has picnic tables, showers and washing up areas.

## Places to Eat
*Le Manapany* (☎ 26 55 58), in Manapany-les-Bains, is rated the best restaurant in Réunion by the *Guide des Piments Bleus*, and bills itself as a specialist in *nouvelle gastronomie créole*. Apart from its splendid location overlooking the sea, it's noted for turtle, seafood dishes, 'Gaelic pineapples' and a fine selection of house rums and punches. Meal prices vary from F120 to F200. It is closed on Sunday and Monday

nights. For Créole cuisine at Manapany-les-Bains, try *Le Lézard Vert* (☎ 56 29 78).

In Vincendo, there's *Le Tajine* (☎ 56 21 30) which specialises in French and North African cuisine. Alternatively, near the port there's *Le Cap Jaune* (☎ 37 31 41) which is open daily for lunch and dinner.

*Mme Gilette Técher* (☎ 37 20 88) offers table d'hôte for F70 up in the hills at Jacques Payet hamlet. Take the turn-off several hundred metres east of Bras Panon village. There's no public transport up this serpentine road so the only access is by private vehicle.

## Getting There & Away
St-Joseph lies on the coastal bus route between St-Pierre and St-Benoît.

## ST-PIERRE
More than 55,000 people make St-Pierre Réunion's third largest *commune* after St-Denis and St-Paul. Although St-Pierre has a pleasantly lively atmosphere, there's little to see in or around the town.

## Information
**Tourist Office** The Syndicat d'Initiative de St-Pierre (☎ 25 02 36) is at 27 Rue Archambaud. It isn't a particularly helpful office but they do have tourist literature and can answer most queries. Be warned, however, that they seem to assume foreigners are only interested in established tourist businesses. For camping, trekking or budget food and accommodation options, you'll have to ask specifically.

**Post** The main post office at 108 Rue des Bons Enfants is open weekdays from 7.30 am to 6 pm, and on Saturdays from 8 am to noon.

**Banks** The Banque de la Réunion at 18 Rue des Bons Enfants and the Banque National de Paris is just opposite. They're open from 8 am to 4 pm during the week.

**Laundry** The *Pressing* automatic laundromat is opposite the town hall.

## Interesting Buildings

There aren't many sights in the centre of town, but if you're near the Hôtel de Ville (Town Hall), it doesn't take five minutes to pop inside and have a look at this 200-year-old building which was restored in 1975. The counter clerk will let you in and upstairs anytime between 8 am and 5.30 pm Monday to Friday.

The public library near the beachfront was once the terminus for the old St-Pierre to St-Benoît railway. In the centre is the *Médiathèque*, a new cultural centre with exhibits.

There is also a mosque in the centre, Mosquée Atyaboul-Massajid, and the Narassigua-Peroumal Hindu temple at La Ravine Blanche on the western end of town. Both of these are open to visitors.

## Grave of Le Sitarane

In the cemetery on Blvd Hubert Delisle is the grave of the African bandit/sorcerer Le Sitarane, marked by a black cross. It represents a shadowy side of Réunion. At the turn of the last century, Le Sitarane and his men raided and robbed numerous homes in the St-Pierre and Le-Tampon areas, killing the occupants and using their remains for purposes of black magic.

Eventually, the gang was surprised while raiding a house. They were caught, identified by objects they'd dropped while fleeing and sentenced to death by hanging. Today, the grave is used for rites and offerings by people hoping to bring misfortune upon others.

## Cockfighting

Although few foreigners will feel compelled to attend the weekly matches at 184 Rue du Four á Chaux, it's interesting to know that cockfighting remains a popular gambling venue in Réunion. Those whose morals stretch to include this rather barbaric pastime can check at the Syndicat d'Initiative for times or ask them to ring the organiser.

## Market

The market beside the gare routière is open Monday to Saturday from 6 am to 7 pm in the summer months (7 am to 6 pm in winter), and 7 am to noon on Sundays and holidays. One can purchase souvenirs and handicrafts as well as food.

## Beach

St-Pierre also has a clean municipal beach protected by a reef and a jetty, making St-Pierre a favourite lair for yachties. Unfortunately, it's subject to strong winds and sunbathers are liable to get a real sandblasting.

## Places to Stay

**Hotels** *Hôtel Sterne* (☎ 25 70 00) on Boulevard Hubert Delisle overlooks the sea. The least expensive single/double rooms cost F390/490 per night, with breakfast an extra F48 per person. On the same street, at No 50, is the smaller *Hôtel Les Hibiscus* (☎ 35 13 10) with single/double rooms costing F350/400; breakfast is F55. Not far from the beach, at 12 Rue François de Mahy, is the centrally located *Hotel Nathania* (☎ 25 04 57). Double rooms begin at F300 and breakfast is an extra F50 per person.

The *Hôtel Le Suffren* (☎ 35 19 10), 14 Rue Suffren, is near the seafront with 18 rooms costing F320/370 for single/double rooms. It is often fully booked by students on special rates.

There are also three cheaper hotels to choose from. The *Hôtel Tropic* (☎ 25 90 70) at 2 Rue Auguste Babet, opposite the Rex cinema, has 12 air conditioned double rooms costing from F170 to F220 per night. Breakfast is an extra F30 per person.

The *Hôtel Star* (☎ 27 20 69) at 88 Condé Ravine des Cabris (on the Ligne des 400 route to Le Tampon) has doubles from F200 to F300, and breakfast for F35.

**Pensions de Famille** The most pleasant inexpensive accommodation in St-Pierre is the *Pension Touristique Chez Papa Daya* (☎ 25 64 87 day, 25 11 34 evening) at 27 Rue du Four à Chaux. It's as if Papa Daya had a manual on how to create a very agreeable travellers' ghetto. For F125/150 a single/double you get a pleasant private room with a

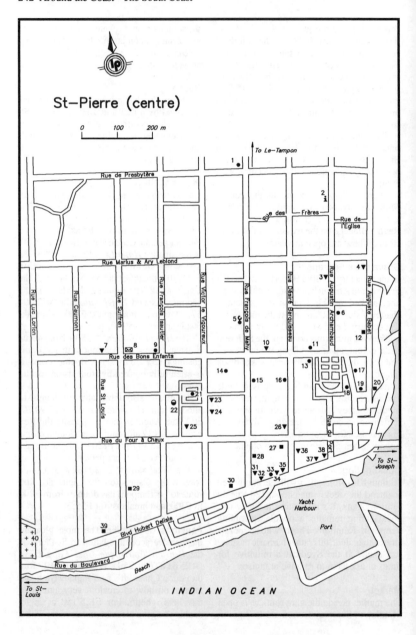

St-Pierre (centre)

| ■ PLACES TO STAY | | 35 | Pizzeria Le Cabanon |
|---|---|---|---|
| | | 36 | Pizza Rapido |
| 12 | Pension Decanonville | 37 | Restaurant Le Margouillat |
| 20 | Hôtel Tropic | 38 | Crêperie St Malo |
| 27 | Pension Touristique Chez | | |
| | Papa Daya | | OTHER |
| 28 | Hôtel Nathania | | |
| 29 | Hôtel Le Suffren | 1 | Le Star Club Disco |
| 30 | Hôtel Sterne | 2 | Tourist Office |
| 39 | Hôtel Les Hibiscus | 5 | Mosque |
| | | 6 | Gendarmerie |
| ▼ PLACES TO EAT | | 8 | Post Office |
| | | 9 | Police |
| 3 | Restaurant Le Bambou | 11 | Banque de La Réunion |
| 4 | Le Grec Restaurant | 13 | Banque National de Paris |
| 7 | Restaurant Cantonnais | 14 | Médiatheque (Cultural Centre) |
| 10 | Café Bar | 15 | Librairie Pointe Virgule |
| 23 | Restaurant Moderne | 16 | Librairie Cazal |
| 24 | Restaurant Canton | 17 | Pressing (Laundromat) |
| 25 | Donald Duck Burger | 18 | Town Hall |
| 26 | Restaurant Le Flamboyant | 19 | Ciné Rex |
| 31 | La Jonque Restaurant | 21 | Market |
| 32 | Brasserie des Îles; Restaurant | 22 | Gare Routière (Bus Station) |
| | L'Origan & Restaurant Yang Tsé | 33 | Bar/Disco L'Acropole |
| 34 | Restaurant Le Retro | 40 | Cemetery & Grave of Le Sitarane |

fan and shared facilities. There's also a kitchen for self-catering and a reading/TV lounge. When I was there, a local artist was in the process of meticulously applying a painted jungle to the outside walls.

There's another pension de famille run by *Mme Fontaine Luline* (☎ 25 50 07) at Rue Rodier 46. She charges F100 per person per night and F1800 for monthly rentals.

Another choice for travellers is the pension de famille of *Mme Decanonville* (☎ 25 04 62) at 17 Rue Auguste Babet. Mme Decanonville is an affable lady who describes her home as *'très, très modeste'*; the main building with its columns and fountain has a crumbling splendour (standards slipped after the revolution) but her prices are right at F40 for a shared room and F60 for a little chalet with shared facilities. A room with a shower is F70 and meals cost F30. If you want to stay there, it's best to book a room in advance; she frequently accommodates teenagers with problems and there isn't always space available.

**Chambres d'Hôte** There are two chambres d'hôte in the area, but none are right in town. One is that of *M Lebon* (☎ 49 73 78) at 11 Chemin Maurice Técher in Ravine-des-Cabris about seven km from St-Pierre. He charges F150 a single or double with an extra F70 for the evening meal.

A bit nearer town is that of *Mme Mireille-Rita Malet* (☎ 25 61 90) at 52 Allée des Aubépines in Bassin-Plat, just three km from town. She charges F95/140 a single/double and F70 for meals.

**Places to Eat – bottom end**
For some reason, St-Pierre is one of the gastronomic centres of Réunion; there's a restaurant on every corner and a few in between so you'll have no shortage of choices.

There are several no-frills cafés around the market and bus station, including the *Donald Duck Burger*, which sells hamburgers for F16 (but not duck!). If you're after a pizza, there's *Pizza Rapido*, which does takeaways, and *Pizzeria Le Cabanon* just around the corner. The latter is owned by a friendly Armenian, a talented conversationalist who will probably speak your language and want to chat about his relatives in Australia. Up on Rue des Bons Enfants, there's a tiny place known simply as *Cafe-Bar* (at least that's all the sign says!) which serves snacks and fresh fruit juices.

A very good and reasonably priced Chinese option is *La Jonque* (☎ 25 57 78) near the corner of Boulevard Hubert Delisle and Rue François de Mahy. It closes on Tuesday. Another cheap but acceptable Chinese restaurant is *Le Canton* at 16 Rue Victor le Vigoureux. They have huge lunch specials for F30 to F40, but don't order anything greasy like spring rolls. Next door is *Le Moderne* (☎ 25 05 40) which serves Créole as well as Chinese cuisine. Finally, there's the no-frills *Restaurant Le Cantonnais* on Rue des Bons Enfants, which is recommended for inexpensive Chinese meals.

For another value-for-money option, try *Les Filaos* (☎ 25 27 85) on the Blvd Front de Mer. It has terrace tables and serves up menu and à la carte Créole and Polish dishes for around F50.

### Places to Eat – top end

There are several beach snack and ice cream stalls, and an especially wide selection of restaurants along Boulevard Hubert Delisle offering a slightly snooty sidewalk café ambience. These include *L'Origan* (☎ 25 44 57), *L'Acropole* and *Le Retro* (☎ 35 33 06) (these also offer reasonable breakfasts).

A recommended option on Boulevard Hubert Delisle is *Le Margouillat* (look for the green gecko!). Just next door at the bottom of Rue du Port is the equally recommended *Crêperie St-Malo* (☎ 25 75 25) which specialises in Breton cuisine and has crêpes for F30 to F50.

A block inland is the highly rated (and expensive) *Le Flamboyant* (☎ 35 02 15), which specialises in French cuisine. Alternatively, try *Le Bambou* (☎ 25 58 66) – no, it's not Chinese – at 15 Rue Augustin Archambaud for *cuisine métro*. Other top of

the range restaurants include the Italian *L'Osteria* (☎ 25 14 15) at Rue Marius & Ary Leblond 16 and *Le Bibelot* (☎ 31 00 25) at Terre Rouge, east of town. For upmarket Greek food, go to *Le Grec* (☎ 25 76 76) at 23 Rue Auguste Babet. It's open for lunch daily except weekends, and for dinner daily except Sunday.

### Entertainment

St-Pierre's main disco is Le Star Club at 36 Rue du Presbytère on the upper end of town. There's another, L'Acropole, at the beach front on Boulevard Hubert Delisle. The Rex cinema is on Rue Désiré Barquisseau.

### Getting There & Away

Buses to and from St-Denis run 38 times daily along the western side of the island via St-Louis and St-Paul, so you shouldn't have to wait too long for transport; the first one leaves at 4 am and the last at 5.30 pm. They also run three times a day to St-Benoît across the centre of the island via Plaine des Palmistes; and four times a day via the south-eastern coast road through St-Joseph and Ste-Anne.

# The West Coast

### ST-LOUIS

You have to go to St-Louis to get the bus to Cilaos but there's really no other reason to visit. The gare routière is isolated on the southern side of town near a couple of snack bars and the church, which is the oldest on the island, dating to 1733.

If you do find yourself stuck for a day or two, there's a scenic 15 km drive up to the hill village of Les Makes, and a further twisting 10 km drive or walk up the Route Forestière 14 to La Fenêtre, (the Window). There, clouds permitting, you'll have a grand view into the Cirque de Cilaos. There's also a two km trip to the coastal lagoon Étang de Gol at Bel Air, where you'll find a pleasant picnic site.

About 1.5 km west of St-Louis, at Le Camp du Gol, is an old sugar refinery (☎ 26

10 02), Le Sucrérie du Gol, probably the most interesting one on the island. Ring to make arrangements for a visit. Behind it stands a château dating to the end of the 18th century.

## Places to Stay
The only accommodation is in Les Makes, a scenic 14 km inland from the main town. *M Georges Leperlier* (☎ 37 92 15) at 41 Rue Paul Herman, Les Makes, and *M Jean-Luc d'Eurveilher* (☎ 37 82 77) further up the road toward La Fenêtre both charge F90/20 a single/double for chambre d'hôte accommodation. Evening meals cost an extra F75.

## Places to Eat
If St-Louis is quiet on a Saturday, it's dead on a Sunday. The only eating house open is the *Restaurant Les Bons Amis* (☎ 26 10 19) on the Route Nationale. On the same drag is *Les Baguettes d'Or* (☎ 26 17 93). St-Louis also has a plethora of Chinese restaurants; at least seven of them! A recommended atmospheric tourist restaurant is *L'Auberge du Vieux-Moulin* (☎ 26 12 45) along the mountain road to Cilaos. It's open daily for lunch and dinner.

## ÉTANG-SALÉ-LES-BAINS
If you're coming from the south, Étang-Salé-les-Bains is the beginning of the holiday coast, though the area remains very much an agricultural community. On weekends, the black sand beach is much quieter than the coast further north around St-Gilles-les-Bains. Étang-Salé-les-Bains itself is sheltered by a coral reef which, with extreme caution, is accessible on foot at low tide (trainers or reef shoes are essential to avoid serious cuts on the coral).

## Information
The Syndicat d'Initiative de l'Étang Salé (☎ 26 67 32) is housed in the old railway station at Rue Octave Bénard. They have information on the entire stretch of coast between St-Louis and St-Leu.

## Le Gouffre
Just off Route Nationale 1, two km south of Étang-Salé-les-Bains, is Le Gouffre, an abyss in the basalt cliffs where the waves dramatically roar in and foam up, sending plumes of spray into the air. Don't venture too close.

## Office National des Forêts Bird Park
On the road from Étang-Salé-les-Bains to Étang-Salé-les-Hauts, just where it forks to the left to go to Les Avirons, is a two hectare bird park operated by the Office National des Forêts. This route is beautifully crimson when all the flamboyant trees are in bloom.

## Sports
On the slopes between Le Gouffre and Étang-Salé-les-Hauts, in the ONF land, is the nine-hole Golf Club de Bourbon golf course (you can hire clubs). There's also a swimming pool nearby and a drop zone for parachutists who've taken off at Pierrefonds airfield.

## Places to Stay
Despite its tendency to consider itself part of the holiday coast, Étang-Salé-les-Bains has no hotel accommodation (admittedly, some people like it that way!) and only one chambre d'hôte, that of *M Richemond-Eugène Savigny* (☎ 26 31 09), Sentier des Prunes 3, in Ravine Sheunon. He charges F80/120 a single/double and F70 for table d'hôte.

## Places to Eat
There are two restaurants in Étang-Salé-les-Bains. *La Louisiane* (☎ 26 63 92) is on the main road and serves Créole cuisine. It's closed Wednesday, Thursday and Sunday nights. The other, *L'Été Indien* (☎ 26 67 33) on Rue Salines Delisle, is open daily. Don't forget the table d'hôte listed in the Places to Stay section.

## LES AVIRONS
Les Avirons (the Oars) is a pretty hill town with commanding views and a reputation, along with Étang-Salé-les-Hauts, for turning

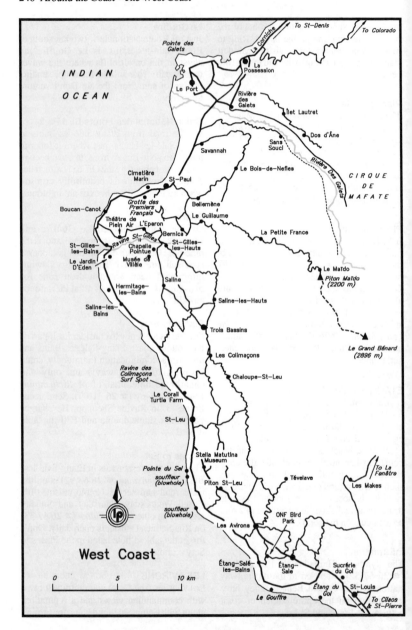

To St-Denis

To Colorado

La Corniche

Pointe des Galets

La Possession

INDIAN OCEAN

Le Port

Rivière des Galets

Îlet Lautret

Dos d'Âne

Sans Souci

Savannah

Le Bois-de-Nefles

Rivière Des Galets

CIRQUE DE MAFATE

Cimetière Marin

St-Paul

Bellemène

Grotte des Premiers Français

Le Guillaume

Boucan-Canot

Théâtre de Plein Air

L'Eperon

La Petite France

Bernica

Ravine St-Gilles

St-Gilles-les-Hauts

St-Gilles-les-Bains

Chapelle Pointue

Le Jardin D'Eden

Musée de Villèle

Le Maïdo
▲ Piton Maïdo (2200 m)

Hermitage-les-Bains

Saline

Saline-les-Bains

Saline-les-Hauts

Le Grand Bénard (2896 m)

Trois Bassins

Les Colimaçons

Ravine des Colimaçons Surf Spot

Chaloupe-St-Leu

Le Corail Turtle Farm

St-Leu

Stella Matutina Museum

Pointe du Sel souffleur (blowhole)

Piton St-Leu

Tévelave

To La Fenêtre

Les Makes

souffleur (blowhole)

ONF Bird Park

Les Avirons

West Coast

Étang-Salé-les-Bains

Étang-Salé

Sucrérie du Gol

Étang du Gol

St-Louis

Le Gouffre

To Cilaos & St-Pierre

0     5     10 km

out artesans specialising in woodcrafts and replicas of French East India Company furniture. They also make distinctive caned chairs known as *de Gol* (no, that's not the Créole name of the former French president!). Their predecessors were said to have originally made the oars for all the island's boats, hence the name of the town. However, one reader suggests the name is derived from the Malagasy word for a high place with a view.

The excursion into the mountains or cirques from Les Avirons is by way of Tévelave and, 11 km up the mountain by way of Route Forestière 6. There are also two performing *souffleurs* (blowholes) in the rocks between the Pointe du Portail and the Pointe au Sel, on the coast road between Les Avirons and St-Leu.

### Places to Stay

The chambres d'hôte are all up in the heights, as usual, and don't cater for the beach crowd. In this case, they're all in Tévelave, 11 km north of Les Avirons. *Mme François Turpin* (☎ 38 04 21) has three rooms and charges F95/120 a single/double, and *Mme Marie-Anne Tipary* (☎ 38 00 71) has two rooms and charges F78/106 a single/double. They both do tables d'hôte meals for F75 per person. At Le Plate (near Tévelave), there's a two bedroom chambre d'hôte belonging to *Mme Darty* (☎ 54 01 94). She charges F95/125 a single/double and F70 per person for an evening meal.

*Mr Jerry Vitry* (☎ 38 03 07) in Tévelave has gîte de France accommodation for between F1000 per week for seven people and F1350 per week for up to 12 people. The nearest gîte to the sea is that of *Mme Augustin Cadet* (☎ 38 01 34) at Chemin Fond Maurice 3, 97425 Les Avirons, three km from the beach. She has accommodation for four people and charges F950 per week.

### ST-LEU

The name St-Leu was derived from the original name 'Boucan-de-Laleu' which appeared on an early map of the island at this site. Historically, the place has had its share

of problems; a violent slave rebellion in 1811 and devastating cyclones in 1932 and 1989. It was, however, the one town on Réunion which was spared the ravages of a cholera epidemic which decimated St-Denis and St-Louis in 1859. In 1978, the people of the nearby village of Stella were unemployed en masse when the sugar refinery ceased operations. Area inhabitants are now more occupied with fishing than farming.

### Hôtel de Ville

The stone Hôtel de Ville on the main road, an old store built by the French East India Company, is worth a look. It has recently been 're-stored'.

### Notre Dame de la Salette

You may want to seek out the chapel of Notre Dame de la Salette, built in the Virgin Mary's honour in 1859 as a plea for protection against a cholera epidemic sweeping the island. It must have worked because St-Leu's populace was spared. Each 19 September, thousands of people make a pilgrimage to the chapel.

### Beach

A few km north of St-Leu the beach changes from black sand to white sand. Swimming is safe and there's a reef for protection. At the mouth of the Ravine des Colimaçons, north of town, there's a break in the reef which serves as a prime surf spot, considered one of the best in the Indian Ocean.

### Conservatoire Botanique de Mascarin

This newly opened garden (☎ 24 92 27) on the old property of Chateauvieux at Les Colimaçons, is planned to become a sort of museum of endemic Réunionnais flora. It's open year round on the first weekend of each month from 10 am to 5 pm. Admission is F15 per person.

### Le Corail Turtle Farm

The Le Corail Turtle Farm is undoubtedly good for the operators, the employees and the local economy, but whether it's good for the green turtle community is debatable. It may be breeding a threatened species, but it is also encouraging their exploitation for food, jewellery and other purposes. Furthermore, it provides an easy answer for vendors of illegal tortoise-shell products: 'It came from St-Leu'. Who's going to check apart from your customs officer back home, and by that time, the illegal turtle trade already has your money and your vote of approval to continue operations.

The conscience-searching over, those interested in a visit can proceed to the farm two km north of St-Leu on Route Nationale 1. Entry costs F10 for adults and F5 for children aged five to 16 years. It's open daily from 8 am to noon and 2 to 5 pm.

The enterprise sustains between 18,000 and 26,000 turtles, covering three generations, and produces up to 7000 individuals each year (well, actually, the turtles themselves do the producing). The original stock was brought to Réunion from the French islands of Tromelin and Europa, the former located between Mauritius and the Seychelles and the latter in the Mozambique Channel between Africa and southern Madagascar.

Inside the tower there's an exhibition of the breeding process and the ritual and symbolic significance of the turtle. Finally, it gushes about the contributions of turtle farming to the causes of conservation, the economy and human health. The non-greasy meat is rich in protein, the oil is used in curing leprosy and Mexican women use the oil for firming their breasts!

On sale in the shop are complete shells ranging from F150 to F2500, spectacle frames, jewellery and other ornamental knick-knacks (accompanied by a certificate for EC customs; North Americans and Australasians, amongst others, may not import turtle products at all). They'll also oblige those who can't leave without sampling the culinary value of turtles.

### Stella Matutina

This quirky museum at the village of Stella, four km south of St-Leu on the inland route toward Les Avirons (known as l'Allée des Flamboyants) tells the agricultural and industrial history of Réunion. It's dedicated primarily to the sugar industry, but does provide insight into the history of the island, and has exhibits on other products known and loved by the Réunionnais: vanilla, orchids, geraniums and vétiver. It's open Tuesday to Sunday from 10 am to 6 pm. Admission is F30.

### Places to Stay

**Camping** There is a camp site near the shore in St-Leu which charges F2 per square metre per day for tent or caravan space plus F10 for electricity. The site is well lit and has a shower and WC block. Bookings may be made through the Service du Garde Champêtre (☎ 34 80 03) at the town hall. It's open only in August. Readers have reported that the site isn't safe; don't leave anything in your tent.

**Chambres d'Hôte** At Colimaçons-les-Hauts, in the hills 10 km north of St-Leu, *Mme Aliette René* (☎ 54 80 81), CD13, Bras Mouton, has three guest bedrooms and a good table d'hôte. Accommodation costs F75 per person.

In St-Leu proper there's *Mme Irène Rangapin* (☎ 34 42 51) at 132 Chemin Dubuisson. Single or double occupancy costs F125. There are no meals available.

In Chaloupe-St-Leu, on the high road between St-Leu and Trois-Bassins, *Mme Julia Maillot* (☎ 54 82 92) at 4 Chemin des Hortensias, runs a chambre and table d'hôte; she has three rooms. She charges F80/120 a single/double. Also in Chaloupe-St-Leu is the chambre d'hôte of *M Ivrin Cadet* (☎ 54 85 00) at 20 Chemin Payet Emmanuel. Rooms cost F80/120 a single/double and meals cost F70 extra.

**Gîtes** There are numerous gîtes de France in the St-Leu area, the majority in the vicinity of Piton-St-Leu 11 km south of town. The nearest to town is a cosy little place in Étang, that of *Mme Crescence* (☎ 34 41 75) which accommodates three people. She charges F895 per week. Another nice option is the gîte of *M Henri René* (☎ 54 80 81) in Bras Moutons. To get there, turn inland just north of the turtle farm and wind your way 10 km or so up the hill (unfortunately there's no public transport heading this way). He charges F900 per week for two people.

**Village Vacances Famille** The 32 studios and bungalows at the VVF holiday village *Le Laleu* (☎ 34 81 43) in St-Leu, range in price from F200 per night for one or two people on weekdays and F350 on weekends. If you're not a VVF associate, look up Mme Jacqueline who will sign you up for F100 per family. Breakfast and other meals are available as well. One reader has advised us that it's exactly 184 steps from the VVF to the beach.

**Places to Eat**
*Le Palais d'Asie* (☎ 34 80 41) at Rue du Général Lambert 127, near the VVF, has been recommended for superb Chinese meals with plats du jour going for as little as F30. It's closed on Tuesday. Near the shore at 36 Rue du Lagon is the Créole restaurant *Le Varangue* (☎ 34 78 45). It's open for lunch and dinner daily except Tuesday.

## ST-GILLES-LES-BAINS
The beach scene may not be what Réunion is all about but at times, you have to wonder. On weekends and during holiday periods, St-Gilles-les-Bains is ridiculously overcrowded. It's pretty much like Brighton, Bondi or Santa Monica on a hot, sunny Sunday with packed restaurants, cramped beaches and all day traffic snarls which seem particularly constipated if you're coming from the St-Denis side. The excitement centres on the 20 km stretch of lagoon and white coral sand beach stretching from Boucan Canot to La Souris Chaude (the hot mouse?!). On either side of this area, the sand is of the black volcanic variety.

In the 1800s, the small fishing village of St-Gilles-les-Bains belonged to the estate of the Desbassyns family. After the road from St-Paul arrived in 1863, however, it was discovered by holiday makers and has been growing more popular ever since.

### Information
**Tourist Information** Tourist information is available from the Syndicat d'Initiative de l'Ouest (☎ 24 57 47) in the Galerie Amandine in the centre of St-Gilles-les-Bains. This is one of the most helpful offices on the island.

**Laundry** Pressing du Lagon has a self-service laundrette in the Score Arcade at Hermitage-les-Bains.

**Bookshops** For newspapers and magazines, go to Maison de la Presse on Rue du Général de Gaulle. You'll also find bookshops in the arcades near the Syndicat d'Initiative and behind the Score supermarket.

### Beaches
Roches Noires, a popular surfing spot, is St-Gilles-les-Bains' main beach area and the French like to call it *Le St-Tropez de la Réunion*. It's rather touristy but is nevertheless a nice place to sit in the sun.

Further south, between St-Gilles-les-Bains and Saline-les-Bains, around Hermitage-les-Bains, the reef is well out from the shore, thus creating stony shallows and calm seas. Watch out for sea cucumbers and sea anemones. This long casuarina-lined stretch of beach, ploughed and scraped regularly, is good for snorkelling and sunbathing.

Topless sunbathing seems almost obligatory for women. Those who want to go bottomless as well should head for the nudist beach just south of Saline-les-Bains where there's a private club for naturists.

North of St-Gilles-les-Bains and seven km south of St-Paul is Boucan Canot, the best beach on the island. With its solitary palm tree, it's the favourite of the Réunionnais. The sea is more animated here than around the sheltered lagoons south of Pointe des Aigrettes, and you can even body-surf when the waves are right. If they aren't, keep in

mind that the lifeguard is on duty only on
Wednesday, Saturday, Sunday and holidays.
For those who prefer docile water, there's a
seawater swimming pool.

Unfortunately, sharks can be a real
problem for surfers and other water enthusiasts along this coast and although it's not as
dangerous as the east coast of the island,
there have been some nasty incidents. Late
afternoons are the most risky, especially offshore of the mouths of rivers and streams;
heed local advice!

### Théâtre de Plein Air

On the road between upper and lower St-
Gilles, the modern Théâtre de Plein Air
(Open-air Theatre) is used frequently for
concerts and plays. The hills rise behind the
audience and the town and sea act as a backdrop. Try to catch a performance by the
Talipot theatre group.

### La Ravine St-Gilles

About one km inland from the open-air
theatre, on the road to St-Gilles-les-Hauts, is
a parking area and a path down to an old
irrigation and water supply system. The area
encompasses a stunning series of waterfalls
and pools which are, from top to bottom:
Bassin Malheur, Bassin des Aigrettes and
Bassin du Cormoran.

Bassin du Cormoran, the most accessible,
is reached along the lower path which cuts
away from the irrigation canal about 10
metres from the car park. When the water
level is right, the falls are excellent for swimming and provide an alternative to the beach
on hot days. On weekends, the area is
thronged with picnickers. The rather stag-
nant pool in the Bassin des Aigrettes is
reached by a slightly precarious 800-metre
walk along irrigation channels and through
two slippery tunnels.

### Musée de Villèle

Near St-Gilles-les-Hauts is the Musée de
Villèle (☎ 22 73 34). Built in 1787, this
colonial mansion became the home of the
wealthy and very powerful Mme Panon-

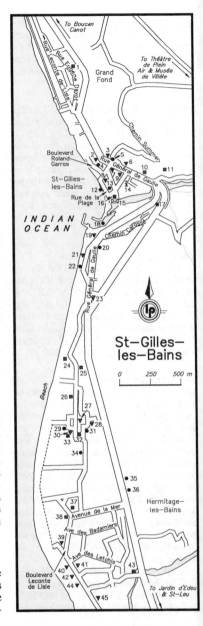

St-Gilles-
les-Bains

0      250     500 m

■ PLACES TO STAY

| | |
|---|---|
| 1 | Hôtel Le Colombier |
| 10 | Hôtel Les Dents de La Mer |
| 11 | Hôtel Les Aigrettes |
| 13 | La Plaza Créole |
| 16 | Caro Beach Hotel |
| 24 | Le Récif Village Club |
| 25 | Les Brisants Résidence du Tourisme |
| 26 | Municipal Camping |
| 32 | Hôtel Alamanda |
| 33 | VVF |
| 37 | Blue Beach Hotel |
| 38 | Coralia Novotel |
| 43 | Résidence Les Bougainvilliers |

▼ PLACES TO EAT

| | |
|---|---|
| 2 | Le Coralys Pizzeria |
| 3 | Restaurant Le Traiteur |
| 6 | Piccolo & Le Bourbon Restaurants |
| 7 | La Canne á Sucre |
| 8 | Le Grand Large Restaurant |
| 9 | Chez Loulou |
| 19 | Le St-Gilles Restaurant |
| 21 | Alpha Centre de Pêche Restaurant |
| 23 | Caltex & L'Escale de Gastronomie Restaurant |

| | |
|---|---|
| 27 | Moulin du Tango Disco & L'Auberge du Bonheur |
| 28 | Restaurant Le Borsalino |
| 30 | Le Chaland Restaurant |
| 39 | Restaurant Les Trois Toches (Chez Go) |
| 40 | Le Toboggan Restaurant & Bar |
| 41 | L'Esquinade Restaurant |
| 42 | La Bobine |
| 44 | Le Père La Frite Restaurant |
| 45 | La Mandibule Restaurant |

OTHER

| | |
|---|---|
| 4 | Police |
| 5 | Maison de La Presse |
| 12 | Roches Noires beach |
| 14 | Tourist Office |
| 15 | Post Office |
| 17 | Disco Le Roche Noire |
| 18 | Yacht Harbour |
| 20 | 'Musée du Coquillage' |
| 22 | Gis Car Hire |
| 29 | Aqua Park |
| 31 | Club Saïn Gym |
| 34 | Score Supermarket |
| 35 | Réunion Air Service |
| 36 | L'Île en Moto |

Desbassyns (the name originated because the family's turf surrounded the Bassins above St-Gilles-les-Bains). She was a coffee and sugar baron who, among other things, held 300 slaves. Legend has it that she was a cruel mistress and that her tormented screams can still be heard from the hellish fires whenever the volcano is erupting. She died in 1846 and her body lies in the Chapelle Pointue, which is visible on the left as you cross the Ravine St-Gilles on the road toward Saline-les-Bains.

A bit further, on the other side of the road, is Mme Panon-Desbassyns' house and the ruins of the sugar mill. Guided tours are available, in French, from the caretakers who conduct a lightning tour unlocking and locking doors as you proceed. Exhibits include a clock presented to the Desbassyns by Napoleon; a set of china from Mauritius

featuring *Paul et Virginie*, the love story by Bernardin de St-Pierre (see Mauritius section); a commemoration of the Réunion-born aviator Roland Garros (1888-1915); an English cannonball (a memento of British rule!); a collection of French East India Company furniture and china; and a Gobelin tapestry depicting Christ.

The well-preserved mansion is open daily except Tuesday from 9.30 am to noon and 2 to 5 pm. Admission to the ground is free but guided tours of the site cost F10 per person.

### Village de L'Eperon

At L'Eperon, near St-Gilles-les-Hauts, is a picturesque old grist mill, L'Usine de l'Eperon. It's now occupied by the Village Artisanale de L'Eperon run by Mr Le Gall (☎ 22 73 01). The shop is open Monday to Saturday from 8.30 am to noon and 1.30 to

6 pm. There's also an interesting Hindu temple nearby.

The only public transport to l'Eperon is the infrequent short-haul bus which travels between Grand Fond and Trois Bassins, passing through l'Eperon.

## Le Maïdo

One of the most superb views of the Cirque de Mafate is available at Le Maïdo viewpoint at 2204 metres above sea level. The name comes from a Malagasy word meaning 'burnt land', probably due to its vulnerability to fire on the dry western slopes of the island. It's a long, winding road up the mountain from Le Guillaume in the heights above St-Gilles-les-Bains, winding through forests and past picnic sites galore.

From Le Maïdo, one can see the island's highest points: Le Gros Morne (2991 metres), Piton des Neiges (3070 metres) and Le Grand Bénard (2896 metres). You'll need to get an early start if you want to see anything, however. The clouds normally obscure the view by 10 am. There's a tough walk along the cirque rim to the summit of Le Grand Bénard (2896 metres). Allow at least six hours for the return trip and be prepared for dramatic changes in the weather.

It's also possible to travel on foot into the Cirque de Mafate from Le Maïdo. A spectacular trip is from the lookout along the western wall of the cirque, high above the Rivière des Galets, to the hamlet of Sans Souci near Le Port. Although the route begins with a steep descent, it's a relatively easy trip because there's very little climbing involved. The problem is that there are no gîtes along the route; to make a two-day trip of it without camping will involve an extremely difficult side trip across the gorge of the Riviére des Galets to reach the Cayenne gîte at Grand Place. For other options, see the Interior chapter.

## Le Jardin d'Eden

If you haven't guessed, the name of this new, self-proclaimed *jardin ethno-botanique* (ethno-botanical garden) means 'The Garden of Eden'. As silly as that may sound, it's a worthwhile visit with sections dedicated to such interesting concepts as the sacred plants of the Hindus, medicinal plants, edible tropical plants, spices, aphrodisiac plants, cactus, aquatic plants and simply 'blue flowers'.

It's open Tuesday to Saturday from 9.30 am to 12.30 pm and 2.30 to 6 pm, and on Sundays and holidays from 10 am to 6 pm. Admission is F25 per person. Exhibits are well-labeled but for an additional F2, you can hire a guide booklet which gives further information on the 500 plant species on display.

## La Petite France

The village of La Petite France on the road to Piton Maïdo is the best place to visit geranium farms and watch the distillation of the oil used in perfumes. The property of Mr Lougnon is open to visitors; for further information, check with the Syndicat d'Initiative in St-Gilles-les-Bains.

## Water Sports

Most agencies offering 'nauti' activities – surfing, deep-sea fishing, sailboarding, boat charters, diving, snorkelling, etc – are based around the harbour south of the river mouth in St-Gilles-les-Bains. For names of clubs which offer instruction or hire equipment, see under Activities – Water Sports in the Réunion – Facts for the Visitor chapter.

Nautique Service and Planche Alizés in Saline-les-Bains hire out sailboards (windsurfers), kayaks and pedalos. A cruise in a glass-bottom boat will cost around F80 for hour; try Société Neptune (☎ 24 07 51). They're open only on weekends and holidays. If you prefer to don a parachute and fly to St-Paul behind a motorboat, get in touch with Sky-Ride (☎ 24 14 78) at the port in St-Gilles-les-Bains.

The best surfing in the area is found at Boucan Canot and Roches Noires beaches (St-Leu further south is said to be Réunion's best). Surfing lessons from any of the surf clubs, including board hire, will cost between F90 and F130 per hour.

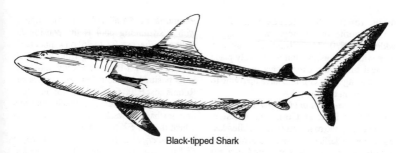

Black-tipped Shark

Dive operators and instructors all charge roughly the same rates. A diving course in St-Gilles-les-Bains will cost F1650 plus equipment rental for one week and divers must have a current medical certificate stating that they have no health problems which would be aggravated by diving. Advanced courses cost F1800 and F2000 plus equipment rental. These prices include classroom instruction, two dives daily, exams and certification. Those who just want to have a go at diving will pay F150 plus equipment rental for one carefully supervised dive. Certified divers will pay the same per dive or F840 for a series of six dives.

For some freshwater splashing and water sliding, go to Aqua Parc in Hermitage-les-Bains. One go costs F5, seven times down costs F20 and all day costs F35 on Wednesday, Thursday or Friday and F50 on weekends. It's open from 9.30 am to 6.30 pm daily except Monday and Tuesday.

### Places to Stay

There's plenty of accommodation choice in the area, but everything is normally booked out during holiday periods and on weekends. Unless you like risks, don't arrive without a reservation.

**Camping** The *Camping Municipal* (☎ 24 42 35) at Hermitage-les-Bains is in a good location beside the beach but isn't as tidy or organised as it could be. Sites cost F40 per day for a 25 square metre patch and use of

the facilities. Additional charges include F6 for water and electricity, F1 per person tax and F3 for vehicle parking. It's open only during French school holidays in July and August. Long-term stays cost F800 per month. On the camp site notice board, you'll normally find lots of 'For Sale' notices for tents, most asking from F1500 to F3000. Robbery is rife at this popular site so don't leave anything in your tent.

If the official site is full and you don't have anything to lose, have a look along the shore between Boucan Canot beach and the turn-off to St-Gilles-les-Hauts. There are a couple of unofficial camp sites lost among the casuarina trees with no attached *Camping Interdit* (Camping Prohibited) signs. Fresh water is available from a roadside pump but there are no other facilities.

**Youth Hostel** At Bernica in the hills behind St-Gilles-les-Bains is a new youth hostel (☎ 22 89 75). IYHF members pay F60 for dormitory accommodation plus F10 for breakfast. Evening meals cost F45 and there are no cooking facilities. Reservations should be made through S/C Arts & Traditions (☎ 45 53 51), BP 127, Rue da la Caverne, 97863 St-Paul.

**Chambres d'Hôte** *Mme Louis Gabriel Grondin* (☎ 22 74 15) runs an excellent, homely establishment at Bernica, five km uphill from St-Gilles-les-Hauts. There is a row of three bedrooms separate from the main house. She charges F92/120 a single/double occupancy, meals cost an additional F70. The Grondins' daughters help with the cooking and it's a lively place at meal times; the Créole chat never stops and years ago, Mr Grondin gave up trying to get a word in edgeways!

*Mme Céline Maillot* (☎ 55 69 83) offers a chambre d'hôte at Coin des Artistes, L'Eperon, on the road between St-Gilles-les-Bains and St-Gilles-les-Hauts. She has three double rooms in her home and charges F90/120 a single/double occupancy. Meals cost F80 per person.

On Chemin Bosse also in Bernica is the chambre d'hôte of *Mme Thérèse Ramincoupin* (☎ 55 69 13). She charges F88/110 a single/double. Nearer the coast at L'Eperon, *Mme Maillot* (☎ 55 69 83) has two rooms for F90/120 a single/double. Meals are available for F80 for the first person and F50 for each additional person.

Far up the mountainside at Petite France above Le Guillaume, on the road to Maïdo, are two chambre d'hôtes. The geranium distiller *M Lougnon* (☎ 32 44 26) has two rooms in a quiet setting for F150 per person. Groups of four can rent both rooms for F125 per person. *Mme Magdeleine* (☎ 32 53 50) also has two rooms for F80/120 a single/double. Meals cost F70 extra.

**Gîtes** The same *Mme Magdeleine* (☎ 32 53 50) who has a chambre d'hôte at Petite France also owns a gîte which accommodates five people and rents for F900 per week. The gîtes of *M Lougnon* (☎ 32 44 26) rent for F1340 and F2350 per week for three and five people, respectively. Both of these are good bases for walks to Le Maïdo and Le Grand Bénard.

*Mme Louis Gabriel Grondin* (☎ 22 74 15) also has a couple of pleasant gîtes, one in Bernica and one in Tan Rouge even further up the hill. The former accommodates seven people and the other has space for 10. For capacity crowds, she charges F1340 and F1450 per week but for a couple, she charges only F925 per week for either one.

**Pensions de Famille** A very nice option with a swimming pool is the pension *Le Bougainvilliers* (☎ 24 44 76) on a quiet back street five minutes walking from the beach at Hermitage-les-Bains. The only drawback is its position beside a fetid sewage canal. Rooms cost F200 for single or double occupancy and extra beds are F50 each. For stays of more than two weeks, there are apartments which rent for F220 per night.

At *Auberge Cadet des Îles* (☎ 24 63 73) at 55 Rue Lacaussade, double rooms cost F200 per night. Breakfast costs F20 and evening meals are F65 extra.

Finally, there's *Les Cytises* (☎ 24 41 55) at 44 Rue Eugène Dayot in Grand Fond near Boucan Canot. An air-conditioned studio accommodating four people costs F290 per day or F7250 per month.

**Hotels – bottom end** Hotel-wise, there's nothing in St-Gilles-les-Bains in any price range that has much character. The best budget hotel accommodation is *Le Dor y Flane* (☎ 24 44 19) at 21 Avenue de la Mer, 100 metres from the Coralia Novotel. For a single/double rooms, they charge F140/180 per night. Air-conditioned studio flats cost F250 and full flats are F300. There are two full kitchens available to guests.

The once popular Hôtel Surf at Roches Noires beach is now *Le Plaza Créole* (☎ 24 42 84) a restaurant and brasserie with four chalet-style rooms out the back, each containing one double and one single bed. Each unit costs F200, excluding breakfast, regardless of the number of occupants.

For a similar price is the nicer *Le Colombier* (☎ 24 00 62) at 28 Rue Eugène Dayot, Grand Fond. It's only 10 minutes walking from Roches Noires beach and there's public access through to Grand Fond beach as well. Single/double rooms cost F220/280 with communal kitchen, swimming pool and facilities. Weekly rates are F1000/1500. Rooms with private bath cost F250/300 a single/double.

*Les Dents de la Mer* (☎ 24 44 64) at 129 Rue du Général de Gaulle is not as pleasant as Le Colombier. It charges F175 a single or double. Lower rates are available for longer stays.

**Hotels – middle** The *Hôtel Alamanda* (☎ 24 51 00) at Hermitage-les-Bains has 58 double rooms for F295/398 a single/double. The *Caro Beach Hotel* (formerly *Le Coryphène*) (☎ 24 42 49) on Avenue de la Mer at Roches Noires beach, charges single/double F440/490. Breakfast is included. The *Hôtel des Palmes* (formerly *Le Nénuphar*) (☎ 24 43 89) on Rue du Général de Gaulle in St-Gilles-les-Bains has rooms for F256/350 a single/double. Breakfast costs and extra F30.

The large and residential looking *Hôtel Blue Beach* (☎ 24 50 25) is just a short walk from Les Filaos beach in Hermitage-les-Bains. They charge F360/470 a single/double.

If you'd like a beautiful little family-run hotel, a reader recommends the new *Hôtel Swalibo* (☎ 24 10 97) south of St-Gilles-les-Bains in Saline-les-Bains. It lies 50 metres up a track between the bus stop and the petrol station on the inland side of RN 1. Single/double rooms cost F300/350; breakfast is an additional F30.

**Hotels – top end** The large *Hôtel des Aigrettes* (☎ 24 55 55) on Chemin Bottard in St-Gilles-les-Bains charges F510/610 a single/double, including breakfast.

The *Le Boucan-Canot* (☎ 24 41 20), near the beach of the same name, charges F580/660 a single/double, including breakfast. A few hundred metres away is the large three-star *Hôtel Coralia Novotel* (☎ 24 44 44) where single/double rooms start at F580/680.

The leading hotel in the area, however, is the four star *Grand Hôtel des Mascareignes* (☎ 24 36 24) at Boucan-Canot which charges F700/800 a single/double and if that isn't enough, they want F75 extra for breakfast. The brand new *Hôtel L'Archipel* is above Grand Fond just a couple of hundred metres along the road toward L'Eperon.

**Bungalows & Holiday Flats** Near the Novotel at 27 Avenue des Badamiers are *Les Bungalows* (☎ 24 46 06) with fully equipped units for F250 a double or F300 for four people. At 76 Rue Lacaussade is a private air-conditioned home (☎ 24 69 92) which accommodates four people and rents by the week for F2800. For a less expensive option, there's a similar home on the Route du Théâtre (☎ 24 43 92) for F250 per night with a minumum stay of one week.

*Le Récif Village Club* (☎ 24 50 51) is a private complex with 10 double rooms and 44 one and two-bedroom, self-catering bungalows. The rooms cost F305/425 a single/double and the latter begin at F540 for two to four people. *Les Brisants Résidence du Tourisme* (☎ 24 50 51) in Hermitage-les-Bains offers fully equipped flats for F430 for up to four people and F590 for up to six people.

**Holiday Villages** The *VVF* (☎ 24 47 47) at St-Gilles-les-Bains is open to VVF affiliates only (annual membership costs F100 per family). There are two and three-room bungalows starting at F200 per night on weekdays and F350 per night on weekends. Readers have suggested that it has a less than friendly atmosphere and isn't as nice as the one in St-Leu.

The *Villa du Lagon* (☎ 24 61 91) at Hermitage-les-Bains is Réunion's Club Méditerranée, but nonresidents can use the facilities for a price. Single rooms range from F380 to F420 per night and doubles from F400 to F460 per night.

**Places to Eat**

There are plenty of snack stalls and rapid repast joints around the beach areas. There are also roadside stands along the Route Nationale selling roast chickens for around F30, but get there early to ensure freshness. Most other restaurants, however good or mediocre in appearance or reputation, have set menus from about F60.

For a no-frills beach munch try the friendly *La Bobine* at Hermitage-les-Bains.

They serve very good grilled fish, lobster and steak & chips for around F30 and you can chew into your meal while seated on the beach surrounded by equally well-done sunbathers. Other swift-serve beach restaurants at Hermitage-les-Bains include *L'Esquinade* (☎ 24 48 79); *Le Père la Frite* (☎ 24 31 49), which serves such Créole specialities as *civet z'ourite* (sea urchin stew); the rather pretentious *Le Toboggan* (on weekends, it reserves all its tables, leaving no space for casual drop-ins from the beach!); and the consistently recommended *Les Trois Roches* (aka *Chez Go)*, which has great Créole meals in an airplane hangar ambience beneath the casuarina trees for around F65. It's closed Monday nights and Tuesdays.

Near the camp site in Hermitage-les-Bains you'll find the Chinese-oriented *L'Auberge du Bonheur* (☎ 24 09 97), which is closed on Monday. Nearby, beside the Aqua Parc, is the recommended upmarket Créole restaurant *Le Chaland* (☎ 24 05 11). Just opposite is the similarly expensive French restaurant, *Le Borsalino* (☎ 24 04 34), which is open every day.

The brasserie at *La Plaza Créole* (attached to the hotel of the same name) on Roches Noires beach is a nice open air restaurant with a friendly ambience and a good view of the beach. They have excellent salads and vegetarian options. They also have a more upmarket restaurant inside. The best of the lot, however, is the equally friendly *Grand Large* on the same street. They also serve breakfast for F30 to F35 including the standard fare plus juice and yoghurt.

There is a plethora of restaurants on the main road in the centre of St-Gilles-les-Bains. At *L'Italiano* (☎ 24 55 33) you'll get a pizza for F40. It competes well with the less friendly *Le Piccolo* on the same street, where solo travellers are apparently unwelcome; I went in alone looking for a meal and they refused to serve me because they preferred to save their tables for larger groups! Another option is the rather odd *Chez Loulou* (☎ 24 46 36) at 42 Rue du Général de Gaulle which has good food and serves breakfast. From the attached takeaway stand, they serve excellent sandwiches to order for F10 to F15, as well as a variety of titbit snacks and a standard takeaway meal of curry and rice for F30. It's closed Mondays. *Le Bourbon* (☎ 24 48 01) at 55 Rue du Général de Gaulle has meals starting at F40; it's closed on Monday.

Toward the north end of St-Gilles-les-Bains is *La Canne à Sucre* (☎ 24 02 56) which specialises in Créole cuisine. It's closed Sunday lunchtimes and all day Mondays. In the same area is another Italian restaurant/pizzeria, *Le Coralys* (☎ 24 49 15). It's open every day for lunch and dinner.

Beside the Circus nightclub in Hermitage-les-Bains is the highly rated but quite expensive *Le Jardin du Flibustier* (☎ 24 45 07). Just down the road, north of the lane which crosses the Ravine de l'Hermitage, is the friendly and recommended *La Mandibule* (☎ 24 44 31). It manages to be cosy without being costly or pretentious. Set-menu meals begin at F60.

*Le St-Gilles* (☎ 24 43 12), at the harbour in St-Gilles-les-Bains, has business people's lunches for F70. It's closed on Monday. For a range of fresh catch of the day options, try the restaurant at Alpha Centre de Pêche (☎ 24 02 02) at the port in St-Gilles-les-Bains. It's open daily from 10 am to 10 pm except Monday and Tuesday lunch.

Saline-les-Bains village has a disproportionate number of restaurants for its size, including *Chez Désiré* ☎ 24 65 43), the Chinese restaurant *Le Palais de L'Orient* (☎ 24 68 90) and *La Bamba* (☎ 24 65 38) with Belgian specialities. A good option for seafood with a great sea view is *L'Espadon* (☎ 24 67 57) at Plage Trou d'Eau. It's closed on Sunday nights and Mondays. For a typically Créole meal in a simple, friendly setting, reader Stephen Clarke recommends *Le Zingade* (☎ 24 58 19), down a little track just off RN 1 between Saline-les-Bains and Hermitage-les-Bains. They do great gratin de chouchou and civet de zourite (sea urchin curry).

If you're at the Musée de Villèle, near St-Gilles-les-Hauts and feel peckish, there's a roadside corner café close by called *Le Snack des Îles*, and at L'Eperon, there's *La*

Top Left: Rivière des Galets, Cirque de Mafate, Réunion (DS)
op Right: Rivière des Remparts from Nez de Boeuf (DS)
Bottom: Créole workers repair narrow track up the edge of the Cirque de Mafate, Réunion (RW)

Top: Choice of routes up to the volcano, Réunion (RW)
Bottom: Looking down the outer crater of the volcano, Réunion (RW)

*Crêperie* (☎ 55 52 70). The latter is closed at lunchtime on Mondays and Tuesdays. There are also a number of table d'hôtes associated with chambre d'hôtes in the area; see under Places to Stay earlier in this section.

## Entertainment

**Casino** As one would imagine, St-Gilles-les-Bains is relatively flush with nightlife, as Réunion goes. There's a casino at the Coralia Novotel (☎ 24 47 00) which is open Monday to Thursday from 9.30 pm to 2 am; on Saturday, Sunday and holidays from 3.30 pm to 3 am; and on Fridays and the evenings before holidays from 8.30 pm to 3 am.

**Discos** St-Gilles-les-Bains area also has a greater density of discos than anywhere else on the island. Some of these include *Le Swing* (☎ 24 45 98) at Grand Fond near the turn-off to St-Gilles-les-Hauts and the open-air theatre. It's open on Friday, Saturday and holidays only. *Le Love's* (☎ 33 67 33) on the road up to L'Eperon operates Tuesday, Friday, Saturday and holidays from 10 pm to 6 am. *Le Circus* (☎ 24 50 18) near the beach at Hermitage-les-Bains is open the same schedule as Le Love's. There's also *Le Privé* night club, which isn't anything out of the ordinary. On weekends, there's a F100 cover charge but reader Julian Burke reports that plenty of local regulars breeze in without paying, missing out on the 'free drink' offered to ticket holders.

*Moulin du Tango* (☎ 24 53 90), also at Hermitage-les-Bains. It operates on Wednesday, Friday, Saturday and holidays and is known for its opening roof and Wednesday singles night. Admission is F70, including the first drink (which would otherwise set you back about F50!). *Dancing des Roches Noires* (☎ 24 44 15) at the road bridge across the Ravine St-Gilles is open only on Saturdays and holidays from 10 pm to dawn; women are admitted without charge so if you're offended by this or what it implies, choose another disco.

**Music** Folk music programs are staged at the Hotel Les Aigrettes (☎ 24 55 55) on Thurs-

day and Saturday nights. On Tuesday evening, there's a performance by the local duo, Interlude. The same group performs at Le Récif Village Club on Thursday.

The Coralia Novotel (☎ 24 44 44) stages a buffet fish BBQ on Monday night, accompanied by live entertainment. On Wednesday, there's a Créole evening and on Saturday, a buffet beef BBQ to the strains of the hotel music ensemble. At Le Récif Village Club (☎ 24 50 51), there's a Réunionnais folk music performance and on Sunday, the noon meal is accompanied by live music. At the restaurant *Le Case Créole* (☎ 24 32 50), there's live entertainment and a Créole program each Wednesday night.

**Pubs** At St-Gilles-les-Bains there's a pub in the restaurant *La Canne à Sucre* and a cocktail lounge called *La Rhumerie*. Both of these are on the main road through town.

### Getting There & Away

St-Gilles-les-Bains lies on the St-Denis to St-Pierre line and buses leave approximately every half hour between 8 am and 6 pm in either direction; the bus stops are along the Route National in both Hermitage-les-Bains and St-Gilles-les-Bains. The trip to St-Denis takes at least an hour – longer if the route is via Le Port and La Possession – and costs F16.80. The St-Paul to St-Gilles-les-Bains leg costs F5.60.

### Getting Around

Bicycles may be hired from Locacycles (☎ 24 49 67), 18 Avenue du Général de Gaulle in St-Gilles-les-Bains for F80/50 for a full/half day plus a F200 deposit. They also hire out motorbikes on a day and half-day basis. A 50cc moped costs F100/85 for a full/half day. A Vespa scooter costs F130/100 and a 125cc trail bike costs F200/150. There's a F2000 deposit on each bike.

There are also a couple of rental firms which hire out scooters and motorbikes. L'Île en Moto (☎ 24 05 63) at 216 Avenue du Général de Gaulle hires out 50cc mopeds and scooters for F110 per day or F480 per week, with a F3000 deposit. For a 125cc machine, they charge F200 per day or F1085 per week with a F5000 deposit.

For information on car hire firms, see under Driving in the Réunion – Getting Around chapter. St-Gilles-les-Bains is also a popular take-off spot for helicopter tours around the island. For details, see under Air, also in the Réunion – Getting Around chapter.

## ST-PAUL

Pleasantly attractive and worthwhile for a few hours of exploration, St-Paul is often bypassed by those scurrying toward the surf and white sand further south. As the original capital of Réunion, it bears a pleasantly tropical and colonial air, with historical buildings along the seaside promenade, lined with cannons and shaded by straggly coconut trees. Most people find the black sand beach pleasant to look at but on closer inspection, the nose reveals its primary purpose for the locals.

In addition to the main attractions described later in this discussion, there are a couple of minor sights. The town hall, built in 1767, is an old French East India Company building. There's also an interesting Hindu temple along Rue St-Louis, dedicated to the god Shiva. On Saturday, there's a rag-tag local market held on the waterfront.

### Information
**Post** The post office is at 38 Rue Rhin et Danube and is open weekdays from 7.30 am to 6 pm, and Saturdays from 8 am to noon.

**Banks** The Banque de la Réunion is found on Rue Rhin et Danube and the Crédit Agricole is at 85 Chaussée Royale. They're both open weekdays from 8 am to 4 pm.

### Cimetière Marin
The only St-Paul site that could be considered a real attraction is the bright and well-kept cemetery near the southern end of town, a great place to wander and recall the island's tumultuous, renegade and mercantile past. It contains the plots and remains of Réunions writers, rogues and respectable gentry. 'Celebrity graves' are well signposted and include those of the poet Leconte de Lisle (1818-94), complete with an epitaph extracted from one of his works, and Eugène Dayot, who lived from 1810 to 1852.

And then there's the grave of Eraste Feuillet (1801-30) who died because he took a sense of remorse too far. Feuillet, a young sea captain, awoke one morning in a hotel and, forgetting he was on dry land, tossed an empty toilet-water bottle out of the window. Unfortunately, it struck an unwitting passerby who became miffed and challenged Feuillet to a duel. Fortunately, the irate adversary's pistol jammed, but unfortunately, Feuillet had a sense of honour and offered his own weapon as a replacement. And the bugger accepted it! Feuillet's epitaph reads simply *Victime de sa générosité* (victim of his generosity).

The cemetery's greatest attraction, however, is the final resting place of the pirate Olivier Levasseur, 'La Buse' (The Buzzard), who came to the Indian Ocean in 1720 in search of easy prey, after the Caribbean and Atlantic trade routes became too well policed. After stealing a fortune in treasure from the Portuguese vessel *La Vierge du Cap*, La Buse based himself on the east coast of Madagascar. He was the last Indian Ocean pirate to be apprehended. He was captured, taken to St-Paul and hanged on 7 July 1730. There are people still searching for his treasure in Mauritius, the Seychelles and Réunion.

La Buse still has disciples. On his grave, marked by the pirates' trademark skull and crossbones, stand recently placed *Remerciement* (thank you) plaques and each night, secret admirers place cigarettes, glasses of rum, fruit and other offerings on the grave; many attribute them to a religious cult. Ironically, the epitaph of the gravestone beside the pirate's reads 'Here lies an honest man', just in case anyone should think the

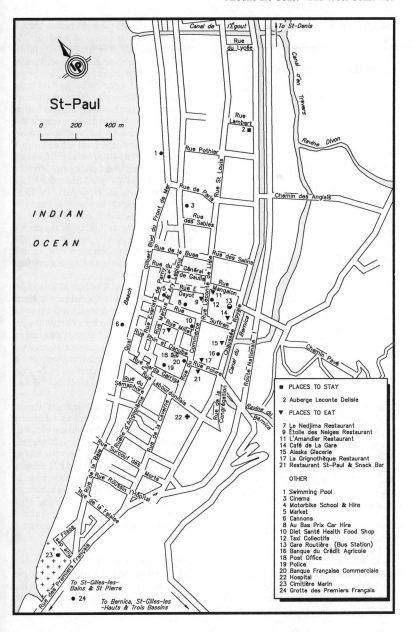

St-Paul

0    200    400 m

INDIAN

OCEAN

■ PLACES TO STAY

2 Auberge Leconte Delisle

▼ PLACES TO EAT

7 Le Nedjima Restaurant
9 Étoile des Neiges Restaurant
11 L'Amandier Restaurant
14 Café de La Gare
15 Alaska Glacerie
17 La Grignothèque Restaurant
21 Restaurant St-Paul & Snack Bar

OTHER

1 Swimming Pool
3 Cinema
4 Motorbike School & Hire
5 Market
6 Cannons
8 Au Bas Prix Car Hire
10 Diet Santé Health Food Shop
12 Taxi Collectifs
13 Gare Routière (Bus Station)
16 Banque du Crédit Agricole
18 Post Office
19 Police
20 Banque Française Commerciale
22 Hospital
23 Cimitière Marin
24 Grotte des Premiers Français

To St-Gilles-les-
Bains & St Pierre

To Bernica, St-Gilles-
-Hauts & Trois Bassins

neighbourhood was the wrong side of the burial ground!

## Grotte des Premiers Français

Across the highway from the Cimetière Marin is a small park in a cave-studded cliff face. The largest cave is said to have sheltered the mutineers from Madagascar who arrived in Réunion in 1646, the first Frenchmen to settle on the island. On one side is the shrine of Notre Dame des Lourdes, which at times becomes waterlogged, and on the other is a cold waterfall suitable for bathing if you don't mind spectators or sharing it with the local lads.

## Chemin de la Tour des Roches & Ravine du Bernica

These two pleasant walks up the slopes directly behind St-Paul are signposted on the Route Nationale just inland from the centre of town. On the paved Tour des Roches path are the remains of an old mill, heaps of coconut and banana trees and a nice view over the town. The dirt track up the Ravine du Bernica where, according legend, La Buse deposited one of his treasures, follows the course of a clear stream up a lovely and quiet gorge.

## Places to Stay

For hotel accommodation, you'll have to head south to Boucan-Canot or St-Gilles-les-Bains. St-Paul's only accommodation is *Auberge Leconte Delisle* (☎ 45 43 92) at Rue Lambert 8 near the north end of town but it suffers from a bit of highway noise. Single/double rooms cost F100/130; breakfast is an extra F20.

## Places to Eat

St-Paul has a few good restaurant options but on weekends nearly everything is dead. For quick takeaway snacks, *Café de la Gare* at the gare routière, or *Restaurant St-Paul* on Rue Poivre are just fine. You'll also find deep-fried goodies at food stalls along the

waterfront. Behind the gare routière, there's a nice sidewalk cafe called *L'Amandier*. *La Grignothèque* on Rue Poivre is classy, popular and, for some items, cheap. Plan on around F30 for a set meal.

At Rue Marius & Ary Leblond 58 is the Indian café/restaurant *Le Maghreb* (☎ 22 59 23) which is open for lunch only and offers coffee, snacks, Middle Eastern cuisine and curries for around F40. A few metres away you'll find Italian food at *Le Jardin d'Emeraude* (☎ 45 49 20). It's open for lunch and dinner except on Sunday and Monday. At Rue Marius & Ary Leblond 94 is a Chinese restaurant, the *Hong Kong* (☎ 45 51 06), which is one of the few places open on Sunday. It's closed on Monday.

Another option for Sunday (or any day but Monday!) is *Leconte Delisle* (☎ 45 43 92), attached to the Auberge Leconte Delisle described under Places to Stay. It specialises in Créole cuisine.

*Le Nedjima* (☎ 22 59 42) at 14 Rue Millet is an upmarket option specialising in North African cuisine. It's open from 8 am to 10 pm daily except Sunday. The *Étoile des Neiges* (☎ 22 54 48), a Chinese restaurant on Rue Leconte de Lisle, has meals starting at F35. There are two Créole restaurants on the same street worth contemplating, *Le Petit Jardin* (☎ 22 60 40) and *Le Poisson Rouge* (☎ 22 55 87).

Way up the Rivière des Galets at Rue des Rosiers 18 in La Plaine is an interesting restaurant called *Le Mangoustan* (☎ 44 22 22) which claims its speciality is *nouvelle cuisine Créole*. They even have a sort of *grande dégustation* known as *Le Mangoustour*, a culinary tour of Réunion with 24 different Réunionnais specialities and a mysterious *digestif* known as *Le Trou Réunionnais*. If you want to take a Mangoustour, reservations are required.

## Getting There & Away

St-Paul lies on the St-Denis to St-Pierre bus route and there are departures more or less half hourly from the gare routière in either town. The fare is F8.40.

## Getting Around

There's a car hire firm called Au Bas Prix (☎ 45 43 36) at 35 Rue Suffren. Moto-Flash (☎ 22 64 92), a motorbike driving school at 75 Rue Marius & Ary Leblond, hires out mopeds for F100 per day and trail motorbikes for F200. They charge a security deposit of at least F2000.

## LE PORT & LA POSSESSION

As they head west out of St-Denis, vehicles are crowded onto the cliff-hugging stretch of coastal motorway known as La Corniche. After 14 km, the highway issues onto open ground at the industrial centre of La Possession, really little more than a suburb of Réunion's main port area, which is known appropriately as Le Port. It was here that Governor Pronis took possession of the island in the name of the French king in 1640. There is little of interest in either place, but the highlands above them are another matter.

## Dos d'Âne

Dos d'Âne village is an alternative starting or finishing point for treks to the Plaine d'Affouches and La Roche Écrite, as well as into the Cirque de Mafate via the Rivière des Galets route. An easy day walking from Dos d'Ane will get you to Cayenne gîte at Grand Place, while a magnificent but more challenging route will take you up the beautiful Bras des Merles to Aurère.

Unfortunately, there's no longer any public transport to Dos d'Âne, so those without a vehicle will have to hitch or take a taxi from the small town of Rivière des Galets, which lies along the St-Denis to St-Pierre bus route.

## Places to Stay

La Possession has a hotel, the *Burotel Les Lataniers* (☎ 22 23 23) at 102 Rue Raymond Mondon. Single/double rooms with showers cost F290/340. Breakfast is an extra F45.

At Dos d'Âne, *M Axel Nativel* (☎ 32 01 47) operates a basic gîte d'étape with space for 30 people. Beds cost F60 per person and meals are available at the table d'hôte (see Places to Eat). It's a good option for trekkers setting to and from the Cirque de Mafate.

## Places to Eat

*Le Viet Nam* (☎ 22 28 32), run by M Nguyen at 301 La Corniche in La Possession, has a terrace with sea views and a swimming pool. After you try one of his meals, which costs around F130, you'll never want to face Chinese takeaways again! Another excellent Vietnamese restaurant in La Possession is the *Haï Phong* (☎ 22 39 80) at Rue Raymond Mondon 32 beside the hotel. Set menus cost around F60 but à la carte is available. It's closed on Sunday.

An inexpensive option is *La Grenouille* (☎ 43 29 28) at Rue de St-Paul 38. Although the name means 'the frog', don't expect any amphibious recipes; it's a Créole and Italian restaurant. It's open from 7 am (for breakfast) to 6 pm daily except Sunday.

For some of the most gourmet fare available in Réunion, go to *Lions de Lyon* (☎ 22 21 41) at 10 Rue Camp Magliore in La Possession. It specialises in cuisine Lyonnaise and with prices starting at about F180 for a meal, you'd have to really appreciate haute cuisine to get the most out of it.

A variety of cuisines, from French and Créole to German and Greek, is available at the reasonably expensive *Chez Georgie* at the corner of Rue du Général de Gaulle and Verdun in Le Port. It's open daily for lunch and dinner except Tuesday night and Wednesday. Also on Rue du Général de Gaulle is *L'Ebène* (☎ 42 07 70) which specialises in French-African cuisine. On Saturday night, they stage a live African music program. The restaurant is closed all day Sunday and on Monday evening.

The rather legendary *Le Poteau Vert* (☎ 32 01 47), the table d'hôte of M Axel Nativel in Dos d'Âne village, is recommended by anyone who's ever eaten there. Not only is it in a superb setting, it's also a welcome option for trekkers entering or leaving the Cirque de Mafate. Meals cost F65 per person.

# The Interior

Réunion's interior is a tremendous tramping ground, an exotic and mountainous terrain that manages to provide outdoor thrills without being too dangerous or overly challenging. With beachcombing limited on the island, the mountain and cirque country provides room to roam and as an additional bonus, the scenery is as breathtaking as the sometimes humid tropical climate.

Undoubtedly the best way to explore this country is on foot. There are hundreds of walks that would take another book to cover in any worthwhile detail, but some of the most popular options will be discussed in this chapter. For planning and information, see the Trekking section in the Réunion – Facts for the Visitor chapter.

# The Cirques

Like leaves of a three-leaf clover, the cirques of Cilaos, Salazie and Mafate dominate the heart of the island. Although they superficially resemble volcanic craters, they are actually the product of the same erosional forces that sharpened the peak of the Matterhorn in Switzerland. The massif was originally one immense volcanic dome known as a shield volcano. After volcanic activity ceased, aeons of erosion scoured out amphitheatres on three sides of the summit, Piton des Neiges, and sculpted the ridge and valley landscape visible today.

It's worth travelling the roads into these amazing amphitheatres for the trip alone. If you go by bus or taxi, the ride can be hairraising; the roads edge along cliffs and gorges, corkscrew up and around mountain sides and hairpin bends, and pass through tunnels and over viaducts. At a contortion called Le Boucle on the trip into Cilaos, the road even makes a complete loop over itself.

Here, the cloud and mist formations provide wonderful special effects, and

during (and just after) the rainy season, the world is green, lush and dripping. The Cilaos and Salazie cirques seem to be enchanted kingdoms and the Cirque de Mafate is wild, secluded and bizarre.

## CILAOS & THE CIRQUE DE CILAOS
The town of Cilaos developed as a spa resort at the end of the 19th century when the thermal baths were constructed. The name, pronounced 'see-LA-oos', is thought to be derived from the Malagasy word *tsy laosana*, a place from which one never returns. Most of the village's inhabitants are descended from settlers who came from Brittany and Normandy in the 1700s.

The area is known for the production of lentils, local embroidery and sweet red and white wines reminiscent of sherry and tawny port, respectively.

### Information
**Tourist Office** The Syndicat d'Initiative (☎ 31 78 03) in the new tourism complex at 2 Rue Mac Auliffe is very helpful and well-stocked with souvenirs and local crafts and products. It's open Monday to Saturday from 8 am to noon and 2 to 5 pm, and on Sundays from 10 am to noon. This is also the Cilaos headquarters for Maison de la Montagne (☎ 31 71 55), which will book gîtes de montagne and provide trekking information.

**Money** There aren't any banks in Cilaos so bring a supply of cash from elsewhere. The post office will cash cheques drawn on French banks but that's about it.

### Sources Thermales
Although they were probably known for some time by escaped slaves hiding out in the cirque, the *sources thermales* (thermal springs) of Cilaos were brought to the attention of the outside world in 1815 by a goat hunter from St-Louis, M Paulin Técher. The

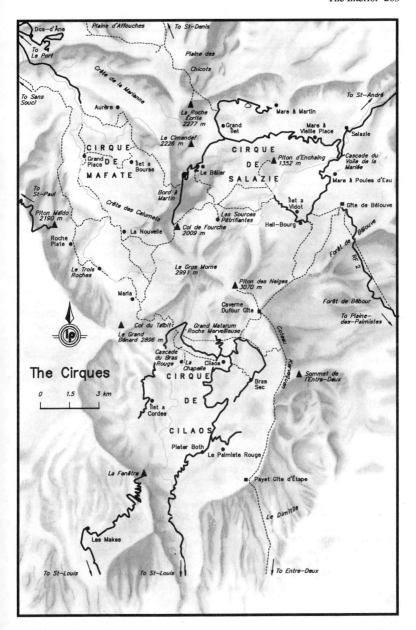

Dos-d'Âne
To Le Port
Plaine d'Affouches
To St-Denis
Plaine des Chicots
To St-André
Crête de la Marianne
Aurère
To Sans Souci
La Roche Écrite 2277 m
Mare à Martin
Grand Îlet
Mare à Vieille Place
Salazie
Le Cimandef 2226 m
CIRQUE DE SALAZIE
Piton d'Enchaing 1352 m
Cascade du Voile de la Mariée
CIRQUE DE MAFATE
Grand Place
Îlet à Bourse
Le Bélier
Mare à Poules d'Eau
To St-Paul
Bord à Martin
Les Sources Pétrifiantes
Îlet à Vidot
Gîte de Bélouve
Piton Maïdo 2190 m
Crête des Calumets
La Nouvelle
Col de Fourche 2009 m
Hell-Bourg
Forêt de Bélouve
RF 2
Roche Plate
Le Trois Roches
Le Gros Morne 2991 m
Piton des Neiges 3070 m
Forêt de Bébour
Marla
Caverne Dufour Gîte
To Plaine-des-Palmistes
Col du Taïbit
Grand Materum Roche Merveilleuse
Coteau Kerveguen
The Cirques
Le Grand Bénard 2896 m
Cascade du Bras Rouge
La Chapelle
La Cilaos
Sommet de l'Entre-Deux
0    1.5    3 km
CIRQUE DE CILAOS
Bras Sec
Îlet à Cordes
Pieter Both
Le Palmiste Rouge
La Fenêtre
Payet Gîte d'Étape
Le Dimitile
Les Makes
To St-Louis
To St-Louis
To Entre-Deux

first track into the cirque was constructed in 1842 and the springs formed the basis of Cilaos' existence as a colonial health resort and hill retreat from the sticky coast. The water gushing from the spring is hot and the active ingredient seems to be bicarbonate of soda with traces of magnesium, iron, calcium, sulphur and a weak radioactivity. It's said to cure rheumatism, among other bone and muscular ailments. The first thermal station to avail its medicinal qualities to the public was constructed in 1896, but the source was ruined in a cyclone in 1948 and not revived until 1971.

Over the years, the baths and walls became heavily stained and it was closed in mid-1987 and turned into a museum. A new complex, using the same source, was opened just uphill from the Hôtel des Thermes. It has a bigger pool, plush private cubicles, a sauna, gymnasium, café and reception area. It's open Monday to Saturday from 7 am to noon and 2 to 5 pm, and on Sundays from 7 am to 2 pm.

If you go, take a towel. A bath at the new Établissement Thermal Irénée-Accot (☎ 31 72 27; fax 31 76 57) costs F40 for 15 minutes, while a five minute shower is F29. Moving upmarket at little, a 20 minute jacuzzi bath will set you back F80 and a sauna of the same duration is F60. If you're after the whole nine yards – two and a half hours of jacuzzi, rolfing massage, seaweed bath, sauna, shiatsu massage, and musicochromotherapy – you'll pay F330 per day or F1580 for six days running!

All this (most of this, anyway) is magic for relaxing after a long hike when your feet are sore and your muscles stiff. If you don't want or need a bath, you can always visit the spring itself. Of the massages, however, one reader has written:

Be warned; don't expect a Créole beauty to give you a massage as a friend of mine did. He was most disappointed when he discovered that the massage he booked at the thermal station was to be performed by a machine!!

**Gillian Chambers**

## Maison de la Broderie

Although the designs and procedures came originally from Brittany, Cilaos' embroidery tradition began at the turn of the 20th century when Dr Jean-Marie Mac Auliffe arrived to practise thermal medicine. His daughter Angèle took up embroidery as a pastime, learning her technique from books and from the sisters who taught the young village girls how to embroider handkerchiefs. Angèle soon organised a small needlework club, which led to an embroidery workshop of 20 ladies and the distinctive Cilaos style evolved. Angèle died in 1908, aged 31, during a measles epidemic in St Denis.

In 1953, however, the sisters of Notre-Dame-des-Neiges opened a workshop and school which continue to operate. There are now more than 120 professional embroiderers at work in Cilaos. The Maison de la Broderie, built under the direction of mayor Irénée Accot in 1984, provides a venue for both teachers and students. Here, they embroider children's clothes, baptism dresses, serviettes, place settings and table cloths for sale and exhibition. The centre is open to the public Monday to Saturday from 9 am to noon and 2 to 5 pm, and on Sunday from 10 am to 3 pm.

## Philippe Turpin's Studio

The signposted studio of Cilaos-born artist and former primary school teacher, Philippe Turpin (☎ 31 73 64), is on Rue Vinceslas Rivière just uphill from Rue des Écoles. Entry is free, and if M Turpin isn't home, his son will show you around. The etchings from copper engravings of Cilaos and other landscapes on Réunion capture the feel of the island perhaps better than the oil-based media normally uses for tropical scenes. Other prints depict fantasy scenes, magical forests and people, star signs and Gothic romances. Prices for his works start at F150.

## Swimming Pool

The public pool on Rue Victorine Séry is open on Thursdays and Fridays from 11 am to noon, and on Wednesdays and Saturdays from 10.30 am to noon and 2 to 4 pm. Admission costs F10. Opening hours are longer during the school holidays.

## Cascade de Bras Rouge

This day walk begins by following the road behind the Maison de la Montagne; turn downhill between the hotel Le P'tit Randonneur and the Refuge Le Sentier. From the end of the road, there's a track which descends to the old thermal station where you'll find the start of the track which traverses the slopes above the Bras des Étangs. After about two hours, you'll arrive at the waterfall Cascade de Bras Rouge.

From the waterfall, the route continues up the side of the cirque to the Îlet à Cordes road and from there up to the Col du Taïbit and into the Cirque de Mafate.

## Bras Sec

The road to Bras Sec village passes through a lovely forest of Japanese cryptomerias. Hikers, however, can take the short cut across the Ravine du Bras de Benjoin. Begin by following the road north from the lake, Mare à Joncs, then taking the right fork at the hospital. After a couple of hundred metres straight on, the road will turn into the unpaved track which descends into the Ravine du Bras de Benjoin, then climbs into the village of Bras Sec. Allow about two hours for this walk.

From the southern end of Bras Sec village, it's possible to continue along the Sentier des Calumets to the village of Palmiste Rouge (at least four hours). The track leaves from the village and climbs to the foot of Bonnet de Prêtre, the 'priest's bonnet'. Here, take the left fork, the Sentier Forestier which traverses the walls of Les Calumets and emerges at Palmiste Rouge. From the village, it's possible to return the way you came, or walk out to the main St-Louis-to-Cilaos road (two km) and catch a bus or hitch back to Cilaos.

Buses run between Cilaos and Bras Sec about a dozen times daily, except on Sunday when there are only three in either direction.

## Roche Merveilleuse

The signposted path off the road behind the Hôtel des Thermes ascends to Roche Merveilleuse in the Forêt du Grand Matarum. The walk takes at least two hours each way; be sure to follow the right fork at the Plateau des Chènes (yes, there are oak trees!) or you'll wind up en route to the Col du Taïbit. Oh, yes – it's also possible to drive to Roche Merveilleuse along Route Forestière 11!

## La Chapelle Cave

A pleasantly and slightly challenging day hike is to La Chapelle. It begins near the village of Bras des Étangs and quickly descends into the Ravine Henri Dijoux. After about three km, the track climbs two hundred metres up and over a crest before plunging into the Ravine de Bras Rouge, and following it upstream to the cave of La Chapelle. An alternative route is via the Cascade de Bras Rouge (described previously), which lies only 500 metres upstream from La Chapelle. Readers have written in a bit of additional information about La Chapelle:

La Chapelle has been featured in a David Attenborough TV nature film because from the end of October through to November, the martins raise their young without nests; the parents – and then their young – simply hang onto the ceiling of the cave. If you go there during the breeding season, please don't disturb the birds!

**Peter & Ginette Scott**

## Coteau de Kervéguen

Those with a great deal of energy may want to consider the day walk to the Coteau de Kervéguen which separates the Cirque de Cilaos from the Forêt de Bébour. It begins from the picnic kiosk along the road to Bras Sec, and climbs nearly 1000 metres to the crest. Plan on at least seven hours for the return trip from the picnic kiosk, longer from Cilaos. This is also an alternative route to use for the Gîte du Caverne Dufour and the climb to the summit of Piton des Neiges; from the crest, turn left and follow the track three km to the gîte.

If you have a few days and would like a

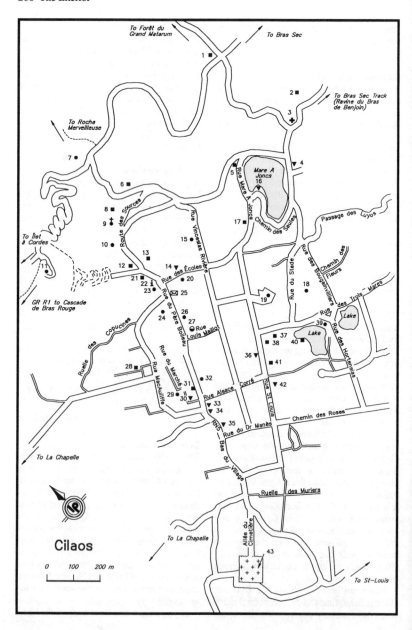

To Forêt du
Grand Matarum

To Bras Sec

1

2

3

To Bras Sec Track
(Ravine du Bras
de Benjoin)

To Roche
Merveilleuse

7

4

5

Mare A
Joncs
16

6

Passage des Luyos

8

9

17

Route des sources

Chemin des Saules

To Îlet
à Cordes

15

10

Rue Vincislas Rivière

Rue Mare A Joncs

Chemin des
Fleurs

Rue des Bougainvilliers

18

13

12

14

20

Rue du Stade

GR R1 to Cascade
de Bras Rouge

11

21

22

23

Rue des Écoles

25

19

des Trois Mares

Lake

26

24

Rue du Père Boileau

27

Rue
Louis Maillot

Lake

37

38

40

Rue des Hortensias

Ruelle des Capucines

36

41

28

Rue du Marché

31

32

Corré

Rue Macauliffe

29

30

Rue Alsace

Rue St-Louis

42

33

34

RN5 Bas du Village

35

Rue du Dr Manès

Chemin des Roses

To La Chapelle

Cilaos

0    100    200 m

Ruelle des Muriers

To La Chapelle

Allée du Cimetière

43

To St-Louis

real challenge, it's possible to continue to Entre-Deux. From the summit, follow the track about another one km, and take a right turn. This track leads to the 2350 metre Sommet de l'Entre-Deux. Then for about five km it follows knife-edge crest between the steep slopes of Les Calumets inside the Cirque de Cilaos and the spectacular Le Dimitile, which slopes dramatically down to Les Hautes Plaines, before descending Le Dimitile into Entre-Deux. Alternatively, from the Coteau de Kervéguen, you can continue straight along to the Plaine-des-Cafres or the Col de Bébour.

### Col du Taïbit

The Col du Taïbit is the trekkers' Cilaos gateway to the Cirque de Mafate, and there are several ways of getting there. The easiest is to take a bus or hitch a lift along the Îlet à Cordes road to the trailhead, which is about six km from Cilaos village. Alternatively, descend from the village to the old thermal station and follow the Cascade du Bras Rouge route described earlier in this section, or begin along the Roche Merveilleuse route, also described earlier, and follow the left fork at the Plateau des Chènes. Either of these options will add about five hours to the walk.

These two routes connect just below the Îlet à Cordes road trailhead. From the trailhead, it's a steep three hour huff up to the Col du Taïbit at the entrance to the Cirque de Mafate.

### Piton des Neiges

Piton des Neiges, the summit of Réunion at 3069 metres, is normally shrouded in cloud after about 8 am, so it's best to allow two days for this trek. The 39-bed gîte at Caverne Dufour is the objective at the end of the first day's walk from either Cilaos (three to four hours) or Hell-Bourg (at least six hours – for a description of the Hell-Bourg route, see under Cirque de Salazie later in this chapter). The ascent early next day to the summit takes up to two hours. Naturally, the trip down is much quicker.

The trip begins at Le Bloc, along the road toward Bras Sec. If you're walking from Cilaos, the quickest way to reach the trailhead is along the road, but it's also possible to walk via Roche Merveilleuse, described previously, then follow the road down to Le Bloc. The climb from the Cirque de Cilaos to Caverne Dufour is extremely steep and if it's been raining, it can get quite slippery. Those who are afraid of heights should think twice about attempting it, although walking downhill is much worse than uphill.

Because this is a popular trip, the gîte at Caverne Dufour fills up quickly on weekends and during school holidays. Book at the Maison de la Montagne in either Cilaos or St-Denis as far in advance as possible. For further information, see under Places to Stay – Gîtes later in this discussion.

Those walking from Piton des Neiges out to the Plaine-des-Cafres using the old IGN 1:25,000 trekking map, *Cilaos 4405R* should beware: the track leading from the ridge between Bras Chanson and the Bras de Ste-Suzanne, along the top of the slope, to the Col de Bébour was omitted. To reach the Plaine-des-Cafres, take the right fork shortly after gaining the ridge.

### Places to Stay

Cilaos is well endowed with accommodation options and although it can become crowded, travellers should be OK for a bed even at the height of the season.

**Camping** The *Camping de Cilaos* and *Gîte d'Étape Eucalyptus* (☎ 31 77 41) in Matarum is a good option, with 120 sites and two small gîtes, one with six bunk beds and one with 16 beds. The site and buildings are clean, and there are showers and toilets as well as a bar & restaurant where three-course meals cost

F60. You'll pay F20 per night for a 20 sq metre tent site, and gîte beds cost F40 per person without sheets.

There's also a 100 site camp site belonging to the Office National des Forêts (☎ 31 71 40) on Rue du Pére Boiteau. Use is free of charge with authorisation from the office.

**Hostels** Just downhill from the Hôtel des Thermes is the rather quirky unofficial youth hostel, the *Auberge du Hameau* (☎ 31 70 94), in the old seminary at 5 Chemin Séminaire. It has 16 bedrooms and caters for clubs, groups and families on a full-board basis only. Singles/doubles are F100 per person, including lots of filling food: breakfast, lunch and dinner.

A recommended option is the convent of the *Soeurs de St-Joseph de Cluny* (☎ 31 71 22), also known as *Notre Dame des Neiges* (Our Lady of the Snows), an ex-boarding school for girls at Rue Père Boiteau 80. They have accommodation for 40 people in partitioned dormitories, with kitchen facilities available and it's rarely crowded. Furthermore, the nuns love to have guests and there are fewer restrictions than in the youth hostels. Dormitory beds cost F50 per person plus F10 for linen, if necessary.

Another hostel, which is actually more like a budget hotel, is the popular *Refuge Le Sentier* (☎ 31 71 54) at Rue du Père Boiteau 63 near the Syndicat d'Initiative. The proprietor M Bruno Sausseau charges just F50 per person but claustrophobes should note that the rooms and windows are tiny.

Finally, there's the *Auberge du Lac* (☎ 31 76 30) at Rue Mare à Joncs 13, just north of Mare à Joncs, Cilaos' largest lake. Single or double rooms cost F200 including breakfast and meals cost F80 each.

**Chambres d'Hôte** Due to high demand, there are numerous chambre d'hôtes in Cilaos. *Mme Léonard Gardebien* (☎ 31 72 15) operates a chambre d'hôte at 50 Rue de St Louis and although it seems less intimate and homely than most, it's not unfriendly. Rooms cost F90/120 a single/double and the meals, which seem to be popular, cost F70.

A conveniently located option is the home of *M Luc Payet* (☎ 31 77 79) at Ruelle des Artisans 1 just west of the centre of town. Rooms cost F120 whether they're occupied by one or two people.

Another chambre d'hôte is run by *Mme Aurélien Nassibou* (☎ 31 71 77) not far from the camp site on the road toward Bras Sec. She charges F78/106 a single/double and F65 for meals. In Bras Sec itself, at 40 Chemin Saül, is *M Christian Dijoux* (☎ 25 56 64) who rents rooms for F90/150 a single/double. Meals cost F65. At number 29 on the same street is another *M Dijoux* (☎ 25 56 45) who charges F80/150 a single/double and F70 for meals. Sounds like friendly family competition! There are numerous buses between Cilaos and Bras Sec.

Way out in Îlet à Cordes at the western edge of the cirque is a chambre d'hôte run by *Mme Hélèe Payet* (☎ 35 18 13). She charges F80/120 a single/double for very basic accommodation. Meals cost F70. There are at least four buses daily (except Sunday and holidays) between Cilaos and Îlet à Cordes.

If you really want to get away from it all, try the chambre d'hôte of *M Camille Ferrère* (☎ 25 69 80) 18 km from Cilaos in Îlet Haute, an oddly named village considering it's at the very bottom of the cirque! The house is an hour's walk uphill from Le Maison Forestière at Le Pavillon. The beds cost F55/110 a single/double.

Other options include *Mme Nella Hoareau* (☎ 31 72 09) at Rue des Chènes 4 up in Matarum (F80/120 a single/double); *M Pascal Maillot* (☎ 31 75 17) at Chemin des Trois Mares 13 in Cilaos (F90/180 a single/double); *Mme Marie-Jeanne Maillot* (☎ 25 57 08) at Chemin Cryptomérias 10 in Bras Sec (F120 single or double); and Mme Flavie Doris (☎ 31 71 23) at Chemin Matarum 8 just outside Cilaos (F80/120 a single/double).

**Gîtes** Conveniently in town at Rue Vinceslas Rivière 2 is the *Gîte-Auberge Le Grand Bénare* (☎ 31 78 29). Either of its two double rooms costs F120 per night.

Two km from town on the main road toward St-Louis is the *Gîte du Cap Noir* (☎ 31 70 52) run by M Grondin. It's fully equipped and will hold up to 14 people. With a capacity crowd, it rents for F1900 per week or F1760 for a weekend. If there are only six guests, the rates drop to F870 for a weekend.

The same *Mme Nassibou* (☎ 31 71 77) who has a chambre d'hôte also owns two gîtes, one for independent travellers and the other for groups. Double rooms cost F90 and dormitory beds start at about F50 per person.

The gîte de montagne at Caverne Dufour (☎ 51 15 26) along the trekking route to Piton des Neiges costs F50 per person. Meals must be booked in advance and cost F70 extra. This is a popular gîte so book as far in advance as possible through Maison de la Montagne in St-Denis or Cilaos.

**Hotels** The clean and friendly *Hôtel Le Marla* (☎ 31 72 33), not far from the lake, is probably the best hotel option for budget travellers. Double rooms with shared shower cost only F125, while singles or doubles with bath cost F150. Breakfast is F15 and immense set menu meals are F60.

Also in the centre is another relatively budget choice, *Le P'tit Randonneur* (☎ 31 79 55) at Rue du Père Boiteau 65. Single/double rooms including breakfast cost F180/230.

The *Hôtel du Cirque* (☎ 31 70 68), in the centre of town at Rue du Père Boiteau 27, has 30 rooms and charges F190/240 a single/double including breakfast. Meals in the restaurant cost between F60 and F70, and at the attached bar are three bowls of punch (F16 per snort) and two small barrels of Vin Cilaos.

The *Hôtel Le Vieux Cep* (☎ 31 71 89) at Chemin des Trois Mares 2 is relatively new and looks more expensive than it is; for single/double rooms including breakfast they charge F230/320. Another mid-range place is the rather basic *Hôtel Le Cilaos* (☎ 31 71 50) at Rue St-Louis 44. Single/double accommodation costs F200/250. There's no restaurant.

Finally, the prestigious three star *Hôtel des Thermes* (☎ 31 70 01; fax 31 74 73), grandly placed behind the church overlooking town, has a top-class restaurant with top-class prices. Room rates are F400/460 a single/double including breakfast. Built in 1936, the Hôtel des Thermes is worth a visit in itself. The tennis courts are meant to be for guests only, but if no-one is playing and you ask nicely after buying a drink or lunch, they may let you hire equipment for F20.

**Holiday Village** Behind the hospital, not far from the camping area, is the VVF *Les Fleures Jaunes* (☎ 31 71 39). There are 280 beds in all, in a variety of rooms ranging from a studio with two beds to a collective dormitory with 20 beds. Whichever room you take, the charge is F230 per person (double occupancy) on weekdays and F320 on weekends, including all meals. Groups of five or six people will pay only F190 per person on weekdays and F220 on weekends. Non-affiliates of VVF must also pay an annual joining fee of F100 per family.

### Places to Eat

The least expensive food option is the pack of mobile food stalls opposite the school. Samosas cost F1.50 and sandwich rolls range from F10 to F12. On the southern end of Rue due Père Boiteau is the snack restaurant *Le Golden Bar*, which is open for lunch only. A more upmarket snack bar is *Crêperie-Salon de Thé La Mousseline* on Rue St-Louis.

Other smaller places include *Chez Noë* (☎ 31 79 93) at 41 Rue du Père Boiteau. The emphasis is on Créole cuisine. Just a few metres away is the *Pizzeria Le Triton* (☎ 31 79 41) which serves Italian and Créole meals as well as pizza. A new restaurant on Rue du Marché, *Chez Miko*, serves Oriental cuisine.

A highly recommended option is *Restaurant du Stade* on Rue St-Louis. It's run by the very jolly Mme Gillette, who serves large (she's used to cooking for her 11 children!) and appetising Créole meals for F50.

The best value restaurant in Cilaos is *La Pensée d'Eau* (☎ 31 71 93) near the Mare à Joncs. Créole meals cost around F50; the fish curry is highly recommended. Across the lake with a great view is *La Grange* (☎ 31

70 38) where prices range from F45 to F60 for a main dish. It's closed on Monday.

The *Refuge Le Sentier* (☎ 31 71 54) in the centre of town also serves meals. The setting is an old Créole hall, and the French/Créole menu ranges from F70 to F150. Although one person has nominated it as the best quality for the price in Réunion, some readers have disagreed. See for yourself.

Another very good restaurant is at *Hôtel Le Marla* (☎ 31 72 33) with a choice of three set menus daily, all consisting of soup or starter, salad, main course and dessert for F60. The emphasis is on Créole but there are occasionally Italian, Chinese and French choices. On cool days, there's a log fire to keep you toasty.

*Hôtel du Cirque* (☎ 31 70 68) has one of the broadest menu ranges in town with Créole, Chinese and French cuisine in a pleasant and popular dining room. It's open every day for lunch and dinner. The other hotels, *Hôtel des Thermes* (☎ 31 70 01), *Le Vieux Cep* (☎ 31 71 89), *Le P'tit Randonneur* (☎ 31 79 55) and *Auberge du Lac* (☎ 31 76 30) all have restaurant facilities, and the chambres d'hôte mentioned in the Places to Stay section offer tables d'hôte as well.

### Entertainment

The only disco, *Le Noctambule* is beside one of the two smaller lakes. There's also a makeshift cinema opposite the church.

### Things to Buy

Cilaos is noted for its lentils and wine. You'll get lentils with most meals, particularly at the chambres and tables d'hôte, and probably a sip of the wine as well.

There are several places in Cilaos and Bras Sec which have signs saying they sell Vin Cilaos. It's also available at the Syndicat d'Initiative for F35 in an officially labelled bottle but on the roadside, it's available in liquor bottles for only F20. Another good place to buy it is at Chez Noë near the market on Rue du Père Boiteau.

Cilaos is also a good place to stock up on groceries for trekking trips through the cirques.

## Getting There & Away

Cilaos lies 112 road km from St Denis and 37 km from the nearest coastal town, St Louis. The road into the Cirque de Cilaos begins at St-Louis and twists and contorts its way steeply into the lofty cirque floor. Le Pavillon, where a road bridge crosses the Bras de Cilaos, marks the spot from which early visitors to the cirque either had to be carried on a palanquin or had to begin walking.

To get to Cilaos from St-Denis, take a bus toward St-Pierre and change buses at St-Louis. From St-Louis, there are eight buses daily on weekdays and Saturdays, and four on Sunday (the Sunday routes run only between St-Louis and Cilaos and don't include St-Pierre). One or two of these services continue on to Îlet à Cordes, useful for reaching the Col du Taïbit trailhead, and quite a few connect Cilaos with the village of Bras Sec. The fare from St-Louis to Cilaos, Îlet à Cordes or Bras Sec is F22.50.

There are also taxi-collectifs running twice daily between Cilaos and St Louis for F25, leaving Cilaos early in the morning and late at night. Enquire at the Syndicat d'Initiative for exact times and pick-up points.

## Getting Around

Mountain bikes can be hired from Cilaos Fun (☎ 31 76 99) at the Place de l'Église. They charge F30 per hour, F70 for a half day and F100 for a full day.

## HELL-BOURG & THE CIRQUE DE SALAZIE

The Cirque de Salazie, the wettest of the three cirques, is busier and more varied than Cilaos, and although it's a bit 'flatter' (although 'flat' is not the first word that will spring to mind when you see it!), the scenery and approach are nearly as awesome. The name is thought to derive from the Malagasy word *salazane*, which means 'sentry stakes'.

The community of Salazie sits at the eastern entrance to the cirque, while Hell-Bourg occupies a beautiful setting nine km further up the slopes. Named after former governor Admiral de Hell rather than the state of the town, it served as a thermal resort until its springs dried up. Visitors can still see the ruins of the old baths and the Hôtel des Salazes which once accommodated the thermal crowd. Hell-Bourg is also one of the best places to see Créole architecture.

Grand Îlet is a perfect introduction to rural Réunion and home to several pleasant and rustic chambres and tables d'hôte. Still further up is Le Bélier, the Cirque de Salazie's main gateway to the Cirque de Mafate.

## Information

The Syndicat d'Initiative (☎ 47 50 14) occupies a minuscule office opposite the Mairie (Town Hall) in Salazie.

## Cascade du Voile de la Mariée

A couple of km from Salazie on the road toward Hell-Bourg, below the turn-off to Grand Îlet, is the Cascade du Voile de la Mariée (Bridal Veil Falls). These towering falls drop in several stages from the often cloud-obscured heights into the ravine at the roadside.

## Mare à Poules d'Eau

On the road from Salazie to Hell-Bourg, at the top of the corkscrew section, is the village of Mare á Poules d'Eau with its superb viewpoint. If you want to see the Mare à Poules d'Eau (Water Chickens Pond) itself, take the road on the right (if you're coming from Salazie) beside the village school. This leads to a track which eventually follows a stream course for about 100 metres before reaching the pond. It's a favourite angling spot for locals but because of nasty algae, it's not suitable for swimming. During the rainy season, the mosquitoes can be overwhelming.

## Anciens Thermes

The old spa at Hell-Bourg is found in the ravine near the western end of town, and it's a nice short walk from the centre. Head downhill from the Hôtel Relais des Cimes along the main street. Where the street begins climbing to the gendarmerie, bear right and follow the track down to the river, where you'll see the blue-tiled ruins of the old baths. There's not much left now, but it's a quiet and leafy spot. Cross the clunky steel bridge and climb the hill and you'll connect with the Îlet à Vidot road.

### Jardin de la Villa des Chataigniers

This late 19th century flower and palm garden at 5 Rue Amiral Lacaze in Hell-Bourg is planted densely around a series of walls, walkways, kiosks, terraces and fountains. You'll find a variety of tropical flowering plants including camellias, orchids, anthuriums, asters, nasturtiums, etc. You can arrange a visit by phoning the owner, M Jean-François Folio (☎ 47 80 98). Admission is F20 per person.

### Élévage de Truites

Near Hell-Bourg is the trout farm Élévage de Truites, also known as the Parc Piscicole d'Hell-Bourg. It was established in 1940 and is now operated by Mr Paul Irigoyen. Entry is F7 per person unless they're fishing, in which case entry is free but self-caught trout cost F60 per kg. Even habitually unlucky or impatient anglers will be able to score a catch here.

### Les Sources Pétrifiantes

These iron-rich hot springs, discovered in 1916 by an illegal hunter, are a popular destination of day hikers from Hell-Bourg. At least many day hikers start out for the springs; quite a few are intimidated by the narrow tracks along precipitous slopes and turn back short of the destination.

Begin by following the variation on the Col de Fourche route described later in this section. After two km on this track, turn left on the track across the Ravine Goyave. It then climbs up and over the ridge before descending to the springs. There are pleasant waterfalls both upstream and downstream from the site.

### Piton d'Enchaing

The 1352 metre high summit of this prominent flat-topped peak, in the heart of the Cirque de Salazie, is a popular day-hiking destination from Hell-Bourg. The peak was named after an escaped slave who took refuge on its summit, from which he was able to survey the entire Cirque de Salazie and report to other fugitives on the presence of pursuers and bounty hunters.

It's a rather steep and difficult walk which concludes with a precipitous gain of 500 metres of elevation, so bring energy snacks and allow plenty of time for rests; at least five hours return from Hell-Bourg. The trip begins at the end of the Îlet à Vidot road. From there, follow the track toward Col de Fourche for about 1.5 km, then take a right turn and begin the long grunt to the peak.

### Forêt de Bélouve & Forêt de Bébour Trek

This is at least a full-day walk – about 20 km – mostly along tracks (the Sentier des Tamarins and Sentier des Mares et des Bois de Couleurs) paralleling the unsealed Route Forestière 2. The IGN 1:25,000 maps to carry (the TOP25 series) are 4402RT (St-Denis) and 4405RT (St-Pierre) – see the Books & Maps section of the Réunion – Facts for the Visitor section. Along the route, hikers will see examples of some of Réunion's most interesting forest habitats, including guava, cryptomeria, tamarins, various orchids, vines and tree ferns and native *bois de couleur*.

The 4.8 km climb from the eastern end of Hell-Bourg on the GR R1 takes about two hours. It's steep but the going is good with concrete steps in places and a wonderful view over the Cirque de Salazie.

At the summit (1480 metres) is the Bélouve gîte (☎ 41 21 23), an especially useful accommodation option if you're coming from the opposite direction (bookings must be made through Maison de la Montagne in Cilaos or St-Denis). With Office National des Forêts clearance, it's possible to drive a vehicle to this point from Plaine-des-Palmistes.

At Bélouve gîte, the GR R1 heads south-west along the ridge of Cap Anglais towards Piton des Neiges and the Cirque de Cilaos, but for the forêts, follow the Route Forestière 2 southward. It forks in several places, but if you follow the map, there shouldn't be any problems. There are also various other signposted tangents. For thorough exploration of the Forêt de Bélouve, you'll need a couple of nights at the gîte. From here, the very adventurous can strike off eastward along the track that traverses the utterly wild and uninhabited Plaine des Lianes and eventually descends to connect with minor roads above Bras-Panon. On the east coast, apart from two basic bivouac gîtes, there's no accommodation along this route.

At the Ravine Misère picnic area, the road is blocked by a locked ONF gate. There's also a parking area where trekkers coming from Plaine-des-Palmistes leave their cars. If you read French, note the ONF sign which philosophically admonishes picnickers and trekkers to respect nature and to preserve and appreciate the silence. Hear, hear!

The picnic area itself offers tables and BBQ pits with wooden rain shelters. From this point, there's a 2.5 km nature walk. Heading south, the route forestière is paralleled by the 2.8 km Sentier des Mares et des Bois de Couleur.

When you reach the lip of the Rivière des Marsouins gorge, you can continue along the RF2 or follow the shortcut path, the Sentier de la Rivière, which entails a steep 100 metre descent to the bottom of the gorge. At the river, it's possible to sidetrack 100 metres upstream to a waterfall with a deep pool that's safe for swimming or 300 metres downstream to Caverne des Hirondelles (where the RF2 crosses the Rivière des Marsouins). Here you'll find a picnic site and quite an impressive waterfall.

Otherwise, the Sentier de la Rivière continues up the southern side of the gorge to rejoin RF2. Thereafter, the route descends through coniferous forest with several picnic sites and, as would be expected, there's

increased traffic, especially on weekends. You can avoid the crowds by cutting off the RF2 at the Plateau de Duvernay picnic site and following the spectacular 10 km Sentier du Bras Cabot track down to Plaine-des-Palmistes. If you prefer to stick with RF2, there's a nice swimming spot at Rivière du Bras Sec about three km from the junction with the cross-island road.

When you reach the main St Benoît-St Pierre road, turn left and, within a few metres, you'll reach a welcome little restaurant called Chez Tante Agathe. Aunty Agathe's meals cost F50 and she specialises in home-made cheese. For further information on the Plaine-des-Palmistes area, see the Les Hautes Plaines section later in this chapter.

## Piton des Neiges

This highly popular trek may be started in either Cilaos (see earlier in this chapter) or Hell-Bourg. From the Élévage des Truites in Hell-Bourg, take the track leading uphill; it's a nearly 300 metre climb up to the sloping plateau known as Terre Plate – and continue across it. After about 4.5 km and a very steep 800 metre ascent, you'll gain the Cap Anglais ridge. Here, the track meets up with another alternative route: the one along the crest of Cap Anglais from the Gîte de Bélouve (see the Forêt de Bélouve & Forêt de Bébour Trek sections earlier in this chapter).

For Piton des Neiges, turn right and continue for about 2.3 km to the Gîte du Caverne Dufour. As the trees diminish in size and the vegetation reduces in variety and density, you'll know you're closing in. For information on accommodation here, see Places to Stay – Gîtes under Cilaos & the Cirque de Cilaos section earlier in this chapter. Despite the times posted, the trek this far will take around six or seven hours, more if you follow the alternative routes through Bélouve.

Most trekkers stay the night at Caverne Dufour, then rise very early in the morning (4 or 5 am) to make the final two-hour assault on the summit and see the entire island spread out below in the first rays of the sun.

There's normally no point in being at the summit after the clouds close in at around 8.30 am.

## Col de Fourche Trek

The Col de Fourche is a popular entrance into the Cirque de Mafate. Although most people opt for the shorter and easier route via Le Bélier (from which there's a motorable road approaching within a few hundred metres of the Col), the main GR R1 route is from Hell-Bourg. You can reach the trailhead by bus from Hell-Bourg, or walk via a shortcut from the gendarmerie in Hell-Bourg, down past the old thermal baths and back up to the road. The track leaves from the end of the Îlet à Vidot road. There's also a variation which turns left a couple of hundred metres before the end of the road – this is the track to use for Les Sources Pétrifiantes – meeting up with the main track at a relatively level spot called Le Grand Sable.

From Le Grand Sable, two hours from the trailhead, the route climbs steadily for about five km up to Col de Fourche. For information on continuing into the Cirque de Mafate, see the Cirque de Mafate discussion later in this chapter.

## Plaine d'Affouches Trek

The access to Plaine d'Affouches (see the St-Denis chapter) is via Grand Îlet in the upper part of the Cirque de Salazie. After two km, follow the road toward Mare à Martin and take the signposted track toward La Roche Écrite. From there, it's a steep 1000 metre climb to the plateau and from the crest, it's two km to the summit of La Roche Écrite and 4.5 to the Plaine des Chicots gîte. Plan on at least five hours from Grand Îlet to the gîte.

## Places to Stay

**Youth Hostel** The *Auberge de Jeunesse* (☎ 47 82 65), well-managed by Isabelle and Thierry, is in a majestic old colonial home, Maison Morange, at Rue de la Cayenne in

Hell-Bourg. Its 20 beds are arranged in a variety of small dormitories and double rooms, and cost F60 per person for card-carrying IYHF members. Non-affiliates can join for F100 (F50 for those under 26).

The kitchen is open to guests who wish to cook their own meals. Alternatively, evening meals are available for F45 and breakfast for F10. There are hot-water showers and laundry facilities, including a washing machine which will be a welcome sight for trekkers just in from the muddy trail.

It's always best to book a bunk in advance. In the high season, the hostel is very popular with trekkers and in the off season, it frequently fills with work camp visitors. If they're full, you may be able to pitch a tent outside for F30.

**Chambres d'Hôte** For inexpensive accommodation, Grand Îlet, with three chambres and tables d'hôte, is better than Hell-Bourg. It's also a good jumping-off point for treks into the Cirque de Mafate. *Mme Jeanine Grondin* (☎ 47 70 66) has three rooms on Rue de l'Église right in Grand Îlet. She charges F80/110 a single/double. *Mme Jeanne Marie Grondin* (☎ 47 70 51) has three rooms and *Mme Christine Boyer* (☎ 47 70 87) has two rooms. Both of the latter rent for F76/108 a single/double. Mme Boyer is a bit difficult to find: get off the bus near the church and walk up the hill signposted to La Nouvelle. Pass the pharmacy and keep going uphill until you reach a restaurant near the top of the hill. Here you turn left down a track and the chambre d'hôte will be on your left near the bottom of the track. All three places provide table d'hôte service as well.

Further into the hills, beyond Grand Îlet towards the Cirque de Mafate at Le Bélier (the name means 'the ram' but Le Bélier is definitely a porcine stronghold!) is the quirky chambre d'hôte of *M Christian Maillot* (☎ 23 51 37). To get there, take the bus to Le Bélier; from the final bus stop, continue walking downhill along the road for several hundred metres. Turn right along the first track and follow it until you see the chambre d'hôte on the right. For trekkers, this is a better option than Grand Îlet because it's an hour's walking nearer Bord á Martin and Col de Fourche.

In Hell-Bourg, try the friendly chambre d'hôte of *Mme Madeleine Parisot* (☎ 47 81 48) who has a rustic annexe right on the main street of Hell-Bourg. For either of her two rooms she charges F70/140 a single/double. It's not a table d'hôte but if you're in need of a meal, ask in advance and she'll arrange something. A bit further from town, 900 metres from Hell-Bourg toward Mare á Poules D'Eau is *Mme Madeleine Laurent* (☎ 47 80 60). She charges F70/120 a single/double and had table d'hôte for F65. Both of these places are highly recommended.

**Gîtes** The 20-bed Bélouve gîte de montagne (☎ 41 21 23), about two hours walking above Hell-Bourg, costs F50 per person and must be booked through Maison de la Montagne. For further information, see under the Forêt de Bélouve & Forêt de Bébour Trek earlier in this discussion. For information on the Caverne Dufour gîte, see Places to Stay – Gîtes under Cilaos & the Cirque de Cilaos earlier in this chapter.

In addition, there are two Gîtes de France in Salazie. In the centre of Hell-Bourg is one owned by *Mme Parisot* (☎ 47 81 48) of chambre d'hôte fame. She charges F950 per week for up to five people, and F1250 per week for up to eight. The other is that of *M Jean-Pierre Robert* (☎ 47 53 13) at Mare à Martin, four km by road above Grand Îlet. He charges F1350 per week for up to seven people. If there are three or fewer guests, the price drops to F900.

**Hotels** The Cirque de Salazie's only hotel is in Hell-Bourg. On the main street, *Hôtel Le Relais des Cimes* (☎ 47 81 58; fax 47 82 11)

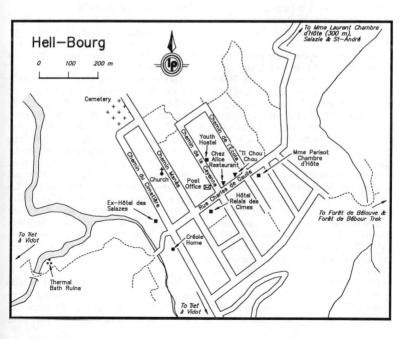

charges F250/320 a single/double, including breakfast. The hotel also offers horseback riding and canoeing activities.

## Places to Eat

While Cilaos is known for its lentils, the name Hell-Bourg is locally synonymous with chou chou, a green, pear-shaped vegetable (known in Europe as *crystophène)* imported from Brazil in 1834. The simple restaurant *'Ti Chou Chou* (☎ 47 80 93), with a varied Créole menu and a cute vegetable mascot, serves up a large number of them in various forms: boiled, shredded, fried, baked in muffins and gateaux, etc. Plats du jour cost between F45 and F65.

Just down the street is the friendly Créole restaurant *Chez Alice* (☎ 47 86 24) and Arlo Guthrie had it right; 'you can get anything you want' it's great, and there's lots of it! Alice serves up hearty plats du jour, including massive salads, massive main dishes and desserts, for F70. Á la carte appetisers cost around F20 and main courses from F40 to F50. It's very popular, especially at lunch hour, but is closed on Mondays.

The restaurant at the *Hôtel Le Relais des Cimes* (☎ 47 81 58) in Hell-Bourg serves Créole and French specialities for F60 to F100. It's open every day for lunch and dinner. For Chinese food in Hell-Bourg, go to *Le Palmier* (☎ 47 82 01) uphill from town on the Îlet à Vidot road. It's closed on Wednesdays. Another option, also uphill from town on Rue Sanglier, is the Créole restaurant *Les Orchidées* (☎ 47 82 18).

At Mare á Poules d'Eau is the *Hong Kong Saigon* (☎ 47 58 34) and the name says it all – they serve Chinese and Vietnamese food. It's open every day for lunch and dinner.

Beneath the waterfall of the same name, *Restaurant Le Voile de la Mariée* (☎ 47 53 54) in Cirque de Salazie, specialises mainly in its fine view but the cuisine is French and Créole. It lies on the road toward Hell-Bourg near the Grand Îlet turn-off.

All of the chambre d'hôtes listed under Places to Stay, with the exception of Mme Parisot in Hell-Bourg, have table d'hôte as

well and provide the restaurants with a bit of competition.

### Getting There & Away

The road alongside the gorge of the Rivière du Mât from St-André to Salazie winds past superb waterfall displays and, in places, swinging bridges cross the chasm to small farms clinging to the slopes. Just above the village of Salazie, the road forks; the left fork goes to Hell-Bourg and Îlet à Vidot and the right leads to Grand Îlet, Mare à Martin and Le Bélier. There are six buses a day in either direction between St André and Salazie, four of which continue on to Hell-Bourg (and two of these continue to Îlet à Vidot) and two that go to Grand Îlet and Le Bélier. The fare to Salazie is F8.40, to Hell-Bourg is F14, to Grand Îlet is F19.70 and to Le Bélier is F22.50.

## THE CIRQUE DE MAFATE

The Cirque de Mafate, the least accessible of the three cirques, is a trekker's paradise. As yet, no roads penetrate it and, in places, the vistas remind one of landscapes from *The Lord of the Rings*.

Foot access into the Cirque de Mafate is via one of six routes: from Le Bélier or Hell-Bourg via Bord à Martin or Col de Fourche; from Cilaos via the Col du Taïbit; from Piton Maïdo down to Roche Plate; from Sans Souci along the Rivière des Galets; from the village of Rivière des Galets up the north bank of the river to Les Deux Bras (unfortunately, this route is currently a road construction destruction zone); and from La Possession via Dos d'Âne (this option also passes through the construction). As a result of the road building in progress, the lower portions of the Cirque de Mafate will soon be accessible by vehicle. If you want to see Mafate in a relatively pristine state, you'd best hurry!

In the Cirque de Mafate, there are gîtes de montagne at Îlet à Bourse, Grand Place (Cayenne), Roche Plate, La Nouvelle and Marla. In addition, there are two gîtes

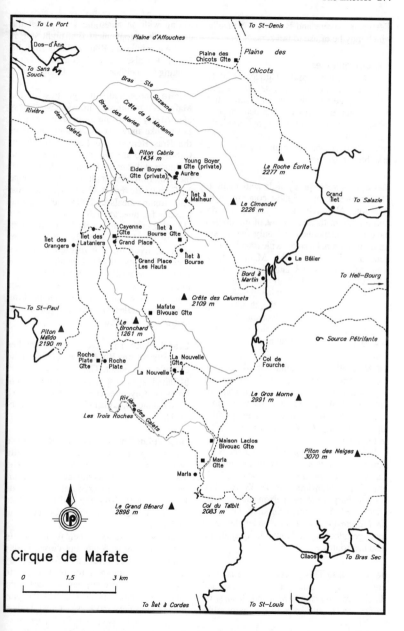

## Cirque de Mafate

0    1.5    3 km

d'étape in Aurère and two at La Nouvelle which may be of use to trekkers.

## The Communities
Despite its remoteness, the Cirque de Mafate is populated and there are several ragged villages large enough to support shops and other minor enterprises. Not much happens in these generally grotty and soporific little places but they do provide reminders of civilisation dropped onto an otherwise formidable landscape.

**Marla** This very quirky little settlement at 1540 metres is the highest community in Réunion. Although there were once forty households in the area, most of the houses have been abandoned and only five or six families remain. Despite its pleasant location beneath the Col du Taïbit, Marla endears itself to few trekkers and several readers who've been booked at the gîte have reported taking one look at it and rushing on to La Nouvelle or Cilaos rather than tarrying there. A recent report, however, indicates that the accommodation is improving, and a nearby store sells basic supplies.

**La Nouvelle** The 'capital' of Mafate, La Nouvelle is the cirque's largest village and supply depot. Its large gîte will accommodate up to 44 people but there is other accommodation – as well as three épiceries and a restaurant, *La Nouvelle* (☎ 43 61 77) – in the village.

If the action at the gîte de montagne is too much for you, there are two private gîtes in La Nouvelle: *Sylvain Bègue* (☎ 43 82 77) and *César Manrique* (☎ 43 43 16). The former charges F50 per person and the latter charges F125 a single or double. *Le Relais de Mafate* (☎ 43 61 77), under the same management as La Nouvelle Restaurant, also has rooms.

**Îlet à Bourse** This pleasant village is probably the tidiest in the Cirque de Mafate and its gîte, which is the newest and cleanest we came across, sits in a lovely garden-like setting with an awesome view down the cirque. It's a convenient first night stop if you're coming over Bord à Martin from Le Bélier. It's also within a couple of hours walking from either Aurère or Grand Place.

**Aurère** Undoubtedly the grottiest of the Mafate communities, Aurère is nevertheless beautifully positioned, perched Machu Picchu-like above the precipitous canyon of the Bras Bémale and beneath the Piton Cabris. There are two private gîtes, owned by father and son; the father's is the nicer of the two. To reserve a place at either, phone M Georget Boyer (☎ 43 28 37). Beds cost F50, evening meals are F60 and there are no cooking facilities available.

Less than one km downhill on the northern side of the Aurère eyrie is a magnificent lookout over the convoluted Bras des Merles; I believe it's the best view in all of Réunion, especially in the late sun. To get there, follow the track marked Sentier Botanique, then turn left at the sign pointing to Bras des Merles. From there, it's about 350 metres to the lookout.

**Grand Place** This two-level village lies above the rushing Rivière des Galets near the cirque's main outlet. The gîte, which is run by the village priest, is in the lower section, known as Cayenne. The village shop lies 15 to 20 minutes walking uphill in Grand-Place-les-Hauts.

**Roche Plate** The community of Roche Plate sits on sloping ground near the western rim of the Cirque de Mafate. Most people who visit Roche Plate are doing the popular four-day route through upper Mafate from Col de Fourche via La Nouvelle and Roche Plate gîtes to Marla, and on over the Col du Taïbit to Cilaos.

The village store is open from 7 am to noon and 1.30 to 5 pm, but closes Friday afternoons and weekends. You can buy tinned and packaged foods. Clean and modern Roche Plate gîte has 24 beds but the consensus among readers is that the *gardienne* considers trekkers a rather bothersome sort and would be happier not having to deal with them at all.

## Cilaos to Roche Plate

You join GR R1 at the old thermal station in Cilaos. The easiest route is along the paved road toward Îlet à Cordes. This is a leisurely, approximately hour-long walk past some impressive waterfall displays. There's also the GR R2 shortcut which takes you deep into the Bras Rouges, past the Cascade du Bras Rouge, and up the other side, to meet up with the road near a picnic site and parking area (see the Cilaos & the Cirque de Cilaos section for further information). This is the GR R1-GR R2 trailhead and here you begin climbing to the entrance of the Cirque de Mafate. It takes about three hours to reach the path's summit, Col du Taïbit, at 2083 metres. That's a climb of nearly 1000 metres from the Cilaos trailhead.

The Marla gîte is near the foot of the Col du Taïbit, lurking over a low hill from the main track toward La Nouvelle, not the route toward Roche Plate. The spartan, 13-bed gîte is south of a little red-roofed school. The caretaker is a neighbouring crofter with a dog of dubious character.

The route from Marla to the Roche Plate gîte is 11.5 km and takes over five hours. For the first few km it is like scrambling down a quarry and you must watch your footing on the loose rocks. Several waterfalls cascade in various ways off the cliffs. The river runs into a lovely, deep, green pool (an ideal bathing spot) and then at Trois Roches, into a deep gorge, where there's a bivouac hut. Thereafter, the path ascends and descends through thick vegetation until you arrive at Roche Plate hamlet. When you reach another bivouac/camp site, the GR R2 branches down towards the Mafate bivouac Gîte on the Rivière des Galets. For Roche Plate gîte, carry on until you reach the school. The gîte, a long, single-storey building with a blue roof, is behind it. In between there is the Office National des Forêts office and the well-stocked Co-op store.

It's also possible to travel from Marla to Roche Plate via La Nouvelle. This involves the steep descent from La Nouvelle to the Rivière des Galets followed by a tiring ascent up the other side to Roche Plate. This route requires about seven hours.

If you're continuing to Grande Place, Îlet à Bourse or Aurère, you really should be on the east side of the Rivière des Galets; the quickest route is past the imposing flat-topped hill Le Bronchard and then steeply downhill to the Mafate bivouac hut (this is also the start of the route to La Nouvelle). Otherwise, head down the cirque from Roche Plate toward the hamlet of Sans Souci, at the mouth of the cirque. This is an incredible route, literally carved out of a sheer precipice for much of the way.

Alternatively, you can tramp more directly up the side of the cirque along the Grand Bord route. It is a 7.5 km uphill climb and takes a gruelling three hours, but the view is spectacular if you have the breath to enjoy it. The peaks and plateaus of Mafate below appear ever tinier as you wind your way up the side of the immense cirque.

At the top, you meet the road coming up from foothill villages above St Paul and St-Gilles-les-Bains. It is 14 km down to the nearest village, via several picnic spots among wooded glades and nature walks. Going up, the road ends at the Piton Maïdo lookout point over the Cirque de Mafate.

## Le Bélier to Cilaos Route (Circuit des Trois Cirques)

Walking from Le Bélier begins with scaling the forestry road to Bord à Martin. Pass the helipad (there's a minor route into Mafate via the Augustave track which turns off just to the right of the helipad). The next turning, which is to the left, leads to La Nouvelle via Col de Fourche, and those without a vehicle should follow this short cut to the Col de Fourche. Those with a vehicle may continue on to either Col des Boeufs or turn left at the fork about 3.5 km beyond Bord à Martin; the end of the road lies about 600 metres from Col de Fourche.

To head for lower Mafate (Îlet a Bourse or Aurère), continue past the first La Nouvelle track near Bord à Martin. After a couple of hundred metres, turn right on the track marked Aurère. This route follows the Sentier Scout and includes a very pleasant descent of the Grand Rein ridge. At times it approaches knife-edge sharpness!

Readers have reported that due to frequent break-ins and theft, it is unwise to leave vehicles at any of the trailheads above Le Bélier.

**Via Upper Mafate** This is the more popular option since it requires the least change in altitude. The easiest access is by vehicle along the Route Forestière du Haut Mafate to the Col des Boeufs, beneath the spectacular Crête des Calumets. From there, the track trends downhill all the way to La Nouvelle. Here you have the option of adding one or two days to the route by circling through Roche Plate, which includes a tough slog into and out of the canyon carved by the Rivière des Galets. Overnights along the longer route would be at Le Bélier, La Nouvelle, Roche Plate and Marla. Alternatively, you can follow the easy route through Marla and over the Col du Taïbit to Cilaos.

**Via Lower Mafate** There are several loop options through lower Mafate. Good first night options from Le Bélier are Îlet à Bourse or Aurère.

On the approach to Aurère from the south (Îlet à Malheur), trekkers are issued across the breathtaking gorge of the Bras Bémale on a small footbridge. Alternatively, you can take the steep and difficult shortcut; turn right at the sign marked Bémale just north of Îlet à Malheur. It's not recommended if you're carrying a pack.

If you opt to stay at Îlet à Bourse, it's either an easy second day to Aurère or directly west around Piton Carré to Grand Place. If you have a bit more energy, follow the spectacular loop through Aurére, down to Rivière des Galets and on to Grand Place. From Grand Place, there's a tiring detour around a landslide and a gruelling climb up to La Nouvelle. On the last day, it's a relatively easy walk out to Cilaos via Marla.

For a real challenge, from Grand Place head back downstream and turn left on the steep track leading down Rivière des Galets. From there, the route ascends almost vertically to Îlet des Lataniers, and on to Îlet des Orangers, before levelling out and continuing to Roche Plate. (This route is all the more interesting because Roche Plate is plainly visible from Cayenne gîte in Grand Place!) From Roche Plate, you can continue directly to either La Nouvelle or Marla on one of the upper Mafate routes.

# Les Hautes Plaines

Réunion's only cross-island route passes through the Plaine-des-Palmistes and the Plaine-des-Cafres, collectively known as Les Hautes Plaines, the high plains. These relatively large open areas actually form the saddle which separates the massif, comprised of the three cirques, from the volcano, Piton de la Fournaise. Because there's a road which approaches within a few km of the summit, nearly all visitors to the volcano arrive from this side. The plains also serve as starting points for trekking excursions into Cirque de Salazie and Cirque de Cilaos.

Because the plains provide a cool retreat for the lowlanders during particularly hot and humid weather, the highway and beauty spots are well attended during weekends and holidays.

## PLAINE-DES-PALMISTES

There were once large numbers of palm trees on the Plaine-des-Palmistes (hence the name) but due to heavy historical consumption of heart-of-palm salad, they've all but disappeared and are now protected. The community is divided into two villages. The main settlement and centre of action, such as it is, is Le Premier, literally 'the first' village for those coming from St Benoît. Le Premier is often referred to simply as Plaine-des-Palmistes.

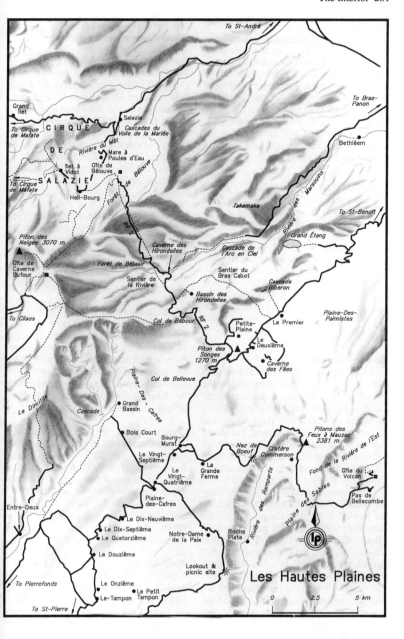

Les Hautes Plaines

## Information

In the centre of Le Premier, opposite the mairie (town hall), is the Syndicat d'Initiative (☎ 51 32 57) kiosk. It's meant to be open Tuesday to Friday from 9 am to noon and 1.30 to 5 pm but despite repeated attempts at contact, I never found it attended during any of these hours. If you're lucky, this is the place to enquire about the latest developments on Caverne des Fées, for instance. Just south-west of Le Premier is (predictably) Le Deuxième.

## Cascade Biberon

The waterfall Cascade Biberon, a great place for a cool swim, lies at the northern edge of the Plaine-des-Palmistes, an easy, two km walk (if the weather is not too wet) from Le Premier. Follow the road north near the north-eastern end of the village and then the first track on the left. It crosses a few streams, but when it reaches the normally dry, boulder-strewn bed of the Ravine Sèche, the path disappears. You must join it upstream where the electricity wires cross to the opposite bank.

## Caverne des Fées

Although the name of this cave means 'cave of the fairies', it is thought to derive from the French word *feux* (fires), a reference to the volcanic soil in the area. People seem to have problems finding it and there have been recent reports that the landowner has closed it to the public thanks to less than thoughtful visitors. Check at the Syndicat d'Initiative in Plaine-des-Palmistes before a attempting a visit.

If it is open, from Le Premier, head along the main road toward Plaine-des-Cafres. At the turn-off in Le Bras Creux, just past Le Deuxième village and just before the road climbs and twists up toward Plaine-des-Cafres, you turn left. After less than 500 metres, the road will turn into a footpath which follows the Bras Creux ravine. About 150 metres from the end of the road, turn left onto the track called Ligne Trois Mille Cinq Cents. Follow it for about 800 metres. At this

point, the Caverne des Fées will be approximately 100 metres to your left.

## Forêt de Bébour

The Forêt de Bébour is a busy weekend picnic and leisure area. Although the Col de Bébour is normally the limit of activity from the southern access, the Route Forestière 2 continues on to the Gîte de Bélouve above Hell-Bourg, paralleled by a series of walking tracks. For a description of the entire route, see under Forêt de Bélouve & Forêt de Bébour Trek in the Hell-Bourg & the Cirque de Salazie section.

## Piton des Songes

On the summit of Piton des Songes is a cross, shrine and small reservoir pond. From the peak, it's possible to see across the plain and down to St Benoît and the sea. Access to the summit is from Bras des Calumets at the top of the winding road leading up from Le Deuxième village.

## Places to Stay

**Camping** There is a private camp site courtesy of *Mme Lucette Ahrel* (☎ 51 36 26) at 37 Rue Pignolet, Chemin de la Petite Plaine, Plaine-des-Palmistes. She charges F10 for the site and an additional F6 per person per day. This is a popular rural area and lies near the end of the Forêt de Bélouve and Forêt de Bébour track from Hell-Bourg.

**Gîtes** At Rue Eugène Rochetaing, north of the cross-island road in Le Deuxième, *Mme Paulette Plante* (☎ 51 33 45) rents a basic four-person gîte for F900 per week. She also runs a table d'hôte. A slightly more upmarket option is the gîte of *M Klébert Cadet* (☎ 51 37 15) on Rue des Rempart in Petite Plaine along the Route Forestière 2 toward Col de Bébour. It accommodates up to 10 people and costs F1570 per week.

**Hotels** In Le Deuxième at 160 Rue de la République, is the *Hôtel des Plaines* (☎ 51 31 97), a three-star hotel with rooms for F280/360 a single/double. A nice option on the Route National in Le Premier, 300 metres from the track to Cascade Biberon, is *Village-Hôtel Les Azalées* (☎ 51 34 24). It has bungalows for F245 a single or double.

On Rue Jean Thèvenin at Petite-Plaine, there's a new set of fairly basic bungalows, *Les Hirondelles* (☎ 51 35 68). A double unit, including breakfast, costs F235.

### Places to Eat

Near the bottom of Route Forestière 2 where it joins the hill road entering Plaine-des-Palmistes, is *Chez Tante Agathe* (☎ 51 35 00). This plain but cosy little cottage restaurant, open daily for lunch, dishes up aunty's own cooking for a very reasonable F50. For an evening meal, you must book in advance. She also sells delicious home-made cheese.

The Créole restaurant *Les Platanes* (☎ 51 31 69) in Le Premier is open for lunch and dinner daily except Monday. It's under the same management as the *Hôtel des Plaines* (☎ 51 31 97) in Le Deuxième, whose in-house restaurant is open daily for lunch and dinner but meals are expensive at F75 to F200. They also serve a special buffet lunch on Sundays.

For Indian food, go to *Le Combava* (☎ 51 35 98) in Le Premier, open from 11.45 am to 8.30 pm daily except Thursday. A broader menu which includes French, Créole and Chinese options is available at *Le Palmiplainois* (☎ 51 40 45) on Rue Henri Pignolet.

If you prefer just a lunchtime snack or a very inexpensive plat du jour, there's a small outdoor snack bar on the left as you head out of Le Premier toward St-Benoît.

Tables d'hôte are offered by *Mme Henriette Grondin* (☎ 51 33 79), 17 Rue Dureau in Plaine-des-Palmistes; *Mr Klébert Cadet* (☎ 51 37 15), Rue des Remparts in Petite Plaine; *Mme Paulette Plante* (☎ 51 33 45), Rue Eugène Rochetaing in Plaine-des-Palmistes; and *Mme Lucette Ahrel* (☎ 51 36 26), 37 Rue Henri Pignolet, Chemin de la Petite Plaine.

### Getting There & Away

Plaine-des-Palmistes lies on the cross-island highway between St-Benoît and St-Pierre. For bus information, see Getting There &

Away under Le-Tampon & The Plaine-des-Cafres.

## LE-TAMPON & PLAINE-DES-CAFRES

The Plaine-des-Cafres, once a refuge for runaway slaves from the coast, serves as a convenient gateway for visiting the volcano but is also pleasantly scenic in its own right. This area of dispersed population and gentle farmland is hemmed in between the two great massifs of the island, the cirques and Piton de la Fournaise, and provides a dramatic contrast to the thick forests on the slopes above and the barren lava desert that surrounds the hulking volcano just 30 km away.

The Plaine-des-Cafres is hazily delimited; it's normally defined as everything between Bras-de-la-Plaine (at the foot of Le Dimitile) to the Rivière des Remparts, from Le-Tampon to the crest of the winding road that descends toward Plaine-des-Palmistes.

The metropolis of the Plaine-des-Cafres, Le-Tampon, loudly proclaims itself the geranium capital of the world but in reality, it's a relatively uninteresting way-station en route to more worthwhile destinations. The absorbant name is derived from the Malagasy word *tampony*, which refers to a small hill.

Most of the Plaine-des-Cafres villages on the cross-island road are named for their distance from the sea. Thus, Le Onzième (11th) just north of Le-Tampon, is 11 km from the sea, followed one km later by Le Douzième (12th) and so on up to Le Vingt-Septième (27th), where Route Forestière 5 turns off to the volcano. Le Trentième, two km beyond the turn-off, is the last numbered village before Plaine-des-Palmistes.

### Grand Bassin

Opposite the church in Le Vingt-Troisième (23rd) village (also known simply as Plaine-des-Cafres), turn north and continue five km to Bois Court. Just before the lookout point at the end of the road, turn left on Rue Roland Hoareau. After 100 metres, you'll see the beginning of the footpath which descends about two km to Grand Bassin, known as *la vallée perdue*, 'the lost valley'.

This picturesque basin in the gorge is formed by the confluence of the Bras Sec, the Bras de Suzanne and the Bras des Roches Noires. It's a quiet community with a lovely waterfall and three gîtes d'étape (see under Places to Stay). From here, there's a beautiful 10 km walking track which descends the Bras-de-la-Plaine all the way to Entre-Deux.

### Volcano Observatory

If you wish to know more about the behaviour of volcanoes in general and Piton de la Fournaise in particular, arrange a visit to L'Observatoire Volcanologique de la Réunion (☎ 27 54 61) on the cross-island road, on the Le-Tampon side of Le Vingt-Septième. Here, scientists keep as close a watch as possible on the volcano's moods, and are prepared to issue warnings to the local populace in case of an impending violent eruption. For further information, check with the university in St-Denis or seek the good services of Alain Mussard, son of Mme Thérèse Mussard (see the following Places to Stay section).

### Notre-Dame-de-la-Paix

Three km beyond Notre-Dame-de-la-Paix village (coming from Le Vingt-Quatrième) where the road skirts the Rivière des Remparts is a picnic and BBQ area and a lookout point. If you happen to be there in late afternoon when the sun is low and the valley is filled with cloud, try standing on the fence for a super special effect: your shadow projected onto the cloud by the sun behind will be encircled by a rainbow ring. Without the clouds, the expanse of the valley below is just as inspiring.

### Places to Stay

**Chambres d'Hôte** It seems that half the chambres d'hôte in Réunion are on the Plaine-des-Cafres so there's no shortage of inexpensive accommodation.

At Le Petit Tampon, five km up a twisting road from Le-Tampon, are two chambres d'hôte run by the Payet family. *Mme Roger Payet* (☎ 57 04 71) has two bedrooms at 163 Route du Petit-Tampon, just uphill from the church on the same side. There's a taxi-collectif stop nearby. Further down the road at number 74 is her sister-in-law *Mme Lucot Payet* (☎ 27 83 15). Both charge F80/110 single double and provide table d'hôte, as well.

In Le-Tampon itself at 64 Chemin Jamerosas is *Mme Huguette Mangue* (☎ 27 36 85) who charges F90/120 a single/double and has table d'hôte for F85. In the upper suburb of Trois Mares near Le-Tampon, at 32 Impasse Georges Brassens, is *Mme Hélène Defaud* (☎ 57 18 06) who has two double rooms costing F80/120 a single/double. There's no table d'hôte but she'll prepare meals for guests for F60. Another option is 58 Chemin Zazo Dassy in Le-Tampon is *Mme Jeanine Mondon* (☎ 27 45 27) who charges the same for rooms as Mme Defaud. For table d'hôte, guests pay F70 while outsiders are charged F100 per person.

Moving up valley to upper Plaine-des-Cafres, *Mme Louise Magnan* (☎ 27 56 91) at Chemin Henri Cabeau 331, Bois Court has one bedroom which she lets for F86/120 a single/double occupancy. This place is also known as the *Restaurant Taureau Noir*. In order to stay at the chambre d'hôte, guests must take their meals here, as well.

Near Le Dix-Neuvième (19th), *Mr Harry Céleste* (☎ 27 59 63), at Chemin Philidor Técher has one bedroom to let. He charges F100/120 a single/double and meals cost F70.

On the Route National at Le Vingt-Deuxième (22nd) is *Mr Jean-Louis Lacouture* (☎ 59 04 91). He has five rooms which cost F90/120 a single/double and he runs a table d'hôte, as well. Also at Le Vingt-Deuxième is *Mme Anne Rivière* (☎ 27 59 78) lets four double rooms upstairs in her home for F80/115 a single/double.

Near Le Vingt-Troisième at Piton Hyacinthe, *Mme Rock Berrichon* (☎ 27 59 49), Chemin des Canas, has rooms for F70/110 a single/double. She also runs a table d'hôte.

On Chemin Notre Dame de la Paix six km from Le Vingt-Troisième, *M Sylvio & Mme*

*Thérèse Mussard* (☎ 27 57 59) have a peaceful farmhouse with two guest bedrooms, great food and terrific family hospitality. They charge F90/120 for a single/double occupancy. Further up the road, beside the gendarmerie, at Le Vingt-Quatrième (24th) is *Mme Anne Tenon* (☎ 59 10 41). Rooms cost F80/120 a single/double and table d'hôte meals are F70.

Finally, in Grande Ferme seven km from Le Vingt-Septième is the recommended chambre d'hôte of *Mme Chantal Guesdon* (☎ 27 59 25). Single/double rooms cost F100/140 and meals are F80. This is a particularly convenient meeting point if you're hoping to hitch up to the volcano.

**Gîtes** On Chemin de Notre Dame de la Paix, just a few km from the Rivière des Remparts lookout, is the rustic, chalet-style gîte of *M Hubert Frédéric Lauret* (☎ 57 60 35). He charges F2200 per week. At Grand Ferme, two km from Le Vingt-Septième, is the gîte belonging to *M Guy Hoareau* (☎ 57 10 44). It holds up to eight people and costs F1250 per week.

Along the road to the volcano, 3.5 km from Bourg-Murat, is the gîte d'étape of *M Jean-Claude Coutant* (☎ 59 03 16). He has space for up to nine people and charges F150 per person, including breakfast and dinner.

On the Chemin du Grand Tampon in Le Petit Tampon, *Mme Joseph Victor Payet* (☎ 27 09 92) has a gîte which she lets for F1350 per week.

There are three gîtes d'étape with table d'hôte in Grand Bassin, a scenic spot in the Gorges de Bras de la Plaine (for more information, see under Grand Bassin earlier in this section). The first, operated by *Mme Jeanne-Marie Nativel* (☎ 27 51 91) has a three dormitory gîte accommodating up to 37 people. She charges F60 per person, including breakfast. Meals are available for F65.

Next, *Mme Marie Josée Sery* (☎ 59 10 66) offers four dormitories with a total of 40 bunks. Beds cost F60 per person including breakfast and meals are F65. The third is the gîte of *Mme Sery-Picard* (☎ 27 51 02), with

three dormitories of 12 bunks each. She charges F50 per person and an extra F25 for breakfast. Meals cost F70.

**Hotels** A good alternative to the gîtes and chambres d'hôte are the hotels, which are surprisingly reasonably priced. In Le-Tampon, the *Hôtel Relais du Tampon* (☎ 27 95 30), at 83 Rue Sarda Garriga near the corner of Rue du Général de Gaulle, is good value. They have 13 rooms at F130 a single or double for up to five nights. Discounted rates are available for longer stays.

The former Hotel Le Métro near the intersection known as Six-Cent, just outside Le-Tampon, is now known as *Le Château Enchanté* (☎ 27 07 90). It's very good value; doubles with bath in the old section (what was Le Métro) cost F130, and in the newly renovated section, they're F200. All rates include breakfast and there's also a small swimming pool for guests' use.

At the bottom of Rue Jules Ferry is the small *Hôtel les Orchidées* (☎ 27 11 15), reasonable value at F200/250 a single/double. Further upmarket in Le-Tampon is the *Hôtel Paille-en-Queue* (☎ 27 47 50) at 14 Rue du Paille-en-Queue. It's a chalet complex with a 14-double rooms costing F570/530 a single/double, including brekkie.

Moving into upper Plaine-des-Cafres, the *Hôtel La Fermette* (☎ 27 50 08) at Rue Raphaël Douyère 48 in Bois Court costs F220, single or double, with breakfast included.

At Le Vingt-Troisième is the *Hôtel L'Allemand* (☎ 27 51 27) which offers singles or doubles for F180. Breakfast is F20 extra. Four km further along the Route National at Bourg-Murat, Le Vingt-Septième, is the popular *Auberge du Volcan* (☎ 27 50 91), which goes for a cosier log-fire and woodsmoke atmosphere. Rooms with showers cost F150 a single or double and breakfast costs an extra F15. Meals average F45 a dish or you can opt for a F50 set menu.

Toward Plaine-des-Palmistes at Le Vingt-Huitième (28th) is another hotel, *La Diligence* (☎ 59 10 10) with two, three and four bed bungalows for F330, F380 and

F460. During the low season, breakfast is included; otherwise, it's F28 extra. Horses are available for hire and the hotel runs short outings and longer treks.

About La Diligence, Stephen Clarke writes 'The bungalows were built by a cross-eyed do-it-yourself amateur with night vision (the rooms have dark corners, brown wallpaper and 40-watt bulbs!) but it is ideally placed for an early start to the volcano. The only trouble is they start breakfast at 7.30 am and it's best to leave earlier. You can choose between skipping breakfast and getting sunburn after a late start.'

### Places to Eat

One of the best restaurants in the area is the Créole dining room at the *Auberge du Volcan* (☎ 27 50 91) at Le Vingt-Septième. It's closed Mondays and Sunday nights. At the Caltex petrol station near the Auberge du Volcan is the *Chez Michel* with a snack bar and a games room.

Several other restaurants also cater to volcano-bound visitors. At Le Vingt-Huitième is *Le Tourne-Broche* (☎ 26 60 57) which has a Sino-Créole menu. *La Bonne Grillade*, on the road from Le Vingt-Septième to the volcano, has set menus for F50. It's closed on Wednesday. The restaurant in the *Hôtel La Diligence* (☎ 59 10 10) at Bourg-Murat, Le Vingt-Huitième, is a slightly more upmarket option for French and Créole cuisine. It's open every day. Further along at Le Trentième is *La Soucoupe Volante* (☎ 27 55 42) which serves good Créole cooking. It's normally open on weekends only; book in advance if you want a meal any other day.

At La Ravine Blanche near Le Vingt-Troisième is *Chez Cocotier* (☎ 59 08 30), which is open every day for lunch and dinner. Nearby, at Le Vingt-Quatrième, is the Créole restaurant *Les Geraniums* (☎ 59 11 06), open for lunch and dinner every day.

*La Fournaise* (☎ 27 19 87) on Rue Marius & Ary Leblond, the main road through Le-Tampon, goes for real French cooking with plats du jour for F60. On the same street are a number of Sino-Créole restaurants with

F40 plats du jour, as well as the Vietnamese restaurant *Le Tonkinoise* (☎ 27 09 14) with plats du jour for F75. Chinese cuisine is available at *Les Délices de Chine* (☎ 57 50 93), Rue Hubert Delisle 273. It's closed on Sundays and Monday evenings.

Le-Tampon's finest restaurants are probably the dining rooms at the hotels *Les Orchidées* (☎ 27 11 15) and *La-Paille-en-Queue* (☎ 27 00 15). The latter, at Rue Hubert Delisle 25, is housed in a traditional Créole home. For Indian cuisine, go to the dining room at *Hôtel Relais du Tampon* (☎ 27 95 30). It's closed on Sunday nights. For something different, try *L'Auberge Alsacienne* (☎ 27 87 41) at Rue Hubert Delisle 460, which specialises in Alsatian dishes.

The chambres d'hôte listed in the Places to Stay section have tables d'hôte too.

### Entertainment

The Thêâtre Luc Donat on Rue de l'Église in Le-Tampon stages many of the musical and theatrical productions which have played in St Denis. Le-Tampon also has a cinema, L'Eden, at Rue Hubert Delisle 72.

At Bois Court near Le Vingt-Troisième is the disco *L'Ouragan* (☎ 58 08 51). It's open on Saturdays and nights before holidays from 10 pm to dawn.

### Getting There & Away

There are three buses a day each way between St-Benoît and St-Pierre via Le-Tampon, Plaine-des-Cafres and Plaine-des-Palmistes. The fare from Plaine-des-Palmistes to Plaine-des-Cafres (Vingt-Troisième) is F11.70, from Le-Tampon to Plaine-des-Cafres, F5 and from Le-Tampon to St-Pierre, F6. Taxi-collectifs operate between Le-Tampon and surrounding villages, costing from F6 to F8 per trip.

### ENTRE-DEUX

This community got its strange name, 'between two', because it lies between two rivers – the Bras de Cilaos and the Bras-de-la-Plaine, which together form the Rivière St-Étienne. This is a fruit and tobacco-growing enclave which is pleasant enough in itself but for tourists, it's used primarily as a staging point for the tough trek up the slopes of Le Dimitile to a super view over the Cirque de Cilaos. Start by taking the Jean Lauret path from Entre-Deux. If you leave at dawn, the ascent and descent of Le Dimitile (1837 metres) can be done in a single day; plan on at least 16 hours.

If you're not a superhuman trekker or you think this is cutting things too closely for a single day, at Le Dimitile there's the gîte d'étape of *M Marc François Payet* (☎ 39 50 19). It will hold 16 people and costs F65 per person. Breakfast is an extra F20. For other options, see Coteau de Kervéguen in the Cilaos & the Cirque de Cilaos section near the beginning of this chapter.

### Places to Stay & Eat
Entre-Deux is now the proud location of a brand new youth hostel along the main road into town. It charges the standard rates: F60 per person for IYHF members. Evening meals cost F45 and breakfast is F10 extra.

There are also three chambres and tables d'hôte which have sprung up in this area. The most central is that of *Mme Josette Grondin* (☎ 39 51 89) at Rue du Commerce 8. She charges F120 a single or double and F80 for table d'hôte meals. There's also *Mme Jacqueline Corré* (☎ 39 53 43) at Grand Fond Intérieur 66 and *Mme Noé Fontaine* (☎ 39 51 21) at Chemin Pifarelli 18. They each have two rooms to let; the former charges F90/120 a single/double occupancy and the latter charges F90/110. Meals cost F75 per person.

### Getting There & Away
There are minor bus lines operating between Entre-Deux and the gares routière in St-Pierre and St-Louis. There's also a bus to and from Le-Tampon.

### PITON DE LA FOURNAISE
This bubbling, smouldering volcano is probably Réunion's most renowned feature and is relatively safe and straightforward to visit. Although the volcano occupies a single massif, there are actually two major craters

– Dolomieu, the largest, and Bory, inactive since 1791 – and a host of smaller barnacle-like craters strewn across the slopes of the mountain. Several of these peripheral craters have erupted over the past few years, thankfully providing more spectacle than tragedy. The most recent eruption was from the small crater called Zoé, on the mountain's southeastern flank, in late 1992.

### Climbing the Volcano
Potential hikers should be aware that temperatures and climatic conditions swing wildly at times, and despite the popularity of this walk, it's still a good haul to the top. Although it may seem harmless enough on a crisp sunny morning, this is a potentially hazardous region. Warm windproof and waterproof clothing are essential. The weather started out as fairly pleasant the day I did the climb but on the return trip, it was sleeting, the temperature hung just above freezing and it was blowing a gale! Furthermore, carry all the liquid you'll be needing (the cold wind can cause rapid dehydration!) as well as a few energy snacks.

When crossing the crater floor, under no circumstances wander off the marked path. The clouds and fog can roll in literally instantaneously, and without reference points the landscape of the crater floor all looks the same. In recent years, there have been several disappearances resulting in fatalities. If you're concerned, carry the IGN 1:25,000 series map 4406RT *Piton de la Fournaise* and perhaps even a compass.

For the best view (potentially, anyway) and most agreeable weather conditions, start as early as possible. The trip begins with a 600 metre walk from the gîte to the Pas de Bellecombe car park and volcano information post at an altitude of 2353 metres. The return walk from the gîte to (and around) the summit is approximately 13 km and takes five hours under optimum conditions.

Begin the walk by turning left at the information post and following the track along the rim. After several hundred metres, the track turns right and begins its steep descent of the sheer wall to the floor of the immense U-

**Piton de la Fournaise Area**

0    1.5    3 km

shaped outer crater, known as l'Enclos Foucqué.

At this point, the route is marked by a dashed white line across the lava, reminiscent of a super highway (and during August, the resemblance is even greater!). En route are pustule-like lava domes and bizarrely sculpted lava formations. After several hundred metres, you'll arrive at a small scoria cone, Formica Léo, which can be explored on foot. Two km beyond it is the bizarre lava formation known as Chapelle de Rosemont. At this point, the route splits. The right fork climbs steeply and directly to the

2632 metre high, 200 metre across, Cratère Bory, while the left fork takes a more gradual route up to La Soufrière, the northern wall of the gaping 900 metre wide Cratère Dolomieu.

Once at the top, you can decide whether to do the circuit around both craters or just traverse the track along the northern rims connecting the Bory and La Soufrière routes. While walking along the rim, beware of large fissures, holes and most of all, overhangs. Stay on the marked track and heed the signs.

## Places to Stay

Although many people opt to stay down at Plaine-des-Cafres, there'll be a much better chance of seeing the volcano with the early start afforded by staying at the *Gîte du Volcan* (☎ 21 28 96). It has 30 beds, and meals, prepared by the talented chef M Jacques Picard, are available for F70 per person if booked in advance. This is an extremely popular gîte so book through Maison de la Montagne in Cilaos or St-Denis as far in advance as possible.

If you're staying a couple of days at the gîte and are looking for an act to follow the volcano, hike from the gîte down the road into the Fond de la Rivière de l'Est. After about two km, the road becomes a track and turns east, following the Ravine Savane Cimetière. In seven km, the track ends with a breathtaking view into the gaping amphitheatre, Rond des Cascades, where the Rivière de l'Est begins its journey to the sea.

## Getting There & Away

For those with a vehicle, getting to the volcano couldn't be easier because there's an all-weather road which winds and climbs from Bourg-Murat in Le Vingt-Septième all the way to Pas de Bellecombe on the crater's outer rim, just a couple of hours walking from the summit. Hitching along the road isn't normally too difficult but naturally you'll have the best luck during the high season (July and August) and on weekends when the weather is fine. Local forestry workers are always a good bet for lifts.

It's also possible to trek up the volcano from the south, up the lava flows from St-Philippe or Tremblet, but this is an extremely arduous route made even more difficult by near constant precipitation. Even in the dry season, there's a good chance of some rain. For more information, see under The South-East Corner in the Around the Coast chapter.

Most hikers prefer to approach by the much, much easier route from the west. If you're walking up from Bourg-Murat the gîte should be the objective of the first day's effort. Leave the summit slog until early the next morning when there'll be a better chance of good weather and views.

The route up from the Plaine-des-Cafres passes the panoramic lookout point at Nez de Boeuf, which gives you a view down the deep valley of the Rivière des Remparts 1200 metres below. It also passes the sinister black hole of an extinct volcano, Cratère Commerson.

About two km downhill from Cratère Commerson is Sentier Josemont, a marvellous two-hour or 6.5 km tramp directly to the Gîte du Volcan and a far more interesting route than the road. Near the start of the trek is a memorial to the forest ranger Josemont Lauret, who died here from exposure one night in October 1887, a 'victim of his own courage and devotion to his companions'. Travellers are asked to pay homage to Lauret by placing a rock and a sprig of branle, a heatherlike plant, at the foot of the stone.

The path moves away from the road and into the giant Caverne des Lataniers, where it then proceeds gently down a cliff edge (experiment with the echoes!). At its foot lies the broad expanse of the moon-like Plaine des Sables. The track across this strange terrain is clearly marked by dobs of paint every few metres. At the end of the plain it's an easy climb up to the Gîte du Volcan.

# Seychelles

# Facts about the Country

The Seychelles have some of the most beautiful islands in the Indian Ocean, if not the
world. This is the glorious, lush, idyllic paradise we see in the holiday brochures and in
the adverts for Bounty Bars. In fact, what you
see on paper or TV is a half-truth: the real
thing is much more stunning.

As usual, beauty has its *frisson* of trouble,
in this case an intriguing and often dangerous
political background to what appears to be a
comfortable, quiet, contented way of life.
Since President France-Albert René grabbed
power in 1977 from the elected leader of the
formerly independent British colony, there
have been periods of turbulence.

Until recently, the Seychelles harboured a
hotbed of spies as well as tourists. The
setting, the plot and the characters could
have graced the pages of a Graham Greene,
Frederick Forsyth or Ian Fleming novel. The
CIA, KGB and MI5 flitted through the
islands during the Cold War era, mixing with
communist troops from North Korea and
Tanzania, Russian advisers, US military personnel from the satellite tracking station,
mercenaries, private detectives, exiled
rebels, diplomats and the Mafia. The political rhythms have currently reverted to a more
relaxed mode, and tourists rarely sense anything untoward.

To exploit its biggest asset (the beauty of
the islands) the Seychelles government has
made a great effort to promote savvy
tourism. By upping prices and cutting
numbers of visitors, the pressures of tourism
on the islands' infrastructure have been
reduced, and the ecological wealth of the
Seychelles has been recognised as an important tourist attraction worthy of protection
and preservation.

Apart from stunning beaches and excellent snorkelling and diving, the Seychelles
can also boast ecological highlights: with its
many wildlife reserves another reason to
visit and risk falling in love with these beautiful islands.

## HISTORY

Until the 17th century, the Seychelles were
uninhabited. There may have been a camp or
two of shipwrecked Arab sailors in the
course of the early centuries; they were possibly responsible for the ancient tombs found
on Silhouette Island, but whoever built them
didn't last long.

Portuguese explorers were the first Europeans to discover the islands. The first
recorded landing was left to a British East
India Company ship in 1609. The skipper
reported that the islands were an ideal spot
for replenishing supplies and energy.

The pirates and privateers who had just
moved shop from the Caribbean came to the
same conclusion and, during lulls in their
maraudings, set up temporary bases on the
islands. Frégate Island is believed to have
been one such base. The name of pirate
Olivier 'La Buse' Levasseur still crops up in
the continual search for his treasure around
Bel Ombre on Mahé.

In 1742, the great Mahé de Labourdonnais, the governor of Mauritius (then
known as Île de France), sent Lazare Picault
to check out the islands. Picault named the
main island after his governor (and the bay
where he landed, after himself) and laid the
way for the French to claim possession of the
islands 12 years later. They were named
Séchelles in honour of the finance minister
to Louis XV, Jean Moreau de Sachelles.

The first batch of the French and their
slaves arrived on Ste Anne Island in 1770.
After a few false starts, the settlers began
growing spices, cassava, sugar cane, coffee,
sweet potatoes and maize, and began exploiting the large colonies of giant tortoises.

When the British started taking an interest
in the islands at the end of the 18th century,
Queau de Quinssy had been installed as governor. Instead of risking life and limb to fend
off British attacks, de Quinssy lowered the
French flag and surrendered to the British
frigates. When the aggressors sailed on, he

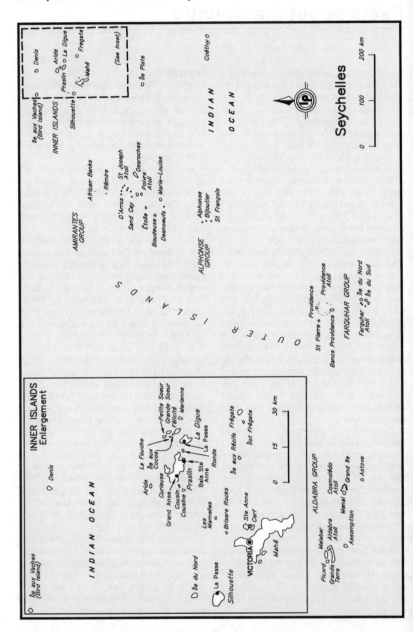

Seychelles

raised the flag again. De Quinssy was to capitulate about a dozen times before the Seychelles became a British dependency of Mauritius, after the Napoleonic Wars and the Treaty of Paris in 1814.

De Quinssy, the 'Great Capitulator', was allowed to remain in charge until 1827. He changed his name to De Quincy in deference to his new masters and lived out his days in the Seychelles. His tomb is at Government House in Victoria, Mahé.

The British did little to develop the islands except increase the numbers of slaves. When slavery was abolished in 1835, the slaves were released. French remained the main language, and French culture too was dominant.

The islands were also used by the British as a five-star jail and retreat for political prisoners and exiles, most of whom had a great time there. They included banished tribal kings, sultans and independence leaders who were chipping away at the British Empire. Among them was Archbishop Makarios of Cyprus, who was housed in the governor's lodge at Sans Souci (on Mahé) in 1956. Later, the Southern Maldivian rebel Abdullah Afif Didi was also imprisoned on the island.

The British also thought of reducing the exclusivity of the jail and turning it into a concentration camp for Boer prisoners of war or Irish republican rebels, but this never came about.

In 1903 the Seychelles became a crown colony administered from London. The country went into the political and economic doldrums until 1964, when political parties were formed. France-Albert René, a young lawyer, founded the Seychelles People's United Party (SPUP). His colleague in law, James Mancham, led the new Seychelles Democratic Party (SDP).

### 1965 Onwards

In 1965, an Australian journalist wrote: 'Hardly anything happens in the Seychelles. People show virtually no interest in politics...the clocks chime twice for those who were not awake the first time'.

The next 20 years saw a complete and stunning transformation of the sleepy, forgotten islands, with events that would wake up the world.

Mancham's SDP, made up of the islands' business people and planters, won the elections in 1966 and 1970. René's SPUP fought on a socialist and independence ticket. In June 1975, a coalition of the two parties gave the appearance of unity in the lead up to independence from the UK, which was granted a year later. Sir James Mancham became the first president and René, the prime minister.

The flamboyant Sir Jim – poet, playboy and grandson of a Chinese immigrant – placed all his eggs in one basket: tourism. He jet-setted around the world with a beautiful socialite on each arm, putting the Seychelles on the map.

The rich and famous poured in for holidays or to stay and party, party, party. Adnan Khashoggi and other Arab millionaires bought large tracts of land on the islands. Film stars and celebrities came there to enhance their romantic, sexy images. *Goodbye Emmanuelle* was filmed on La Digue.

But in the opinion of René and the SPUP, the wealth was not being spread evenly or fairly and the country was no more than a rich person's playground. René said that poor Créoles were little better off than slaves.

So on 5 June 1977, barely a year after independence, René and a team of Tanzanian-trained rebels carried out an almost bloodless coup while Mancham was in London attending a conference of Commonwealth leaders. As Mancham said at the time: 'It was no heroic deed to take over the Seychelles. Twenty-five people with sticks could seize control.' Tanzanian and North Korean soldiers were brought in by René to make sure that any opposition would need more than that to take over the country.

An attempt to do so came in November 1981, when a band of mercenaries, led by ex-Congo 'dog of war' Colonel Mike Hoare, bungled a chance to invade the country. The group posed as a South African rugby club on an annual binge, but a customs officer discovered weapons in one of the suitcases. Two people died in a shoot-out at the airport before the mercenaries beat a hasty retreat by hijacking an Air India plane back to South Africa. Five mercenaries, the advance guard, were rounded up, tried and sentenced to death. They were later released and deported. In 1992, the South African government paid the Seychelles government eight million rupees as compensation for the coup.

René had already deported many of the members and supporters of the outlawed SDP party. Opposed to René's one-party, socialist state, these *grands blancs* (rich whites) set up 'resistance movements' in the UK, South Africa and Australia.

The country fell into disarray as the tourist trade dried to a trickle. In 1982 there was a mutiny of NCOs (non-commissioned officers) in the Seychelles army, and a coup plot by Seychelles expatriates was discovered taking place in a London hotel room. Bombings and murders on the islands continued into 1983 as part of a campaign of civil disruption.

In December 1984 thorough intelligence gathering by the Seychelles government foiled another coup plot in the early stages of planning in South Africa. A year later, Gerard Hoareau, the immigration chief under Mancham and leader of the Seychelles resistance movement in the UK, was machine-gunned to death by persons unknown outside his London home. In 1986 there was another attempted coup by majors from within the Seychelles army.

During the early '90s, René started to rethink his adherence to one-party rule and in December 1991 he surprised his opponents by legalising opposition parties within a multiparty system. Quite possibly, this move might have been prompted by hints from European countries that continued aid would be linked to democratic developments.

Multiparty elections to a 23-member commission were held in July, 1992, under the watchful eye of Commonwealth observers. René and his party, the Seychelles People's Progressive Front (SPPF), won 58.4% of the votes. Mancham, who had returned to the Seychelles with a suitably hefty SAS security team, fielded 33.7% for his Democratic Party (DP) and contested the results as rigged and unfair.

In November 1992, the draft constitution prepared by the commission was thrown out after a referendum failed to achieve the required 60% of votes in favour. The opposition, most notably Mancham's Democratic Party, campaigned successfully against proposed linkage between presidential election results and the allocation of national assembly seats.

## GEOGRAPHY

'Unique by a Thousand Miles' is the Seychelles tourist slogan. That's how far the centre of this archipelago lies off the coast of East Africa, its nearest neighbour. There are roughly 115 islands, with a combined area of only 455 square km, situated between the equator and the 10th parallel south.

The central islands are granite, the main three being Mahé, Praslin and La Digue. The outlying islands are coral atolls. The granite islands, which do not share the volcanic nature of Réunion and Mauritius, appear to be peaks of a huge submerged plateau which was left behind by India when the continental plates shifted about 65 million years ago. The highest point in the islands is Morne Seychellois (905 metres) on Mahé.

## CLIMATE

The great news here is that the islands lie outside the cyclone zone, which makes them a safer bet than Mauritius or Réunion for visits during the November to April period.

The seasons are defined by the beginning and end of the south-east trade winds, which usually blow from May to October. During the rest of the year, the islands experience the north-west monsoon winds which bring the rain, especially in January. The turn-round periods between the two winds are the calmest.

The rain generally comes in sudden, heavy squalls. Mahé, the most mountainous

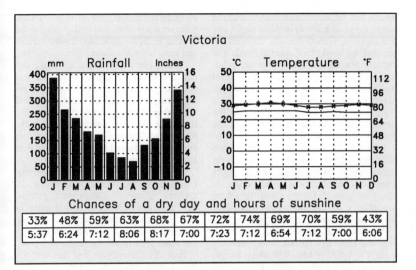

Victoria

| | Chances of a dry day and hours of sunshine | | | | | | | | | | |
|---|---|---|---|---|---|---|---|---|---|---|---|
| 33% | 48% | 59% | 63% | 68% | 67% | 72% | 74% | 69% | 70% | 59% | 43% |
| 5:37 | 6:24 | 7:12 | 8:06 | 8:17 | 7:00 | 7:23 | 7:12 | 6:54 | 7:12 | 7:00 | 6:06 |

island, and lofty Silhouette get the highest rainfall. January is the wettest month by far while July and August are the driest. The temperature is constant throughout the year, between 24°C and 31°C, as is the humidity, at around 80%.

## FLORA & FAUNA

The islands are a haven for wildlife, particularly for birds and tropical fish. The government's conservation policies, which include the formation of several marine and nature reserves, seem to work well alongside and within the tourist industry.

### Flora

As you would expect from the lush praises heaped on the islands' beauty, the Seychelles are rich in vegetation – but not that rich. Christopher Lee wrote in his book *Political Castaways* (see the Books & Maps section):

If there is one criticism to be levelled at the scenery of the Seychelles, it is one of little variation in the colour of its plant life...Possibly because of the most idyllic reputation of the islands, one expects that a blaze of strong colour will cover the stark granite environment. It doesn't. To the knowing eye there

may be a subtle difference in shade, but there is definitely a gap between the often imagined tropical paradise of travel brochures and film locations and the real thing.

He has a point, but only up to a point, for the islands *are* used widely as film and advertisement locations, and the travel brochures, if anything, don't do the place justice. If anyone has difficulty appreciating the scenery, I'd refer them to the 'knowing eye' of Michael Adams' paintings.

The coconut palm and casuarina are the most common trees on the islands. There are a few banyans (a giant one shades the road at Ma Constance, about 3.5 km north of Victoria), screw pines (or *vacoas*), bamboo and tortoise trees (so named because the fruit looks like the tortoises that eat it). Virgin forest now only exists in the higher parts of Mahé and Silhouette, and in the Vallée de Mai on Praslin, one of only three places in the world where the giant coco de mer palm grows. The other two are Silhouette and Curieuse islands.

Out of about 200 plant species, 80 are endemic. These include the *bois rouge*, which has broad, reddish leaves and red wood, the giant and very rare *bois de fer*, and the *capucin*, named because its seed resembles the hood of a Capuchin monk. The capucin features prominently in the paintings of Marianne North, the English artist who visited the islands in 1883 to paint their plant life. Her work was donated to Kew Botanical Gardens in London and the Seychellois collection is on view in the North Gallery there.

In the high, remote parts of Mahé and Silhouette islands, you may come across the insect-eating pitcher plant, which either clings to adjacent trees or bushes or sprawls along the ground. On the floral front there are plenty of orchids, bougainvilleas, hibiscuses, gardenias and frangipani.

The Botanical Gardens in Victoria are well kept and provide a pleasant and interesting walk. The Vallée de Mai on Praslin is a must. And for chance discoveries, get yourself away from the beach for a day and head into the hills on Mahé, Silhouette or Praslin.

### Fauna

Common mammals and reptiles around the islands are the fruit bats or flying foxes *(chauves souris)*, geckos and skinks. Electric wires cause problems for bats: on Mahé you may see their electrocuted cadavers hanging between the wires. There are also some small snakes, but they are not dangerous.

Insect life on the Seychelles is represented by more than 3000 species. Amongst the more interesting insects are the lumbering rhinoceros beetle whose larvae cause considerable damage by feeding on young shoots of coconut palms; the giant tenebrionid beetle, a bizarre amalgamation of legs and knobbly body, unique to Frégate Island; and the various kinds of wasp, which excel in creating mud pots attached to vegetation, rocks, or walls. Despite their impressive appearance, the giant millipedes, palm spiders and whip scorpions are not life-threatening, but you can expect a nasty reaction if you handle them.

**Bird Life** Because of the islands' isolation

and the comparatively late arrival of humans, there are many species of birds unique to the Seychelles. Some are plentiful, some are rare and some are now extinct.

Almost every island seems to have one rare species to its name. On Frégate and Aride are the magpie robins (known as *pie chanteuse* in Créole), on Cousin you'll find the bush warbler, La Digue has the paradise flycatcher (or *veuve)* and Praslin has the black parrot. The bare-legged scops owl and the Seychelles kestrel live on Mahé, and Bird Island is home to millions of fairy terns.

In general there are plenty of herons, fodies, sunbirds, lovebirds, egrets, owls, mynahs, sparrows, shearwaters, petrels, plovers, boobies, sooty terns and gulls. In fact, there are so many barn owls that the government offers a Rs 30 reward for each one slain. Mynahs are also a plentiful pest.

Four of the islands are bird sanctuaries – Bird, Cousin, Aride and Frégate. The Vallée de Mai National Park on Praslin and the Veuve Reserve on La Digue are also protected reserves.

**Marine Life** Four areas around Mahé and Praslin have been designated marine national parks – Port Launay, Baie Ternay, Ste Anne Island and Curieuse. Ste Anne, off Victoria, is well patrolled by the tourist glass-bottom boats. More than 150 species of tropical reef fish have been identified. You have only to snorkel off any reef-protected shore to get an eyeful of beautiful fish and 30 species of coral.

Dolphins and porpoises are common sights in the channels between the islands, and pods occasionally become beached. Whales are rare after excessive hunting around the turn of the century. (Victoria was used as an American whaling port.) Sharks and barracuda are about, but attacks on humans are rare. Now humans get the better of marlin, swordfish and other big-game fish. Historically, people have also posed a threat to green and hawksbill turtles, but, hopefully, that slaughter will prove a thing of the past and turtle numbers will increase.

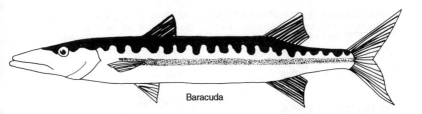

Baracuda

**Tortoises** The French and English wiped out the giant land tortoises early on from all the islands except Aldabra, where there are still a few thousand left. Several tortoises have been brought to the central islands and now munch their way around pens at hotels and guesthouses. There is a free-roaming colony on Curieuse and perhaps the biggest daddy of all is in the Cousin Island bird reserve (although Bird Island's operators also claim that distinction for Esmeralda!). The giant tortoise, central to the Seychelles coat of arms, is endemic to only two regions in the world. One is the Seychelles, the other is the Galapagos Islands, off Ecuador.

## GOVERNMENT

The Seychelles is a republic. The current president, Mr France Albert René, heads a cabinet of 10 ministers with specific portfolios. Following the introduction of multiparty politics in 1992, there has been intense discussion about changes to the constitution.

## ECONOMY

The Seychelles are very Westernised islands with most of the trappings of a Western economy. The minimum wage, however, is still around Rs 1500 (US$250) per month.

The mainstay of the islands' economy is tourism, as it was before the socialist revolution or coup of 5 June 1977. The coup itself and the subsequent shenanigans had an adverse effect on the holiday industry. The new government made matters worse by trying to reduce the nation's dependency on tourism too quickly and proceeded to build up other less servile enterprises. But it wasn't long before President René realised that the country really couldn't do without tourism. After hiring a series of overseas specialists, the industry is now back in full swing. It employs 20% of the workforce and accounts for half the country's gross national product. The government continues to invest heavily in tourism development.

In 1986, 66,780 tourists came to the Seychelles. The figures rose to 86,000 in 1989 and increased to 103,000 in 1990 when the income from tourism amounted to Rs 646 million.

Fishing and agriculture have also come a long way in the past 10 years or so by making better use of natural resources. The Seychelles' 320 km Exclusive Economic Zone, proclaimed in 1977, gave the country control of waters rich in tuna. Victoria is turning into a busy port for foreign trawlers, and provides a number of support services. A fishing port has been built along with a tuna processing and canning plant. Fish is the staple diet of the Seychellois, but that is changing with the greater availability and choice in agricultural produce.

The Seychelles Marketing Board (SMB) is responsible for all aspects of the agricultural sector, including production, processing, packaging and distribution of products. It sets and controls prices across the board. Copra and cinnamon have traditionally been the main agricultural exports but, although production of these has been further developed, the government's first concern is to become self-sufficient in food.

Other industries include the manufacture of paint, detergents, plastics and packaging products, and joint foreign ventures in TV-set assembly.

The islands were, and still are, labelled an

idyllic paradise with plenty of fish in the sea and fruit on the trees; a place where traditional work patterns are very different from Western ones. With the René government's importation of foreign skills and workers, these patterns are changing.

## POPULATION & PEOPLE

The population of the Seychelles is less than 70,000 and there's no more racially integrated society in the world. Every shade and hue of skin and hair imaginable exists in the Seychelles, arising out of a mixture of European, African, Indian, Chinese and Arab genes. No creed or colour can be said to dominate since the 1977 coup, when most of the *grands blancs* were dispossessed. Over 67% of the population is under 30 years of age.

The racial harmony of the Seychelles is more likely due to liberal morals than liberal politics. The islands used to have a reputation for being a haven of free love. This was based on the high illegitimacy rate. At one stage during the 1970s, more than 50% of the population was illegitimate. The reasons given were that marriages were expensive and married couples did not stay together long (even though most of the people are Catholic).

During the early days of tourism under James Mancham's promotion, the local promiscuity enhanced an image of a Garden of Eden with all the associated lust, temptation and sin.

That image has been 'cleaned up' by the socialist government and the tourist board now promotes packaged weddings and honeymoons on the islands, leaving any erotic suggestiveness to the famous coco de mer nut.

In general, the Seychellois are less open and friendly to visitors than Mauritians and the colonial backlash is still evident. With the increase in national pride and identity that developed after independence and the coup, came a more aloof attitude to visitors. At first it was as if the local population resented having to rely on tourism for its livelihood.

The locals felt they had been exploited, so the standards of service and hospitality reached rock bottom for a while, until they realised the financial benefits of the tourism industry. And now they're exploiting the tourists!

## EDUCATION

The education system has developed considerably since René's takeover. Nowadays, between the ages of 3½ and 5½, children can attend a non-compulsory creche education programme. Primary and secondary level schooling is compulsory up to the age of 15½.

The most significant and controversial aspect of the Seychelles education has been the National Youth Service (NYS), which was until very recently compulsory for school-leavers. During their two-year service, they continued their academic studies and trained in agricultural and industrial work at camps at Port Launay, Ste Anne Island and Cap Ternay. At first, the children were locked away in this communist finishing school for months on end, unable to see their parents, and given overdoses of Marx and Engels courtesy of Cuban, Russian and Angolan teachers. Since the early '90s, the NYS system is no longer compulsory, lasts 12 months, and has become more practical than political.

The Polytechnic at Mont Fleuri provides a wide range of academic, technical, and vocational courses for students between the ages of 16½ and 20½.

## CULTURE & ARTS

There is no indigenous culture in the Seychelles and little of African or Asian origin has survived – apart, that is, from the *séga* and *moutia* dances.

The government has formed the National School of Music and the National Cultural Troupe (NCT) to foster a Créole cultural identity and tradition. So far, much of it is nationalistic jingoism with 'liberation' songs such as 'Hail, 5th June', but coming through are some fine singers, dancers and writers.

There are regular performances by the NCT at the Polytechnic Theatre, Mont Fleuri, in Victoria, or at the theatre at Anse Royale, 20 km south of the capital.

## Dance

The sombre *moutia* is the typical dance of the Seychelles, with strong African and Madagascan rhythms. The songs are prayers which the slaves turned into work chants, similar to the early black gospel music of the USA. They are accompanied by slow, repetitive dance routines. It is a popular communal dance which normally is danced around a fire and serves as the primary evening entertainment. European influences are evident in the *contredanse*, which has its roots in the court of Louis XIV of France, the Sun King, as well as the *mazok*, reminiscent of the French waltz and the *kosez*, a type of quadrille.

The Seychelles version of the séga differs little from that of Mauritius. Séga dance displays are held at most of the large hotels at least one night a week and you may even be lucky enough to stumble onto a more spontaneous celebration.

## Art

In the past 20 years several artists and craftspeople have settled in the Seychelles and spawned a local industry to cater for the souvenir-hungry tourists. The best known is 51-year-old painter Michael Adams, whose home and studio are at Anse aux Poules Bleues in the south-west of Mahé. His paintings are incredible and convey the beauty of the Seychelles better than any photograph or film. This is what he says about his work:

I'm basically a jungle person. Every time you look at it, you see a different way of painting it. But the sea is perhaps the main feature of the Seychelles' beauty. The colour is almost edible, but it is hard to capture. It's like trying to remember tastes or a love from a long time ago.

I try and turn objective reality into abstract hieroglyphics, but never leave realism behind. I try to create the same vibrancy you get in 3-D. And because I use water colours, I have to make those colours shout.

Adams' work is featured on local calendars and promotional material.

Other paintings to look out for are those by Seychellois artist Christine Harter, of Praslin. She painted the big mural in the reception hall of the Beau Vallon Hotel, which took her more than a year to complete. Another local artist is Donald Adelaide of Baie Lazare, a former pupil of Adams.

Less admirable are the works of local entrepreneur Gerard Devoud, whose studio is at the Mamelles in Victoria. The paintings seem remarkably similar in style, although not quality, to those of Mr Adams. Mr Devoud also runs the Budget Car Rental.

Lorenzo Appiani is responsible for the new sculptures on the roundabouts at either end of 5th June Ave in Victoria. The Freedom Square monument is said to be three wings or birds – Twa Zwazo – representing the continents of Africa, Europe and Asia, each of which has played a part in the development of the Seychelles' people.

One of the best art galleries in Victoria is Christy's Art Gallery in de Quincy St.

## Music

The Indian, European, Chinese and Arabic backgrounds of the Seychellois people are reflected in their music. The accordion, banjo and violin music brought to the islands by the early European settlers has blended with that of the *makalapo*, a stringed instrument with a tin sound box; the *zez*, a monochord sitar; African skin drums, and the *bom*, a bowed instrument.

Patrick Victor is the best known musician on the islands for Créole pop and folk and is now head of the National Music School. You can get his records in most souvenir and music shops. Other popular local stars are David Philoe, Jonise Juliette, Serge Camille, Jones Camille and Hudson Dorothe. Another popular singer, Raymond Lebon, died recently.

On a more traditional level are the roving *camtole* bands featuring a fiddle, banjo, accordion and drums. They also accompany contredanses.

## Theatre

The Créoles once performed impromptu street theatre plays known as *sokwe*, but the practice has all but disappeared and theatre arts aren't yet popular with the Seychellois; public performances these days concentrate on music and dancing. However, the recent success of the Créole comedy *Bolot Feray* is encouraging greater interest in play writing and theatre performance.

## Sport

Soccer, as on all Indian Ocean islands, is the only game which can truly be called a national sport. Within the busy league programme there are occasional international matches against visiting teams at the National Stadium in Victoria. Réunion is the biggest rival.

Volleyball, basketball and hockey are also very popular. Athletics and boxing are gaining in strength, with the country sending teams to the last three Olympic games.

## RELIGION

Most Seychellois are Catholic and the majority of them are avid churchgoers, but there is a widespread belief in the supernatural and in the old magic of spirits known as *gris-gris*. Sorcery was outlawed in 1958, but there are a number of *bonhommes* and *bonfemmes di bois*, medicine men and women, practising their cures and curses and concocting potions for love, luck and revenge. These rituals and beliefs resemble those of Caribbean voodoo, but are practised only on a limited scale.

## LANGUAGE

English and French are the official languages and both are spoken by most people, although French Créole is the lingua franca. *Kreol seselwa* was 'rehabilitated' and made semiofficial in 1981 and is increasingly used in newspapers and literature. There are several novels and poetry collections in Créole for general sale.

Seychelles Créole is similar to that of Mauritius and Martinique, but differs remarkably from that of Réunion. In the local patois, the soft pronunciation of certain French consonants is hardened and silent syllables are dropped completely. The soft 'j' becomes 'z', for example (see the Mauritius section on Créole for suggested usage). The following phrases may help you venture into Créole:

| | |
|---|---|
| Good morning/ afternoon? | *Bonzour.* |
| How are you? | *Comman sava?* |
| Fine, thanks. | *Mon byen, mersi.* |
| What's your name? | *Ki mannyer ou appel?* |
| My name is... | *Mon appel...* |
| Where do you live? | *Koté ou resté?* |
| I don't understand. | *Mon pas konpran.* |
| I like it. | *Mon kontan.* |
| This is very beautiful. | *Sa i byen zoli.* |
| Where is...? | *Ol i...?* |
| How much is that? | *Kombyen sa?* |
| I'm thirsty. | *Mon soif.* |
| Can I have a beer, please? | *Mon kapa ganny en labyer silvouplé?* |

# Facts for the Visitor

## VISAS & EMBASSIES

You don't need a visa to enter the Seychelles, just a valid passport, an onward ticket, booked accommodation and sufficient funds for your stay.

Upon arrival by air, you will be given a visitor's visa for up to a month, depending on the departure date printed on your onward ticket.

If you don't have a ticket on a flight out of the country, you could be asked to deposit money for one with the immigration authorities. If you haven't booked accommodation, just name any hotel or guesthouse on your disembarkation card and hope it hasn't closed down! If that fails, an immigration officer will escort you to the travel agency counter while you make a booking.

If you arrive by yacht, you will be issued a visitor's permit for two weeks by the Port Authority. If staying longer, you must apply for an extension. You may be politely approached by a 'security officer' who will further enquire about your visit. The government is still on guard for potential coup planners and political agitators.

For a while after one counter-coup attempt, a citizen of South Africa would be treated as a *persona non grata*, but now South Africans are welcome again.

### Seychelles Embassies & Consulates

Seychelles has diplomatic representation in the following countries:

Australia
Seychelles Consulate, 271 Canning Rd, Les Murdie, Perth, WA 6076 (☎ (9) 291 6570)
France
Seychelles Embassy, 5ème etage, 53 bis, Rue François 1er, 75008 Paris (☎ (01) 47 23 77 02)
UK
Seychelles High Commission, PO Box 4PE, 2nd floor, Eros House, 111 Baker St, London W1M 1FE (☎ (071) 224 1660)
USA
Seychelles Embassy, Suite 927F, 820 Second Avenue, New York, NY 10017 (☎ (212) 6879766)

There are also Seychelles consulates in Austria (Vienna), Belgium (Brussels), Greece (Athens), India (New Delhi), Italy (Rome, Milan), Japan (Nagoya), Madagascar (Antananarivo), Netherlands (Huizen), Spain (Barcelona, Madrid), Sweden (Stockholm), Switzerland (Zürich) and Germany (Munich, Hamburg).

### Visa Extensions

If you wish to extend your visa, apply at the Immigration Office (☎ 322881), Independence House, on the corner of Independence and 5th June Avenues in Victoria.

Again, you may need proof of sufficient funds and an onward ticket. You will have to fill in a form and leave it, along with two passport photographs and your passport. The extension will be processed within the week.

You can extend the visa by up to three months free of charge. Thereafter it is Rs 200 per extension, for a further three months. You can only stay one year on a visitor's visa.

### Working Holidays

There are many foreigners working in the Seychelles, most of whom are employed on a contract basis by the government or work in the tourist industry.

If you get a job with the government your work permit will be arranged. If you are offered a job by a private company, it must apply for a permit on your behalf, with a convincing case for not employing a Seychellois. Direct application for a permit is permitted only if you set up your own business and only after you have received appropriate licences, which are issued if you have a suitable work site, accommodation and qualifications.

## Foreign Embassies & Consulates in the Seychelles

Following are the addresses of the major foreign embassies and consulates:

French Embassy
    PO Box 478, Mont Fleuri (☎ 224523)
Madagascar Consulate
    Box 68, Plaisance (☎ 344030)
Netherlands
    PO Box 372, Glacis (☎ 261200)
Sweden
    New Port (☎ 224710)
German Consulate
    PO Box 132, Mont Fleuri (☎ 322306)
UK High Commission
    3rd floor, Victoria House, State House Ave, Victoria (☎ 225225); open Monday to Friday from 8.30 am to 1.30 pm
US Embassy
    4th floor, Victoria House, State House Ave, Victoria (☎ 225256); open Monday to Friday from 7.30 am to 3.30 pm

China, Cuba and the Russian Federation also have embassies, and there is an Indian High Commission. Belgium, Cyprus, Denmark, Mauritius, Monaco and Switzerland also have consular representation.

## CUSTOMS

The international airport is 10 km south-east of Victoria. Entry formalities are quick and uncomplicated, although you may be questioned more fully, but politely, at customs. You are permitted to bring in one litre of spirits and one litre of wine; up to 200 cigarettes or 250 grams of tobacco; 125 ml perfume; and 250 ml of eau de toilette. Spearguns, along with other weapons and ammunition are forbidden, as is any food or agricultural produce.

When leaving the Seychelles do not take any shells, corals or preserved fish, turtles, etc. The illegal purchase of rare and endangered species directly contributes to their extinction. Tourists who illegally possess or transport these items should also be aware that the items are liable to confiscation on leaving the Seychelles, and to combined fines and confiscation by customs officials

in most Western countries which have signed agreements on endangered species.

If you are taking home a coco de mer nut, make sure you have the requisite export certificate.

## MONEY

### Currency

The Seychelles unit of currency is the rupee (Rs), which is divided into 100 cents (c). Denominations of notes come in Rs 10, 25, 50 and 100; and coins in Rs 1, 5 and 1c, 5c, 10c and 25c.

The Seychelles rupee (Rs) is tied to an account unit of the International Monetary Fund known as the Special Drawing Right, which also includes the British pound, US dollar, German Deutschmark, French franc and Japanese yen. Although the rates of exchange fluctuate daily, the rupee is generally strong and stable.

### Exchange Rates

The rate of exchange is set by the Central Bank of the Seychelles and is approximately:

| | | |
|---|---|---|
| US$1 | = | Rs 5.04 |
| A$1 | = | Rs 3.38 |
| UK£1 | = | Rs 7.6 |
| C$1 | = | Rs 3.95 |
| DM1 | = | Rs 3.1 |
| Fr1 | = | Rs 0.92 |

You'll get a better rate for travellers' cheques than for cash. Barclays Bank issues a list of the rates at the beginning of the week. Rates are also published daily in the newspaper 'Nation'.

No restrictions apply on the amount of rupees you can take into or out of the country. There are few places you can buy or sell Seychelles rupees abroad – not that any visitor would want to. Obviously the best rates of exchange are in the Seychelles.

Victoria, the capital, is well endowed with banks, including the Seychelles Savings Bank, Banque Française Commerciale, Bank of Baroda, Habib Bank and Standard Bank. The main bank is Barclays Bank, which has branches on La Digue (at Grande

Anse) and Praslin (at Baie Ste Anne) and around Mahé (Beau Vallon; airport). The bigger hotels change money, if you need cash on a Sunday for instance, but their rates do not compare favourably with those of the banks.

In 1991, as part of a global crackdown, the expansive offices of the Abu Dhabi-based Bank of Credit & Commerce International (BCCI) in the centre of Victoria were closed following worldwide investigation of the biggest bank fraud in history. During its 20-year history of financial mayhem BCCI is estimated to have defrauded over a million investors of many billions of dollars and is reported to have been involved in a dazzling network of organised crime. In 1992, these offices were officially requisitioned.

### Credit Cards

All major credit cards are accepted in most hotels, restaurants and shops, and the banks give cash advances against the cards. Credit cards are not accepted on Silhouette Island.

Barclays Bank (☎ 224101) represents Visa; Diners Club is represented by J.K. Parcou (☎ 225303), 1st floor, Victoria House, Victoria; and MasterCard and American Express are represented by Travel Services Seychelles (TSS) Ltd (☎ 322414; emergency assistance ☎ 344378), in Victoria.

### Costs

For information on costs in the Seychelles see the Costs section in the introductory Facts for the Visitor chapter.

### Tipping

Tipping is welcomed but not obligatory. A 10% service charge is added to your bill in hotels and restaurants.

### Bargaining

In general, there's a relaxed approach to bargaining. We found that gentle prompting could produce discounts for car rental, but the prices marked in shops are seldom negotiable.

### WHEN TO GO

The best times to visit really depend on what you like to do. Windsurfing and sailing are best at the start or end of the south-east trade winds (May to October), which can sometimes be up to two months late. The rain can fall in short torrents during the wet season, yet it can be overcast for days during the cooler, drier periods. Some beaches are better during the monsoon season, others during the south-east trade winds. Then there are the busy holiday seasons of December to January and July to August that you must also take into account.

### TOURIST OFFICES
### Local Tourist Offices

The Seychelles Tourist Board, or STB, (☎ 225333) has its head office at Independence House, PO Box 92, Victoria. It has a public information office full of brochures and assistance nearby, among the shops down from the Pirates Arms. There is no STB counter at the airport. The welcome and accommodation booking service there is provided by the National Travel Agency.

### Overseas Representatives

There are STB offices at the following addresses overseas:

France
  Seychelles Embassy, 32 Rue de Ponthieu, 75008 Paris (☎ (01) 42 89 85 33)
Germany
  Kleine Bockenheimer Strasse 18A, D-6000 Frankfurt am Main 1 (☎ (069) 292 064)
Italy
  Centro Cooperazione Internazionale, Piazza Giulio Cesare (Fiera), 20145 Milan (☎ (02) 49 85 795)
Japan
  Jingu 12-3, OTSU 620 (☎ (81) 775 22 3072)
Kenya
  3rd floor, Jubilee Insurance Exchange, PO Box 30702, Nairobi (☎ 225103)
Madagascar
  Seychelles Consulate, PO Box 1071, Antananarivo (☎ 20949)
UK
  2nd floor, Eros House, 111 Baker St, London W1M 1FE (☎ (071) 224 1670)

USA
820 Second Avenue, Suite 927, New York, NY 10017 (☎ (212) 6879766)

## BUSINESS HOURS & HOLIDAYS
### Business Hours
Offices and shops keep British rather than French hours, opening at 8.30 am, lunching between noon and 1 pm and closing at 4 pm (government offices) and 5 pm (shops). On Saturdays, many shops are open in the morning. Some shops even stay open through lunch and all day on Saturday. In the villages, shops are open until around 9 pm.

In Victoria, the banks are open Monday to Friday from 8.30 am to 12.30 pm and 2 to 3.30 pm, and on Saturdays from 8.30 to 11.30 am. The branches keep shorter hours. At the airport, bank counters are open to meet incoming international flights.

See individual island chapters for details of post office hours.

### Holidays
Some dates to remember in the Seychelles include:

*New Year* – 1 & 2 January
*Good Friday & Easter* – March or April
*Labour Day* – 1 May
*Liberation Day* – 5 June
*Independence Day* – 29 June
*Corpus Christi* – May or June
*Assumption* – 15 August
*La Digue Festival* – 15 August
*All Saints' Day* – 1 November
*Immaculate Conception* – 8 December
*Christmas* – 25 December

## POST & TELECOMMUNICATIONS
### Postal Rates
Airmail postcards to all international destinations cost Rs 3. Airmail letters weighing up to 10 grams cost Rs 3.50 to Europe or Australia; Rs 4 to the USA or Canada; and Rs 3 to Indian Ocean or African destinations. Aerogrammes cost Rs 2.50.

### Sending & Receiving Mail
The mail service is reliable and reasonably quick, and there is a free poste restante service at the Central Post Office in Victoria.

### Telephone
The telephone system, run by Cable & Wireless, is one of the world's most modern. Despite protestations from the company, phone bugging is a very open secret in the Seychelles. Originally, the bugging was performed by official request, but the tables were turned a few years ago when a stirring conversation between the President and his mistress was recorded and illicitly broadcast on Seychelles Radio.

Telephone cards, known as Phonocards, can be purchased at the airport, Cable & Wireless offices, and from shops and post offices on the major islands. Cards are available for Rs 30 (30 units), Rs 60 (60 units), Rs 100 (120 units), and Rs 200 (240 units).

**Local Calls** There are public phone boxes all over Mahé, nine on Praslin, and one each on La Digue, Silhouette and Cerf.

Local calls cost Rs 0.80 for up to six minutes. Long-distance calls within Mahé, from Victoria to Anse Royale for instance, cost Rs 0.80 for 45 seconds. From Mahé to Praslin or La Digue, calls cost Rs 0.80 for 25 seconds. Calls to the outlying islands of Desroches, Coétivy and Farquhar cost Rs 10 for one minute.

If you wish to contact vessels at sea, within the vicinity of the Seychelles, dial 376733. These radio telephone calls are charged at the rate of Rs 2.50 per minute.

**International Calls** You can make international calls direct using international direct dialling (IDD). The rate per minute for a call to the UK, the USA, Australia or Canada is Rs 25.16; and to Germany the equivalent rate is Rs 29.26. If you are tempted to phone from your hotel room, remember that hotels often add a large mark-up to this rate.

Direct operator services, such as USA Direct, UK Direct, and KDD Direct are also available at phone locations with the requisite signs.

Some useful international dialling codes are: Seychelles 248; Mauritius 230; UK 44; USA 1; Australia 61; New Zealand 64; Réunion 262; Madagascar 261; Comoros

269; and South Africa 27. Dial 999 for emergency services; 18 for international directory assistance; and 15 for the international operator.

### Fax, Telex & Telegraph
Telegram, telex and telefax services are also available through Cable & Wireless on Francis Rachel St, Victoria.

### TIME
Seychelles time is four hours (three hours during the European summer) ahead of Greenwich Mean Time (GMT) and Universal Time Coordinated (UTC), one hour ahead of Madagascar time and two hours ahead of South African time. So when it is noon in the Seychelles it is 8 am in London; 3 am in New York and Toronto; midnight in San Francisco; 6 pm in Sydney or Melbourne; and 7 pm in New Zealand. It is in the same time zone as Mauritius and Réunion.

### ELECTRICITY
The current is 240 volts AC. The plugs in general use are square pins and have three points.

### LAUNDRY
Laundry services are widely available at guesthouses and hotels.

### WEIGHTS & MEASURES
The metric system is used in the Seychelles, but it's still common to find references to British standards, such as miles, feet and inches.

### BOOKS & MAPS
#### History
There are a couple of interesting books on the Seychelles worth reading before or after you go to the islands for a comparison with the recent past, attitudes and life style of the country. The more picturesque of these is *Forgotten Eden* by Atholl Thomas (Longmans, London, 1968). It's long out of print, but is still considered to be one of the best books on the country. More politically biased (on the side of the first president James Mancham) but still quite informative and a good read, is *Political Castaways* by Christopher Lee (Elm Tree Books, London, 1976).

A more recent account is Mancham's own story of his rise and fall in *Paradise Raped* (Methuen, London, 1983). The book is not available in the Seychelles, but Mancham's locally published collection of poetry *Reflections & Echoes from Seychelles* (1972) is still available from the library in Victoria. President René doesn't mind Mancham waxing lyrical about the beauties of the islands.

France-Albert René has his say about the history of the Seychelles United People's Party, the revolution and the necessity of a one-party state in *Seychelles: the New Era* (Seychelles National Printing Co, 1982). This follows his collected speeches and writing in *The Torch of Freedom* (1981). The government has also published the *White Book*, which gives full details of the failed mercenary coup attempt by 'Mad Mike' Hoare on 25 November 1981. It's a fascinating account of how to plan a coup or, in this case, how not to plan one. These books are available from the National Bookshop on Albert St, Victoria.

Mad Mike's own version of the bungled coup attempt *The Seychelles Affair* (Bantam, London, 1986) adopts a more novelistic approach. It is also available in a Corgi paperback.

For the studious, there is *Men, Women & Money in Seychelles* by Marion & Burton Benedict (University of California Press, 1982). Less academic is Guy Lionnet's *Seychelles* (David & Charles, London, 1972) in the 'Islands' series.

Leslie Thomas includes a chapter on the Seychelles and Mauritius in his *A World of Islands* (Michael Joseph, London, 1983). In *The Treasure Seeker's Treasury* by Roy Nevill (Hutchinson, London, 1978), the author expounds on the hunt for the treasure of the pirate Olivier 'La Buse' Levasseur at Bel Ombre on Mahé. (Atholl Thomas has more of the story in *Forgotten Eden*, as he talked to the late Reginald Cruise-Wilkins, who spent most of his life looking for the treasure at Bel Ombre.) In *Island Home* (Hale, London, 1970) Wendy Weevers-Carter writes about life on Rémire Island in the isolated Amirantes group of atolls. Don't forget Auguste Toussaint's *History of the Indian Ocean* (Routledge & Kegan Paul, London, 1966) for an overview of the Indian Ocean.

### Fiction

The only novel I found set around the Seychelles looks to be of little merit, but that's just on the basis of a quick perusal. It's called *Adrift* and was written by Dion Divigny (Collins & Harvill, London, 1981).

### Cookbooks

Sir James Mancham may have fallen out of favour in the Seychelles, but his mum's recipes have not. Eveline Mancham's *La Cuisine Seychelloise* (St Fidèle, Victoria, 1960) is now in its fourth edition.

### Flora & Fauna

There are eight books in the series of *Seychelles Nature Handbooks*, which deals with most aspects of nature on the islands – shells, coral reef life, natural history, birds, fish and plant life. Another relevant title is Francis Friedmann's *Flowers & Trees of Seychelles* (Department of Finance, Seychelles, 1986).

The life and work of artist Marianne North, who visited the Seychelles in 1883 to paint the flora, is set out in *A Vision of Eden* (Webb & Bower, Exeter, 1980).

Guy Lionnet is a well-known Seychellois naturalist and historian. About 20 years ago he wrote a small book on the unique coco de mer palm, called *Romance of a Palm*. It has been reissued and is widely available in souvenir shops and newsagents (L'Île aux Images, Mauritius, 1980).

Ornithologists will be interested in *The Birds of Seychelles and the Outlying Islands* (Harper Collins, 1992) and *Birds of the Republic of Seychelles* (ICBP, 1990).

*Aldabra Alone* by Tony Beamish (Allen & Unwin, London, 1970) looks at life among the giant tortoises, robber crabs, and other

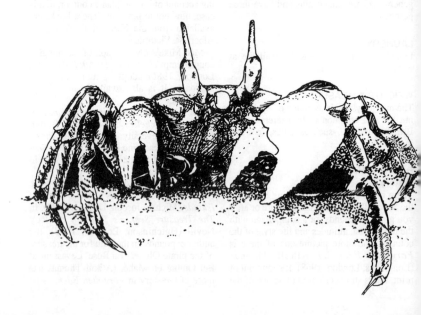

incredible natural phenomena during an expedition to the Aldabra group.

From tortoises to turtles and terrapins, American scientist Jeanne Mortimer has produced an educational booklet on the creatures and the need to protect them. It's called *Turtles, Tortoises & Terrapins of the Seychelles* and is published by the World Wildlife Fund. If nothing else, you'll at least learn the difference between the T's.

There are still copies available of Al Venter's *Underwater Seychelles* (Gordon Verhoef, London, 1972). Dr F D Ommanney writes a fair bit about the Seychelles and Mauritius in an account of a fisheries expedition entitled *The Shoals of Capricorn* (Longmans, London, 1952).

*Beyond the Reefs* (Century Travellers, 1990) by William Travis is, in fact, a reprint in one volume of the author's two works: *Beyond the Reefs* and *Shark for Sale*, first published in 1959 and 1961 respectively. The first work describes Travis' attempts to start a commercial venture diving for shells, and the second details his career move into shark fishing. Travis and his crew have some amazingly close brushes with marine danger in the Seychelles.

### Bookshops
The main bookshop is the SPACE Bookshop in Albert St, Victoria. It has all the government publications and is also the place to look for foreign newspapers, magazines, novels and books. In the shopping arcade inside Victoria House, there is a small shop which sells a few foreign novels.

### Libraries
The National Library is housed in a new building on Francis Rachel St. It is open Monday to Friday from 8.30 am to 5 pm, and on Saturdays from 8.30 to 11.45 am. You can borrow a book by leaving a deposit of Rs 50 and are allowed to take out two books at a time. For more specific research, contact Alain Lucas at the National Archives & Museum at La Bastille, Union Vale, just north of Victoria on the coast road. In early 1994, there are plans to relocate the archives

and museum collection to the new library complex. There are also public libraries on Praslin and La Digue.

### Maps
Good tourist maps of Mahé as well as Praslin and La Digue, based on British Ordnance Survey maps, can be purchased for Rs 20 each from the map division of the Information Office, Independence House, 5th June Ave, Victoria.

### MEDIA
### Newspapers & Magazines
The daily paper is the government-controlled *Nation*. It costs Rs 2 (Rs 5 for a weekend edition); contains stories in English, French and Créole; and carries cinema, TV and radio programmes and adverts.

SPACE bookshop gets the Sunday papers from the UK off the London flight on Monday, if you want to keep up with the soccer results. *Time*, *Newsweek* and many other magazines are also on sale here and at the shops in the major hotels.

Two recently launched political publications are *Regar* and *La Verité*, both are trilingual and published biweekly. Other local publications include *Seychelles Today*, a monthly news review in English published by the government's Central Information Service; the political *People*, published bimonthly in three languages by the Seychelles People's Progressive Front; and the bimonthly *L'Echo des Îles*, also trilingual, published by the Catholic Mission.

The *Seychelles Island Journal* is published in England and covers political and general news about the islands. It's available from The Indian Ocean Publishing Company (☎ (344) 50814), 6 Wantage Close, Harmans Waters, Bracknell RG12 3NL, UK.

### Radio & TV
The Seychelles Broadcasting Corporation (SBC) provides daily radio broadcasts until 8 pm on weekdays and 10 pm on weekends. There is a daily, 20 minute news bulletin in English at 7 pm.

The Far East Broadcasting Association (FEBA) is a radio station specialising in religious programmes for the Far East, Asia, and some Middle Eastern countries.

SBC provides television broadcasting each evening from about 6 to 11 pm. Programmes include films from France and Germany, the occasional comedy show from England and nature specials, as well as short news bulletins (in English at 6 pm). The latest news is supplied to SBC by CNN (Cable News Network International). The up-market hotels have TV sets in every room and run in-house video movies.

## FILM & PHOTOGRAPHY

As always, it's best to stock up on film from duty free shops before you arrive. If not, there's a plentiful supply here and several decent developing studios. Photo-Eden, next to the Pirates Arms in Victoria, and at Mont Fleuri, sells Kodak Gold (36 exposures) for Rs 30 and charges Rs 118 for developing and printing. Slide film available here includes Ektachrome 100 for Rs 51 and Kodachrome 64 for Rs 50. Across the street Fujicolor boasts a one-hour printing service at Rs 3 per print; it also runs lots of discounts.

## HEALTH

After all that talk about the vagaries of the weather, don't throw yourself at the mercy of the sun every chance you get, even if it's probably the only time you'll see it all year. I saw a lot of British visitors doing great lobster impressions. As they say in Australia, 'slip, slop, slap' (slip on a shirt, slop on some cream and slap on a hat).

No vaccination certificates are required for entry into the Seychelles. The islands are free of malaria, yellow fever and other nasties. You don't need to take malaria tablets if you are visiting only the Seychelles, but the mosquitoes are still best avoided, so bring cream, coils and sprays if you react badly to bites.

The biggest health hazards, after the sun, are the speeding drivers on the roads on Mahé, and to a lesser extent on Praslin. The half dozen motor vehicles, couple of ox carts and several dozen bicycles on La Digue can hardly be considered lethal. Be careful when driving or walking on the roads after dark, especially on the busy, twisting hill route between Victoria and Beau Vallon. Accidents are common. If the locals are not going too fast, the tourists in their hired Mokes are going too slowly.

The sea is more benign. Here the danger comes only when snorkelling, diving or swimming, from stinging and razor-sharp coral.

If you do get ill, you can see a local doctor for a basic consultation fee of Rs 75 under the National Medical Service. You must pay for prescribed medicines or drugs at the pharmacy. The main outpatient clinic is at Mont Fleuri, Victoria (near the Botanical Gardens). The casualty unit (☎ 234400) at the hospital is open 24 hours. There are several European doctors working in the Seychelles and the standard of treatment and medical equipment is reasonably good. The tourist board hopes to import doctors to provide treatment at the big hotels.

Other districts in Mahé have clinics, as do Praslin and La Digue islands. There is no chemist on Praslin, but the hospital at Baie Ste Anne (☎ 233333) fills prescriptions. The shops also sell aspirin, tampons and the like.

If you have dental problems, contact the Mobile Dental Unit through Mont Fleuri Hospital. It has a fully qualified, English-speaking aid dentist in charge.

### Water

Tap water is safe to drink, although it has more of a 'chlorinated' taste on Mahé than on Praslin.

## WOMEN TRAVELLERS

There are no real restrictions on women travelling alone in the Seychelles and foreign women will probably receive less attention from local men than they would in North America or most European countries. As anywhere, you'd be advised not to hitch alone or walk alone at night in the unlit neighbourhoods of Victoria, but even so, the risks are minimal.

Because tourism in the Seychelles is geared primarily to couples, however, anyone travelling alone – male or female – is bound to get some incredulous looks in tourist-oriented hotels and restaurants.

## DANGERS & ANNOYANCES
Break-ins and burglaries, sometimes violent ones, are a problem throughout Mahé, so most houses have a guard dog or dogs (which can be a barking nuisance during the wee small hours). Hotel and guesthouse residents are not at a great risk, but long-term visitors should take extra security measures.

Petty theft is very common. Don't take valuables to the beach and *never* leave belongings unattended on the beach – even if you're just going in for a quick dip. Although many beaches may appear deserted when you arrive, it's surprising how quickly someone can materialise from the bushes to casually loiter past. Similarly, nothing of any value should be left in your rental car, especially if it's a Mini-moke (the lock-box at the back is useless and a favourite target for petty thieves).

Most hotels offer safe deposit facilities to their guests. If you place valuables in a hotel safe, remember to get a receipt. Make sure you package your valuables in a small, double-zippered bag which can be padlocked, or use a large envelope with a signed seal which will easily show any tampering. Count money and travellers' cheques immediately before and after retrieving them from the safe.

The most intrepid burglary award must go to the gang of thieves who waded across to the island hotel of l'Islette at dinner hour and cleaned out the rooms whilst the guests were busy eating!

### Security
As a tourist, you won't generally be hampered by the defence or police forces, unless you give them reason to be suspicious. The army keeps a lower public profile these days. There are a few out-of-bounds areas such as the NYS camps at Cap Ternay, Port Launay and Ste Anne Island, and the Long Island prison.

## ACTIVITIES
### Water Sports
For visitors the main pursuits are water sports – water-skiing, paragliding, snorkelling and the like. There are plenty of water sports experts around to teach holiday-makers.

At Beau Vallon Bay Hotel on Mahé, the Aquatic Sports Centre (☎ 247141, extension 825) offers paragliding, water-skiing, canoeing, minisailing, sailboarding and snorkelling. Equipment can be hired and instruction is available for most of these water sports. The centre also provides diving and game fishing expeditions. You get a 20% reduction if you're a Beau Vallon Bay Hotel guest.

On the beach nearby is Leisure 2000, which offers similar activities.

Although other hotels can offer some of these activities, few can match the wide range available at Beau Vallon.

**Snorkelling** Snorkelling in the Seychelles must be rated as a highlight or 'must do' for any visitor.

The best spots around Mahé are: the marine national parks at Ste Anne (from a boat) and Port Launay (from the shore); the rocks near the Northolme Hotel; Anse Soleil in the south-west and Petite Anse just south of it; and Île Souris, just south of Pointe au Sel.

Off Praslin, try around Chauve Souris Island within wading distance of Anse Volbert beach. Alternatively, there's Petite Soeur Island near La Digue, if you can get out there by boat.

Most hotels and diving schools sell or rent snorkelling gear (daily rates around Rs 25 for a mask and snorkel, Rs 25 for fins), but bring your own if possible. Flippers are heavy and space-consuming to pack. Spear fishing is strictly forbidden.

When snorkelling, remember to wear flippers or canvas shoes to protect your feet, a T-shirt to protect your back and shoulders from sunburn; and never reach into a crevice with your bare hand.

**Diving** Diving in the Seychelles, particularly around the outlying islands, is considered world class. Next to the Maldives, the Seychelles offers the best location in the Indian Ocean to take up or pursue diving. The best time for diving is between April and November. During the rest of the year, the sea is rougher and the water cloudier.

**Certificates** Certificates are generally issued by the internationally recognised PADI (Professional Association of Diving Instructors) or FAUI (Federation of Australian Underwater Instructors).

**Diving Courses** An introductory course for a total novice (minimum 12 years of age) lasts a day and includes theory tutorial, a pool training session, and a boat dive on a shallow coral reef with an instructor. Instruction is usually available in English, French, German, Afrikaans, and various other languages. The price is around Rs 400, including equipment rental. Subsequent accompanied resort dives cost around Rs 250 each.

For Rs 2200 you can take the course for an International PADI Open Water Certificate, which requires four days on an intensive course, including five theory tutorials, five pool training sessions, and four qualifying dives.

For qualified divers, dives can be arranged at prices starting around Rs 170/230 per dive, depending on whether you rent only cylinder and weights or full equipment. The more dives you take, the bigger the discount.

Also on offer are advanced diver training courses in specialist areas such as night diving, deep diving, natural and compass navigation, and search and recovery diving. The minimum duration is two days and prices start around Rs 1500.

Hawksbill Turtle

**Diving Schools** There are several schools offering courses from novice to divemaster and underwater photography. Equipment is available for hire or purchase.

The Underwater Centre (☎ 247357; fax 344223), run by British couple David Rowat and Glynis Sanders, is at the Coral Strand Hotel and has diving instruction contracts with several of the major hotels. Marine Divers (☎ 247141 ext 8133; fax 247809), run by Peter Driessel, is based at Beau Vallon Bay Hotel and has branches at the Northolme Hotel, Auberge Sun Hotel, and on La Digue. Diving in Paradise (☎ 232148; fax 232244), run by Bernard Camille, is based at the Praslin Beach Hotel on Praslin.

The Baobab Pizzeria on Beau Vallon beach runs a school called Le Diable de Mer, 'Devil of the Sea' (☎ 247167).

**Dive Sites** The diving schools mentioned in the previous section have a wide choice of favoured dive sites. The schools based on Mahé, for instance, provide clients with a map and annotated list of over 30 sites. The following are just a few sample descriptions taken from the Underwater Centre's list:

*Coral Gardens* 16 metres deep, 10 minutes by boat. An immense soft coral area with frequent sand patches. A mixture of soft and hard corals with numerous reef fish. Excellent for photography. Suitable for all divers.

*Vista Do Mar Granite Massif* 15 metres deep, 15 minutes by boat. '*The* site for photographers. Amazing walls completely encrusted with blazing soft tree corals and fans of white gorgonias provide a spectacular backdrop for the myriads of iridescent blue damsels and flamboyant anthias, not to mention at least four forms of lion fish.' Suitable for all divers.

*Whale Rock* A large, submerged granite outcrop, just off shore. Large archways and overhangs make it an excellent site for Moray eels, stingrays and octopi. Suitable for all divers.

*L'Îlot* Off the northern tip of Mahé, 25 minutes by boat. A picturesque 'Desert Island' complete with palm trees hosts some remarkable submarine scenery. Sheer walls cut by gulleys, archways and crevices attract large shoals of shade-loving fish. Visited by large pelagic fish, grouper and occasional reef shark. Experienced divers (some current).

*Ennerdale* Wreck of a British tanker lying at 30 metres in three sections, about 45 minutes by boat from Beau Vallon. Home to shoals of golden snapper and a giant grouper. A long-range dive for experienced divers only.

*Shark Bank* About five km off shore. A rock pinnacle and feeding area for many fish, including the large predators. Immense stingrays. A long-range dive for experienced divers only.

*Brissare Rocks* About 35 minutes by boat. 'An amazing carpet of fire coral' with 'some of the most prolific fish life in the islands'. Among the fish life are shoals of batfish, massive Napoleon wrasse, eagle rays and cruising reef sharks. A long-range dive for experienced divers only.

Further afield, 250 km to the south-west of Mahé, there is great diving around the Amirantes islands, particularly St Joseph's Atoll, Poivre and Desroches. Assomption Island in the Aldabra Group has been descrived as one of the world's best dive sites.

**Windsurfing** is popular on Mahé, and Praslin. If you fancy yourself as a good windsurfer there is a 40 km open race from Mahé to Praslin each year. The record time is one hour 20 minutes. If you're on La Digue, look up Reverend Bos, the local priest. He's a keen windsurfer and has several sailboards for hire or loan.

**Surfing** There probably are several good spots around the islands, but few people bring their boards to discover them. There are no surfboards for hire and few for loan in the Seychelles.

**Sailing** The MCA has several yacht owners among its members who charter cruises around islands near and far. There are also a few 'rogue' operators undercutting the rates. See the Seychelles – Getting Around chapter for more details.

**Deep-Sea Fishing** For those who are not content with watching fish and want to kill them, the Seychelles hotels and boat charters are happy to oblige. As they boast: 'There are records for the taking.'

Minimum half day/full day charter rates start around Rs 1700/2800. You may be able to negotiate cheaper prices directly with some of the 30 or so members of the Marine Charter Association (MCA) (☎ 322126; fax 224679), which is next to the Yacht Club in Victoria.

There is a sponsored National Fishing Competition each year about March. Contact the MCA for details.

### Hiking

The Tourism Division of the Ministry of Tourism & Transport has produced an excellent set of ten hiking brochures for the Seychelles which describe individual hiking routes, the islands' natural history and points of interest along the way, with lively and informative material on fauna and flora. The brochures are available for Rs 10 each from the tourist office in Victoria. Some of the major hikes will be described individually in several of the following chapters.

**Organised Walks on Mahé** Basil Beaudoin (☎ 241790), an experienced guide, organises mountain walks on Mahé. He charges Rs 200 per person and offers trips to Mont Sebert (five hours); La Reserve (two to six hours); Les Trois Frères (three to six hours); Congo Rouge (three to six hours); Anse Major (two to four hours); Copolia (one to two hours); and Morne Seychellois (six to eight hours).

### Land Sports

The Reef Hotel (☎ 376251) at Anse aux Pins has a golf course, and hotel guests can play for free if they have a 'fun card'. Nonresidents must pay green fees and can hire clubs, golf balls, and caddies (registered only). The Barbarons Beach hotel also has a small golf course.

Horse riding is only available at the plush Barbarons Estate (☎ 378339, 378577) on the west coast of Mahé, near the hotel of the same name.

Tennis courts are available at most of the major hotels.

**Rock Climbing** Because of the Inner Islands' stark granite nature, there are some fine challenges for rock climbers. A few travellers have made the trip for this purpose alone. The best block and cliff-face climbs are on Praslin and La Digue.

On Praslin, the sites to tackle are en route from Baie Ste Anne over the hill to Anse Marie-Louise, behind Anse Lazio; and at the end of the Anse Kerlan road at Pointe Ste Marie. For cliff climbs on Praslin, go to Anse Possession, just west of La Reserve hotel; Anse Citron on the inland side of the road; and between Anse Gouvernement and Anse Matelot.

Blocks for climbing on La Digue can be found at Anse Caiman, Anse Pierrot, Pointe Source d'Argent, Pointe Belize (between Grande and Petite Anses), Anse Grosse Roche and Anse Patates. There are also good cliff climbs at Pointe Jacques and L'Union, behind the government lodge and copra factory.

## HIGHLIGHTS
### Beaches
Carana (Mahé – Glacis); Anse Lazio (Praslin); Anse Patates (La Digue); Anse Victorin (Frégate)

### Activities
Diving; snorkelling

### Walks
La Reserve & La Brulée (Mahé); Vallée de Mai (Praslin); La Passe to Anse Cocos (La Digue); Frégate Island

### Ecological Interest
Cousin Island; Bird Island; Vallée de Mai (Praslin); Aldabra & Assomption

### Scenic Drives
Forêt Noir (Mahé)

### Accommodation
Colibri Guest House (Praslin); Patatran (La Digue); Félicité; Les Bougainvilliers (Mahé); Fisherman's Cove (Mahé); Frégate; Château St Cloud (La Digue)

### Restaurants
Kaz Kreol (Mahé); Bon Bon Plume (Praslin); Chez Gaby (Round Island); Patatran (La Digue)

### Arts
Michael Adams' Studio

## ACCOMMODATION
The Seychelles tourist industry is heavily controlled by the government. The Seychelles has more than 40 guesthouses, small hotels or bungalow complexes, 29 large or luxury hotels and four self-catering apartment or chalet villages.

About 75% of the accommodation is on Mahé and it is registered and regulated by the Seychelles Tourist Board (STB). This is advantageous in that a consistently high and relatively affordable Western standard of service and facilities is maintained, but it does cut out the budget end of the market. The STB does not want any losmens, 'native accommodation', pensions de famille, youth hostels or Indian doss houses. Camping is forbidden everywhere on the islands.

### Hotels & Guesthouses
A guesthouse without a licence that takes and charges guests is operating illegally and will be reported by other guesthouse operators. Some owners can't afford to make the necessary renovations to meet STB standards, and have to let rooms on the sly to 'friends who make a donation'. Others get round the officialdom.

Virtually all the luxury hotels and a couple

of the guesthouses charge higher rates for the three peak periods (high season) over Christmas and New Year, Easter, and July to August. Low season prices generally apply from late April to late July, and from early September to mid-December.

Accommodation is limited on La Digue and it is always best to book and to confirm before arrival. Often, the operators will meet you at the boat.

Prices given in this edition for hotels and guesthouses in the Places to Stay sections are expected to rise by 5% each year.

### Houses & Flats

If staying long term, it is better to look for a house or flat to rent. You can expect to pay between Rs 2000 and Rs 3000 per month. There are 'To Let' adverts in the *Nation* newspaper. Ask at the bungalows next to the Baobab Pizzeria on Beau Vallon beach or ask any of the expat workers, many of whom are young British teachers on one-year contracts.

### FOOD

The Seychelles is the best of all Indian Ocean islands for Créole cuisine. Fish and rice are the staple foods, but for once the rice takes a back seat while more imaginative use is made of fruit, vegetables, herbs and spices. What the cooks do with fish is exceptionally good.

With more than 35 guesthouses trying, encouraged by the tourist authorities, to put on the best in home cooking, the standard and variety of Créole dishes has come out of the closet during the past five years. The Seychelles Hotel & Tourism Training School at Bel Ombre is also playing a part in this renaissance by turning out young chefs for the hotels and restaurants.

The range of fish and seafood available is huge and you'll probably be able to try shark, barracuda, kingfish, octopus, squid, jack fish, red snapper *(bourgeois)*, cordonnier, parrot fish and grouper *(vielle)* cooked in several different ways. Other Créole dishes standard to the region are the *daube*, a sweet sauce or stew; *rougaille*, a tomato-based

sauce used with fish, sausages or as a side dish; *carri coco*, a mild meat or fish curry with coconut cream; fish marinaded in lemon; and *brèdes*, a local variety of spinach or Chinese cabbage.

Two delicacies served in some restaurants are fruit bat and turtle. However, fruit bat is not widely available, and eating turtle is grossly selfish and should be taboo due to the endangered status of the green turtle. La Sirène restaurant at Anse aux Poules Bleues on Mahé has 'curried bat' on the menu. Don't expect it to taste fruity. You can also get the 'millionaire's salad' or heart-of-palm served up at normal prices in some guesthouses. The heart, or the 'apical bud', of the palmiste palm is used, causing the tree to die.

The Créoles are big on soups. The *tec-tec* soup, which contains small shells, is delicious. On the meat side, pork is becoming more popular. Chicken fricassee and chicken curry are other favourites.

There is also a wide choice of fruits (and vegetables to a lesser extent), and a fair bit of imagination goes into making desserts. I once had sliced onion and orange – mixed. Sweet potatoes, cassava and breadfruit form a big part of the daily Créole diet. Among the more exotic selections are jamalacs, custard apples *(coeurs de boeuf)*, golden apples, corassols, passion fruit and guavas. Bananas come in various kinds – you get the giant St Jacques variety used in cooking or for chips, and the stubby little ones for sweets.

### Eating Out

There are about four price levels from which to choose. The cheapest places to eat are the takeaway counters in Victoria where you can fill up for Rs 25. Then there are a few economy restaurants where you can eat for between Rs 40 and Rs 50.

Some of the guesthouses, such as the Bougainville near Anse Royale, do good set-menu meals for around Rs 75. At hotels and higher-class restaurants expect to pay at least Rs 100 for a modest meal.

Choose from Créole, Chinese, Italian and French restaurants and your palate *must* be subjected to the variety of Créole fish dishes.

The Beau Vallon Bay Hotel does vegetarian meals.

The Seychelles Hotel & Tourism Training School at Bel Ombre has a restaurant, but sadly it's not as cheap as you'd expect for the pleasure of letting students experiment on you. Another alternative, if you're staying around Victoria, is to join the Yacht Club for RS 350 per month. It has the cheapest restaurant on the islands.

### Self-Catering

The markets are no longer the colourful affairs of old, but the prices and stocks are a lot more consistent thanks to the control of the Seychelles Marketing Board (SMB). The SMB also runs the main supermarket on Albert St in the centre of Victoria. Ironically, it was the store belonging to ousted president James Mancham's family. There you can buy most imported foodstuffs, household items, wines and spirits. A packet of biscuits costs Rs 7, processed cheese is Rs 8.50, long-life milk is Rs 4, a loaf of bread is Rs 5 and cakes are 70c. You can buy fish down at the fishing port near where the schooner ferries leave for Praslin and La Digue.

There are bakeries on Praslin and La Digue where you can buy bread and cakes; in Victoria, choose from a number of patisseries. It is hard to buy fresh fruit and vegetables on islands other than Mahé because most of the produce is home-grown for household needs only.

### DRINKS
### Nonalcoholic Drinks

For those who don't trust the water, there is Eau de Val Riche mineral water at Rs 8 for a small bottle and Rs 12 for a large one.

Seybrew makes a range of soft drinks, such as bitter lemon, fruit cocktail, tonic, and ginger ale, under the Seypearl label.

### Alcohol

**Beer** The local lager beers, Seybrew and EKU, are excellent. They are brewed under German supervision on Mahé. Bottles of Seybrew cost Rs 6 in shops, but double or more in hotels and restaurants. EKU costs

Rs 8 in shops. The Seychellois also like their Guinness, for around Rs 7.50 per bottle.

Most village stores stock cold beer which you can drink there or take away. All bottled drinks include Rs 1 deposit, so your empty bottles are worth taking back.

**Wine** The cheapest retail wines available are Greek and South African. You can get a litre of South African red or white at the stores for about Rs 50. The Greek plonk is less palatable. The house wine served in restaurants seems very rough.

**Toddy** Toddy from the coconut palm is not common because toddy-tappers must have a licence, which is hard to come by.

You've a better chance of finding toddy on Praslin than on Mahé. Look for ladders disappearing up the palm trunks. The toddy is cheap from the source at about Rs 4 per bottle. It ferments quickly and must be drunk shortly after tapping.

Bacca rum, made from cane spirit and 'other things', is the other local hooch, along with Lapuree, which is made from fruit and 'other things'.

### ENTERTAINMENT
### Cinemas

Movie outlets are limited to the Deepam Cinema at the north end of Albert St in Victoria; the American Cultural Centre (☎ 225170) on Francis Rachel St; and the Centre Culturel Français, or CCF, (☎ 322268), above the Pirates Arms restaurant on Independence Ave. The Deepam shows a good selection of English and American films, and seats cost Rs 8 and Rs 10. The billing is advertised in the *Nation* newspaper.

The American Cultural Centre is open Monday to Friday from 11.30 am to 3.30 pm. It shows films on Mondays, and news programmes on Tuesdays and Thursdays. The centre also has a magazine and research library.

The CCF shows modern and classic French films three times a week. The centre also puts on occasional rock and folk concerts, art exhibitions, videos of French TV news, sports programmes and fashion shows. It is open Monday to Friday from 8.30 am to 1 pm and 1.30 to 4 pm, and on Saturday from 10 am to noon.

## Discos & Nightclubs

The Seychellois go to the local discos, including the *Lovenut* and the *Barrel* bar & disco in Victoria, and the *Katiolo*, just south of the airport. Only Friday and Saturday nights are worth trying. Another hotspot is the *Black Parrot* in Beau Vallon.

There are dances with a live band at the end of the month at the Anse Gaulettes dance hall on the south-west corner of Mahé and at the Horizon bar on Praslin, among other places. These are much livelier, friendlier affairs than the discos. Look for posters advertising them.

The main hotels are the focus of the nightlife for tourists. There are discos every other night and most of the large hotels put on séga shows once a week.

Next to the Pirates Arms in Victoria is the Seychelles Artistic Productions box office (☎ 322731), where you purchase tickets to shows by the National Cultural Troupe and visiting companies at the Polytechnic (Mont Fleuri) or Anse Royale theatres.

The Beau Vallon Bay, Sheraton and Plantation Club hotels each have a casino, for tourists only.

## THINGS TO BUY

Most of the general traders in Victoria are of Indian or Chinese descent. There are lots of traders named Chetty or Pilay.

### Paintings

Refer to the Culture section in the Seychelles – Facts about the Country chapter for more information about artists. You can visit the painter Michael Adams' studio gallery (☎ 371106) most times during the day when the family is at home (ring first to check). There is a large sign on the roadside before you leave the coast to go up the hill to Baie Lazare village. The Victoria-Takamaka bus will take you there and back.

In a less tropical and more personal vein

than Adams' work are the paintings of Italian artist Lorenzo Appiani. His studio (☎ 247 432) is at Mare Anglaise, near Beau Vallon.

Christine Harter is a Seychellois artist whose paintings you should look out for.

You can buy the artists' works from their studios, or at Christy's Art Gallery on de Quincy St. There are Christine Harter prints for sale in the Home Industries craft shop in Victoria.

### Batik

There are three places to buy batik around Bel Ombre, Mahé. On the Beau Vallon beach, near the pub/restaurant, is the studio of South African-born Ron Gerlach. On the road to Bel Ombre, past the entrance to the Beau Vallon Bay Hotel, is Mike Gouffe's studio. Up the hill towards the Auberge Sun Hotel, at Danzilles, is the Studio Oceana.

### Pottery

The crockery at the Pirates Arms restaurant in Victoria is made by Seypot, the Seychelles Potters' Cooperative. There are other examples in a display case at the restaurant and the crockery is sold by several shops. For the best prices and selection go to the pottery workshop itself (☎ 344080), which is at Les Mamelles, opposite the old Isle of Farquhar boat. You can get nice little pieces for as little as Rs 15. They also have a 'seconds' shelf.

### Clothes

There are a number of shops in Victoria, such as Sunstroke Design Studio, that sell fashionable beachwear and flimsy things with considerably more thought and flair to them than an 'I've been to Seychelles Too' T-shirt. They're also considerably more expensive.

Ron Gerlach's batik studio on the beach at Beau Vallon has dresses (Rs 250), shirts (Rs 175), sarongs (Rs 110) and other garments designed by him in silk or cotton. Gerlach came from South Africa to the Seychelles almost 20 years ago. You can watch him at work and see the dyed cloth hanging out to dry.

## Model Ships

There is only one workshop in the Seychelles compared to about a score on Mauritius, so the prices for a model Victory or Bounty are a lot dearer here. The factory, La Marine, is at La Plaine St André, near Anse aux Pins. It's run by Christine Diaz and the models range from Rs 3000 to Rs 25,000, about twice the price of the Mauritius ones. Make sure they are well packed, and check up on all possible freight and duty fees at the other end.

## Handicrafts

The Seychelles company for handicrafts development, Compagnie pour Le Developpement de L'Artisanat (CODEVAR) has set up a craft village at Anse aux Pins and a shop in Victoria. Please don't buy jewellery or knick-knacks, such as key rings, made from tortoiseshell – refer to the Conservation section about marine products in the introductory Facts for the Visitor chapter.

Across from the museum on Independence Ave is the Home Industries craft shop, which sells a variety of carved-wood and coconut crafts, prints, souvenirs and nature's little wonders.

Making boxes from local wood and shell is a new craft. Guy César, whose workshop is about half a km up Buxton Lane on the north side of Victoria, is an expert. He makes little cigarette and jewel boxes inlaid with mother-of-pearl, and made-to-order backgammon and domino sets.

There's also a small craft shop near Bernique Guest House on La Digue, which sells carved wooden sculptures suitable for hanging on walls for between Rs 250 and Rs 300.

## Stamps

The stamp tradition of the Seychelles, as in Mauritius, is still healthy, with a variety of new colourful issues released regularly to commemorate everything from the Pope's visit to the coco de mer nut. There's nothing quite as rare as the Mauritian Blue, but most of the early Seychelles stamps are valuable collector's pieces. There is a special counter for philately sales, including first-day covers, at the main post office in Victoria.

## Coco de Mer Nuts

You can read more about this famous nut of nuts in the Vallée de Mai section of the Praslin Island chapter. But in case you don't know much about the nuts and are confronted with an assortment of 'buttocks' on the tourist souvenir stalls in Victoria, here are a few tips about buying.

The best place to buy coco de mer nuts is at the Forestry Division store on the road up to the Vallée de Mai from Baie Ste Anne, Praslin. Only the female nuts take the erotic shape most buyers are after. The male nuts are (appropriately) a bit more phallic! They are all in their natural, dirty, husky state from the store and you have to clean and polish them yourselves. They each cost around Rs 450 whether they are big, small, hairy or bald, rotund or oblong. This compares to the Rs 600 to Rs 800 you'll pay at the tourist shops.

When you buy here, you are given an export permit, which is a must. This is to save any unscrupulous sale and exploitation of the rare coconut. Your purchase may be confiscated at the airport if you don't have a permit.

Authorised sellers should also issue a receipt. The nuts are extremely heavy in their natural state, so be prepared for baggage problems. The 'processed' souvenir nuts are polished, lacquered and hollowed out and often aren't coco de mer at all. The miniature ones certainly are not.

Coco de Mer Nuts

## Spices & Tea

The Home Industries craft shop and some other general stores sell packets of vanilla, patchouli, cinnamon leaf, nutmeg, other spices and tea. Seychelles tea comes in several flavours. You can also get it from the lofty tea factory and restaurant on the Sans Souci road between Victoria and Port Glaud.

## Souvenirs

There is a cluster of souvenir stalls opposite the post office in the centre of Victoria and countless shops dotted around the three main islands. It's a shame to deny the Créole traders a living, but read the Conservation section about marine products in the introductory Facts for the Visitor chapter before contemplating going back home with a set of shark dentures, a sprig or two of coral, fishbone personal adornments and a crustacean work of art that looks better in the sea than on your mantelpiece. As for walking sticks made out of sharks' backbones...well, there's no accounting for tastes. The palm frond hats-and-mats business has been slow to take off here.

# Getting There & Away

## AIR

The number of airlines flying to the Seychelles has increased during the 1990s in line with the upturn in tourism.

The regulars are Air France, British Airways, Kenya Airways, Air Seychelles and Aeroflot. In addition, there are chartered flights from Europe about once a week during the high season, mainly from Italy.

### To/From the UK & Europe

Most tourists arrive on hotel-flight package holidays from Europe.

The cheapest advance purchase fare from London to the Seychelles on British Airways costs UK£674. However, package deals for seven nights begin at UK£730. These can be extended to take in Mauritius and Kenya. On Air Seychelles the advance purchase fare from London is Rs 7093 (around UK£780). Aeroflot is cheaper (Rs 6400), although you may have to suffer a day or two in Moscow and do without an in-flight movie and other frills.

If direct flights from Europe are full, visitors may be re-routed via Nairobi.

### To/From Mauritius & Réunion

There are no cheap return flight deals from the Seychelles to Réunion or Mauritius and vice versa. You would be better off taking the Seychelles as a stopover en route from Europe to Mauritius or other countries.

## SEA

Cruise liners regularly call into Victoria, but there are no passenger services directly to the Seychelles. Plenty of yachts visit during the cruising season from April to October.

If you do arrive by yacht, you must wait off Victoria lighthouse, switch to VHF Channel 16 and wait for a customs and health clearance to proceed to the inner harbour. You are given a two-week visa. The authorities will permit pets only if they are kept on board. Any firearms or spearguns must be handed over for safekeeping, to be collected on leaving. Don't make the mistake of trying to bribe officials.

If you want to leave the Seychelles by yacht, there are a few each year looking for crew members. Check the notice board at the Yacht Club in Victoria.

## TOURS

Seychelles tourist offices can supply lists of international tour operators, of which there are many.

## LEAVING THE SEYCHELLES

The departure tax is reportedly Rs 100. At the time of research there were plans to introduce a 'green tax'.

Top: La Brulée, Mahé, Seychelles (DS)
Bottom: Anse Source d'Argent, La Digue, Seychelles (RS)

Top: Central Victoria, Mahé, Seychelles (RS)
BottomLeft: Maritime porker feeling sick as a pig, Seychelles (RS)
Bottom Right: Impending rainstorm, Baie Ste Anne, Praslin, Seychelles (RS)

# Getting Around

## AIR

### Local Air Services

Air Seychelles (☎ 373101) takes care of all inter-island flights operating out of Mahé International Airport. There are regular flights only to Praslin, Frégate, Desroches, Bird and Denis islands.

Air Seychelles puts on extra flights to meet demand and runs charter flights to D'Arros Island in the Amirantes group. It also provides 30 minute sightseeing tours for Rs 250 per person.

There are airstrips on the outer islands of Marie-Louise, Coétivy and Île Plate, as well as on Farquhar, Assomption and Cosmolédo atolls. Flights with turbo-prop aircraft are operated by the Islands Development Company (IDC) (☎ 224640).

The Aero Club (☎ 376520) at the international airport on Mahé caters for people who wish to charter planes or learn to fly.

Check-in time is 30 minutes before departure and the usual luggage limit is 10 kg, but the rules may be stretched if you are connecting with an international flight.

Bookings can be made at the office in Victoria House by the clock tower in Victoria. The planes are 20-seat Twin Otters, nine-seat Britten-Norman Islanders and 17-seat Trislander aircraft. The following sections deal with routes and return fares.

**Mahé to/from Praslin** There are frequent daily flights. The 15 minute trip costs Rs 340.

**Mahé to/from Frégate** There are flights twice daily (except Thursday & Saturday). The trip takes 15 minutes and a return ticket costs Rs 410.

**Mahé to/from Desroches** There are flights three times a week. The trip takes one hour. Only excursion packages are available for a minimum of two nights, including the flights and full board, for Rs 2339 per person.

**Mahé to/from Bird Island** There are daily flights, but bookings can only be made locally. The trip takes 30 minutes. Only excursion packages are available for a minimum of one night, including the flights and full board, for Rs 990 per person.

**Mahé to/from Denis Island** Only excursion packages are available for a minimum of three nights, including the flights (flight time 25 minutes) and full board, for Rs 4211 per person. However, it is possible on a last-minute basis – subject to availability – to book for just one or two nights at a price per person of Rs 2130/3170.

## BUS

An extensive bus service operates throughout Mahé. A limited service operates on Praslin. The fleet consists of small Italian Iveco buses, which fill up quickly at the terminus in Victoria and are often difficult to board at other stops in town. It is always best to board at the bus station if you can. Some conductors allow standing room, others don't.

The minimum fare is Rs 2 and the maximum Rs 5. When you want to get off you shout *Dévant!* Nothing else. 'Stop', 'Whoa' or 'Arrêtez' don't work. If the driver doesn't hear you, make sure the conductor does. People generally don't stand up until the bus comes to a halt. On Mahé and Praslin the bus stops have signs and there are also markings on the road.

There are 26 routes on Mahé. The main ones are Victoria-Anse aux Pins, Victoria-Beau Vallon and Victoria-Les Mamelles. There's a bus each hour on most routes from early morning until around 7 pm. Timetables and maps of each route are posted at the central bus park in Victoria.

A night service operates in both directions on the Victoria, Anse aux Pins, Takamaka, Port Glaud, Victoria circuit, and the Victoria, Anse Étoile, Glacis, Beau Vallon, Bel

Ombre, Victoria circuit from 8 pm until around midnight.

On Praslin, the basic route is from Anse Boudin to Anse Kerlan (via Anse Volbert, Baie Ste Anne and Grande Anse). Buses run each direction every hour from 6 am to 5.30 pm. Some go via Anse Consolation and others via the Vallée de Mai. Fares range between Rs 2 and Rs 4. Unlike those on Mahé, the Praslin buses are rarely full.

## TAXI

The taxi fares on Mahé and Praslin are set by the government. On Mahé you pay Rs 15 for the first km and Rs 3.80 for each additional km regardless of the number of passengers. Between 8 pm and 6 am, the charge is Rs 16 for the first km, then Rs 4.20 for each additional km. There is also a charge of Rs 11 for each 15 minutes of waiting time and drivers can also charge Rs 5 for each major piece of luggage and for the outward journey to a pick-up point.

Some examples of day/night fares are: Victoria to airport Rs 55/60, Victoria to Beau Vallon Rs 35/40, Victoria to Baie Lazare Rs 115/130 and airport to Grande Anse Rs 85/90.

Alternatively, you can hire a taxi for a set period and arrange a fee with the driver. If you want to query any fare, get a receipt from the driver and contact either the Director of Land Transport (☎ 376247), PO Box 47, Victoria, or the head of the Taxi Operators' Association (☎ 323895), Olivier Maradam St (near the Catholic cathedral), Victoria.

On Praslin, the taxis cost Rs 18 (Rs 19 at night) for the first km, and Rs 4.50 for each additional km (Rs 5 at night). Luggage and waiting charges are the same as on Mahé. Therefore, from the Baie Ste Anne jetty to the Paradise Sun Hotel at Anse Volbert is Rs 51 during the day and Rs 61 at night; from the airport to Vallée de Mai is Rs 45; and from Baie Ste Anne jetty to Baie Ste Anne village is Rs 24.

There is one taxi on La Digue, where the prices are the same as on Praslin.

## CAR & MOTORBIKE

Most of the road network on Mahé is sealed and in good shape. The worry is not the road surface so much as the bends and the speed at which some drivers take them. On Praslin, most of the major roads are surfaced, but on La Digue or the other islands none of them are.

### Road Safety

When driving, do so on the left, the British way, and beware of drivers with fast cars and slow brains – especially late on Friday and Saturday nights. The speed limit is supposed to be 65 km in Victoria and villages, but no-one sticks to it. Driving at night you may be startled by running over something that explodes like a pistol shot. Giant African snails, imported by the French, are the cause of the noise.

On Mahé, petrol stations are found in Victoria: opposite the airport; at Anse Royale (opposite Kaz Kreol restaurant); Beau Vallon and the Sheraton Hotel (Port Glaud).

On Praslin they're only found at Baie Ste Anne and Grande Anse. Petrol costs Rs 6.5 a litre. As a rough guide for Mini Moke petrol consumption and reasonable mileage, reckon on eight litres and 140 km a day.

### Car Rental

Mini Mokes are *the* hire cars in the Seychelles. 'Moking is not a wealth hazard' is the motto of one car hire firm. But at more than Rs 300 a day, I'm afraid it is.

Most of the Mokes have some sort of mechanical defect. Make sure that basic essentials such as brakes, steering, gears, lights, etc actually work – and don't be shy about asking for something to be fixed or to have the car replaced with another one...which might at least have more acceptable foibles!

Mokes are built for outdoor driving and if you travel in one, you should be prepared to welcome the elements inside. Those little plastic covers that purport to keep the rain out are no match for a thunderous downpour, particularly if a sidewind neatly whips it all through one side of the car and out the other – soaking the occupants en route. During very humid spells, it's really quite refreshing!

We recommend that you *never* leave any valuables unattended in your vehicle. Mokes have a useless trunk box (use your own padlock) and anything left inside the vehicle is clearly an easy target for petty theft.

Make certain you have the hire company's out-of-office hours telephone number in case of a breakdown.

There are more than 25 car hire companies, all about the same size and charging roughly the same prices. The government limits each firm to a certain number of vehicles, so none of the companies gets too big. Six of the companies are represented on Praslin.

The standard daily rate for a Moke is Rs 300 plus Rs 40 for insurance. There is no per km rate. The daily rate is reduced the longer you hire the car. You can get it down to Rs 250 or even Rs 200 per day if you rent for three days or more, and most companies will make offers if you approach them individually. The best place to 'bargain' is at the temporary car hire counters in the Beau Vallon Bay Hotel, which are open to meet international flights.

After the Moke, Suzuki open jeeps are the most popular vehicles and not much more expensive at Rs 325. Sedan cars are available at Rs 350 or Rs 375 (with air-con), as are chauffeur-driven vehicles for around Rs 180/700 per hour/day inclusive.

The most reliable and one of the oldest hire firms is Victoria Car Hire (☎ 376314), near the Reef Hotel at Anse aux Pins. Also good is M S Car Rental (☎ 376522), at Le Cap. The manager, Mark Albert, is very helpful.

The carelessly named RAM Car Hire (☎ 323443) is known to provide special reductions, particularly if you take a Moke for a week. The office is at English River on the coast road, just north of Victoria. Jean's Car Hire (☎ 322278), at St Louis on the Victoria-Beau Vallon road, has also been recommended. Avis and Hertz are both represented but seem to be no different or better than the others.

On Praslin, try Karl d'Unienville's Prestige Car Hire (☎ 233226) at Grande Anse. Mr d'Unienville is a local 'character' and name-dropper extraordinaire. He has hired cars to people such as Roman Polanski, Richard Chamberlain, Michel Platini and Walter Matthau, to name a few.

### Motorbike

There is no official motorcycle or moped hire in the Seychelles. It is forbidden by the tourist board for safety reasons. When you see the locals whizzing about on the narrow twisting roads, you'll appreciate why. If you still want to pursue the matter, try St Louis Motors (☎ 322270) or Low Hong (☎ 322 278) both in St Louis.

### BICYCLE

There are only a couple of places to arrange bicycle hire on Mahé, but lots on Praslin and La Digue. See individual island chapters for details.

If you are a keen cyclist, don't bring your bike to the Seychelles. One poor tourist had his bike impounded by customs for most of his stay while he waited to get a licence and a bell!

### HITCHING

It's OK to hitch on Mahé or Praslin. You'll have few problems getting a lift from local drivers. If you have hired a car, be sure to return the favour. Again, beware of walking on the narrow roads after dark.

### BOAT
#### Inter-Island Ferries

Schooner ferries run regularly between Mahé, Praslin and La Digue. As well as passengers, they carry supplies and mail for the islands. For all other islands you have to charter a boat, take tours or hitch a ride on a government vessel or fishing boat. The schooners are fast and elegant, but you can easily get wet and/or seasick. So take seasickness pills and don't wear your best clothes.

**Mahé to Praslin** There are three schooners sailing Monday to Friday on the Mahé-Praslin route. The trip takes three hours, depending on sea conditions, and the one-way fare is Rs 50. If you're leaving from Praslin or La Digue, buy your ticket on the boat. There are no booking arrangements – just be there on time.

*La Belle Praslinoise* sails from Praslin to Mahé on Monday, Wednesday and Friday, departing at 5.30 am. The return trip from Mahé is made on the same days at 11 am.

*Cousin* sails from Praslin to Mahé at 5.30 am on Monday, and at 6 am on Tuesday, Thursday and Wednesday. It returns from Mahé at noon on Tuesday and Thursday, and at 1 pm on Monday and Wednesday.

*La Bellone* sails from Praslin at 5.30 am on Monday only. It returns from Mahé at 11 am.

On Praslin, the schooners usually sail to and from the Baie Ste Anne jetty – tides permitting, the Grande Anse jetty may also be used.

In Victoria tickets are available at the ferry pier, north of Independence Ave, at 9.30 am on the morning you leave. If it's expected to be a busy day, get there early or try to book the day before. Also, board early to make sure of a good seat. Check to see if there's a choice of schooners going to Baie Ste Anne or Grande Anse and take the one which is closer to your booked or intended accommodation.

**Mahé to La Digue** There is one schooner, *La Belle Edma*, operating Monday to Friday between Mahé and La Digue. The schooner departs from La Digue at 6 am and returns from Mahé at 1 pm (noon on Tuesday and Thursday). The journey takes 3¼ hours and the one-way fare is Rs 50.

Between the months of May and October this route is notorious for heaving even the most travel-hardened stomachs – the soft option is to fly to Praslin and take the calmer, shorter boat ride from there.

**Praslin to La Digue** Two schooners, *Silhouette* and *Lady Mary* run daily (except Sunday) for the 30 minute trip between Praslin and La Digue. The ticket costs Rs 30.

On Monday and Saturday there are departures from Praslin at 7 am and 5 pm; and from La Digue at 7.30 am and 5.30 pm. On Wednesday there are departures from Praslin/La Digue at 9.30/10 am; on Thursday from Praslin/La Digue at 10.30/11 am; and on Friday from Praslin/La Digue at 2.30/3.30 pm.

### Charters

The Marine Charter Association (☎ 322126; fax 224679), beside the Yacht Club in Victoria, has about 30 members who offer a variety of boats for hire for a variety of purposes and at a variety of high prices. There are schooners, yachts, launches and motor cruisers for cruising, ferrying, fishing and diving. The best months for cruising are April and October. The worst are January, July and August.

Most of the boat owners are English, Australian and South African. They charge around Rs 3000 per day for the vessel on overnight trips, or around Rs 375 per person for a day trip with a minimum of six people. They will drop the rates during quiet periods.

One of the old salts of the yacht club is an Australian known as Brownie. He has a 24 metre ocean cruiser called *My Way* which can take up to 40 people on a day trip or 10 people on an overnight trip. For an overnight trip with 10 persons, he charges Rs 7000.

South African Brian Laaks runs a large catamaran called *Encounter* (which was used in the film *Castaways*). He charges Rs 375 per person (minimum six, maximum 12 persons) for a day trip; and Rs 3000 per day for a group of up to four persons.

There is a 1936 Dutch-built trawler which has been converted into a brigantine schooner called the *Seypirate*. She does evening, supper and cocktail sails around the Ste Anne Marine National Park from 5 to 11 pm. Make bookings through Mason's Travel (☎ 322-642).

The *Laura B* does day trips for Rs 6000

(maximum 35 persons); excursions to the inner islands for Rs 8000 per day (maximum eight); and long range trips to Amirantes and Aldabra for Rs 10,000 (maximum eight) per day.

On Praslin, Michel Gardette (☎ 233972; fax 233015) is a specialist diving operator and marine archaeologist who runs King Bambo Charters & Aqua Diving Services. Michel can arrange trips on his catamaran to the outer islands, Amirantes, and Aldabra. Clients can choose to save time by flying to Assomption Island and then sailing and diving in the region before flying back to Mahé. A maximum of eight persons can specially charter the presidential plane for Rs 35,000/110,000 one-way/return.

Michel is also a qualified PADI diving instructor and offers a full 21-day sailing trip to Amirantes, Aldabra, and the Outer Islands for Rs 80,000 (maximum six persons), including full board and two dives per day, but excluding drinks.

There are also one or two independent boat operators, usually Seychellois, who pick up charters where they can. A number of small boat owners, attached to various hotels, run 'taxi' services to nearby islands such as Silhouette, Cerf, Moyenne, and Thérèse islands (from Mahé); and to Curieuse, Cousin, Coco and Felicité (from Praslin and La Digue). Alternatively, you can approach local fishermen at Bel Ombre, Port Glaud, Baie Ste Anne, etc and negotiate a price.

### Outer Island Services

Schooners take supplies to the outer islands every few months, but they do not take passengers. You may be able to get a berth as a paying or nonpaying crew member. Contact the skippers at the ferry piers at Victoria, Praslin and La Digue.

The Islands Development Corporation (☎ 224640) in New Port, Victoria, also runs a ship called the *Argo* to the Aldabra group and other islands en route; it carries government workers and scientists. To go, you need permission from the Ministry of National Development at Independence House, Victoria.

### WALKING

Because the islands are small and the roads little travelled (away from North Mahé), walking is a pleasurable activity just about anywhere in the Seychelles and there are still lots of wild hilly and mountainous areas where you can escape the crowds, appreciate the islands' natural scenery and enjoy some of the alternatives to beach-oriented activities.

To facilitate things, local naturalist Katy Beaver, working in conjunction with the Ministry of Tourism and Transport, has come up with a series of hiking guides to interpretive nature trails on Mahé and La Digue. These are available at the tourist office in Victoria for Rs 10 each, and at several hotel bookshops for a bit more.

None of the routes is more than a few km, so you won't need to bring cooking or camping equipment, but you should carry energy-rich snacks and more water than you expect to need; you'll sweat buckets climbing in this humidity. Also, carry a sun block and a hat or other head covering as protection from the equatorial sun. If you have a camera or other valuables, place them in a waterproof container to protect them from the frequent tropical downpours which occur throughout the year. Good treaded footwear is also essential since the almost perpetually muddy mountain tracks turn to ski slopes after rain.

From the environmental point of view, keep to the trail as much as possible; carry out all your rubbish; don't pick or damage plants; and don't try to capture or worry wild creatures (although it's difficult to avoid the immense palm spiders which booby trap everything in the forest; you'll constantly be picking sticky silk out of your nose and eyes!).

If you prefer to try a guided walk, get in touch with local mountain guide Basil Beaudouin (☎ 241790) who leads hiking and birdwatching trips of varying difficulties into the Mahé backcountry, including

Copolia, Morne Seychelloise National Park, Les Trois Frères, Congo Rouge and Anse Major. These walks take anywhere from two to eight hours and cost an average of Rs 200 per person.

## LOCAL TRANSPORT
### To/From the Airport
A taxi to Victoria from the airport costs between Rs 40 and Rs 50. From Beau Vallon to the airport, expect to pay Rs 85. Large pieces of luggage incur an extra charge of Rs 5. If you arrive during the day and have no mobility problems with your luggage, there is a bus stand about 20 metres away, directly opposite the airport gates near the petrol station. Buses run about every hour between 6 am and 7.30 pm. The fare to Victoria is Rs 3.

### Ox Cart
Only available on La Digue, these are a bit of hype for the tourist image and photo opportunities, on the same level as donkey rides at the beach, but they're not part of everyday life.

Michelin runs the ox carts and charges Rs 15 for one short trip, say from the pier to the Island Lodge. Tours of the island lasting two to three hours cost Rs 250 for two to four people. There are also trips from the Island Lodge at 9.30 am and 3.30 pm for Rs 25.

## TOURS
Travel Services Seychelles – (TSS), Mason's Travel, and the National Travel Agency (NTA) run extensive tour programmes involving flights, coaches, boats and accommodation. Most tours include a guide, lunch, entrance fees and transfer to and from your hotel. These tour operators cater for most hotel residents, but some hotels, such as the Paradise Sun on Praslin, also run their own tours.

The cheapest and perhaps most popular tours are the glass-bottom boat trips around the Ste Anne Marine National Park off Vic-

toria, which run most days of the week, but to a different island each day. A TSS full day excursion with lunch on Cerf or Round Island includes a chance to go swimming and snorkelling and costs Rs 360/190 per adult/child.

If you contact Patrick at the Marine Charter Association (☎ 322126; fax 224679) you can arrange to charter a small boat for almost half the price and with the added advantage of a small group – a minimum of two persons – whilst the group tours may have as many as 40 passengers on a glass-bottom boat. A half day trip costs Rs 125 per person, a full day costs Rs 175 per person, including snorkelling equipment, but excluding lunch.

TSS bus tours of Mahé cost Rs 190 for a full day. An NTA day trip by boat to Praslin and La Digue is Rs 570 – more if you complete the outward or return journey by air. Trips can also be arranged to Silhouette (Rs 475 per person), Bird (Rs 990 per person, including overnight stay), Frégate (Rs 595 per person), Cousin (Rs 785 per person), and Aride (only from April to October).

### Tour Operators
The main tour operators and travel agents in the Seychelles are all based in Victoria:

Travel Services Seychelles
　　Victoria House (☎ 322414; fax 321366)
National Travel Agency
　　Kingsgate House (☎ 224900; fax 225111)
Mason's Travel
　　Revolution Ave (☎ 322642; fax 225273)
Bunson Travel Ltd
　　Revolution Ave (☎ 322682)

TSS, NTA and Mason's are the largest operators; independent tourists or travellers use them mainly to arrange trips to the smaller islands and snorkelling tours of the Ste Anne Marine National Park. Otherwise, these operators are busy with hotel package tourists.

# Mahé

Mahé was named by the French in honour of the 18th-century governor of Mauritius, Mahé de Labourdonnais, and is by far the largest of the Seychelles' islands. It is home to the country's capital, Victoria (no prizes for guessing who that was named after), and about 88% of the country's 70,000 people. It is 27 km long and between three and eight km wide, so you can motor around it easily in a day.

A range of granite peaks runs through the centre of the island from north to south. The highest peaks are in the north of the island and include Morne Seychellois (905 metres), which overlooks Victoria.

About 85% of the country's tourist accommodation and restaurants are on Mahé, so many visitors leave without visiting any of the other quieter, less developed islands.

Not that Mahé is overcrowded. It's top-heavy to the north-east around Victoria, but the further south and west you go the more peaceful it becomes. If you want to get away from everybody, just head into the hills. There are also good beaches and snorkelling points evenly spread around the coast. Beau Vallon is the busiest and one of the largest beaches, although not the best.

Moving south from the centre of Victoria along the coast road, you pass through the suburbs of Le Chantier, Mont Fleuri, Plaisance and Mamelles.

From this route, two main roads head across the mountains to the west coast. The first is the Sans Souci or Forêt Noire road across to Port Glaud, which goes through the districts of Bel Eau, Bel Air and Hermitage before coming to Sans Souci. The second hill road is the La Misère route across to Grande Anse. It begins at Plaisance and goes through the La Louise district of Victoria.

The route north out of Victoria passes through the districts of English River and Union Vale. The steep winding road leading directly west out of the centre of Victoria to Beau Vallon and Bel Ombre goes via the hill district of St Louis. The other hill routes out of town go to Mont Buxton and Belonie.

The international airport is 10 km southeast of Victoria.

## VICTORIA

About 27,000 people live in Victoria, the only major port in the Seychelles. As it's one of the world's smallest capital cities, you should find it difficult to get lost.

Victoria is the only 'town' in the country; the rest of the settlements are 'villages'. The town centre is marked by the clock tower or *l'horloge*, a replica of the clock tower on London's Vauxhall Bridge, brought to Victoria in 1903 when the Seychelles became a crown colony. The islanders bought it as a memorial to Queen Victoria.

The courthouse and post office stand solid and untouched since colonial days, although most of the streets emanating from the clock have been rebuilt over the past 20 years, giving the centre a clean and modern look. There are no giant office blocks or other ugly complexes.

Francis Rachel St, named after one of the victims, or 'martyrs', of the 1977 coup, and Albert St (named after Victoria's hubbie rather than President France-Albert René) still contain a few old houses and shops, but barely enough to give Victoria any real character.

According to historians and writers, Victoria was never a particularly pleasant place. All of them said it had little character and some called it a shanty slum. So today's Victoria is probably the nicest it's ever been.

### Information

**Tourist Office** The tourist office (☎ 225333) on Independence Ave has a selection of brochures and limited information for visitors. If you're interested in hiking, this is the place to stock up on the excellent guides for individual routes.

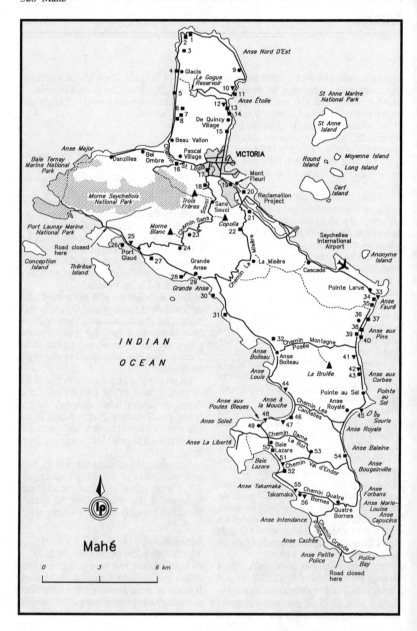

Mahé

■ PLACES TO STAY

| | |
|---|---|
| 1 | North Point Guesthouse |
| 2 | Chez Jean Guesthouse |
| 3 | Vista Bay Club Hotel & Danielle's Restaurant |
| 4 | Sunset Beach Hotel |
| 5 | Northolme Hotel |
| 6 | Pti Payot Guesthouse |
| 7 | Vacoa Village |
| 8 | Panorama Guesthouse |
| 11 | Manresa Guesthouse |
| 13 | Calypha Guesthouse |
| 14 | Maxim's Jade House Guesthouse |
| 15 | Sea Breeze Guesthouse |
| 16 | Le Niol Guesthouse |
| 17 | Bel Air Guesthouse |
| 18 | Mountain Rise Hotel |
| 19 | Sunrise Guesthouse |
| 20 | Harbour View Guesthouse |
| 21 | Auberge Louis XVII & La Suisse Restaurant |
| 22 | La Louise Lodge |
| 26 | L'Islette Guesthouse |
| 27 | Seychelles Sheraton Hotel |
| 28 | Equator Hotel |
| 30 | Le Meridien Barbarons Beach Hotel |
| 31 | Château d'Eau Guesthouse |
| 32 | Auberge d'Anse Boileau |
| 34 | Carefree Guesthouse |
| 35 | La Retraite Guesthouse |
| 37 | Reef Golf Club Hotel |
| 38 | Lalla Panzi Guesthouse |
| 39 | La Roussette Guesthouse |
| 40 | Casuarina Beach Hotel |
| 46 | Blue Lagoon Self-Catering Bungalows |
| 50 | Plantation Club Hotel |
| 52 | Lazare Picault Guesthouse |
| 54 | Residence Bougainville |

▼ PLACES TO EAT

| | |
|---|---|
| 10 | Étoile de Mer Restaurant |
| 12 | Kyoto Restaurant |
| 25 | Sundown Restaurant |
| 29 | Marie Galante Restaurant |
| 33 | Katiolo Restaurant & Discotheque |
| 41 | Village Artisanal & Pomme Cannelle Restaurant |
| 42 | Ty-Foo Restaurant |
| 44 | Oscar Au Capitaine Rouge |
| 45 | Kaz Kreol Restaurant |
| 47 | Anchor Café & Pizza |
| 48 | La Sirène Restaurant |
| 51 | Anse Gaulettes Restaurant |
| 55 | Chez Batiste Restaurant |
| 56 | Le Reduit Restaurant |

OTHER

| | |
|---|---|
| 9 | Kreol Fleurage |
| 23 | Mission Lodge Ruins & Viewpoint |
| 24 | Tea Factory |
| 36 | Golf Course |
| 43 | La Marine Model Boats |
| 49 | Michael Adams Studio |
| 53 | Val d'Andorre Pottery |

**Money** Victoria is well endowed with banks, including the Seychelles Savings Bank, Barclays Bank, Banque Française Commerciale, Bank of Baroda, Habib Bank and Standard Bank.

The banks here are open Monday to Friday from 8.30 am to 12.30 pm and 2 to 3.30 pm, and on Saturdays from 8.30 to 11.30 am.

**Post** The main post office in Victoria is open Monday to Friday from 8 am to 4 pm and on Saturdays from 8 am to noon.

**Telephones** The Cable & Wireless office on Francis Rachel St is open 24 hours a day for cable, fax, telex, and phone services.

**Airlines** The Air Seychelles office (☎ 321548) is in Victoria House, near the clock tower. British Airways (☎ 224910) is at the National Travel Agency, Kingsgate House, and Air France is at the Travel Services Seychelles office (☎ 322414), also in Victoria House. Aeroflot (☎ 225005) has an office in the Pirates Arms arcade on Independence Ave and Kenya Airways (☎ 322989) is on Revolution Ave.

### National Museum

The National Museum is next to the post office, right in the heart of town. It is open Monday to Friday from 9 am to 5 pm and on

Saturdays from 9 am to noon. Admission is free.

At the entrance to the museum is the Stone of Possession, laid in 1756 by Corneille Nicolas Morphey to commemorate French possession of the islands. Inside are some unusual nature exhibits, including bones of the extinct Seychelles crocodile, the giant coconut or robber crabs (see Aldabra section) and some very dried-out grotesque fish; there's also a grossly deformed piglet in a jar – it seems to have a trunk like an elephant. There are shells, butterflies, stuffed birds, crabs, corals, urchins, turtles, centipedes and scorpions.

Other displays include wreckage of a ship which came to grief off the Amirantes in 1570; an American whaler sunk in 1828; a captured WW I German machine gun and helmet; a voodoo or gris-gris display of letters, cards, dominoes, seeds, potions, statues and hair; and an amazing musical contraption called a *bombe*.

### Sir Selwyn Clarke Market
Despite what the tourist brochures say, the central market is not the bustling, colourful place it used to be. Produce and prices are controlled by the Seychelles Marketing Board and most people buy from the SMB store. All you'll find in it are bus loads of tourists figuring out how best to spend the hour they've been allotted. The produce also attracts flocks of cattle egrets, known to locals as Madame Paton, which perch on the stalls and pick off unattended morsels.

The market was previously known as Sir Selwyn Clarke Market after perhaps the best remembered of the British governors.

### State House
You can't visit the former British governors' residence, now the offices of the president, unless you have government permission. Enquire at the entrance gate guard post.

Intriguingly, it is said to have been designed by the wife of a governor early this century who, after construction had begun, discovered she had forgotten to put any staircases in the plan!

The 'great capitulator', Le Chevalier Jean Baptiste Queau de Quinssy (or De Quincy), is buried in the grounds. He arrived in 1794 as the French governor and remained in charge through British occupation until he died in 1827.

### Botanic Gardens
The gardens are next to the hospital, just past Le Chantier roundabout and the Sans Souci road exit, at the south end of town. They are open daily and are highly recommended for short and shady walks among a variety of native and introduced trees.

Some of the trees are identified by discs, most are not. Among those identified are elephant apple trees (from Malaysia), the Rose of Venezuela, pandanus, palmiste palms and cocos de mer from Praslin.

Within the gardens is a cafeteria, a pen of giant tortoises, an orchid garden and a boutique. There is also a restaurant called Le Sapin.

Entrance to the gardens as a whole is free, but the orchid garden costs Rs 10. It is open daily from 9 am to 6 pm and contains other tropical plants as well as orchids, whose blooms are staggered throughout the year. The best time to visit is between June and August and the worst is during December and January, when the blossoms are hammered by heavy rains.

### Bel Air Cemetery
You'll find the cemetery at the beginning of the Sans Souci road in Bel Air, not by spotting the gravestones, but by the washing laid out to dry upon them and the surrounding overgrown grass. The cemetery, said to be the first on the islands, is not a standard tourist attraction and has been neglected by authorities.

It is said to contain the grave of a teenage Seychellois giant who was over three metres tall. His memorial stone is the obelisk of the same height. He was gentle and handy for carrying fishing pirogues to and from the water, but the local people feared him and believed he would grow bigger and terrorise the island. He was poisoned in the 1870s, so the story goes. If only there had been a basketball team.

The pirate Jean François Hodoul is also said to be buried here among the remains of the family tombs on the higher level of the cemetery. But the stones are so old and worn that no inscriptions are legible.

## SPUP Museum

If you are intrigued by the Seychelles' perpetual celebration of 'revolution' and 'liberation', pop into the Seychelles People's United Party (SPUP) headquarters and museum on Francis Rachel St. There is an exhibition of photographs covering the history of the party since it was founded by René in 1964. Exhibits include guns and riot shields used to put down early demonstrations and the suitcases (yes, suitcases!) used in the 1977 coup to overthrow President Mancham. The SPUP has now been replaced by the Seychelles People's Progressive Front (SPPF).

## La Bastille

This old house at Union Vale, on the outskirts of Victoria, is not a prison. It currently houses the National Archives & Museum, but there are plans to move in early 1994 to larger premises at the new National Library site on Francis Rachel St. The archives contain ancient documents of the Seychelles and newspaper files, as well as a library of reference books and the statue of Queen Victoria which used to stand outside the courts. Call Alain Lucas on ☎ 321931 or 321330 if you have a special interest you'd like to follow up.

## Cappucin Friary

The friary next to the cathedral on the north side of town was built in 1933 according to a Portuguese design. It is home to several aged friars who are members of a Swiss order. They used to run the mission school across the road. The priests are still allowed into primary schools to give lessons and talks, but not into secondary schools.

## Cathedral of the Immaculate Conception

The Roman Catholic cathedral next to the friary is more to be heard than seen. It has a clock which chimes twice for every hour and has always done so. It could be a mistake which was never rectified. Or perhaps it was designed that way for the local population: the first chimes woke them up and the repetition told them what time it was. There is also the theory that certain Swiss clocks strike the time twice in order to provide a double check for busy business people.

## Monuments

The new 'revolutionary' sculptures are described in the Culture section in the Seychelles – Facts about the Country chapter. As for the old ones, there aren't many left. A statue of Pierre Poivre (Peter Pepper) stands outside the courthouse opposite the post office. Poivre introduced spices to Mauritius and the Seychelles back in the 18th century. The bust of Queen Victoria is kept in the National Archives building, La Bastille, at Union Vale.

## Places to Stay

**Guesthouses** There are several guesthouses in the suburbs, none near the town centre. All rates include breakfast and a room with a bathroom, as per tourist board regulations. Some offer seasonal rates and some take credit cards; most offer laundry services.

Among the best is *La Louise Lodge* (☎ 344349), formerly the Eureka Relais des Îles at La Louise, run by Rose Marie and France Adrienne. The house is a bit of a climb up La Misère hill, three km from Victoria, but the four double bedrooms are modern and fully furnished. The rates are Rs 200/300 for a single/double, including breakfast, or Rs 275/400 for half board. There are views over Ste Anne marine park, but no patio from which to enjoy them.

Nearby in La Louise, is the grander and more expensive *Auberge Louis XVII* (☎ 344411; fax 344428). It has sea views, a swimming pool, bar lounge, wine cellar and

10 twin rooms. Single/double/triple rooms cost Rs 395/502/753, including breakfast; Rs 470/652/910 for half board; or Rs 545/802/1053 for full board.

The Auberge is named after the son of King Louis XVI and Queen Marie-Antoinette of France. Louis XVII was born in 1785 and is reputed to have escaped to the Seychelles during the French Revolution. The royalist governor was sympathetic to his plight and the refugee was able to live in Mahé under the assumed name of Poiret until his death in 1856, when his true identity was revealed.

High above Victoria, in the hills of Sans Souci, is *Mountain Rise Hotel* (☎ 225145; fax 225503) a recently renovated family mansion with superb views, cool breezes, a swimming pool, extensive gardens, organic fruits, and its own mountain water. The owners can arrange walks to Trois Frères, excursions to other parts of the island, and diving trips.

There are five large rooms, almost the size of a separate apartment, each furnished with antiques. Rates for a single/double/triple start at around Rs 380/550/710 (B&B) and Rs 467/800/1000 for half board. BBQs are

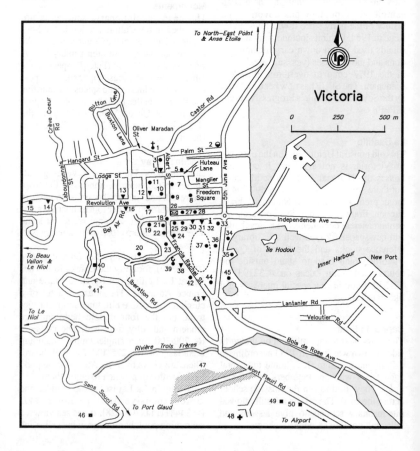

arranged on Friday night and for Sunday lunch.

Down on the coast road, in Mont Fleuri district, are the Beaufond Lane Relais des Îles, the Sunrise, and the Harbour View guesthouses.

The *Beaufond Lane Guest House* (☎ 322-408) has three air-conditioned double rooms for single/double Rs 225/300, including breakfast. Meals cost an additional Rs 60. The position near the main road is not the best, but it is close to the centre of town.

The *Sunrise Guest House* (☎ 224560) is run by the Chung Faye family. It has seven air-conditioned rooms for single/double

Rs 300/375 per night. Créole and Chinese meals cost Rs 75.

This is a very friendly place, long established as a favourite for visiting traders, expatriate employees and businessfolk, many of whom have interesting backgrounds. When we visited, the guests included a Belgian dentist, a Sri Lankan doctor, an Italian media advisor, a Chinese violin teacher, a family of French yachties, a North Korean construction crew, a Kenyan preacher and an Indian textile salesman.

The *Harbour View Guest House* (☎ 322-473) is on the sea wall, but swimming is out of the question. It has eight rooms for single/double Rs 320/450 per night. Meals cost Rs 70.

Behind the Marie Antoinette Restaurant on Serret Rd, off the road to Beau Vallon, is the *Hilltop Guest House* (☎ 323553) run by Fulbert Green. It has eight rooms, a bar and a terrace. A single/double/triple room costs Rs 250/350/500, including breakfast. Meals cost Rs 75 per person.

Behind State House, on the road to Bel Air and Sans Souci, is the *Pension Bel Air* (☎ 224416) – a favourite with resting aircrews. It is an old colonial house, built on a rise, with six rooms for single/double/triple Rs 430/580/750, including breakfast. It also has an annexe on the road to Beau Vallon with eight more rooms. Meals cost Rs 80 and the manager, Roland Rassool, organises fishing trips and loans snorkelling gear.

**Hotels** The first hotel in the Seychelles was the Equator, on what is now Francis Rachel St. It closed many years ago and none has replaced it in town.

**Apartment Rental** The only option close to Victoria is *Michel Holiday Appartements* (☎ 344540), between the Seypot pottery and the Seybrew brewery at Mamelles. There are 16 self-catering flats, but the location leaves a lot to be desired – they're too close to the road and town. Traffic is busy and there are no nearby beaches. A studio for two adults and two children costs Rs 2800 per week.

**Places to Eat**
**Budget End** Victoria is slightly better off than other areas for restaurants. It is the only place on the island for cheap eats.

*The* place to meet, see and be seen, if not to eat, is the *Pirates Arms* (☎ 225001) on Independence Ave. This open-fronted café/restaurant used to be a hotel and has been the centre of the island's social activity for many years.

The staff are friendly and efficient and the atmosphere is lively. It's a good place for a coffee, or a beer and sandwiches. More substantial lunches and dinners are available for between Rs 35 and Rs 90. The Pirates Arms

is not only convenient as a meeting place for coffee and snacks, it has good, modern and clean semipublic toilets to the rear of the arcade and restaurant. It's closed on Sunday.

*L'Amiral*, also on Independence Ave, is a quieter place with similar prices and menu options. It's open daily, except Sunday.

For inexpensive snacks, try the café at the Marine Charter Association.

There are several takeaway food shops in the centre of town where you can get fish and chips, sausage and chips, curry and rice, and a variety of other fried or curried foods for Rs 20; soft drinks and sweets are also available. Try *Bon Appetit* on Francis Rachel St or *Sandy's* on Revolution Ave.

In the walkway under Independence House, down the street from the Pirates Arms, a food counter does a busy lunchtime trade in hamburgers, samosas, sausage rolls, and ham, salad and cheese rolls, and soft drinks.

*Delite* on Market St, off Albert St, sells good ice cream.

**Speciality Restaurants** The place with the best reputation for food and location in Victoria, and in fact one of the best on the island, is the Créole restaurant *Marie Antoinette* (☎ 323942) in St Louis, on the main Victoria-Beau Vallon hill road. The building, a beautiful old Créole house set in lovely grounds, is worth visiting in itself.

Set meals here cost Rs 80, but make sure you do not book the same night as a tour party, otherwise you will get second-best service. The fish dishes are excellent. Parrotfish, tuna steaks and curries are all served as part of the menu, along with tec-tec soup. The restaurant is closed on Sundays. Otherwise it is open for lunch between noon and 3 pm and for dinner between 7 and 10 pm.

For Chinese food, there's *King Wah* (☎ 323658) on Benezet St. It is plain and the family often sits around empty tables chatting or making up takeaway boxes. You can get a three-course meal here for Rs 70. The main courses cost between Rs 35 and Rs 50 for good-size helpings.

Also highly recommended, providing you have transport, is the restaurant at the Mountain Rise Hotel (see Places to Stay). It is essential to phone in advance for a reservation. Créole and international dishes are served for lunch and dinner.

**Clubs** If you're going to be spending a lot of time in Victoria, it would be worth joining the *Yacht Club* (☎ 322362) at Rs 250 per month. (The fee is waived if you are already a member of an associated yacht club.) It's not posh – anyone can join and take advantage of the cheap menu. Breakfast, lunch and dinner are offered. Meals cost Rs 35. You can also get coffee, tea and snacks between meals.

Another club, for ex-servicemen, with a cafeteria that's cheap is the *Tobruk Club* (☎ 322475); it's on Freedom Square behind Independence Ave. Here you don't have to be a member. Sit down to fried fish or meat curry and have a beer. It is open for lunch only, from Monday to Saturday between 11 am and 3 pm. The hall also is rented out to various organisations for discos and dances. Both the hall and club come under the control of the Ministry of Social Services.

### Entertainment
See under Entertainment in the Seychelles – Facts for the Visitor chapter.

### Things to Buy
See under Things to Buy in the Seychelles – Facts for the Visitor chapter.

### Getting There & Away
For information on bus routes around Mahé and transport to other islands, see the Seychelles – Getting Around chapter.

### NORTH MAHÉ
North of an east-west line from the airport to Grande Anse is the more populated and elevated half of the island. South of Victoria, between the town and the airport, the government has reclaimed land from the sea and has started constructing highways. It is also hoping to lease parts of the reclaimed zone to international industry.

### Beau Vallon Beach
One of the largest and certainly the most popular beach in the Seychelles, Beau Vallon beach is fronted by both the Beau Vallon Bay Hotel and the Coral Strand Hotel. The sand is good, clean and relatively free of rocks or coral inshore. The waves can sometimes be large as there is a big break in the reef.

Off the Coral Strand Hotel are two platforms you can swim out to. Nonresidents can mix freely with residents, even to the point of using the beach loungers. The snack and drinks bars of both hotels are handy, and there are two large water sports enterprises and three diving schools operating from the beach.

Towards the north end of the beach are restaurants, a supermarket, and a couple of shops. There is plenty of parking space.

In Beau Vallon village, where the road from Victoria forks to Bel Ombre (west) and Glacis (north-east), is a petrol station, a Barclays Bank (open Monday to Friday from 9 am to noon and on Saturdays from 9 to 10.45 am), souvenir shops and the police station.

Buses leave somewhat regularly from Victoria to Beau Vallon, either the long way around via Glacis or straight over the hill via St Louis. There is also a night bus service between 8 pm and midnight along these routes.

### Victoria to Beau Vallon Walk
It's possible to walk between Victoria and Beau Vallon – in fact a friend of ours walked it to and from work each day! The route is quite easy but it passes through an inhabited area, following the main road part of the way, so you must watch out for traffic which is relatively heavy.

In Victoria, the route begins at the central taxi stand near the clock tower (on the Beau Vallon side, it begins at the police station). Follow Revolution Ave west through town. When it turns sharply to the left near the Marie Antoinette restaurant, continue straight ahead along Serret Rd until it ends

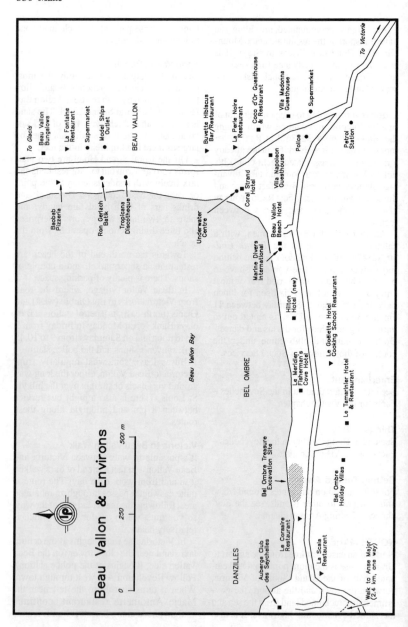

# Beau Vallon & Environs

To Glacis

To Victoria

**BEAU VALLON**

Beau Vallon Bungalows
La Fontaine Restaurant
Supermarket
Model Ships Outlet

Baobab Pizzeria
Ron Gerlach Batik
Tropicana Discotheque

Underwater Centre

Coral Strand Hotel
Buvette Hibiscus Bar/Restaurant
La Perle Noire Restaurant
Coco d'Or Guesthouse & Restaurant
Villa Madonna Guesthouse
Supermarket

Villa Napoleon Guesthouse
Police
Petrol Station

Beau Vallon Beach Hotel
Marine Divers International

*Beau Vallon Bay*

Hilton Hotel (new)

**BEL OMBRE**

Le Meridien Fisherman's Cove Hotel
Le Gaulette Hotel Cooking School Restaurant
Le Tamarinier Hotel & Restaurant

Bel Ombre Treasure Excavation Site

Bel Ombre Holiday Villas

**DANZILLES**

Auberge Club des Seychelles
Le Corsaire Restaurant
La Scala Restaurant

Walk to Anse Major (2.4 km, one way)

0    250    500 m

near the main road about 500 metres further along.

Turn right and carefully follow the road over the crest of the hill, watching out for traffic. At Le Niol junction, abandon the main road, taking the right fork and continuing down through Pascal Village. After 200 metres, follow the left fork which soon rejoins the main road. From there, it's about 700 metres to Beau Vallon police station, where you need to fork right and continue about 500 metres further to reach Beau Vallon Beach.

## Bel Ombre Treasure Site

This is not a tourist attraction yet, because few tourists know the story behind the site and the government is keeping quiet until it sorts out the maze of claims and counterclaims with regard to the land and exploration rights. The tale is a fascinating one in the best tradition of pirate adventure.

Olivier Levasseur, known as 'La Buse' (The Buzzard), was one of the last and most infamous of the 18th century pirates hovering around the Indian Ocean in their privateers. He crops up in the histories of Réunion, Mauritius and Madagascar, as does his seizure, along with English pirate John Taylor, of the Portuguese ship *Vierge du Cap*. This prize yielded a fortune in treasure. When La Buse was finally caught and hanged in Réunion in July 1730, he is said to have tossed a piece of paper into the crowd and shouted 'Find my treasure, he who can.'

As La Buse was bound to have called into the Seychelles for rest and recuperation from the raping and pillaging, there was a fair chance his treasure was buried there. In 1941, a retired English guardsman, Reginald Cruise-Wilkins, came to Mahé from Kenya for the sake of his health – he suffered from malaria. Seven years later he began a search at Bel Ombre for La Buse's treasure that was to last until he died a few years ago.

A cryptogram which belonged to an old Norwegian whaling skipper, old documents from the archives and strange markings on the shore rocks at Bel Ombre led him, as it had done others, to take up the challenge

issued by the pirate. It turned into an obsession for Cruise-Wilkins which cost him thousands of pounds and perhaps his life.

Cruise-Wilkins believed La Buse to be a learned man who had based his treasure-hunt puzzle on Greek mythology and astrology. The markings on the rocks supported this. The pirate, it seems, wanted the seekers to undertake the 12 labours of Hercules. Cruise-Wilkins nearly moved mountains and excavated underground tunnels and steps. But apart from the odd coin, piece of pottery or weapon, he found nothing.

His sons John and Godfrey still live in Bel Ombre and have vowed to carry on where their father left off. The government has now cordoned off the site and put the search on hold until a suitably serious and remunerative solution presents itself. At present there is no move to prolong and exploit the myth, but its tourism value may eventually be realised.

The treasure excavation site is at the first set of rocks heading west along the shore past Le Corsaire Inn. You can see Cruise-Wilkins' retaining walls and the area where the site has been fenced off by the authorities. There are no markings visible on this section, apart from bore holes.

A little 'treasure' has been found elsewhere on the Seychelles islands (see the sections on Ste Anne, Thérèse, Silhouette and Astove islands), but there have been no spectacular finds. There seems to be a myth that every pirate buried treasure like a jealous dog or a crazy hermit. Mind you, there couldn't have been a lot to spend it on.

## Danzilles to Anse Major Walk

This easy and pleasant three hour return walk follows the coastline between the village of Danzilles and Anse Major, west of Beau Vallon, passing some fine examples of glacis rock formations. Most of the walk lies within Morne Seychelloise National Park. Drive or take a bus to Danzilles, then follow the road up the hill; about 100 metres from the coast, you'll see the trail marker.

The vegetation along the route is typical of the coastal areas of the Seychelles. The ruins at Anse Major are said to have been the property of a wealthy French widow who left her estate to the Catholic mission. The mission established a small agricultural settlement at Anse Major, growing cinnamon, vanilla, patchouli and fruit trees. Anse Major has since been taken over by the government. During calm weather, the beach is good for swimming and snorkelling. Return to Danzilles by the same route.

### Kreol Fleurage

Founded by Mr Hugelmann, a German microbiologist who arrived in the Seychelles in 1978, Kreol Fleurage is a small centre for the production of essential oils and perfumes. Local plants form the basis for many of these products which are on sale here.

### La Gogue Reservoir

La Gogue Reservoir, which could be loosely considered the Seychelles' only mountain lake, is a pleasant wet spot in the centre of Mahé's northernmost peninsula. You can reach it either by the parallel concrete tracks (which are just passable for mini-mokes) climbing from the east coast near the Manresa Guest House, or on foot from near the Northolme Hotel on the west coast. If you're walking, the latter route is steeper but it passes through less populated areas and is the more enjoyable.

### Sauzier Waterfall

Not many people know about this beauty spot near Port Glaud on the west coast. Take a bus to Port Glaud from Victoria. If you have a car, park opposite the small island known as L'Islette and take the track inland alongside the church. Walk straight ahead past the Créole homes for about 10 minutes and when you hear the waterfall, turn left towards it. The cascade is magnificent, the surroundings are peaceful and the water is clean (no washing) and deep enough to swim.

A reader wrote to say that a lady in one of the Créole homes asks people to sign a book indicating their name, nationality, and current hotel address – it seems there have been walking accidents in the area. Another reader says that a local farmer has labelled the plants and trees around the waterfall and set up a pen with tortoises.

### US Tracking Station

It's not hard to see the giant 'golf balls' (the white plastic protective domes) of the satellite tracking station run by the US Navy. The turn-off to the station is four km up the La Misère road from La Louise, Victoria. Visits are possible with permission from the US Embassy in Victoria. Often base personnel invite friends up to sample the entertainment facilities.

The USA pays a massive rent to the Seychelles government for the tracking station, built in 1963. Its purpose is not supposed to be military, but rather to collect information from circling research satellites and relay it to the headquarters in California. But many believe it keeps an eye on warship movements about the Indian Ocean on behalf of its colleagues at Diego García.

### Trois Frères Peak Walk

Trois Frères Peak, which forms the mountain backdrop for Victoria, lies in Morne Seychellois National Park. The steep walk to its 699 metre summit begins at Sans Souci Forest Station on the Forêt Noire route, about five km from Victoria. After you pass the FEBA radio station and the Forestry Division offices, look for the right turning, 50 metres before the military checkpoint. Continue along this road for about 250 metres to the trailhead car park.

Although the climb to the peak is only about two km each way, it is all steeply uphill from the car park and extremely slippery after rain, so plan on at least two hours up and one hour down. Follow the posts dabbed with yellow paint and the arrows on the rough bits. About 1800 metres from the car park, the summit track cuts off to the right of the main track and climbs to the peak, which is frequently wrapped in cloud.

The major attractions on the route are the stand of *nepenthes pervillei* (pitcher plants) atop a rock face about mid-way to the summit, and the potentially incredible view from the peak. Although most people return the way they came, those who would prefer a traverse can tackle the rough track which continues from the summit cutoff for about five km down to the village of Le Niol, between Beau Vallon and Victoria.

## Copolia Walk

Further along the Forêt Noire route is the start of a short and steep but wonderful walk to the summit of the 510 metre peak, Copolia. Although the walk is just 250 metres each way, it leads to the most accessible stand of pitcher plants on Mahé.

The walk begins at Val Riche about six km from Victoria; watch for the signpost on the left side of the road. It is marked by posts dabbed with blue paint and is easy to follow, despite a couple of indistinct forks. The summit of Copolia is a large area of glacis, exposed granitic rock, and if the weather is clear, it's interesting to explore. However, beware of the super-duper dropoff at the end of it!

## Port Launay Marine National Park

This is a pretty, sheltered bay with some secluded beaches and good areas for snorkelling. Get a bus to Port Glaud from Victoria and walk or drive the four km up to Port Launay bay. The road ends at the National Youth Service camp gates before Ternay and you can't go further without permission.

## Tea Factory

The tea factory and restaurant is on the Sans Souci road between Victoria and Port Glaud, about four km from the latter in the shadow of Morne Blanc mountain. It is open Monday to Saturday from 8 am to 4 pm. A variety of Seychelles teas is on sale (orange, vanilla, lemon, etc) at the tea tavern. You can also buy toasted sandwiches from Rs 25 and lunches for around Rs 50. Ice cream is Rs 10. There are souvenirs and postcards for sale

and you can enquire here about visits to the nearby tea plantation itself.

## Tea Factory to Morne Blanc Hike

The imposing white hulk of 667 metre Morne Blanc and its almost sheer 500 metre face make a great hiking destination. Although the track is only 600 metres long, it is quite steep, climbing 250 metres from start to finish. Unless you're very fit, plan on about an hour for the trip up.

The beginning of the route is signposted 250 metres up the road from the tea factory, along the Forêt Noire cross-island road, and the trail is marked by intermittent yellow splotches of paint on trees. The return is via the same route.

## Rivière Cascade Walk

From Cascade village, near the airport, take the road up past the church until it ends when it crosses the river, and follow a path up the left-hand side of the nearest house for about half a km. Then ask directions along the way. The people are helpful even if you do walk through their gardens (be careful not to trample anything)! The path passes waterfalls and sluices to eventually break away from the river and head for the US satellite tracking station and the La Misère road.

## Places to Stay

There is a large concentration of hotels and guesthouses in the north of Mahé, but there's nothing available for less than single/double Rs 140/225 per night. The standards of service and facilities are consistent, as demanded by the tourist board, so visitors generally choose a place because of the surroundings or the friendliness of the proprietors or staff.

The following rundown of guesthouses and hotels is given under village locations, in order, from Victoria around North Point and along the coast to Beau Vallon and Bel Ombre, back over the St Louis road to Victoria, across the Sans Souci road to Port Glaud and down the west coast to Barbarons

Estate. All rates include breakfast, unless otherwise specified.

**Pointe Conan** First on the road at Pointe Conan, about three km from Victoria, is the *Sea Breeze Guest House* (☎ 241021), run by Justin Morin. It is a modern complex with six air-conditioned chalets, each with a private terrace for single/double Rs 275/330. Créole meals cost Rs 60 to Rs 75.

*Maxim's Jade House* (☎ 241489; fax 241888) is further up the coast. This unassuming guesthouse, run by a friendly Chinese couple, has six double rooms with air-con and private bath. Rates for single/double/triple occupancy are Rs 350/425/500, or Rs 425/575/725 for half board.

**Ma Constance** Next in line at Ma Constance, 3.5 km north of Victoria, is *Calypha Guest House* (☎ 241157), run by Claude and Florienne Brioche. The house, food and hospitality are first rate and the owners manage to keep the price down to single/double Rs 140/225 per night. Meals cost Rs 75. Calypha is a modern, airy house with a balcony and good views. It has five double rooms, but no air-conditioning. In terms of value for money, it's a lot better than guesthouses that cost twice the price.

To get there, turn west up the hill at the first opening north of the giant banyan tree, on the main road heading north. If taking the bus, get off at the FEBA (Christian) radio station. Close by is the Kyoto, a Japanese restaurant.

At the other end of Anse Étoile bay at Pointe Cèdre, is the *Manresa* (☎ 241388). This guesthouse has five twin bedrooms (three with air-conditioning). All the rooms are named after birds and have balconies; some also have good views across to Ste Anne Island. Rates for a single/double room are Rs 300/350; Rs 380/470 for half board; or Rs 430/575 for full board. Meals cost Rs 75. Manresa has a restaurant called L'Étoile and a bar called La Mer and is run by Nicholas Mederick.

From the bus stop outside the guesthouse, buses run every half hour to and from Victoria throughout the day. Although the views are good, the sea here is not great for bathing here. You have to get round North Point to the west side before the good coves and beaches begin.

**Machabée** At the north end of the island is the *North Point* (☎ 242339), run by Gilbert Hoareau. This guesthouse has eight rooms and is popular with independent travellers. The rates for a single/double room are Rs 275, without meals (no single rate, minimum stay of three days); Rs 275/330, including breakfast; or Rs 330/412 for half board. Self-catering bungalows with two rooms cost Rs 330.

A little further around the point, at Machabée village, is *Chez Jean* (☎ 241445; fax 225430) guesthouse, which charges single/double Rs 200/300, or Rs 275/440 for half board. Long term Mini Moke rental can be arranged for guests for two weeks or more at a cost of Rs 200 per day.

You can also rent a house nearby known as *Les Manguiers* (☎ 241455) for Rs 300 per day (maximium of five persons) or one of six double rooms in two neighbouring houses for a negotiable rate. You have some jet-setting neighbours – an Arab sheik has a mansion here and there are some other exclusive properties. There is also the local Créole bar called the Kakao.

**Glacis** Working down the coast into the Glacis community, you come to the first of the hotels, the *Vista Bay Club Hotel* (☎ 247351; fax 247621). This is a modern, terraced beach hotel with 33 rooms and all the extras. Singles/doubles cost Rs 770/850 for B&B and Rs 930/1200 for half board. The hotel is set away from the shore and has an elevated pedestrian crossing to Danielle's, an elegant thatched restaurant with a great view over wild waves. There's also a cove for snorkelling, but no beach as such.

The next hotel, two km south, is the Dutch-managed *Sunset Beach Hotel* (☎ 247227; fax 247521). This is an exclusive holiday village stuck on a rock promontory with a nice cove beach on one side. Rates for a single/double room start at around Rs 1105/1280, including breakfast; and rise to Rs 1332/1660 for half board. Meals cost about Rs 200. If you feel like spending more, there are also more expensive suites and a luxury villa.

The *Northolme Hotel* (☎ 247222), one km further down the coast, is the oldest of the current Seychelles hotels. Famous writers such as Ian Fleming and Compton MacKenzie have stayed here and waxed lyrical from their rooms with a view. The trees, rocks, and general windswept feeling might remind Californians of Carmel-by-the-Sea, but the beach isn't outstanding.

The hotel has 36 rooms and a large garden. The rocks nearby are an excellent snorkelling site. From June to early December, singles/doubles cost Rs 990/1300 for half board. These rates increase by around 15% during the rest of the year.

**Beau Vallon** At Mare Anglaise, just north of Beau Vallon, is the newly constructed *Pti Payot Guest House* (☎ 261447) which is a complex of three self-catering chalets perched on a hillside with excellent views across Beau Vallon beach. Each chalet can accommodate a maximum of three persons – children are welcome. The price per chalet is Rs 550/600 during high/low season. The manager, Evans Calva, is a former water sports instructor. Baby-sitting and laundry facilities are available and there's a weekly BBQ. The garden contains plenty of fruit trees, including an enormous mango tree.

On the outskirts of Mare Anglaise village you come to the *Vacoa Village* (☎ 261130; fax 247606), a 'Spanish-style self-catering complex' surrounding a pool and gardens. The use of giant boulders and almost troglodyte accommodation is quite pleasant. The rates are Rs 760 per day for a studio; Rs 900 per day for a one-bedroom apartment; and Rs 1215 per day for a two-bedroom apartment.

More affordable is the *Panorama Guest House* (☎ 247300), a modern house with eight rooms just off Beau Vallon beach, run

by Sheila Smith. Doubles/triples cost Rs 395/510 for B&B; singles/doubles/triples cost Rs 410/535/710 for half board and Rs 460/650/835 for full board. This place has a good reputation, and behind it there's a walking track up to 417 metre Mt Signal.

Nearby, across from the Baobab Pizzeria, are Janine Mancienne's *Beau Vallon Bungalows* (☎ 247382). This place looks less tidy and more run-down than most guesthouses, but the family is friendly and the single/double/triple rooms are good value at Rs 250/350/450, including breakfast, or Rs 350/450/550 for half board. Discounts may apply the longer you stay.

The empty or dilapidated bungalows across the road from the main stretch of beach are what remains of the old Hôtel des Seychelles.

At the corner where the road kinks inland to Beau Vallon village and Victoria is the *Coral Strand Hotel* (☎ 247036; fax 247517) which is unpretentious and popular with the young crowd after beach fun and frolics. It offers 103 rooms for single/double Rs 890/1055 (B&B), Rs 1055/1285 (half board) and Rs 1155/1485 (full board) per night. These daily rates are greatly reduced if you come on a package holiday, as most of the guests seem to do. The hotel is always very busy and, like the Pirates Arms in Victoria, it is a popular gathering spot for expatriate residents, workers and their friends, particularly on weekends.

The pool bar is a step off the beach and does good snack lunches as well as more expensive meals. The bar is open from 10 am to 6 pm. The Seychelles Underwater Centre diving school is also based at the hotel.

Just up the hill from the Coral Strand is a cluster of guesthouses. The cheapest and homeliest is the *Villa Madonna* (☎ 247403) run by Adeline Port-Louis (she's the mother of Sheila Smith, the Panorama proprietor). Singles/doubles cost Rs 220/275 on a B&B basis only. There are no other meals.

The more commercial *Coco d'Or* (☎ 247331; fax 247454) offers eight rooms for single/double/triple Rs 415/495/625, including breakfast, or Rs 455/605/835 for half board. The manager, Rama Vital, accepts credit cards.

On the other side of the road is the *Villa Napoleon* (☎ 247133), with two houses that each have three double rooms. Rates are single/double Rs 215/340.

**Bel Ombre** The large *Beau Vallon Bay Hotel* (☎ 247141; fax 247107), sometimes abbreviated to BVB, is on Beau Vallon beach, but the main entrance is on Bel Ombre road. It has 184 rooms and is kept busy with package tour groups.

Singles/doubles/triples cost Rs 1005/1325/1780 (half board) and Rs 1095/1415/1870 (full board). Attached to the hotel is a water sports centre, the Marine Divers centre, a casino, tennis courts, car hire desks and shops. Nonresidents can mix freely for coffee, drinks, snacks, meals and occasionally entertainment. The beach is better towards the Coral Strand end. Meals cost around Rs 120 and you can even order from a vegetarian menu.

At the time of writing, plans had been announced for the construction of a Hilton hotel on a site between the BVB and Fisherman's Cove Hotel.

Within walking distance, by beach and road, of the BVB Hotel is *Le Meridien Fisherman's Cove Hotel* (☎ 247252; fax 247450). The palm-thatched cottages, gardens, sealed-off pool and rock area place it a cut above the Coral Strand and Beau Vallon Bay hotels.

The rates for a single/double room are Rs 1055/1470 for B&B; and Rs 1235/1830 for half board. There is a daily supplement per person of about Rs 550 during peak periods. Meals cost at least Rs 200. More expensive suites and deluxe rooms are also available.

On the other side of the road, beyond the church and up a concrete lane called Marie Laure Drive, is *Le Tamarinier* (☎ 247611, 247429; fax 247711), run by France M Hoareau. This is a smart, modern guesthouse with seven rooms. Rates for a single/double/triple room start at Rs 330/500/580 for B&B;

Rs 400/590/645 for half board; and Rs 475/710/810 for full board.

At Danzilles, the end of the road and bus route, is the *Auberge Sun Hotel* (☎ 247550; fax 247703) The 40-odd thatched huts are scattered about the headland in a leafy garden leading down to the shore. There's an attractive terrace restaurant with a sea view.

Rates for single/double/triple rooms are Rs 580/900/1200 for half board. The management organises a weekly walk to Anse Major with a 'Robinson Crusoe Picnic' and return transport by boat.

The *Bel Ombre Holiday Villas* (☎ 247-616), in Bel Ombre village, are good value at Rs 300 per day for a villa (maximum four persons) or Rs 600 (maximum six). An extra bed costs Rs 50 per day. The villas look substantially better than thatched huts.

**Le Niol** Less than one km up the side road to Le Niol peak from the top of the Victoria-St Louis-Beau Vallon road is *Le Niol Guest House* (☎ 323262). At the edge of the Morne Seychelloise National Park forest, it's a bit of a doss house, with four very basic rooms. At Rs 150/195 for a single/double room, the place is not good value. When we visited, the entire place seemed to be operating as a digs for foreign workers.

**Port Glaud** On the west coast, about 1.5 km north of Port Glaud, is the tiny island simply named L'Islette. Four separate thatched bungalows and a restaurant, also known as *L'Islette* (☎ 378229), take up most of the space among the granite boulders and palms.

The islet is only 200 metres from the Mahé mainland and a little outboard boat can be summoned (using the whistle hanging on a tree) to ferry residents and diners back and forth throughout the day. Three resident tortoises happily cruise their tiny domain, munching fallen palm leaves. Run by brothers Max and John Maurel, the islet has 'idyllic' stamped all over it, and is popular for 'paradise weddings' and honeymoons. The proprietors occasionally hold a séga or camtole dance.

Singles/doubles/triples cost Rs 550/630/

900 with half board. Perhaps the most appealing room is No 11, which consists of two tiers, including two separate rooms, and a terrace with a stunning view.

Approximately the same distance south of Port Glaud, where the road turns away from the coast, is the 173-room *Seychelles Sheraton Hotel* (☎ 378451; fax 378517). Previously known as the Mahé Beach Hotel (a good disco spot), the multi-storey white edifice broke the tradition that all hotels on the islands should be no taller than the height of a palm tree. Single/doubles cost Rs 940/1210, including breakfast. During the Christmas and Easter seasons, prices increase by around 30%.

**Grande Anse** Just north of Grande Anse bay and village, a side road leads off towards the sea and the *Equator Sun Hotel* (☎ 378228, 378212; fax 378244). This 60-room hotel is built into the cliff face on various levels and is worth visiting to see the architectural drop to the swimming pool and bar, if nothing else.

The rates for single/double/triple rooms are Rs 1006/1368/1749 (half board). Rates increase at least 15% during high season. There is some good swimming and snorkelling to be done between the hotel and Île aux Vaches.

On the other side of Grande Anse is *Le Meridien Barbarons Hotel* (☎ 378253; fax 378484). This 125-room hotel is run by the French Meridien (Air France) group. The pool seems to dominate the complex, despite a near perfect beach. Single/double rooms cost Rs 840/1040 (B&B) and Rs 980/1330 (half board).

Finally, arguably the most exclusive guesthouse on the islands is the *Château d'Eau* (☎ 378339) on the Barbarons Estate. Rates are single/double Rs 530/680 for B&B and Rs 700/940 for half board. The five-bedroom chateau, like L'Islette, also has its sights set on honeymooners. The manager, Renée Troian, can arrange tennis, squash or horse riding, as well as fishing, diving or snorkelling trips from the owner's yacht, *Laurentia*.

**Places to Eat**

Of the guesthouses mentioned so far, the ones which double as restaurants are *Manresa*, *L'Islette*, *Le Tamarinier* and the *Coco d'Or*; main dishes at these places cost between Rs 60 and Rs 80. There is little incentive to try the hotel restaurants if you are not a guest at the hotel, as there are ample private restaurants offering a variety of styles and prices.

**Ma Constance** The *Kyoto* (☎ 241337) is the only Japanese restaurant on the islands. The setting is simple but elegant and, in the Rs 100 range, may provide a break from saucy Créole fare. It's open for lunch and dinner from Monday to Saturday; closed on Sundays.

**Beau Vallon** The licensed restaurant *Baobab Pizzeria* (☎ 247167), which has a sand floor, is right on the beach. It's the most popular and cheapest place in the north of the island. The pizzas are good and properly baked, and cost around Rs 35. Pastas, ice creams and salads are also available. The atmosphere manages to be lively, yet intimate, and the restaurant is always cooled by the sea breezes. Get there before 8 pm to be sure of a seat, especially on weekends. It is open every day.

Across the road is *La Fontaine* restaurant, which serves Créole food. Main dishes start around Rs 45.

*La Perle Noire* (☎ 247046) is opposite the Coral Strand Hotel. The manager, Lambert Bonne, is an island 'personality' and may be more in demand in some quarters than the food. The restaurant has a French and Créole à la carte menu and main dishes start around Rs 140.

**Bel Ombre** The *Seychelles Hotel & Tourism Training School* (☎ 247414) has a restaurant, *La Goëlette*, where trainee chefs and waiters can try out their new-found skills on the public. Unfortunately, the prices are not as low as you would expect from a government-funded college venture. Main courses cost between Rs 60 and Rs 90. If you paid half that price, you'd be prepared to be a guinea pig and taste-test first attempts. But as it is, why not go to a 'qualified' restaurant for the same price? The school restaurant is open Tuesday to Friday from noon to 1.30 pm for a set-menu lunch. It's also closed during school holidays.

At Bel Ombre village you'll find *Le Corsaire* (☎ 247171) restaurant in a large steep-roofed chalet right on the waterside. Main dishes start around Rs 180. It's closed on Monday.

Up the hill towards the Auberge Sun Hotel is the *Restaurant La Scala* (☎ 247535), run by the Torsi family. It specialises in Italian food (raw fish in green lemon?) and seafood, and is expensive at around Rs 180 per meal. It opens for dinner at 7 pm from Monday to Saturday; it's closed on Sundays and throughout the month of September.

**Port Glaud** Opposite L'Islette is the *Sundown Restaurant* (☎ 378352). Situated on the water, it's a nice place for an intimate, romantic dinner. Créole meals are about Rs 100 per person. The restaurant is closed on Sunday.

**Grande Anse** *La Marie Galante* (☎ 378-455) restaurant specialises in Créole food. Main dishes start around Rs 100.

**La Louise** About three km from Victoria, up the Les Mamelles hill road, is *La Moutia* (☎ 344433), formerly known as La Suisse. It specialises in seafood, and main dishes cost around Rs 150.

## SOUTH MAHÉ

The southern half of Mahé is less mountainous and less populated than the north. 'Moking' tourists can cover the region effortlessly, but there are scores of bays around the coast and it never gets crowded.

In the hilly interior, there are some pleasant walks and hikes around Chemin Les Cannelles and Chemin Val d'Endor.

### Beaches

Beaches are the main attraction in the south of the island. Starting with Anse Royale, south of Pointe au Sel (also known as Fairyland Point), the beaches along the east coast are smaller, quieter and prettier than most in North Mahé. They're best for relaxing, lagoon swimming and snorkelling, as almost the whole coast is fringed by the reef.

The nicest area for swimming and snorkelling is opposite tiny Île Souris. Although the crowds descend on weekends, it's fairly empty during the week. Continuing south, there are good stretches of beach at Anse Bougainville, Anse Parnel, Anse Forbans (also called Pirates' Bay) and Anse Marie-Louise.

On the west coast, both Anse Boileau and Anse à la Mouche have reef beaches, but are not really suitable for sunbathing or swimming. They are too shallow and too public. The secluded beaches begin at Anse Soleil and Petite Anse, but the coast here fronts open sea and that means waves, rips and the need to take additional care when swimming.

There is a rough 2.5 km road down to Anse Soleil and Anse Petite, which a Mini Moke can just about manage with great risk to the underside. Jeeps are better. The trip is almost impossible in a private sedan. The rewards, however, are worth the effort: there's a palm-fringed beach to laze on and granite boulders to dive or snorkel from (with extreme caution!). You can see some wonderful marine life, including barracuda and small sharks.

At Baie Lazare, the Plantation Club Hotel has snaffled the best bit of beach, but there is a nice stretch at Anse Takamaka, where the road heads inland and east.

There is a lovely, wild stretch of beach at Anse Intendance at the end of a good secondary road leading down from Quatre Bornes village. Anse Intendance is the wildest beach on Mahé and great for surf watching. Swimming is not allowed due to the violence of surf and currents.

The road from Quatre Bornes continues a couple of rough km past Anse Cachée and Anse Corail, but is blocked off for security reasons before you come to the aptly named Police Bay. The beach at the end of the public road is wild and beautiful, with high frothing surf, but rogue currents make it unsuitable for bathing.

The bus service from Victoria provides access to most of the island as far south as Takamaka and Quatre Bornes villages; there's even a night service between 8 pm and midnight (see the Seychelles – Getting Around chapter.)

## La Brulée Walk

At the Cable & Wireless station, near the crest of the Montagne Posée cross-island route between Anse aux Pins and Anse Boileau, is the start of an easy but highly rewarding walk to three spectacular vantage points overlooking the west coast of Mahé. Note the inedible wild pineapples behind the signpost at the trailhead.

The track is well marked and easy to follow, first descending through groves of mahogany to cross a stream, and then climbing through dense forest to a small forested plateau area. The routes to the three viewpoints can get a bit confusing so it's wise to carry the *La Réserve and Brulée #7* hiking brochure and map, available at the tourist office in Mahé. If you prefer to have a go on your own, the main circular route is marked with green splotches; Viewpoint No 1 has yellow splotches; for Viewpoint No 2 they're red on yellow; and those for Viewpoint No 3 are green on yellow.

Viewpoint No 1 is the best of the three, with a fabulous view over a precipice down to the west coast. Nearer at hand, look for the fruit bat roost down in the valley below; we were there at midday and were surprised to find it bustling with activity. The most remote of the overlooks, Viewpoint No 3, offers the best views of the 501 metre peak of La Brulée, as well as a glimpse of the east coast, and Viewpoint No 2 offers the most wide-ranging west coast panorama.

## Craft Village (Village Artisanal)

The rather contrived crafts village at Anse aux Pins is a collection of craft shops grouped around a restored colonial building and restaurant. Visitors can browse through the crafts on display but please don't buy marine products made from endangered species – see the Conservation section in the general introductory chapter.

## Anse Royale

In addition to having a good beach, Anse Royale is home to the new national theatre, where you can see cultural concerts or shows by visiting artists. The Banque Française Commerciale in the village exchanges currency; there is also a petrol station.

## Michael Adams' Studio

Michael Adams' studio, at Anse aux Poules Bleues, should not be missed. The painter's work is explained in more detail in the Arts & Culture section of the Seychelles – Facts about the Country chapter, and for directions in getting to the studio, see Things to Buy in the Seychelles – Facts for the Visitor chapter. Adams' wife, Heather, usually looks after visitors. The shop sells T-shirts, silkscreen prints, B&W lineblocks, and postcards. Packing and posting for overseas orders can be arranged.

## Chemins Dame Le Roi & Val d'Endor

These are two cross-country lanes leading from Baie Lazare on the west of Mahé through the valley to Anse Bougainville on the east. For the most part, the Chemin Val d'Endor follows the Rivière Bougainville and the Rivière Baie Lazare. Chemin Dame Le Roi runs in a wide loop from Baie Lazare village before joining Chemin Val d'Endor – there's a small pottery just before the junction. Like any other forest walks, these two lanes provide an admirable alternative to lazing around the beach all day.

## Places to Stay

**East Coast** The closest guesthouse to the airport is the *Carefree* (☎ 376237), just past Pointe Larue on Anse Faure. It has four rooms, some with air-conditioning, for single/double/triple Rs 250/295/420. Meals cost Rs 80. It's right on the road and next to the sea, although the beach from here down to Pointe au Sel is not too inviting. The Carefree also has a good restaurant.

In Anse aux Pins village, near the school and the bus station opposite the Savings Bank, is *La Retraite* guesthouse (☎ 376816). Hélène Etienne has only three rooms and is less houseproud about sand and beach towels lying around the verandah than some of the other overly spic n' span guesthouses. She is also a specialist in craftwork. Her room rates are among the island's lowest at single/double Rs 160/220. Meals cost Rs 80. Nearby is the local Cantina bar.

*Lalla Panzi* (☎ 376411), at Anse aux Pins, is a small guesthouse run by a German/Seychellois couple. There are four rooms and guests can use the facilities of the nearby Reef Hotel. Singles/doubles cost Rs 200/265 (B&B). Meals are not provided. The Zulu name was given to the establishment by a previous South African owner.

On the other side of the road, at the end of a lane, are the three chalets of *La Roussette* (☎ 376245), which has recently been renovated. Rooms have individual verandahs, air-con, fridge and phone. Single/double/triple rates are Rs 400/550/650 (B&B) or Rs 490/750/940 (half board). The restaurant and bar are only for residents.

The *Reef Hotel* (☎ 376251; fax 247606) is one of the more established hotels on Mahé, with a pool, tennis courts and a golf course opposite. Like its sister hotel, the Beau Vallon Bay (guests can do meal exchanges), it tends to cater for down-market package tourists. Rates for single/double/triple rooms start around Rs 760/1100/1400 for half board.

It's a good spot for meeting people or for a night out; it has plenty of discos, séga nights and camtole bands, and there are singers in the lounge bar. It has a jetty for boats and fishing, and sailboards for hire, but a poor beach. The Reef hotel is one of the few places on Mahé where you can rent a bike. There are discounts for long-term rental and you can even have a bike delivered to another hotel if you hire it for more than four days.

Next door is the *Casuarina* (☎ 376211) hotel, which has been renovated and expanded to provide 35 rooms. This quiet and relaxing place has a colonial house as an annexe, and a swimming pool. Rates for single/double/triple rooms start at Rs 330/440/620 and increase to Rs 415/590/700 for half board. The restaurant is open to nonresidents.

The last guesthouse south along the east coast is the most impressive on the islands – the *Residence Bougainville* (☎ 371334), owned by Tessie Ellinas. It is an old plantation house with eight bedrooms upstairs, surrounded by a wooden verandah. Each room has a stable-style door and period furniture and fittings. The rooms to the front of the house overlook the sea at Anse Baleine. Single/double/triple rooms cost Rs 325/415/580 (B&B) or Rs 400/535/700 for half board. If you can afford it, it's worth the extra to stay here. If not, at least try a meal. A good set-menu meal costs Rs 80. There is also a bar and the atmosphere is generally pleasant. Anse Bougainville and Anse Parnel are nearby for swimming.

**West Coast** The *Auberge d'Anse Boileau* (☎ 376660) is more noted for its restaurant, Chez Plume, than its guesthouse. The eight bedrooms in the thatched units surrounding the restaurant cost single/double/triple Rs 350/375/400 (B&B) or Rs 450/575/700 (half board).

The *Blue Lagoon* (☎ 371197), at Anse à la Mouche, is a small complex of four self-catering bungalows, each with two double bedrooms, a kitchen and a lounge. There are boats available for diving with an instructor, as well as deep-sea fishing expeditions. Windsurfing and water-skiing are also provided to get you away from the retirement village surroundings. A bungalow costs Rs 5840 per week for four people; and Rs 480 per week for an extra bed for a child.

The *Lazare Picault* (☎ 371117), on the hillside overlooking the Baie Lazare, provides similar thatched luxury for single/double Rs 325/450 (B&B) or Rs 395/580 for half board.

Out towards Pointe Lazare, on the north side of the bay, is the *Plantation Club* (☎ 371588; fax 371517) with 206 rooms and suites and a casino. A room on a twin-share basis costs Rs 920 per person. Various categories of suites are also available at prices ranging from Rs 2000 to Rs 5000.

### Places to Eat

Of the guesthouses in the south of the island, the ones with restaurants are the *Résidence Bougainville, Auberge d'Anse Boileau (Chez Plume), Lazare Picault, Casuarina Beach* and *Carefree*. Chez Plume reportedly has the best food on the island but it's pricey. Try the *capitaine rouge* fish in passion fruit sauce. The Résidence Bougainville has the best surroundings as well as being reasonably cheap, at Rs 65 for a main dish.

**East Coast** The *Katiolo* (☎ 376453), just past the airport at the dip in the road approaching Anse Fauré, doubles at night as a disco. It cooks up a Créole seafood treat, but the place is a bit of a barn.

The *Ty-Foo* (☎ 371485), at Le Cap, is the southern equivalent of the Baobab Pizzeria for popularity and bargain meals. Here you can order large helpings of soup, fish curry, and sweet and sour pork. It has a separate bar and there are pool tables. Open for lunch and dinner until midnight each day, it offers a good atmosphere.

In Anse Royale village is *Kaz Kreol* (☎ 371680), which offers excellent Créole cuisine. Main dishes start around Rs 75. We'd recommend the raw fish with ginger or grilled croisant (a type of red snapper) with ginger, followed by jamalac (a local fruit) dessert.

**West Coast** There are two restaurants on Anse à la Mouche. At the southern end is the *Anchor Café & Pizza* which does cheap snacks, juices, sandwiches, and hamburgers from 11 am to 11 pm daily – except Monday. At the northern end is the *Oscar Au Capitaine Rouge* (☎ 371224) which serves French cuisine. Main dishes cost around

Rs 150 and the restaurant is closed on Wednesday.

Just before you come to Michael Adams' studio, where the road turns inland, is Bob Noddyn's *La Sirène* (☎ 371339). It has the simplest and most basic setting under thatch on the sand, but the Créole food is good. Fish and bat are the specialities. The cost of an average meal is Rs 120 to Rs 150, so there must be overheads somewhere. Further south, on Baie Lazare, is *Anse Gaulettes* restaurant. It's attached to a dance hall and offers Chinese and Créole food. Main dishes cost around Rs 75. There is a good dance here at the end of each month.

*Chez Batiste* (☎ 371535) on Anse Takamaka is popular for Créole food. *Le Reduit Restaurant*, on a small promontory overlooking the southern end of Anse Takamaka, also offers Créole cuisine.

### STE ANNE MARINE NATIONAL PARK

There are six islands lying within the park a few km off Victoria. All are inhabited, save Le Cachée Island, which is a nature reserve, but visitors are permitted to land only on Cerf, Round and Moyenne. Long Island houses a prison, and Île Ste Anne, the site of a National Youth Service camp, is off limits to visitors.

The snorkelling in the park is most impressive and highly recommended. We particularly enjoyed the audible underwater crunch of parrot fish chomping into coral and the inquisitive damsel fish clustering round our masks to get a closer look at us.

Mason's, TSS and NTA travel agencies run glass-bottom boat day trips to each island (see the Tours section of the Seychelles –

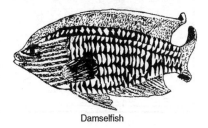

Damselfish

Getting Around chapter). Only Mason's runs tours to Moyenne, which it extols in brochures as an 'exclusive Mason's product'. For details about hiring your own boat from Marine Charter Association see the Tours section of the Seychelles – Getting Around chapter. There are no ferry services.

## Ste Anne Island

Ste Anne Island, the site of the first settlement on the Seychelles back in 1770, recently housed a National Youth Service camp. Visitors are not permitted to land, but there is a good snorkelling site off the southern coastline and an abandoned whaling station nearby.

A chess set belonging to settlers or pirates was found on the island several years ago and there were rumours about buried pirate treasure, but unlike the mysterious hoards at Bel Ombre, somebody is supposed to have surreptitiously swiped the lot about 20 years ago. There's also good snorkelling along the north-east coast.

## Moyenne Island

Moyenne is said to be the best of the marine park islands to visit. It is owned by Bernard

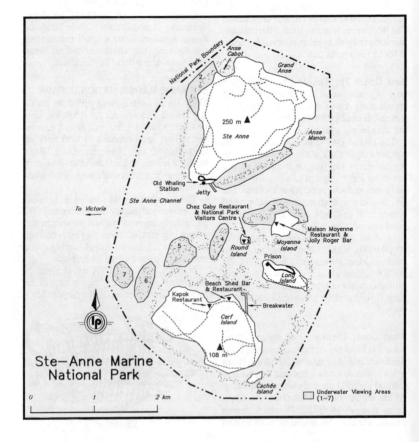

Ste—Anne Marine National Park

0    1    2 km

Underwater Viewing Areas (1–7)

Grimshaw, a retired journalist, and is open to tour parties from Mason's Travel Agency three days per week. The Marine Charter Association can sometimes arrange tours to the island providing you give several days notice.

On the island you may be told about buried treasure and ghosts; and shown the ruins of the 'House of Dogs', a home built at the turn of the century by an eccentric English woman as a refuge for stray dogs. There is a marked trail through the Moyenne's 9 hectares – taken at a leisurely pace, the hike lasts about 45 minutes. Grimshaw has spent many years regenerating the fauna and flora. You'll come across many species of endemic Seychelles flora, including coco de mer, bwa de fer, the dragon tree, and Wright's gardenia. Apart from Grimshaw's two dogs, Emma and Coconut, the most noticeable animals are the giant land tortoises, the oldest two being 60-year-old Derek and 50-year-old Julia.

Moyenne also has a couple of excellent snorkelling sites and you can relax afterwards at the *Jolly Roger* bar and the *Maison Moyenne* (☎ 322414) restaurant in a renovated Créole house. Main dishes cost around Rs 75.

### Round Island

This island, like Curieuse Island near Praslin, was once home to a leper colony. The chapel of the 80-year-old building is now occupied by the kitchen and bar of the *Chez Gaby* (☎ 224209) restaurant. If Moyenne is the best island to visit, Round has the best restaurant – a culinary highlight for the Seychelles. Chez Gaby is run by the Calais family and is open for lunch daily except Monday and Friday. A meal for two costs around Rs 160.

A typical meal has been described thus: 'Specially marinated, BBQ'd tuna steaks with fresh salad and fried aubergine, followed by heaped servings of octopus curry, chicken curry, vegetables and rice. Dessert is a fresh fruit salad with grated coconut mixed with caramelised sugar, orange juice and brandy, topped with coconut milk and served with strongly brewed coffee.'

Only the island ranger lives on Round; the Calais have to commute daily from Cerf Island.

If you're visiting the restaurant, take a few minutes to follow the tree-shaded circle island track, and don't miss the national park visitors' centre just a few metres from the restaurant.

### Cerf Island

About 40 people live on Cerf, including Wilbur Smith, the South African novelist, who occasionally visits his holiday home here. Wills and Andrée Gardner offer Créole cuisine at the *Beach Shed* (☎ 322126) restaurant. It is open for lunch only on Monday, Tuesday, Thursday and Sunday. Advance reservations are essential. An average meal for two costs Rs 160. There's also a new restaurant, the *Kapok*, on the same beach as the Beach Shed.

The island is popular for weekend excursions and you can either go there as part of an organised excursion with a travel agency or hire a boat from the Marine Charter Association.

### Thérèse Island

Thérèse is the more interesting of the two islands on the north-west coast of Mahé (the other is known as Conception Island). It is uninhabited now, apart from the residents of an ancient cemetery. From the top of the small hill (160 metres) you can see across to the huge granite steps on Pointe l'Escalier, the southern head of Port Launay bay. One theory is that the steps were carved out for religious rites by Malay-Polynesians at about the same time they settled the Maldives, but before they reached Madagascar and the Comoros.

The island belongs to the Sheraton hotel, which operates day trips for Rs 300 per person. On Thérèse there's a water sports centre with facilities for big game fishing, windsurfing, diving, canoeing, etc. Thérèse is also a good snorkelling site, with a large lagoon on its north shore.

## Silhouette Island

Romantics believe that Silhouette received its name because, from Beau Vallon, it appears in silhouette when the sun sets behind its high profile. Historians trace the name to that of a French minister. Watching the sunset from Beau Vallon beach is the pre-dinner thing to do. If the island looks dark and mysterious from Beau Vallon, the impression is confirmed upon landing and visitors have described it as 'eerie' and 'mystical'.

This large granite island, almost 20 km from Mahé, rises steeply from around the shore up to three peaks, of which Mt Dauban is the highest (750 metres). The west side of the island is shielded by a reef that has a small break to allow boats to pass to and from Anse La Passe – the site of the island's only hotel. The protected waters are good for beach-bumming, swimming and snorkelling. Silhouette is under the control of the Islands Development Company, which is developing livestock and agricultural production on the island – follow your nose to the poultry farm beyond the hotel.

About 250 people live on the island, formerly the property of the Dauban family. The family mausoleum is at Pointe Ramasse Tout, near the main landing spot at Anse la Passe. A few hundred metres south of Anse Lascars are the remains of what are believed to be Arab tombs, possibly of early shipwrecked seafarers.

Pirate Jean François Hodoul made the island his base – and again, there's gold in 'them thar hills', or so the tourist publicity would have you think. If you want to search, there are caves to explore. If nothing else, they contain stalagmites and stalactites.

Getting into and up to the centre of the island through the dense native virgin forest is difficult and provides a good pioneering challenge for visitors.

**Swimming** Silhouette's best swimming beach is in front of the hotel, but it's a bit shallow at low tide. Other high tide possibilities – although far from ideal – are at Anse Lascars and Anse Patate, both of which have large and chunky fields of coral on the bottom.

**Anse La Passe** Just south of Anse La Passe village is an antiquated but interesting – and functional – copra press in a shed. It's worth a look as you're passing by.

**Anse Mondon** The route around the northeast end of the island runs from La Passe, north through the hotel grounds, past the odiferous poultry farm and over Belle Vue Pass to Anse Mondon. There, you'll find a small settlement and some reasonably sheltered snorkelling. Baie Cipaille is also meant to offer snorkelling opportunities. At Anse Mondon, you'll find a pineapple, guava and avocado farm/plantation which was abandoned due to rumours of haunting by phantoms.

**Mont Pot à Eau Walk** To visit the summit of magnificent 630 metre Mont Pot à Eau and see its namesake phenomenon, the bizarre carnivorous pitcher plant, will require the better part of a day. Wear light, cool clothing and carry some salty biscuits and lots of water – you'll sweat a lot and will frequently have to replenish salts and liquids.

From the hotel, head into the village and past the school, where you'll take a very sharp right at the intersection of tracks (There's also a route connecting to this track just south of the bridge near the hotel but it's obscure and passes through peoples' gardens.) Follow this track until it begins to lose altitude. There you'll find a concrete spur leading off to the left into a patch of grass. Turn here and follow this track to a T-junction, where you'll turn left again. The track then climbs steadily through intermittent coconut trees and rainforest.

At about 200 metres elevation, there's a fork in the track. The left fork will take you over the relatively easy traverse to Grand Barbe on the western shore. For Pot à Eau, take the right fork. The track will continue to climb, crossing the Grande Rivière and passing a stand of coco de mer palms with immense fan-shaped leaves (for further

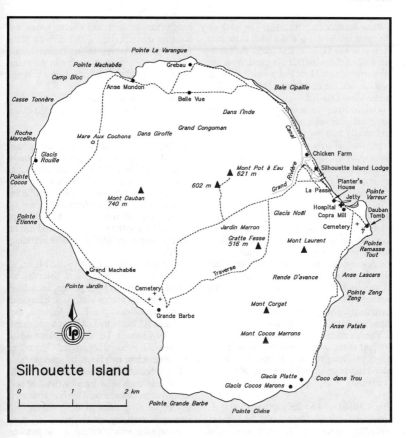

**Silhouette Island**

0        1        2 km

Pointe La Varangue
Pointe Machabée
Grebau
Camp Bloc
Anse Mondon
Belle Vue
Baie Cipaille
Casse Tonnère
Dans l'Inde
Roche Marceline
Mare Aux Cochons
Dans Giroffe
Grand Congoman
Glacis Rouille
Chicken Farm
Silhouette Island Lodge
Pointe Cocos
Mont Pot à Eau 621 m
Grand Rivière
Planter's House
Pointe Varreur
602 m
La Passe
Jetty
Mont Dauban 740 m
Glacis Noël
Hospital
Copra Mill
Dauban Tomb
Pointe Étienne
Jardin Marron
Cemetery
Gratte Fesse 516 m
Mont Laurent
Pointe Ramasse Tout
Grand Machabée
Traverse
Anse Lascars
Pointe Jardin
Cemetery
Rende D'avance
Pointe Zeng Zeng
Grande Barbe
Mont Corgat
Anse Patate
Mont Cocos Marrons
Glacis Platte
Coco dans Trou
Glacis Cocos Marons
Pointe Grande Barbe
Pointe Civine

information on the coco de mer, see Vallée de Mai under Praslin). Careful not to tread on the monstrous millipedes, slugs and African snails that inhabit the forest floor!

At 400 metres elevation, the track steepens and climbs to a 500 metre high crest, near which a track branches off to the right. It's accessed by passing beneath an immense fallen log. The track climbs gently at first, then enters very thick vegetation where larger trees have fallen, and the resulting sunlight on the forest floor has allowed a profusion of undergrowth. The track disappears at times into dense vegetation; look for the machete blazes on larger trees. At one stage, hikers must balance on a series of slippery logs.

Where the vegetation begins to thin out again, you'll gain a minor summit. From there, look around to your right for a faint track leading downhill, across the valley which separates you from Mont Pot à Eau. Once you find the track, it's fairly easy to reach the summit of Pot à Eau; the track loses 50 metres of altitude, traverses a small saddle and then climbs steeply to the summit.

Once you've reached the summit, with pitcher plants blooming all around, look for a small boulder on your right. The track on the other side of this boulder leads to the best view down to the hotel and across the southern half of the island. If it's clear, from the opposite side of Mont Pot à Eau's summit, you can see the spectacular summit of 745 metre Mont Dauban.

Guides from the hotel, who work for the Seychelles development corporation, are technically free but you can tip them whatever you feel they're worth. Don't attempt this trip for at least two days after heavy rain; much of the way is over red clay and it can be impossibly slippery, especially on the steep bits.

**Grande Barbe** The best route to Grande Barbe is the relatively easy southern route over the mountain, which takes about three hours one way from La Passe. For access, see the description under Mont Pot à Eau. From Grande Barbe, a rough track continues north to the foot of Grand Machabée, a rocky outcrop, but since camping is illegal, you'd have to get a very early start in order to get there and back in a single day.

There's no coastal route around the northern part of the island, as is marked on many maps, although you can cross to Anse Mondon via an inland route past Mare aux Cochons.

**Place to Stay** The only place to stay is *Silhouette Island Lodge* (☎ 224003; fax 344178), which has 12 bungalows and charges Rs 1300 for full board in a standard bungalow. The price for full board in an executive bungalow is Rs 1540, and there is a Rs 850 single room supplement. Some of the bungalows are not beside the sea – be sure you specify your choice.

In the restaurant, barred ground doves exasperate the staff and charm guests by ambling over the tables and filching rolls from breakfast tables. In the evening, fruit bats squabble and crash around in the palm trees above; and a pair of Seychelles kestrels placidly nests above the bar.

Although the food is good, the bungalows are overpriced in relation to the facilities on offer.

**Getting There & Away** There are no air connections from Mahé and no sealed roads on the island. To get there you can join a tour, arrange a package deal with the hotel, or find your own boat (see the Charters section in the Seychelles – Getting Around chapter).

The coral reef makes for tricky access to the island. Once their boat has arrived inside the reef, visitors are ferried to shore in zodiac dinghies.

Tour operators, such as TSS and Mason's, run day trips on Monday and Saturday to Silhouette for Rs 475 per person, including lunch. The boat leaves Victoria at 8 am and returns around 4.30 pm. From Victoria, the trip takes 1½ hours by fast launch and three hours by schooner. The crossing from Beau Vallon to Silhouette takes around 45 minutes by fast launch or two hours by schooner.

If you book accommodation at the hotel, you should book your transfer (Rs 440 per person) at the same time. This hotel transfer service only operates in the morning on Sunday, Wednesday and Friday.

To organise your own trip, ask at Marine Charter Association, or make arrangements with the fishermen around the Corsair restaurant or at Cima boat-building in Bel Ombre. If agreeable, they will take you across for Rs 80, if time, tide, wind and sea conditions are suitable. Make arrangements around 4 pm the day before you want to go.

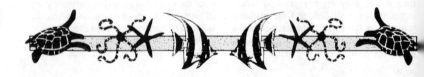

Top: View from La Misère, Mahé, Seychelles (DS)
Bottom: Anse Gaulettes, La Digue, Seychelles (DS)

Top: Anse Source d'Argent, La Digue, Seychelles (DS)
Bottom: La Passe seen from Mont Pot à Eau, Silhouette, Seychelles (RS)

# Praslin

Praslin, the second largest Seychelles island, is about 35 km north-east of Mahé. It is 12 km long, and five km across at its widest point. Lazare Picault, the French navigator, named it Île de Palme (Palm Island) when he stepped ashore in 1744. In 1768, just before the first settlement on Ste Anne Island, a stone of possession was set up at Anse Possession, across from Curieuse on the north of the island. It was renamed in honour of the Duc de Praslin, a French minister of state, who was later guillotined.

The island, like Mahé, has a granite mountain ridge running east-west down the centre. The highest point is Praslin Island Peak (367 metres), which marks the edge of the island's main attraction, the Vallée de Mai, home of the unique coco de mer palm.

The pace of life on Praslin is much slower than on Mahé. The people also seem friendlier towards visitors. There is little traffic and no towns. The 5000 inhabitants are scattered around the coast in a series of small settlements. Anse Volbert, Grand Anse and Baie Ste Anne are the main communities. Ferry schooners from Mahé arrive at the latter two.

## Information

**Post** The main post office on Praslin is next to the police station at Grand Anse. It's supposed to be open Monday to Friday from 8 am to noon and 1 to 4 pm, but is often closed by 3 pm.

**Money** Barclays Bank has branches at Baie Ste Anne and Grand Anse. The branch at Baie St Anne is open Monday to Friday from 8.30 am to 1 pm and on Saturdays from 8.30 to 11 am. The branch at Grand Anse is open Monday to Friday between 9 am and noon and on Saturdays from 9 to 10.45 am.

## Vallée de Mai

When General Gordon, of Khartoum, did a reconnaissance of Praslin in 1881 and wandered through the Vallée de Mai, which lies between Baie Ste Anne and Grand Anse, he thought he had discovered the original Garden of Eden. He devised a coat of arms for the then-British colony of the Seychelles in which a coco de mer palm stood on the back of a giant tortoise. Around the palm a snake was entwined, signifying Eden. The republic has retained the coat of arms, but the snake has gone!

The coco de mer, Gordon believed, was the tree of good and evil knowledge used to test Adam and Eve. Its fruit, he wrote, 'externally represents the heart, while the interior represents the thighs and belly, which I consider as the true seat of carnal desires...'

When these amazing nuts originally reached other continents, they were thought to have come from large submarine trees. Hence the name coco de mer (sea coconut). They inspired several different legends and theories when they were washed up on the shores of Indonesia, Sri Lanka, Malaysia, India, the Maldives, Mauritius and other countries. The Indonesians thought the tree might be the home of the mythical garuda bird, and the Indians attributed healing powers to the nuts. Several of the nuts were made into drinking vessels, decorated in gold and silver, by European rulers and now lie in various museums, including the British Museum.

Because of the female nuts' voluptuous feminine shape, some people believed they had aphrodisiac qualities. The elders of Praslin still hold that they do, if you soak the kernel of the nut overnight and boil it for drinking.

To add to the erotic nature of the tree, propagation only takes place when the female tree, which bears the nuts, is close to the male tree, which has a long, brown, dangling catkin that resembles a you-know-what. Local folklore is full of stories about people actually seeing or hearing the trees

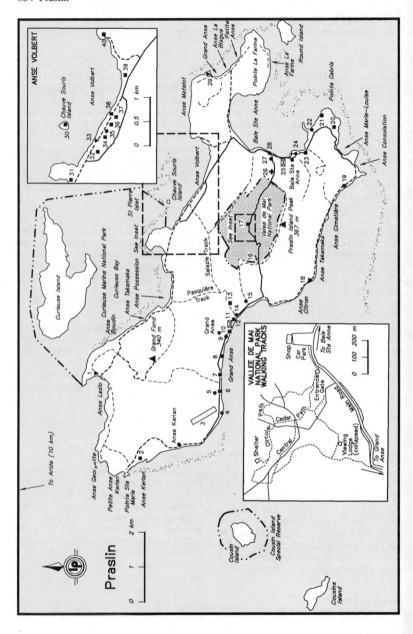

mate, and being cursed for looking! Actually, insects or the wind are responsible for pollinating the trees.

The coco de mer palm grows naturally only on Praslin, Silhouette and Curieuse islands. It is one of about nine varieties of palms and screw pines growing in the Vallée de Mai. The palm only starts to bear fruit after 25 years, and then it takes seven years for a nut to mature. The trees can then live up to 1000 years. Some of the ones in the Vallée de Mai national park are 45 metres high and about 800 years old. In the park you'll see many hollow 'bowls' in the ground; these are the sites of dead palms and can last 60 years after the tree has fallen.

There are approximately 4000 palms in the Vallée. The female palm produces about 20 fruits, of which three to five reach maturity. They each weigh up to 200 kg, making them the heaviest fruit in the world. The harvesting of the coco de mer nuts is strictly controlled by the government. Some of the younger, green nuts are eaten after they are a year old. The mature ones sell for Rs 400 and upward.

The best place to buy one is at the Fond Boffay Forestry Division store, about one km from Baie Ste Anne on the road to the Vallée de Mai. Cut in four, the nuts make good serving bowls. Cut in half, sideways, they can be turned into fruit baskets. See the Things to Buy section in the Seychelles – Facts for the Visitor chapter for further information.

Together with their admission ticket, visitors are given a 'nature trail' guide with thorough notes on most of the trees and plants. One of them is called the 'dumb cane' because it produces a toxic juice which can cause paralysis of the tongue and throat muscles. It was said to have been used to punish slaves who talked back to their masters. Mme Raville Lesperance, of the

Orange Tree guesthouse, said it was later used on mothers-in-law!

Other interesting plants are the wild (red) pineapple, wild coffee and the allspice bush, which produces a sort of variety pack of spices used in Créole cooking.

The palms consist of the palmiste, latanier, splayed traveller's palm and Chinese fans. Their collective fronds provide a designer's or artist's dream: the way the sunlight filters through the forest ceiling and hits the various greens and oranges of the leaves is really something. You can appreciate the wonder of Michael Adams' paintings more after you've been to the Vallée de Mai. Also look out for the Seychelles black parrot which, like the coco de mer, exists only on Praslin.

A viewing tower marked on the guide fell down several years ago. There are a number of paths you can find yourself without going through the entrance gate, but they are not as beautifully staged as the official ones. You can also see a little waterfall on the road to Grand Anse, just past the car park. A sign says no swimming, bathing or drinking, but you wouldn't want to anyway.

The Vallée de Mai is open daily from 8.30 am to 5.30 pm. Entry costs Rs 25 – admission is free for children under 12 years old. There is a souvenir shop at the entrance gate which sells soft drinks, T-shirts, postcards, books, etc.

## Beaches

The best beach on Praslin is Anse Lazio, 6.5 km from Anse Volbert on the north-west side of the island; the sublimity here is thick in the air, especially in the late light – glorious white sand, a few rounded granite boulders and a lively line-up of waves. There's also a more sheltered area with good snorkelling opportunities at the rocky ends of the bay. Where the road arrives at the beach, there's an excellent restaurant known as Bon Bon Plume (see Places to Eat).

The bus route extends as far west as Anse Boudin, from where it's possible to walk or drive the rather rough 1.5 km up and over the hill to Anse Lazio. En route, the beaches at

Anse Boudin and Anse Takamaka (not to be confused with the beach of the same name on the south coast of Praslin) are also inviting. Cyclists will have to walk their bikes over this hill. Around Anse Lazio is the only bit of Praslin not shielded by a coral reef.

The quality of Anse Lazio is consistent, but not so for other island beaches. For half the year (May to September), the north coast beaches around Anse Volbert are better than those on the south coast around Grand Anse, while the opposite is true from October to April.

The long stretch of beach in front of the Paradise Sun, Praslin Beach and Côte d'Or hotels at Anse Volbert is good for sunbaking and bumming about. The whole beach, in fact, is called the Côte d'Or (Gold Coast). The lagoon is shallow and a bit like a bath at times. Walk or wade out to Chauve Souris Island and try snorkelling around there.

On the south coast, the reef is much further out and the beaches tend to be less attractive. The best are found in the extreme west around Anse Georgette, Petite Anse Kerlan (one of the locations for the film *Castaway* with Oliver Reed) and Anse Kerlan, and to the extreme east at Anse Consolation and Anse Marie-Louise. There is a nice tide pool and small beach at Anse Marie-Louise where the road winds uphill and inland. Buses from Anse Kerlan village go past Anse Consolation.

Anse Georgette is wilder than Anse Lazio and very remote. To get there from Anse Lazio, you must walk 2.5 km south along an overgrown path which runs parallel to the coast. It's also accessible from the south via the track leading north from Anse Kerlan.

## St Pierre Islet

Also good for snorkelling and some sloshing around are the waters around the tiny St Pierre Islet, about one km seaward from Chauve Souris Island (see Places to Stay). Boat trips organised by the Paradise Hotel, Praslin Beach Hotel and private operators cost Rs 40 per person.

## Grand Fond

The road from Anse Boudin up to 340 metre Grand Fond hill, the second highest summit on Praslin, can be done by car or Mini Moke, but it is nicest on foot. The reward is a fine view across Praslin and the surrounding islands and if you've managed to push a bicycle all the way to the top, you're in store for a great run down. Alternatively, descend along the track which heads south from Grand Fond and hits the south coast at the Catholic mission, just west of Maison des Palmes hotel on Grand Anse.

## Pointe Cabris

This rocky headland on the north-east tip of the island used to be the home and estate of a rich American woman. The ruined house overlooking the sea and steps stands testimony to a romantic but rough existence. You get there by taking the track down to the sea immediately before the Château de Feuilles lodge. However, the owners of the lodge do not want visitors strolling round the gardens or stopping en route for picnics.

## Walking Routes

There are two long and leisurely forest tracks which traverse the island. The five km Salazie Track runs from Anse Volbert village to Grand Anse village, and the three km Pasquière Track connects Anse Possession on the north coast with Grand Anse on the south coast.

There are also a couple of 'unofficial' walking routes around the perimeter of Vallée de Mai National Park (to walk the organised routes costs Rs 10 per person). The most interesting is probably the ascent of 367 metre Praslin Island Peak, the highest point on the island. The route is a traverse which begins 800 metres inland from Baie Ste Anne and follows the park boundary to Nouvelle Découverte Estate near Grand Anse.

Near the end of the south coast road at the westernmost point of the island, a track takes off over the hill to the coast at Chevalier Bay, then turns east and continues all the way to Anse Lazio. From Anse Kerlan to Anse Lazio is about five km and takes less than two hours.

For good views of Round Island and La Digue, follow the road from the northern end of Baie Ste Anne two km east to the shore at Anse La Blague. Continue on foot east along the shore past Petite Anse, then up the hill and through the village toward Anse La Farine. The path is overgrown to begin with, but it clears near the summit. Local people are happy to help with directions.

## Places to Stay

In recent years there has been a large increase in numbers of hotels and guesthouses. This has stabilised the prices for cheaper accommodation and has attracted visitors to use Praslin, rather than Mahé, as a base during their stay in the Seychelles.

## Places to Stay – bottom end

**Baie Ste Anne** The delightful *Orange Tree* (☎ 233248), perched on a hilltop above Baie Ste Anne, is reached via a steep and winding track. It is run by Mme Raville Lesperance and has six rooms for single/double Rs 200/300, including breakfast.

The atmosphere is traditional and homely, although Mme Lesperance's English is not too hot. The Orange Tree has a pen of tortoises, a dog that barks at night and a gaggle of related children who gather to watch TV. The rare Seychelles black parrot has even been spotted here. One of the tortoises died recently and proved too heavy to remove – it was buried in its pen.

**Pointe Cabris** Tucked away on Pointe Cabris is *Colibri* (☎ 233902). This guesthouse is recommended as a Seychelles highlight. Run by Daniella and Robert Maurer – Robert is Swiss and once worked for Swissair – Colibri has six rooms in a tranquil setting with a grand view of Baie Ste Anne. For a real treat, try the 'Honeymoon Suite'. There's a beachfront terrace and plenty of opportunity for snorkelling and swimming nearby. To keep the kids happy, there's also a video and compact disk library. Be sure to try the excellent food prepared by a renowned local chef. Rates for a single/ double room are Rs 320/420 (B&B) or Rs 370/550 for half board.

**Grand Anse** *Cabanes des Pêcheurs* (☎ 233-320) offers four bungalows, with verandahs fronting the sea. Rates for single/double/ triple occupancy start around Rs 275/350/ 400 (B&B) or Rs 350/500/575 for half board. The bungalows are close to the pier in Grand Anse.

Also nearby is *Beach Villas* (☎ 233445), run by Mr Auguste Confait. He has two bungalows, each with a fridge and hot water for single/double/triple Rs 230/320/400, including breakfast. Mr Confait can also arrange trips to Curieuse or St Pierre islet.

On the same stretch is the *Indian Ocean Fishing Club* (☎ 233324; fax 233911), with 16 rooms for single/double Rs 450/800 for half board. This hotel offers plenty of boat trips and hires out bikes for Rs 25/50 per half day/full day.

Close to the church in Grand Anse is *Britannia* (☎ 233215; fax 233944) guesthouse and restaurant. Service seems decidedly lacklustre, but the rooms are pleasant. Prices for a single/double/triple room start around Rs 300/380/455 (B&B); Rs 380/490/580 (half board); and Rs 430/ 650/750 (full board).

*Villa de Mer* (☎ 233972; fax 233015) is a new complex of six self-catering chalets, each with separate verandah. Prices for single/double/triple occupancy are Rs 330/ 440/605 (B&B). Maid services are supplied for laundry and daily cleaning. A BBQ area is available for grill parties. Light meals and dinner can be supplied on request and the Maison des Palmes hotel next door offers 20% discount to Villa de Mer guests. The owner's son, Michel Gardette, runs King Bambo Charters & Aqua Diving Services, which offers yacht charters and diving trips – for full details refer to the section on charters in the Seychelles – Getting Around chapter.

**Anse Volbert** In the centre of Anse Volbert is *Laurier* (☎ 232241), a new guesthouse and

bungalow complex with five rooms and two chalets. Rates for a single/double room are Rs 280/380 – single rate only applies if you stay longer than one night. The rate for double occupancy of a chalet is Rs 425 – no discount for single occupancy. The complex includes a restaurant and a boutique.

Close by is the *Duc de Praslin* (☎ 232-252), a similar complex containing three chalets and a restaurant. Rates for single/double occupancy are Rs 350/425 (B&B) or Rs 425/575 for half board.

**Anse Kerlan** At Anse Kérlan, there's the new *Islanders* (☎ 233224) complex which includes a restaurant, boutique, two self-catering chalets and four self-catering apartments. The friendly owners, Miet and Patrick Godley, are happy to accommodate families with extra beds for children. Rates for single/double occupancy start around Rs 290/400 (self-catering); Rs 310/440 (B&B); Rs 390/600 (half board); and Rs 470/760 (full board). For each additional person, there's a charge of Rs 50 (self-catering); Rs 70 (B&B); Rs 150 (half board); and Rs 230 (full board).

### Places to Stay – top end
**Anse Volbert** The *Praslin Beach* (☎ 232222; fax 247606) has 77 rooms, self-catering flats, a pool and the usual extras. The rates are single/double/triple Rs 690/ 1295/1350 for half board.

There are plenty of excursions to neighbouring islands (including Mahé) as well as around Praslin. Nonresidents can also organise deep-sea fishing trips, or hire sailboards, through the hotel. Bernard Camille operates a diving centre here.

The *Côte d'Or* (☎ 232200; fax 232130), at the east end of Anse Volbert, is used extensively, almost exclusively, by the Italian holiday tour company Club Vacanze, which also uses the associated *Chauve Souris Island Lodge* (☎ 232003; fax 232130).

The Côte d'Or offers 28 rooms. Rates for single/double/triple rooms start around Rs 680/950/1250 (B&B); Rs 750/1090/

1450 (half board); and Rs 850/1290/1720 (full board).

The Chauve Souris Island Lodge is a four-suite lodge on a tiny island opposite Anse Volbert village. For a minimum stay of three days, daily rates for single/double/triple occupancy are Rs 1300/1100/1050 (half board) and Rs 1450/1250/1200 (full board). There are discounts of around 10% for one week stays, and further discounts if you stay outside the peak months between December and May.

The *Village du Pêcheur* (☎ 232030; fax 232185), diagonally opposite the Praslin Beach Hotel at Anse Volbert, offers 10 rooms. Rates for a single/double/triple are Rs 632/770/1260 (B&B) and Rs 702/907/1358 (half board). The bar and restaurant are also open to nonresidents. On Saturdays there is a BBQ.

Rates at the *Paradise Sun Hotel* (☎ 232255; fax 232019), at the west end of Anse Volbert beach, are currently Rs 1113/1443/1806 for a single/double/triple room on half board. Major renovation is planned as part of the takeover of this hotel by the Sun Hotel group. It runs a range of excursions to nearby islands.

At the other end of the Côte d'Or beach, on Anse Gouvernement, is *L'Archipel* (☎ 232242; fax 232072). Singles/doubles in the well-spaced and well-situated bungalows cost Rs 1340/1600 for half board. The hotel has 6.5 hectares of tropical vegetation, a secluded beach, and many water sports facilities.

*La Réserve* (☎ 232211; fax 232166) at Anse Petite Cour is surrounded by lush scenery. It has three rooms in the main building and 12 bungalows. The single/double/triple rooms cost Rs 710/890/1220 (B&B); Rs 840/1150/1610 (half board); and Rs 930/1130/1860 (full board). The hotel also has an excellent restaurant.

**Grand Anse** At the western end of Grand Anse are two upmarket hotels. The *Flying Dutchman* (☎ 233337; fax 247606) has attractive, palm-thatched bungalows. Rates for single/double/triple occupancy are Rs 950/1200/1650 (half board). The *Maison des Palmes* (☎ 233411; fax 233880) has similar accommodation with single/double/triple rooms for Rs 695/750/855 (B&B); Rs 815/990/1180 (half board); and Rs 875/1110/1395 (full board). On Wednesdays there's a grill night, and on Saturdays there's a Créole buffet with singing and dancing – nonresidents may be admitted for a charge of Rs 120.

**Anse Cimitière** *Coco de Mer* (☎ 233900; fax 233919) is a new hotel with 30 chalets set in lush gardens fronting the hotel beach. Single/double rates are Rs 1020/1250 for half board, and an extra adult/child costs Rs 450/350 per day. Hotel guests have free use of windsurfers, canoes, bicycles, and a games room. There are two bars and an excellent restaurant. The Black Parrot bar offers nightly entertainment. There are also plans to set up a nature trail with marked sights of interest in the hills above the hotel grounds. The full walk will take between two and four hours and admission will be free to guests, but nonresidents will pay around Rs 10 per person.

**Pointe Cabris** *Château de Feuilles* (☎ 233-316; fax 233916), on the Pointe Cabris estate south of Baie Ste Anne, caters for those in search of exclusivity. All bookings should be made through *No Problem* (☎ 43 27 99 30), 243 Boulevard Raspail, 75014 Paris, France. There are two signs at the head of the driveway, one that says 'Consulat de Monaco' and the other 'No Visitors'.

Rooms, apartments, bungalows, and suites are available at prices ranging from

Fairy Tern

Rs 1000 for a double room, including breakfast, to Rs 1800 for four persons sharing a suite, including breakfast.

## Places to Eat

Most of the guesthouses and virtually all of the hotels on Praslin are open to nonresidents for meals. There are also several restaurants which cater to hotel guests in search of a change.

*Bon Bon Plume* (☎ 232136) restaurant on Anse Lazio does excellent food in a perfect setting. House specials include fish, lobster, and sorbets. A meal for two won't leave much change out of Rs 250. It's closed on Monday. *Rocky Bay Restaurant*, at the northern end of Petite Anse, is another isolated eatery in a great position. Main dishes cost around Rs 75.

The *Laurier Restaurant* (☎ 233241) on Anse Volbert is open for snacks and light meals. The lunch and dinner à la carte menu, however, is expensive.

The *Britannia* at Grand Anse does lunches for Rs 80 and dinners for Rs 90 per head.

**Self-Catering** Providing your own meals on Praslin will require a visit to the supermarket in Grand Anse or to the small stores in Grand Anse and Baie Ste Anne, which are stocked with a limited variety of imported tinned and packaged foods. Fresh vegetables and fruit are hard to come by, as the people only grow enough for their own needs.

Some stores have a selection of pastries and cakes for a few rupees or you can go to the bakery at La Réserve Hotel at Anse Petite Cour. You can also meet the fishermen coming in near the police station at Baie Ste Anne. A horn announces their arrival.

## Entertainment

Most of the large hotels, such as the Flying Dutchman, Praslin Beach and Paradise Sun hold dances at weekends.

The *First & Last Bar* at the end of the pier at Baie Ste Anne has a friendly atmosphere. There's a table football machine. One of the Gappy family, who own the bar, will pass the time of day and can cook you a meal for Rs 60. Occasionally, locals hold a disco here.

Mr Gappy Jnr runs the *Horizon Bar* at the far end of the bay which also runs discos and dances with live bands. A sign outside proclaims 'Visitors Welcome'!

## Getting There & Away

**Air** The airport terminal is three km from Grand Anse. See the Seychelles – Getting Around chapter for flight details.

**Boat** You can get to the island by schooner from Mahé and La Digue. See the Seychelles – Getting Around chapter for details of routes, times and prices for these schooner ferries.

Apart from the schooner ferries, all island-hopping, for example to Curieuse, Cousin, St Pierre and Aride is done by boat charter, either privately or through the hotels and tour operators. For more details, see the separate sections in this chapter for each of these islands.

The Praslin Beach and Paradise Sun hotels have the most extensive tour programmes. The tour operators TSS, Mason's, and NTA all have offices and representatives on the island.

## Getting Around

**Bus** There is a good bus service on the island; see the Seychelles – Getting Around chapter for details.

**Taxi** Details about taxi services and prices are provided in the Seychelles – Getting Around chapter.

**Car Rental** For car hire, try Solace Car Hire (☎ 233525), Prestige Car Hire (☎ 233226) or Austral Car Rental (☎ 232015). There are petrol stations at Baie Ste Anne and Grand Anse. For more details about car rental, see the Seychelles – Getting Around chapter.

**Bicycle** Bikes are popular on Praslin. The main bike hire operator is Côte d'Or (☎ 232071), at the entry road to the Praslin Beach Hotel in Anse Volbert village. It rents roadster bikes, ladies' and kids' models for Rs 25/50 per half day/full day.

The Indian Ocean Fishing Club hotel at Grand Anse also rents bikes for Rs 50 per day. The Praslin roads, however, can be heavy going on a bike and most people are saddle-sore after one day.

**Boat** Most of the hotels, guesthouses and tour operators can arrange boat hire. You can also contact Mr Louis Bédier (☎ 232192), who operates regular boat excursions to neighbouring islands. For more adventurous boat charters contact Michel Gardette (☎ 233972; fax 233015) who runs King Bambo Charters & Aqua Diving Services – for full details refer to the section on charters in the Seychelles – Getting Around chapter.

**Walking** Several walks and hikes are described in this chapter. TSS offers the following guided walks: Salazie track; Bassin Loulou/Grand Fond; Serimon/Anse Lazio;

and Fond Ferdinand. Contact TSS for more information.

**CURIEUSE ISLAND**

This island, just 1.5 km off the north coast of Praslin, was a leper colony from 1833 until 1965. The ruins of the leprosarium still stand on the south coast around Anse St José, like rows of gutted pit cottages or an early holiday village.

At Anse St José itself, and still very much intact, is the old doctor's house, a Créole home with a spacious verandah looking across to Praslin. It has been declared a national monument by the government.

The only inhabitants of Curieuse at present are the island manager and his family, who live in a large house on Laraie Bay, and several park wardens. Roaming the island are a couple of hundred giant tortoises, each marked with a number and a yellow cross. Attempts to preserve and increase this colony of giant land tortoises introduced

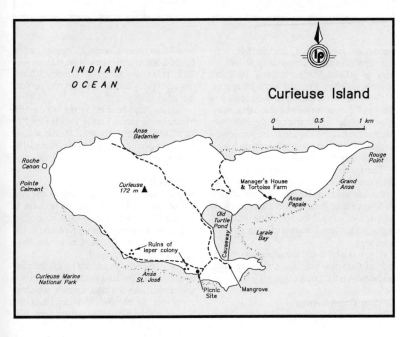

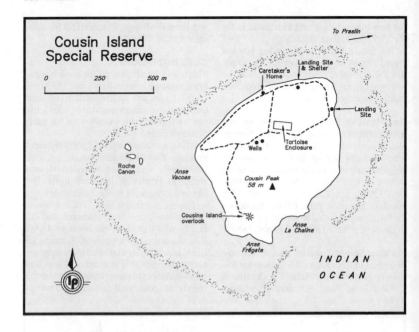

Cousin Island
Special Reserve

0        250        500 m

To Praslin

Caretaker's
Home

Landing Site
& Shelter

Landing
Site

Roche
Canon

Anse
Vacoas

Wells

Tortoise
Enclosure

Cousin Peak
58 m ▲

Cousine Island
overlook

Anse
La Chaline

Anse
Frégate

INDIAN
OCEAN

from Aldabra have been hampered by poaching. The island and surrounding waters are now an official Marine National Park and visitors are given a guided tour by wardens.

From the picnic site on Anse St José, you are guided over a rise and through a mangrove swamp before crossing the causeway to the manager's house. The causeway encloses the turtle pond, which is no longer used for breeding turtles.

There are some stunning granite rock sculptures en route. Look for the 'clash of the dinosaurs' at Laraie Bay and the 'pig' at Anse St José (where there is also a good beach). Beware of tiny blood-sucking seaweed gnats, which leave masses of little spots on your legs.

There is also a track leading around the side of Curieuse hill (172 metres) to Anse Badamier on the north coast.

### Getting There & Away

Most visitors to Curieuse arrive on a 'Three

Islands' day trip (Cousin, Curieuse, and St Pierre Islet) organised by NTA, Mason's or TSS. This trip operates on Tuesday, Thursday and Friday and costs Rs 400 per person, including lunch.

You may also be able to arrange a day trip by enquiring at the Praslin Beach Hotel or Paradise Sun Hotel. The return fare is around Rs 80 per person. The trip across takes 10 to 15 minutes.

### COUSIN ISLAND

Approximately one km in diameter and two km off the south-west coast of Praslin is Cousin Island, which used to be a coconut and cotton plantation, and is now one of the major highlights for visitors to the Seychelles – not to be missed!

The island was purchased by the International Council for Bird Preservation in 1968 and turned into a nature reserve, which is supported by the World-Wide Fund for Nature and the Seychelles government. It is the home of several endangered species, and it's also a breeding site for sea birds and turtles. It's an amazing experience to walk through thick forest with birds seemingly nesting on every branch. Undaunted by humans, birds create a constant flurry whilst gathering twigs, leaves, and anything else that looks suitable for nesting material.

A small booklet, sold for Rs 3 on the island, explains the different species of birds, reptiles, insects and vegetation you'll see. There are thousands of skinks and geckos, and plenty of guano. The rarest bird to be seen is the brush warbler – Cousin is its only natural habitat. The most common birds are the black noddies.

You may also have the opportunity to see the *paille en queue*, or white-tailed tropic bird, at close quarters. This long-tailed bird graces the emblems of Réunion and Mauritius but is not often seen on those islands. The island is also home to the oldest giant tortoise outside Aldabra, although Esmeralda on Bird Island also claims that distinction. Keep an eye open for George and Georgina, carapaces spotted with guano,

who diligently plod after visitors in the hope of having their leathery necks stroked.

Six volunteer ICBP staff live on the island and take turns conducting guided tours. Roby Bresson, a lively local character, has spent much of his life on the island and has amassed a wealth of knowledge about the fauna and flora as well as a bunch of anecdotes. He walks with a slight limp, the result of almost losing a leg to an irate needlefish which he'd unintentionally rammed whilst windsurfing across to Praslin!

You have to go on a tour, which takes about 1½ hours at a comfortable rate. You cannot visit without advance notice and you cannot do your own thing when you get there. You can get close enough to the birds to photograph them nesting, but tripods and close-up lenses are not allowed.

At the end of the tour it may be possible to go for a dip, but official regulations forbid this. There are soft drinks and postcards on sale. If you want more information on the ICBP and its work, sign the visitors' book or write to them at 219C Huntingdon Rd, Cambridge, CB3 0DL, UK (☎ (0223) 27 7318).

## Noddies

Cousin hosts around 100,000 pairs of black (lesser) noddies during the southeast monsoon. They prefer to nest in pisonia trees, but will make do with casuarina and other forest trees. At the height of the nesting season their smell pervades the island and their droppings drop so regularly that at this time of year you're strongly advised to wear a wide brimmed hat while walking the island foot trails.

When mating season approaches, noddies go through an elaborate mating ritual. The female bird sits in the tree where the nest will be built while the male carefully selects an appropriate leaf to use for building the nest. Having checked the leaf from every perspective he reverently hands it to his potential mate who disdainfully discards it. This process is repeated until a pile of discarded leaves litters the ground. Finally he hands her the right leaf, and she defecates on it! This leaf then forms the keystone of the nest, constructed from the previously discarded leaves cemented together with droppings.

The ritual far exceeds the quality of the resulting nest, however. No way about it, noddies build a shoddy nest. Into the shallow depression on this grotty little nest a single egg is laid and incubated for an average 35 days. That is if the egg doesn't simply fall out of the nest. If that happens they just start all over again. Unfortunately chicks are also prone to falling out of the noddies' slipshod nest and in that case they, too, are simply abandoned. A storm during nesting time can wreak havoc upon a noddy colony.

Once the chicks are old enough to leave the nest they wander round in groups known as creches. During the day their parents venture far out to sea hunting small fish which swim close to the surface. When they return at night they call to their offspring, which recognise their parents' call and break away from the creche to be fed on regurgitated stomach contents. ■

## Getting There & Away

You can make arrangements to visit Cousin on a half day or full day tour through any of the hotels, or through TSS, Mason's or NTA tourist agencies. Cousin is only open to visitors on Tuesday, Thursday and Friday. To make the most of Cousin, we recommend a full day tour, which costs Rs 275. A half day tour costs Rs 265, or you can take a 'Three Island' (Cousin, Curieuse, and St Pierre Islet) tour for Rs 400. If you charter a boat or arrange a private visit, you will have to pay a landing fee of Rs 75 per boat. This fee is included in the price of group tours. In addition there is an admission fee of Rs 75 per person, also included in the cost of group tours.

The boat ride from Grand Anse to Cousin takes about 15 minutes, but the landing sites vary depending on the time of the year. There is no jetty and often visitors have to be ferried from the launch to shore in a zodiac dinghy. This can be fun or harrowing, depending on the size of the swells.

## COUSINE ISLAND

From the modest heights of Cousin you can see across to Cousine, a privately owned island which is not open to the public. The present owner, a South African millionaire who shelled out US$5 million for the island, is busy building a villa.

## ARIDE ISLAND

Aride Island lies 10 km to the north of Praslin. The island was purchased for the Royal Society for Nature Conservation in 1973 by Christopher Cadbury (of chocolate fame).

Aride, the most northerly of the granite islands, rises to 135 metres, and is partly surrounded by a coral reef. It has been declared a nature reserve, as it has the greatest concentration of sea birds in the area,

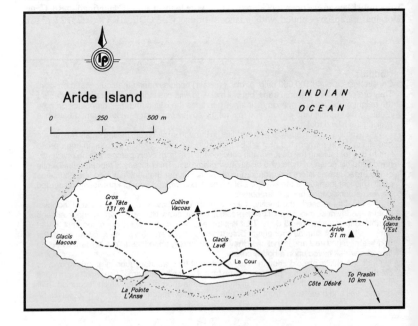

## Wedge-tailed Shearwaters

While the noddies nest in trees, wedge-tailed shearwaters breed in burrows, from October to March. The male shearwaters return first to exactly the same burrow as in previous years, and clean things up in preparation for the arrival of their mates.

Shearwaters mate for life and when their companion, unseen for the past year, turns up all hell breaks loose. From dawn to dusk they shriek, wail, groan and howl to each other. The whole colony seems to get together on this and the noise builds up to an absolute crescendo then suddenly ceases. A single groan will recommence the whole symphony. It's said that sailors became convinced that certain islands were haunted. All night long this horrible, almost human-like noise would be heard, but come dawn the island would be found empty. The shearwaters had set out just before dawn to spend the day fishing.

Wedge-tailed shearwaters have a wingspan disproportionately large compared to their body size. This makes for easy flying but difficult takeoffs and landings. The birds have well-defined 'runways' where they line up to make their pre-dawn departure. When coming in to land, once they're committed on their final approach they have great difficulty in making changes of direction and have been known to collide with objects in their path.

The single egg is incubated for about 50 days and the chick is fed so energetically that it may eventually grow to be bigger than its parents! Then the parents abandon their offspring and fly off, leaving their well-fed chick to survive on its body fat, learn to fly and follow its parents. It's been suggested that shearwaters' lousy takeoff and landing abilities is not unrelated to the fact that their parents leave them to learn this vital skill by trial and error! ■

including large colonies of the lesser noddy, roseate terns and the frigate bird (noted for its giant wing span). The strangely perfumed, white and purple-spotted Wright's gardenia, which grows nowhere else in the world, is also found here.

It can be reached by boat between April and October only. The rest of the year the winds and seas make landing difficult and dangerous on the island's southern coast, Côte Désiré. Recent problems with management and poor weather have hampered access for visitors.

Booby Island, just off the coast of Aride, is reputed to have received its name because of an anatomical resemblance! (Well, it might have been named for the bird...)

### Getting There & Away

Between April and October, the larger hotels on Praslin and TSS, Mason's, and NTA tour agencies run day trips up to four times a week – usually on Wednesday, Thursday, Friday and Sunday. The price per person is around Rs 350, including lunch, drinks and landing fee. The journey takes about an hour – don't forget to pack your gear in a waterproof bag.

For more information about Aride on a regular basis, subscribe to the quarterly *Aride Island Nature Reserve Newsletter* available from Ron Gerlach, PO Box 207, the Seychelles. You can also contact the International Council for Bird Preservation (ICPB – address details supplied in the Cousin Island section in this chapter).

# La Digue & Other Inner Islands

## LA DIGUE

La Digue Island is beautiful and remains virtually unspoilt by either the local inhabitants, who number only 2000, or the tourists, whose numbers remain low due to the small number of hotels. If you thought the pace of life on Praslin was relaxed, you'll find La Digue even more easygoing.

The island, which is about four km east of Praslin, was once a big coconut plantation. The main settlement stretches from the harbour area at La Passe down the west coast to L'Union.

The central granite ridge of the island reaches an altitude of 300 metres. Surrounding the island is a profusion of giant naturally sculpted granite boulders which would do credit to Henry Moore. Together with the

La Digue

| 0 | 0.5 | 1 km |

**PLACES TO STAY & EAT**

1 Patatran Restaurant & Bungalows
3 Anse Sévère Bungalow
11 Choppy's Bungalows
13 La Digue Island Lodge
15 Le Romarin Guest House
16 Bernique Guest House
17 Sitronnel Guest House
18 Château St Cloud

**OTHER**

2 Cemetery
4 Pier & Bicycle Hire
5 Bakery
6 Post Office & Police Station
7 TSS & Tarosa Cafeteria
8 Market
9 Hospital
10 Mason's Travel
12 National Travel Agency
14 Barclays Bank & Gregoire's Shop
19 Shop
20 La Digue Veuve Reserve
21 School & National Library
22 Phoenix Store & Ice Cream Parlour
23 Church
24 Petrol Station
25 Old Cemetery
26 Plantation House
27 Public Water Tap
28 Abandoned settlement

Anse Patates
Good swimming & snorkelling
Anse Sévère
Good beach at high tide
Anse Gaulettes
Pte Cap Barbi
Good swimming beach
Ferry to Praslin
Anse Grosse Roche
La Passe
Nid d'Aigles
Anse Banane
Anse Fourmis
Anse la Réunion
La Réunion
Belle Vue
La Digue Island Peak 333 m
Anse Caiman
L'Union
Roche Bols
Fond Piment
Pte Ma Flore
Anse Union
l'Union Estate Copra Plantation
La Retraite
Anse Cocos
Pte Source d'Argent
Citadel 150 m
Pte Turcy
Petite Anse
Anse Source d'Argent
Passable only at low tide
Pte Belize
Grand Anse
Anse Songe
Anse Pierrot
Pte Canon Grand l'Anse
Anse aux Cèdres
Anse Bonnet Carré
Grand Cap
Pte Camille
Pte Jacques
Anse Marron

brilliant white sand, the turquoise sea and the greenery of the palms, the scenes are some of the most picturesque in the Seychelles.

## Information
**Post** The post office is next to the police station, near the pier at La Passe. It is open Monday to Friday from 8 to 11 am and from 1 to 3 pm. There is one mail collection per day.

**Banks** Barclays Bank has a branch opposite the Island Lodge Hotel, next to Gregoire's Boutique. It is open on Monday, Wednesday and Friday from 10.30 am to 2 pm. There is also a Seychelles Savings Bank, opposite the hospital, which is open Monday to Friday from 8.15 am to 1 pm and from 2 to 3.30 pm, and on Saturdays from 9 to 11 am. You can change money at both these banks.

## Beaches
On the south-eastern shore of La Digue are several white sandy bay beaches, swept by waves which have broken past the reef. Beware of dangerous undercurrents. A 3.5 km road crosses the island from La Passe to Grand Anse, the largest and one of the busiest beaches – if you can call any place on La Digue busy. Look carefully and you may see the rock formation known as Le Roi Triste (sad king). To continue from there to the next cove, Anse Cocos, requires a little effort to find the path (a full description is given under Grand Anse & East Coast Walk later in this chapter).

Near La Passe, there is a nice path from L'Union down the coast to Anse Source d'Argent. The track leads through variously shaped granite boulders – look out for the 'turtle's head' and the 'big fort' rocks – to the splendid beach at Anse Source d'Argent, setting for many of the sets for the film *Crusoe*. During high tide, the trail can be impassable.

Anse Patates in the north of the island must rate as one of the Seychelles' finest and most beautiful swimming beaches, and further down the east coast is another magical stretch of beach at Anse Gaulettes.

## Diving
The diving centre at La Digue Island Lodge can arrange diving instruction and expeditions.

## L'Union Estate & Copra Factory
The estate management now charges visitors Rs 10 to visit the copra factory and grounds at L'Union. The factory still operates between 7 am and 4 pm during the week and tours are available. Enquiries should be made at the office.

Beside the factory is the State Guest House, which is used for presidential guests, and was also a location for the film *Goodbye Emanuelle*. Behind the factory office is a craft shop specialising in wooden carvings. The grounds also have a boatyard, a vanilla plantation and tennis courts for the workers.

North of the estate is an old colonial cemetery. Most of the headstones are now illegible, but you can still make out a couple dating to the 19th century.

## Veuve (Paradise Flycatcher) Reserve
This narrow strip of forest alongside the central road into the interior of the island serves as a bird sanctuary. It was established by British conservationists Tony Beamish and Christopher Cadbury, who also own the Aride Island bird sanctuary.

The bird in question is the black paradise flycatcher *(Terpsiphone corvina)*, which the Créoles call the *veuve* (widow) because the male bird appears to be in mourning with its streaming black tail feathers. Endemic to the Seychelles, there are thought to be fewer than 50 pairs left, with just five or six nesting pairs in the reserve itself.

Most of the trees in the reserve are takamaka and badamier. Watch out also for frogs, moorhens and the rare terrapins described under Grand Anse and East Coast walk.

## Grand Anse & East Coast Walk
**La Passe to Grand Anse** The first part of the walk, between La Passe and Grand Anse, follows the road and may be negotiated on either on foot or bicycle.

Begin by walking south out of La Passe. After a little more than one km, just before the colonial government cemetery, bear left and head inland through the copra plantation. Less than one km later, you'll reach the Mare Soupape, a low marshy area where you'll be able to see moorhens, dragonflies, frogs and even two very rare freshwater terrapins, the yellow-bellied terrapin and the star-bellied terrapin. These are known to the Créoles as *torti soupape*, hence the name of the marsh.

Past the marsh, follow the bend around to the left, then to the right, and continue to a T-junction. Here, take a right and follow the road as it slowly climbs up and across the spine of the island. After less than two km, you'll reach the east coast at Grand Anse, which is a great place for a picnic but isn't ideal for swimming due to high surf and dangerous currents.

At Grand Anse, you can either decide to return to La Passe the way you came or continue to Petite Anse, Anse Cocos and beyond.

**Grand Anse to Anse Fourmis** If you're going on, follow the prominent track north along the coast, past the marshy areas. It will then turn inland and climb a short steep route over a rocky ridge before descending to Petite Anse, with dangerous bathing but nice views of the foaming breakers.

From there, the track continues, slightly inland behind the front row of trees and scrub along the beach, emerging at a track intersection near the northern end of Petite Anse. Here, you should turn left and cross two small bridges into a cattle pasture. Beyond it is a small farmstead (to be avoided – the owners don't appreciate being asked directions!).

About 15 to 20 metres beyond the second bridge (ie into the cattle pasture), you'll see a very faint track leading off to the right and into a clump of trees. Once amongst the trees, the track becomes quite prominent – good solid stone steps – and climbs over another small, rocky ridge. Near the top of the ridge,

you'll pass through a gate and descend along a very well-defined track.

At the foot of the hill, it turns seaward and leads out to the shore at Anse Cocos. Follow the beach northward toward the cluster of abandoned buildings and old rotting wooden boats. This was once a lively spot and served as an agricultural enterprise as well as a storage and transport point for copra from surrounding plantations. At the northern end of Anse Cocos is an enclosed rock pool which provides a calmer dip than the strong waves on the open beach.

From here, the route becomes rougher and more difficult, so if you aren't up for an adventure, return to Grand Anse the way you came. Otherwise, continue to the end of the beach, but avoid the fairly obvious track leading out to the rocky point (keep seaward of the swamp of bulrushes) and search in the trees for the track which climbs to the summit of the ridge. Once you're on the track, it'll be obvious, but at times you may have to search around in the grass to locate the route. Once over the ridge, the track drops to an abandoned building at the south end of Anse Caiman.

Here, strike off through the vegetation along a very faint track leading north along the coast. Resist any temptations to venture inland, especially at a muddy area where the track seems to disappear. Instead, search in the boulders ahead; the route is marked by splotches of white paint, placed at intervals of about five metres. You'll have to scramble a bit, but the route is marked.

At the north end of Anse Caiman, you'll arrive at a formidable-looking barrier of granite boulders. The route from here across to Anse Fourmis is very difficult so don't attempt it unless you're an agile scrambler. The only possible route through is marked by splotches of white paint on boulders, and keeps to within about 10 metres of the sea (at high tide). Again, don't be tempted inland – there's no way across the ridge higher up! After about 150 metres of rock-hopping and scrambling on all fours, you'll arrive at Anse Fourmis and will see the road about 50 metres away, straight ahead.

If you're trying to access this route from the north, don't follow the faint track leading uphill, inland from the end of the road; it's a dead end. Instead, walk straight ahead (ie parallel to the coast). You'll see an opening in the trees ahead and just beyond, the first white paint splotch (a very large one, like a bulls-eye) on the boulder marking the route's beginning.

## La Digue Island Peak

To reach the highest point on La Digue, head up to 333 metre La Digue Island peak in the centre of the island. Take the only road leading uphill from the main route near Château St Cloud and follow it to its end. From there, you'll find a track leading up to and along Nid d'Aigles ridge. A right turn at the ridge will eventually get you to the peak but the going can get tough and the view obscured due to the profusion of French plum trees. There are a few isolated properties in the area.

## Places to Stay – bottom end

Places to stay on La Digue are limited, so you should always book ahead. There is one major hotel and a growing number of guesthouses and bungalow complexes. Often there is a vacancy for a short time only. If you do get stuck, some of the small hotel owners have friends who will put you up temporarily (and unofficially) for the same fee, but don't rely on that.

*Château St Cloud* (☎ 234346) used to be *the* place for travellers to stay in the Seychelles and, with low prices and recent renovations, it is still a great deal. The atmosphere is relaxed, friendly and informal – buffet meals are eaten together at a long table.

The château is a former plantation house which hasn't changed much since it was built – the slave quarters are still in evidence. It has 10 recently renovated rooms each with a bathroom. Rates per person are Rs 100 per night on a half-board basis only.

Just along the road from Château St Cloud is the pleasant and friendly *Bernique Guest House* (☎ 234229), run by Mme Jeanne

Legge. The guesthouse has six double rooms, arranged in small bungalows. Prices for a single/double/triple are Rs 200/300/400, including breakfast; or Rs 275/400/600 for half board. There are also a couple of older rooms in the main house which cost around 10% less.

The restaurant serves excellent food and is a pleasant place to relax and watch livid green geckos beside the lights patiently waiting for the arrival of their insect dinner. On Tuesday and Saturday nights, a local musical group with no name rolls up in an ambulance for an evening of Créole hits, as well as John Denver, and Paul Simon 'golden oldies'.

Just south of Bernique is *Le Sitronnel* (☎ 234230), a friendly guesthouse, run by Madame Adrienne, who offers three double rooms. At Rs 365 for a double room with half board, this place represents good value.

Just north of Bernique is *Le Romarin* (☎ 234115), run by Madame Bailey. This modest guesthouse has three rooms and the rate is Rs 200 per person on half board basis.

*Choppy's Bungalows Guest House* (☎ 234334), on the shore near La Passe, has four rooms in two bungalows. One of the bungalows faces the sea. Across the road is the bar and reception area in what used to be the island's Odéon cinema. The restaurant is an open, thatched shelter near the shore and food is carried over from the cinema. Choppy's is fading at the edges and the prices are relatively high. Singles/doubles cost Rs 335/460 on half board basis or Rs 415/615 for full board.

To rent *Anse Sévère Bungalow* on Anse Sévère, contact Odette de Comarmond (☎ 247354).

## Places to Stay – top end

*Patatran Village* (☎ 234333; fax 234344) is a spiffy complex of seven chalets in a superb position at Anse Patates. The chalets, named after flowers, are clean, bright and enjoy good views across to the Soeurs islands and Félicité. Just a couple of metres away is perhaps the most picturesque beach on the Seychelles – Anse Patates. Rates for a single/double room are Rs 610/850 on half board basis or Rs 680/1000 for full board. The restaurant serves snacks, set meals, and à la carte dishes.

*La Digue Island Lodge* (☎ 234233) is an amalgamation of the former Gregoire's Island Lodge and the Cabanes des Anges. Accommodation in this large, resort-style hotel, is provided in A-frame chalets, round chalets, and colonial villas. Prices for single/double occupancy of the chalets start around Rs 880/1270 on a half board basis or Rs 945/1390 for full board. Slightly cheaper are single/double rooms in the lodge's annexe which cost Rs 580/835 on a half board basis or Rs 660/985 for full board. The restaurant offers a good set menu or you can order a snack at the poolside bar. The hotel also has a small beach and a diving centre, and can organise a variety of tours around La Digue or to neighbouring islands. Guests are given free use of snorkelling equipment and bicycles. Glass-bottom boat tours and water sports facilities are also available.

The hotel arranges day trips to Félicité three times a week for Rs 300 per person, including BBQ lunch and time for snorkelling.

### Places to Eat
There are no independent restaurants on La Digue and places to eat are limited, so you should make advance reservations. All the places to stay will take bookings from non-residents for meals.

At the *La Digue Island Lodge* restaurant, beside the entrance, you can order a large grilled fish for Rs 50 – good value and delicious. *Bernique* is also recommended – a set dinner costs Rs 75 per person. *Patatran* restaurant is good for inexpensive snacks, such as omelettes or sandwiches, or you can splurge Rs 95 on a four course set meal. For a cheaper treat try the fish marinaded in lemon for Rs 35.

If you want to buy food or snacks, there are a couple of food shops and a bakery close to La Passe pier. *Gregoire's Boutique*, near the Island Lodge, is the largest shop on the island, but tends to be more expensive than

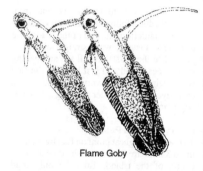

Flame Goby

the smaller, older stores near the pier. They all sell wine, beer, spirits, long-life milk, biscuits, jams, souvenirs, etc.

### Getting There & Away
You can only get to La Digue by boat from either Mahé or Praslin. See the Seychelles – Getting Around chapter for details about schooner ferry services.

### Getting Around
**Taxi** See the Seychelles – Getting Around chapter for details about the taxi service on La Digue.

**Bicycle** Everyone walks or cycles on La Digue. Only essential vehicles are permitted on the islands. There are hundreds of bikes to rent, with several operators offering daily rates of Rs 25 (without gears) and Rs 35 (with gears). Check the bikes carefully, many are in poor condition and the gears often don't work. If you hire a bike for more than one day, ask for a discount.

Bicycle rental people line up to meet tourists at the ferry. This was the only place in the Seychelles we found people actually pushing to sell you a service. Keep in mind that there are no sealed roads, that visitors often find they have enough time on their hands and that the island is small enough to cover comfortably on foot.

**Walking** Several walks and hikes are described in this chapter.

**Boat** Boat hire or charter is limited on La Digue. The Island Lodge offers boat trips; alternatively, check the guesthouses for contacts.

**Ox Cart** The ox carts are for pleasure trips and are not a practical or cheap alternative. An official tour of L'Union estate costs Rs 10 per person.

**Tours** NTA, Mason's, and TSS have offices on La Digue. Day trips can be arranged to Grande Soeur Island (Rs 450 per person); Frégate (Rs 600 per person); and Cousin, Curieuse and St Pierre Islet (Rs 400 per person). La Digue Island Lodge arranges day trips to Félicité.

## FÉLICITÉ ISLAND
This mountainous island, 3.5 km north-east of La Digue, has good walking trails and excellent snorkelling sites.

The island's main entrepreneur, Gregoire Payet (who runs the supermarket and Island Lodge on La Digue), has renovated two French plantation houses for use as luxurious accommodation, complete with air-con and deluxe bathrooms. Each house has two bedrooms and can accommodate up to four. Close to the houses is the beach of La Penice – a motor cruiser is provided for fishing or snorkelling excursions. Planned walking tracks lead guests to discover the fauna and flora, including giant land tortoises and many bird species. A tennis court is also available. For evening entertainment you can either soak in the peace and quiet or watch TV or videos.

The island is rented out according to the motto, 'an island of your own'. The minimum number of guests is two and the maximum is eight. Once a reservation has been confirmed, no other reservation is allowed to overlap with the confirmed stay of the guests on the island. Group bookings are accepted only for families and groups of friends wishing to spend their holiday together.

The minimum length of stay is three days.

Full board only is provided and all drinks are included. Also included in the rates are the transfer – 30 minutes by boat – from La Digue or Praslin. Children under 12 years old stay free of charge.

Rates for a three-day stay start around Rs 12,240 for two persons, Rs 2950 for four persons, and Rs 35,700 for eight persons. For bookings, contact La Digue Island Lodge (☎ 234232; fax 234132), which also arranges day trips to Félicité at Rs 300 per person.

## COCOS ISLAND
This is a tiny island just to the north of Felicité Island and closer to La Digue than to Praslin. It was once considered to be the best place for snorkelling in the area. However, the government closed it to visitors in 1987 because coral and shells were being damaged and pilfered at an alarming rate by tourists and locals. The island will continue to remain off limits until the coral has recovered.

## PETITE & GRANDE SOEUR ISLANDS
These two islands are north of Félicité and Cocos islands. Grande Soeur has good beaches, a forest of coconut palms, and dramatic outcrops of huge granite boulders. NTA, Mason's, and TSS arrange trips to Grande Soeur Island from La Digue for Rs 450 per person, including snorkelling and a BBQ lunch.

## FRÉGATE ISLAND
This privately owned granite island, 56 km east of Mahé and about 20 km south of La Digue, was once reputed to be a pirate lair – today it's a stronghold for the birds.

Where La Digue has the only black paradise flycatchers, Praslin the only black parrots and Cousin the only brush warblers, Frégate has the only magpie robins. It is also the last home of the tenebrionid beetle! There once were Java deer on the island, which the French introduced from Mauritius, but these died out in the 1950s. The giant land tortoises are still around.

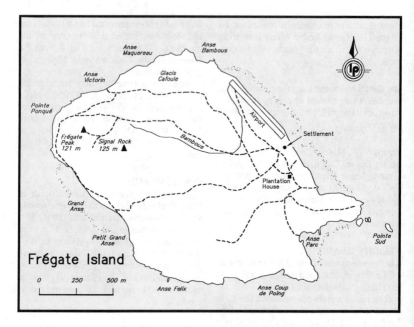

Frégate Island

| 0 | 250 | 500 m |

Anse Maquereau · Anse Bambous · Anse Victorin · Glacis Cafoule · Airport · Pointe Ponqué · Frégate Peak 121 m · Signal Rock 125 m · Bambous · Settlement · Plantation House · Grand Anse · Petit Grand Anse · Anse Parc · Pointe Sud · Anse Felix · Anse Coup de Poing

Attractions include superb beaches, such as Anse Victorin (considered one of the best beaches in the Seychelles), bird watching, hiking along wooded paths, and treasure hunting. There are caves around the island and, as at Bel Ombre, some rocks bear mysterious markings awaiting someone to decipher them.

### Place to Stay

The only place to stay is the *Plantation House* (☎ 224789), a picturesque hotel entered through the roots of a giant banyan tree. There are 10 rooms and rates for a single/double room are Rs 940/1225 on a full board basis. An extra bed costs Rs 610.

The house is managed by Mrs Marlene Lionnet, the former managing director of the National Travel Agency. Bookings can be made through travel agencies or direct with the Frégate office (☎ 323123; fax 225169) on Revolution Ave, Victoria.

### Getting There & Away

Air Seychelles operates flights twice daily (except Thurs & Sat) to and from Mahé. The trip takes 15 minutes and a return ticket costs Rs 410. TSS, Mason's and NTA travel agencies offer day trips for Rs 600 per person, including flights, lunch and guided tour.

### BIRD ISLAND

In contrast to the central granite islands of the Seychelles, this is a coral island – flat, covered in palms and ringed by a white coral beach. As the name implies, the entire island is dominated by birds, birds, birds. For most visitors it's an awesome and immensely enjoyable experience, but it takes a while to become accustomed to the sights, smells, and noises of the bird world.

The privately-owned island, 96 km north of Mahé, is one km long and two km wide. Apart from being an obvious magnet for ornithologists, Bird Island is also good for

**Bird Island
(Île aux Vaches)**

weight stakes when he made it into the 1990 Guinness Book of Records.

### Place to Stay

*Bird Island Lodge* (☎ 344449) has 25 wooden bungalows with twin-bed rooms and verandahs facing the sea. Singles or doubles cost Rs 990 for the first night on obligatory full-board basis, including the flights. Rates for single or double rooms become less expensive when booked for longer stays. For example, the rates per person for two/four/seven days are Rs 1150/880/760 with full board and including return flights.

### Getting There & Away

Air Seychelles (☎ 373101) flies in and out of Bird Island every day of the week, but you must book an excursion package for a minimum of one night. You can also get to the island by boat from Mahé. The trip takes up to eight hours, compared with 30 minutes for the flight.

### DENIS ISLAND

Denis Island is similar in size and everything else to Bird Island, but is more exclusive. The island was named after the French navigator Denis de Trobriand, who 'discovered' it in 1773.

Now Denis supports a population of 50 and belongs to French couple Pierre and Suzanne Burkhardt, who bought it in 1975.

The Burkhardts' brochure says: 'Denis Island is not – does not pretend and does not want to be – a hotel. Welcomed as personal guests by the island owner, his family and his friends who joined the family, the guests participate in the accomplishment of a dream: the dream to be themselves, for a few days, the owners of an isolated island in the middle of the Indian Ocean'.

Having said that, the island attracts and plays to the big-game fishing set more than any other group. The coral island is southeast of Bird Island and about 80 km from Mahé. There are far fewer sea birds than on Bird and the vegetation is richer and thicker. The Burkhardts make their own suntan oil from the coconuts that grow on the island.

snorkelling, swimming, diving, windsurfing, deep-sea fishing, playing tennis and simply lazing around. Check where you swim, as there are dangerous currents in some parts.

Bird Island is also called Île aux Vaches (Cow Island), probably derived from the local name for 'sea cows' or dugongs. The island takes its present name from the vast colonies of fairy terns, common noddies and millions of sooty terns which nest at one end. The sooty terns arrive between April and May and breed around October.

Large numbers of turtles also breed on the island. Out of 500 baby turtles born to each female, only 30 may survive to adulthood.

Bird Island claims to have the oldest tortoise in the Seychelles, if not the world. Esmeralda is believed to be over 150 years old, weighs around 300 kg, and, despite the name, is a male. The Cousin Island people maintain that their resident giant tortoise is older, but Esmeralda officially topped the

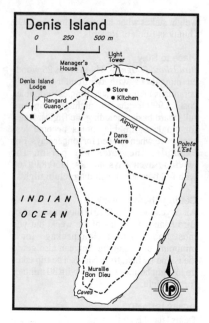

# Denis Island

0    250    500 m

Manager's House
Light Tower
Denis Island Lodge
Hangard Guano
● Store
● Kitchen
Airport
Dans Varre
Pointe L'Est

INDIAN OCEAN

Muraille Bon Dieu
Caves

## Place to Stay

The *Denis Island Lodge* (☎ 344143), which 'does not pretend to be a hotel', has 24 luxuriously thatched, roomy and secluded bungalows. Singles/doubles cost Rs 1330/1936 on a full board basis. The minimum booking is three days – daytrippers are not allowed – and you must deposit 30% of the fee within eight days of making a reservation.

Excursion packages are available from travel agents for the minimum of three nights, including the flights and full board, for Rs 4211 per person. However, it is possible on a last-minute basis – subject to availability – to book for just one or two nights for Rs 2130/3170 per person.

## Getting There & Away

Air Seychelles flies daily between Mahé and Denis. The flight takes 25 minutes.

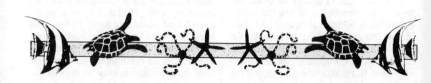

# Outer Islands

The majority of the Seychelles islands, all of them coral, are spread out over hundreds of km to the south-west of the main Mahé group and fall into three main groups – the Amirantes, Farquhar and Aldabra groups.

Let's face it, you would need to have a lot of time and money to go to these islands as a visitor. Or you would need to have a special scientific interest and authoritative or financial backing to persuade the Seychelles government to let you ride along with the workers and supply boats. For private boat charter, contact the Marine Charter Association (☎ 322126; fax 224679) in Victoria (for more details refer to the Seychelles – Getting Around chapter).

Only a few of the 70 islands are inhabited, by about 500 fishermen, research and agricultural workers employed by the Islands Development Company (IDC). The rest of the islands are too small to be productive, although one day some may end up as Maldives-style resorts.

The main industry of these islands is copra. More than 2500 tonnes are produced annually. Livestock has also been introduced.

The IDC is responsible for managing Coétivy, Desroches, Marie-Louise, Desnoeufs, Plate and Alphonse in the Amirantes group; Providence and Farquhar in the Farquhar group; and Cosmolédo and Astove in the Aldabra group.

Seven of the IDC islands have airstrips and the company also runs three schooners – the *Argo*, *Lady Esme* and a 35 metre fibreglass schooner from Italy which can carry 24 passengers. For prices and permission to visit the islands contact the IDC (☎ 224640) at New Port, Victoria.

## AMIRANTES GROUP

The largest of the three groups, the Amirantes, lies 200 km to 330 km south-west of Mahé. The islands were named Ilhas do Amirante (Admiral Islands) in 1501 by Vasco da Gama, the Portuguese explorer.

To charter a boat to the Amirantes, contact the Marine Charter Association in Victoria or Michel Gardette of King Bambo Charters & Aqua Diving Services (see the Seychelles – Getting Around chapter). *Scuba Safaris* (☎ 071-4980003) at 14/11 Park House, South Bank Commercial Centre, 140 Battersea Park Rd, London arranges one-week cruises to the Amirantes on the luxury dive vessel, Fantasea, for around UK£2500.

## Desroches Island

The main island in the group is Desroches which, having been exploited for timber, is now a tourist destination with a resort offering water sports, fishing, diving, and excursions to other islands in the Amirantes.

**Amirantes Group**

African Banks
Rémire Island
Rémire Reef
D'Arros Island
Residence Island
Fouquet Island
St Joseph Island
Paul Island
Pelican Island
Poivre Island
Florentin Island
Desroches Island
South Island
Carcassaye Island
Etoile Island
Boudeuse Island
Chien Island
Marie-Louise Island
Desnoeufs Island

0     50     100 km

Alphonse Island
Bijoutier Island
St François Island

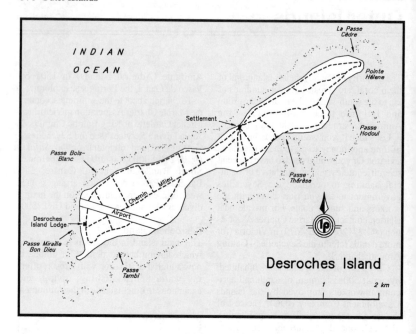

Desroches Island

The best time for diving is from September to May.

After being flattened by a freak cyclone in 1990, the *Desroches Hotel* (☎ 229002) is back in action with 20 chalets. Excursion packages only are available for a minimum of two nights, including the flights and full board, for Rs 2339 per person.

There are flights three times a week between Mahé and Desroches. The trip takes one hour.

### Poivre Island

Poivre Island is named after Pierre Poivre, the French governor of Mauritius from 1763 to 1772, who later introduced spices to Mahé. Poivre is accessible on 10-day yacht charters for up to eight people for around Rs 35,000. Contact the Marine Charter Association (☎ 322126; fax 224679) in Victoria for more information.

Boat transfer from Desroches takes two hours, but the crossing has to be made at high

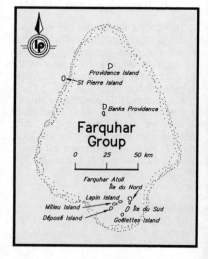

Farquhar Group

## Stingrays & Manta Rays
Rays are essentially flattened sharks but their feeding habits are quite unsharklike. Stingrays are bottom feeders, equipped with crushing teeth to grind the molluscs and crustaceans they sift out of the sand. They are often found lying motionless on the sandy bottom of their favourite shallow bays. It's fun to wade across such a bay, watching them suddenly rise up from the bottom and glide smoothly away. Just make certain you do scare them up, for stingrays are less than impressed when a human foot pins them down to the bottom, and that barbed and poisonous tail can then swing up and into your leg with painful efficiency.

Manta rays are amongst the largest fish found in the Indian Ocean, and a firm favourite of scuba divers. There's nothing quite like the feeling of sensing a shadow passing over the sun and looking up to see a couple of tons of manta ray swooping smoothly through the water above you. They are quite harmless, feeding only on plankton and small fishes, and in some places seem quite relaxed about divers approaching them closely. Manta rays are sometimes seen to leap completely out of the water, landing back with a tremendous splash.

Despite their shy nature rays do have one shark-like characteristic in that they generally give birth to live young. A baby manta ray is born neatly wrapped up in its bat-like wings. ■

tide when the reef surrounding Poivre is covered with sufficient water.

### D'Arros Island
D'Arros Island, about 40 km to the north of Poivre, is privately owned. It has an airstrip but offers no accommodation.

### FARQUHAR GROUP
This group of islands – Farquhar Atoll, Providence and St Pierre – is another 400 km south-west of the Amirantes. The lagoon of Farquhar Atoll is a popular resting point for yachts and schooners. Copra production and fishing are carried out by the few inhabitants. Île du Nord has an airstrip.

### ALDABRA GROUP
This is the best known, most remote and most interesting of the outer island groups. Aldabra lies more than 1000 km from Mahé

– in fact it's closer to Madagascar (400 km) and Africa (650 km) than its own capital.

It is thought to have been discovered around the 9th century by Arab seafarers who called it Al Khadra, and through the centuries and various European pronunciations this became Aldabra.

When it was part of the British Indian Ocean Territory (along with Farquhar), Aldabra was fancied by the Americans for a military base, but fears of a run-in with conservationists put them off and they eventually decided on Diego García. (The poor Diego Garcíans had no powerful lobby to protect them.)

### Aldabra Atoll
Aldabra Atoll is one of the world's largest coral atolls. It stretches for 22 km east to west and contains four major islands – Picard (west), Polymnieli, Malabar (middle) and Grand Terre (south) – which enclose a huge

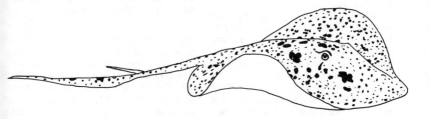

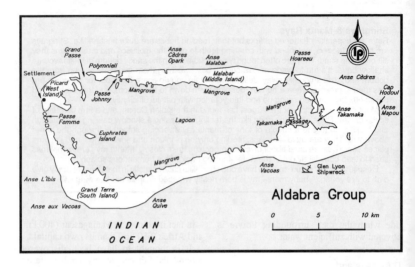

Aldabra Group

INDIAN OCEAN

tidal lagoon. Grand Passe, the main entrance to the lagoon, can be dangerous, particularly after low tide when the incoming tide rushes in at eight to 10 knots. Tiger sharks and manta rays also enter with the tide and water activities are not recommended at this time!

Aldabra is the original habitat of the giant land tortoises. There are about 200,000 of them on the atoll now, although at the turn of the century they were almost killed off. Marine turtles lay their eggs on the atoll and flocks of migratory birds, including flamingo, ibis, heron and frigate, fly in and out in their thousands. The white-throated rail is the sole remaining species of flightless bird in the Indian Ocean. Aldabra was declared a nature reserve some years ago by the Seychelles government and it is now listed as a World Heritage site.

Aldabra Atoll is inhabited only by scientists, and only for three months of the year. There is a scientific station, with generator-powered electricity, situated there. The Seychelles government is keen to see more scientists making use of the station.

The fishing settlement huts on West Island can be used by visiting scientists. There is no electricity. One major problem is the presence of giant 'robber' coconut crabs which scuttle about pinching anything they can lay their claws on and have been known to run off down burrows with cameras and clocks. If you catch a coconut crab, they are tasty to eat, but make sure you get rid of the poisonous large intestine.

### Cosmolédo Atoll
The Cosmolédo Atoll (which includes Astove Island) is a ring of 12 tiny islands, 110 km east of Assomption in the Aldabra Group. The largest of these is Wizard Island (Grand Île) with less than two square km.

The islands have been more or less ignored by outsiders and still serve as nesting sites for terns, boobies and the rare red-tailed tropicbird. Cosmolédo is managed by the Island Development Company.

### Assomption Island
Sausage-shaped Assomption Island, 27 km south of Aldabra, was once one of only two islands in the world with a population of the Abbot's booby (the other is Christmas Island in the Eastern Indian Ocean). It was also a stronghold of the flightless rail, but both

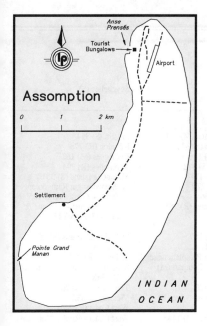

## Assomption

0    1    2 km

Anse Prensés

Tourist Bungalows

Airport

Settlement

Pointe Grand Manan

INDIAN OCEAN

today, fewer than 200 females come ashore annually to lay their eggs.

Underwater, however, it's a different world and it was here that Jacques Cousteau came to film much of his documentary, *The Silent World*. Although he'd dived throughout the world, he reported that he'd never seen any other place on earth with the same clarity of water or such colourful and extensive reef life.

Assomption was recently provided with an airstrip, so tourists can fly from Mahé, then take a three-hour boat trip to Aldabra. A small group of bungalows provides tourist accommodation in the north of Assomption. There's a small tree planting effort going on in the immediate area of the bungalows.

### Getting There & Away

If you wish to go to Aldabra as a tourist, contact the Marine Charter Association in Victoria or Michel Gardette of King Bambo Charters & Aqua Diving Services (see the Seychelles – Getting Around chapter). A popular alternative to the long yacht trips from Mahé is to fly to Desroches and pick up a schooner or yacht charter from there.

*Scuba Safaris* (☎ 071-4980003) at 14/11 Park House, South Bank Commercial Centre, 140 Battersea Park Rd, London arranges two-week cruises to Aldabra on the luxury dive vessel, Fantasea, for around UK£3500.

The schooner *Argo* arrives every three months. It takes five to seven days to reach the island by boat from Mahé.

these slow-moving birds were wiped out early on. Rich in guano, the island was exploited for its wealth in fertiliser but in the process it was stripped of vegetation and, as a result, was rendered uninhabitable to the birds which produced the guano. By the 1920s, it was practically bereft of plant or animal life. Furthermore, the green turtles which nested regularly on the island had been hunted to the brink of extinction and

# Index

## ABBREVIATIONS

Mauritius (M)　　　　　　　Réunion (R)　　　　　　　Seychelles (S)

## MAPS

## TEXT

# LONELY PLANET PHRASEBOOKS

**Nepali** phrasebook

**Ethiopian** Amharic phrasebook

**Latin American Spanish** phrasebook

**Ukrainian** phrasebook

**Greek** phrasebook

**Vietnamese** phrasebook

*Building bridges,*
*Breaking barriers,*
*Beyond babble-on*

*Listen for the gems*

*Speak your own words*

*Ask your own questions*

*Master of your own image*

- handy pocket-sized books
- easy to understand Pronunciation chapter
- clear and comprehensive Grammar chapter
- romanisation alongside script to allow ease of pronunciation
- script throughout so users can point to phrases
- extensive vocabulary sections, words and phrases for every situations
- full of cultural information and tips for the traveller

*'...vital for a real DIY spirit and attitude in language learning'* – Backpacker

*'the phrasebooks have good cultural backgrounders and offer solid advice for challenging situations in remote locations'* – San Francisco Examiner

*'...they are unbeatable for their coverage of the world's more obscure languages'* – The Geographical Magazine

---

Arabic (Egyptian)
Arabic (Moroccan)
Australia
  Australian English, Aboriginal and Torres Strait languages
Baltic States
  Estonian, Latvian, Lithuanian
Bengali
Burmese
Brazilian
Cantonese
Central Europe
  Czech, French, German, Hungarian, Italian and Slovak
Eastern Europe
  Bulgarian, Czech, Hungarian, Polish, Romanian and Slovak
Egyptian Arabic
Ethiopian (Amharic)
Fijian
Greek
Hindi/Urdu

Indonesian
Japanese
Korean
Lao
Latin American Spanish
Malay
Mandarin
Mediterranean Europe
  Albanian, Croatian, Greek, Italian, Macedonian, Maltese, Serbian, Slovene
Mongolian
Moroccan Arabic
Nepali
Papua New Guinea
Pilipino (Tagalog)
Quechua
Russian
Scandinavian Europe
  Danish, Finnish, Icelandic, Norwegian and Swedish

South-East Asia
  Burmese, Indonesian, Khmer, Lao, Malay, Tagalog (Pilipino), Thai and Vietnamese
Sri Lanka
Swahili
Thai
Thai Hill Tribes
Tibetan
Turkish
Ukrainian
USA
  US English, Vernacular Talk, Native American languages and Hawaiian
Vietnamese
Western Europe
  Basque, Catalan, Dutch, French, German, Irish, Italian, Portuguese, Scottish Gaelic, Spanish (Castilian) and Welsh

# LONELY PLANET JOURNEYS

JOURNEYS is a unique collection of travel writing – published by the company that understands travel better than anyone else. It is a series for anyone who has ever experienced – or dreamed of – the magical moment when they encountered a strange culture or saw a place for the first time. They are tales to read while you're planning a trip, while you're on the road or while you're in an armchair, in front of a fire.

JOURNEYS books catch the spirit of a place, illuminate a culture, recount a crazy adventure, or introduce a fascinating way of life. They always entertain, and always enrich the experience of travel.

---

### THE RAINBIRD
### A Central African Journey
### *Jan Brokken*
### translated by Sam Garrett

*The Rainbird* is a classic travel story. Following in the footsteps of famous Europeans such as Albert Schweitzer and H.M. Stanley, Jan Brokken journeyed to Gabon in central Africa. A kaleidoscope of adventures and anecdotes, *The Rainbird* brilliantly chronicles the encounter between Africa and Europe as it was acted out on a side-street of history. It is also the compelling, immensely readable account of the author's own travels in one of the most remote and mysterious regions of Africa.

*Jan Brokken* is one of Holland's best known writers. In addition to travel narratives and literary journalism, he has published several novels and short stories. Many of his works are set in Africa, where he has travelled widely.

---

### SONGS TO AN AFRICAN SUNSET
### A Zimbabwean Story
### *Sekai Nzenza-Shand*

*Songs to an African Sunset* braids vividly personal stories into an intimate picture of contemporary Zimbabwe. Returning to her family's village after many years in the West, Sekai Nzenza-Shand discovers a world where ancestor worship, polygamy and witchcraft still govern the rhythms of daily life – and where drought, deforestation and AIDS have wrought devastating changes. With insight and affection, she explores a culture torn between respect for the old ways and the irresistible pull of the new.

*Sekai Nzenza-Shand* was born in Zimbabwe and has lived in England and Australia. Her first novel, *Zimbabwean Woman: My Own Story*, was published in London in 1988 and her fiction has been included in the short story collections *Daughters of Africa* and *Images of the West*. Sekai currently lives in Zimbabwe.

 *This project has been assisted by the Commonwealth Government through the Australia Council, its arts funding and advisory body.*

# LONELY PLANET TRAVEL ATLASES

Lonely Planet has long been famous for the number and quality of its guidebook maps. Now we've gone one step further and in conjunction with Steinhart Katzir Publishers produced a handy companion series: Lonely Planet travel atlases – maps of a country produced in book form.

Unlike other maps, which look good but lead travellers astray, our travel atlases have been researched on the road by Lonely Planet's experienced team of writers. All details are carefully checked to ensure the atlas corresponds with the equivalent Lonely Planet guidebook.

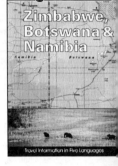

The handy atlas format means no holes, wrinkles, torn sections or constant folding and unfolding. These atlases can survive long periods on the road, unlike cumbersome fold-out maps. The comprehensive index ensures easy reference.

- full-colour throughout
- maps researched and checked by Lonely Planet authors
- place names correspond with Lonely Planet guidebooks
  – no confusing spelling differences
- legend and travelling information in English, French, German, Japanese and Spanish
- size: 230 x 160 mm

***Available now:***
Chile & Easter Island • Egypt • India & Bangladesh • Israel & the Palestinian Territories •Jordan, Syria & Lebanon • Kenya • Laos • Portugal • South Africa, Lesotho & Swaziland • Thailand • Turkey • Vietnam • Zimbabwe, Botswana & Namibia

---

# LONELY PLANET TV SERIES & VIDEOS

Lonely Planet travel guides have been brought to life on television screens around the world. Like our guides, the programmes are based on the joy of independent travel, and look honestly at some of the most exciting, picturesque and frustrating places in the world. Each show is presented by one of three travellers from Australia, England or the USA and combines an innovative mixture of video, Super-8 film, atmospheric soundscapes and original music.

Videos of each episode – containing additional footage not shown on television – are available from good book and video shops, but the availability of individual videos varies with regional screening schedules.

***Video destinations include:*** Alaska • American Rockies • Australia – The South-East • Baja California & the Copper Canyon • Brazil • Central Asia • Chile & Easter Island • Corsica, Sicily & Sardinia – The Mediterranean Islands • East Africa (Tanzania & Zanzibar) • Ecuador & the Galapagos Islands • Greenland & Iceland • Indonesia • Israel & the Sinai Desert • Jamaica • Japan • La Ruta Maya • Morocco • New York • North India • Pacific Islands (Fiji, Solomon Islands & Vanuatu) • South India • South West China • Turkey • Vietnam • West Africa • Zimbabwe, Botswana & Namibia

*The Lonely Planet TV series is produced by:*
**Pilot Productions**
The Old Studio
18 Middle Row
London W10 5AT UK

**For video availability and ordering information contact your nearest Lonely Planet office.**

***Music from the TV series is available on CD & cassette.***

# PLANET TALK

### Lonely Planet's FREE quarterly newsletter

We love hearing from you and think you'd like to hear from us.

**When...**is the right time to see reindeer in Finland?
**Where...**can you hear the best palm-wine music in Ghana?
**How...**do you get from Asunción to Areguá by steam train?
**What...**is the best way to see India?

**For the answer to these and many other questions read PLANET TALK.**

Every issue is packed with up-to-date travel news and advice including:

- a letter from Lonely Planet co-founders Tony and Maureen Wheeler
- go behind the scenes on the road with a Lonely Planet author
- feature article on an important and topical travel issue
- a selection of recent letters from travellers
- details on forthcoming Lonely Planet promotions
- complete list of Lonely Planet products

*To join our mailing list contact any Lonely Planet office.*

**Also available: Lonely Planet T-shirts. 100% heavyweight cotton.**

---

# LONELY PLANET ONLINE

### Get the latest travel information before you leave or while you're on the road

Whether you've just begun planning your next trip, or you're chasing down specific info on currency regulations or visa requirements, check out Lonely Planet Online for up-to-the minute travel information.

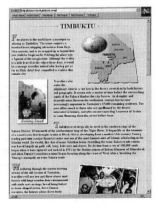

As well as travel profiles of your favourite destinations (including maps and photos), you'll find current reports from our researchers and other travellers, updates on health and visas, travel advisories, and discussion of the ecological and political issues you need to be aware of as you travel.

There's also an online travellers' forum where you can share your experience of life on the road, meet travel companions and ask other travellers for their recommendations and advice. We also have plenty of links to other online sites useful to independent travellers.

And of course we have a complete and up-to-date list of all Lonely Planet travel products including guides, phrasebooks, atlases, Journeys and videos and a simple online ordering facility if you can't find the book you want elsewhere.

### www.lonelyplanet.com
### or
### AOL keyword: lp

# LONELY PLANET PRODUCTS

Lonely Planet is known worldwide for publishing practical, reliable and no-nonsense travel information in our guides and on our web site. The Lonely Planet list covers just about every accessible part of the world. Currently there are eight series: *travel guides*, *shoestring guides*, *walking guides*, *city guides*, *phrasebooks*, *audio packs*, *travel atlases* and *Journeys* – a unique collection of travel writing.

## EUROPE

Amsterdam • Austria • Baltic States phrasebook • Britain • Central Europe on a shoestring • Central Europe phrasebook • Czech & Slovak Republics • Denmark • Dublin • Eastern Europe on a shoestring • Eastern Europe phrasebook • Estonia Latvia & Lithuania • Finland • France • Greece • Greek phrasebook • Hungary • Iceland, Greenland & the Faroe Islands • Ireland • Italy • Mediterranean Europe on a shoestring • Mediterranean Europe phrasebook • Paris • Poland • Portugal • Portugal travel atlas • Prague • Russia, Ukraine & Belarus • Russian phrasebook • Scandinavian & Baltic Europe on a shoestring • Scandinavian Europe phrasebook • Slovenia • Spain • Spanish phrasebook • St Petersburg • Switzerland • Trekking in Greece • Trekking in Spain • Ukrainian phrasebook • Vienna • Walking in Britain • Walking in Switzerland • Western Europe on a shoestring • Western Europe phrasebook

## NORTH AMERICA

Alaska • Backpacking in Alaska • Baja California • California & Nevada • Canada • Florida • Hawaii • Honolulu • Los Angeles • Mexico • Miami • New England • New Orleans • New York, New Jersey & Pennsylvania • Pacific Northwest USA • Rocky Mountain States • San Francisco • Southwest USA • USA phrasebook • Washington, DC & the Capital Region

## CENTRAL AMERICA & THE CARIBBEAN

Bermuda • Central America on a shoestring • Costa Rica • Cuba • Eastern Caribbean • Guatemala, Belize & Yucatán: La Ruta Maya • Jamaica

## SOUTH AMERICA

Argentina, Uruguay & Paraguay • Bolivia • Brazil • Brazilian phrasebook • Buenos Aires • Chile & Easter Island • Chile & Easter Island travel atlas • Colombia • Ecuador & the Galápagos Islands • Latin American Spanish phrasebook • Peru • Quechua phrasebook • Rio de Janeiro • South America on a shoestring • Trekking in the Patagonian Andes • Venezuela

*Travel Literature:* Full Circle: A South American Journey

## ANTARCTICA

Antarctica

## ISLANDS OF THE INDIAN OCEAN

Madagascar & Comoros • Maldives• Mauritius, Réunion & Seychelles

## AFRICA

Africa on a shoestring • Arabic (Moroccan) phrasebook • Cape Town • Central Africa • East Africa • Egypt • Egypt travel atlas• Ethiopian (Amharic) phrasebook • Kenya • Kenya travel atlas • Malawi, Mozambique & Zambia • Morocco • North Africa • South Africa, Lesotho & Swaziland • South Africa, Lesotho & Swaziland travel atlas • Swahili phrasebook • Trekking in East Africa • West Africa • Zimbabwe, Botswana & Namibia • Zimbabwe Botswana & Namibia travel atlas

*Travel Literature:* The Rainbird: A Central African Journey • Songs to an African Sunset: A Zimbabwean Story

Lonely Planet products are distributed worldwide. They are also available by mail order from Lonely Planet, so if you have difficulty finding a title please write to us. North American and South American residents should write to Embarcadero West, 155 Filbert St, Suite 251, Oakland CA 94607, USA; European and African residents should write to 10 Barley Mow Passage, Chiswick, London W4 4PH; and residents of other countries to PO Box 617, Hawthorn, Victoria 3122, Australia.

## NORTH-EAST ASIA

Beijing • Cantonese phrasebook • China • Hong Kong • Hong Kong, Macau & Guangzhou • Japan • Japanese phrasebook • Japanese audio pack • Korea • Korean phrasebook • Mandarin phrasebook • Mongolia • Mongolian phrasebook • North-East Asia on a shoestring • Seoul • Taiwan • Tibet • Tibet phrasebook • Tokyo

*Travel Literature*: Lost Japan

## MIDDLE EAST & CENTRAL ASIA

Arab Gulf States • Arabic (Egyptian) phrasebook • Central Asia • Iran • Israel & the Palestinian Territories • Israel & the Palestinian Territories travel atlas • Istanbul • Jerusalem • Jordan & Syria • Jordan, Syria & Lebanon travel atlas • Middle East • Turkey • Turkish phrasebook • Turkey travel atlas • Yemen

*Travel Literature:* The Gates of Damascus • Kingdom of the Film Stars: Journey into Jordan

## ALSO AVAILABLE:

Travel with Children • Traveller's Tales

## INDIAN SUBCONTINENT

Bangladesh • Bengali phrasebook • Delhi • Hindi/Urdu phrasebook • India • India & Bangladesh travel atlas • Indian Himalaya • Karakoram Highway • Nepal • Nepali phrasebook • Pakistan • Rajasthan • Sri Lanka • Sri Lanka phrasebook • Trekking in the Indian Himalaya • Trekking in the Karakoram & Hindukush • Trekking in the Nepal Himalaya

*Travel Literature:* In Rajasthan • Shopping for Buddhas

## SOUTH-EAST ASIA

Bali & Lombok • Bangkok • Burmese phrasebook • Cambodia • Ho Chi Minh City • Indonesia • Indonesian phrasebook • Indonesian audio pack • Jakarta • Java • Laos • Lao phrasebook • Laos travel atlas • Malay phrasebook • Malaysia, Singapore & Brunei • Myanmar (Burma) • Philippines • Pilipino phrasebook • Singapore • South-East Asia on a shoestring • South-East Asia phrasebook • Thailand • Thailand travel atlas • Thai phrasebook • Thai audio pack • Thai Hill Tribes phrasebook • Vietnam • Vietnamese phrasebook • Vietnam travel atlas

## AUSTRALIA & THE PACIFIC

Australia • Australian phrasebook • Bushwalking in Australia • Bushwalking in Papua New Guinea • Fiji • Fijian phrasebook • Islands of Australia's Great Barrier Reef • Melbourne • Micronesia • New Caledonia • New South Wales & the ACT • New Zealand • Northern Territory • Outback Australia • Papua New Guinea • Papua New Guinea phrasebook • Queensland • Rarotonga & the Cook Islands • Samoa • Solomon Islands • South Australia • Sydney • Tahiti & French Polynesia • Tasmania • Tonga • Tramping in New Zealand • Vanuatu • Victoria • Western Australia

*Travel Literature:* Islands in the Clouds • Sean & David's Long Drive

# THE LONELY PLANET STORY

Lonely Planet published its first book in 1973 in response to the numerous 'How did you do it?' questions Maureen and Tony Wheeler were asked after driving, bussing, hitching, sailing and railing their way from England to Australia.

Written at a kitchen table and hand collated, trimmed and stapled, *Across Asia on the Cheap* became an instant local bestseller, inspiring thoughts of another book.

Eighteen months in South-East Asia resulted in their second guide, *South-East Asia on a shoestring*, which they put together in a backstreet Chinese hotel in Singapore in 1975. The 'yellow bible', as it quickly became known to backpackers around the world, soon became *the* guide to the region. It has sold well over half a million copies and is now in its 9th edition, still retaining its familiar yellow cover.

Today there are over 240 titles, including travel guides, walking guides, language kits & phrasebooks, travel atlases and travel literature. The company is the largest independent travel publisher in the world. Although Lonely Planet initially specialised in guides to Asia, today there are few corners of the globe that have not been covered.

The emphasis continues to be on travel for independent travellers. Tony and Maureen still travel for several months of each year and play an active part in the writing, updating and quality control of Lonely Planet's guides.

They have been joined by over 70 authors and 170 staff at our offices in Melbourne (Australia), Oakland (USA), London (UK) and Paris (France). Travellers themselves also make a valuable contribution to the guides through the feedback we receive in thousands of letters each year and on our web site.

The people at Lonely Planet strongly believe that travellers can make a positive contribution to the countries they visit, both through their appreciation of the countries' culture, wildlife and natural features, and through the money they spend. In addition, the company makes a direct contribution to the countries and regions it covers. Since 1986 a percentage of the income from each book has been donated to ventures such as famine relief in Africa; aid projects in India; agricultural projects in Central America; Greenpeace's efforts to halt French nuclear testing in the Pacific; and Amnesty International.

*'I hope we send people out with the right attitude about travel. You realise when you travel that there are so many different perspectives about the world, so we hope these books will make people more interested in what they see. Guidebooks can't really guide people. All you can do is point them in the right direction.'*

– Tony Wheeler

# LONELY PLANET PUBLICATIONS

**Australia**
PO Box 617, Hawthorn 3122, Victoria
tel: (03) 9819 1877  fax: (03) 9819 6459
e-mail: talk2us@lonelyplanet.com.au

**USA**
Embarcadero West, 155 Filbert St, Suite 251,
Oakland, CA 94607
tel: (510) 893 8555  TOLL FREE: 800 275-8555
fax: (510) 893 8563
e-mail: info@lonelyplanet.com

**UK**
10 Barley Mow Passage, Chiswick,
London W4 4PH
tel: (0181) 742 3161  fax: (0181) 742 2772
e-mail: 100413.3551@compuserve.com

**France:**
71 bis rue du Cardinal Lemoine, 75005 Paris
tel: 1 44 32 06 20  fax: 1 46 34 72 55
e-mail: 100560.415@compuserve.com

**World Wide Web: http://www.lonelyplanet.com**